D0938814

HISTORY OF THE CHURCH

VIII

HISTORY OF THE CHURCH

Edited by
HUBERT JEDIN
and
JOHN DOLAN

Volume VIII

THE CHURCH
IN THE AGE
OF LIBERALISM

by

ROGER AUBERT

JOHANNES BECKMANN

PATRICK J. CORISH

RUDOLF LILL

Translated by

Peter Becker

CROSSROAD · NEW YORK

1981

The Crossroad Publishing Company

18 East 41st Street

New York, N.Y. 10017

Translated from the *Handbuch der Kirchengeschichte*

Vol. VI/I *Die Kirche in der Gegenwart: Die Kirche zwischen Revolution*

und Restauration, chapters 22 through 44, 2d edition

© Verlag Herder Freiburg im Breisgau 1971

Printed in the United States of America

Library of Congress Cataloging in Publication Data

Main entry under title:

The Church in the age of liberalism.

(History of the church; v. 8)

"Translated from the Handbuch der Kirchengeschichte,

vol. VI, 1, Die Kirche in der Gegenwart: Die Kirche

zwischen Revolution und Restrauration, chapters 22

through 44, 2d edition."

Includes bibliographies and index.

1. Catholic Church—History—19th century.

I. Aubert, Roger. II. Series: Jedin, Hubert, 1900–

ed. Handbuch der Kirchengeschichte. English; v. 8.

BR145.2.J413 1980, vol. 8 [BX1386] 282'.09'034 80-25830

ISBN 0-8245-0011-3   Previously: 0-8164-0447-X

CONTENTS

Preface to the English Edition ix

List of Abbreviations xi

PART ONE: BETWEEN THE REVOLUTIONS OF 1830 AND 1848

SECTION ONE: THE CONTINUATION OF CATHOLIC RENEWAL IN EUROPE
(Roger Aubert) 3

Chapter 1: The Progress of Ultramontanism and the Growth of the International
Orders 3
  Progress of Ultramontanism 3
  The Large Orders 9

Chapter 2: Old and New in Pastoral Care and Moral Theology 14
  The Modernization of Ecclesiastical Institutions 14
  The Methods of Catechetical Instruction 16
  Pastoral Theology and Pastoral Practice 20
  The Reaction of Moral Theology to the Rationalism of Enlightenment
  and Rigorism 27

Chapter 3: Catholic Thought Searching for New Ways 31
  The Hermesian Controversy 32
  Rise and Fall of Güntherianism 35
  Tübingen and Munich 39
  The Catholic University of Louvain 43
  Tentative Attempts by the Catholic Intellectuals in France 45
  The Growth of the Catholic Press 53

SECTION TWO: THE ASCENSION OF PIUS IX AND THE CRISIS OF 1848
(chs. 4, 5, 6/II: Roger Aubert; ch. 6/1: Rudolf Lill) 57

Chapter 4: The First Years of the Pontificate of Pius IX: From the Neoguelf
Mythos to the Roman Revolution 57

Chapter 5: The Consequences of the Events of 1848 in France 66

Chapter 6: The Consequences of the 1848 Revolution in the States of the
German Confederation and the Netherlands 70
  The States of the German Confederation 70
  The Netherlands 77

CONTENTS

PART TWO: THE CATHOLIC REACTION TO LIBERALISM

Introduction: Pius IX after 1848 83

SECTION ONE: THE TEMPORARY IMPROVEMENT IN THE SITUATION OF
THE CHURCH (chs. 7, 9/II, 10, 11: Roger Aubert; ch. 8: Rudolf Lill; ch. 9/I:
Patrick J. Corish) 91

Chapter 7: The Seeming Success of the Church in France during the Second
    Empire and the "Moral Order" 92
    The Privileged Status of the Church 92
    The Ambivalence of the Actual Religious Situation 98

Chapter 8: The States of the German Confederation and Switzerland,
    1848–70 104

Chapter 9: The Rise of Catholicism in the Anglo-Saxon World 121
    England 121
    Scotland 125
    Ireland 126
    The United States 130
    Canada 138
    Australia 142

Chapter 10: The Easing of Tensions in the Iberian World 143
    Spain 143
    Portugal 148
    The Spanish-American Republics 149
    Brazil 153

Chapter 11: The Catholic Church in the Orthodox World 154
    Unionist Prospects in the East 154
    The Russian Empire 158
    The Slavs in Austria-Hungary 165
    Progress of Catholicism in Southeastern Europe and the Levant . . 167
    The Eastern Patriarchates 171

SECTION TWO: THE MISSIONS BETWEEN 1840 AND 1870
(Johannes Beckmann) 175

Chapter 12: The Strengthening of the Gregorian Restoration 175
    The Weakening of the Portuguese Patronage and the Reorganization of
    the Asian Missions 178
      In the British Sphere of Influence 178
      In the French Sphere of Influence 186
    Philippines, Indonesia, Oceania, Africa 193

Chapter 13: The First Vatican Council and the Missions 199

SECTION THREE: LIGHT AND SHADOWS OF CATHOLIC VITALITY
(Roger Aubert) 208

Chapter 14: Regular and Secular Clergy 208
    Orders and Congregations 208
    The Diocesan Clergy and Pastoral Work 213

Chapter 15: The Growth of Piety 218

Chapter 16: The Backwardness of Religious Studies and the Controversy about
    the "German Theologians" 228
    Religious Studies Outside of Germany 228
    Scholastics and Germanics vs. the "German Theologians" 237

CONTENTS

SECTION FOUR: THE ALTERCATION BETWEEN CATHOLICISM AND
LIBERALISM (chs. 17, 18, 20: Roger Aubert; ch. 19: Rudolf Lill) 248

Chapter 17: The Roman Question 248
   From the Papal Restoration to the Italian War 248
   From the Establishment of the Kingdom of Italy to the Occupation
   of Rome 250

Chapter 18: The Offensive of the Liberal Governments in the Non-German
   Speaking Countries 255
   The Secularization Policy in Italy 255
   Anticlericalism in Belgium and in the Netherlands 262
   The Confused Situation in the Iberian Peninsula 267
   Regalistic Liberals and Freemasons in Latin America 269

Chapter 19: Preliminary Phases of the *Kulturkampf* in Austria, Bavaria, Baden,
   and Switzerland 272

Chapter 20: Internal Catholic Controversies in Connection with
   Liberalism 283
   Catholicism and Liberalism after 1848 283
   The Division of the Catholics in France 285
   Catholic Liberalism outside France around 1860 289
   The *Syllabus* and its Consequences 293
   Antiliberalism and Social Catholicism 299

SECTION FIVE: THE VICTORY OF ULTRAMONTANISM (chs. 21, 22:
Roger Aubert; 23: Rudolf Lill) 304

Chapter 21: Ultramontane Progress and Final Gallican Resistance 304
   The Ultramontane Movement around 1850 304
   Rome's Systematic Activity 306
   The Excesses of Neo-Ultramontanism and the Reaction in Germany
   and France 312

Chapter 22: The Vatican Council 315
   Preparation 315
   Infallibilists and Anti-Infallibilists 318
   First Council Debates 322
   Agitation concerning Papal Infallibility 325
   The Constitution *Pastor Aeternus* 328

Chapter 23: The Rise of the Old Catholic Community 330

BIBLIOGRAPHY 335
   General Bibliography 337
   Bibliography to Individual Chapters 349

INDEX 383

PREFACE TO THE ENGLISH EDITION

The decision to entitle this volume of the *History of the Church The Church in the Age of Liberalism* was not arrived at without taking into account the fact that the decades of the nineteenth century examined here witnessed a waning of much of what the expression "liberalism" signified: freedom of thought, laissez-faire in economics, and representative and parliamentary government. All of these declined in the face of nationalism, Romanticism, and especially political democracy. Yet in the Church it was the struggle over liberalism that overshadowed all else and it was Pio Nono who, holding the see of Rome longer than any other Pontiff, in opting for the Middle Ages treated all liberals as revolutionaries and all revolutionaries as devils. To many the anathemas of the *Syllabus Errorum* against all forms of Enlightenment-inspired liberalism were no less vituperous than Voltaire's *écrasez l'infâme.*

It is ironic that the temporal power of the papacy, based to a large extent on the slogans of Gregory VII on *libertas,* should have witnessed in its final moments an unprecedented attack on the same basic concept. Ironic also that the same Pope, who so vehemently denounced democracy as a form of government, was forced, due to a lack of evidence, to proclaim his infallibility on the basis of a plurality vote, albeit seemingly coerced from the cardinals. The notion of tradition was required to produce what it had not preserved.

Lord Acton, who was the outstanding spokesman of liberalism during this period, was angered not by the feeling that infallibility was a theological error but by the belief that it enshrined in the Church a monarchical autocracy which could never maintain itself apart from crime committed or condoned. The same author also maintained that almost every writer who really served Catholicism fell sooner or later under the disgrace or suspicion of Rome. This is certainly true of two of the great minds of the time, Döllinger and Newman. It is the genius and personality of the latter that is both the embodiment and the contradiction of the period. He, as Christopher Dawson writes, realized with perception and clarity of vision the new dangers which threatened the Christian faith and the whole traditional order of Christian civilization. At the same time he discovered and investigated the internal principle of development in the life of the Church by which what is already implicitly contained in Christian faith and tradition is unfolded and applied to meet the needs of the age, so that every new challenge to the faith becomes an opportunity for the conquest of new truths and reveals unsuspected depths of meaning in truths that are already familiar.

Newman saw that it was only in history that the divine process of progressive revelation and spiritual renovation could be fulfilled. "The Church does not teach that human nature is irreclaimable, else wherefore should she be sent?" For Newman, who along with Acton brought to the Church the long overdue influence of the Anglo-Saxon world once resplendent with the works of Bede, Anselm, Scotus, and More, if not for Pius, *ecclesia subjectos non habet ut servos, sed ut filios.*

John P. Dolan

LIST OF ABBREVIATIONS

ADRomana   *Archivio della Deputazione Romana di Storia Patria,* Rome 1935seqq. (1878–1934: *ASRomana*).

AFP   *Archivum Fratrum Praedicatorum,* Rome 1931seqq.

AGKKN   *Archief voor de Geschiedenis van de Katholieke Kerk in Nederland,* Utrecht 1959seqq.

AHPont   *Archivum historiae pontificiae,* Rome 1963seqq.

AHR   *The American Historical Review,* New York, 1895seqq.

AHRF   *Annales historiques de la Révolution française,* Paris 1924seqq.

AHSI   *Archivum historicum Societatis Iesu,* Rome 1932seqq.

AHVNrh   *Annalen des Historischen Vereins für den Niederrhein, insbesondere das alte Erzbistum Köln,* Cologne 1855seqq.

AIA   *Archivo Ibero-Americano,* Madrid 1914seqq.

AkathKR   *Archiv für Katholisches Kirchenrecht,* (Innsbruck) Mainz 1857seqq.

Albers, *Herstel*   P. Albers, *Geschiedenis van het herstel der hiërarchie in de Nederlanden,* 2 vols., Nijmegen and The Hague 1903–04.

Albers, *Lib. saec.*   [P̄. Albers] *Liber saecularis historiae Societatis Iesu ab anno 1814 ad annum 1914,* Rome 1914.

Ammann   A. M. Ammann, *Abriβ der ostslawischen Kirchengeschichte,* Vienna 1950.

AMrhKG   *Archiv für mittelrheinische Kirchengeschichte,* Speyer 1949seqq.

Anthropos   *Anthroposophische Internationale Zeitschrift für Völker- und Sprachenkunde,* Mödling 1906seqq.

Antonianum   *Antonianum,* Rome 1926seqq.

AÖG   *Archiv für österreichische Geschichte,* Vienna 1865seqq.

AOP   *Analecta Sacri Ordinis Praedicatorum,* Rome 1892seqq.

ArchSR   *Archives de Sociologie des religions,* Paris 1956seqq.

ArSKG   *Archiv für schlesische Kirchengeschichte,* K. Engelbert, ed., I–IV, Breslau 1936–41; VIIseqq., Hildesheim 1949seqq.

ASRomana   *Archivio della Reale Società Romana di Storia Patria,* Rome 1878–1934 (*ADRomana* after 1935).

ASS   *Acta Sanctae Sedis,* Rome 1865–1908.

AstIt   *Archivio storico Italiano,* Florence 1842seqq.

Aubert, *Pie IX*   R. Aubert, *Le pontificat de Pie IX* (A. Fliche and V. Martin, eds., *Histoire de l'Église depuis les origines jusqu'à nos jours* 21) Paris 1962.

Aubert, *Vat*   R. Aubert, *Vaticanum I,* Mainz 1965.

Aubert-Martina   R. Aubert, *Il pontificato di Pio IX,* translated by G. Martina with notes and supplement, Turin 1969.

Backmund   N. Backmund, *Monasticon Praemonstratense* I–III, Straubing 1949seqq.

Bastgen   F. Bastgen, *Die römische Frage*, 3 vols., Freiburg i. Br. 1917–19.

Baunard   L. Baunard, *Un siècle de l'Église de France 1800–1900*, Paris 1902.

Becqué   M. Becqué, *Le cardinal Dechamps*, 2 vols., Louvain 1956.

Bellesheim, *Irland*   A. Bellesheim, *Geschichte der Katholischen Kirche in Irland*, 3 vols., Mainz 1890–91.

Bellesheim, *Schottland*   A. Bellesheim, *Geschichte der Katholischen Kirche in Schottland*, Mainz 1883.

Belvederi   R. Belvederi, *Il papato di fronte alla Rivoluzione ed alle conseguenze del Congresso di Vienna (1775–1846)*: P. Paschini and P. Brezzi, eds., *I Papi nella storia* II, Rome 1951, 767–930.

Bernasconi   A. M. Bernasconi, *Acta Gregorii Papae XVI, auspice cardinal Vanutelli recensita*, 4 vols., Rome 1901–04.

BIHBR   *Bulletin de l'Institut historique belge de Rome*, Brussels and Rome 1919seqq.

Bihlmeyer-Tüchle   K. Bihlmeyer and H. Tüchle, *Kirchengeschichte* I: *Das christliche Altertum*, Paderborn 1955; II: *Das Mittelalter*, Paderborn 1955; III: *Die Neuzeit und die neueste Zeit*, Paderborn 1968.

BLE   *Bulletin de littérature ecclésiastique*, Toulouse 1899seqq.

BnatBelg   *Biographie nationale. Publiée par l'Académie de Belgique*, 35 vols., Brussels 1866–1970.

Boudou   A. Boudou, *Le Saint-Siège et la Russie. Leurs relations diplomatiques au XIXe siècle*, 2 vols., Paris 1922–25.

Brugerette   J. Brugerette, *Le prêtre français et la société contemporaine*, 3 vols., Paris 1933–38.

BStBiS   *Bolletino storico-bibliografico subalpino*, Turin 1896seqq.

BullRomCont   *Bullarii Romani Continuatio*, A. Berberi and A. Spetia, eds., 19 vols., Rome 1835–58.

Burnichon   J. Burnichon, *La Compagnie de Jésus en France. Histoire d'un siècle*, 4 vols., Paris 1914–22.

Cath   *Catholica. Jahrbuch (Vierteljahresschrift) für Kontroverstheologie*, (Paderborn) Münster 1932seqq.

CathEnc   *The Catholic Encyclopedia*, C. Herbermann, ed., 15 vols., New York 1907–12.

Catholicisme   *Catholicisme. Hier-Aujourd'hui-Demain*, G. Jacquemet, ed., Paris 1948seqq.

CH   *Church History*, New York and Chicago 1932seqq.

CHR   *The Catholic Historical Review*, Washington 1915seqq.

ChStato   *Chiesa e Stato nell'Ottocento. Miscellanea in onore di P. Pirri*, ed. by R. Aubert, A. M. Ghisalberti, E. Passerin d'Entrèves, 2 vols., Padua 1962.

Cîteaux   *Cîteaux. Commentarii cistercienses*, Westmalle (Belg.) 1950seqq.

CivCatt   *La Civiltà Cattolica*, Rome 1850seqq. (1871–87 Florence).

CodCanOrFonti   S. *Congregazione per la Chiesa Orientale. Codificazione Canonica Orientale. Fonti*, 3rd ser., Rome 1931seqq.

Colapietra   R. Colapietra, *La Chiesa tra Lamennais e Metternich*, Brescia 1963.

ColLac   *Collectio Lacensis: Acta et Decreta sacrorum conciliorum recentiorum*, ed. by Jesuits of Maria Laach, 7 vols., Freiburg i. Br. 1870–90.

CollFr   *Collectanea Franciscana*, Rome 1931seqq.

CPF   *Collectanea Sancta Congregationis de Propaganda Fide* I (1622–1866), II (1867–1906), Rome 1907.

D   H. Denzinger, *Enchiridion Symbolorum, Definitionum et Declarationum de rebus fidei et morum*, Freiburg i. Br. 1967.

DACL   *Dictionnaire d'archéologie chrétienne et de liturgie*, F. Cabrol and H. Leclercq, eds., 15 vols., Paris 1903–53.

Daniel-Rops   Daniel-Rops, *L'Église des Révolutions*, 2 vols., Paris 1960–63.

Dansette   A. Dansette, *Histoire religieuse de la France contemporaine*, 2 vols., Paris 1948–51.

DBI   *Dizionario biografico degli Italiani*, A. M. Ghisalberti, ed., Rome 1960seqq.

DDC   *Dictionnaire de droit canonique*, R. Naz, ed., 7 vols., Paris 1935–65.

Debidour, *Histoire*   A. Debidour, *Histoire des rapports de l'Église et de l'État en France de 1789 à 1870*, 2 vols., Paris 1891.

Debidour, *IIIᵉ République*   A. Debidour, *L'Église catholique et l'État sous la Troisième République, 1870–1906*, 2 vols., Paris 1906.

de Clercq   C. de Clercq, *Conciles des Orientaux catholique* (Histoire des conciles XI), 2 vols., Paris 1949–52.

Delacroix   *Histoire universelle des missions catholiques*, S. Delacroix, ed., 4 vols., Paris and Monaco 1957–59.

de Montclos   X. de Montclos, *Lavigerie, le Saint-Siège et l'Église, 1846–1878*, Paris 1965.

DHGE   *Dictionnaire d'histoire et de géographie ecclésiastiques*, A. Baudrillart, ed., Paris 1912seqq.

DictEngCath   *A Literary and Biographical History or Bibliographical Dictionary of the English Catholics from 1534 to the Present Time*, by J. Gillow, 5 vols., London and New York 1885seqq.

DSAM   *Dictionnaire de Spiritualité ascétique et mystique. Doctrine et Histoire*, M. Viller, ed., Paris 1932seqq.

DThC   *Dictionnaire de théologie catholique*, A. Vacant and E. Mangenot and É. Amann, 15 vols., Paris 1930.

Dupeux   G. Dupeux, *La société française 1789–1960* (Collection U, Histoire contemporaine), Paris 1964.

Duroselle   J.-B. Duroselle, *Les débuts du catholicisme social en France 1822–1870*, Paris 1951.

DVfLG   *Deutsche Vierteljahresschrift für Literaturwissenschaft und Geistesgeschichte*, Halle 1923seqq.

ECatt   *Enciclopedia Cattolica*, 12 vols., Rome 1949–54.

ED   *Euntes docete* (Commentaria urbana), Rome 1948seqq.

EEAm   *Enciclopedia Universal Ilustrada Europeo-Americana*, 70 vols., Barcelona 1908–1930.

Éfranc   *Études franciscaines*, Paris 1909–40; n.s. 1950seqq.

Ellis, *AmCath*   J. T. Ellis, *American Catholicism* (The Chicago History of American Civilization), Chicago 1956.

Ellis, *Documents*   *Documents of American Catholic History*, J. T. Ellis, ed., Milwaukee 1956.

Engel-Janosi   F. Engel-Janosi, *Österreich und der Vatikan*, 2 vols., Graz 1958–60.

EnI   *Enciclopedia Italiana di scienze, lettere ed arti*, 35 vols., Rome 1929–37, Supplement 1938, Index volume 1939, 2 Supplements (1938–48), Rome 1948–49.

ÉO   *Échos d'Orient*, Paris 1897seqq.

EThL   *Ephemerides Theologicae Lovanienses*, (Bruges) Gembloux 1924seqq.

Études   *Études*, Paris 1856seqq. (until 1896: *Études religieuses*).

Feine, *RG* H. E. Feine, *Kirchliche Rechtsgeschichte* I: *Die katholische Kirche,* Graz 1964.

Fliche-Martin *Histoire de l'Église depuis les origines jusqu'à nos jours,* published under the direction of A. Fliche and V. Martin, Paris 1935seqq.

FreibDiözArch *Freiburger Diözesan-Archiv,* Freiburg i. Br. 1865seqq.

Friedrich J. Friedrich, *Geschichte des Vaticanischen Conzils,* 3 vols., Nördlingen 1877–87.

FZThPh *Freiburger Zeitschrift für Theologie und Philosophie* (before 1914: *Jahrbuch für Philosophie und spekulative Theologie;* 1914–54: *DTh*), Fribourg.

Goyau G. Goyau, *L'Allemagne religieuse au XIXe siècle,* 4 vols., Paris 1905–09.

Gr *Gregorianum,* Rome 1920seqq.

Grabmann *G* M. Grabmann, *Die Geschichte der katholischen Theologie seit dem Ausgang der Väterzeit,* Freiburg i. Br. 1933.

GregMC *Gregorio XVI. Miscellanea commemorativa* (*Miscellanea historiae pontificiae* XIII/XIV), 2 vols., Rome 1958.

Grimaud L. Grimaud, *Histoire de la liberté d'enseignement en France,* 6 vols., Grenoble and Paris 1944–54.

GRM *Germanisch-Romanische Monatsschrift,* Heidelberg 1909–42 and 1951seqq.

Gurian W. Gurian, *Die politischen und sozialen Ideen des französischen Katholizismus 1789–1914,* Freiburg i. Br. 1929.

Hagen *R* A. Hagen, *Geschichte der Diözese Rottenburg,* 3 vols., I, Stuttgart 1957.

HAHR *Hispanic American Historical Review,* Durham (N.C.) 1918seqq.

Hajjar J. Hajjar, *Les chrétiennes uniates du Proche-Orient,* Paris 1962.

Hales *Pio Nono, A Study in European Politics and Religion in the 19th Century,* London 1954.

Heimbucher M. Heimbucher, *Die Orden und Kongregationen der katholischen Kirche,* 3 vols., Paderborn 1907–08.

Hermelink H. Hermelink, *Das Christentum in der Menschheitsgeschichte von der Französischen Revolution bis zur Gegenwart* I–III, Stuttgart and Tübingen 1951–55.

HistCathFr A. Latreille, J. R. Palanque, É. Delaruelle, and R. Rémond, *Histoire du catholicisme en France* III: *La période contemporaine,* Paris 1962.

HJ *Historisches Jahrbuch der Görres-Gesellschaft,* (Cologne 1880seqq.) Munich 1950seqq.

Hocedez E. Hocedez, *Histoire de la Théologie au XIXe siècle,* Brussels and Paris, I, 1948; II, 1952; III, 1947.

Hochland *Hochland,* Munich 1903seqq.

Holzapfel H. Holzapfel, *Handbuch der Geschichte des Franziskanerordens,* Freiburg i. Br. 1909.

HPBl *Historisch-politische Blätter für das katholische Deutschland,* F. Binder and G. Jochner, eds., 171 vols., Munich 1838–1923.

HRSt *Historical Records and Studies of the United States Catholic Historical Society,* Philadelphia 1884seqq.

HS *Hispania Sacra,* Madrid 1948seqq.

Hurter H. Hurter, *Nomenclator literarius theologiae catholicae,* 6 vols., Innsbruck 1903–13, F. Pangerl, ed.

IER *The Irish Ecclesiastical Record,* Dublin 1864seqq.

Irénikon *Irénikon,* Amay and Chevetogne 1926seqq.

JEH   *The Journal of Ecclesiastical History*, London 1950seqq.

Jemolo   A. C. Jemolo, *Chiesa e Stato in Italia negli ultimi cento anni*, Turin 1963.

JLW   *Jahrbuch für Liturgiewissenschaft*, Münster 1921–41 (now: *ALW*).

JP   *Jus pontificium de Propaganda fide, Pars I complectens Bullas, Brevia, Acta Sancta Sedis*, R. De Martinis, ed., 7 vols., Rome 1888–97.

Jürgensen   K. Jürgensen, *Lamennais und die Gestaltung des belgischen Staates. Der liberale Katholizismus in der Verfassungsbewegung des 19. Jahrhunderts*, Wiesbaden 1963.

Katholik   *Der Katholik*, Mainz 1821seqq.

KuD   *Kerygma und Dogma*, Göttingen 1955seqq.

Latourette, *Christianity*   K. S. Latourette, *Christianity in a Revolutionary Age. A History of Christianity in the Nineteenth and Twentieth Centuries*, 5 vols., New York 1958–62.

Latourette, *Expansion*   K. S. Latourette, *A History of the Expansion of Christianity*, 7 vols., New York and London 1937–45.

Le Bras S   G. Le Bras, *Études de sociologie religieuse*, 2 vols., Paris 1955–56.

Lecanuet   E. Lecanuet, *L'Église et l'État en France sous la Troisième République*, 4 vols., Paris 1907–30.

Leflon   J. Leflon, *La crise révolutionnaire 1789–1846* (*Histoire de l'Église depuis les origines jusqu'à nos jours* 20, A. Fliche and V. Martin, eds.) Paris 1949.

LJ   *Liturgisches Jahrbuch*, Münster 1951seqq.

Lösch   S. Lösch, *Döllinger und Frankreich. Eine geistige Allianz, 1823–1871*, Munich 1955.

LThK   *Lexikon für Theologie und Kirche*, Freiburg 1957–68.

Maaß   F. Maaß, *Der Josephinismus. Quellen zu seiner Geschichte in Österreich* I–V, Vienna 1951seqq. (*Fontes rerum Austriacarum* II/71–74).

MAH   *Mélanges d'archéologie et d'histoire*, Paris 1880seqq.

Mansi   J. D. Mansi, *Sacrorum conciliorum nova et amplissima collectio*, 31 vols., Florence and Venice 1757–98; reprinted and continued by L. Petit and J. B. Martin, eds., in 60 vols., Paris 1899–1927.

Mathew   D. Mathew, *Catholicism in England*, London 1936.

McAvoy   T. McAvoy, *A History of the Catholic Church in the United States*, Notre Dame 1969.

MCom   *Miscelánea Comillas*, Comillas/Santander 1943seqq.

MD   *Maison-Dieu*, Paris 1945seqq.

Mellor   A. Mellor, *Histoire de l'anticléricalisme français*, Paris 1966.

Mercati   A. Mercati, *Raccolta di Concordati su materie ecclesiastiche tra la Santa Sede e le autorità civili*, 2 vols., Rome 1919–54.

Meulemeester   M. de Meulemeester, *Bibliographie générale des écrivains rédemptoristes* I–III, Louvain 1933–39.

MF   *Miscellanea francescana*, Rome 1886seqq.

MH   *Missionalia Hispanica*

MIÖG   *Mitteilungen des Instituts für österreichische Geschichtsforschung*, (Innsbruck) Graz and Cologne 1880seqq.

MiscMercati   *Miscellanea Giovanni Mercati*, 6 vols., Rome 1946.

Mollat   G. Mollat, *La Question romaine de Pie VI à Pie XI*, Paris 1932.

Moroni   G. Moroni, *Dizionario di erudizione storico-ecclesiastica*, 103 vols., Venice 1840–61.

Mortier	A. Mortier, *Histoire des maîtres généraux de l'ordre des frères prêcheurs*, Paris 1903seqq.
MÖSTA	*Mitteilungen des Österreichischen Staatsarchivs*, Vienna 1948seqq.
MThZ	*Münchener Theologische Zeitschrift*, Munich 1950seqq.
NAG	*Nachrichten von der Akademie der Wissenschaften in Göttingen* (until 1940: *NGG*), Göttingen 1941seqq.
NDB	*Neue Deutsche Biographie*, Berlin 1953seqq.
NRTh	*Nouvelle Revue Théologique*, Tournai, Louvain and Paris 1849seqq.
NZM	*Neue Zeitschrift für Missionswissenschaft*, Beckenried 1945seqq.
ÖAKR	*Österreichisches Archiv für Kirchenrecht*, Vienna 1950seqq.
ÖBL	*Österreichisches Biographisches Lexikon*, Graz and Cologne 1954seqq.
OrChrP	*Orientalia Christiana periodica*, Rome 1935seqq.
Pastor	L. von Pastor, *Geschichte der Päpste seit dem Ausgang des Mittelalters*, 16 vols., Freiburg i. Br. 1885seqq.
Pouthas	C. Pouthas, *L'Église catholique de l'avènement de Pie VII à l'avènement de Pie IX* (Les Cours de Sorbonne), Paris 1945.
PrJ	*Preußische Jahrbücher*, Berlin 1858seqq.
PrOrChr	*Le Proche-Orient chrétien*, Jerusalem 1951seqq.
QLP	*Questions liturgiques et paroissiales*, Louvain 1921seqq.
RACHS	*Records of the American Catholic Historical Society*, Philadelphia 1884seqq.
RAM	*Revue d'ascétique et de mystique*, Toulouse 1920seqq.
Rémond	R. Rémond, *La Droite en France, de la Première Restauration à la Ve République*, Paris 1963.
RevSR	*Revue des Sciences Religieuses*, Strasbourg 1921seqq.
RF	*Razón y Fe*, Madrid 1901seqq.
RGB	*Revue générale belge*, Brussels 1945seqq.
RH	*Revue historique*, Paris 1876seqq.
RHE	*Revue d'histoire ecclésiastique*, Louvain 1900seqq.
RHEF	*Revue d'histoire de l'Église de France*, Paris 1910seqq.
RHLR	*Revue d'histoire et de littérature religieuse*, Paris 1896–1907.
RHM	*Revue d'histoire des missions*, Paris 1924seqq.
RHPhR	*Revue d'histoire et de philosophie religieuses*, Strasbourg 1921seqq.
RhVJBll	*Rheinische Vierteljahresblätter*, Bonn 1941seqq.
Rigault	G. Rigault, *Histoire générale de l'Institut des Frères des Écoles chrétiennes*, 9 vols., Paris 1936–53.
Ris	*Risorgimento*, Brussels 1958seqq.
ROC	*Revue de l'Orient chrétien*, Paris 1896seqq.
Rogier *KG*	*Geschichte der Kirche*, ed. by L. Rogier, R. Aubert, and D. Knowles, IV, Einsiedeln 1966.
Rogier, *KathHerleving*	L. Rogier, *Katholieke Herleving. Geschiedenis van Katholiek Nederland sinds 1851*, The Hague, 1956.
RömHM	*Römische Historische Mitteilungen*, Graz and Cologne 1958seqq.
Roskovany	A. de Roskovany, *Romanus Pontifex tamquam Primas Ecclesiae et Princeps civilis e monumentis omnium saeculorum demonstratus*, 20 vols., Nitra 1867–90.

RPol	*Review of Politics,* Notre Dame 1939seqq.
RQ	*Römische Quartalschrift für christliche Altertumskunde und für Kirchengeschichte,* Freiburg i. Br. 1887seqq.
RQH	*Revue des question historiques,* Paris 1866seqq.
RRosm	*Rivista Rosminiana,* Stresa 1906seqq.
RSIt	*Rivista storica Italiana,* Naples 1884seqq.
RSoc	*Recherches sociographiques,* Quebec 1960seqq.
RSPhTh	*Revue des sciences philosophiques et théologiques,* Paris 1907seqq.
RSR	*Recherches de science religieuse,* Paris 1910seqq.
RSTI	*Rivista di storia della Chiesa in Italia,* Rome 1947seqq.
RStRis	*Rassegna storica del Risorgimento,* Rome 1913seqq.
RStT	*Rassegna storica toscana,* Florence 1955seqq.

Saeculum	*Saeculum. Jahrbuch für Universalgeschichte,* Freiburg i. Br. 1950seqq.
Salvatorelli	L. Salvatorelli, *Chiesa e Stato dalla Rivoluzione francese ad oggi,* Florence 1955.
SC	*Scuola Cattolica,* Milan 1873seqq.
Scheffczyk	*Theologie in Aufbruch und Widerstreit. Die deutsche katholische Theologie im 19. Jahrhundert,* ed. by L. Scheffczyk, Bremen 1965.
Schmidlin *PG*	J. Schmidlin, *Papstgeschichte der neuesten Zeit* I–IV, Munich 1933 39.
Schmitz *GB*	P. Schmitz, *Histoire de l'ordre de Saint Benoît* IV and VII, Maredsous 1948 and 1956.
Schnabel *G*	F. Schnabel, *Deutsche Geschichte im 19. Jahrhundert,* Freiburg i. Br. I, 1948; II, 1949; III, 1954; IV 1955.
Scholastik	*Scholastik,* Freiburg i. Br. 1926seqq.
Schrörs, *Braun*	H. Schrörs, *Ein vergessener Führer aus der rheinischen Gestesgeschichte des 19. Jahrhunderts, Johann Wilhelm Joseph Braun,* Bonn 1925.
Schulte	J. F. von Schulte, *Geschichte der Quellen und der Literatur des kanonischen Rechts,* 3 vols., Stuttgart 1875–80.
SE	*Sacris Erudiri. Jaarboek voor Godsdienstwetenschapen,* Bruges 1948seqq.
Seppelt-Schwaiger	F. X. Seppelt, *Geschichte der Päpste von den Anfängen bis zur Mitte des 20. Jahrhunderts* I, II, IV, V, Leipzig 1931–41.
Simon, *Rencontres*	A. Simon, *Rencontres mennaisiennes en Belgique* (Académie royale de Belgique, Mémoires de la Classe des Lettres, LVI/3), Brussels 1963.
Simon, *Sterckx*	A. Simon, *Le cardinal Sterckx et son temps,* 2 vols., Wetteren 1950–51.
SM	*Studien und Mitteilungen aus dem Benediktiner- und Zisterzienserorden bzw. zur Geschichte des Benediktinerordens und seiner Zweige,* Munich 1880seqq.
Sommervogel	C. Sommervogel, *Bibliothèque de la Compagnie de Jésus* I–IX, Brussels and Paris 1890–1900; X (Supplements by E. M. Rivière), Toulouse 1911seqq.; XI (*History* by P. Bliard), Paris 1932.
SourcesHist.rel.Belg.	*Sources de l'histoire religieuse de la Belgique. Époque contemporaine. Colloque Bruxelles 1967* (Centre interuniversitaire d'histoire contemporaine, Cahiers 54), Louvain and Paris 1968.
SpAzLCIt	*Spiritualità e Azione del laicato cattolico italiano,* 2 vols. (Italia sacra 11/12), Padua 1969.
Spini	G. Spini, *Risorgimento e protestanti,* Naples 1956.
SPM	*Sacrum Poloniae Millenium,* Rome 1954.
StdZ	*Stimmen der Zeit* (before 1914: *Stimmen aus Maria-Laach*), Freiburg i. Br. 1871seqq.
StL	*Staatslexikon,* ed. by H. Sacher, Freiburg i. Br. 1926–32.
StMis	*Studia Missionalia,* Rome 1943seqq.

Streit   *Bibliotheca Missionum*, started by R. Streit, continued by J. Dindinger, (Münster and Aachen) Freiburg i. Br. 1916seqq.

StudFr   *Studi francescani*, Arezzo and Florence 1903seqq.

SZG   *Schweizerische Zeitschrift für Geschichte*, Zurich 1951seqq.

ThGl   *Theologie und Glaube*, Paderborn 1909seqq.

ThJ   *Theologische Jahrbücher*, Leipzig 1842seqq.

ThQ   *Theologische Quartalschrift*, Tübingen 1819seqq.; Stuttgart 1946seqq.

TThZ   *Trierer Theologische Zeitschrift* (until 1944: *Pastor Bonus*), Trier 1888seqq.

Villoslada   R. G. Villoslada, *Manual de historia de la Compañía de Jesús*, Madrid 1954.

Walz   A. Walz, *Compendium historiae Ordinis Praedicatorum*, Rome 1948.

Weill, *Cath. lib.*   G. Weill, *Histoire du catholicisme libéral en France 1828–1908*, Paris 1909

Weill, *Idée laïque*   G. Weill, *Histoire de l'idée laïque en France au XIXe siècle*, Paris 1929.

Winter, *Byzanz*   E. Winter, *Byzanz und Rom im Kampf um die Ukraine*, Leipzig 1942.

Winter, *Rußland*   E. Winter, *Rußland und das Papsttum* II: *Von der Aufklärung bis zur Oktoberrevolution*, Berlin 1961.

WiWei   *Wissenschaft und Weisheit*, Düsseldorf 1934seqq.

WZ   *Westfälische Zeitschrift. Zeitschrift für vaterländische Geschichte*, Münster 1838seqq.

ZAGV   *Zeitschrift des Aachener Geschichtsvereins*, Aachen 1879seqq.

ZBLG   *Zeitschrift für Bayerische Landesgeschichte*, Munich 1928seqq.

ZGObrh   *Zeitschrift für die Geschichte des Oberrheins*, Karlsruhe 1851seqq.

ZKG   *Zeitschrift für Kirchengeschichte*, (Gotha) Stuttgart 1876seqq.

ZKTh   *Zeitschrift für Katholische Theologie*, (Innsbruck) Vienna 1877seqq.

ZMR   *Zeitschrift für Missionswissenschaft und Religionswissenschaft* 34seqq., Münster 1950seqq. (*Zeitschrift für Missionswissenschaft* 1–17, Münster 1911–27; *Zeitschrift für Missionswissenschaft und Religionswissenschaft* 18–25, Münster 1928–35; *Zeitschrift für Missionswissenschaft*, 26–27, Münster 1935–37; *Missionswissenschaft und Religionswissenschaft* 28–33, Münster 1938–41, 1947–49).

ZRGG   *Zeitschrift für Religions- und Geistesgeschichte*, Marburg 1948seqq.

ZSKG   *Zeitschrift für schweizerische Kirchengeschichte*, (Stans) Fribourg 1907seqq.

PART ONE

Between the Revolutions of 1830 and 1848

The Continuation of Catholic Renewal in Europe

CHAPTER 1

The Progress of Ultramontanism and the Growth of the International Orders

Progress of Ultramontanism

The fifteen years of the pontificate of Gregory XVI saw significant steps toward the victory of ultramontanism,[1] and the weakening of ecclesiastical influence upon civil society turned the Church inward. During the Restoration period, the influence of these internal forces was already noticeable throughout Europe and in particular in France and Germany. From this time forward, the ultramontane movement enjoyed increasing encouragement even from Rome itself.

Resistance to the interference of the Roman Curia in the life of the national Churches continued far beyond the middle of the century, but increasingly it met with countervailing opinion. Many of the scholars and theologians in England, such as historian J. Lingard, archeologist M. A. Tierney, liturgist D. Rock,[2] and E. Cox, the director of the seminary of Saint Edmund's, clung fiercely to the concept of the national Church and rejected new customs coming from Italy and the doctrine of the personal infallibility of the Pope. Wiseman, on the other hand, supported by the first generation of liberal Catholics and Italian missionaries, developed contacts with Rome and favored the "new" continental exercises of piety. Thus the situation gradually changed. In Piedmont, where Josephinistic tendencies were still very much alive in the theological departments and seminaries, a number of young clergymen and militant Catholics began to charge that such tendencies consti-

---

[1] In contrast to Pius VII, who was trained in a slightly Jansenist environment, Mauro Cappellari became an adherent of the strictest ultramontanism. His *Trionfo della Santa Sede,* written in 1799, articulated the strictly papalist point of view according to which the entire church is subjected to the Pope without any collegial aspects (see Y. Congar, *L'ecclésiologie au XIXe siècle,* 92f., 96ff.). Reissued after the elevation of its author to Pope, the book was translated into French and German in 1833 and contributed to the spread of ultramontane ideas among the clergy.

[2] *The Church of Our Fathers,* 3 vol. (1849–53).

tuted an expression of the despised Austrian influence and to represent an orientation toward Rome as an affirmation of membership in the Italian nation.

After 1830, true Gallicanism had few defenders in France. Relations between the bishops and the Holy See, however, remained at best tentative. That part of the clergy which had not been won by Lamennais continued to maintain the position of the bishop within the hierarchy as well as to adhere to special ecclesiastical customs, particularly in the liturgical and canonical areas. In order to promote unifying elements with Rome, Lamennais's former adherents used this particularism in the field of Church discipline to complain about what they not unjustifiably regarded as functional Gallicanism. It was in this atmosphere, then, that during the July Monarchy the ultramontane campaign gained ground quickly and simultaneously at many different levels and in many different areas.

Abbé Combalot,[3] a diocesan missionary, made himself the champion of Roman ideas among the lower clergy. On the other hand, the campaign for a Roman liturgy,[4] led by Dom Guéranger with the support of some young priests, was directed chiefly against the Gallican sympathies still harbored by some members of the upper clergy. The fact that even before 1848 many dioceses rejected modern French liturgies seemed to be a victory for ultramontanism over ecclesiastical particularism. In the years between 1842 and 1849, Abbé Rohrbacher[5] realized his intention to revise Fleury's *Histoire ecclésiastique* in an ultramontane direction for use by the young generation of clerics. Assisted by Father Gaultier,[6] a scholarly member of the Congregation of the Holy Spirit, he did so with more good intention than critical acumen. Rohrbacher's cell was the "Roman salon of Paris," and his library well represented that Gallican position. Two of the most zealous defenders of the ultramontane

---

[3] Théodore Combalot (1797–1873), until 1833 one of the strongest supporters of Lamennais's movement in southeastern France, won great influence as a retreat master (biography by Ricard [Paris 1891]).

[4] On Dom Guéranger and the founding of Solesmes, see below, n. 17. Guéranger was neither the first nor the only one demanding a return to the Roman liturgy, but only after the publication of volume 2 of his *Institutions liturgique* (1842) did the movement go beyond the circle of a few intimates. Guéranger bitterly opposed what he called the "antiliturgical heresy." More than sixty bishops protested his attack, complaining about the tone and attitude of Lamennais's school and his lack of respect for the bishops.

[5] Concerning René-François Rohrbacher (1789–1856), the former companion of Lamennais and professor at the seminary of Nancy as well as author of a *Histoire de l'Eglise* in 28 volumes, see A. Ricard, *Gerbet, Salinis et Rohrbacher* (Paris 1886), 269–365.

[6] *Notice sur le R. P. Gaultier* (Paris, n.d.). On Gaultier's circle, see also F. Cabrol, *Le cardinal Pitra*, 205f.

movement in the French episcopate, Monsignor Gousset and Monsignor Parisis, stayed with him on the occasion of their journey to Paris. Monsignor Gousset's efforts were directed chiefly toward making theological principles clearer to the common man. Monsignor Parisis promoted the desire of the Holy See that the French dioceses give up their customary privileges and regularly consult the Roman congregations in matters of religion and church discipline; a position which caused great dismay on the part of those who had long been opposed to the intervention of the Curia in the internal affairs of France.

Many factors worked in support of the ultramontane campaign. Loyalty to the monarchy, that very foundation of Gallicanism, had lost much of its meaning with the fall of the Bourbons, and the anticlericalism of the July Monarchy was an added reason to look for support from Rome. In addition, the lethargy of certain bishops in the struggle for educational freedom also favored the Roman position. Montalembert and his friends won the Catholic masses to ultramontanism with the aid of the newspaper *L'Univers*. From this time on ultramontanism found enthusiastic support among the elite of French laymen. Another decisive factor was that the lower clergy disliked accepting the unlimited power of the bishops and desired nothing more than to have the Roman congregations provide protection against episcopal capriciousness. Even the bishops recognized the de facto privilege of the Holy See to intervene in doctrinary or disciplinary questions concerning the Church of France. This was particularly evident when they asked the Pope to intervene against Lamennais. The nunciature intervened ever more openly. While Monsignor Garibaldi, who was interested in keeping relations with the government as good as possible, considered it best to let Gallicanism die out by itself, his successor, Fornari, supported the militant ultramontanes fully even when their conduct was questionable. Not satisfied with opposing the demands of some bishops for independence in the liturgical and canonical areas, Fornari supported the vehement reactions which these demands evoked in many priests or monks. This was especially evident with regard to some of the former students of Lamennais, who adopted an arrogant stance toward the bishops whom they suspected of moderation.

In 1844, Montalembert could announce: "I would wager that among the eighty French bishops there are not three supporters of the Four Articles." The general approval which met the condemnation of the *Manuel de droit ecclésiastique* by Dupin in 1845 proved that political Gallicanism was completely discredited in France. The changes in the church treatise used at this time by Saint Sulpice,[7] which was especially

---

[7] De Montclos, 40–58; A. Castellani, *Il b. Leonardo Murialdo* (Turin 1966), 769–74; M. de Hédouville, *Monseigneur de Ségur* (Paris 1957), 177–207.

strongly tied to the traditions of the old France, as well as the revisions of the commonly used catechisms and handbooks[8] were also symptomatic of the decline of theological Gallicanism. In practice, however, moderate Gallicanism continued to enjoy considerable sympathy. Several pastoral letters lauding Bossuet, the attitude of Monsignor Affre to the exemption of the cloistered clergy, and the position of the bishops in the conflict with Dom Guéranger over the introduction of the Roman liturgy witness areas of continuing Gallican commitment. Prelates reacting in this fashion were only a minority by the end of Gregory's pontificate and were regarded with mistrust by the younger clergy. The sympathies of a number of older priests, however, remained attached to the traditions of the old French clergy and its specific concepts of hierarchy, liturgy, and piety. These advocates became the most serious obstacle to the complete victory of Roman ideas in France, but the group lacked a cohesive core. In this respect the failure to reestablish the old theological departments destroyed by the Revolution was of great significance; had they succeeded, the encounter with the history of Christian antiquity could have resulted in a concept of the church according to the Gallican model.

In Germany, an analogous but much slower development took place. Here there was much more resistance than in France. Although Liebermann, in his textbook in 1831, modified the views of the Pope in a more Roman direction, Klee, a teacher of dogmatics in Bonn, presented papal infallibility as "highly deserving of respect," and G. Phillips, professor of canon law in Munich, defended with enthusiasm the ideal of the greatest possible centralization of the Church around the Roman Curia. Many theologians, however, continued to defend a moderate episcopalism, which in their eyes seemed to correspond better to the organization of the old Church as well as to the German concept of authority and society. They viewed this position as less influenced by Roman law and thus more patriarchal and corporative. They saw the relationship between the Pope and the bishops from the organic perspective of the Holy Roman Empire, where sovereign and feudal lords cooperated together in the Diet. In addition, a large number of bishops continued to act independently from the Roman congregations. Knowing from experience that the congregations generally failed to take into account the true situation in the Protestant areas, they tried to reserve decisions for themselves in cases which the Holy See regarded as its province. This was true the more so because the frequent appeals

---

[8] See the tendentiously interpreted information supplied by E. Michaud, *De la falsification des catéchismes français et de manuels de théologie par le parti romaniste* (Paris 1872). Among others, the *Institutiones thelogicae* were corrected by Bailly in 1842.

to Rome were often made by men notable for neither intelligence nor moderation. Such men as Binterim, who once had been regarded as a champion of Catholic renewal in Germany,[9] denounced to Rome without consideration of justice and truth all those with whom they disagreed.

Many of the opponents of the planned centralization of Catholic life in the Roman Curia resisted this development for various reasons both theoretical and practical. They were outmaneuvered, however, by those who believed that this resistance gave aid to a number of fearful and neglectful ecclesiastics and to governments that wanted to prevent the escape of the Church from their tutelage. Thus, as it had happened in France, albeit with a ten-year delay, a genuine ultramontane party was formed in Germany to which clerics as well as such laymen as Buß and Andlaw could belong. The spiritual center of this party was at Mainz, where the influence of Maistre and Lamennais[10] joined with a development arising from the Catholic Action. The leaders at Mainz, trailblazing in the area of the apostolate and clearly aware of the demands of the modern world, sensed that traditional ecclesiastical particularism was no longer tenable in a world which ignored national borders. They were convinced that the destructive power of the antireligious forces could be countered only through a mobilization of the masses, who were guided strictly and uniformly. Only the Holy See was capable of providing this guidance. As Schnabel very astutely demonstrated, this was less a case of national opposition between the Germanic spirit and the Roman influence than a conflict of generations. Under the pressure of increasingly complex problems, Germany was developing from the collegiate and corporative system of the Old Regime toward modern centralization.

Strengthened by the so-called "Germanists," the former students of the German College in Rome which was reopened in 1824, this ultramontane party published its ideas in *Der Katholik* and experienced an increase of its reputation as a result of two circumstances. They gained the trust of the masses because the ultramontane bishops and priests successfully intervened with Protestant governments for greater religious freedom of the Catholics. The opponents of the ultramontanes, sympathizing with the doctrines of Hermes, lost their standing in the eyes of the faithful when these doctrines, after years of discussion, were

---

[9] See his biography by C. Schoenig, *A.J. Binterim (1779–1855) als Kirchenpolitiker und Gelehrter* (Düsseldorf 1933), which corrects the picture.

[10] One of the most important links was the Alsatian Räß, professor of dogmatics in Mainz before he became Superior of the seminary of Strasbourg in 1829. But he was not the only one. In *Die Gemeinsamkeit der Rechte,* whose first volume appeared in 1847, Buß cited several French writings, especially those by Montalembert.

finally condemned. Thus, the movement spread and new centers were formed. In Cologne a center formed around Archbishop Geissel, who was inspired by the principles which had been taught to him at the seminary of Mainz, and in Speyer, Bishop Weis, the successor to Geissel in 1841, also formed a center in the spirit of Mainz. In Munich, also in 1841, the Germanist Karl August von Reisach, a personal friend of Cardinal Cappellari, became coadjutor and for twenty years remained one of the most active representatives of Roman influence in southern Germany. He was skillfully supported by Monsignor Viale-Prela, nuncio to Vienna.

In Austria ultramontanism developed even more slowly than in Germany. It is characteristic of the Austrian movement that as late as 1842, when four bishops were consulted whether to lift the ban of 1781 forbidding seminarists to study in Rome, two were opposed to a change and another had serious objections.[11] But in Austria also the consciousness of the Church awakened, and the opposition of the militant Catholics, even though they were still in a minority, began to shake the foundations of the Josephinist system. A decision in 1833, probably made through the intervention of Bishop Wagner of Sankt Pölten directly with the Emperor, to withdraw from use in the educational system the textbooks of canon law and church history which had been placed on the Index in 1820, was an almost revolutionary turning point. A few years later the Austrian ambassador drew Metternich's attention to the growing threat to Austrian influence in Rome. He pointed out that the civil service in Vienna was determined to curtail the relations between the Holy See and the Church of Austria at a time when, as the Curia emphasized at every opportunity, France was in the process of relinquishing this antiquated system.

Rome, aware of its growing strength, no longer hesitated to influence and encourage firmly a movement which pointed both faithful and clergy toward the center of Catholicism. At times, as it did in Austria, Rome attempted to loosen the regalistic policies of governments; at other times, the nuncios supported the work of the ultramontane clerics and tried to increase the number of ultramontane seminarists at Roman colleges. In order to break down resistance, and to encourage the efforts of some and to hasten the development of others, a systematic policy was employed with great skill. This policy included direct and indirect pressure with a scale of finely differentiated expressions and briefs of approval and disapproval, tailored in each case to the special circumstances. It also included the awarding of benefices as well as the delay of

[11] Maaß op. cit., 673f.

honors and rewards. Rome's policy was developed by Pius IX, but it was inaugurated during the last years of Gregory XVI with increasing benefit.

The Large Orders

The Generals of the large international orders had since the Middle Ages had their seat in Rome and actively had assisted in the Roman centralization as well as provided able members for the congregations.[12] Even if the mendicant orders recuperated only slowly and played only a secondary role in this connection, the pontificate of Gregory XVI was marked by a triple phenomenon whose consequences were of significance for the efficiency of the Holy See during subsequent pontificates. It consisted of the rapid growth of the Society of Jesus, the new impulse which the Dominicans received from Lacordaire, and the founding of the Benedictine congregation in France by Dom Guéranger.

Once the Society of Jesus had overcome its developmental crisis of the first decade, it experienced a remarkable growth under the generalate of the Dutchman Philipp Roothaan[13] (1829–53). Roothaan was able to skillfully employ his great influence on Gregory XVI for the benefit of his order, while also fashioning it into a marvellously reliable instrument in the service of Roman unity and ultramontane ideals. In a very short time the Jesuits grew in numbers from 2,137 in 1830 to 4,757 in 1847. They reestablished their former provinces: in 1831 in Piedmont, in 1832 in Belgium, in 1833 in America, in 1836 a second house in France, and in 1846 in Austria. They exerted growing influence upon the direction of ecclesiastical studies and piety in these countries in a post-Tridentine sense, that is, contrary to the spirit of the eighteenth century. In the Roman congregations they also gradually acquired a position which, as a consequence of the decline of the mendicant orders, soon surpassed their position in the Old Regime; a condition which gave rise to complaints even in Rome. Father Roothaan also urged the Jesuits in 1833 to devote themselves to missions among the heathens as they had done under the Old Regime. Thus, to the old missions in India and the Missouri region, there were added within a few years missions in Bengal (1834), Madeira and Argentina (1836), Jamaica (1837), China, Algeria, and the Rocky Mountains (1840), Australia (1849), and California and Guatemala (1851). In 1851, there

---

[12] Concerning the damaging consequences for the Holy See of the crisis which the orders experienced since the end of the eighteenth century, see the letter by Lambruschini of 6 July 1829, quoted by L. Manzini, *Lambruschini* (Vatican City 1960), 151.
[13] On his election, see P. Grootens in *AHSI* 33 (1964), 235–68.

were 975 Jesuits active in mission work, a fifth of the total membership of the society.

Father Roothaan provided pious as well as skillful leadership for the society. He has been called its "second founder." Systematically promoting the external development of his order and adapting (with limited success) the *Ratio studiorum* (1822) to the new conditions, he endeavored at the same time to intensify the order's internal life. He strove to reawaken in it the full spirit of its founder. He interpreted the spirit more narrowly, however, by placing emphasis more upon ascetic exercises than on mystical enthusiasm. Roothaan saw to it that the two years of the novitiate and the third year (terciate) were served under normal conditions. Beginning in 1832, he convened a meeting of all procurator generals regularly every three years in order to achieve a strict observance of the rules. More frequently than any other general before him, Roothaan directed letters to all members of the society in order to keep awake in them the religious spirit peculiar to the Jesuits.

But the remarkable successes which the Society of Jesus experienced within only a few years were not without repercussions. Some bishops, especially in Belgium, regarded the society as too aggressive. The liberals in particular were uncomfortable with their rapid rise. What appeared to many as the Jesuits' tendency "to confuse revolutionary disorder with the inevitable tendency of the modern world to replace absolute monarchy with the principle and practice of national sovereignty" (Montalembert) provided their enemies with an easy pretext to incite the public against them. In 1834 the Jesuits again were expelled from Spain and Portugal. In 1845 the order experienced a general attack. In France this occurred upon the occasion of the controversy concerning freedom of education, but with very limited practical results. In Switzerland the radicals used Jesuit mistakes in the Wallis to persuade the Swiss Diet to expel them from the whole of Switzerland (3 September 1847) and then to confirm this ban in a separate article of the new constitution drawn after the end of the Sonderbund War. In Italy the accusation against the order was that it was in league with Austria and constituted an obstacle to a harmony between religion and modern society. This accusation was formulated by V. Gioberti in his *Il Gesuita moderno* (1847). Finally, although the order retained fervent adherents, the Jesuits were expelled from the Kingdom of Naples, from Piedmont, and, at the beginning of 1848, from the Papal State. But the storm was only of short duration; favored by the conservative reaction following the crisis of 1848, the progress of the Society of Jesus was even more rapid than before.

The mendicant orders, however, only slowly recovered from the crisis which had overcome them at the end of the eighteenth century. This was especially true because the Iberian peninsula, in which they had been able to retain their strong position,[14] was now being shaken by the secularizations being conducted by Madrid and Lisbon between 1833 and 1837. The Augustinian Hermits disappeared forever from Portugal, where they once had possessed about fifty monasteries. In Spain they only retained the missionary college of Valladolid.

The Franciscans, counting about ten thousand members in Spain, were reduced to a few hundred; this enabled the Italians once again to regain their leading position in the order, the more so as the monasteries of Poland and Russia, having escaped the dissolution measures of 1831, suffered from the decline to which the tsarist government condemned them. The development of the order in the German-speaking and Anglo-Saxon countries became significant only in the second half of the century.

The Dominicans were reduced in numbers in Mexico, Russia, Portugal, Cuba, and especially Spain, where 221 monasteries were dissolved. A number of monks found refuge in the missions in the Far East, and the seminary of Ocana, their source of growth, remained open. Even the provinces of Italy, constituting 40 percent of the membership of the order,[15] did not display great vitality. But under the pontificate of Gregory XVI a change of fortunes occurred. In 1838, Abbé Lacordaire,[16] who had received great acclaim from the students of Paris as a result of his Lenten sermons at Notre-Dame, announced his intention to reestablish the order in France. His objective was a diverse intellectual apostolate in keeping with the movement of rejuvenation started by Lamennais and the Congregation of Saint Peter. Lacordaire envisioned sermons in town and country, the instruction of the young, and, in keeping with the temper of the time, the writing of religious and profane tracts from an apologetic perspective. After contacting Master General Ancaroni, Lacordaire published his *Mémoire pour le rétablissement en France des Frères Prêcheurs,* (7 March 1839), appealing to the

---

[14] At least quantitatively. Immediately before the catastrophe, Gregory XVI in June 1833 had asked the nuncio in Madrid to undertake the very necessary reform of the discipline in the Spanish monasteries and convents after the mode of election of their higher superiors had been changed.

[15] In 1844, of 4,562 Dominicans 1,709 were in Italy (and Malta), 1,048 in Spain and the Philippines, 709 in Russia, and 626 in Latin America (Walz, 576).

[16] On Henri Lacordaire (1802–61), Lamennais's supporter in the campaign of *L'Avenir,* see the biographies by B. Chocarne (2 vols., Paris 1866), T. Foisset (2 vols., Paris 1870), P. Baron, *La jeunesse de Lacordaire* (Paris 1961; until 1830), and *Le testament du Père Lacordaire,* ed. by C. de Montalembert (Paris 1870; autobiography to 1851). Complementing bibliography: *Catholicisme* VI, 1572. Works: *Oeuvres complètes du R. P. H.-D. Lacordaire* (9 vol., Paris 1911–12), and *Lacordaire journaliste (1830–48),* ed. by P. Fesch (Paris 1897).

country for freedom for the orders. He finished his novitiate in Italy and, armed with papal encouragement, returned to France, where the government, after some hesitation, treated him with benign neutrality. In 1850 he had a sufficient number of adherents to enable him to establish a French Dominican province. In the same year, one of Lacordaire's companions, Alexander Jandel, was appointed Vicar General by Pius IX (he became Master General in 1855), with the charge of reorganizing the order.

Another French initiative in the second half of the century led to an almost simultaneous rejuvenation of the Benedictine order, an event which met with a certain amount of resistance by the Curia, but eventually was supported by Gregory XVI. Moved by a romantic longing for the medieval past and the desire of Lamennais to reestablish the centers of cloistered scholarship so lacking in postrevolutionary France, Prosper Guéranger,[17] together with three companions, ignored all legal hindrances and settled in the former priorate of Solesmes. In 1837 the Pope confirmed Solesmes as an abbey and recognized it as a focal point for a new Congregation of France. The constitutions approved by the Pope were essentially similar to those of the Maurists. Only on two points did Dom Guéranger go back to the old tradition which had been abandoned almost everywhere else: these were the autonomy of each house and the appointment of abbots for life, a request approved by Rome only after long hesitation. These positions, as paradoxical as they may seem, did not prevent him from becoming one of the strongest proponents of liturgical centralization and the most extreme ultramontane theses. Dom Guéranger had to overcome numerous difficulties: distrust because of his earlier connection with Lamennais and because of his vocal support of the ultramontane movement; the enmity of the bishop of Le Mans against the monastic exemption; repeated financial worries; and the internal disputes among his students, which were aggravated by his administrative mistakes. But Dom Guéranger's persistence succeeded in overcoming these obstacles. His abbey of Solesmes, in spite of its moderate size, became a beacon of influence toward a return to the traditions of the past, an influence which was felt during the subsequent decades throughout the various branches of the Benedictine family. Of course, such a tradition contained the danger of artificially

[17] Concerning the very controversial personality of Dom Guéranger, the panegyrical but well-documented biography by P. M. Delatte, *Dom Guéranger, Abbé de Solesmes* (2 vols., Paris 1909–10) was complemented critically by E. Sevrin, *Dom Guéranger et Lamennais* (Paris 1933) and A. Ledru, *Dom Guéranger et Monseigneur Bouvier* (Paris 1911). He had great faults (narrow, combatant, excessive spirit, lack of critical sense), but his indomitable energy enabled him to effect lasting changes in many different areas. Sevrin, who otherwise is very critical of him, is of the opinion that except for Lamennais no one else had a greater effect on the Catholic life of his time.

reawakening a monastic life which had been created in a social and economic context totally different from a Europe in the process of developing an industrial society.

It was precisely this effort to meet the religious needs of a changing society which explains the success of the congregations devoted to education and the care of the sick. The educational congregations, in particular, experienced a marked revival during the course of the first decades of the century. Old congregations like the Daughters of Charity, whose number between 1807 and 1849 increased from 1,600 to 1,800, experienced a new bloom. Many new congregations were founded also: in 1830, the Vincentian Brothers of Abbé Glorieux; in 1839, the Brothers of Our Lady of Mercy of Monsignor Scheppers in Belgium; in 1832, the Sisters of Charity of Lovere of Saint Bartolomea Capitanio and in 1833, the Sisters of Providence of Rosmini in Italy. Many more followed, among them, in 1840, the Brothers of the Immaculate Conception; in 1844, the Brothers of Our Lady of Mercy in the Netherlands; in 1841, the Little Sisters of the Poor of Jeanne Jugan; and in 1849, the Sisters of the Most Holy Savior, the so-called Niederbronn Sisters, in France. The growth of these congregations contributed its part to the progress of Roman centralization. While under the Old Regime each convent and numerous smaller congregations founded during the first quarter of the century remained autonomous and subject only to the local bishop, Rome now encouraged the tendency to gather the novices and concentrate the members under the authority of a General Superior. It was an authority which, in spite of the protests of the diocesan bishops, frequently resulted in liberation from the supervision of the bishops and in direct submission to the authority of the Congregation of Bishops and Orders in Rome.[18] This congregation, aware of the great dissimilarity of objectives and local conditions, very carefully refrained from forcing a uniform type of constitution upon the smaller congregations and convents, but left to each the formulation of its rules, as long as it could control them and suggest changes. Thus, there gradually came into being a new canon of members of orders, codified only much later, whose development after the second quarter of the nineteenth century occurred under the vigilant control of Rome. On the other hand, the increasingly important role assigned to the superiors of these new congregations in comparison to that of their ordinary members favored the development of a mentality which facilitated the progress of ultramontanism by placing emphasis more on authority and obedience than on collegial responsibility.

[18] See F. Callahan, *The Centralization of Government in Pontifical Institutes of Women* (Rome 1948), 48–62.

CHAPTER 2

Old and New in Pastoral Care and Moral Theology

The Modernization of Ecclesiastical Institutions

Historians have noted the lasting effect of Napoleonic institutions in a large part of Europe: wherever the French introduced them, they were generally retained, and occasionally they were imitated even in countries which did not experience any French occupation. This development was nothing more than the legal recognition of an irreversible economic and social evolution. The development in the ecclesiastical area was similar. Gradually the profound changes resulting from the nationalization of the estates of the Church and from the concordat of 1801 spread. The concordat turned the bishop into a "violet prefect." Geissel in the Rhineland, Sterckx in Belgium, and Mathieu and Bonald in France were characteristic of the new bishop's generation. These bishops had come to acknowledge that the restoration of disturbed Catholic life and the increasing complexity of problems needing solution demanded much more in the way of organization and administrative work than had been the case during the Old Regime. Clearly cognizant of their episcopal authority as it had been determined by Napoleon's Organic Articles, they were eager to systematically guide the pastoral activity of their priests. Abbé Combalot, contemporary witness of this change of the episcopal office into a centralized and bureaucratized ecclesiastical activity, bitterly suggested the alteration of the phrase used in the ordination of bishops from "Accipe baculum pastorale" into "Accipe calamum administrativum, ut possis scribere, scribere scribere usque in sempiternum et ultra."

In parallel fashion, the situation of the lower clergy also changed fundamentally. The priest without a precisely defined task became a rarity, in contrast to their high numbers under the Old Regime. The decline occurred less rapidly in the southern countries, where there were still too many clergy. Some of the priests continued to exercise their apostolate on the fringes of the diocesan clergy as preachers and private or public teachers. But most of them were now employed in the incumbency, where they began to constitute a parish clergy whose social status completely changed within a few years. Instead of receiving income from a benefice, the clergy in most countries were paid by the state. At the same time they were to a high degree exposed to the capriciousness of the bishops. Indeed, officialities and diocesan courts frequently played a much less distinctive role than at the time of the Old

Regime, and in many countries most of the pastors had to endure being transferred against their will from one parish to another. In Austria, Bavaria, and southern Europe the obligation of advertising vacant positions continued and the canonical principle of being irremovable remained. Some bishops in Spain and Italy circumvented this rule, however, by declaring that they were the only irremovable pastors. Geissel managed to persuade the Prussian government to accept the removability of parish priests which had been introduced in France and Belgium with the concordat of 1801.[1] This facilitated control of the administration of the parishes, but the system also gave rise to abuses which—especially in France—led to serious discontent. Only a few bishops, like Monsignor Sibour, the bishop of Digne, were interested (from a collegial point of view) in creating safeguards for their priests.[2] By the middle of the century, a few bishops began to establish pension funds for their old priests.

The chapters also lost much of their independence and importance. Their members, personally selected by the bishop from the diocesan curia officials, were only subordinates and did not have the faintest intention of risking a conflict with their superiors. Besides, the tasks once carried out by the canons were more and more assumed by the secretaries, who, in conjunction with the vicars general, became the real assistants of the bishops.

Furthermore, the bishop, whose jurisdiction over his clergy was so strongly expanded, to an increasing degree was elected without any participation of the clergy. The concordats of the early nineteenth century generally granted the right of nomination to the governments, whose choice ordinarily was more influenced by administrative than by pastoral criteria. Suggestions by Rosmini in Italy (in his *Cinque piaghe*) or Affre in 1848 in France to change this procedure fell on deaf ears in the Roman Curia.[3] In countries like the United States or Belgium,[4] where the governments were not interested in participating, the bishops selected the nominees without consulting the priests of the diocese in question. And even where, such as in parts of Germany or Switzerland, a chapter election, or, as in Ireland, a limited participation of the clergy was retained, the Holy See gradually took such suggestions less into account, a practice which was increasingly adopted after the middle of

---

[1] See *DDC* I, 492–500; also IV, 895–96.
[2] His *Institutions diocésaines* (2 vols. [Paris 1845–48]; see Montclos, 246 and 251, n. 4) found only a slight echo among the episcopate.
[3] See G. Martina in *RRosm* 62 (1968), 384–409, especially 394–98.
[4] Concerning the United States, see *ColLac* III, 47–48, 153 (decrees of 16 June 1834 and 10 August 1850); concerning Belgium, see Simon, *Sterckx* II, 280–90.

the century.[5] It must be said, however, that Rome generally chose genuine pastors from all walks of life. Yet the weight of the past was such, especially in countries where a violent break with the Old Regime had not occurred, that the upper clergy was more concerned with the sensibilities of the governing class than with those of the common people. Still, in fulfilling its pastoral obligations, the upper clergy remained interested in a limited independence from state officials. The bishops were also aware of the necessity to coordinate their actions with respect to the governments and their activity on the pastoral level. For this reason they attempted to revive the old practice of synods, which had fallen out of use because of the suspicion by the states and the Roman Curia. The Organic Articles denied the French bishops any collective action, and only after the revolution of 1848 was it possible for the first provincial councils to meet again. On the other hand, the primate of Hungary as early as 1822 called a national council at Bratislava, and the American bishops regularly held their councils at Baltimore. Other episcopates preferred the more subtle formula of informal annual gatherings. This was the case with the Irish bishops after the emancipation of 1829 and the Belgian bishops after independence. The German bishops followed this example in 1848.[6]

The Methods of Catechetical Instruction

The transformations at the end of the eighteenth century occasioned profound and lasting changes not only in the area of institutions, but also in the various aspects of pastoral care. Added to them were the influences of the new currents of thought. This explains why the catechism, especially in the German states and in France, became the object of several revival efforts.[7]

The introduction of compulsory education in Germany resulted in the transfer of catechetical instruction from the Church to the school. While this made it possible to devote more time to religious instruction, it changed this instruction to nothing more than another academic subject which was taught in a profane environment. Thus there was the danger of infection by the intellectualism and naturalism prevailing in the atmosphere of the Enlightenment. But it was the influence of the

[5] See, for example, J. H. Whyte, "The Appointment of the Catholic Bishops in 19th Century Ireland," *CHR* 48 (1962–63), 12–32.
[6] R. Lill, *Die ersten deutschen Bischofskonferenzen* (Freiburg i. Br. 1964), 5–8. See also A. Simon, *Réunions des évêques de Belgique* (Louvain 1960); J. Ahern in *IER* 75 (1951), 385–403, 78 (1952), 1–20.
[7] In other countries there were only a few publications on the question of catechisms before the middle of the century. In Italy several catechisms were placed on the Index in 1817 (see H. Reusch, *Der Index* [Bonn 1885], 1056).

16

Enlightenment which caused educators to include biblical history in catechetical instruction and to adopt the Socratic method in order to accommodate themselves to the intellectual receptivity of the children. This method avoided the need to introduce concepts which had not been explained properly before, but it also held the danger of overlooking the transcendental character of God's word. The consequence was that at the beginning of the nineteenth century the dogmatic substance of ecclesiastical doctrine was almost eliminated from many catechisms, which were governed by moralism and more directed toward man than toward the gospels. During the first half of the century there was a reaction which attempted to deepen and to evolve the valuable impulses of the Enlightenment, but to exclude a too rationalistic way of thinking. The first to choose this path was Bernard Overberg from Westphalia. His main works (published in 1804), the *Katechismus* and the *Christ-katholische Religionshandbuch,* were used for decades in the dioceses of northern Germany and in 1824 were adopted by Vienna and translated into Dutch. His *Biblische Geschichte* (1799) underwent several revisions in almost one hundred editions.[8] The largest influence on the overcoming of the Enlightenment without discarding its positive elements was exercised by Johann Michael Sailer. He shared the interest of the people of his time in all aspects of education and emphatically underscored the importance of the personality of the catechist by pointing out that not even the best instruction book could replace a pious and dedicated teacher. More than Overberg he was also concerned with the educational content of the catechism, gave it a stronger biblical and dogmatic foundation, and demanded that it be concerned with the message of salvation.

In Austria the legal situation of the state before the signing of the concordat in 1855 made it difficult to replace the official catechism of 1777. But efforts were made on the methodological level. Galura, one of the pioneers of modern catechetical revision, urged the use of biblical stories and emphasized the necessity of orienting religious instruction toward the idea of God's empire.[9] Milde, the future archbishop of Vienna, very much concerned with the catechetical education of his clergy, emphasized psychological aspects in his *Lehrbuch der allgemeinen Erziehungslehre* (1811–13). Archbishop Gruber of Salzburg in the catechetical instructions for his clergy *(Praktisches Handbuch der Katechetik,* 2 vols. [Salzburg 1832–34]), inspired by Augustine's *De catechizandis rudibus,* exhorted the catechists to present themselves to the children as the deputies of God. In contrast to the Socratic method of the Enlightenment the catechists were to act as messengers of God,

[8] W. Sahner, *Overberg als Pädagoge und Katechet* (Gelsenkirchen 1949).
[9] J. Hemlein, *B. Galuras Beitrag zur Erneuerung der Kerygmatik* (Freiburg i. Br. 1952).

and he demanded that catechesis transmit more than pure knowledge in order to bring to full bloom in the child the three chief Christian virtues.[10]

In Germany the thoughts of Sailer and others were translated into practice by Christoph Schmid. He was the author of catechisms (1801, 1836, 1844–45) and a *Biblische Geschichte*, which was in use for several generations. He also wrote Catholic children's literature with edifying stories in order to point out the hand of God in man's life.[11] Sailer's ideas were most strongly employed by J. B. Hirscher.[12] From 1817 to 1863 Hirscher was professor of pastoral and moral theology, first in Tübingen, then in Freiburg. He criticized as too abstract the catechisms inherited from the Counter-Reformation, such as the so-called *Mainz Catechism,* adapted from the French by Räß and Weis, and demanded a greater consideration of the emotional side of the child. He emphasized as chief goal of catechesis the religious instruction and not the transmittal of an overly large body of knowledge. Throughout his entire life he urged that Christianity be presented as a message of salvation, as a doctrine of God's realm emerging from the biblical stories. He attempted to apply his principles in practical terms and for this purpose wrote a large and a small catechism (1842–47) for the diocese of Freiburg, in which he emphasized the organic and communal aspects of the realities of faith. But the presentation of these thoughts was too compact and the theological precision occasionally inadequate. The main obstacle was that Hirscher's program presupposed a level of education that far exceeded the powers of the average clergy of that time.

Hirscher attracted some enthusiastic students like Ignaz Schuster and G. Mey, who helped to make a place for the Bible in religious instruction for the next several decades. But Hirscher's promising beginning was negated within a few years by the new Scholasticism and the tendency once again to emphasize the doctrinal differences among the Christian denominations. In this kind of atmosphere the bishops, looking for uniformity in catechisms, accepted the catechism of the Jesuit Deharbe. It offered a short survey of scholastic theology with clear and precise formulations, was concerned more with theological accuracy than with educational adaptation, was very strongly apologetic and anti-Protestant, and was free from all biblical and kerygmatic perspectives. After its appearance in 1847 and a revision in 1853, it was initially

---

[10] F. Ranft, *Fürstbischof A. Gruber. Ein Beitrag zur Geschichte der katholischen Religionspädagogik* (Innsbruck 1938).

[11] See *LThK* IX, 432–33.

[12] F. Bläcker, *Johann Baptist von Hirscher und seine Katechismen* (Freiburg i. Br. 1953); W. Nastainczyk, *Johann Baptist von Hirschers Beitrag zur Heilpädagogik* (Freiburg i. Br. 1957).

adopted by the Bavarian bishops, then adopted by most of the German dioceses, and used until 1924. During the second half of the century it was used also in several other countries: in England, the United States, Austria, and the missions in India and in China. After 1850, the practice of discussing the problems of the concepts and the content of the catechism was ended, and only purely didactic and educational questions were raised.

In France there were no chairs for pastoral theology and theoretical problems were much less debated there than in Germany. But on the practical level many interesting efforts were undertaken. The most interesting one started at the seminary of Saint Sulpice. J.-A. Émery, who had started Saint Sulpice again, returned to the tradition of J. -J. Olier and initially introduced young clerics to pastoral care by way of catechetical exercises in the parish. This method was adjusted to the new times by a few priests who understood the psychology of children. They knew how to make catechetical instruction come alive through the use of approving letters and other rewards and by interspersing it with songs and prayers. Notable among them were Teysseyrre, Frayssinous, de Quélen, and Borderies, the author of "Adeste fidelis" and director of the catechists in the parish of Saint Thomas Aquinas from 1802 to 1819.[13] The essential aspects—especially the recesses—were summarized in the *Méthode de St-Sulpice dans la direction des catéchismes,* published in 1832 by Abbé Faillon. The direct heir of these innovators was Dupanloup, who was inspired by their example and their spirit and who added his own educational genius. Even if the old clergy accused the young vicar of adding too much drama and profane accents to his catechetical instruction at La Madeleine in Paris (1826–34), his method, aiming equally at the training of the religious sensibililities and the theoretical knowledge of the child, was gradually accepted. The works in which he commented[14] upon his method became for several generations the breviary of catechists in the world outside of the German states.

On the whole, the French province lagged behind during the first decades of the new century. Only when the group of the Paris catechists was dispersed across the country as a consequence of successive bishops' promotions, did the catechetical movement spread there also. It was then anchored in the decrees of the provincial councils which met after 1848. But here and there interesting initiatives had been undertaken before. One needs to think only of the extraordinary success achieved

[13] See F. Dupanloup, *La vie de Monseigneur Borderies* (Paris 1905), especially 61–67, 89–185.
[14] *Manuel de catéchismes* (1831); *Méthode générale de catéchisme,* 2 vols. (1839); and especially *L'oeuvre par excellence ou entretiens sur le catéchisme* (1868).

before 1830 by the catechists of the Curé d'Ars, who stood out because of their continual attempt to speak a language which was understood by the common people. His bishop, Monsignor Devie, was inspired by his example and published several works on teaching the Christian doctrine which, in his time, were very successful. During the Second Empire, Abbé Timon-David in Marseille and Father Chevrier in Lyon were similarly engaged in simplifying religious instruction. Timon-David frequently relied on biblical stories, insisting on "education through the heart"; Chevrier added pictures to catechetical instruction and no longer employed the traditional organization in use since the sixteenth century (truths of the faith, obligatory commandments, and means of grace), instead concentrating on three concrete topics: God, Jesus Christ, and the Church.

Without a doubt, important catechetical work was being done in France during the time between the First and Second Empire. But it was hampered by a much too individualistic view of religion as the means to "achieve salvation"[15] and the lack of a connection with liturgical life; its chief deficiency was that it was directed at the young communicants, in spite of the efforts at developing "catéchismes de persévérance" for young men and women. During the July Monarchy first communion was dressed up as a spectacular celebration, which doubtless underscored its importance, but also produced the impression in children and parents alike that catechetical instruction was more a preparation for the rite of first communion than an introduction to the daily life of a Christian. The result was that after first communion many ceased practicing. Catechetical instruction, on which so much effort had been spent, was not adequately integrated into the totality of pastoral care.

Pastoral Theology and Pastoral Practice

So far we have only a few monographs on pastoral theology in the nineteenth century, but it can be said that its situation corresponded pretty much to what was already noted about catechetical instruction. In the theological departments of German universities emphasis was placed on theoretical considerations of how the Catholic Enlightenment could be overcome without doing away with its positive aspects. France was more concerned with practical initiatives, even if they were hesitant, unsure, and much more isolated. Their aim was accommodation to the new situation as it had resulted, on the one hand, from the transformations of the political revolution and the decisively changed position of the clergy in the nation, and, on the other hand, from the industrial

[15] See E. Germain, *Parler du salut? Le catéchèse du salut dans la France de la Restauration* (Paris 1968).

revolution, gradually presenting astute Catholics with the completely new problem of pastoral care for the urban proletariat.

Moralism and the anthropocentric inclination of the Enlightenment left their mark on the first suggestions for pastoral theology in Germany. This was particularly true for the Church, which saw its mission from an almost exclusively sociological perspective. Sermons and catechesis were seen as nothing more than mere instruction according to the rules of the profane world, and liturgy was reduced to an exercise in the virtue of religion. From this perspective, the essentially Christian and supernatural aspect was lost sight of and pastoral theology was narrowed to a professional ethic for the use of the clergy, whose function seemed to be limited to the moral and cultural education of the parish members. This view continued to dominate the textbooks like the *Systema theologiae pastoralis* (1818) by T. Powondra. A change came with Johann Michael Sailer at the turn of the century.[16] As professor of pastoral theology at Dillingen from 1784 to 1794 and at Landshut from 1800 to 1822 he exerted great influence on the clergy of southern Germany, strengthened by the success of his *Vorlesungen aus der Pastoraltheologie*.[17] His teaching effected a break with the naturalistic pastoral of the Enlightenment, but he tried to retain the positive elements developed in reaction to the Jansenist mentality, the pietistic anthropology, and the excessive objectivism of the post-Tridentine pastoral. Although Sailer was also interested in an improvement of homiletics, he was primarily concerned with the content of the sermon, to which he devoted the entire second volume of his *Vorlesungen*. Instead of moralizing and dogmatically poor observations he demanded the preaching of the fundamentals of Christianity, free from scholastic formulations which went beyond the understanding of the people and consisted of nothing more than scholarly commentaries on theological concepts. The best method to achieve the ideal consisted for him of direct and continual contact with Holy Scripture. For this reason he devoted the first volume of his *Vorlesungen* to an "Introduction to the Practical Study of Holy Scripture." Initially, the Bible interested him only as a collection of edifying examples, but gradually he arrived at a view oriented toward the Passion and Salvation of Christ in which Christianity functioned primarily not as a doctrine but as an event, as the story of God's activity in the world.

In spite of everything, Sailer was still strongly tied to the influence of the sentimental individualism of the "Sturm und Drang" period and the

---

[16] Concerning his influence in the German Catholic movement at the beginning of the nineteenth century, see vol. VII, pp. 216f.

[17] Three volumes (Munich 1788); 2nd edition 1794; 3rd edition 1812; 4th edition 1820.

contemporary Protestant theology of "experience." The Tübingen School represented a step forward, as it emphasized the positive and historical character of Christianity as well as the ecclesiastical perspective from which the pastoral theology needed to be derived. Hirscher already had taken this path, but had stopped short: convinced that the kerygmatic function was by far the most important aspect of the pastoral office—one sees here the didactic intention of the Enlightenment—he confined his efforts at rejuvenation to the preaching of the faith and neglected the sacramental side. His student and successor Anton Graf[18] expanded the views of his teacher by adding to the function of pastoral theology of sermon and catechesis the task of treating the entire range of activities by which the Church rejuvenates itself thanks to the work of the constantly present Holy Spirit, active among God's people. Unfortunately, the expectations maturing around 1840 at Tübingen failed to bear fruit, in part because Hirscher's school was dispersed, in part for more general reasons. After 1850, the ecclesiological direction which Graf had wanted to impart to pastoral theology was neglected, and it became more and more a science of practical work in which psychological, ascetic, and canonical considerations won out over the theological aspects. This was the case with J. Amberger's[19] *Pastoraltheologie* (1850–57), and the textbooks of subsequent years, such as that by the Austrian I. Schüch, which between 1865 and 1924 came out in twenty editions, followed the same line. Another indication of the development of this time, damaging the efforts at biblical and theological rejuvenation in Germany, was the success gained around the middle of the century by German versions of French works with characteristic titles. They were chiefly designed to supply the parish clergy with "recipes": *Pflichten des Priesters* by F. Hurter (1844), *Anleitung zur Selbstprüfung für Weltgeistliche* by T. Katerkamp (1845), and *Der praktische Seelsorger* by H. Dubois, adapted by a priest from Mainz (1856).

As long as it was not a matter of purely theological consideration of the pastoral, but one of practical realization, France was indeed the country which set the pace until, beginning with the middle of the century, the "movement of union" pushed Catholic Germany into the forefront. Increasingly, priests and laymen concerned with the rejuvenation of the forms and methods of the apostolate turned to the movement.

---

[18] On Anton Graf (1811–67), professor of pastoral theology at Tübingen, and author of a noteworthy *Kritische Darstellung des gegenwärtigen Zustands der praktischen Theologie* (1841), see F. X. Arnold, *Seelsorge aus der Mitte der Heilsgeschichte,* 178–94.
[19] See H. Schuster, *Handbuch der Pastoraltheologie* I, 63–66.

The pastoral, as it was understood by the French priest and his helpers during the first half of the nineteenth century,[20] was filled with a longing for the past, governed by the desire to rejuvenate the Christian community and the express feeling of hostility toward the world. It was in fact a pastoral of preservation, which attempted not to lose all those who still clung to the Church, i.e., chiefly women and children. This emphasis was not without consequences. The center of gravity of pastoral care moved increasingly to the world of women and children, attested to during this time by many church songs, pictures of saints, statues, and religious paintings.

All too frequently priests were tempted to concentrate on the small loyal group of followers who were willing to bow to their authority without resistance. Yet they did not totally ignore the lost sheep. For this purpose they employed the missions to the people or parish missions from the preceding period. Gradually these had developed into a coherent system using instruction, exercises, and ceremonies to reach their limited goal. The new conditions imposed some accommodations, but essentially the system remained true to its tested traditions. After an interruption of several years toward the end of the Empire, these popular missions were immediately resumed in France after the return of the Bourbons. At first they were under the leadership of secular priests, then their place was taken by preachers who were supplied by the congregations specializing in the apostolate. The July revolution stopped this movement, which often had assumed a political character; gradually it was resumed with less fanfare but with greater emphasis on depth.

In Italy also the parish missions had developed into firm fixtures and were resumed almost everywhere after the end of the revolutionary upheavals. In the Papal State, Pius VII in 1815 entrusted a reliable priest, Gaspare del Bufalo (1786–1837), with the task. Bufalo was later canonized; in Umbria be founded a congregation of priests which was to be important in the future. This congregation, the Society of the Precious Blood,[21] was introduced in 1840 by Franz Brunner[22] into Switzerland, where, at the beginning of the 1820s, Father Roothaan had encouraged the Jesuits to become active in the missions to the people.

---

[20] See among other reference books J. S. Dieulin, *Le bon curé au XIXe siècle,* 2 vols. (Paris 1842; four printings between 1845 and 1864) or *Rituel du diocèse de Belley,* 3 vols., by Mgr. Devie (1830–31), dealing extensively with the question of the administration of parishes and sacraments.

[21] See G. de Libero, *S. Gaspare del Bufalo* (Rome 1954), and Heimbucher II, 611–13.

[22] See J. J. Simonet, *F.S. Brunner und seine Mutter* (Chur 1935).

Italians like the Rosminian L. Gentili and the Passionist Dominicus Barberi[23] introduced such missions into England and Ireland after 1843. As a result of the limitations imposed by the governments, the missions in the German states were not very successful until the middle of the century. But after 1840 they were permitted to spread in Austria and after 1848 also in Germany.[24] In the United States an Austrian Jesuit, F. X. Weninger (1805–88), conducted about eight hundred missions after 1848.[25]

The organization of a mission was always an extraordinary event, and in between them the priests had to search for suitable means of drawing the people into the churches, where they could learn how to fulfill their obligations, to avoid sins, and to gain salvation. The parish priests of that time viewed their task in this formalistic fashion. A high point of the year was first communion, establishing a connection, strengthened by folklore, between parish, school, and family. An attempt was made to transform the ceremony into a kind of popular mission in order to induce indifferent families once again to partake of the sacraments.

But the popular missions were not the only institutions which the French priests of the nineteenth century, in admiration of the traditions of the old French clergy, wished to revive. They also tried to restore a number of former confraternities such as the Black and White Penitents in the south of France, and the confraternity of the Sacred Childhood of Jesus in Burgundy, which was restored in 1821 by the bishop of Dijon and raised to the rank of an archconfraternity by Pius IX in 1855. But it was above all the Marian congregations which experienced a lively revival in similar forms. They had been dissolved in France in 1760 under pressure from the Jansenists, but in the nineteenth century enjoyed the advantages of the veneration of Mary. Among them were the classic congregations associated with Roman *Prima Primaria,* which, after the decree of 7 March 1825 by Leo XII, no longer needed to be associated with Jesuit settlements and which during the first decades of the century increased annually by a thousand: the Association of Sons of Mary the Immaculate, which, between 1820 and 1830, was founded by the Daughters of Charity for the children of their boarding schools, but which after the appearances of Mary to Catherine Labouré and their official acknowledgment by Pius IX in 1847 became a worldwide phenomenon without regard to social class (six hundred thousand members

[23] See D. Gwynn in *IER* 70 (1948), 169–84; C. Charles in *JEH* 15 (1964), 60–75.
[24] See E. Gatz, *Rheinische Volksmission im 19. Jahrhundert* (Düsseldorf 1963); K. Jockwig, "Die Volksmission der Redemptoristen in Bayern von 1843 bis 1873," *Beiträge zur Geschichte des Bistums Regensburg* I (Regensburg 1967), 41–408.
[25] F. Weiser, *Apostel der Neuen Welt* (Vienna 1937).

by the end of the century); and the Association of Ladies of the Children of Mary, which was founded in Lyon in 1832 for the former pupils of the boarding schools of the Religious of the Sacred Heart and quickly spread among upper-class women in Europe and America.[26]

In addition to these traditional forms, there were others which endeavored to take into account the new needs of an increasingly urban society. Of chief importance in this connection were the juvenile homes which attempted to compensate for the lack of moral and religious instruction among the common people. They were established in different forms and countries: in France by J. J. Allemand (1772–1836) and his student Timon-David (1821–91), supported by energetic laymen like Armand de Melun;[27] in Piedmont under the leadership of Don Bosco; in Belgium; and in the Rhineland, where Kolping with his developed understanding of the needs of a modern industrial society expanded this pastoral arrangement by founding the Catholic Association of Journeymen in 1849.

In France and Belgium such protective pastoral organizations developed especially under the influence of the Society of Saint Vincent de Paul. The Vincentians, started by young French laymen, the best known among them being Frédéric Ozanam,[28] had given themselves three goals: assistance for the poor, not only materially, but also psychologically through contacts between human beings; strengthening of the faith of the members through the common exercise of charity; and apologetic witness before the world by attesting to the viability of Catholicism through action. Founded in 1833 in Paris, the Vincentians quickly spread in France (39 conferences in 1839, 141 in 1844, and 282 in 1848) and subsequently in other countries as well: in 1844 in Italy, in 1845 in Germany and the United States,[29] and by 1848 they counted 108 branches outside of France.

The Vincentian Conferences were an enterprise in which laymen played the primary role. The increasingly large role played by laymen in the service of the Church was one of the most significant innovations in the pastoral of the nineteenth century, in the course of which this trend became more pronounced. The lay movement is connected with a num-

---

[26] See *Un centenaire. Enfants de Marie du Sacre-Cœur,* 2 vols. (Paris 1932).

[27] See Duroselle, 183–97, and 548–604 for the rise in the third quarter of the century.

[28] Concerning the beginnings of the "Conférences de St. Vincent de Paul," see A. Foucault, *Histoire de la société de S. Vincent de Paul* (Paris 1933), *Livre du centenaire,* 2 vols. (Paris 1933), and J. Schall, *A. Baudon* (Paris 1897); also *Lettres de Frédéric Ozanam 1819–40,* ed. by L. Celier (Paris 1960).

[29] See B. Kühle, *Der Münchener Vincenzverein* (Wuppertal 1935); F. Molinari, "Le Conferenze di S. Vincenzo in Italia," *Spiritualita e Azione del laicato italiano* (Padua 1969), 59–103. A first attempt had taken place in Rome in 1836.

ber of famous names: Princess Gallitzin, Görres and Buß in Germany; Montalembert, Melun, Veuillot, and Pauline Jaricot in France; Cesare d'Azeglio in Piedmont, O'Connell in Ireland; and Donoso Cortés in Spain. They were the men and women, generally from the social elite, who placed their wealth or their active interest in the service of the parishes in order to preserve already existing institutions or to help with the creation of new ones. Year by year the number of journalists and parliamentarians increased who often quite selflessly defended the interests of the Church with word and pen. In a world which within a few decades had changed fundamentally, in which large numbers of people had distanced themselves from the Church while simultaneously the number of priests and monks had decreased together with the support once given to the clergy by the state, astute people recognized that attracting laymen was an absolute necessity. Laymen were necessary in order to regain contact with the world through the presentation and defense of the faith in a language understood by all. The use of laymen as mediators for the purpose of representing the Church in the nerve centers of the new society was imperative. (The theology of the time had not yet understood that laymen, in fact, are the Church.) These centers were located in parliamentary bodies, in the offices of the civil service, in communal administrations, and in the editorial offices of newspapers. In 1820, Ferdinand de Bertier, one of the leaders of the movement, wrote: "I am convinced that priests are no longer the most effective apostles." Chaminade in Bordeaux had recognized this fact twenty years earlier. It was even better understood by Vincent Pallotti (1795–1850), who in 1835 in Rome attempted to create the Society for the Catholic Apostolate by calling upon Catholics—not only notables, but also craftsmen, teachers, servants, farmers, housewives, and mothers—to spread the principles of Christianity in their neighborhoods and their places of work.[30] But the intentions of this man, whom Pius IX characterized as the "Pioneer and Champion of the Catholic Action," met with violent resistance by the ecclesiastical authorities who thought that the apostolate should remain a monopoly of the clergy. In the same way, the activities of Montalembert and Veuillot in France about ten years later in the interest of Catholic education were regarded by the episcopates and the old clergy as an interference in the traditional rights of the hierarchy. In spite of complaints and lamentations based on old habits difficult to shed and on a too narrowly inter-

---

[30] See G. Ranocchini, *Vincenzo Pallotti, antesignano e collaboratore dell'Azione cattolica* (Rome 1943) and H. Schulte, *Priesterbildner und Künder des Laienapostolates, Vinzenz Pallotti* (Limburg 1967).

preted ecclesiology,[31] the people who looked to the future with awareness hesitated less and less to identify themselves with Lacordaire when
he wrote: "The layman has a mission; he must add whatever the secular
clergy and the religious orders lack. The faithful must join in their
efforts to defend truth against the continual influence of bad doctrines;
their love must work together in order to repair the breaches in the
Church and the social order."[32]

The Reaction of Moral Theology to the Rationalism of Enlightenment and Rigorism

As in so many other areas, moral theology and pastoral theology often
have been characterized by the contrasting views of decadence on the
one hand and restoration on the other in connection with the period of
the Enlightenment and the first half of the nineteenth century. In reality, the reaction of numerous moralists of the eighteenth century against
the reduction of moral theology to casuistry or against the discussions
about probabilism also contained many positive values and justified
objectives. But all too frequently there was the tendency to lose sight of
the peculiar nature of Christian morality in comparison to a purely
philosophical morality and to lend more weight to psychological considerations than to the biblical and ecclesiastical foundations of moral
theology. This antidogmatic tendency was encountered in a number of
German moralists of the first decades of the nineteenth century, such as
J. Salat, guided by F. H. Jacobi, H. Schreiber, whose *Lehrbuch der
Moraltheologie* (1831–34) was strongly influenced by post-Kantian rationalism, and the students of Hermes, P. Elvenich and G. Braun. There
was also the parallel development both in moral theology and dogmatic
theology of a growing reaction to rationalism. But even if the German
moralists endeavored to seek their primary source of inspiration in
Holy Scripture and increasingly to respect the entire range of doctrines
of the Church, they were much more concerned with developing syn-
theses in close contact with the philosophy and the problems of their time
than were their colleagues in the Latin countries.

Rejuvenation was only weakly in evidence in the case of G. Riegler
(1778–1847). His *Christliche Moral* (1825; 1836) was merely an
amplification in German of the *Ethica christiana universalis* (1801) by

---

[31] An ecclesiology with which most of the laity itself was imbued. The following lines by
Montalembert from the year 1834 may serve as proof: "I am only a layman and therefore am responsible to Church and God only for my personal salvation" (*Lettres de
Montalembert à Lamennais,* ed. by G. Goyau [Paris 1932], 209).
[32] *Le Journal de Bruxelles,* 27 April 1849.

Maurus von Schenkl[33] and like it lacked a deeper understanding of the supernatural order. The matter was much clearer with the Austrian J. A. Stapf (1785–1844), who in his *Theologia moralis,*[34] in contrast to Kant, emphasized the importance of dogma as the root of morality and who gave credit to the great moralists of the past, even though he himself employed a more modern and more synthetic method. But even in this context reference must be made to the work by Sailer and Hirscher,[35] whose productive intuitions developed in part in contact with other contemporary Protestant theologians such as Heß, Schwarz, and Schleiermacher.

In their argument with the naturalism of the preceding generation, they tried to restore biblical morality with its original force and to point out the intimate ties existing between it and the dogmas. But they also turned against the classical moral theology which seemed to limit itself to drawing the line between mortal and venial sins. As far as they were concerned, it was the function of moral theology to present the ideal of a Christian life in its totality. They did not consider the methods and the language of jurisprudence as suitable for a morality based on the gospel. Thus, Sailer's *Handbuch der christlichen Moral* (1817), written without much system and in an elevated style, yet filled with a host of original ideas, was a kind of introduction to a life of devotion. It was designed, as the subtitle explained, primarily for future Catholic pastors and secondarily for every educated Christian. In the reaction against the casuistry of the Jesuits and also against the rationalism predominating in the universities toward the end of the eighteenth century, Sailer traced the essential nature of Christian law to the love of God without, however, adequately delineating the subjective conditions of this love. Hirscher, whose accomplishments in the area of moral theology have already been mentioned, surpassed his predecessor "in the acuteness of psychological observation, by the greater actuality and contemporaneity, and not least through the cohesiveness of the systematical presentation, even if he does not always reach Sailer's mystical drive" (B. Häring). It was his

---

[33] Concerning this book, which was not without merit, see C. Schmeine, *Studien zur "Ethica christiana" M. von Schenkls und zu ihren Quellen* (Regensburg 1959).

[34] Four vols. (Innsbruck 1827/31). He compiled his thoughts in his *Compendium,* 2 vols. (Innsbruck 1832), which was in use in Austria for many years. In 1841 he published *Die christliche Moral,* 4 vols., reflecting the influence of Hirscher.

[35] Concerning its contribution to moral theology with respect to Sailer, see, in addition to H. J. Müller, op. cit., P. Klotz, *J.M. Sailer als Moralphilosoph* (Paderborn 1909); J. Ammer, *Christliche Lebensgestaltung nach der Ethik J.M. Sailers* (Düsseldorf 1941); with respect to Hirscher, J. Scharl, *Freiheit und Gesetz. Die theologische Begründung der christlichen Sittlichkeit bei Johann Baptist Hirscher* (Munich 1941); A. Exeler, *Eine Frohbotschaft vom christlichen Leben, die Eigenart der Moraltheologie Johann Baptist Hirschers* (Freiburg i. Br. 1959).

intention to reconstruct morality on the biblical concept of "God's realm"[36] just as Drey had done with dogmatics.[37] It should be noted, though, that he did not really derive his concept of God's realm from the New Testament but from his teachers as they had understood it from the Romantic perspective of the period.[38] A critical examination reveals other inadequacies as well without, however, detracting from his great achievement.

One finds traces of the influence of Hirscher, Sailer, and Möhler in the writings of several authors of the subsequent generation such as Magnus Jocham, Bernhard Fuchs, Martin Deutinger, Karl Werner, and Ferdinand Probst. These authors, with their chief works appearing around 1850, partially returned to the classical tradition so strongly criticized by their predecessors, but they inherited from the Tübingen professors the concern of providing moral theology with its own organic unity in contrast to a merely external systematization. They also gained from them the conviction that the unique foundation of Christian morality must lie "in the nature of God's children, sanctified by the sacraments" (Jocham). Additionally, they emphasized the idea of development inasmuch as they show a moral life not based statically on fixed definitions and standards but rather dynamic, as a battle between grace, encouraging the perfect life, and the earthly forces pulling toward the darkness of sin.

Most of these moralists neither aimed at an approximation of morality with ascetic and mystical theology nor desired to have their books viewed narrowly as a guide for fathers confessor but wanted them to be regarded as useful scholarly works of edification for catechists, preachers, and educated believers.

The situation was totally different in the Latin countries. Here the classical form of the seminary textbook of a canonical-pastoral type was retained, designed to educate future fathers confessor and assembling a dry codification of obligations and sins on a casuistic basis. Here the innovation consisted of the replacement of the rigoristic or at least probabilistic principles by the moderate equiprobalistic doctrine of Saint Alphonsus Liguori in the French-speaking countries. This development, taking place in the second quarter of the century, was "one of the chief events of French Church history during the nineteenth century" (Guerber). It was in fact one of the primary factors for the victory of ultramontanism over the Gallican tradition. It also facilitated access

---

[36] Die christliche Moral als Lehre von der Verwirklichung des göttlichen Reiches in der Menschheit, 3 vols. (Tübingen 1835; 5th printing 1851).

[37] See J. Geiselmann in ThQ 111 (1930), 116.

[38] J. Stelzenberger, "Biblisch oder romantisch ausgerichtete Moraltheologie," ThQ 140 (1960), 291–303.

to the sacraments for the faithful and revitalized Christian life.

The adherence by the moralists and the clergy to Liguori's system was promoted by the frequent favorable indications given it by the Roman authorities: the Congregation of Rites in 1803; Pius VII in 1816 on the occasion of the blessing of Alphonsus Liguori; Leo XII in 1825 in a letter to the publisher of his collected works; Pius VIII in 1829; the "Sacred Penitentiary" in 1831 in a reply confirmed by the Pope; and Gregory XVI in 1839 with the bull of canonization.[39] Liguori's victory over the rigorism taught by the Sulpician seminaries was due primarily to Abbé Gousset, a seminary professor at Besançon, as it was he who had occasioned the reply of the Penitentiary in 1831. But he was not the only one—as has been asserted—to spread Liguori's doctrines in France: aside from three French editions of the *Theologia moralis* during the restoration period, there were published in Lyon in 1823 and 1824 two anonymous pamphlets by the priest Pio Bruno Lanteri of Turin in defense of the Liguoristic position against the criticism of the rigorists; in 1828 the brothers Lamennais in their curriculum for the Congregation of Saint Peter made Liguori's work the basis for moral theology; and in 1830 Monsignor Devie praised it in his *Rituel du diocèse de Belley.* Yet it touched only small groups and the clergy in the countryside were hardly influenced by the movement. But when Abbé Gousset in 1832 published his *Justification de la théologie morale du bienheureux Alphonse de Liguori,* he created a deep impression and during the following decade more than thirty thousand copies of Liguori's *Theologia moralis* were sold in France. After he became archbishop of Reims, Gousset added to this success by publishing a *Théologie morale à l'usage des curés et des confesseurs,* in which he presented Liguori's doctrines simply and impressively. The work saw seventeen editions in France, was reprinted in Switzerland and in Belgium, and was translated into Italian, German, Polish, and Latin. In addition to this simply written work for the parish clergy, J. B. Bouvier with his widely distributed *Institutiones theologicae* opened the doors of the seminaries for Liguori. The same was done a short time later by the Jesuit P. Gury, who had discovered Liguori during his years of study in Rome. His *Compendium theologiae moralis,* partially inspired by Gousset, was used at Vals after 1833, within a few years saw twenty editions, and was adopted by many seminaries in France and other countries.

Probabilism was the prevailing doctrine in Belgium until the end of the eighteenth century. A few priests who had emigrated to Germany

---

[39] See *Vindiciae Alphonsianae* I (Paris-Tournai 1874) LXXVIII–LXXX. While the Holy See applauded Liguori's doctrine, it carefully avoided taking a position against probabilism (see O. Fusi-Pecci, *La vita del papa Pio VIII* [Rome 1965], 157–60).

during the revolution there discovered Liguori's *Theologia moralis,* of which two editions were published in Mechelen and Antwerp in 1822. The settling of the Redemptorists in the country contributed to the success of Liguori's doctrine among the clergy in spite of persistent resistance in the seminaries and by the old clergy. As in France, it was accepted in Belgium between 1830 and 1840, thanks especially to the support given it by the theology department of the University of Louvain.

At the same time Liguori also was accepted in Germany, where he had always had a number of followers. A portion of the clergy became interested in good casuistic works in addition to the more synthetic ones mentioned earlier. In 1839 the Franciscan A. Waibel published his *Moraltheologie nach dem Geiste des heiligen Alphons von Liguori mit reichlicher Kasuistik,* and after 1844 K. Martin, professor of moral and pastoral theology at the University of Bonn, also introduced Alphonsus Liguori to the university curriculum. Several editions of the *Theologia moralis* were published during the following years in Mainz, Regensburg, and other cities. Incidentally, the textbook by Gury, reprinted several times, ultimately was more successful than those of native moralists. Just as in other areas, so also in moral theology parallel to the growing success of ultramontanism, a return to increasingly traditional positions could be noted. It was at the expense, of course, of the frequently interesting attempts at innovation. These had matured in the atmosphere of the Enlightenment and of Catholic Romanticism and were now smothered for almost a century.

CHAPTER 3

Catholic Thought Searching for New Ways

As in the preceding fifteen years, attempts were continued under the pontificate of Gregory XVI to guide Catholic thought into channels more suitable to the modern way of thinking than Scholasticism. The result of such efforts was uneven in Germany, France, and Italy. The defenders of tradition resisted innovations passionately, and the Holy See, whose authority was growing firmer, after a long interval once again began to censor those Catholic theologians and philosophers whose writings it regarded as threatening the faith. Most of the theological discussions took place in Germany, such as the posthumous controversies over the theories of Hermes, the admiration for Günther and the attacks against him, and the influence of the schools of Tübingen and Munich. But the Catholic University of Louvain also rose as a new center of higher education in Belgium. The failure of Lamennais and Bautain in France must not let one forget that numerous, often hapless, often interesting initiatives were taken. They were a testament to the efforts of open-minded Catholic intellectuals to leave the old worn-out paths and to accommodate themselves to the thinking of their contemporaries. One of the most notable indications of such efforts is the growth of the Catholic press; not of dailies as yet, but of journals and periodicals. It is especially noteworthy that this phenomenon characterized all of western Europe.

The Hermesian Controversy

After the death of Georg Hermes on 26 May 1831, at the height of his fame, criticism immediately became stronger and more virulent. This was especially the case with the new scholastics of the Mainz *Katholik,* but also with the groups espousing the Romantic theory of experience. They lacked the intellectual force for a precise limning of his errors, but they sensed that Hermes had assigned reason too high a place in the doctrine of faith. In order to be able to answer the accusations of Pelagianism, Socinianism, and rationalism, the students of Hermes, on their part accusing their opponents of fideism, in 1832 founded the *Zeitschrift für Philosophie and katholische Theologie.* An increasingly bitter and often confused polemic was carried on in periodicals and anonymous pamphlets without any notable result, until Anton Josef Binterim (after 1805 pastor in Bilk near Düsseldorf), one of the bitterest opponents of Hermes, succeeded in convincing the nuncio in Munich to warn the Roman authorities. Until then they had relied on the Cologne Archbishop Count Spiegel, who had defended the orthodoxy of the Bonn professor. But in consequence of the report by the nuncio, the *Philosophische Einleitung in die christ-katholische Theologie* was placed before the Index congregation. Toward the end of 1833 two German-speaking theologians, the Alsatian Kohlmann and the future Cardinal Reisach, were asked to translate the contested passages into Latin and to evaluate them. The nuncios in Munich and Vienna were requested to obtain the testimony of experts and to forward it to Rome. The Munich nuncio turned to two bitter enemies of Hermes, C. H. Windischmann and Binterim, the latter of whom was hardly competent to make a judgment. The Vienna nuncio consulted the Güntherian J. E. Veith, who was favorably inclined towards Hermes, but also the theologically untrained jurist K. E. Jarcke (cofounder of the *Historisch-politische Blätter für das katholische Deutschland),* who was very hostile to Hermes.

In Germany the controversy was renewed when J. A. Achterfeld in 1834 posthumously published the hitherto unpublished first volume of

Hermes' *Dogmatik*. With public opinion being agitated, the examination of Hermes' doctrines continued. Father Giovanni Perrone played a large role in the proceedings, even though his ignorance of the German language was a hindrance in arriving at a judgment. In view of the extent assumed by the controversy it was decided not to be satisfied with a simple indication. On 26 September 1835 a sharply worded papal brief[1] globally condemned Hermes' writings as "absurda et a doctrina Catholicae Ecclesiae aliena." Branded were numerous errors concerning God, grace, original sin and ecclesiastical tradition, especially the method of using positive doubt as the foundation of all theological inquiry, and the rationalistic principle which sees reason as the only means of obtaining knowledge of supernatural truth. The papal document, distributed through the nuncios in Brussels and Munich, filled Hermes' opponents with joy and prompted them to demand the immediate dismissal of his students from all university teaching posts. But aside from the bishops of Osnabrück and Posen, the bishops took no action, as the brief had not been transmitted through governmental channels. The chapter vicar of Cologne even imposed total silence about the brief on his priests.

The Hermesians, totally unprepared for the condemnation and thunderstruck by the judgment as well as by the harsh language used in connection with their revered master, quickly went over to the counterattack. They declared that Hermes' doctrinal opinions had been badly interpreted and that the papal brief attacked only a heresy of the imagination. They asserted that the recent condemnation of Bautain's fideism by the bishop of Strasbourg justified Hermes and proved at the same time the weakness of the position of their opponents. The last was a point valid for many of the involved. For no matter how bitter their attacks, they still were not able to write a decisive refutation (the first really serious criticism philosophically was leveled by A. Kreuzlage in 1838, theologically by J. Kuhn in 1839 and especially by the Austrian Franz Werner in 1845). In contrast, the leading Hermesian, P. J. Elvenich, succeeded with his extraordinarily well written *Acta Hermesiana* (1836) in creating a deep impression.

The controversy raged again after the appointment of Archbishop Droste zu Vischering. In his youth he had belonged to the circle around the Princess Gallitzin with its mystic and Platonic tendencies. Now, quite unjustly, he suspected the Hermesians of making common cause with the Prussian government in order to secretly undermine Catholi-

---

[1] Bernasconi II, 85ff. This papal brief was supplemented by another one on 7 January 1836 condemning the last two volumes of the *Dogmatik,* which had appeared in the meantime.

cism. The archbishop also intended to destroy the influence of the department of theology at the University of Bonn and to replace it with the diocesan seminary in Cologne.[2] He demanded from the professors an express submission to the papal brief and from all ecclesiastical candidates a sworn agreement with the eighteen theses in which the errors condemned by the Pope were even more sharply formulated; they were in fact very tactlessly phrased.[3] According to the anti-Hermesian Franz Werner, Droste also was guilty of a number of mistakes: he was incapable of recognizing what was correct in some of the scholarly demands of the Hermesians. But primarily he lacked the pastoral tact and the conciliatoriness which would have allowed the Hermesians a graceful retreat. He wanted to drive them to an unconditional surrender, but instead only succeeded in embittering them and confirming them in their excessive adherence to the doctrines of their teacher, of which they did not want to change one iota. They also were contemptuous of the archbishop's magisterial office, which desired to contradict with arguments of authority a philosophical system whose spirit it had evidently not grasped at all.

Toward the end of 1835 F. X. Biunde, professor at the seminary at Trier, established contact with Rome in order to enable the Hermesians to explain the meaning of the condemned writings, which, according to their opinion, had been misunderstood by the Roman censors. The result was that at the beginning of 1837 two delegates went to Rome. They were P. J. Elvenich, layman and philosopher, fully acquainted with the Hermesian system and also a capable Latinist, and J. W. Braun, a theologian of great erudition, "the best mind of the Bonn faculty" (Schrörs), with good connections in Rome. They were initially well received—much better than Lamennais—and asked to discuss their case with the Jesuit general Roothaan, who spoke German. But they quickly discovered that everything rested on a misunderstanding: The Roman authorities were solely interested in determining whether the Latin translation which the censors had used was correct, while Elvenich and Braun wished to explain the essential nature of the doctrines in order to justify them. The Index congregation refused to consider this approach and did not even wish to see the Latin summary, *Meletemata theologica,*[4]

---

[2] The importance of these nontheological aspects in the Hermesian controversy—not to mention the personal rivalries which occasionally poisoned the atmosphere even more—were underscored by H. Schrörs, according to whom the Cologne events were "basically more caused by Hermesianism than by the question of mixed marriages" (*Geschichte der katholisch-theologischen Fakultät zu Bonn* [Cologne 1922], 69, n. 1).

[3] *ThG1* 21 (1929), 316–28.

[4] I.e., "Theological Studies." Concerning the weaknesses of this study, first published in Latin and then, after the return of the two to Germany also published in German, see Schrörs, *Braun,* 272–73.

34

which the two had prepared. Other misunderstandings and the intervention of Metternich, who saw in rationalism a danger to the principle of authority and feared that the religious ferment could degenerate into political disturbances,[5] served to discredit them entirely. With the departure from Rome of Capaccini and the Prussian envoy Bunsen they lost two valuable supporters, and their eleven-month stay ended in total defeat. Because they insisted that they agreed with the Pope in condemning all of the errors which he had cited, including the method of positive doubt, but denied that Hermes' writings contained such errors, Secretary of State Lambruschini in a letter of 6 April 1838 accused them of lacking obedience and of taking recourse to the Jansenist differentiation between *quaestio iuris* and *quaestio facti*.[6] The letter, immediately published by their opponents, hastened the decline of Hermesianism which had begun two to three years earlier. Although the Hermesians active in pastoral care delivered excellent service, the majority of the clergy and the militant Catholics, who were increasingly ultramontane, distanced themselves completely from these "ivory tower theologians" who openly opposed the Holy See. The intellectuals began to turn to Anton Günther, the new rising star, who also attracted some of the best speculative minds among the Hermesians. After a renewed attempt by the Breslau Church historian Ritter in 1845–46 in defense of Hermes failed even to reach Rome, the bishops had no difficulty in gradually purging the main centers of Hermesianism at the universities of Bonn, Munich, and Breslau, and the seminary of Trier. Nor were the rearguard actions by the uncompromising Hermesians, among others Braun and Achterfeld, to any avail. They believed to have reasons for hope when Pius IX in his inaugural encyclical *Qui pluribus*,[7] directed against the fideists, emphasized the importance of the rational basis of the act of faith. The Hermesians interpreted the passage as a revocation of the brief of 1835. But the Pope put a quick end to this tactical maneuver.[8] The time of the Hermesians was gone irrevocably.

Rise and Fall of Güntherianism

Anton Günther (1783–1863), like Hermes a pious and concerned priest, attempted to reconcile faith and reason and to enable Catholic

[5] With respect to the political importance which the Austrian chancellor attached to the Hermesian controversy and his intervention in the matter in Rome after 1833, see J. Pritz, op. cit., 133–35 and H. Bastgen, op. cit., 27, 408.
[6] After their return to Germany, Elvenich and Braun published all documents concerning their negotiations in Rome under the title *Acta Romana* (1838).
[7] Text in *Acta Pii IX* I (Rome 1854), 4–24.
[8] Letter to the archbishop of Cologne, 25 July 1847. See H. J. Stupp, *Pius IX. und die Katholische Kirche in Deutschland mit besonderer Berücksichtigung des Hermesianismus* (Solingen 1848).

intellectuals to remain in the Church while they confronted the great philosophical currents of their time. Like Hermes he became the revered teacher of a whole generation of philosophers and theologians who rejoiced that Catholic speculation was exploring new paths better suited to the modern mentality. And like Hermes he was accused—not without grounds—of semirationalism. But the differences between the two thinkers were considerable. Hermes endeavored to overcome Kantian criticism and to create a rational basis for the acceptance of revelation. Günther dealt with Hegel's pantheistic idealism and Feuerbach's materialistic monism in order to work out a philosophical justification of the great Christian dogmas. The differences between the two men were even greater when one considers their intellectual background. Hermes and his followers were late representatives of the dry rationalism of the Enlightenment of the eighteenth century, while Günther and most of his enthusiastic students were deeply influenced by the Catholic romanticism of the restoration period. P. Wenzel characterized their system as a kind of gnosis of romanticism and added that their semirationalism was also a type of semi-irrationalism.[9]

Günther was born in northern Bohemia and received his philosophical education in the rationalistic atmosphere of Prague, where he studied under Bernhard Bolzano.[10] After surviving a personal crisis of faith, caused by studying the idealistic German philosophers, he developed an intense religiosity and began the study of theology with the help of the Redemptorist Clemens Maria Hofbauer. In 1821 he became a priest and settled in Vienna, where he lived as a private scholar until his death. He failed to obtain a teaching position in Vienna and rejected all offers coming from Germany. He lived surrounded by like-minded admirers, clerics, and laymen, who were equally attracted to his apostolic temperament, his metaphysical genius, and the charm of his discourse. Among them were the Cartesian naturalist J. H. Pabst, Günther's chief collaborator, and the famous preacher J. E. Veith, a former Jew.[11]

With his numerous books,[12] written in a very personal, sometimes

---

[9] H. Witetschek is also of the opinion that Günther "connected theology with a radical belief in reason as well as with irrational romantic aspects" (*HJ* 86 [1966], 110).

[10] Concerning Bernhard Bolzano (1781–1841), a priest with progressive ideas who quickly became suspect to the defenders of the Catholic restoration, a religious philosopher who was primarily notable as a precursor in the area of logic and mathematics, see E. Winter, *Bernhard Bolzano und sein Kreis* (Leipzig 1933); E. Winter, *Bernhard Bolzano, ein Denker und Erzieher im österreichischen Vormärz* (Vienna 1967); E. and M. Winter, *Der Bolzanokreis 1824–33* (Vienna 1970).

[11] Among Günther's followers were a good number of Jewish converts.

[12] Index, *LThK* IV, 1277.

very condensed, sometimes free and humorous style, Günther's influence reached far beyond this personal circle. Without much system they offered original and often far-seeing observations and astute criticisms of the most important philosophical systems, especially of Hegelianism. There is no doubt that Günther recognized the intellectual greatness of Hegelianism, but he also recognized the danger it presented much more clearly than most of the other theologians of his time. He was also convinced that Scholasticism was not only outdated but, like any philosophy of concepts, was connected to a kind of semipantheism, and therefore he devoted himself with unusual intellectual enthusiasm to a new scholarly proof of theology with an anthropological base. He presented Catholic dogma in the language of the "phenomenology of the mind" and tried to show how it is possible to understand creation through the Trinity and the Trinity through human self-consciousness. As in all of German idealism, the accent was placed on the concept of man as "nature and mind." Worked out between 1822 and 1835, Günther's essential thought was contained in his *Vorschule zur spekulativen Theologie* (1828–29). From that point onward, his influence superceded that of Hermes. During the 1840s Günther dominated the German Catholic intellectual world, the more so as the Prussian government appointed numerous Güntherians to philosophical and theological university teaching posts. It wanted to avoid appointing Hermesians in order not to anger the ecclesiastical hierarchy, but it also did not wish to appoint men who were compromised by the Catholic reaction to the Cologne events.

The chief centers of the movement were Vienna, Silesia, and the Rhineland. In Silesia, Güntherianism dominated the theological department at the University of Breslau, thanks to the protection of Prince-Bishop Diepenbrock, the former Hermesian Baltzer, and J. H. Reinkens, the future Old Catholic bishop. In the Rhineland, there was formed a "German Port-Royal" (P. Wenzel) by F. Knoodt and H. Nickes. The brothers Wolter, who founded the abbey of Beuron, also belonged to their circle. In the atmosphere of a romantic mysticism they dreamed of overcoming the rationalism around them through the combined effect of Güntherian speculation and a return to the monastic Middle Ages. In addition to enthusiastic and frequently intolerant adherents, there were also numerous sympathizers elsewhere. Among them were Professor Löwe in Prague, the future Cardinals Schwarzenberg and Tarnoczy, the bishop of Ermland, A. Thiel, several professors in Trier and Bamberg, the Benedictine abbot Gangauf in Augsburg, Görres in Munich, Zukrigl in Tübingen, as well as a good number of Protestants. The Güntherians had an eager protector even in Rome in the person of Pappalettere, the abbot of Monte Cassino, who saw in them the agents for Germany's liberation from rationalism.[13]

But soon there were also opposing voices. The philosophers whom Günther had criticized mercilessly, especially the students of Baader and those who favored a return to Scholasticism, were the first ones to counterattack. Then theologians became involved, accusing Günther of claiming to provide a rational proof of supernatural mysteries. The philosopher F. J. Clemens and the jurist K. E. Jarcke in *Katholik* and *Historisch-Politische Blätter* wrote of his disregard of the great thinkers of earlier times. The arrogance of Günther's students, many of whom did not share the deep religiosity and the apostolic dash of their teacher and who, as is often the case, emphasized the debatable aspects of many of his thoughts, only magnified the discontent. By 1845, the old front of the anti-Hermesians, who rigorously rejected any compromise with modern philosophy, deployed itself against Güntherianism, especially in the Rhineland, where Knoodt, having made of Bonn a very active center of the movement, managed to arouse the ire of Archbishop Geissel. After the crisis of 1848, during which the Güntherians played a predominant role in the Catholic movement, they founded the new philosophical journal *Lydia* (1849–54) for the purpose of spreading their views, but the absolutist reaction in Austria, accusing them of sympathy for the liberal tendencies of the time, was ill-disposed toward them. The position of the Güntherians was endangered by the appointment in 1853 of Rauscher as archbishop of Vienna; for the past twenty years he had been their enemy. This happened precisely at a time when attacks against them increased on the doctrinal level. These were started in 1851 by the Benedictine Sorg, in 1852 by Dieringer and Schwetz, in 1854 by Michelis, and especially by F. J. Clemens, their bitterest enemy, whose pamphlet *Die spekulative Theologie Anton Günthers und die katholische Kirchenlehre* (1853) found a great echo and started a war of pamphlets. When the controversy passionately agitated Germany's and Austria's theologians and philosophers, surpassing in acidity the dispute over Hermesianism fifteen years earlier, the archbishop of Cologne submitted the problem to the Holy See. Günther had powerful protectors, who were grateful to him for having freed Catholic intellectuals from their fascination with Hegel and who sensed the danger of offending the universities, which already viewed the official Church hierarchy with mistrust. Matters probably could have been settled satisfactorily had not Baltzer and Knoodt, authorized to defend their system in Rome directly, spoiled everything by their cool attitude toward the Jesuits and

---

[13] On the support which Günther received from Simplicio Pappalettere, abbot of Subiaco since 1846, see P. Wenzel, *Der Freundeskreis um Anton Günther*, 133–245.

the contempt which they showed for the development of Roman philosophy. Still, Rome hesitated two years before it finally decided to act. The opponents of the Güntherians did not cease their attacks, especially the authoritarian Archbishop Geissel, who made condemnation a point of prestige. Finally, in January 1857, Pius IX decided to place Günther's works on the Index, even though he paid strong compliments to the person and the intentions of the author.[14] Günther submitted despite his deep disappointment. But many of his friends asserted that it was perfectly all right to continue to teach the essentials of his system, as the papal decree had not condemned a single one of his theses. Geissel, supported in Rome by Cardinal Count von Reisach, therefore extracted a papal brief which defined the condemnation.[15] The moderate Güntherians submitted, while the radical ones, like Baltzer, Knoodt, and Reinkens, refused, arguing that it was a matter of academic integrity. They continued the controversy for many more years and provided the most active support for Old Catholicism after 1870.

Tübingen and Munich

Theological life in the German-speaking countries was not limited to the activity of the Hermesians and Güntherians and the controversies which they caused. Even in Bonn, one of their citadels, not all professors agreed with their teachings. H. Klee (1800–40), "the outstanding mind of the first Mainz circle" (Lenhart), taught there from 1829 to 1839 and in 1843 Archbishop Geissel succeeded in placing F. X. Dieringer (1811–76) on the chair of dogmatics. He was a priest strongly engaged in the Catholic movement which in 1844 founded the *Katholische Zeitschrift für Wissenschaft und Kunst* in response to the journal of the Hermesians. Klee[16] lacked speculative acumen, but he had a very pronounced feeling for the supernatural character of revealed religion and was also one of the rare Catholics capable of holding his own in comparison with his Protestant colleagues. His unusual patristic scholarship enabled him to write a *Lehrbuch der Dogmengeschichte* (2 vols. [1832]), one of the first written by a Catholic and of value. Dieringer[17] had studied in Tübingen and was better known for his inspired love of the Church and the ingenious clarity of his teaching than for his creative powers or his depth. The honorary doctoral degree awarded to him by

---

[14] E. Winter, op. cit., 232 ff. and supplement B, provides a wealth of documentation on the trial.

[15] Papal brief *Eximiam tuam,* 15 June 1857, in *Acta Pii* II, 585–90.

[16] See the biographical sketch in volume 1 of the *Katholische Dogmatik* (Mainz 1844), XXIII–XLIII and *LThK* VI, 324.

[17] See J. Wetzel in *FreibDiözArch* 72(1952), 198–212, and *NDB* III, 657.

the University of Munich was a response to his book *System der göttlichen Thaten des Christentums* (1841).

In southern Germany, theological life was concentrated chiefly in the theological departments of the universities of Tübingen and Munich. The generation of the founders gradually disappeared in Tübingen—Möhler and Herbst in 1836, Hirscher in 1837, and Drey in 1846—and their places were taken by younger men. There was A. Graf, who as holder of the chair for pastoral theology developed remarkable ecclesiological points of view; he left the university too early in 1843, a victim of the tensions existing for about ten years between a number of the faculty and the Württemberg government over church political issues;[18] K. J. Hefele, who took Möhler's place as professor of church history and demonstrated his abilities after the middle of the century; and J. E. Kuhn,[19] professor of dogmatics after 1839, who for forty years remained the uncontested head of the school, impressing his students and the readers of his many books[20] by the clarity and depth of his thoughts and the brilliance of his dialectic. In his evolutionary view, Scholasticism was a useful phase in the history of Christian thought, but now outdated. Inspired by Hegel's method, he tried to get to the bottom of the Christian mystery; but his faith-rooted speculation was based on the facts of revelation and took account of the history of dogma. Kuhn remained faithful to the principles of the Tübingen School and was also a talented metaphysician and thoroughly familiar with the Greek Church Fathers and Saint Augustine. He also was an able exegete and in 1832 published his *Leben Jesu wissenschaftlich bearbeitet* to counteract the book on the life of Jesus by David Friedrich Strauß. Kuhn was less tied to romantic idealism than his teachers and placed the concept of mind, spirit, intellect before that of life. In him and his younger colleagues of the Tübingen School "the movement gained speculative depth and systematizing power" (Scheffczyk).

The influence of the Tübingen School extended to other universities. To Münster, where Anton Berlage,[21] a student of Drey and Möhler,

---

[18] On this conflict, see M. Müller, op. cit.

[19] Concerning Johann Evangelist Kuhn (1806–87), see in addition to *LThK* VI, 656–57, A. Hagen, *Gestalten aus dem schwäbischen Katholizismus* II (Stuttgart 1948–54), 59–95, and J. R. Geiselmann, *Die lebendige Überlieferung als Norm des christlichen Glaubens dargestellt im Geiste der Traditionslehre Johann Evangelist Kuhns* (Freiburg i. Br. 1959).

[20] His major book, *Lehrbuch der Dogmatik,* appeared in three volumes between 1846 and 1868. As early as 1832, he had presented his views in an article of the *ThQ,* "Über den Begriff und das Wesen der spekulativen Theologie."

[21] On Anton Berlage (1805–81), see *LThK* II, 231. He also was under the influence of Hermes and Günther and in Munich also under that of Baader, Schelling, and Görres. His *Christ-katholische Dogmatik* (7 vols. [1839–64]), together with Liebermann's *Institutiones,* became one of the most widely used reference books in ecclesiastical circles.

40

became professor of moral theology and dogmatics in 1835; but especially to Gießen and Freiburg im Breisgau. The department of theology at Gießen[22] was established in 1830 as a substitute for the Mainz seminary in spite of the protest of the chapter. From the beginning two Tübingen-educated professors left their imprint: Kuhn, holding the chair for New Testament studies from 1832 to 1837, and Franz Anton Staudenmaier,[23] who taught dogmatics from 1830 until 1837, when he moved to Freiburg. In Freiburg he was joined by Hirscher, another respected Tübingen-educated professor. After its reorganization in 1832, the theology department at Freiburg had gone through a crisis which was ended with the arrival of these two. There was also Alban Stolz (1808–83), who in 1847 assumed Hirscher's chair of pastoral theology. The influence of Staudenmaier, long neglected by historians of theology, was not any less than that of the Tübingen people. In his time his *Geist des Christentums* (1835), which saw eight editions within half a century and was a seminal work in liturgical theology, was even compared to Chateaubriand's[24] *Génie du christianisme*. His *Christliche Dogmatik* (4 vol. [1844–52]) also was a very personal work, in which the central ecclesiological perspectives are grounded in a trinitarian theology and in a history of theology which replaces Hegel's dialectical philosophy of history with the living and free working of God among men as revealed by revelation.

In Munich it was the lay professors who initially played a role. Görres remained the center of the group until his death in 1848. Inspired by the native initiative of Sailer as well as the influence of Tübingen, especially Möhler's presence from 1835 to 1838, the department of theology also improved over time. Of course, not all areas were equally well covered. Work in dogmatics remained tentative in spite of the contributions made by A. Buchner between 1827 and 1838, and moral theology remained inadequately taught for a long time. Canon law,

---

[22] It existed only for a short time, for in 1851 Ketteler stopped its students from attending by reopening the seminary at Mainz. The undeniably rationalistic tendencies of two professors (L. Schmid and A. Lutterbeck) provided him with a good pretext. See F. Vigener, "Die katholisch-theologische Fakultät in Gießen und ihr Ende," *Mitteilungen des oberhessischen Geschichtsvereins,* n.s. 24 (1922), 28–96.

[23] Concerning Franz Anton Staudenmaier (1800–56), see F. Lauchert, *Franz Anton Staudenmaier* (Freiburg i. Br. 1901); P. Weindel, *Das Verhältnis von Glauben und Wissen in der Theologie Staudenmaiers* (Düsseldorf 1940); A. Burhart, *Der Mensch, Gottes Ebenbild und Gleichnis. Ein Beitrag zur dogmatischen Anthropologie Staudenmaiers* (Freiburg i. Br. 1962); P. Hünermann, *Trinitarische Anthropologie bei Staudenmaier* (Munich 1962); A. Scholz in *ThQ* 147 (1967), 210–39.

[24] See W. Trapp in *Liturgische Zeitschrift* 4 (1931–32), 52–54, and F. X. Arnold, *Grundsätzliches und Geschichtliches zur Theologie der Seelsorge* (Freiburg i. Br. 1949).

however, did not escape the influence of George Phillips,[25] who as a member of the law school opened new avenues by employing the methods of historical law in the service of his ultramontane views. After the rather lackluster Joseph Franz von Allioli[26] retired in 1835, exegesis was given new life by Möhler, who was equally interested in finding a firm philological base and in confronting Protestant views; his successors Reithmayr and Haneberg continued the trend. Church history gradually acquired a scholarly character through the young Döllinger and Franz Michael Permaneder,[27] who during the Lola Montez crisis between 1847 and 1849 assumed Döllinger's place. Under Möhler's prodding, the theological faculty at Munich gradually moved away from the intoxicating speculations of Baader and Schelling and adopted a genetic view of history.

After 1826, Döllinger[28] belonged to the faculty to which he had been appointed in consequence of Sailer's help. Connected in his youth with the Mainz group, he had become acquainted with Görres and for two decades stood in the forefront of the journalistic polemic for religious and academic freedom. He had a remarkable talent for dogmatic analysis, which he displayed in his doctoral thesis, *Die Lehre von der Eucharistie in den ersten drei Jahrhunderten*. Regarding university teaching as an apostolate, he turned to church history in the awareness that the Catholics were far inferior to the Protestants in this area. After initial work on Hartig's textbook he published his own *Lehrbuch der Kirchengeschichte* (2 vols. [1836–38]), which was acclaimed for the clarity of his presentation and the originality of his thought. Not merely chronicling events, it treated the development of ecclesiastical institutions in

[25] Volume I of his *Kirchenrecht* appeared in 1845.

[26] On Joseph Franz von Allioli (1793–1873), see *LThK* I, 352, and J. Zinkl, *Magnus Jocham* (Freiburg i. Br. 1950), 54ff. He became known chiefly through his Bible translation, the notes for which were taken from the best commentaries of the time (6 vols. [1830–32]); it was approved by numerous German and Austrian bishops and by the Pope in 1838 and of all German versions was the most widely read.

[27] Concerning Franz Michael Permaneder (1794–1862), see *LThK* VIII, 279–80. He taught canon law and church history at the high-school for girls in Freising and published a reliable *Bibliotheca patristica* (2 vols. [1841–44]), which introduced into Catholic education the Protestant differentiation between "patrology" (literary history of early Christian writings) and "patristics" (theological treatment of doctrines).

[28] Of Ignaz von Döllinger (1799–1890), one of the most remarkable personalities of German Catholicism in the second and third quarter of the nineteenth century, there exists as yet no satisfying biography. See J. Friedrich, *Ignaz von Döllinger*, 3 vols. (Munich 1899–1901); F. Vigener, *Drei Gestalten aus dem modernen Katholizismus* (Munich 1926), 108–88; S. Lösch, *Döllinger und Frankreich. Eine geistige Allianz* (Munich 1955); G. Schwaiger, *Ignaz von Döllinger* (Munich 1963); *DHGE* XIV 553–63. His correspondence is widely dispersed and so far only a small portion has been published.

the areas of religion, discipline, and constitution. The book was quickly translated into other languages: into English in 1840–42, French in 1841, and Italian in 1845. In 1837 Döllinger was elected as a member of the Bavarian Academy of Sciences. In 1842 he founded an Archive for Theological Literature as the organ of expression of the professors of the theology department.

In the course of the following years he was affected by the hardening of the denominational fronts which under the influence of the converts Jarcke and Phillips superceded the indifferentism of the Enlightenment as well as Sailer's irenism and Möhler's dialogue. His first great work, *Die Reformation, ihre Entwicklung und ihre Wirkung* (3 vols. [1846–48]) was an anti-Protestant polemic. It was designed to refute the assertions made by Ranke in his *Deutsche Geschichte im Reformationszeitalter*. Based on a considerable number of primary sources drawn from the reformers, he attempted to show the destructive character of the Reformation and its unfortunate cultural consequences; yet he also tried to indicate the reasons for it. This portrait of Lutheranism was rejected by the Protestants because it only treated the dark side of the Reformation, but it caused Catholics to look upon the author as one of the outstanding champions of the Church and to regard Munich as the shining center of Catholic scholarship.

The Catholic University of Louvain

Soon after the creation of the Kingdom of Belgium, the episcopate, suspicious of the moral and religious atmosphere of the state universities, started an experiment which during the nineteenth century frequently attracted the attention of foreign Catholics. In October 1832 it decided to establish a Catholic university with academic freedom and two years later translated this decision into reality. In the attempt to avoid the impression among the liberals that profane education was subject to Rome, the episcopate refused to make it into a papal university. The decision was quite contrary to the usage under the Old Regime and worried the Holy See. Its fears that the new institution could grow into a citadel of Catholic liberalism were confirmed by the appointment of several of Lamennais's followers, among them the university president Xavier De Ram,[29] the metaphysician Gerhard Ubaghs, and especially the Frenchman Charles de Coux, a former editor of *L'Avenir*. Considering the lack of qualified personnel in the country, it was neces-

---

[29] Concerning Xavier De Ram (1804–65), the real organizer of the new university which he headed for thirty-one years, see *LThK* VIII, 982–83.

sary to turn to foreign professors.[30] They were won with salaries equivalent to those paid by the state universities. Although the faculty included several autodidacts, it became possible from the beginning to provide students with an education qualitatively comparable to that of the other universities of the country. The medical school, for example, opened the first clinic for ophthalmology in Belgium. During its first period, the university became particularly well known for its Middle Eastern studies. In 1841–43 the Dutchman T. Beelen, a Hebraicist, published a *Chrestomathia rabbinica et chaldaica*, which displayed an originality rare for its time, and his research was augmented by that of F. Nève, a specialist in Sanskrit. The president, a sound scholar, was the first to remove national church history from a hagiographic and edifying emphasis and instead based it on a study of the original sources. Thanks to his intervention, the Belgian Jesuits were able in 1837—after an interruption of half a century—to continue the work of the Bollandists.[31] Twenty years later Renan assigned this enterprise first place among the products of the Catholic renaissance of the nineteenth century which he considered serious.

In the theology department, which quickly attracted students from the neighboring countries, the outstanding person was Jean-Baptiste Malou,[32] professor of dogmatics from 1837 to 1849. He displayed his patristic scholarship in the book which he published a few years later on *L'Immaculée Conception de la bienheureuse Vierge Marie* (1857). Educated in Rome, he became at Louvain the defender of Scholasticism against his ontological and traditionalist colleagues Arnould Tits[33] and Ubaghs.[34] Their views were published in the *Revue catholique,* established in 1843 by the professors at Louvain, and read in the seminaries and by educated laymen, but met growing resistance by the Jesuits and the opponents of Lamennais. The rather lively dispute ultimately was decided by Rome. Ubaghs's *Théodicée* and *Logique* were sent to the Congregation of the Index by Nuncio Fornari, and on 23 June 1843 the congregation came to the conclusion that several theses needed to be corrected. But the Holy See considered it advisable not to publish this

---

[30] Two eminent converts came from Germany: W. Arendt for Greek and Roman antiquity, and J. Moeller, a student of Niebuhr's, for history. Windischmann joined the medical school.

[31] See H. Delahaye, *L'œuvre des Bollandistes* (Brussels 1959), 129–35.

[32] On Jean-Baptiste Malou (1809–64), the future bishop of Bruges, see B. Jungmann in *Katholik* 46 (1866) I, 716–41, II, 74–90, 129–56.

[33] Concerning Arnould Tits (1807–51), professor of fundamental theology since 1840, who died early but left a lasting impression, and whom Monsignor De Ram compared to Klee, see *Annuaire de l'Université catholique de Louvain* 16 (1852), 171–94.

[34] On Gerhard Casimir Ubaghs (1800–75), professor of philosophy from 1834 to 1866, see H. van Grunsven, *Gerhard Ubaghs* (Heerlen 1933) and *LThK* X, 427–28.

decision, in order not to hurt the Catholic university. Thus Ubaghs felt justified in continuing his courses in the same vein, which he regarded as more suitable than traditional Scholasticism to ward off the perils of rationalism. After Malou became bishop in 1849, he reopened the case and obtained an unequivocal condemnation from Rome. Ubaghs obediently submitted and resigned his professorial chair.

Tentative Attempts by the Catholic Intellectuals in France

While Germany retained the considerable lead of the first decades of the century and even enlarged it, the Latin countries on the whole presented a sad picture.

In Spain, with the Church suffering the aftereffects of the chaotic political situation, theological studies stagnated.[35] But the training of the clergy in the seminaries was clearly superior to that in France and Italy, even though it was limited to reading the great writers of the sixteenth and seventeenth centuries. Any openness to modern problems was lacking, with the result that Spanish theologians exerted no influence outside of Spain before the Thomist renaissance during the last third of the century. The only exception—aside from the essayist Donoso Cortés, a layman who in 1851 published the strictly conservative monograph *Essai sur le catholicisme, le libéralisme et le socialisme*—was the Catalan priest Jaime Balmes (1810–48), a prolific author of philosophical, historical, and apologetic books. His work was seminal in several areas, but precisely for that reason he found only limited reception among the Spanish clergy.[36] His fame was based on a refutation of Guizot; his *El Protestantismo comparado con el catolicsismo en sus relaciones con la civilizacion europea* (1842) was immediately translated into French.

Italy enjoyed three advantages: the scholarly tradition of the eighteenth century was not totally disrupted by the revolutionary events; it had in Rosmini a Christian philosopher of great stature; and the Roman College was for some of its theologians the means by which they attained international acclaim. But other scholars were not able to work within the framework of famous universities and this could not but have an impact on the quality of their work, no matter how meritorious it was. A case in point was Cardinal Angelo Mai,[37] the tireless editor of classical and patristic texts.

---

[35] This judgment by Hocedez II, 185, is confirmed by the very small number of Spanish authors of the nineteenth century cited in the *DThC* (see *Tables générales,* 1226).

[36] Concerning the limited degree to which he became a precursor of Neo-Thomism, see Hocedez II, 195–97.

[37] On Angelo Mai (1782–1854), see *LThK* VI, 1289–90; *DACL* X, 1196–1202; G. Gervasoni, *Angelo Mai* (Bergamo 1954).

Rosmini was admired by the educated public as well as in the Lombard seminaries, where he contributed to freeing instruction from Febronian tendencies. But after 1840 he saw his doctrines passionately attacked.[38] In the area of philosophy he was accused by Gioberti[39] and his students and the adherents of the Scholastic tradition of ontological inclinations; theologically he was attacked by the Jesuits, who, reacting sharply to the criticism to which Rosmini had subjected probabilism in his *Trattato della coscienza morale* (1840), polemicized against what they regarded as his erroneous concept of original sin, in which they saw the basis of his moral doctrines.[40] Although Gregory XVI, asked by the Jesuits to intervene, in 1843 imposed silence on both parties, the spreading of Rosmini's thought in the Catholic circles under the influence of the Jesuits suffered in consequence of these polemics.

The Roman College, closed to innovation in methods and the perception of problems, offered a qualitatively disappointing education. The German professors complained about it and so did the general of the Jesuits.[41] In philosophy the authors of the preceding century were studied without any originality, and the pioneers of the Thomist renaissance were ignored, as for example Father Taparelli with his work on natural law.[42] In the field of theology, only two names stand out from the general mediocrity. They were F. X. Patrizi, professor of exegesis, a conscientious scholar whose *De interpretatione Scriptuarum sacrarum* (1844) was the first Catholic monograph on the typological interpretation of the Bible, and Giovanni Perrone,[43] from 1824 to 1848 professor of dogmatics, whose *Praelectiones theologicae* (9 vols. [1835–42]) saw thirty-four editions. He was a vulgarizer without much originality who much preferred the dispute with the Protestants and the rationalists to genuine theological reflection. But it was to his credit that the relatively

[38] New documentation in G. Martina in *RRosm* 61 (1967), 130–70.

[39] Gioberti, whose influence was great among a portion of the Italian clergy, in 1841 published a bitter indictment, *Degli errori di Antonio Rosmini,* which started a long controversy.

[40] F. Ruffini, *La vita religiosa di Alessandro Manzoni* II (Bari 1931), 247ff., justifiably pointed out that the conflict between the Society of Jesus and Rosmini was based not only on the competition between two religious congregations, active in the same field, but also on profoundly differing doctrinal and spiritual concepts.

[41] See P. Pirri, *P. Giov. Roothaan* (Isola del Liri 1930), 306–7, citing a letter of 20 December 1842.

[42] On Luigi Taparelli d'Azeglio (1793–1862), whose principal book *Saggio teoretico di Diritto naturale appoggiato sul fatto* dates from 1840, see R. Jacquin, *Taparelli d'Azeglio* (Paris 1943), B. Armando, *Il concetto di proprieta nel Padre Taparelli* (Pinerolo 1960), and Aubert-Martina, 299, n. 20.

[43] On Giovanni Perrone (1794–1876), see *DThC* XII, 1255–56, and Hocedez II, 353–55.

new treatment of the relationship between reason and faith was introduced into classical theology. He also sensed the importance of positive
theology, which during the pontificate of Pius IX came to full bloom in
the Roman College under his students Carlo Passaglia and Johannes
Franzelin.

In France around 1830 there had been two hopes for renewal of
Catholic thought: the School of La Chênaie and Malestroit under
Lamennais and, on a much more modest level, the School of Molsheim
near Strasbourg under Louis Bautain. Lamennais's condemnation was
especially disastrous for his school because the Holy See had condemned both his church-political theories and his philosophical system,
which constituted the basis for his program of renewal. In addition, of
course, the vague and moderate condemnation[44] was exploited extensively by his enemies.[45] It did not immediately curtail the influence of
philosophical traditionalism, especially not in Belgium, the Netherlands, Germany, Italy, Spain, and Poland.[46] But after 1835 most of
Lamennais's students preferred practical work to now suspect speculations. Thus the changing of the guard which the school of La Chênaie
had promised ultimately did not take place and instruction was
mediocre, not least because Bautain's work, undertaken completely
independently from Lamennais, gradually atrophied.

In 1832 Bautain[47] published a pamphlet on *L'enseignement de la
philosophie en France au XIXᵉ siècle* which became the manifesto of his
school. He criticized in it both the eclecticism of Victor Cousin and the
Cartesian Scholasticism reigning in the seminaries. Bautain's numerous
opponents asked the bishop of Strasbourg, Monsignor Le Pappe de
Trévern, to intercede. His opponents consisted of Sulpicians offended
by his attacks against their methods of instruction, Jesuits, among them
the influential Father Rozaven, followers of Lamennais who did not care
for his criticism of the philosophy of common reason, a portion of the
Strasbourg clergy, who regarded him as an interloper, and the seminary
teachers of Besançon who were jealous of the competition by the Molsheim group. In the spring of 1834, Monsignor de Trévern, who for six
years had had no complaints about Bautain, submitted to him six questions on the relationship between faith and reason. There is no doubt

---

[44] See L. Le Guillou, *L'évolution de la pensée de F. Lamennais* (Paris 1966), 197–98.
[45] Ibid., 213–22.
[46] See Hocedez II, 83–112. Concerning Germany, see Schrörs, *Braun,* 289–95, 426.
[47] Concerning the controversy of 1834 to 1840, see F. Ponteil in *RH* 164 (1930),
225–87 and especially P. Poupard, *L'abbé Louis Bautain* (Tournai-Paris 1961), 181–226;
concerning his stay in Rome in 1838, see P. Poupard, *Journal romain de l'abbé Louis
Bautain* (Rome 1964), also the letters from Rozaven (*Bulletin critique* 23 [1902],
194–98, 353–60) and from Roothaan (*CivCatt* [1929] III, 316–19).

that Bautain, lacking adequate theological training, presented fairly correct views on religious knowledge in terms seemingly incompatible with traditional formulations, and that under the influence of Kantianism he was inclined to denigrate human reasoning. But the questions of the bishop were also unfortunately framed. The consequence was a dialogue among deaf people, carried on for years and worsened by personal dislikes. After the bishop had deemed Bautain's answers unsatisfactory, he published a notice on 15 September 1834 and sent it to the Holy See and to all bishops in France. He desired Roman intervention against the "new Lamennais." But the exploitation of the notice by the Hermesians in favor of their semirationalistic views caused Rome to react circumspectly.

Bautain was convinced that the bishop was exceeding his jurisdiction, as in his opinion it was not a problem of dogmatic but only of philosophical questions. In addition he failed to comprehend how a philosophical doctrine based on faith could be accused of "destroying religion." He published a comprehensive work, *La philosophie du christianisme,* in which he presented the essence of his thought in the form of letters to his students. Except for some small exceptions, it was accepted by Möhler at Tübingen, which awarded him the title of doctor of theology.[48] Toward the end of 1835 everything seemed to calm down when Bautain indicated his willingness to sign statements modified with the help of the suffragan bishop of Nancy, Monsignor Donnet. But the Strasbourg bishop insisted that the new sentences were not really any different from his earlier formulations and sent Bautain's writings to Rome so that with the help of his friend Rozaven they would be placed on the Index. Following Lacordaire's advice, Bautain traveled to Rome in order to defend himself personally.

He was received politely, as Rome did not wish to give the Hermesians new food for thought. He also made an excellent impression during his three months in Rome with his declared willingness to submit himself to Rome's decision, so different from the arrogance of the German professors. The authorities limited themselves to requesting him to correct a few passages of his book and of a new one which he carried with him in manuscript form. Bautain was more than willing to do so, as the discussions with Roman theologians had revealed to him where he was exaggerating and as he had also discovered that condemnation of rationalism was a far cry from condemnation of reason. He acknowledged that it was possible to regard reason as a first step toward faith without denying the necessity of grace for the awakening of the soul.

[48] See P. Poupard in *RSPhTh* 42 (1958), 455–82; also *ThQ* 17 (1835), 421–53.

From this perspective he published his *Psychologie expérimentale* (2 vols. [1839]), on which he had labored for longer than eighteen years and which he considered as the major achievement of his life. But the old bishop of Strasbourg refused to reinstate Bautain and his followers in their former positions in spite of a request from Rome. On 8 September 1840, Bautain signed a more refined version of his questionable propositions, drafted by Monsignor Räß, the new suffragan of Strasbourg,[49] and retired to Paris. There, for a quarter of a century, he was active as a respected lecturer and preacher. But the long debate over a single point of his system diverted attention from the importance of his attempt to rejuvenate apologetics. Additionally, he failed to raise the standards of priestly education with respect to the problems caused by modern currents of thought.

Most of the seminaries clearly ignored these problems. Especially at Saint Sulpice "the cult of modesty and caution prevented any attempt at a spiritual rejuvenation" (X. de Montclos). The only notable exception was Charles Baudry,[50] a great patristic scholar who liked to be innovative. In the episcopate as well there was only one man with any sensitivity for these questions: Monsignor Affre, who in 1840 became archbishop of Paris. Results, unfortunately, corresponded little to his intentions.[51] He succeeded as little as his predecessor in breathing new life into the department of theology at the Sorbonne,[52] and he was able only to plan a graduate school of ecclesiastical studies, subordinated to the archbishop. Newman detected in this plan the seed for a future Catholic university, but actually the plan found little echo in France.

Yet the overall balance of the July Monarchy was not only negative. Some—in view of the contemporary circumstances even much—of the vitality and originality of Lamennais's movement survived. It had the goal of reaching the intellectual standards of the Protestants and the faithless and to establish a new humanism in which Catholic dogma was

---

[49] The text of the various proposition lists is in P. Poupard, *L'abbé Louis Bautain*, 393–96. In 1844, on the occasion of a canonical approbation by the *Congregatio Episcoporum et Regularium* of a congregation founded by him, Bautain was requested to sign a number of new statements revised by P. Perrone. They were even more refined than the statements worked out in 1840 in Strasbourg.

[50] On Charles Baudry (1817–63), see de Montclos, 64–75, 605–6.

[51] See R. Limouzin-Lamothe, J. Leflon, *Monseigneur D.-A. Affre* (Paris 1971), 179–87.

[52] On this question which repeatedly surfaced during the second third of the nineteenth century, but was never resolved owing to the mistrust of the Holy See, see R. Limouzin-Lamothe, *Monseigneur de Quélen* (Paris 1955–57) I, 263–66, II, 247–52; R. Limouzin-Lamothe, "Monseigneur d'Astros et la réorganisation des facultés de théologie en 1838–39," *BLE* 52 (1951), 178–86; de Montclos, 108–10; J. Maurain, *La politique ecclésiastique du Second Empire* (Paris 1930), 104–10, 688–92; G. Bazin, *Vie de Monseigneur Maret* (Paris 1891) I, 397–419, II, 9–21, III, passim; *Annales de philosophie chrétienne* 26 (1843), 72–80.

to be the guide for all manifestations of intellectual life without putting the mind in a straitjacket. Even if the plan to send a number of young Catholic intellectuals to Munich (1833–34) was dropped again within a few months, it at least led to important translations. They enabled the French public to become acquainted with some characteristic writings from beyond the Rhine, among them Möhler's *Symbolik* (1836) and Döllinger's *Lehrbuch der Kirchengeschichte* (1841). The good reputation which Lamennais's followers gained for German Catholic scholarship survived among French Catholics for a long time. It encouraged a few clerics—unfortunately much too few—to study at German universities. One who did so was Henri Maret, one of the few great French theologians of the next generation.

The attempt by Gerbet to reconstitute in the college of Juilly a part of the group from Malestroit failed to have a lasting effect. But with the help of some of them he founded in 1836 the periodical *L'Université Catholique*,[53] with the intent of interesting a wide readership. It had a circulation of 1,600, a considerable figure for that period, among them Germans and Englishmen. Because a university independent from the state analogous to the Catholic University of Louvain could not be established in France, the founders of the journal wanted to offer the educated public the equivalent of lectures and presentations in the spirit of Lamennais: research capable of enriching the interpretation of dogma, and critical studies with the aim of refuting rationalistic propositions through extensive reliance on German research, especially that of the Munich School. One of the chief contributors of the new journal was Augustin Bonnetty, who also continued to publish his *Annales de philosophie chrétienne*.[54] With prodigious amounts of labor he collected gigantic numbers of historical documents for the defense of Christianity. He became a precursor of comparative religious studies and his findings and documents were used by other authors for their successful books. Chief among them were the *Histoire du monde depuis sa création* by Henri de Riancé (4 vols. [1838–44]) and the *Études philosophiques sur le christianisme* by Auguste Nicolas (4 vols. [1843–45]; twenty-six editions in forty years). Enthusiasm in the service of truth and the acknowledgement of the central importance of history in intellectual studies unfortunately did not provide for these self-taught writers the critical spirit and methodical discipline, the lack of which was one of the chief deficiencies of French Catholicism until the end of the century. Such deficiencies were quite evident in the voluminous *Histoire universelle de l'Église catholique* by René-François Rohrbacher (29 vols. [1842–

[53] See C. de Ladoue, *Monseignieur Gerbet* II (Paris 1872), 118–46.
[54] On Augustin Bonnetty (1798–1879), see *DHGE* IX, 1058–60, and N. Hötzel, op. cit., XVI–XVIII and 140–369 passim.

49]). A great number of the French clergy regarded this work as a monument to scholarship, but compared to Döllinger's writings it was a sad enterprise. Similar deficiences explain the naivety of the short-lived *Société hagiographique,* founded in 1836 with the aim of completing within a span of ten years, with three volumes per year, the *Acta sanctorum* of the Bollandists.

In the absence of genuinely scholarly works, it was nevertheless to the credit of French Catholics under the July Monarchy that they reissued the classical writers of ecclesiastical scholarship. Advised by clerics, a number of Catholic publishers issued collections of old texts, added fresh commentaries, and hoped to adapt traditional instruction to the progress of modern society. Among them were Antoine de Genoud,[55] also a former follower of Lamennais, who published twelve volumes with excerpts from 196 writers of the preceding four centuries with the aim of providing an apologetics (*La Raison du christianisme* [1834–35]) and seven volumes of translations of the Church Fathers (1835–49). Another one was Jacques-Paul Migne.[56] With the help of a number of excellent scholars and thanks to his own business acumen, Migne published three parallel series as tools for the clergy. These were: the most important Bible commentaries of the seventeenth and eighteenth centuries (25 vols. [1834–40]); a number of theological tracts of the sixteenth to nineteenth centuries (28 vols. [1839–45]); and the most important apologists from Tertullian to Wiseman (16 vols. [1842–43]). He also published a *Collection universelle et complète des orateurs sacrés* (99 vols. [1844–66]), an *Encyclopédie théologique* (52 vols. [1844–52], supplemented from 1851 to 1866 by another 119 volumes) which combined updated excerpts from old encyclopedias (like that by Bergier) with articles by contemporary authors, and finally the two famous Patrologia series (the *Series Latina,* 217 vols. [1844–55], and the *Series Graeca,* 161 vols. [1857–66]). The last was the more meritorious, as a similar project in Italy a few years earlier with the financial support of Gregory XVI had foundered.

To a large degree Migne was able to publish the two Patrologia series owing to the assistance of a monk from Solesmes, Dom Jean-Baptiste Pitra,[57] a scholar of high caliber. Unfortunately, Pitra remained an exception among the French Benedictines. Dom Guéranger, in his youth an adherent of Lamennais's ideal of a rejuvenation of ecclesiastical

---

[55] Concerning the journalist Antoine de Genoude (1792–1849), who in 1835 after the death of his wife became a priest, see *CThC* VI, 1225f.

[56] On Jacques-Paul Migne (1800–75), see F. de Mely in *Revue apologétique,* 5th ser. 2 (1915), 203–58; *DThC* X, 1722–40; *DACL* XI, 948–57.

[57] Concerning Jean-Baptiste Pitra (1812–89), see the two complementing biographies by F. Cabrol (Paris 1891) and A. Battandier (Paris 1896).

scholarship in France, intended to fashion his abbey into a workshop in which the tradition of the Maurists, albeit with an anti-Gallican orientation, could again blossom. Unfortunately, he was not able to gather the necessary qualified people, and even Dom Pitra's work was handicapped by the financial difficulties of the monastery. Guéranger's own works, his *Institutions liturgiques,* of which the first two volumes appeared in 1840 and 1841,[58] and even more his *Histoire de Sainte Cécile* (1849) suffered, like all writings of French theologians at that time, from a fundamental lack of sound scholarship. On the other hand, he started an original and remarkable undertaking in 1841 when he published the first volume of his *Année liturgique,*[59] at first not very successful, but later regarded as a true monument of Christian culture through the ages. Eventually it contributed more than any other work to the rejuvenation of Catholic piety.

On this level of Catholic culture, the French could be proud of a number of other original and contemporary achievements. Lamennais's former student Alexis-François Rio[60] was concerned with the essence of Christian culture, for which he became what Winckelmann had been for the art of classical antiquity. His book *De la poésie chretiénne* (1836), in reality an introduction to early Italian art in which Schelling's aesthetics can be seen, had only limited success in France, but found great acclaim in Italy and Germany. With all of its preconceived apologetic opinions and methodological weaknesses, his book tried to demonstrate that the paintings of the Middle Ages were inseparably connected with a definite Christian view of man and life. Surpassing the *Génie du christianisme,* it wished "to cause a revolution in aesthetics equal to that which metaphysics based on original revelation had tried to cause in the area of philosophy" (Derré). Montalembert started a similar work in the field of Gothic architecture. He fought the demolition of monasteries and in his *Histoire de Sainte Élisabeth de Hongrie* (1836) he wrote a poetic hagiography in honor of the Christian Middle Ages. He intended to demonstrate the atmosphere of medieval piety through a representative which German romanticism had made accessible to him. At the same time he devoted pages of panegyrics to the Marburg Elizabeth Church, connecting the achievement of Gothic art with the religious sentiments of the contemporaries of Saint Francis of Assisi and Saint Louis. His book was similar to that which Ozanam, with greater scholarship, wrote on the

[58] Volume I was translated into German in 1854.
[59] Nine volumes appeared between 1841 and 1866; they were later completed by the students of Guéranger. See O. Rousseau, *Histoire du mouvement liturgique* (Paris 1945), 45–53.
[60] On Alexis-François Rio (1797–1874), see M. C. Bowe, *F. Rio, sa place dans le renouveau catholique en Europe* (Paris, n.d.), and J. R. Derré, op. cit., 615–69.

literature of the Middle Ages. In his lectures at the Sorbonne on Saint Francis of Assisi, in his two books on Dante (1838 and 1839), and in his *Études germaniques* (1847–49) Ozanam, within the framework of comparative literature, always also taught religion and made "the long and arduous education which the Church imparted to modern peoples" the central topic.

It was another accomplishment of Ozanam that at the age of twenty he persuaded the archbishop of Paris to introduce at Notre-Dame on the occasion of Lent a style of preaching designed for the young intellectuals and radically different from usual sermons; additionally he convinced the archbishop to assign these Lent sermons to Abbé Henri Lacordaire,[61] in spite of the prevailing preconceptions about this former follower of Lamennais. As a romanticist who completely grasped the attitude of the new generation, Lacordaire introduced a new style of preaching in 1835 and followed new avenues in apologetics. To a generation captured by the picturesque and by emotions, he offered the eloquence of paintings, colors, enthusiasm, and indignation. He knew how to speak of eternity in everyday language without fruitless bemoaning of the lost past and without condemning the values held by his audiences. Instead of offering methodically a philosophy of spiritualism in the fashion of Frayssinous, proceeding from there to a presentation of the facts of revelation, he allowed himself to be guided by the experience of his own conversion. He accepted Christianity and the Church as givens by attempting to show how much they corresponded to the needs of the present as well as to the essential needs of human nature. His success[62] indicated that he had found the right approach.[63]

The Growth of the Catholic Press

The picture of Catholic achievements in the intellectual sphere is not complete without reference to newspapers and periodicals. Many of them have been mentioned earlier. But it is useful to summarize the

---

[61] Lacordaire preached the Lent sermons in Notre-Dame de Paris in 1835 and 1836, and after his return from Rome, having become a Dominican, he preached the Advent sermons from 1843 to 1846 and the Lent sermons from 1848 to 1851. From 1837 to 1846 his place was taken by the Jesuit de Ravignan, an excellent but more classical orator.

[62] He did not find approval everywhere. By the old clergy as well as by the rationalists, this "Savonarola of the modern pulpit" was accused of acting more like a religious tribune than like a theologian.

[63] At the same period there were in Italy some similar but less famous attempts to adapt sermons to modern concerns. This was the case, for example, with the young Franciscan Arrigoni (see M. Maccarrone, *Il concilio Vaticano e il "Giornale" di Monsignor Arrigoni* I [Padua 1966], 15–17).

essence of these publications in order to show the universality of this phenomenon which started during the first quarter of the century and increasingly grew after 1830. In 1844, the *Revue des deux mondes* noted: "In order to preach more freely on topics other than morality and charity, the press was employed. Priests in large numbers entered the new arena; laymen became theologians and theologians turned into journalists. Today, journalism has become for some members of the clergy a branch of the pulpit in the recognition that the power of the press is mightier than sermons." This observation was true not only for France, but for all of western Europe.

In Germany some astute leaders of the Catholic movement like Lennig and Döllinger quickly grasped the importance of the press. Yet at first great obstacles had to be overcome, not only because there was a dearth of qualified people and of money, but also because of administrative red tape and the hostility of a part of the clergy which was apprehensive about the interference of journalists in internal Church matters. Quickly there appeared a number of journals which addressed themselves to clerics and educated laymen.[64] Among them were *Der Katholik*,[65] founded in Mainz in 1821 "for instruction, warning, and defense against attacks on the Church"; because of state censorship (Görres as editor strove for greater discipline, more careful selection, and reliable expertise), the journal moved to Strasbourg in 1823, where it remained until 1827, then moving to Speyer and publishing there until 1844 under the editorship of Dieringer, finally returning to Mainz in 1844, when it became a weekly; the journal *Eos,* edited by Görres in Munich and transformed by him into the organ of conservative Catholicism in southern Germany, treating both literary questions and church-political problems, although it was published only from 1828 to 1832; the *Zeitschrift für Philosophie und katholische Theologie*,[66] founded in 1832 in Bonn by Braun, a few other Hermesians, and a few bishops in order to provide Catholicism in Prussia with a respectable publication in place of the banned *Katholik,* even though after a few years it adopted an increasingly hostile stance toward the hierarchy; the *Historisch-Politische Blätter* of Jarcke and Phillips in Munich, more accessible to the broad public but, in the view of Prussian Catholics, edited from a too strongly southern German perspective; and the *Rheinisches Kirchenblatt*,[67] founded in 1844 in Düsseldorf as a monthly and converted into a

---

[64] Not mentioned there were scholarly theological journals like the *Theologische Quartalschrift* in Tübingen. Its index is listed in *CathEnc* XI, 678.

[65] See H. Schwalbach, *Der Mainzer "Katholik" 1821–50* (diss., Mainz 1966).

[66] See Schrörs, *Braun,* 153–87.

[67] See R. Pesch, *Die kirchlich-politische Presse der Katholiken in der Rheinprovinz vor 1848* (Mainz 1966), 25–82.

weekly in 1848 in order better to spread Archbishop Geissel's views. The daily press, on the other hand, especially in the Rhineland, had a difficult beginning and for a long time was limited to papers with purely local circulation, edited in pronounced anti-Protestant, apologetic fashion.[68] They only came into their own during the second half of the century.

In France there also appeared a few notable periodicals: the *Annales de philosophie chrétienne* (since 1830) and the *Université Catholique* (since 1836); also the *Revue européenne,*[69] which between 1831 and 1834 took the place of the *Correspondant* and after the demise of *L'Avenir*—with the exception of political aims—served as forum for the followers of Lamennais; and *Le Correspondant* itself, reappearing in 1843 in order to support Montalembert in his struggle for freedom of education. There were also journals of more popular bent, such as the *Journal des personnes pieuses,* founded by P. d'Exauvillez and Abbé Glaire. With the exception of *Le Correspondant,* the French periodicals were more concerned with the problems of ideas than with church-political questions. Such questions were treated in the daily press and especially in *L'Univers,* founded in 1833 by Abbé Migne. In 1843, Louis Veuillot became its dynamic and pugnacious chief editor.[70] The fact that France in the 1830s could boast of several Catholic dailies with a national circulation must not be misread, however. It was at best a modest beginning, for their combined circulation was less than that of a single large liberal paper. Besides, they were scarcely read in Paris, the center of intellectual and political movements and controversies.[71]

In Belgium also there were a number of Catholic newspapers in the provinces, but hardly in the capital. But in 1834 the layman Pierre Kersten founded in Liège a journal of general interest, the *Journal historique et littéraire.*[72] This excellently edited monthly found readers even beyond the borders of the country. Shortly afterwards there appeared in the Netherlands the monthly *De Katholiek* (1842) and the daily *De Tijd* (1845), both of which were to have a long and productive life.[73]

---

[68] Ibid., 197–226, with a chronological listing of the Catholic newspapers of Germany.

[69] See J. R. Derré, op. cit., 500–528 and passim.

[70] Concerning the beginning period, see C. de Ladoue, *Monseigneur Gerbet* II (Paris 1872), 91–118, and A. Trannoy, *Le romantisme politique de Montalembert* (Paris 1942), 437–56; on the role of Veuillot, see E. Veuillot, *Louis Veuillot* (Paris 1899seqq.) I, 282–90, 313–25, II, passim.

[71] A few figures are given in the *Revue des deux mondes* 25 (1844), 355–56.

[72] See A. Vermeersch, *Bijdrage tot de Geschiedenis van de Belgische Pers 1830–48* (Louvain 1958), 36–44.

[73] Concerning the beginnings of *De Tijd,* see Rogier, *KathHerleving,* 257–61.

In Great Britain, the first Catholic monthly appeared in 1831; but the regular Catholic press really began to appear only between 1835 and 1840. At first there was the *Dublin Review,* founded in 1836 by Wiseman with the support of two Irish laymen, Daniel O'Connell and M. Quin, as a counterweight to the strongly anti-Catholic *Edinburgh Review.* It was followed by the monthly *The Tablet,* founded in 1840 by the convert F. Lucas.[74] These were joined by a few less important publications.[75] In 1846 *The Lamp* was founded as an inexpensive paper for the workers.

Religious periodicals also appeared in the Mediterranean countries. In Italy this was due chiefly to the labors of the *Amicizia cattolica.* In Spain, thanks chiefly to Balmes, there appeared in 1830 in quick succession *La Civilizacion, La Sociedad,* and *El Pensamiento de la Nacion.*[76]

Even if the history of the Church in the nineteenth century in many areas was a series of missed opportunities, it must be noted that the Catholics in most countries quickly recognized that the press was destined to play a large role in modern society. But it must also be mentioned that owing to a lack of material and intellectual means, the journalistic achievements, especially with respect to the daily press, were only second-best compared to the freethinking press.

---

[74] See J. J. Dwyer, *English Catholics,* ed. by G. A. Beck (London 1950), 475–76, 482–84. The participation of the converts of the Oxford movement in the Catholic press was weak before the turn of the century (see J. Altholz, *The Liberal Catholic Movement in England* [London 1962], 7).

[75] See T. Wall, "Catholic Periodicals of the Past," *IER* 101 (1964), 206–23, 234–44, 289–303, 375–88, 102 (1964), 17–27, 86–100.

[76] See *CathEnc* XI, 690.

The Ascension of Pius IX and the Crisis of 1848

CHAPTER 4

The First Years of the Pontificate of Pius IX: From the Neoguelf Mythos to the Roman Revolution

When Gregory XVI died on 1 June 1846, the religious situation of the Church posed no problems, but the political condition of the Papal State was tense. In view of the administrative and constitutional attempts at reform and the desire of patriots to free Italy from the tutelage of Austria, the regime represented by the late Pope and Secretary of State Lambruschini was at the nadir of its prestige. For this reason internal political considerations were of primary concern in the conclave, the more so as it was decided in view of the serious political situation to open the conclave immediately, without waiting for the arrival of the foreign cardinals. The intransigents favored the election of Lambruschini, as it would guarantee the continued support of Austria in the suppression of revolutionary elements. Others, led by Cardinal Bernetti, considered a few concessions to public opinion necessary and were in favor of a Pope from the Papal State in order to manifest their independence from foreign influences. The preferred candidate of this second group was Cardinal Mastai. Gizzi was regarded by many as too progressive.[1] On the first ballot, Mastai received fifteen votes, Lambruschini seventeen. Those who feared a victory of Lambruschini then rallied behind Mastai, who received a two-thirds majority on 16 June, the second day of the conclave.

Giovanni Maria Mastai-Ferretti was relatively young; in memory of his benefactor Pius VII he chose the name Pius IX. He was born on 13 May 1792 in Senigallia in the Marches, and from the beginning of his clerical career demonstrated piety, pastoral concern, and administrative ability. A journey to South America (1823–25), undertaken as auditor of the apostolic delegate to Chile, provided him with insight

[1] It should be noted that the Austrian veto was not directed against him but against Bernetti. It allows the conclusion that Metternich was less concerned with the Italian problem than with the fear of French influence on Rome. (Engel-Janosi I, 15–16).

into the new dimensions of missionary problems and into the difficulties which liberal, regalistically oriented governments could cause for the Church. But as archbishop of Spoleto (1827–32), and as bishop of Imola he succeeded in gaining the respect of the area's very active liberals. He was full of charity toward the members of his diocese, regardless of their views, he was open-minded, and he seriously tried to improve the antiquated nature and the police-state aspects of the government of the Papal State.[2] Yet these administrative reforms were not designed to allow the public actively to participate in affairs of state, as this seemed to him incompatible with the religious character of the papal government. On the other hand, there is no doubt that he was open to the stirring of Italian patriotism. Contrary to the widely accepted view, he thought it impossible to implement the neoguelf program and thought that the Pope as the spiritual head of all Christians should not play the role of the president of an Italian federation. But he intensely felt the national enthusiasm which was being fed by the romantic movement, and the brutalities of which the Austrian troops were accused deeply hurt his generous soul. They brought him into agreement with the forces which desired Italy's liberation from the foreign yoke.

The first decision of the new Pope seemed to confirm the "liberal" attitude of which Rome's reactionaries accused this enlightened conservative: On 17 July he decreed a generous amnesty; he appointed Cardinal Gizzi, wrongly suspected of being a representative of Massimo d'Azeglio's ideas, as secretary of state;[3] he selected Monsignor Corboli-Bussi, a young prelate with an open mind for new ideas, as his confidential adviser; he was generous to Father Ventura, the eloquent follower of Lamennais; he kindly received a number of persons known for their connection with the moderate liberals; and he fully agreed to some long-desired reforms, even though they were not part of a comprehensive concept.

In this heated atmosphere and at a time, just before 1848, when the romantic concepts of Catholicism joined with the goals of democracy, even these very limited gestures of the Pope received the acclaim of the masses. Ignoring the encyclical *Qui pluribus* of 8 November 1846, which again condemned the basic principles of liberalism,[4] people pre-

---

[2] In 1845 he had even drafted a characteristic reform program (see G. Soranzo in *Aevum* 27 [1953], 22–46). It was more a reform of abuses than a change of structures, either administratively or politically.

[3] On the true personality of Gizzi (1787–1849), who basically was conservative and antiliberal, see the revealing remarks by A. Simon, *Documents relatifs à la nonciature de Bruxelles 1834–38* (Brussels 1958), 51–91.

[4] Text in *Acta Pii IX* I, 4–24. See A. Latreille, *L'explication des textes historiques* (Paris 1944), 228–230.

ferred to see in Pius IX "a messenger of God sent to complete the great work of the nineteenth century, the alliance between religion and liberty" (Ozanam). Metternich, on the other hand, whose initial response to the attitude of the Pope had been favorable, was beginning to worry that the Church was headed by a man "with the fire of the heart, but weak in planning and without any real ability to lead." All of liberal Europe responded positively, even such countries as England,[5] which could not be said to be harboring any papist sympathies.

For several months the authority of the papacy was at a peak, the more so as at the same time a reconciliation between Rome and the Ottoman Empire seemed possible and the negotiations with Russia, begun in 1845 after a visit of Tsar Nicholas I to Gregory XVI, led to the signing of a relatively favorable treaty.

In Italy, where all demonstrations against the rule of the Austrians or against reactionary governments were accompanied by shouts of "Long live Pius IX," enthusiasm reached a high point. The myth of the "liberal Pope" acted like a catalyst for the disparate elements which before 1848 held progressive opinions; former opponents of the Church, Catholics won over to modern ideas, and the patriotic clergy,[6] all were temporarily united in a common hope. Their disappointment was so much greater when facts began to speak and the actions of the Pope failed to fulfill the hopes which had been placed in him.

The disenchantment began in the area of internal reforms. Pius IX had to take account of the growing opposition on the part of most of the Curia prelates; although he was seriously concerned with an improvement of the situation of his subjects, he himself was not prepared to go beyond the limits of what can be called ecclesiastical paternalism. He was afraid that by relinquishing a part of his priestly kingdom to laymen he would limit the independence which the Holy See required for the fulfillment of its spiritual tasks. Quazza in his book *Pio IX e Massimo d'Azeglio nelle vicende romane del 1847* shows in great detail that Pius IX, even during the period of the most trusting cooperation with Massimo d'Azeglio, when he appeared to approve of the daring opinions of Father Ventura, never went beyond a limited benevolent despotism. He remained far from a liberal attitude toward people and society and by no means wished to change the Papal State into a constitutional and modern state based on the precepts of 1789. A few activists, playing with great skill on his desire to be popular, succeeded in pushing him in this direction, without, however, changing his basic convictions. The

[5] In the United States as well the reaction to the election was enthusiastic. See H. R. Marraro: *CH* 25 (1956), 42–44.
[6] See, for example, B. De Giorgio, *Aspetti dei moti del 1847 e del 1848 in Calabria* (Reggio 1955).

results were freedom of the press, freedom of assembly, formation of a council of twenty-four notables in October 1847, and introduction of a lay element into the government in January 1848. Gradually he agreed to several concessions and also immediately attempted to circumscribe them as much as possible. But after the fall of Louis-Philippe in France he was forced to a hasty approval of the constitution which had been demanded for months.[7] Even this decision appeared only as a half-measure and agitated more than it satisfied the increasingly impatient public opinion.

Such hesitation on the part of the Pope, who constantly wavered between advice from the right and the left and thought that he could avoid offending anyone with his decisions, was displayed also and with grave consequences in his attitude toward the Italian movement. On the one hand it is impossible to agree with many historians of the *Risorgimento* that Pius IX initially supported the liberal program of Italian unification, only to abandon it later; it would be equally incorrect to assert, as has been done by many Catholic historians, that the Pope never had a clear Italian policy and only made a few meaningless gestures to which more significance was attached than they warranted. The truth lies between the two extremes. Pius IX evidently could not accept Mazzini's idea of a unified Italian republic, as it would mean the suppression of papal sovereignty; equally unacceptable was the neoguelf program.

Still, after a period of tentative moves he agreed with some moderates who wanted to reduce Austrian influence in Italy and who wanted to establish the prerequisites for such a development through strengthening the bonds among the various Italian states. Therefore the Pope tried to give a political direction to the negotiations which began in August 1847 with the objective of establishing a customs union with Tuscany and Piedmont. The idea of a union of the Italian sovereigns in a defensive league, sponsored by Florence and supported by the Pope's chief adviser, Monsignor Corboli-Bussi, was also very agreeable to him. This solution automatically would have associated the Papal State with a national resistance in case of military intervention by Austria for the suppression of revolts which were threatening everywhere, without directly forcing the Pope into a declaration of war. But the ambitions of Piedmont, desirous of claiming for itself all of the advantages accruing

---

[7] Text of the "Statuto" of 14 March 1848 in *Atti del S. Pontefice Pio IX* V/1 (Rome 1857), 222–38. See L. Wollenberg in *RStRis* 22 (1935), 527–94, and A. Ara, *Lo statuto fondamentale dello Stato della Chiesa* (Milan 1966; also G. Martina in *RSTI* 21 [1967], 131–46). The latter clearly demonstrates the vain attempt to change the Papal States into a constitutional state.

from a war of liberation, prevented the formation of the league. There-after, events quickly overtook Pius IX.

What has been called the "miracle of 1848" rested in part on a misunderstanding; but for a few months it actually existed. A few re-marks by Pius IX, contradicting the negative attitude of Gregory XVI, sufficed to awaken in many Italians the conviction that the new Pope was willing to implement the entire national program and was prepared, according to a promise by Gioberti, to place himself at the head of a crusade in order to drive the Austrians from the peninsula and to effect national unification. Such illusions were also nourished by the evident reserve which Pius IX since the beginning of his pontificate had exer-cised toward the Austrian ambassador; this reserve, however, stemmed not only from his sympathy for the Italian cause, but also from his dissatisfaction with the Josephinist religious policy of the Empire, espe-cially in Lombardy. When on 10 November 1848 Pius IX in a public address attempted to lessen belligerency but at the same time implored God's blessing for Italy, public enthusiam reached its zenith. Convinced that the Pope was on their side, the clergy as well as the faithful in all of Italy during the subsequent weeks of national agitation lent a large degree of support to the national uprisings.[8] When the Piedmontese government went to war against Austria in support of the nationalists, it was expected that the papal troops would follow suit. A number of papal advisers in Rome encouraged such a step in order to avoid the displeasure of the people. But the majority of the Curia theologians and cardinals spoke out for neutrality, which seemed more fitting for the head of the Church. Pius IX himself, overcome by the events, was in conflict between his genuine Italian patriotism and the awareness of his religious responsibility, which went beyond national concerns. In order to clear the air, the Pope made his famous speech of 29 April, whose recently discovered draft allows us a direct glimpse at his contradictory feelings.[9] In the first version of the speech the Pope said that while he could not intervene against Austria militarily because its subjects like his own were his spiritual sons, he had full sympathy for the Italian demands. The published text, however, probably corrected by Cardinal

---

[8] The clergy, including the upper clergy, in the north provided strong and in the central part (except for Rome proper) considerable help. In the Kingdom of Naples the bishops on the whole continued to support the Bourbons, but although the lower secular and regular clergy were divided, the majority favored the national cause. A good number of bibliographical references can be found in *Rassegna storica toscana* 4 (1948), 277, n. 28. Not even the Jesuits everywhere assumed the reactionary position generally ascribed to them. See G. De Rosa, *I Gesuiti in Sicilia e la rivoluzione del '48* (Rome 1963).
[9] Text in *Acta Pii IX* 1, 92–98. See J. Muller, *Die Allokution Pius' IX. vom 29. April 1848* (Basel 1928); M. Monaco in *Studi Romani* 3 (1955), 175–94; especially G. Mar-tina in *RStRis* 53 (1966), 527–82, 54 (1967), 40–47.

Antonelli, placed the chief emphasis on the first point and left the second one obscure. In his simplicity, Pius IX was unaware of the consequences of these changes, and when a few days later in response to the angry reaction of the Italian opposition he explained that his words had been designed to clarify the special position of the Pope and were in no way to be a disapproval of the national struggle, it was too late.[10] The equivocal epithet of "liberal pope" was replaced by the equally erroneous designation of "antinational pope."

The progressives in Rome immediately tried to benefit from the deep disappointment, caused by what many considered to be traitorous conduct, at the expense of the moderate liberals, who were discredited by the trust which they had placed in the Pope.

The situation was aggravated by the discontent caused by the economic crisis affecting the Papal State and all of Europe. It made the people an easy prey of agitators. Anarchy continued to spread. At the end of March, public demonstrations forced the Pope to ask the Jesuits to leave the Papal State. They were generally thought to be reactionary and pro-Austrian. In May he had to accept a lay ministry exposed to the continuous pressure of radical elements. Political assassinations increased. To establish mastery over such a volatile situation would have required the abilities of an extraordinary statesman. Pius IX, however, very receptive to superficial suggestions, wavered between the reformatory advice tendered him by the likes of Rosmini[11] and the fear of losing his religious independence. It was a fear fed by the reactionary party at the papal court and the result was a growing lack of morale. He finally consented to entrust the administration to the energetic Count Pellegrino Rossi,[12] who wanted to form a constitutional government after the model of France. But he was unpopular with both the parties of the right and the left and was assassinated shortly after his appointment.

Now things happened quickly: The revolutionaries besieged the Pope in the Quirinal Palace and demanded the convocation of a constituent assembly and a declaration of war on Austria. In the city, cardinals and prelates were exposed to all kinds of threats. Under these circumstances the Pope decided on 24 November, primarily advised by Cardi-

[10] On 3 May he sent a letter to the Austrian chancellor (see F. Gentili in *Nuova Antologia* 256 [1914], 458–59), in which he advised him to forgo imposing Austrian domination on the Italian provinces by force and thus implicitly to acknowledge the superiority of the right of nationality over the divine right of kings or the unassailable character of treaties. Concerning the imperial reply, see F. Engel-Janosi in *RömHM* 10 (1967), 244–48.
[11] Consult F. Traniello, *Societa religiosa e societa civile in Rosmini* (Bologna 1966), 283–335.
[12] See M. Ruini, *La vita di Pellegrino Rossi* (Milan 1962).

nal Antonelli, who feared that the Pope could be pressured into making ill-considered concessions, to leave Rome Disguised, he went to the Neapolitan port of Gaeta[13] in order to board ship for France. He was dissuaded, however, by those who feared that he would fall under the influence of a republican country, and instead accepted the invitation of the king of Naples to seek refuge in his kingdom, where he stayed for seventeen months. Two days after his flight Pius IX dissolved the government which he had left behind and placed Cardinal Antonelli at the helm of the papal administration with the title of prosecretary of state. For the next twenty-five years, Antonelli was in charge of the fate of the Holy See.

Antonelli[14] was an easy-going prelate, ambitious and avaricious, and in spite of his genuine faith more a man of the world than a man of the cloth. He was industrious and energetic and possessed a limited intelligence, but without any perspicacity. He had those abilities peculiar to excellent civil servants, and in fact he had risen quickly in the papal administration, successful on each rung of the ladder. Sensitive and observant, cunning and winning in his ways, a diligent pupil of Bernetti, but without any convictions of his own, he now showed himself as a nimble diplomat. But his ability consisted primarily in finding excuses, in adjusting to the conditions of the moment, and in avoiding difficulties, rather than in attacking a problem at its roots and finding new solutions. He was by no means a reactionary and initially supported the reform movement introduced by Pius IX. But events convinced him that a partial laicization and liberalization of the government of the Papal State would not produce results and that the independence of the Pope as head of the Church could be guaranteed only by the return to a theocratic form of government. He thus decided to pursue a hard-line policy toward the politically active in Rome, and placed all of his hopes in a foreign intervention which would return the Pope to his throne. While Rosmini advised the Pope not to burn his bridges to the Roman parliament, Antonelli emphatically refused to receive a Roman delegation which wanted to ask the Pope to return to the capital. On 4 December he urged the European powers to use force in order to return the Pope to his temporal position. He then advised the Pope against a proclamation in the conciliatory form drafted by Rosmini and encouraged him to disavow the provisional government officially. Rosmini,

[13] About the flight to Gaeta see, complementary to the article by G. Mollat in *RHE* 35 (1939), 266–82, the treatments by P. Pirri: *Miscellanea P. Paschini* II (Rome 1949), 421–51 and F. L. Berro in *Studi romani* 5 (1957), 672–82. See also *Positio super introductione causae* I, 59–60, 69, 117–26, 336, 878–80.
[14] On Giacomo Antonelli (1806–76), see *Dizionario biografico degli Italiani* III, 484–93. A definitive study has not yet been written.

who clearly recognized the disadvantages of a connection of the papal cause with Austria and the conservative powers, in vain advised the Pope to seek a solution with Piedmont as intermediary rather than through the aid of foreign troops. Antonelli, determined to achieve a solution through force, easily succeeded in exploiting the prejudices of Pius IX against the government of Turin and after a few weeks the rivalry between Rosmini and Antonelli ended with a complete victory of the latter. The Pope valued the devotion and skill which he displayed during the critical November days.

In Rome, where the flight of Pius IX made a very bad impression, Antonelli's inflexibility completely discredited the moderates and allowed the radicals to gain the upper hand. The constituent assembly, elected on 21 January 1849 with 134 against 123 votes, declared the Pope devoid of all claims to political power over the Roman state and proclaimed a republic. The government was entrusted to a triumvirate under the leadership of Guiseppe Mazzini. Ghisalberti accurately described the peculiarly Roman character of the republic; it was much more the work of the Roman people than of agitators from other Italian states. Moreover, the people had been won over less because of the republican ideology than because of extreme irritation with the "government of priests" and the abuses associated with it. Of the three phases of this six-month republic, only the second one can be regarded as influenced by Mazzini. But Mazzini's role had great significance, for it was he who, like a prophet, made Rome the focal point in the struggle for Italian rejuvenation, a role which it had not played during the time of Gregory XVI. It was now the ideological capital of the Risorgimento.

Joint military action by Austria, Spain, Naples, and France within a few months put an end to the republican government. The Catholics in France, encouraged by the events in Austria, were able to persuade Louis Napoleon to undertake the Roman campaign despite the opposition of the democratic elements.[15] The conference of Gaeta (30 March to 22 September 1849) established the foundation for the restoration of papal power. The French government desired the restoration to take place in a liberal atmosphere. But while Antonelli considered a return to the form of government of 1848 impossible, he untiringly worked to prevent the implementation of the statute of March 1848 which the Pope had conceded. He was supported by the diplomats of the conservative powers; contrary to expectations, Austria's representative was not the most obstinate; in fact, he was very much aware of the dangers of an

---

[15] After an initial failure in April, the occupation of Rome finally took place on 3 July 1849 under the leadership of General Oudinot.

excessive reaction. The end result was the motu proprio[16] of 12 September 1849, which promised great freedom on the communal level and reforms of the judiciary and the administration, but which brought no political freedom. The regulation, which in effect merely implemented the recommendations of the memorandum of 1831, was "about eighteen years behind the requirements of the present" (Ghisalberti). Even so, there was a large number of cardinals who considered even this regime as too progressive. They were supported by the Neapolitan court in their delay of the implementation of the recommendations of the motu proprio. They undertook repressive measures in an atmosphere of passionate prejudices, totally justifying Monsignor Corboli-Bussi's description of the papal restoration as reactionary and inept.

Even more remarkable than the obsolete character of the political restoration was the change in the attitude subsequently demonstrated by Pius IX. At Gaeta, in contrast to the people around him, his concern for a religious revival predominated and was the real cause for the ideas of political reaction. It is well known to what extent people can be influenced by disappointed illusions. His advisers missed no opportunity to keep alive in his impressionable soul the memories of the bloody Roman revolution and especially the murder of Pellegrino Rossi, the defender of a far-reaching liberalization of institutions, by radical elements. Aside from the psychological level, the opinions of Pius IX also hardened, especially his distrust of principles whose dangerous consequences had become evident. More than ever before he was now convinced of the connection between the principles of 1789 and the destruction of traditional social, moral, and religious values. As A. M. Ghisalberti noted with respect to the address by Pius IX on 20 April 1849,[17] the entire *Syllabus* was embryonically present in these experiences. The new orientation began with the placing on the Index on 30 May 1849 of the works in which Gioberti, Rosmini, and Ventura had presented their reform program.[18] The *Civiltà cattolica* became for the Pope, who very much encouraged its founding by a group of Jesuits under the leadership of Father Curci,[19] an instrument of doctrine and a carrier of propaganda effective far beyond the borders of Italy.

---

[16] Text in *Atti del S. Pont. Pio IX* V/1, 286–90 (cf. 293–94).

[17] Text in *Acta Pii IX* I, 167–94. See also A. Gambaro, *Ferrante Aporti nel I° centenario della morte* (Brescia 1962), 235–50.

[18] See R. Rensch, *Der Index der verbotenen Bücher* II (Bonn 1885), 1132–41, and G. Martina, "La censura romana del 1848 alle opere di Rosmini," *Rivista rosminiana* 62 (1968), 384–409, 63 (1969), 24–49.

[19] On the beginnings of the *Civiltà cattolica,* see *CivCatt* (1949) II, 5–40; P. Pirri, *Il P. Roothaan* (Rome 1930), 463ff.; A. Dioscoridi in *RStRis* 42 (1955), 258–66.

CHAPTER 5

The Consequences of the Events of 1848 in France

French Catholics initially were chagrined by the news of the abolition of the monarchy, evoking in them sad memories of the Terror. But then they noted with joy that the new government harbored no hostile sentiments and that the revolutionaries even displayed a respectful attitude toward the Church. It would be too simplistic, of course, to equate the insults hurled at priests in 1830 or the destruction of the residence of the archbishop in Paris with the appeal of 1848 which asked the clergy to bless the liberty trees, for the short period of friendship between Church and Republic was essentially limited to Paris. Yet there is no doubt that a change of mind had taken place since 1830 and that many people in 1848 as heirs of romanticism were motivated by a kind of Christian sentimentalism and were taken by the evangelical message of brotherly love and human equality. They were also impressed by the liberal stance taken by Pius IX at the beginning of his pontificate and by the fact that the clergy, less involved in politics than during the restoration period and even occasionally treated with coldness by the authorities, had come closer to the people. Thus, clergy and flocks, after a momentary disquiet, were calmed by the thought that religion flourished in the American republics and accepted the new government with sympathy. Numerous clerics, regarding themselves as successors to the priests of 1789, became candidates for the constituent assembly, which confirmed their initial hopes. Through the introduction of the universal franchise in a country in which many peasants were still under the influence of the clergy, the Church was assured of a larger political role than under the earlier class voting arrangement.

But the revolution of 1848 posed a much more difficult problem for the conscience of French Catholics than the simple acceptance of the Republic: it was its socialistic character which exercised a disturbing influence on the broad masses of the Catholics, especially in the rural areas, and among the petite bourgeoisie and the landowners. There were also a few groups who under the July Monarchy had become concerned with the problems of the workers. From the beginning these people favored the socialistic tendencies of the young republic. A few clerics and laymen, among them Ozanam and Lacordaire, were even willing to support them actively, and with the approval of the archbishop of Paris, Monsignor Affre, they founded the newspaper *L'Ère Nouvelle,* designed to defend not merely the principles of 1789 and the republican ideal, but also various social reforms, some of which were still rather daring at this time.

The program also found an echo in some Catholic newspapers in the provinces and initially was somewhat successful chiefly among the young clergy. But a large majority of Catholics were above all interested in the maintenance of order and the inviolability of property. Their worries, caused by financial impositions designed to pay for the initial social legislation, turned into panic after the June disturbances which were caused by the closing of the state-run workshops. They convinced the French Church for the next twenty years that religion, morality, and the traditional social order were threatened. Confirmed in its fears by the events in Rome, it essentially returned to a conservative position, and because of its fear of the socialists was prepared for all kinds of compromises. While the bishops painted democracy as the heresy of the nineteenth century and Louis Veuillot began to attack socialism, to which were attributed the areligious antifamilial tendencies of some of its leaders, Montalembert became the leader of the countermovement against the radicals, in whose aims he saw a threat to the true concept of freedom.

This rapid development was favored by the Orleanist bourgeoisie, which now was perfectly willing to make common cause with the Church for the purpose of defending property. To be sure, Montalembert and Falloux,[1] together with Thiers and Molé, the leaders of the large "party of order," were concerned about the preservation of the interests of religion and obtained significant advantages for the Church; but their clever calculation on the parliamentary level took insufficient account of the dangers inherent in this pact between religion and capitalist interests. On the other hand, French Catholics strongly supported the increasingly antidemocratic measures with which the National Assembly in 1849 and 1850 attempted to reduce the influence of the left. Thus they appeared not only as antisocialists but as antirepublicans as well and their attitude toward Louis Napoleon Bonaparte reinforced the impression. Without a doubt, they preferred him to Cavaignac as president because he promised them the freedom of secondary education and the support of France for the restoration of the secular power of the Pope. To the same degree that he revealed himself as dictator, clergymen flocked to him, as the traditionalist movement increased their sympathies for the authoritarian forms of power.

The attitude of the Catholics to the coup d'état of 2 December 1851 was therefore predictable. With a few exceptions—among them Lacor-

---

[1] On Alfred de Falloux (1811–86), who played a significant role during this period, see *DHGE* XVI, 1499–1513.

daire, Ozanam, Dupanloup, and the small group of Christian Democrats—they agreed after brief hesitation with Veuillot: "There is only a choice between Bonaparte as Emperor and the socialistic republic." Montalembert exhorted people to vote "yes" in the plebiscite "in order to defend our churches, houses, and women against those whose greed does not respect anything." The legitimist Monsignor Clausel de Montals was not the only bishop who regarded the coup d'état which drove away the specter of a red republic "as the greatest miracle of God's benevolence known to history." But the praises to God which the clergy sang in public on the occasion of the coup d'état aroused the anger of the republican leaders. Unceasingly they denounced the "alliance between saber and aspergillum" and gradually imbued their followers with their violent anticlericalism.

For the moment, however, the four years of the Second Republic had clearly been positive for the French Church. The tactic employed by Montalembert during the July Monarchy had borne fruit. The Catholics, well represented in the parliament and needed against the left, succeeded in obtaining a number of institutionally and administratively favorable decisions. They were not able, as they had hoped initially, to do away with the so-called Organic Articles which limited the freedom of the Church,[2] but the new constitution quite satisfactorily regulated some points important to the Catholic interests. Favored by generous legislation, orders expanded quickly.[3] Relations with the authorities were easy and often even friendly, and the reconstruction of parish churches increased. Three new dioceses for the Antilles and Réunion Island were established. Advised by Dupanloup, Falloux appointed excellent bishops and they, strictly supervised by the nuncio, gradually grew accustomed to dealing directly with Rome without interference from the government, which in any case granted them more freedom than they had had under the monarchy. After brief hesitation, the government even gave in to the importunings of Monsignor Sibours and

---

[2] Monsignor Affre, archbishop of Paris, supported by some other bishops, planned an even more radical reform which intended to renounce the advantages of the concordat in order to assure the independence of the Church from the government. The election of the bishops by the bishops of their church province further was to replace the appointment of bishops by the government. A letter from the Pope, inspired by the nuncio, put an end to the plan. On the fruitless efforts of the *Comité des Cults,* see P. Pradie, *La question religieuse en 1682, 1790, 1802 et 1848* (Paris 1849) and E. Ponteil, *Les institutions de la France de 1814 à 1870* (Paris 1966), 328–30; on the initiative of Monsignor Affre, see J. Leflon in *Revue des travaux de l'Académie des sciences morales* 121 (1968) I, 221–28.

[3] There were 207 new authorizations within three years compared to 384 during the eighteen years of the July Monarchy, and the total number of regular clergy rose from 28,000 in 1848 to 37,357 in 1851.

permitted the convocation of provincial synods, last held in 1727. These councils regulated a number of ecclesiastical administrative problems which had been left unattended for more than fifty years. They also provided proof for the clergy that large portions of the population had become estranged from the Church and that new methods of pastoral care needed to be employed.

The major advantage for the Church during the Second Republic was in the field of education. Fear of the "socialist danger" and apprehension of the elementary school teachers, many of whom seemed to be enamored of socialism, drove the middle class to the Church which it had fought for so long. Thiers was willing to entrust the entire primary school education to the clergy, whose expectations had been far lower. In secondary education, however, designed for the children of the bourgeoisie, there were still numerous defenders of the monopoly of the state. At all costs they were determined to achieve a series of conditions which seriously would have restricted the freedom promised in ARTICLE 9 of the constitution. For four months the matter was discussed in a special committee created by Secretary of Education Falloux, but finally the skill of Abbé Dupanloup, Thiers, and Cousin succeeded in winning substantial concessions. The draft developed by the commission was adopted on 15 March 1850 by the Chamber of Deputies in spite of the opposition of university professors and the left. The Falloux Law,[4] for thirty years the basis of a dual school system, brought about a total reform of the state and private systems of education. It was based on two principles: freedom of private education, producing some very favorable conditions for schools run by the Church, and influence by the Church on the education system of the state.

The Falloux Law promoted an increase in the number of Catholic schools and perforce gradually deepened the gap which ideologically separated the former pupils of the ecclesiastical colleges from the high schools of the state and the former pupils of the school brothers from the lay schools. By increasingly making the Church a rival of the state in the area of education, this law contributed to the formation of a broad anticlerical movement, which half a century later led to drastic measures against the orders, through which it was hoped to deliver a mortal blow to Catholic education. For the moment, however, the law was a great victory for the Church after forty years of a monopoly by the university.

But it was also a victory for Catholic liberalism. The tactic inspired by Montalembert had made success possible. On the other hand, the ac-

---

[4] Text in H. Michel, op. cit., 484ff. By this time Falloux was no longer secretary of education, but his name remains connected with the law whose real creator he was.

ceptance of this compromise law meant for the Church the official renunciation of its claims to the monopoly of education which it had had
under the Old Regime and of which many still dreamed. A portion of
the clergy, supported by intransigent journalists led by Louis Veuillot,
regarded this "Edict of Nantes of the nineteenth century" (Lacordaire)
as an unacceptable capitulation, signifying in an essential point the end
of the system of an established religion. The discussions soon grew so
heated that the Pope, warned by Montalembert and Dupanloup, had
to force the episcopate to accept the law. It made the split in the
Catholic bloc final and any small incident could not but deepen it. This
was demonstrated, for example, in the discussion of the ideas of Abbé
Gaume concerning the treatment of pagan classics in the Catholic colleges.[5] Initially a bagatelle, it quickly grew with the aid of the newspaper
L'Univers into a controversy between lay journalists and the bishops,
and sharpened the contrast between Gallicans and ultramontanes.

[5] See *DThC* XV, 2807–8.

CHAPTER 6

*The Consequences of the 1848 Revolution in the States of the German
Confederation and the Netherlands*

The States of the German Confederation

Buoyed by the news from France of the revolution in February 1848,
the liberal movement in Germany in March 1848 could have either
taken over the government in various German federal states or gained a
degree of participation. After general elections, the National Assembly
met in Frankfurt in May, confronted with the double responsibility of
creating a unified state and a liberal constitution. It wrote the constitution, but by the time it was passed in March 1849 the Assembly no
longer had the strength to withstand the individual states, which had
regained much of their power. In the larger states by this time the
governments had managed to impose constitutions of their own—in
Prussia in December 1848, in Austria in March 1849—and while these
realized many liberal demands, they actually started a counterrevolu-
tionary phase.

Most of the German Catholics greeted the changes in March 1848
with approval. Brought up in the tradition of empire, they desired
national unification and welcomed the fall of police state administrations
which had oppressed the Church. The old ecclesiastical demands for
freedom could be articulated effectively within the framework of the

March movement and the leaders of the Catholics immediately took advantage of the recently decreed principles of freedom of the press, association, and assembly. From now on they pursued two large goals: The Church in Germany was to gain effective unity of action and lasting autonomy with respect to the governments; and in the desired national state the Catholics were to regain their proportional influence, lost after the secularization. Catholic activity was focused on the three new areas of associations, parliaments, and joint actions of the episcopate. Once again laymen and lower clergy were in the vanguard.

The first impulses which pointed the way were generated in Mainz. In March, Adam Franz Lennig,[1] cathedral chapter member, together with Professor Kaspar Riffel, Pastor Moufang and Chaplain Heinrich,[2] founded the "Pius Association for Religious Freedom," whose program was publicized by the *Katholik* and the *Mainzer Journal* (editor Franz Sausen),[3] founded in the spring of 1848. Several other associations followed, first in the Rhineland, in Westphalia, and in Baden, where Andlaw and Buß were the organizers, then also in Bavaria, Tyrol, and the east (Breslau and Danzig). By September there existed seven central associations and several hundred branches, many of them directed by laymen. In addition to religious freedom, the associations demanded social measures and some, especially in the Rhineland, also favored political liberalism.[4] The most important daily papers founded in 1848 were the Greater-German federalist *Deutsches Volksblatt* (Stuttgart) and the *Rheinische Volkshalle* (Cologne), with the motto: "Freedom for everything and for everyone."

During the elections for the National Assembly, the associations, together with Catholic election committees and the active support of the clergy, worked for the election of Catholic candidates. When the role of religion was debated in Frankfurt in the summer of 1848, the associations generated a flood of petitions which made the public aware of the Catholic demands.

In Prussia, the movement was led by Archbishop Geissel. In consultation with his suffragans he adopted Lennig's suggestion of a synod of all German bishops and pursued it diligently. He drafted a religious policy

---

[1] Adam Franz Lennig (1803–66), in 1845 cathedral chapter member in Mainz, and after 1848 one of the most influential leaders of the Catholic association movement, decisively involved in the elevation of Ketteler as bishop of Mainz, his vicar general since 1852 (see, besides the biography of Brück, G. Lenhart: *StL* III, 924ff.; L. Lenhart in *LThK* VI, 944).

[2] Kaspar Riffel (1807–56), professor of moral theology at Gießen, forced to retire in 1842, in 1851 professor at the new clerical seminary in Mainz.

[3] H. J. Wieseotte, "F.J. Sausen und die Gründung des Mainzer Journals," *AMrhKG* 5 (1953), 267–98.

[4] See the program of the Cologne election committee: Heinen I, 115–19.

program which attenuated the desire of liberal Catholics for a separation of church and state and held fast to a continued parallelism to the extent that it was useful for the Church. It demanded autonomy but simultaneously also the maintenance of protection by the state and of legal privileges for the Church. It had great significance for the future development of the Church in Germany.

The active Catholics among the Frankfurt delegates worked for the realization of this program. They belonged to different political factions and were therefore not yet a regular party but only a working group under the name of "Catholic Club." Its leading members were the bishops Diepenbrock, Geritz (Ermland), Müller (Münster), and Sedlag (Kulm); the clerics Döllinger, Ketteler, and Beda Weber; and the laymen Buß, Gagern, Lasaulx, Linde, Müller (Würzburg), Osterrath, Phillips, Radowitz, and August Reichensperger.

Geissel, attempting skillfully to coordinate these forces, was a member of the Prussian Diet, where he led the Catholic representatives, among them Peter Reichensperger and the Bonn law professors Walter and Bauerband. At the same time the archbishop followed the path of direct negotiations with the government. As parliamentary work in Berlin made only slow progress and there were strongly anticlerical forces on the left, this way was realistic as well as programmatic. Most of the Church leaders wanted greater freedom, but they also wanted to maintain the alliance between throne and altar. Alternatives were not considered. Geissel was not in favor of cooperation between Rhenish Catholics and political liberalism, and he and Diepenbrock defended the threatened authority of the crown. In this matter Geissel was a tough politician: he demanded a price for the services which he offered the state.

In Frankfurt the position of the Church also was debated vigorously, but in September a compromise was found which satisfied central demands of the Churches.[5] In the section on basic rights, all Germans were guaranteed freedom of religion and of conscience; all groups were permitted the public exercise of religion, and civil rights were neither a precondition of nor limited by religion. The greatest success of the Churches consisted of being granted the right to regulate and administer themselves within the framework of general laws. Autonomy was achieved and separation from the state was avoided. Combined with the freedom for Churches was their equality; the privileged existence of some denominations was abandoned. The liberal parliamentary majority also insisted on some core demands of its concepts of state and

---

[5] *Reichsverfassung* Section VI, ARTICLE V, pars. 144–51, ART. VI, pars. 152–54. Text: Huber, *Dokumente* I, 319f.

society, in the face of which the Churches were pushed into a helpless defensive. Civil marriage was introduced, and all public education was placed under the authority of the state, with the exception of religious instruction. Private schools, however, were permitted.

In spite of the failure of the National Assembly, the religious policy compromise of the constitution was significant and even influenced the Weimar constitution. It also had direct results, thanks to Geissel's exertions. The Frankfurt concessions to the Churches became part of the Prussian constitution imposed by the King. It renounced the right of approval, the right of the state to participate in the filling of clerical positions, and it facilitated the founding of orders.[6] The revised constitution of January 1850 confirmed these rights.[7] Under the influence of the conservative reaction it also accepted the Christian religion as the basis of all those state institutions which were connected with religion. It was generally assumed that this basis was provided by the two major denominations. The regulation of civil marriage was postponed until later (it was introduced only during the *Kulturkampf*), and for elementary schools consideration of denominational conditions was accepted. The relaxation of tension in the relationship between church and state thus reached its zenith and the religious paragraphs of the Prussian constitution were regarded justifiably as the Magna Carta of religious freedom.

During the celebration of the building of the Cologne Cathedral in August 1848, an affair equally ecclesiastic and national, Lennig's suggestion of a national meeting of the representatives of Catholic associations met with general approval. At the beginning of October the first German Catholic Conference took place in Mainz; it was characteristic for its structure that it was presided over by a layman, Buß, and that the bishop of Mainz, Kaiser, did not take part in the proceedings. Twenty-three representatives came from Frankfurt, and Döllinger made a programmatic speech in which he demanded a greater degree of freedom for the Church than the National Assembly had granted. He pleaded for a uniform, nationally and historically based organization of the German Church; it would not limit papal primacy, but it would give the Church the weight it deserved. While the majority applauded the speech, the ultramontanes began to have their first doubts. They did not know how to reconcile such autonomy with their centralistic concept. Ketteler, confronting the assembly with the social problems facing the Church, received undivided approval.

[6] Constitution imposed by Prussia, II, ARTICLES 11–21. Text: Huber, *Dokumente* I, 386f.
[7] Prussian revised constitution, II, ARTICLES 12–24. Text: Huber, *Dokumente* I, 402f.

The Mainz Catholic Conference was the start of a lasting integration of German Catholicism. The most important concrete results were the creation of a central organization, the "German Catholic Association," and religious decisions which were directed not against the thrones but merely against the concept of established Churches, demanding freedom of religion as well as guarantees under law. The Catholic Association was to be led by laymen and to pursue national goals, very much like O'Connell's Irish Catholic Organization. But the increasing anticlericalism of many liberals, the failure of the Frankfurt National Assembly, and the subsequent rise of a revolutionary radicalism allowed the growth of uncertainty with respect to political goals. The two Catholic conferences in Breslau and Regensburg in 1849 agreed on political neutrality and on concentration of energies on ecclesiastical concerns. The Regensburg conference declared religious freedom to be the prerequisite for national unity and accused the Frankfurt National Assembly of not having considered this historical truth adequately.

In 1848 Archbishop Geissel managed to convince most of his colleagues to convene a bishops' conference and to invite eminent theologians, among them Döllinger, and laymen as advisers. He designed a tentative program, calling for freedom of religion and reforms in ecclesiastical structure and preaching. Reiterating Döllinger, the archbishop came out in favor of a structural unity of the German Church, which measure was not to be understood as directed against Rome but only against tutelage by the state. He also favored greater rights for the lower clergy and laity and greater use of German in liturgy.

The first German bishops' conference took place from 22 October to 16 November 1848 in Würzburg under Geissel's chairmanship and largely adopted his program. Of the Austrian bishops, only Cardinal Schwarzenberg (Salzburg) participated.[8] In an extensive memorandum to all German governments the conference formulated its religious demands, thus placing the episcopate in the lead of the ecclesiastical movement for freedom. The memorandum contained a consistent maximal program for the emancipation of the Church from the state and

---

[8] Friedrich Prince zu Schwarzenberg (1809–85), 1836 archbishop of Salzburg, 1842 cardinal, 1850 archbishop of Prague, as a defender of Bohemian autonomy opponent of Viennese centralism, remained in Prague, where in 1860 a general meeting of German Catholics took place. In the 1860s Schwarzenberg occasionally was active as a mediator between Rome and German theologians. In 1869–70 he belonged to the most vocal opponents of the dogma of infallibility (see, in addition to the biography by Wolfsgruber, Wurzbach, 33, 71–78; E. Winter, *Die geistige Entwicklung Anton Günthers und seiner Schule* [Paderborn 1931]; K. zu Schwarzenberg, *Geschichte des reichsständischen Hauses Schwarzenberg* II [Neustadt/Aisch, 1964]).

thereby determined the direction for future disputes, especially in southern and southwestern Germany. After lively discussions the majority of the bishops voted in favor of a national organization under the leadership of a primate as well as for timely reforms of church regulations and liturgy. The Pope was asked for permission for a formal national council which was to implement the decisions.

The papal reply was half a year in coming and was negative. The novel initiative of the German bishops had caused suspicion and doubts in the Curia; in fact, Rome had tried to torpedo the conference. Pius IX was not prepared to grant the bishops supradiocesan responsibilities and in ignorance of the people active in Germany (including Döllinger!), shades of Febronius and of the Ems Congress were conjured. Suspicion was awakened and fed persistently by the intransigent Munich internuncio Sacconi[9] and Archbishop Reisach, who closely cooperated with him. Their criticism was focused on the plans for a national church organization and the liturgical reforms and clearly presaged the internal divisions of the Church during the subsequent two decades.

The German bishops accepted the papal decision postponing a national council for an indefinite period of time. After all, they had not intended an action unacceptable to the Pope, and besides, national enthusiasm had considerably diminished in the meantime. Once again the Church had to deal with the individual states after the revolutions. Geissel therefore distanced himself from some of his reform proposals, in part because they had contributed to some far-reaching demands for codetermination by his clergy under the leadership of Pastor Binterim. In southwestern Germany as well the old demands for diocesan synods were strongly raised in the wake of the revolution.[10] Perhaps Geissel and the majority of his colleagues realized only during the period of disenchantment in 1849 that the organizational concentration without the participation of intermediate levels was inseparable from the authoritarian restoration which they also regarded as necessary.

[9] Carlo Sacconi (1808–89), in 1845 envoy in Florence, in 1847 internuncio, in 1851 nuncio in Munich and in 1853 in Paris, in 1861 Curia cardinal. (Schmidlin, *PG* II, 162, 302, 338ff., 345f.; Aubert, *Pie IX,* 110f.; Lill, *Bischofskonferenzen,* 17–51).

[10] The Freiburg professor and cathedral chapter member J. B. Hirscher, with his sensational pamphlet *Die kirchlichen Zustände der Gegenwart* (Tübingen 1849), pleaded for the introduction of synods at which clergy and laymen should jointly formulate canon law. At the same time he attacked Catholic associations, which he accused of superficiality and lack of concern for the real tasks of the Church. He thus assumed an antipolitically motivated position, connected with the polemicism of F. X. Kraus and his pupils against political Catholicism. On the synodal movement under the Rhenish clergy, see especially H. Schrörs in *AHVNrh* 105 (1921), 106 (1922).

Thanks to the bold efforts of Anton Günther, Sebastian Brunner (1814–93),[11] and Emanuel Veith (1787–1870),[12] the association movement in 1848 spread to Austria. The leaders of restoration Catholicism were compromised by their connection with Metternich, and the majority of bishops remained silent for Josephinist reasons. Cardinal Schwarzenberg, a disciple of Günther's, in August 1848 conducted a conference with his suffragan bishops and sent petitions to the Reichstag; after his return from Würzburg he intensified his efforts for the activation of the episcopate. Only when there was no longer any doubt about the victory of the counterrevolution did the Josephinist Viennese archbishop Vincenz Milde (1777–1853) ask the young Emperor Franz Joseph for the convocation of an all-Austrian bishops' conference. The Emperor, who in the Patent of 4 March appended to the Constitution had granted all Christian denominations the right to the autonomous regulation of their affairs, and the government led by Prince Felix Schwarzenberg, a brother of the Cardinal, agreed to the project. The conference took place in Vienna between 27 April and 17 June 1849; its chief participants were Schwarzenberg, Rauscher (prince-bishop of Seckau and administrator of Leoben since 1849),[13] and Diepenbrock, entitled to participate because of the Austrian part of Breslau. Basing itself on the Patent of 4 March, the conference appealed to Emperor and government for the dismantling of Josephinist legislation and for a concordat for the border areas. From now on, this was a persistent demand by the bishops. Franz Joseph, a pupil of Rauscher's, quite in keeping with the recommendations by Metternich, was desirous of assuring his restoration policy through an agreement with the Church. His decrees of 18 and 23 April 1850 satisfied the most important demands of the bishops (among others lifting of the *placet,* freedom of communication with Rome, free exercise of episcopal disciplinary powers),[14] thus starting the Church policy which led to the concordat of 1855.

[11] On Brunner, the founder (1848) and editor of the *Wiener Kirchenzeitung,* see especially K. Ammerl, *Sebastian Brunner und seine publizistische Stellungnahme in der Wiener Kirchenzeitung* (diss., Vienna 1934); J. Treimer, *Sebastian Brunner als Historiker* (diss., Vienna 1945); E. Alker in *NDB* 2, 683f.; *ÖBL* 1, 121f.
[12] C. Wolfsgruber, *Veith als Homileth* (Vienna 1911); E. Hosp, *Das Erbe des heiligen Klemens Maria Hofbauer* (Vienna 1953).
[13] Rauscher owed his bishopric to Schwarzenberg, who as archbishop of Salzburg had the right of appointment for three of his suffragan bishoprics (Lavant, Seckau-Loeben, Gurk).
[14] Text: Walter, *Fontes,* 276–80.

The Netherlands

The support given to Thorbecke's liberal party by the Catholic middle class in the northern provinces made a peaceful revolution possible, leading to the constitution of 1848. The Catholics, desirous of complete freedom in education, had to be satisfied with a compromise, but received full satisfaction in all other areas. Owing to freedom of assembly, the last obstacles were removed for religious orders. In spite of the efforts of the conservatives among the Reformed to give the country the character of a "Protestant nation," the new constitution proclaimed the equality of all religious denominations before the law and the right of each denominational community to regulate its own affairs.

The restoration of a regular episcopal organization, on the agenda for longer than thirty years, had to appear as the crowning point of this complete and legal emancipation. But in reality it was not desired by many priests. In the rural south they were satisfied, ever since in 1842 the vicars apostolic had assumed the character of an *Ordinarius loci,* and in the cities of the north the archpriests and regular clergy feared the loss of their autonomy. The laymen of the north, supported by a few priests of the group clustered around Warmond and the bishop of Liège, Van Bommel, who was of Dutch descent,[15] pleaded with Rome for real bishops. Their main reason was their wish to have a local authority capable of guiding them in all political questions touching the interests of the Church.

They all agreed in principle, but differed in the modalities. Those who were close to the office in The Hague responsible for the Catholic religion would have preferred a concordatory solution or at least an agreement with the state negotiated on the basis of the Mechelen School; the strongly liberal group of the young Papo-Thorbeckians of the *Tijd* chiefly desired the independence of the Church from the state, even at the cost of complete separation. The demands of the government, which had to take into account the rejection by the Protestants of the establishment of dioceses in the north, forced the Holy See to accept the second solution and to decide unilaterally how to restore the hierarchy. In order to offend the Protestants as little as possible, it was at first planned, in agreement with the suggestions of the inter-nuncio and vicar apostolic of 's-Hertogenbosch, Monsignor Zwijsen, to establish only one diocese in the north and three in the south, including the see of the metropolitan. But the prefect of the Propaganda, on the occasion of a visit, convinced himself not only of the numerically growing importance of Catholicism in the north, but also of its dynamic

---

[15] See A. Manning, *De betekenis van C. Van Bommel* (Utrecht 1956), 218–60.

nature,[16] and it was finally decided in a kind of restoration of the pre-Reformation hierarchy to make Utrecht the archepiscopal see and to add four suffragen dioceses: Haarlem for the large coastal cities, Breda, 's-Hertogenbosch, and Roermond for Brabant and Limburg.

The establishment bull of 4 March 1853 caused a wave of protest on the part of the Protestants which became known as the "April Movement," but it had a more political than religious nature. The prejudices of many Calvinists against the Pope were exploited by the reactionaries opposed to the liberal cabinet which had made the Roman decision possible. These attempts to place in question the favorable articles of the constitution of 1848 nevertheless failed because of the hesitant attitude of King Willem II. The King held no sympathies for the Roman Church, but considered it dangerous for the unity of the country to drive the Catholics to the extreme. In spite of a few offending decrees, ultimately everything ended with a rather harmless law on the exercise of religion.[17]

Disregarding the Protestant agitation, the new bishops, under the directorship of Zwijsen,[18] who was appointed archbishop of Utrecht, immediately began to rewrite Church regulations according to canon law. He was an industrious pastor, had no interest in intellectual pursuits, but possessed common sense and strength of character. During this difficult period these virtues were of use, but they also contributed their healthy share to the ultramontane ghetto character of Dutch Catholicism for the next one hundred years.

Under the strict leadership of an episcopate whose authority was limited by neither government nor traditions, surrounded by a pious, active and steadily growing clergy,[19] and ministered to by regular clergy of both sexes, whose growth was even greater, the faithful had hardly any opportunity to make efforts of their own. Like the Irish Catholics they accepted this clericalism, unthinkable in any other environment,

---

[16] Among others, through the immigration of a number of enterprising Germans from the Münster area.

[17] Among others, it raised the small Jansenist Church with about ten thousand members to the rank of an officially recognized religious community. The bishops of this Church—with seats in Utrecht and Haarlem—lodged protests with the government against the appointments by Rome of prelates to sees already occupied by "regular" successors of the former bishops (see B. Moss, *The Old Catholic Movement* [London 1948], 161–68, and Albers, *Herstel* I, 253–57, II, 433–34).

[18] On the other hand, because of the impossibility of cooperation between the internuncio Vecchiotti and the Dutch bishops it was not until 1865 that the first provincial council took place (see J. van Laarhoven, *Een Kerkprovincie in concilie* [Utrecht 1965]).

[19] The number of priests under the pontificate of Pius IX rose from 1,500 to 2,200, while the Catholic population increased by only 15 percent (1,439,137 in the year 1878, i.e., 35.86 percent of the total population; in 1840 it was 38.28 percent).

without any hesitation and supported the clergy with remarkable generosity. For all areas of life the Catholics founded associations. Thus they guaranteed the maintenance of religious life, and nonpracticing Catholics, aside from the workers, remained an exception. But at the same time these social organizations contributed to keeping the Catholics away from most expressions of national life.

The isolation was noticeable especially on the cultural level. While a small body of Catholic intellectuals came into being among the urban middle class, intellectual life on the whole stagnated, especially in comparison to the ferment of the 1830s. While Catholics were well represented in music and architecture—here as everywhere else the Neo-Gothic was in full flower—their contribution to literature was minimal. Much more serious was the fact that their shortsighted suspicions of educational literature mired them in an almost total ignorance of the great literary movements of the time. In philosophy and theology, Catholic Dutch publications hardly rose above the level of reference books for seminaries or popular apologetic writings. Only a few exceptions stood out from the prevailing mediocrity. There were Theodor Borret,[20] who on the basis of his knowledge of Christian archeology became the first Catholic member of the Royal Academy; Willem Nuyens,[21] a talented polemicist who undertook a reassessment of the history of the religious wars of the sixteenth century; and especially Joseph Alberdingk Thijm,[22] the author of scholarly works on art history and Dutch literature. His sympathetic understanding and his intellectual qualities gained him recognition outside of Catholic circles and for many years he alone acted as the mediator between Catholics and Protestants. Only around 1870 did a moderate rejuvenation begin, finding expression primarily in higher academic standards of the *Katholiek* and in the founding of a new journal, *De Wachter*. The latter was especially concerned with those problems which resulted from the participation of Catholics in public life. It was the beginning of a new phase in the gradual emancipation of the Catholics.

[20] Concerning Theodor Borret (1812–90), see P. Dessens in *De Katholiek* 99 (1891), 4–35; a more detailed presentation is given by Rogier, *KathHerleving*, 239–41.
[21] On Willem Nuyens (1823–94), see G. Gorries, *Willem Nuyens* (Nijmegen 1908).
[22] On Joseph Alberdingk Thijm (1820–89), see W. Bennink, *Alberdingk Thijm* (Utrecht 1952) and G. Brom, *Alberdingk Thijm* (Utrecht 1956).

PART TWO

The Catholic Reaction to Liberalism

INTRODUCTION

Pius IX after 1848

Pius IX was still relatively young when at the age of fifty-four he was
chosen Pope by cardinals chiefly concerned with a solution of the political problems of the Papal State. Yet in this very area he failed completely. On the other hand, his unusually long pontificate (1846–78)
profoundly and lastingly affected the fate of the Catholic Church.

He was not at all a strong personality, such as his successor Leo XIII.
But in contrast to his predecessor, Gregory XVI, who lived isolated
from the world and whose influence did not reach beyond the narrow
circle of his immediate collaborators, Pius IX managed rather ef-
fortlessly to win a large number of the clerics and of the faithful for his
ecclesiastic, theological, and spiritual concepts.

His contemporaries were unanimous in agreeing on his fascinating
charm. He loved being in contact with people and increased the number
of audiences, during which with loving good nature he received not
only a few notables, as his predecessors had done, but also numerous
priests and laymen, who, owing to the improvement of transportation,
flocked to Rome in ever greater numbers. The visitors, taken by their
kind reception, after returning to their home countries broadcast their
impressions, and consequently there developed a real papal adulation in
the Catholic world, whose excesses, according to inclination, generated
either smiles or irritation. The adulation facilitated to a high degree the
enthusiastic agreement of many to an increasingly centralized leadership of the Church and to a coordination of the regional Churches with a
certain type of Catholicism preferred by Rome.

The Pope, because of his fervent piety, trust in providence, and
strength of soul in adversity, praised by many as a saint during his
lifetime, appeared to others, including many clerics and many a militant
layman whose devotion to the Church was unquestioned, as no more
than a vain autocrat or a puppet maneuvered by insensitive reactionaries. Both impressions are one-sided and simplistic. It is possible to
arrive at a realistic portrait, in spite of the absence of a good biography
going beyond the framework of a naive hagiography, and to show both
man and Pope as a concrete and differentiated personality.

Pius IX labored under three handicaps. In his youth he suffered from
epileptic attacks which left him with an extreme excitability. It makes
understandable many of his summary declarations and the fact that he
frequently changed his mind according to the opinion last heard. Con-

83

sequently, many observers regarded him as a hesitant and indecisive person. Only when he was convinced that it was a matter of consequence did he demonstrate unshakable resolution and boldly defended his position. The second handicap was that like most of the Italian clerics of his age, raised during the first two decades of the nineteenth century with the upheavals of the Napoleonic era, his education was rather inadequate. His superficial training often did not permit him to recognize the complexity of problems or the implications of many statements which he was expected to judge. This lack was partly compensated for by his Italian shrewdness, which allowed him to understand much without being very erudite. Thus Pius IX was able to apply common sense in assessing concrete situations, at least as long as they were reported to him accurately. Unfortunately, and that was his third handicap, his staff was not always able to inform him with the required care. His trusted advisers were generally conscientious and industrious, but also rather exalted and often viewed matters with the uncompromising attitude of theoreticians out of touch with contemporary views. Under these circumstances it is not surprising that Pius IX failed to adapt the Church to new conditions. These were on the one hand the profound evolution which was in the process of completely altering the structures of bourgeois society, and on the other the totally changed perspectives by which certain theological positions needed to be viewed in light of the progress made in the natural sciences and historical research.

If the capabilities of Pius IX had undeniable limits, especially regrettable in a superior who increasingly was compelled to make solitary decisions in many areas, he must also be credited with qualities and achievements which cannot be regarded as small. This was first of all true on the personal level. Pius IX was a genuinely unpretentious and good person,[1] equipped with a sensitivity which permitted him to make charming gestures and have happy ideas, without excluding, if he considered it advisable, a sometimes rude frankness. He was sufficiently supple to make occasional concessions which at first sight looked dangerous, because more than the tacticians in his environment, he relied on trust built on personal relations. Father Isaac Hecker, who regretted that Pius frequently allowed himself to be guided more by impulses than by judgment, also thought that his impulses were great,

---

[1] With two provisos: the excessive receptivity for impressions stemming from the illness of his youth occasionally drove him to fits of anger, as violent as they were sudden, but they never lasted long and had few consequences for those who had occasioned them. To this was added toward the end of his life a predisposition for flattery and the inability to be contradicted. But it would not be just to take account only of the weaknesses of an eighty-year-old man when assessing the personality of Pius IX.

noble, and universal.[2] He was not an intellectual, but was interested in all kinds of problems, and in his youth had read extensively.[3] After he became Pope, he kept abreast of modern inventions. He knew how to pray, and the depth of his religious sentiments was undeniable, even if in this area, as in others, he combined weaknesses with virtues. He attached too much weight to prophecies and other manifestations of the miraculous, and tended to see in the political convulsions which involved the Church a new episode in the great battle between God and Satan instead of realistically subjecting the events to a technical analysis.

At the beginning of his priestly life, at a time when most young clerics are concerned with making a career, he completely renounced ecclesiastical honors and devoted himself to orphans and other poor. As bishop he impressed the people of his diocese by the apostolic strength with which he rose above party struggles in order to minister to everyone, including the enemies of the papal government. Even after he became Pope, his chief concern was to act as priest and pastor, responsible before God for the defense of Christian values, which were jeopardized by rationalism and the increasing ungodliness of laicism. He increasingly encouraged the ultramontane movement, but not for reasons of personal ambition or love of theocracy, which tempted him less than his successor Leo XIII. He was ultramontane only because this movement appeared to him as the prerequisite for a rejuvenation of Catholic life wherever the intervention of governments in the Church seemed to throttle it, and because he saw it as the best means to coordinate all vital forces of Catholicism for the struggle against the rising flood of anti-Christian liberalism. This attitude explains his resistance to liberalism and his ever more violent condemnation of it. The Pope was part of the political philosophy of the traditionalistic type prevalent among Catholics during the middle of the nineteenth century. As such he was incapable of differentiating among the confused strivings of his time between those of positive value, which actually prepare the ground for a stronger spiritualization of the Catholic understanding of faith, and senseless concessions to fleeting fashions or even unconscious compromises with ideologies which failed to correspond to the Christian spirit. Above all he lacked realism in his church-political ideal, which throughout his entire pontificate he chased with an uncontrollable energy better

[2] Quoted by W. Elliot, *Vie du Père Hecker* (Paris 1897), 250. Many contemporaries emphasized the degree to which Pius IX allowed himself to be guided "by impressions and the heart."

[3] See L. Sandri, "La biblioteca privata di Pio IX," *RstRis* 25 (1938), 1426–32. Concerning the interest of Pius IX in scientific problems, see L. v. Pastor, *Tagebücher,* ed. by W. Wühr (Heidelberg 1950), 362.

expended on a worthier cause. As P. Martina pointed out astutely, it was "a historical impossibility to achieve at one and the same time complete freedom for the Church and the support of the state: a choice needed to be made."[4]

In contrast to these doubtlessly grave defects and missed opportunities, which we can easily see from today's perspective, stands the fact that the long pontificate also had great positive effects. Many things changed in the world and in the Church after Pius IX became Pope. The strongest ecclesiastical change took place with respect to the quality of the average Catholic life, beginning with the spiritual and pastoral standards of the clergy, the chief instrument of preaching the faith in the view of that century. Without a doubt, many elements contributed to this development, but Pius IX also contributed a considerable share, primarily by providing his contemporaries with his personal example of piety and Christian rebirth, which characterized the second third of the nineteenth century. Even more important than his personal example was Pius's activity. Determined and conscious of his authority, he devoted a great deal of his time and of his energy to the activation and promotion of the slow development which started immediately after the great revolutionary crisis. Because a tough attitude in practical and doctrinal terms appeared to him as indispensable for complete success, he forced himself, in spite of a personal inclination to mediation and mitigation, to the reiteration of principles which constituted the basis of his doctrine. Occasionally he did so with a deplorable lack of subtlety.

No Pope, no matter how active and independent, can perform without advisers. Of those who for many years enjoyed the confidence of Pius IX there were chiefly Monsignor Borromeo, Monsignor Ricci, and Monsignor Stella, devoted and scrupulous men, yet without great vision and guided by reactionary tendencies. Of greater weight were two foreigners, Monsignor George Talbot,[5] an Englishman related to Borghese, and Monsignor Xavier de Merode,[6] half Belgian, half French, who together with Prince Gustav von Hohenlohe[7] were appointed in 1850 after the return of Pius IX to Rome for the purpose of underscoring the

---

[4] *Pio IX e Leopoldo II* (Rome 1967), 50.

[5] On George Talbot de Malahide (1816–86), see *Wiseman Review* no. 502 (1964), 290–308.

[6] Concerning Xavier de Merode (1820–74), see L. Besson, *F.F.X. de Merode* (Lille 1908) and R. Aubert in *Revue générale belge* (May and June 1956), 1102–43, 1316–34.

[7] Prince Gustav Adolf Hohenlohe (1823–96) was liked by Pius IX because of his modesty and was useful because of his linguistic skills, but he exercised no political influence; he became a cardinal in 1866, but fell into disgrace because of his relationship to the opposition during the First Vatican Council (see Hubert Jedin, "Gustav Hohenlohe und Augustin Theiner," *RQ* 66 [1971]).

international role of the papacy. Talbot and Merode were intelligent men, holding less simplistic views with respect to modern society than was generally the case in Rome. But in their judgments both failed to consider the pros and cons and more than once encouraged the Pope, who placed great confidence in them, to assume an intransigent stance. Talbot did so in connection with English persons and affairs, in which his views generally were identical with those of Manning, and Merode did so with respect to the Roman Question and the French prelates with good connections to the government of Napoleon III.

While Pius IX's immediate entourage thus played a larger, if unofficial, role than that of his predecessors and successors—"influence without responsibility" Dom C. Butler called it—a noticeable reduction in the importance of the College of Cardinals took place, both with respect to the secular administration of the Papal State and the religious direction of the Church. With respect to the Papal State, Antonelli conducted affairs; concerning the cardinals, their selection occurred under new criteria. When in 1850 Pius IX created ten foreign and only four Italian cardinals, he signalled clearly that the essential task of the Sacred College was no longer that of administering the Papal State. The internationalization of the College of Cardinals continued. At the time of the death of Gregory XVI there were eight foreign and fifty-four Italian cardinals; when Pius IX died, there were twenty-five foreign and thirty-nine Italian cardinals.[8] The Italians by themselves were no longer able to produce the two-thirds majority required for the election of a Pope. The internationalization went hand in hand with another change. The representatives of the Roman aristocracy and the high functionaries in important administrative and political positions, who in the past had constituted the majority in the College of Cardinals, were gradually replaced by men of the Church of often modest background who excelled in pastoral work, theological knowledge, or ultramontane zeal. But in spite of this development the role of the College of Cardinals in the religious leadership of the Church grew smaller to such a degree that on the eve of the council the French ambassador wrote: "Never before was the role of the cardinals so modest and their influence so insignificant as today." The reason was in part the lack of personalities of high caliber, noted by many contemporary observers, but primarily it was Pius IX's personal style. He liked to inform himself directly about matters and did not hesitate, in the process of reaching a decision, to ignore regular channels. Unfortunately, all too often he relied on in-

[8] Of the 123 cardinals created by Pius IX, 71 were Italians and 52 were foreigners, including 16 Frenchmen, 12 Spaniards, 11 Austrians, 4 Germans, and 3 Portuguese.

formants who were partisan or who lacked a sense for the complexity of concrete situations daily facing the Church.[9] While the meetings of the consistories and commissions of cardinals for the discussion of problems touching upon the Church became rarer, individual cardinals personally played a significant role. Some of them headed primary agencies—the most important of them were Giacomo Antonelli,[10] secretary of state from 1848 until his death in 1876, and Alessandro Barnabo, the competent and energetic head of the Congregation for the Propagation of the Faith from 1856 until 1874—others simply enjoyed the personal confidence of the Pope. Among the latter were Cardinals Gaude and Bilio, in charge of dogmatic questions, Mertel for legal affairs, Franchi for church-political problems, and Reisach for the concerns of German-speaking countries but especially there was Cardinal Patrizi, a friend of the Pope, who for thirty years had unhindered access to him. Patrizi was an example of virtue and piety, but with a rather narrow mind.[11]

The continuing centralization of the Church naturally enlarged the importance of the nunciatures and of the Roman congregations. But most of the contemporary observers noted with regret the frequent mediocrity of the staff of both institutions. The men concerned were generally very respectable concerning their morals and piety and well versed in the subtleties of canon law and the theology of reference books, but overwhelmingly they lacked an understanding of the modern world and its developments. They "favored everything that was old, from dress to opinions, from labels to theology," Cochin wrote in 1862. They displayed a hostility toward critical methods which expressed not only their distrust of the new direction of philosophy, history, and natural sciences, but also the thoughtlessness with which they accepted and even encouraged denunciations of all who intellectually and reli-

[9] See, for example, G. Martina, *Pio IX e Leopoldo II,* 375.
[10] During the first two years of the pontificate, one secretary of state replaced another one in quick succession: Gizzi (8 August 1846–7 July 1847); Ferretti (17 July 1847–20 January 1848); Bofondi (1 February–9 March 1848); Antonelli (10 March–2 May 1848); Orioli, *ad interim* (4 May–2 June 1848); Soglia (3 June–29 November 1848). See also G. de Marchi, *Le Nunziature apostoliche dal 1800 al 1956* (Rome 1957), 10–11, and L. Pasztor in *Annali della Fondazione italiana per la storia amministrativa* 3 (1966), 314–18. After the death of Antonelli (6 November 1876) Pius IX appointed Cardinal Giovanni Simeoni (1816–92) as his successor (on him see L. Teste, op. cit., 257–61). Pius IX is supposed to have explained this appointment which created great astonishment as follows: "This is not going to be for long and I thus leave to my successor and to the conclave full freedom of action by selecting a cardinal who is destined for neither the papacy nor for political office" (quoted by Aubert, *Pie IX,* 498).
[11] Concerning Costantino Patrizi (1798–1876), see L. Teste, op. cit., 73—81, and M. Maccarrone, *Il concilio Vaticano I* (Padua 1966 I, 399–400 and n. 2.

giously failed to share their conformist views. This well-meant but short-sighted attitude merely postponed the solution of problems, and the more open-minded approaches under Leo XIII often came too late. These could not completely make up for lost time, so that, even recognizing the positive aspects, the actual roots of the crisis of modernism go back to the pontificate of Pius IX.

There were numerous positive sides. Already mentioned as one of the most important was the intensification of Christian life, in which, in addition to local efforts, Pius IX and some of his collaborators had a large personal share. At the expense of many valuable traditions which once had made up the prestige of the French clergy or Sailer's school, but whose quality seems to have affected only a small elite, there now arose a large movement of popular piety and priestly spirituality. It has often been accused of too much superficiality, but this simplifying condemnation is contradicted by the flowering of church activities and the tremendous growth of orders. At the same time, during these three decades, the Church also became stronger externally. Promoted by the colonial expansion of Europe, there was on all five continents a missionary expansion under the centralizing impulse of the Vatican. The immigration of Catholics led to the creation of new Churches in Canada, Australia, the United States, and Latin America. The old Churches, existing under difficult conditions since the Reformation, were reorganized in England, the Netherlands, and above all in Germany. The resistance recorded during the *Kulturkampf* demonstrated the vitality which this Church was able to develop within a few years through its connection with the Holy See. For together with the quantitative expansion of the Catholic Church[12] went its closer ties with the Pope. The growth of Roman centralization, solemnly sanctioned by the Vatican Council, without a doubt represented one of the most striking phenomena of this pontificate. It caused bitter regret among those who knew the advantages of pluralism, but had positive effects where the regalistic traditions of the Old Regime had weakened the Churches.

The triumph of ultramontanism caused the reaction of governments which did not like the removal of the local clergy from their influence. Additionally, the parties of the left mobilized against the Church in the wake of its compromises with the antirevolutionary systems, underscored by sensational condemnations of liberalism. Thus the last years of the pontificate were darkened by numerous conflicts. At the moment of Pius IX's death (7 February 1878) it was easy to assume at first sight that the Church was totally stranded in a sea of hostile public opinion.

---

[12] Between 1846 and 1878, Pius IX established 206 new dioceses and apostolic vicariates.

But in reality it was not only consolidated internally, but had begun, precisely at the moment when the disappearance of the Papal State eliminated the papacy from the traditional diplomatic chess board of Europe, "to become a world power of which every policy must take account" (H. Marc-Bonnet). This was demonstrated at the start of the pontificate of Leo XIII.

The Temporary Improvement in the Situation of the Church

The Church appeared to have emerged with flying colors from the crisis of 1848, so worrisome to its officials, on two levels. In part it profited from a turn toward conservatism, which, concerned about the rise of democratic demands, expected from it assistance in stabilizing the bourgeois order. After all, Tocqueville's statement that "the fear of socialism has the same effect on the bourgeoisie as the Revolution had on the aristocracy," applied not only to France. At the same time the Church benefitted from the concessions to liberalism of which governments were compelled to take account through a moderation of their regalistic policies or even through the granting of complete independence to the Church. This stabilized condition enabled the Holy See to arrange a number of favorable concordats.[1] The most spectacular one was that signed with Austria in 1855. Recognition of freedom of religion, already in effect for Belgium, Great Britain, and the United States, was also incorporated in the new constitutions of Prussia and the Netherlands and produced the same beneficial results for the growth of Catholicism in these states. Finally, systematically resumed missionary work, in conjunction with European colonial expansion, resulted in noticeable successes after the middle of the century. They permitted the impression that the Church had overcome the great crisis of the past one hundred years and could look optimistically to the future. But the euphoria was of short duration. The situation worsened again after the 1860s and again brought home the truth that it was always a mistake for the Church to rely too much on institutional advantages which it had obtained through nothing more than good fortune. Yet the favorable condition almost everywhere in evidence during the first years of the pontificate of Pius IX made possible the stabilization and spiritual intensification of the Catholic renaissance. In spite of the uncertainties in many countries this condition must therefore not be underestimated

---

[1] In 1851 with Spain, Tuscany, and Bolivia; in 1852 with Costa Rica and Guatemala; in 1855 with Austria; in 1857 with Portugal, Württemberg, and the Duchy of Modena; in 1859 with the Grand Duchy of Baden; in 1860 with Haiti; in 1861 with Honduras and Nicaragua; in 1862 with San Salvador, Venezuela, Ecuador, and Brazil. This policy of concordats was only resumed much later in 1881.

when one attempts to form an exact picture of the religious situation during the final quarter of the nineteenth century.

CHAPTER 7

The Seeming Success of the Church in France during the Second Empire and the "Moral Order"

The Privileged Status of the Church

The favoritisms extended to the Church under the Second Republic were increased at the beginning of the Second Empire. The Emperor and his advisers were not particularly interested in giving preference to the Church, but as conservative opportunists they were aware of the advantages of the moral and social force of religion in checking revolutionary propaganda. Moreover, association with the Church seemed to them a good way of binding legitimist circles to the Empire.

The government visibly enlarged the religious budget, made virtually no attempt to apply the Organic Articles, closed its eyes to the rapid growth of orders, suppressed antireligious tendencies in public education, and looked for opportunities to let the Church share in the prestige of the state. In response to the revolutionary excesses a good number of the middle class—and not only property owners—returned to the Church, seeing in it an effective guaranty for the maintenance of the social order. Having gradually regained its influence on the leading elements since the beginning of the century, the clergy now also obtained the assistance of many high officials. In an authoritarian regime their power was not to be underestimated and through them the benevolent attitude of the government toward the Church found strong expression. In addition, the universal right to vote, introduced in 1848, provided the lower clergy, which had maintained close contact with the people in the rural areas and small towns, a power which it had not yielded before.

But the clergy failed to exercise restraint, and to the extent that revolutionary threats diminished the government began to be suspicious of the growing importance of clerics in public life. The tactless policy of Nuncio Sacconi (1853–61) and the systematic efforts of the ultramontane party to exclude completely any influence of the government in ecclesiastical matters led to a reawakening of the Gallican tradition of a Ministry of Religion. The crisis, present in embryo after 1856, erupted with the development of the Roman Question after the Italian War (1859). The leaders of the Catholic movement, having until now hailed Napoleon III as a latter-day Charlemagne, were very disappointed when the Emperor agreed to a division of the Papal State. They tried to raise a wave of protest in the country, but did not have much success. This convinced the government that the people no longer followed the lead of the clergy as much as before. It decided to deal with the advances of the Church by introducing a plan worked out by Minister Rouland. It appointed bishops who refused to accept the increasing interference of the Roman Curia in France, stopped the further growth of orders and religious communities, and gave preference to the public schools. It increasingly resorted to chicanery in order to destroy the influence of the clergy, but ostensibly continued to promote religion in and outside of the country[1] so as not to lose the confidence of the Catholic population.

The policy, moderated by the benevolent neutrality of many Catholic civil servants, created indignation among the clergy. It also succeeded in drawing a number of notables to the side of the opposition. The growth of the Republican Party after 1863 therefore persuaded the government to return to a less hostile policy in order to regain the good will of the "Clerical Faction."[2] While the cabinet continued to tolerate the attacks of the anticlerical press against the Church, it tried in other ways to regain the confidence of the clergy. It hoped that after the appointment of a number of Gallican-oriented bishops[3] the clergy would less compliantly adhere to the increasingly intransigent positions of the Vatican with respect to problems of modern civilization.

Owing to the Roman Question and the convention of September 1864, this pacification policy did not have immediate results. But after the intervention of French troops in Mentana (1867) nothing stood any longer in the way of the reconciliation desired by both sides. The joint fear of the republican opposition led the two powers to cooperation. Once again it tied the declining Empire to the conservative force of the clergy, which, in turn, was apprehensive of the anticlericalism displayed by the republicans.

[1] In Syria, where French troops protected the Maronites; in China and Indochina where they defended the persecuted missionaries; in Mexico, where they attempted to replace the anticlerical republic of Juárez with the Catholic empire of Maximilian, the Emperor appeared as the defender of the Church, whose interests happened to coincide with those of France.

[2] With the exception of a few areas, the clergy was without a doubt increasingly less able to influence the majority of the voters; this fact was pointed out by Maurain and confirmed by L. M. Case (*French Opinion on War and Diplomacy during the Second Empire* [Philadelphia 1954]). But the vote of the followers of the clergy nevertheless in many instances was a significant factor.

[3] On this policy, applied especially by Minister Baroche, see numerous references in J. Maurain, op. cit. and recent more detailed indications, especially about the important role played by Lavigerie, in de Montclos, 288–99.

The reputable standing of religion and the improvement of the material and moral condition of the rural clergy, which until the middle of the century stood on the sidelines of Christian intellectual life, soon had its effects on the number of priests. This increase was also affected by the Falloux Law. The number of ordinations in France climbed by more than a third,[4] and the total number of priests rose from 46,969 in 1853 to 56,295 in 1869. The increase enabled the bishops to fill numerous vicariates, to raise the number of clerics in public service from 1,541 to 2,467, and to establish 1,600 new parishes. This made the Second Empire appear as the "high point between a period of moderate development during the July Monarchy and a period of hastening decline under the Third Republic" (Pouthas).

The training of the clergy, however, remained deficient. In spite of the efforts of a few discerning bishops—Cardinal de Bonald in Lyon, Dupanloup in Orléans, and Lavigerie and Foulon in Nancy—seminary instruction, imparted by insufficiently educated teachers, hardly rose above the level of a catechism taught in Latin. The priests trained in them were virtuous,[5] but more inclined to minister to the "converted" than to make contact with the increasingly indifferent populace or to counter the prejudices of upwardly mobile people. It is not surprising, therefore, that the clergy—with the exception of a numerically limited elite—regarded Louis Veuillot as their model. With absolutely uncritical zeal they followed the directions of *L'Univers,* a paper which fed the clergy's ultramontane enthusiasm and its mistrust of the "modern world."

If the majority of the lower clergy after the 1850s became ultramontane, they did so primarily in the hope of gaining in the Roman Curia a counterweight to the authoritarian stance of the bishops. While the majority of the bishops did not openly agree with Cardinal de Bonnechose, who compared himself to a general in charge of a regiment, they nevertheless displayed a decided bent for the centralization of diocesan administrations. They strengthened controls, transferred personnel without consideration of their personal desires, put out detailed regulations on Church discipline and pastoral work, and left little ini-

---

[4] This favorable development was not universal, however, and in the center of the countries concerns were being raised over the decline of applications.

[5] Only a small elite, which was at the same time a social elite, attended the French Seminary opened in Rome in 1853 (see Y. -M. Hilaire in *ArchSR* 23 [1967], 135–40) or the seminary of Saint Sulpice in Paris, whose standards by no means equalled those of clerical training in Germany, but which was clearly above those of the provincial seminaries (details in A. Castellani, *Il beato Leonardo Murialdo,* I [Rome 1966], 767–806).

tiative to their priests. This systematic and dutiful activity[6] resulted from their wish to guide their dioceses in the best interest of religion, but in most cases their efforts regrettably were not matched by pastoral sensitivity. On the whole, the upper clergy was extremely colorless and—with a few exceptions, such as Dupanloup or Freppel—not at all the belligerent episcopate depicted by the anticlerical press. Instead of thoroughly rethinking the methods of the apostolate, the bishops were satisfied with the institutionalization of those methods which had proved effective during the first half of the century. Thus, disregarding the migration of people resulting from the industrialization, positions in the countryside were increased while there was a crying need for additional parishes in the burgeoning cities.[7]

The work of the bishops and the clergy was much facilitated by the assistance of the orders. For them the Second Empire was a time of growth; this was especially true for the female congregations, which were favored by the law of 31 January 1852. Between 1851 and 1861 the number of nuns increased from 34,208 to 89,243. During the same period, membership in the male orders rose from 3,000 to 17,656.

The rapid growth of orders and congregations provided the Church with the necessary manpower for reaching two goals. These were entry into public education and free education. The Church was not satisfied with the exercise of supervision of the teachers by the pastors; the practice was made possible by the Falloux Law, but gave rise to frequent friction. The Church wanted to obtain from communal councils, which were often kindly disposed toward the Church, permission to entrust public schools to the supervision by members of orders. Simultaneously, advantage was taken of a favorable tax law facilitating gifts of money and property to increase the number of Catholic schools and colleges. By preferentially admitting students from socially prominent families they attracted the attention of the middle class and contributed to a change in its attitude. Between 1850 and 1875 the number of children educated by teachers of orders rose from 953,000 to 2,168,000, while the number of students in the lay schools rose only from 2,309,000 to 2,649,000.

[6] The best-known case is that of Dupanloup in Orléans, thanks to the researches of Madame Marcilhacy. But he was not alone. On the French episcopate around 1870, see the well-documented description by J. Gadille, op. cit. I, 15–45.

[7] Two typical cases: Paris, where in 1861 there was one priest for 2,498 inhabitants of the parishes in the center, and one priest for 4,955 inhabitants in the parishes of the suburbs, inhabited by the common people (see Y. Daniel, *L'équipement paroissial d'un diocèse urbain, Paris 1802–1956* [Paris 1957]); Lille, where in spite of the population explosion only one church was built before 1870 and after 1854 in some parishes there were more than four thousand people for one priest (see P. Pierrard, op. cit., 372–78).

The dubious character of this achievement was clearly recognized by A. Latreille: "The kind disposition of the government of Napoleon III to congregations and their schools must be regarded as the most significant fact of the history of French Catholicism between 1830 and 1880. It provided the Church with a large degree of satisfaction and possibilities of influence which it had been denied ever since the Revolution. But more than anything else it contributed to the growing distrust of the Church." This distrust became militant especially after 1870, but even during the Second Empire the desire to stop the progress of the Church grew stronger among those who suspiciously watched the influence of the "clericals" (the expression was coined during this period). After a few years, during which public education in view of the republican sympathies of the public teachers consciously had been neglected, Rouland undertook his reorganization in order to fashion public schools into a viable competitor for the schools maintained by the congregations. In spite of repeated protests by the episcopate, Victor Duruy after 1863 with varying success obstructed the development of free Catholic education and freed public schools from the influence of the Church.[8] His ministerial policy found a ready echo as the success of the *Ligue française pour l'enseignement public* attested. This organization was founded by Jean Macé in 1866 and by 1870 counted one thousand eight hundred members.

Although the government was not willing to allow the Church to drive it out of charitable work, it nevertheless pointedly requested the Catholics to participate in this social work. Thus, in addition to poorhouses and hospitals, Catholic facilities of all kinds were established. There were welfare associations and works for poor sick people; mutual help associations, especially in southern France; youth homes and other organizations devoted to young laborers, although their growth was a slow one (in 1866 there were only 165 homes in all of France). The initiators of these enterprises generally were religious congregations (some of them founded expressly for this purpose), laymen from the rural nobility, and wealthy people from the middle class. Many of them were branches of the Society of Saint Vincent de Paul, whose legitimist orientation on the part of some of its leaders in 1861 occasioned sensational interference by the Ministry of the Interior, or of the *Société d'économie charitable*. The latter, reorganized in 1855, had as its chief sponsor Vicomte Armand de Melun, whose name—in addition to that of Monsignor de Segur—was closely connected with the French Caritas movement until his death in 1877.

[8] J. Rohr, op. cit., 163–75. Although the opposite has been asserted, Duruy, anticlerical but not sectarian-oriented, can hardly be regarded as the precursor of the defenders of lay schools in the Third Republic.

In addition to these charitable actions there were many others which, while very active, were too fragmented to achieve a national stature. There were apologetic works, directed against the "bad press"; missionary works which enjoyed particular popularity; and works of piety (eternal adoration, nocturnal adoration, priest associations, congregations of the Most Blessed Virgin, etc.), all of which showed that beyond the social utility of religion an elite of the French middle class rediscovered genuine Christian values. Finally, one event in the France of the Second Empire must not be forgotten: Lourdes in a very short time "became not only the most visited object of pilgrimage in a country already rich in historical holy places, but the world center of prayer and active charity" (Latreille).

This apparently magnificent condition was hardly affected by the fall of the Empire in 1870. The seizure of power by the republicans, almost without exception anticlerical and Freemasons, initially worried the Catholics, but the excesses of the Commune led, just as in 1848, to a shift to the right. The National Assembly, consisting largely of conservative rural nobility and upper bourgeoisie, was especially friendly to the Church. The government of the "Moral Order," whose leaders were friends of Monsignor Dupanloup, tried, much to the dismay of the paper *L'Univers*, to present Catholicism more as a useful social force than as the official state religion. But it did not at all object to the desire of the Church to infuse the state's institutions with a Christian spirit. Disregarding the republican concept of secularization, it strengthened the influence of the clergy in the army, public welfare, and education. Dupanloup succeeded in thwarting the plans of Jules Simon, which were to be the first steps toward the laicization of elementary education. Dupanloup in 1875 obtained freedom of higher education; soon several Catholic universities opened their doors, even though this legislation only barely passed the National Assembly.

The Church was able to exploit its legal advantages because it could call on more personnel. There was also a dark cloud, however: except for a few secluded areas like the Jura or the southern part of the central region of the country, the number of seminarists was declining. Inasmuch as the mortality rate of the clergy was still low and the number of active priests increasing, the threat was not yet perceived. In 1870 the ratio of priests to flock was 1 : 730, by 1876 it was 1 : 654. Membership in the orders grew so much that M. Pouthas regarded the growth of the congregations as a characteristic of the Church during the beginning years of the republic. In 1877 there were 30,287 male and 127,753 female members of orders, a three-fold increase from the year 1789. It enabled France to provide by far the strongest contingent of missionaries for the evangelization of the pagan peoples.

This large number of people alone, coming from all walks of life and signifying more than mere social climbing, together with the continued rise in piety and good works on the regional and national level, would be sufficient proof that the impression of a powerful Church was anything but a facade and that it still commanded large reserves of Christian strength. Actually, the religious awakening in 1870 extended far beyond this elite. Many people viewed the military defeats and the tragic convulsions of the Commune as divine punishment or at least as the logical consequence of the spread of "socialistic atheism" and the frivolity displayed by the Second Empire. The religious awakening found expression in more faithful attendance at Sunday services, greater morality, and in the growth of popular literature devoted to the adoration of the Sacred Heart of Jesus, Mary, and the saints. More spectacularly it was displayed in large pilgramages of faith and repentence centered on the shrines of Lourdes, La Salette, and Paray-le-Monial. Under the direction of the dynamic Assumptionists thousands of pilgrims visited them under the motto *Gallia poenitens et devota.* It was through the efforts of the Assumptionists that Catholicism in these years again became popular and developed into the religion of the people. They took a long-range approach, addressed a broad public, moved the masses, and talked to them in plain language. After an interval of fifty years they resumed the work of the missions of the period of restoration. The visible crowning of their efforts was the construction of the cathedral of Sacre-Cœur on Montmartre.

The Ambivalence of the Actual Religious Situation

The just-described favorable conditions should not obscure the truth, however. There was no doubt that the successes of the established Church—accompanied especially on the local level by the clergy's will to dominate—were matched by a religious intensification. It found expression in pious fraternities, in the rise of the veneration of Mary and the Eucharist, in the growth of the comtemplative and missionary orders, and in the great number of outstanding Christians and saints. But at the very moment when contemporaries were able to record these achievements, the signs of that religious crisis began to appear which was to emerge fully during the final quarter of the century. The seemingly brilliant condition of the institutions on one hand and the effects of a small spiritual elite on the other tended too often to conceal the actual condition of the great mass of the people, which, after all, was the important ingredient of the Church. Thanks to the sociological and historical research inspired by G. Le Bras and conducted during the recent past on the regional level, we have a detailed, if incomplete, image of the situation.

First of all, geographical differences must be considered. A large part of the west, the central region, the Alps, and the Jura, remained closely tied to their faith until the end of the century. Religion was practiced there by many men, the supply of recruits for the priesthood, missions, and orders was abundant, and the new types of piety were received well, especially in the rural areas. The populace, increasingly well integrated with a growing number of priests and a network of Catholic schools, resisted fairly well the blandishments of a society which tried to laicize it.

In other areas, even under the July Monarchy in the process of becoming alienated from Christianity, considerable efforts were undertaken to win them back. The efforts were guided by active bishops such as Dupanloup in Orléans, Dupont des Loges in Metz, and Parisis in Arras. These prelates were actively assisted by people specially trained for preaching in the parish missions. This intensive missionary activity during the Second Empire has been inadequately studied. These efforts, spurred on by the administration and high notables, in some cases resulted in a considerable revival of religious practices, at least before 1870. But in essence they touched only the middle class of small towns and the stale parishes in devout areas. Elsewhere, the differences between the sexes became more pronounced. The women tended to take their religion seriously, while the men largely stayed away from Sunday and Easter services.[9]

The situation was worse in the area of Paris, in the departments of the Charente, in the southeast, and in Provence, where religious practice, weak even before 1848, sank to a level below the present one, in spite of hundreds of missions which had been conducted there. In some parishes not a single soul attended Easter services; the religious practice of the men was close to zero; about half of all marriages took place in front of a civil registrar only; many boys no longer went to their first Communion; and processions were molested. As the years went by, such conditions became more widespread.

Seen as a whole, a considerable part of France fell prey to religious indifference, notwithstanding the efforts of the regular and secular clergy, an indifference generally accompanied by a relentless hostility to the Church. In the countryside the hostility was strengthened by the

---

[9] Thus, in the diocese of Orléans the receipt of the Easter sacrament by men rose from 3.8 percent in 1852 to 5.8 percent in 1868. Frequent Communion by women, on the other hand, was habit with 28 percent of them (detailed information in C. Marcilhacy, op. cit., [II], 239–339).

growth of the means of communication and the more intimate contacts with the new urban civilization which they facilitated. There was also the systematic drumfire of the anticlerical newspapers, only feebly countered by the Catholic press, which was not sufficiently popular. It was further encouraged by the frequent conflicts erupting in the villages over the establishment of Catholic schools and the expensive building of parsonages. Frequently a role was played by the clergy's lust for power and money, their identification with the legitimist landlords,[10] and their rigoristic and negative habit of preaching morality.

The world of artisans and laborers, still a minority but visibly growing, adhered to a kind of Christian atavism; in most areas of the country their alienation from the Catholic Church grew more pronounced.[11] Separated from their rural roots, the workers easily succumbed to the immorality and the anticlericalism of the burgeoning cities.[12] Generally, the clergy neglected them. Scheduling of services and ecclesiastical customs were not fitted to the working conditions of the industrial proletariat. The proletariat was being pushed to the sidelines of the Church, and many priests of rural background were discouraged by the difficulties of the workers' environment. The active religious participation of these people, aside from a small female minority, was limited to the chief events in life. The *Oeuvre des cercles* in which Albert de Mun and Abbé Maignen wanted to gather the workers after 1870 lasted only briefly, as they failed to reach the real laborers. Doubtlessly, the workers were also repulsed by the paternalistic attitude of the middle class to social problems. While the mass of the workers had not yet articulated its discontent, the militants accused the Church of hindering the social rise of the working class. Priests and bishops, in their own view tied to a divinely inspired static and hierarchical concept of society, condemned the attempts to improve the lot of the working class as "antisocial" and only emphasized in their sermons that earthly miseries would be rewarded in the next world. The outbreaks of violence directed against the clergy after the fall of the Empire in Paris, Lyon, and along the Mediterranean coast, all in sharp contrast to their indulgent behavior in 1848, was an indication of the rapid change in the attitude of the workers. The proletariat increasingly developed its own class consciousness, felt alienated socially and psychologically from traditional Catholicism, and began to regard the priests as enemies in the battle

---

[10] It must be noted that most Catholic-influenced regional newspapers (there were about fifty) were legitimist.

[11] Without, however, turning to Protestantism, which appeared to them as a "religion of aristocrats," insufficiently affable, and too sober (see G. Duveau, "Protestantisme et prolétariat en France au milieu du XIXe siècle", *RHPhR* 31 [1951], 417–28).

[12] See G. Duveau, *Histoire du peuple français* IV (Paris 1953), 72–141.

against the conservative forces. Only a few areas were spared this development. In Lille and other municipalities in the east small but strong Christian workers' associations were formed, and around the turn of the century their membership constituted the first Christian labor unions.

While the Church lost ground among the mass of the people, especially in the cities, it could console itself with gains among the middle class. But even here the situation was not entirely satisfactory. To be sure, a large part of the middle class, especially in the provinces in which the population remained faithful to the Church, returned to a genuine Christianity, generously gave of its time and money for Catholic works, and provided young people for the orders. But many others returned to the Church only because romanticism had made cathedrals fashionable and because, after the great fear of 1848, they saw in the Church a guarantee for social stability. Their attitude was more clerical than believing and contributed to exposing the Church in the eyes of the people, the more so as its morality, castigated by Veuillot in his *Odeurs de Paris,* left much to be desired.

On the other hand, religion, especially in the provinces, became an external sign of respectability, even though the professions largely continued to remain anticlerical. In fact, especially among the left, which was angered by the agreement between Church and the Bonapartist government, anticlericalism was on the rise. Among the important reasons for this attitude were the anachronistic character of the Papal State, stoutly defended by the clergy, and the publication of the *Syllabus,* which was seen as the manifesto of the unreasonable demands of traditionalistic Catholic circles on society. Even more serious was the fact that the intellectuals—writers, scientists, historians, and philosophers—influenced by rationalism and positivism, which had taken the place of romanticism, became alienated not only from the Church but from the Christian faith and religion itself. The success of the book *La vie de Jésus* by Renan (1863) was symptomatic. Especially devastating around 1870 was the spiritualism of Jules Simon.

At about the same time the spiritualistic Freemasons adopted that hostility to religion which was to become characteristic for them. The lodges, increasing from 244 to 392 between 1857 and 1870, became the active centers of the idea of laicization. Based on the progress of science, it was not only to free society from the clerical yoke but also to liberate the human spirit from the fetters of dogma and the false belief in supernaturalism.[13]

The men responsible for the fate of the Church in France began to be concerned, but they failed to grasp the true situation and, especially

[13] An example: A. Bouton, *Les luttes ardentes des francs-maçons manceaux pour l'établissement de la République* (Le Mans 1966).

after 1870, their views lagged far behind the developments in their country. Most of them believed that all difficulties would cease if only the government gave stronger support to the Church. This was the view of all those who agreed with Monsignor Pie and Louis Veuillot; basically, however, Monsignor Dupanloup and other bishops did not see things differently.[14] Even the small group of liberal Catholics around the *Correspondant,* which was aware of the illusory character of state protection, was unable to go beyond considerations of principles. They did not initiate actions comparable to those started at the same time by German and Belgian Catholics.

The deficiencies of French Catholicism were also evident in its intellectual life. Catholicism seemed to be incapable of countering lack of faith in its very own bailiwick of philosophy and the history of Christian origins. Apologetic literature as well as episcopal pastoral letters and sermons were characteristic of a vague and romantic phraseology, marked by the total absence of introducing the clergy to a critical spirit and the new methods of scholarship. The bishops refused to acknowledge the necessity of such acquaintance, and with few exceptions they feared that by attending universities no longer under the control of the Church the priests would absorb dangerous ideas.[15] The negotiations for the reestablishment of theological departments at universities, on the other hand, were stalled because of the distrust by the Holy See of the continuation of Gallican tendencies in France. A. J. Alphonse Gratry, conscious of the necessity to confront philosophical and religious problems, tried to give body to an idea held before him by Lamennais and Bautain. He wanted to select a few qualified priests for a kind of "apologetic workshop," but the Oratory of France, reestablished in 1852, was diverted from its original aim by the more practical enterprises of its superior. Only with the founding of Catholic universities, made possible by the law of 1875, was a serious attempt made fifty years later to remove the intellectual deficiencies of the Church.

A further weakness of the Church in France during the Second Empire was the increasingly bitter disagreements of Catholics in various areas. The opponents of an excessive Roman centralization, clinging to the traditional habits of the old French clergy, were worried about the aggressive stance of the defenders of neo-ultramontanism. Many who earlier had favored the ultramontane activity of Lamennais because they wanted to see the Church liberated from the heavy hand of the state, now moved closer to Gallicanism again because they feared that the papacy was developing into a despotic authoritarianism. Liberal

---

[14] See the astute observations by J. Gadille, op. cit., 81–89.
[15] Monsignor Meignan and Monsignor Lavigerie especially.

Catholics, convinced that the Church could regain the respect of the new leading elements through being more open-minded, and intransigent Catholics, seeing in modern liberties the reason for the decline of religious practice, accused one another of being responsible for the worsening of the situation, but failed to seek concrete ways to alleviate it. Liberal Catholics condemned the ultramontane integralism, but could not agree among themselves. While the friends of Monsignor Dupanloup and Montalembert missed no opportunity to present themselves as unreconcilable opponents of the government of Napoleon III and defenders of the secular power of the Pope, many Catholics replied to them that the rights of modern man, still totally unacknowledged by the archaic institutions of the Papal State, were adequately guaranteed by the imperial constitution. Consumed by such internal disputes, the majority did not realize that not only the future of Catholicism but of religion itself was at stake and that it was most urgent to close ranks in intellectual and social areas, where delay had worsened the situation since the time of Monsignor Affre.

The convulsions of 1870–71, far from opening the eyes of the responsible people, contributed to a further intensification of opposing views. The most agitated element of French Catholicism, confirmed in its authority by the defeat of the minority at the Vatican Council, wanted to connect the movement of religious revival with a two-fold restoration from which it expected the secular and spiritual salvation of France. These were the elevation of the Count of Chambord to the throne of the Bourbons and the installation of Pius IX in his restored Papal State. In an atmosphere of providentialistic historical interpretation and of an illuminism which reads from the calamities of today the triumphs of tomorrow, and seeing both positions threatened by the same enemy, they believed in miracles with a childlike confidence which took the place of political awareness.

The tactless manner in which this restoration was promoted, less so by the bishops, who remained relatively reserved,[16] than by the lower clergy and militant Catholics, quickly mobilized the moderates. They saw in the "most Christian King" a herald of theocracy and feared that France would be driven to "make war for the Pope." The friends of Dupanloup and Duke de Broglie recognized the danger and disavowed the anachronistic goals of the radicals. But their moderate approach, diametrically opposed to that of the ultras, angered many adherents of "political supernaturalism," who condemned such a policy as spineless-

---

[16] And not only on the liberal Catholic side. J. Gadille, op. cit., has clearly demonstrated that Monsignor Pie, for example, was a far less intransigent legitimist than presented by his first biographer, Baunard.

ness. The dispute between liberal Catholics and intransigent Catholics grew even more bitter than it had been under the Empire.

While the clergy in this fashion involved itself in noisy and fruitless controversies over the ideal political form of government, it continued to ignore the real problems of the hour: the training of modern-minded laymen, capable of effectively serving the Church in a society undergoing rapid secularization;[17] the definition of its position with respect to the material and intellectual progress which the Church, to the great dismay of the multiplying admirers of scientific discoveries, was disregarding; and finally, and possibly foremost, the problem of social development. As A. Latreille has pointedly noted, most of the Catholics and the leaders of the Church reacted to the rise of anticlericalism "like moralists and not as sociologists." They were convinced that the anticlerical movement had not come about spontaneously. They believed that it had been thought up by a radical intelligentsia and was not a reflection of the actual feelings of the French people, whom they saw as still strongly tied to their religious customs. They concluded that the intellectual crisis could be ended through censorship of the press. They failed to see the close connection which after 1870 in a kind of "messianic hope for the egalitarian, fraternal, and laicistic republic"[18] developed between the militant, radical, and anticlerical wing of the republican middle class and the progressive elements of the urban and agrarian working class. The workers actually remembered only with hate the brutal suppression of the Commune, for which they also held the clergy responsible, as it was sociologically related to the conservative classes. The peasants suspected the clergy of wishing to reintroduce the tithe of the Old Regime together with the restoration of the monarchy. The middle class, finally, was more than ever convinced of the incompatibility of modern society with a Church which looked upon the *Syllabus* as its ideal. The anticlerical offensive started in 1878 with the seizure of power by the radicals thus encountered a well-prepared soil.

[17] E. d'Alzon was one of the few who concerned themselves with it before 1870, but he did not arrive at a precise formulation (C. Molette, *L'Association catholique de la Jeunesse Française* [Paris 1968], 12).
[18] *HistCathFr*, 391; f. 363.

CHAPTER 8

The States of the German Confederation and Switzerland, 1848–70

The years 1848–49 showed that the partial alliance between Catholics and liberals rested on a weak foundation. Political and philosophical liberalism were difficult to separate. The same liberals who were engaged in the struggle for greater freedom, which was also of benefit for the Church, in their majority also asked for separation of Church and state, civil marriage, and public schools. Thus, they fought against positions regarded by the Church as unalterable. Furthermore, economic liberalism hurt the lower middle class and the peasants who were still loosely tied to the Church. These opposing views and the reliance of Catholics on the Roman Curia with its reactionary concepts had grave consequences after 1848. While the leaders of German Catholicism were eager to preserve the freedoms obtained in 1848 and extend them to all German states, they also turned away from liberalism and democracy and toward patriarchal conservatism. The consequence of the failed German revolution for the Church was that once again it was compelled to negotiate with the restored states and to take account of their reactionary policies during the subsequent decades.

Following the Roman example, the German bishops and leaders of the lay movement became convinced that only a monolithic Church would be able to counteract the prevailing liberalism, rationalism, and atheism. They also therefore tried to erect barriers against the intrusion of new ideas; while these barriers succeeded in preserving much of ecclesiastical substance, they also promoted the very isolation desired by opponents. The Church could think of nothing better to counter the turn to political liberalism, experienced by most of the German states toward the end of the 1850s, than an authoritarian defense. Catholics no longer participated in Germany's intellectual development, which was increasingly influenced by the technical and historical sciences.[1] Anyone who adopted the new historical view of the world came in conflict with the scholastic-juridical concepts promoted by Rome.

The leadership of the Catholic movement more and more was taken over by the circles in Mainz and Munich which most thoroughly turned away from liberalism and most effectively propagated their departure in Heinrich's and Moufang's *Katholik* and Jörg's *Historisch-politische Blätter*. Only the Rhenish Catholics remained relatively close to political liberalism; they had ties with progressive western Europe and, as a minority in the Prussian state, could expect benefits from the application of liberal principles.

In the national question as well, of tremendous concern to a large number of people, an unbridgeable rift developed in the 1850s between liberals and Catholics. The majority of the liberals were predominantly in favor of a Little German-Prussian solution. The liberals hailed

---

[1] The only notable exceptions were Adalbert Stifter in literature and Anton Bruckner in music. See L. Nowak in *Große Österreicher* XI (1957), 144–53; H. Cysarz in *Große Österreicher* XV (1963), 48–61.

the Italian unification (1859–60), whose fundamental principles were their own, regardless of the fact that implicitly it was directed against Austria and the Papal State. It encouraged their own activity,[2] and they denied the inherent validity of the Catholic protests against the Pope's loss of territory. The majority of the Catholics continued to cling to the concept of a Greater Germany, even though hopes for unification under Austria's auspices were increasingly improbable.

In Prussia, thanks to the constitutions of 1848 and 1850, the Church gained a new stature and new life, which affected other German states. Geissel and Diepenbrock, the most important persons in the Prussian episcopate, were created cardinals in 1850, but Diepenbrock was able to devote himself to the solution of old and new problems only for a few more years, as he died in 1853. After that date, leadership was completely in the hands of Geissel, dynamic organizer and church politician. He tried to preserve and enlarge the legal position obtained in 1848, to intensify religious life with the aid of ultramontane forms of piety, and to coordinate pastoral care and fresh activities of laymen. He also promoted uniformity of action by the episcopate and was able to hold a provincial council in 1860 in which most of the bishops of northern and western Germany participated. Through the assistance of the bishops the association movement was able to spread, and religious orders and congregations returned, thus permitting the establishment of hospitals, orphan homes, and schools. Sacramental and rosary prayers, pilgrimages and processions were reintroduced, and the dogma of 1854 encouraged the veneration of Mary.[3] The orders also enabled Geissel to revive the missions to the people, which had languished since the Enlightenment.[4] They deepened religious knowledge and interest in the Church among the lower classes. After initial distrust, the missionaries were assisted by some state officials, as the preachers also defended conservative authority and spoke against revolution, socialism, and democracy. But the missionaries did not really have any helpful alternative suggestions for the workers mired in the proletariat. In general, the social efforts of Geissel and his people did not go beyond the traditional limits of charity; this was only done by Ketteler, who at first agreed with much of Geissel's activity and eventually grew into his position of leadership.

[2] See E. Portner, *Die Einigung Italiens im Urteil liberaler deutscher Zeitgenossen* (Bonn 1959).
[3] G. Müller, "Die Immaculata Conceptio im Urteil der mitteleuropäischen Bischöfe," *KuD* 14 (1968), 46–70.
[4] E. Gatz, *Rheinische Volksmission im 19. Jahrhundert, dargestellt am Beispiel des Erzbistums Köln* . . . (Düsseldorf 1963).

The reactionary ministry of Manteuffel (1850–58) applied specifically Prussian and therefore often anti-Catholic traditions of state, and the largely Lutheran state bureaucracy continued to prevent the full implementation of constitutional parity. In 1852, Friedrich von Raumer, minister of religion, decreed a ban on studying at the Collegium Germanicum in Rome, established state supervision of foreign clerics and of parish missions, and confined the latter to purely Catholic areas. The decrees were primarily directed against the Jesuits, as a result of whose activities a reduction in the number of Lutherans was feared. Geissel and Bishop Müller of Münster protested immediately. In addition, a political opposition came into being, leading in 1852 to the formation of a "Catholic Faction" with sixty-two representatives in the Prussian Diet. Under this dual pressure the government moderated Raumer's decrees in a way acceptable to the Catholics. Subsequently the Catholic Section in the Ministry of Religion, headed by Matthias Aulike, successfully worked toward a better understanding between state and religious interests, but the increasing gravity of the differences between Catholicism and liberalism as well as between the two denominations began to hinder its work in the 1860s. The government tried to interfere in the election of the Cologne archbishop after Geissel's death (1864), when it was called upon for help by the liberal chapter minority against the ultramontane chapter majority, but ultimately it accepted Bishop Melchers of Osnabrück, who had the approbation of the Roman Curia.[5] In Gnesen-Posen as well, Rome was able to place its candidate, Count Ledóchowski.[6]

The leaders of the Catholic Faction[7] (called "Faction of the Center" after the assignment of seats in the Diet), August and Peter

[5] Paulus Melchers (1813–95), in 1857 bishop of Osnabrück, in 1866 archbishop of Cologne, as such leader of the Prussian episcopate during the *Kulturkampf*. He was imprisoned in 1874 and after 1875 guided his diocese from exile. In the interest of religious peace, he resigned in 1885 and became a Curia cardinal (biography by H. M. Ludwigs [Cologne 1909]; A. Franzen, *LThK* VII, 251).

[6] Mieczyslaw Halka Count von Ledóchowski (1822–1902), in the papal diplomatic service after studies at Warsaw and Rome, in 1861 nuncio at Brussels in 1866 archbishop of Gnesen-Posen, in 1875 cardinal. Ledochówski was arrested in 1874, expelled from Prussia in 1876, after which he lived in Rome and resigned his position in 1886. After 1885 he was secretary of the briefs, in 1892 he became prefect of the Congregation for the Propagation of the Faith (biography by W. Klimkiewicz, 2 vols. [Cracow 1938–39]; G. Maron in *RGG* IV, 261f.; B. Stasiewski in *LThK* VI, 874).

[7] Bachem (*Zentrumspartei* II, 96–220) is basic for the history of the faction and its influence on the formation of other Catholic parties (renewed founding of the Center Party in 1870). See also H. Donner, *Die katholische Fraktion in Preußen 1852–58* (diss., Leipzig 1909); L. Bergsträßer, *Geschichte der politischen Parteien in Deutschland* (Munich 1960), 110f.

Reichensperger[8] and Hermann von Mallinckrodt,[9] were interested in developing a general political party. The immediate goal of the faction was the defense of ecclesiastical freedom, and it was only sensible to argue for the observance of the consitution as a whole. This led to the splitting off of a number of noble representatives who began to support the Catholic-conservative movement propagated in Mainz and Munich. In its church policy and its Greater German attitude the Catholic Faction differed from the liberals, in its constitutionalism it differed from the conservatives. Together with the liberals it fought against the reactionary tendencies of the 1850s; in this connection it also favored equality for the Jews. But together with the conservatives it fought bitter battles after 1859 with the liberals against the introduction of civil marriage and for the preservation of the organic unity of Church and elementary schools. Its inability to formulate for all of its members a common position during the great Prussian constitutional conflict (1862–67), however, led to its demise. The decline of the Pius Associations and the resignation of many Catholics because of the political developments contributed considerably to its decline.

In Austria, Emperor Franz Joseph, steadfastly converting his restoration policy after 1850 to a neo-absolutism, in religious questions also remained on the path taken in 1848–49. He started negotiations for a concordat, headed on the part of the state by Josef Otmar von Rauscher, who had become archbishop of Vienna; the negotiator for the Curia was Viale-Prela. Franz Joseph and his representative regarded the Catholic Church as the unifying factor in holding together the multinational state, and they also wished to make of Austria the preeminent political power of Catholicism; for this reason the Emperor strongly desired a concordat at any price.[10] The Curia exploited this desire and successfully created a precedent for its negotiations with other states. The concordat was signed on 18 August 1855; it not only liquidated Josephinism and fulfilled justified ecclesiastical expectations, but it derived these from ultramontane principles.[11] Throughout, it reflected the militantly defensive antiliberalism of both contracting partners. Literally duplicating the Bavarian concordat of 1817, the Catholic Church in the entire monarchy was guaranteed all rights to which it was entitled in

[8] Biographies by L. v. Pastor and F. Schmidt. See also E. Deuerlein in *StL* VI, 777f.
[9] Biography by O. Pfülf. See also E. Deuerlein in *StL* V, 519f.
[10] Against the objections of the Hungarian episcopate, which, under its primate Cardinal Scitowski, favored the continuation of Hungary's special religious status (Weinzierl-Fischer, *Konkordate,* 73f).
[11] Text: Weinzierl-Fischer, *Konkordate,* 250–58. Text of the concordat and pertinent documents: Walter, *Fontes,* 280–303; Mercati I, 821–44.

keeping with "the divine order and canonical statutes" (ARTICLE 1), laws conflicting with the concordat were repealed (ART. 35), and all religious issues not specifically treated by the concordat were to be settled according to the doctrines of the Church and its regulations as authorized by the Holy See (ART. 34). The Emperor assured the Church and its institutions of his special protection (ART. 16), and he retained his right of nomination to episcopal sees (ART. 19) and most of the cathedral canonships (ART. 22). The appointment of bishops was clearly designated as a papal privilege; the permission to correspond freely with Rome was justified with the jurisdictional primacy of the Pope by divine right. The Catholic Church retained considerable influence on the education system: In general, instruction in the schools was to coincide with Catholic doctrine, and elementary schools were placed under the control of the Catholic Church (ARTS. 5,7,8). The state agreed to the suppression of all books antagonistic to the Church (ART. 9), and marriages were subjected to canon law (ART. 10).

The legal monopoly of the Catholic Church engendered passionate opposition among liberals, Protestants, and Josephinist Catholics. Yet the Curia and the majority of the bishops believed that they had won a great victory. They failed to recognize that less would have been more and that this concordat could not but generate new and profound controversies.

Cardinal Rauscher, who in 1856 gathered the bishops of the monarchy in Vienna and subsequently guided the episcopate in authoritarian fashion, saw to it that the concordat was strictly implemented. Through it he wanted to preserve the Christian character of all public institutions. He was convinced that he was safeguarding ecclesiastical and state interests alike. But the cardinal and the like-minded minister for religion and education, Count Thun, were faced with growing difficulties. The ratification of the concordat also saw the beginning of the struggle for its repeal or changes in it, a struggle which was to burden domestic Austrian politics for the next fifteen years. When in the 1860s Austria started on a path of liberalization (October Patent of 1860, February Patent of 1861),[12] its leading politicians realized that the concordat had pushed the state into a dead-end street; but their attempts to ameliorate the marriage and education articles, ultimately supported partially even by Rauscher, met the obstinate and short-sighted resistance of the Curia.

The domestic and foreign policy defeats of the conservatives in 1866 intensified the controversies. Beust, the new chancellor, pointed to the

[12] No calming of the waters in the battle over the concordat occurred as a result of the patents published on 1 September 1859 and 8 April 1861, granting autonomy to Austria's Protestant Churches (texts: Walter, *Fontes,* 303–22).

concordat and its propagandistic exploitation by the liberals in Germany and Italy as one of the causes of Austrian defeat. As it was his intention to gain new respect and influence in German affairs through a liberal Austrian policy, he closely cooperated with the liberal parliamentary majority.[13] In the spring of 1868 denominational laws were passed which once again subjected marriage and education to the state and guaranteed the free choice of religion. The most important clauses of the concordat were thus liberally modified.[14]

While the revolution and its results in the two major states of the German Confederation produced liberalization of the legal position of the Church, the other German states continued to adhere to the practice of state regulation. Maximilian II, who became King of Bavaria in 1848, was a confirmed Catholic, but he also regarded himself as the guardian of parity and tolerance.[15] He was determined to preserve the sovereign rights of the state, and disliked ultramontanism and its representative Reisach. He pursued moderate, liberal education and religious policies, but consulted advisers of different persuasions, among them C. A. von Abel, whose influence on the liberal-conservative ministry of von der Pfordten effected some concessions to the reactionaries. Only after Pfordten's resignation in 1859 was Bavaria's domestic policy guided by liberalism. King Ludwig II (after 1864) also was a liberal.

Archbishop Reisach attempted to satisfy the demands of the Würzburg bishops' conference in Bavaria. At a Bavarian bishops' conference in Freising (October 1850) a memorandum drafted by Reisach and Windischmann was passed, demanding the complete realization of the concordat and the repeal of the religious edict. Disregarding Döllinger's warnings—in spite of his differences with Reisach he still acted as adviser to the bishops—the conference also raised educational demands, such as participation in the filling of positions, which were unacceptable for a state pledged to parity.[16]

---

[13] See H. Potthoff, *Die deutsche Politik Beusts von seiner Berufung zum österreichischen Außenminister 1866 bis zum Ausbruch des deutsch-französischen Krieges 1870–71* (Bonn 1968).

[14] The controversies over these laws are treated in connection with the tensions of the late 1860s which constituted the beginnings of the *Kulturkampf*.

[15] H. Rall, "König Max II. von Bayern und die katholische Kirche," *HJ* 74 (1955), 739–47; H. Rall, "Ausblicke auf Weltentwicklung und Religion im Kreise Max' II. und Ludwigs II.," *ZBLG* 27 (1964), 488–522.

[16] Döllinger was also firmly opposed to Windischmann's suggestion to establish episcopal theological teaching institutes because it was directed against the departments of religion at universities (see Friedrich, *Döllinger* III, 90–99).

The Freising demands caused a protracted debate. The government realized that the old system could not be maintained as it was and therefore looked for an acceptable compromise. The royal decisions[17] of 8 April 1852 and 9 October 1854 met the bishops' demands with respect to priest seminaries and control of schools. In return for the concessions the government asked for the removal of Reisach, a request which Pius IX eventually granted. In December 1855 the archbishop became a Curia cardinal and in his new position had great influence on German religious affairs; his successor in Munich was the Benedictine Gregor von Scherr.

The Bavarian bishops met again in 1864 for the purpose of weighing defensive measures against the government's liberal religious and education policies; even in Catholic Bavaria, the Church had become rather isolated because of its undifferentiated resistance to the prevailing thought of the time. Also in 1864 it came to a conflict with the government leading to the closing of the seminary at Speyer which Bishop Weis had established.[18]

Under the chairmanship of Freiburg Archbishop von Vicari, a conference of the Upper Rhenish bishops in March 1851 sent a memorandum to the government which was based on the Würzburg demands. It was published and seen as a fundamental attack against the concept of a state church. The government did not respond until two years later, when it offered a number of concessions, which, however, a further joint declaration of the bishops characterized as inadequate.

Inasmuch as the governments refused to give in or to accept the conference of bishops as a negotiating partner, the five bishops were compelled in the succeeding years to negotiate individually. In electoral Hesse, Bishop Kött of Fulda achieved a temporary agreement. In Hesse-Darmstadt, Ketteler, bishop of Mainz since 1850, had considerable success.[19] He displayed an unusual degree of assurance, but also supported the government in its Greater German conservative policies and its battle against liberalism and democracy. Their mutual aversion to these movements produced an alliance, prudently employed by the

---

[17] Text: Walter, *Fontes,* 233–39. See *AkathKR* VIII, 403ff., 430ff.

[18] L. Stamer, "Der Streit zwischen Staat und Kirche um den Ausbau des Speyrer Priesterseminars 1864," *AMrhKG* 16 (1964), 249–80.

[19] The majority of the Mainz cathedral chapter in 1849 elected the moderate liberal Gießen theology professor Leopold Schmid; he was sharply opposed by Lennig and his friends and upon their instigation was not confirmed by Pius IX. The Hessian government, eager to avoid conflicts, gave in, and under pressure from Rome and Darmstadt the chapter eventually agreed on a list of three non-Hessian clerics. One of them, as a result of Lennig's intervention, was Ketteler.

bishop and his advisers Lennig, Heinrich, and Moufang[20] in the service of religious freedom. In 1851 Ketteler opened a theological studies institute at the Mainz seminary, thereby removing the reason for the existence of the state's institute at Gießen. The Dalwigk government lodged only a verbal protest. In 1854 Ketteler and Dalwigk signed an agreement which took account of the interests of both sides and kept religious peace for longer than a decade.[21] The Curia in the meantime had begun to insist on the Pope's exclusive right to negotiate concordats and was irritated by the bishop's unauthorized action and his failure to make maximum demands; Ketteler succeeded in obtaining Rome's consent only after further concessions by the government. Such success was denied to the Rottenburg Bishop Lipp, who with the aid of his vicar general Oehler in 1854 negotiated a similar agreement with the government of Württemberg; the Curia insisted on opening negotiations for a concordat, which after 1856 took place in Rome.

The development in Baden was much more discordant. To attempts by Vicari to exercise his episcopal rights without reference to the demands of the government, the government reacted with repression. Temporarily it placed the archbishop under house arrest and punished clerics who obeyed him. Vicari responded by excommunicating several members of the High Consistory. In order to settle the resulting conflict, which was widely publicized, the Baden government in 1854 began negotiations for a concordat.

In the negotiations with the governments of Württemberg, Baden, and Nassau,[22] the Holy See, represented by Cardinal Reisach, was able to obtain some central objectives analogous to the concordat with Austria. This, however, went too far again: The concordats with Württem-

---

[20] Johann Baptist Heinrich (1816–91), in 1851 professor of dogmatics at the new Mainz seminary, in 1855 member of the cathedral chapter, in 1867 cathedral dean, in 1869 vicar general, from 1850–90, together with Moufang, editor of *Katholik* (see, in addition to the biography by Pastor, H. Lenhart in *AMrhKG* 5 [1953], 325–59; L. Lenhart in *LThK* V, 204).—Franz Christoph Moufang (1817–90), in 1851 regent and professor of moral philosophy and pastoral care at the Mainz seminary, after 1854 also member of the cathedral chapter, after Ketteler's death administrator of the bishopric from 1877 to 1886, and representative in the Hessian parliament after 1863 (see, in addition to the biography by Götten, K. Forschner, *Hessische Biographien* I [1918], 241–47; L. Lenhart in *Jahrbuch für das Bistum Mainz* 5 [1950], 400–441; L. Lenhart in *AMrhKG* 19 [1967], 157–91; G. May in *AMrhKG* 22 [1970], 227–36).

[21] Text: Walter, *Fontes*, 359–63. See Vigener, *Ketteler*, 258–61.

[22] The Nassau government, after 1857 again negotiating with the Limburg Bishop Blum, on 25 May 1861 published a provisional regulation for religious affairs (text: Brück, *Oberrheinische Kirchenprovinz*, 550). Only the annexation of the duchy by Prussia (1866) produced a brief period of religious freedom (see Höhler, *Geschichte des Bistums Limburg*).

berg[23] (1857) and Baden[24] (1859) required parliamentary consent, which was obtained in neither state. After heated debates, the Baden concordat was rejected in 1860, that with Württemberg in 1861.

Subsequently, both states regulated the affairs between Church and state unilaterally in keeping with their prevailing liberal orientation. The legislation of 9 October 1860 in Baden[25] for the first time reflected liberal goals in a German state; the compromise clauses of the National Constitution of Frankfurt, which served as a model, were interpreted to the disadvantage of the Church. The Churches were granted a position as public corporations and the autonomous regulation of their affairs (ARTICLES 1,7), but otherwise they remained subject to the laws of the state; ecclesiastic regulations which affected "the rights of citizens" required the consent of the states (ARTS. 13,15). Evidence of a "general academic education" became a prerequisite for the holding of a Church office; the government was entitled to reject applicants of whom it did not approve for "civic or political reasons" (ART. 9). Property of the Church was administered jointly by the Church and state agencies (ART. 10), the establishment of religious orders was subject to state approval (ART. 11). The entire system of public education was placed under the control of the state (ART. 6), even though the Church was empowered to establish parochial schools (ART. 12). Religious legislation in Württemberg,[26] passed on 30 January 1862, rested on the same principles, but in a few points was more favorable to the Church.

Many of the new regulations were ambivalent; it all depended on how they were applied. In Württemberg, thanks to the conciliatory conduct of King Wilhelm and to the moderate attitude of Bishop Lipp and his successor Hefele, often misunderstood by zealots among the clergy, battles were avoided. In Baden, the administration of August Lamey (1860–66) was equally conciliatory, but the subsequent ministry of Julius Jolly (1866–76) used the legislation to start the first fundamental conflict between a liberal state and the Catholic Church in Germany.

Between 1850 and 1870, seventeen Catholic Conferences continued the work begun by the previous ones. They served to unite the Catholic

---

[23] Text of the Württemberg concordat and official supplements: Walter, *Fontes,* 363–76; Mercati I, 853–75.

[24] Text of the Baden concordat and official supplements: Walter, *Fontes,* 376–404; Mercati I, 880–920.

[25] Text (with the pertinent laws, also passed on 9 October 1860): Walter, *Fontes,* 405–10; Friedberg, *Staat und katholische Kirche im Großherzogtum Baden seit dem Jahre 1860* (Leipzig 1874), 237–40; M. Stadelhofer, *Der Abbau der Kulturkampfgesetzgebung im Großherzogtum Baden 1878–1918* (Mainz 1969), 392ff.

[26] Text: Golther, *Staat und Kirche in Württemberg,* 541–47.

forces, and enabled them to look at the associations, the press, and pastoral care; to an unprecented degree, laymen became involved in ecclesiastical affairs.

Most of the associations were founded at the Conferences, such as in 1848 in Mainz the Vincent Association by August Reichensperger, and the Boniface Association in 1849 at Regensburg upon the suggestion of Döllinger. The Vincent Association devoted itself to charity;[27] the Boniface Association, whose first president was Count Josef Stolberg (1804–59), the son of the famous convert, assisted the communities of the Diaspora.[28] Active support was also given to the journeymen associations. Their founder, Adolf Kolping (1813–65), a practical-minded educator, after 1848 developed them into a network for young craftsmen, covering all of Germany and Switzerland. When they finished their training, the journeymen often joined these associations. Kolping's concern for craftsmen and skilled workers characterizes the middle class origin of the Catholic social movement, which one encounters also in the contemporary Catholic press and in Alban Stolz's apologetics. It was an attempt to preserve the old social order by improving it and by fighting against liberalism, capitalism, and socialism. Unfortunately, the movement had no solutions for the novel problems of an industrial society and its proletariat. Ketteler was the first one to address this problem and to say that traditional methods of charity were inadequate.[29] He called for a state social program which would also engage the Church,[30] and at the same time pointed to new areas of activity for it. He singled out such matters as pastoral care for the workers, diocesan workers' associations directed by the local bishop, and social-pastoral instruction for theology students. In 1869 Ketteler confronted the entire German episcopate with the problem of the workers, but failed to induce it to make a decision along the line of his suggestions. The bishops at the time were absorbed by the problems and controversies which had arisen after the announcement of the Vatican council; the plight of the workers took a second seat behind the struggle for papal infallibility.

[27] H. Bolzau, *Vinzenzverein und Vinzenzgeist* (Cologne 1933); H. Auer, "100 Jahre Vinzenzverein in Deutschland," *Vinzenz-Blätter* 33 (1950), 40–54.

[28] *In heiliger Sendung. 100 Jahre Diaspora-Arbeit*, ed. by Generalvorstand des Bonifatiusvereins (Paderborn 1949); *Handbuch des Bonifatiusvereins* (Paderborn 1953).

[29] Especially with his book *Die Arbeiterfrage und das Christentum* (Mainz 1864, 1890), countless sermons, and in his report at the Fulda bishops' conference (September 1869) on "Fürsorge der Kirche für die Fabrikarbeiter" (Vigener, *Ketteler*, 435–70, 552–61; Lenhart, *Ketteler* I, 92–118; Lill, *Bischofskonferenzen*, 91f.).

[30] Important suggestions in this respect were made at the Frankfurt Catholic Conference (1863) by the Cologne religion teacher Christian Hermann Vosen (1815–71), a collaborator of Kolping.

Other organizations inspired by the Catholic Conferences were art associations, even though one-sidedly and retrospectively they clung to the examples of the Nazarenes and Neo-Gothics, as well as a Catholic Academy, which, while it was first suggested in 1852, was realized only partially in 1876 with the founding of the Görres Society.[31] In the same context belongs the project of a Catholic university, discussed during the conferences of the 1860s and promoted by the bishops. It was an understandable reaction to the snubbing of Catholics by the universities outside of Austria and Bavaria, but in view of the attitude of the governments it was impossible to realize.

The Catholic Conferences adhered to the decision made in 1849 not to become involved in everyday politics, but, interested in achieving the broadest possible effect by their attempt at rejuvenation, they voiced their opinions with respect to fundamental questions of public life. Defending the ecclesiastical status quo and opposing the spreading secularization, the Catholic Conferences and associations were increasingly pushed into the defensive by liberals and their Protestant comrades.

Controversies over the national question and the Papal State intensified the differences. The Conferences came out in favor of a Greater Germany.[32] In a Germany which included Austria, the Catholics were in the majority and therefore in a better position to obtain the rights denied them by individual German state governments; contrary to liberal polemics, the Catholic Church was an intimate part of many national traditions and wished to participate actively in the nation's unification. But Döllinger's logical call for national ecclesiastical cooperation was met with reserve which grew to decided resistance with the gradual merger of German Catholicism and ultramontanism.

The combination of ultramontane religiosity and Greater German objectives was unable to make headway, because the non-Catholic majority in the non-Austrian German states favored a Little Germany and an alliance with liberalism. The German National Association (after 1859) organizationally and ideologically modeled itself on the Italian Risorgimento. Resignation spread among the Catholics and many Pius Associations were dissolved. The Catholic Conference of 1858 at Cologne shifted the emphasis of the movement to the area of social charity, and Moufang's Greater German Party (1862) was nothing more than an episode.

[31] H. Finke, "Gründung, Entwicklung und Erfolge der Görres-Gesellschaft," *Jahresberichte der Görres-Gesellschaft 1937* (Cologne 1938), 68–73; A. Allgeier, "Geschichtlicher Rückblick," *Jahresberichte der Görres-Gesellschaft 1937*, 1–62; W. Spael, *Die Görres-Gesellschaft 1876–1941* (Paderborn 1957). See also J. Spörl in *StL* III, 1007f.
[32] Five of the Catholic Conferences between 1850 and 1870 took place in Austrian cities.

In this situation the defense of the Papal State, clearly enunciated for the first time by the Catholic Conference in 1861 at Munich, assumed an integrative character. Leaders and members of the movement were guided by their special feeling of solidarity with the Pope, a solidarity derived from the ultramontane concept of the Church. The activity of the Michael Confraternity (after 1860), the "Peter's Pence," pilgrimages, and demonstrations provided the Pope with material and spiritual assistance. With dangerous oversimplification, only comprehensible against the background of the liberal attacks on papacy and Church, the liberty of the Church was seen as dependent on that of the Pope, and his, in turn, dependent on that of the Papal State. In the course of the actual injustices inflicted on the Pope it was overlooked that the Roman priest state went counter to the political and legal principles of the century. The defense of its continued existence, which the liberals inherently denied, could not but bring further isolation and divert attention from the urgent problems of the time. Modifying statements like those of Döllinger, who doubted the necessity of the Papal State, were rejected out of hand;[33] they only fed the mistrust of the intellectual minority which objected to the growing Romanization of German Catholicism. The Catholic Conference in 1862 at Aachen merely intensified the activity. It also inspired the Club movement; it brought together Catholics of the upper and middle classes in social clubs which also in the 1860s in many areas became bases for the Catholic movement to counter the strength of the liberals through increased voting.

The reaction of the *Syllabus* (1864) was characteristic of the intellectual orientation of the Catholic movement. Without reserve the Catholics accepted the summary condemnation, in some points unjustified, in others inadequately reasoned, of ideological and political liberalism, even though a moderate interpretation, taking account of Germany's situation, was necessary. New disputes became unavoidable, for the papal document created tremendous excitement among liberals and Protestants, to be exceeded only by the dogma of infallibility. Although the *Syllabus* did not say anything new, it was seen as a declaration of war on the modern state and modern science, in view of its claim to authority and the sharpness of its formulations.

The political decisions of 1866 accentuated the contrasts further. Prussia's destruction of the German Confederation and exclusion of Austria from German affairs put an end to the political hopes of the Catholics. At first they looked upon the events more as a revolutionary break with legitimate tradition than as the beginning of a new form of

---

[33] See the controversies over Döllinger's Munich Odeon lectures (1860); Friedrich, *Döllinger* III, 233–69; Conzemius, *Briefwechsel Döllinger-Acton* I.

national unity. The removal of Austria as a great power from the concerns of Germany and Italy was also a defeat of Catholicism. In the new North German Confederation the Catholics were only a minority; the Italian national state required only the remainders of the Papal State for its completion, whose disappearance was thus only a question of time. The change in Germany was heightened by the fact that liberal and Protestant publicists viewed the events as a victory of Protestantism; with dangerous simplification they viewed Prussia as the embodiment of progress and disposed of the Austrian Empire as a relic of the Middle Ages.[34]

In 1867 the Catholic Conference took place at Innsbruck, and, employing the example of Tyrol to demonstrate the synthesis of Germandom and Catholicism, it once more came out in favor of a Greater Germany. But soon the realization gained ground that an effective representation of Catholic interests could only be made on the basis of the new realities and that national unification could be achieved under Prussia's auspices only. The first to plead impressively for the integration of Catholics with the North German Confederation was Ketteler;[35] of the politicians only Peter Reichensperger seconded him.[36] This integration during the subsequent years was much more of a fact than the polemics of the 1860s against what were called the "enemies of the nation" indicated. It was facilitated by Prussia's adherence to its friendly policy toward the denominations. Initially, Bismarck wooed the Catholics and for their sake denied Italy, Prussia's ally in the war against Austria, any assistance in Italy's hostile stance to the Papal State. But Bismarck's policies in 1866 also initiated his alliance with the National Liberals, which during the succeeding decade decisively influenced Prussian-German domestic politics and steered it into the *Kulturkampf*.

The political transformation and the announcement of the Vatican Council gave birth in the German episcopate to the desire for closer cooperation and to the plan of a joint conference like that of 1848. This realistic plan encountered objections only in Rome, but Cardinal Rauscher succeeded in removing them. The centralism of Pius IX refused to concede initiatives and jurisdictions to the bishops which tran-

---

[34] See J. C. Bluntschli, *Denkwürdiges,* ed. by R. Seyerlen, III (Nördlingen 1884), 145; F. Gregorovius, *Römische Tagebücher 1852–74* (Stuttgart 1892), entry 8, 14 July 1866; H. von Treitschke, *Aufsätze, Reden und Briefe,* ed. by K. M. Schiller, III (Meersburg 1929), 311, 312–30, 331–39, 360 f. Also K. G. Faber, *Die nationalpolitische Publizistik Deutschlands von 1866 bis 1871* II (Düsseldorf 1963), nos. 581, 583, 591f., 596f., 599, 603, 608, 610, 612, 615ff.

[35] In the sensational book *Deutschland nach dem Kriege von 1866* (Mainz 1867).

[36] August Reichensperger withdrew from active politics; Mallinckrodt and Windthorst in Diet and Reichstag remained very reserved toward Prussia but nevertheless loyal to the constitution.

scended the borders of their German states. In September 1867 the bishops from the North German Confederation and the south German states met at Fulda; the most important outcome of their deliberations was the institutionalization of the bishops' conference, which was to be held every two years.[37]

The gathering of Germany's Catholic scholars in 1863, suggested by Döllinger and observed with fearful mistrust by Rome, produced no understanding between the representatives of historical and Neo-Scholastic theology; the *Syllabus* and the announcement of the Vatican Council only served to intensify the contrasts. The monopolization of Neo-Scholasticism, eagerly promoted by Rome, was propounded by Heinrich, Moufang, and Paul Haffner (1829–99, after 1886 bishop of Mainz); they saw in Scholasticism the best ideological basis for their own antiliberal concentration. The Cologne seminary professor Matthias Joseph Scheeben (1835–83), who far surpassed his collaborators in speculative talent, and the Würzburg professors Joseph Hergenröther (1824–90, in 1879 prefect of the Vatican Archives and cardinal) and Franz Hettinger (1819–90) worked in the same direction. The writings of the German Jesuit Joseph Kleutgen (1811–83), who taught at Rome, and the Jesuit-directed theology department at the University of Innsbruck also established Roman Neo-Scholasticism.

But the larger majority of the German theology professors, including Döllinger, who had fought for religious freedom during the 1850s, resisted the Roman uniformity of thought with theological, historical, economic, and religious arguments. They feared that the extreme ultramontanism imposed on the Church by Pius IX's Curia would destroy legitimate religious structures and traditions and would produce an intensification of the conflict with the liberal forces which was as dangerous as it was unnecessary. In contrast to the Neo-Scholastics who were harking back to an idealized past, they sought a dialogue with other scholars and a reconciliation with modern thought in general. In addition to Döllinger there were two Tübingen professors, the dogmatist Johannes E. Kuhn (1806–87) and the historian Karl Joseph von Hefele (1809–93, after 1869 bishop of Rottenburg), and the Munich abbot Daniel Bonifaz von Haneberg (1816–76, after 1872 bishop of Speyer). Friedrich Michelis (1815–86) and Döllinger's student Johannes Friedrich (1836–1917) acted very polemically. Next to Bishop Maret's French neo-Gallicans, the German theology professors were regarded as the most dangerous opponents of the Curial movement.

[37] The invited Austrian bishops were unable to attend the meeting at Fulda because of domestic difficulties, especially the concordat controversy, which required their presence in Austria.

Their enemies, with the Catholic masses behind them, fought, defamed, and largely isolated them. The Munich nuncio accused them frequently of rebellion against authority and of sympathies for Protestanism.

In Switzerland, the liberals consistently exploited to their advantage the victory of 1846–48 over the Catholics. Their policy, designed to narrow further the freedom of movement of the Catholic Church, was viewed as exemplary by the liberals of other countries and was imitated in the religious battles during the 1860s and 1870s; the first state to do so was neighboring Baden. After 1848 as well, a good number of monasteries and religious schools were closed, the curricula of the remaining schools and the administration of ecclesiastical property were placed under cantonal control, and the clerics were compelled to swear an oath promising to uphold the laws; some cantons suppressed religious instruction entirely. But the constitutional guarantee of freedom of religion made possible the establishment of religious communities in the Protestant cantons, aided by gifts from foreign Catholics.

Bishop Marilley of Lausanne-Geneva was the first to be involved in a basic conflict. The governments of the five cantons of Berne, Fribourg, Geneva, Neuenburg, and Waadt, which his bishopric encompassed, in 1848 concluded a concordat in which they regulated religious problems unilaterally and in disregard of ecclesiastical principles. In the concordat the governments demanded the right to designate bishops and the adaptation of religious laws to those of the state; candidates for ecclesiastical offices had to undergo an examination before cantonal officials. Marilley's protests and his order to his clerics not to swear loyalty to the laws of the state were answered by the governments first with his arrest and then with his expulsion. A large majority of the clerics and laity remained loyal to their bishop, and under pressure from public opinion the governments in 1852 began negotiations with the Vatican. By 1856 these led to an agreement. Additionally, an agreement was reached two years later in Fribourg concerning Church property.

The radical behavior of the governments met the approval of only a minority of the Catholics which had continued to develop Wessenberg's reforms in a democratic direction and which believed that it could do so in continued cooperation with the governments. Groups with such aims continued to exist in most of Switzerland's cantons and eventually joined the Old Catholic protest movement against the dogma of papal infallibility. Those antiultramontanes who remained in the Church were isolated, and such men of compromise as the Lucerne politician Anton Philipp von Segesser[38] were unable to make their voices heard as

[38] E. F. J. Müller-Büchi in *ZSKG* 56 (1962), 185–200, 301–31, 60 (1966), 76–102, 275–304, 368–98, 64 (1970), 328–69; *Conzemius, Katholizismus ohne Rom,* 72f.

mediators between the hardened fronts. The liberals asserted to be fighting not against the Church as such, but only against hierarchism and ultramontanism, but actually their attitudes helped the growth of the movements to which they objected.

The closest possible cooperation with Rome seemed to be the best guarantee for development and continuation of religious life, and ultramontane activists like Gaspard Mermillod (1824–92) dominated the situation.[39] Mermillod worked in Geneva, where the number of Catholics increased substantially in consequence of immigration from Savoy. As the federal constitution did not permit the establishment of additional bishoprics, Pius IX in 1864 appointed Mermillod as suffragan bishop for Geneva; it seems that the Pope harbored totally unrealistic expectations of "converting" the city of Calvin.

The pressure exerted upon the Church strengthened the need for organization, which often was set up according to the German example. After the 1850s, Pius Associations and other charitable organizations sprung up, the latter under the guidance of the Capuchin Theodosius Florentini,[40] the founder of the Menzing and Ingenbohl congregations of sisters.

The predominantly agrarian structure of the Catholic cantons, which burdened the struggle with the urban liberals with additional social tensions, did not permit much intellectual activity. Only Fribourg and the abbey of Einsiedeln under the leadership of Abbot Heinrich Schmid were productive. Independent scholarly work was done by Bishop Karl Johann Greith of Saint Gallen,[41] the educator and historian Gall Morel, an Einsiedeln Benedictine,[42] and the politician and journalist Count Theodor von Scherer-Boccard.[43]

---

[39] Mermillod, who after his appointment as apostolic vicar of Geneva (1873) was exiled by the Federal Council, in 1883 became bishop of Lausanne-Geneva, and in 1890 was created Curia cardinal. Mermillod combined great social activity with extreme efforts on behalf of papalistic church doctrine (see Aubert, *Pie IX,* 303; biographies by L. Jeantet [Paris 1906] and C. Comte [Paris 1924]; C. Massard, *L'oeuvre sociale du Cardinale Mermillod* [Louvain 1914]; A. Hammann in *LThK* VII, 310).

[40] P. V. Gadient, *Der Caritasapostel Theodosius Florentini* (Lucerne 1946); A. von Wolfenschießen, *Die industriellen Unternehmungen von Pater Theodosius Florentini* (diss., Rome 1956), B. v. Mehr in *LThK* IV, 170.

[41] J. Oesch, *Karl Johann Greith* (St. Gallen 1909); J. B. Villiger in *LThK* IV, 1220.

[42] B. Kuehne, *Pater Gall Morel* (Einsiedeln 1875); R. Henggeler in *LThK* VII, 628.

[43] J. G. Mayer, *Graf Theodor von Scherer-Boccard* (Fribourg 1900).

CHAPTER 9

The Rise of Catholicism in the Anglo-Saxon World

England

In 1840 the number of vicars apostolic was raised from four to eight, but the solution of the problems of the Catholic Church in England, resulting from the growing number of Irish immigrants to the industrial cities, was possible only through the establishment of a diocesan episcopate. After the elevation of Pius IX, representatives of the vicars apostolic asked Rome in 1847 and in 1848 to give them immediate relief. But the Roman revolution and the exile of the Pope delayed a decision until 1850. In the meantime, the arrival of great numbers of destitute Irishmen following the great famine of 1847 burdened the ecclesiastical organization heavily.

The papal brief of 29 September 1850 established in England and Wales a Catholic hierarchy, with Westminster as the metropolitan see and twelve suffragan bishops. Wiseman was named archbishop and cardinal. A few days before journeying from Rome to England, he addressed a pastoral letter to all English Catholics in which he expressed his tremendous joy "that Catholic England once again was placed in its orbit in the ecclesiastical heavens." He was by nature effusive and optimistic, but his letter merely confirmed many Catholics in their conviction that Wiseman basically did not understand the English situation and the English character. The news of the establishment of the hierarchy generally had been well received, but his letter caused irritation. The press reacted with an outburst of bigotry, and there were street demonstrations against what was called "papal aggression," as illustrated by Wiseman's claim to govern the counties of Middlesex, Hertford, and Essex as bishop. In the process of choosing the twelve suffragan bishops mention of the Anglican dioceses had been tactfully avoided, but the designation of Westminster as residence of the archbishop caused indignation. Even though Westminster was not an Anglican diocese, the abbey was regarded as a national shrine.

Wiseman poured oil on the waters, which he had roiled unwittingly, with his skillful and effective *Appeal to the Reason and Good Feeling of the English People,* published shortly after his return to England. Even though in August 1851 an Ecclesiastical Titles Bill became law, imposing a penalty of one hundred pounds sterling on anyone accepting title to a non-existing episcopal see in the United Kingdom, the law was not enforced and was repealed twenty years later.

There were still conversions, but only in small numbers. The most notable one was that of Henry Edward Manning. He belonged to a group of people who in 1851 left the Anglican Church because of the Gorham decision. It involved the decision of a council of state committee which overruled an Anglican bishop who had refused to install the Rev. J. C. Gorham because his belief in the efficacy of baptism was in question. But the primary concern of the hierarchy was not the proselytization of England, but the creation of a system of parishes and the construction of churches and schools for the impoverished Catholics in the industrial areas. More than half of all Catholics lived in Lancashire (dioceses of Liverpool and Salford), whose population had swelled as a result of the strong influx of Irishmen after the famine of 1847. The rest was concentrated in London (dioceses of Westminster and Southwark) and in the industrial area of the Midlands (chiefly the diocese of Birmingham). In the remaining part of England Catholics lived so dispersed and in such small numbers that it was almost impossible to establish a diocesan organization for them.

Much, however, was achieved at the three provincial synods of 1852, 1855, and 1859, convoked by Wiseman.[1] The parish missions received their final status and the problem of obtaining priests for them was tackled. Some priests, of course, came from Ireland. In addition, Wiseman continued to employ regular clergy. This led to some difficulties, as the interests of the exempt regular clergy did not always coincide with those of the bishops. The cardinal himself founded a diocesan organization, the Oblates of Saint Charles, and appointed Manning as their superior. Additional problems resulted from the tendency of Wiseman and Manning to promote seminaries with strict Tridentine principles. Until then, it had been English practice to train candidates for the priesthood and candidates for lay occupations together. After an upsetting period of doubt and of changing methods, tradition finally won out.

Wiseman's state of health was rather bad during the last years of his life, and in 1855 George Errington from Plymouth was appointed his coadjutor. But the natures of the two men were so contrasting that Wiseman leaned more and more on Manning. When Wiseman died on 15 February 1865, it was the personal decision of Pope Pius IX to designate Manning as his successor, even though the chapter had chosen Errington for the post.

Manning, a man of iron will and firm determination, remained archbishop for twenty-seven years. Almost immediately after his conver-

---

[1] At this synod, Newman delivered one of his most important sermons: "The Second Spring." It indicated that his imagination also was fired by the hope for a conversion of England, even though temperamentally he was far more subdued than Wiseman.

sion he had been ordained a priest and had then spent three years in Rome. There he developed extreme ultramontane views, but yet became a national figure in Victorian England. His social conscience and his concern for the poor were probably the outstanding features of his activity. This tendency had become clear even before his conversion and reached its zenith with his successful mediation during the great London dock strike in 1889. His life was also filled with the battle to obtain a fair proportion of public funds for Catholic elementary schools when, as a result of the Education Bill of 1870, public schools came into being. His genuine sympathy for Ireland also was of benefit for his pastoral care, as 80 percent of the English Catholics were of Irish descent.

Manning had a firm grasp of the intellectual problems of his age, but also a deep distrust of their effect on the Catholic faith. Although supported in the matter by almost all of the bishops, it was he who was responsible for the absolute ban on Catholics studying at Oxford or Cambridge. In 1874 he founded a Catholic university in Kensington, but it was a failure and closed its doors eight years later. Three years after his death in 1885 the prohibition on Catholics attending state universities was lifted.

The problem of university attendance led to discord between Manning and Newman. It was only a part of the underlying tensions between the so-called "Old Catholics" and the "converts." The "Protestant" tendencies of Newman agreed with much of traditional English Catholicism; Newman and the Old Catholic group were brothers under the skin and viewed with distrust the enthusiastic ultramontanism of Manning and other converts. Even though these divisions disappeared by 1880, the personal animosities between Manning and Newman continued.

After his conversion, Newman had studied theology in Rome. There he had become aware of his spiritual affinity to the oratory of Saint Philipp Neri, and after his return he founded the first English oratory in Birmingham. Its growth faced many obstacles. In view of the tensions between him and Frederick William Faber, the oratories in Birmingham and London developed independently from one another and even with a certain degree of hostility. In 1852, Newman accepted the invitation of Archbishop Cullen to go to Dublin as president of Dublin University. But his tenure was not very successful and in 1858 he resigned his position. But he left a lasting memorial to his presidency in the form of a series of lectures which he had given in May 1852 and which were published under the title *The Idea of a University*.

Returned to England, he founded the oratory school in 1859 and thus made a notable contribution to the tradition of Benedictine and Jesuit education.[2] In the same year, his bishop, Ullathorne of Birmingham, asked him to take over the *Rambler,* a journal founded in 1848 by John Moore Capes. In 1854, Richard Simpson had become its publisher, and in 1858 John Acton[3] had become a partner. The reason for Newman's appointment was ecclesiastical suspicion of the *Rambler,* but his own contribution to the July issue of 1858[4] was denounced by Rome, and George Talbot, the Pope's English informant, characterized Newman as the most dangerous man in England. During the next five years his attitudes were questioned, he was treated with disrespect, and became a man without influence. His earlier position was restored with the publication of his *Apologia pro vita sua.* It appeared in 1864 in monthly installments as a reply to accusations by the Rev. Charles Kingsley that Newman and the Catholic clergy did not regard "truth for its own sake" as a virtue.

The core of the reply bears the title: "A history of my religious opinions," and the honesty displayed by Newman was a very effective defense of his personal honor. He could hardly hope to have a similar success in 1864 when he attempted to refute the assertion that Catholic theologians were severely handicapped in their scholarly work. Two years later, Ullathorne offered him a church in Oxford, but the suggestion was blocked by Manning, Ward, and Talbot, who did not consider Newman sufficiently orthodox. In the following year, the Congregation for the Propagation of the Faith prohibited Catholics from attending public universities.

In 1870 Newman published *A Grammar of Assent.* He had spent twenty years on it, and it is perhaps his only work which was not written as an immediate response but was the fruit of long reflection.[5] Its theme was the fundamentals of certainty and, more specifically, the reasons of faith: How can one believe something that is beyond comprehension or

---

[2] Another important date in the development of higher education for boys is the year 1855, in which the Salesians in London opened Clapham College, the first of its kind for the middle class.

[3] John Emmerich Edward Dalberg Acton (1834–1902) was one of Döllinger's most significant students at Munich. As a political liberal and defender of freedom of religion he fought actively against ultramontanism. Unlike Döllinger he did not break with the Church after the First Vatican Council but retired to a strictly academic life. In 1886 he founded the *English Historical Review.* In 1895 he was appointed Regius Professor of Modern History at the University of Cambridge. During his final years he planned the *Cambridge Modern History* (published 1901–11) (see U. Noack, *Katholizität und Geistesfreiheit nach den Schriften von John Dalberg-Acton* [Frankfurt 1936]; G. E. Fasnacht, *Acton's Political Philosophy* [London 1952].

[4] Later published separately as "On Consulting the Faithful in Matters of Doctrine."

[5] See H. Tristram, ed., *John Henry Newman, Autobiographical Writings* (London 1956), 273.

proof? His approach—the more interesting as it takes place independently from the scholastic tradition—is essentially a psychological analysis of "moral proof, of a collection of probabilities,"[6] not a single one of
which is proof in itself, but which as a whole can produce an act of faith
based on what Newman calls the "illative sense," the ability of reason to
draw conclusions and arrive at judgments.

Also in 1870 there was a growth of tension between Newman and
Manning with respect to the definition of papal infallibility. Newman
had no difficulties with the dogma as such—in fact, in a very real sense it
had been a motive for his conversion—but he feared that a formal
definition would create hostility outside of the Church and discontent
within it, especially if it were to be pronounced in the extreme form
which he had reason to believe would be used. He had no difficulty with
accepting the doctrine as defined by the council.

In 1877 he returned to Oxford after thirty years in order to accept
the first honorary fellowship awarded by Trinity College. Two years
later Leo XIII created him a cardinal with the unusual privilege of
residing in Birmingham, even though he was only a priest. There he
spent the last eleven years of his life in peace. His gravestone bore the
inscription, which he had written himself: "Ex umbris et imaginibus in
veritatem."

Scotland

The number of Catholics in Scotland also grew noticeably as a result of
Irish immigration to the industrial areas. In 1851, 18 percent of the
population of Glasgow were Irish. Most of the immigrants came from
the province of Ulster and brought with them the tension existing there
between Catholics and Protestants. In addition, they encountered the
hostility of the Scottish Presbyterians and were incapable of adjusting
themselves to the native Catholics. Ever since the days of O'Connell the
Irish Catholics in Glasgow were very nationalistic. Many of their priests
came from Ireland and there was discord between Irish and Scottish
priests. In 1851, the Irish in Glasgow started a newspaper, the *Free Press,*
whose incessant polemics against Dr. Murdoch, the vicar apostolic,
probably hastened his death. Murdoch's successor was John Gray, his
former coadjutor. Rome suggested that Gray should choose his own
coadjutor and hinted that an Irish priest would be suitable. But Gray
was unwilling to do this and was supported by the other vicars apostolic,
who, in the case of an Irish appointment, feared a general worsening of
the situation of the Church in Scotland.

[6] *Grammar of Assent,* 217.

At the urging of Archbishop Cullen of Dublin the president of the Irish College in Paris, James Lynch, C.M., was finally appointed Gray's coadjutor. Regrettably, but unavoidably, the appointment increased tensions in Glasgow, where the Irish clergy followed Lynch and the Scottish clergy followed Gray. In 1867, Archbishop Manning was named apostolic visitor.[7] He suggested the transfer of both Gray and Lynch and thought that the Scottish problems could be solved only through the establishment of a diocesan hierarchy. But the government regarded such a step as premature and relayed its reservations to Manning and Rome.

Consequently, Rome hesitated to establish such a hierarchy in Scotland. The selection of the metropolitan see also proved difficult. Two-thirds of the three hundred fifty thousand Catholics lived in the metropolitan area of Glasgow. The next larger concentration was Edinburgh, Scotland's capital; Saint Andrews, the seat of the medieval archbishopric, was only a small town with very few Catholics. When the hierarchy was finally established in March 1878, an attempt was made to take all of these considerations into account. The metropolitan see was established in Saint Andrews and Edinburgh with four suffragan bishoprics, and Glasgow as archbishopric without suffragan sees was subordinated directly to the Holy See.

Ireland

It is generally taken for granted that the great famine of 1847 was a decisive turning point in the modern history of Ireland. It marked the beginning of a strong emigration which possibly raised the standard of living in Ireland slightly, but nevertheless still left behind a large agrarian proletariat, which had little hope of improvement as long as the laws concerning landownership remained unchanged. In spite of many developments which seem to point to progress, such as the construction of new churches and an increase in ecclesiastical institutions, the emigration after the famine left behind a Catholic population without any self-confidence and exposed to constant economic and political shocks.

Catholics constituted almost 80 percent of the population. The majority of the Protestants were concentrated in Ulster, while in most of the south and the west the population was almost totally Catholic. The predominant Protestants gave up their essential monopoly of wealth and political power only slowly. In 1873, a very important court judgment stated that papal jurisdiction in Ireland was still illegal, according

---

[7] V. A. McClelland, "The Irish Clergy and Archbishop Manning's Apostolic Visitation of the Western District of Scotland 1867," *CHR* 53 (1967), 1–27, 229–50; "A Hierarchy for Scotland 1868–78," *CHR* 56 (1970), 474–500.

to an unrepealed statute from the sixteenth century. In practice, however, civil courts respected the jurisdiction of the Church, as its decisions were easily accepted by the Catholics.

Under the force of the Penal Code and during the days of O'Connell,
a feeling of closeness had developed between the Catholic clergy and
the laity; it became stronger during the nineteenth century as a consequence of the fact that the large majority of the parish clergy was
educated in Ireland, chiefly at Maynooth. Only a small minority attended the few seminaries on the continent which had been reopened
after the French Revolution.

In 1849, Paul Cullen, head of the Irish College at Rome, was appointed archbishop of Armagh. In 1852 he was transferred to Dublin
and in 1866 became the first Irish cardinal; he dominated the Irish hierarchy until his death in 1878. He was equipped with the authority of an
apostolic delegate and thus empowered to convoke a national synod at
Thurles in 1850. There, Church discipline and religious practices were
adapted to common canon law and the prevailing ultramontane tendencies, the planned Queen's Colleges were condemned, and the political
activity of the Irish clergy was restricted.

Attempts to define these restrictions were only partially successful
and resulted in the complete alienation of Cullen and the influential
Archbishop MacHale of Tuam. After 1860, there was the revolutionary
movement of the Fenians, which, according to Cullen's conviction,
posed the same threat to the Church in Ireland as the revolutionaries on
the continent or in Italy. But Cullen was wrong, for even though the
Fenians refused to continue to recognize the leadership of the clergy in
Irish politics, they were not unbelievers.

In his opposition, Cullen was supported by the bishops, but the clerics
in some instances hesitated to follow him, as they shared the anti-British
sentiments of the people. But it was not easy for them to find a theological justification for the rebellion at the very time of the *Syllabus,* and
therefore on the whole they refrained from openly supporting the revolutionary movement. After a failed uprising in 1867, many Fenians were
imprisoned; now the clerics acted less restrained and participated in the
public demonstrations of sympathy for the prisoners. In order to
counter this threat, Cullen in 1870 managed to obtain a formal Roman
condemnation of the Fenian movement.

In 1869, Odo Russell, the unofficial British representative at Rome,
reported that Cardinal Antonelli had informed him that the "conditions
in Ireland filled him with distaste and pain and that he did not understand the Irish character."[8] Five years earlier, Cullen had accepted a

[8] Odo Russell to the Earl of Clarendon, Rome, 5 May 1869; quoted in N. Blakiston,
The Roman Question (London 1962), 363.

cautious participation in politics and in spite of his Roman training and early history had shown himself to be the type of liberal Catholic which Antonelli had difficulty in understanding. Ultimately, Cullen was prepared to cooperate with the Liberal Party, then in the process of formation under the leadership of Gladstone, even though it was hostile to an ultramontane papacy.

English liberals and Irish Catholics were in agreement that the Protestant Church in Ireland should be disestablished. Both parties wanted to distribute its property to all Churches in Ireland. But Cullen insisted that no Church be subsidized by the state and that each should instead be a voluntary association before the law, just as the Catholic Church had been since the Reformation. This principle was embodied in the Irish Church Act of 1869.

Cullen's association with the English liberals remained more in the area of common interests than in common principles, and his support of a "free Church in a free state" was primarily based on his Irish thought and not on any principles of liberalism. This became clear in the question of education. After 1850, the developments in the system of non-denominational elementary schools introduced in 1831 gave the bishops reasons for concern, and they tried repeatedly to gain the support of the government for a system of denominational schools. They were not able to effect such a change, but in practice it became quite denominational, as almost all children in Ireland attending public schools were Catholic. The system of secondary schools had always been established on the basis of private denominational schools. In 1878 the Intermediate Education (Ireland) Act granted small salaries for principals and stipends for students according to the scores achieved on state examinations.

University education had long been a source of conflict. In 1850 the synod of Thurles had prohibited Catholics from attending interdenominational universities, known as Queen's Colleges. Cullen returned from Rome with the charge of establishing a university modeled on Louvain. Newman accepted the invitation to become its president, but the institution was always in trouble. There were many reasons. The government was unwilling to accredit the institution, and its degrees were therefore not recognized. The Irish Catholic middle class, which was ready to send its sons to this university, was numerically too small, and Newman's hope to erect in Dublin a Catholic university for all of Great Britain and Ireland was unrealistic. Some of the bishops denied the new university their active support, and MacHale was soon its bitter enemy. This aspect was particularly grave, as the finances of the university depended on church collections. With respect to practical matters, Newman could deal solely with Cullen, but the temperaments of the two men were too different.[9] After Newman's departure in 1858 the Catholic University was constantly in difficulties. The government still refused to grant it a constitution, even though in 1879 it installed the Royal University of Ireland as a supervisory agency which examined the students of the Catholic University together with those of all other colleges for the granting of degrees.

The frailty of the Catholic University and the concentration of seminary training in Maynooth led to a strictly clerical orientation of the Catholic professors in Ireland. Two of the Maynooth theologians deserve mention. They were Patrick Murray, whose *De ecclesia Christi* (3 vols. [Dublin 1860–66]) revealed the ultramontane orientation of the college, and George Crolly, who, in his *De iustitia et iure* (3 vols. [Dublin 1870–77]), was the first one to discuss this topic within the context of British law. Cullen's nephew, Patrick F. Moran, the future archbishop of Sydney, was the first person to utilize the papal archives in his numerous publications. Together with Cullen he was responsible for the founding of the monthly *Irish Ecclesiastical Record* (1864).

Experience taught Cullen that it was impossible for a priest or bishop in the Ireland of the nineteenth century not to become involved in politics. But the involvement of the clergy in politics had a particularly sad consequence. The Protestants concluded that an independent Ireland would be ruled by the Catholic clergy and that "Home Rule" would in fact mean "Rome Rule." After 1860, the Orange Order, started in 1795 as an instrument of Protestant domination, was revitalized.

The break between the Irish Catholics and the Protestant Liberals over the question of university education in 1873 led to the fall of Gladstone's government. After six years of political instability, a number of bad harvests at the end of the decade once again raised the problem of the tenant farmers. Charles Stewart Parnell, a Protestant, acted as the leader of a strong parliamentary group which demanded agrarian reform and a limited degree of autonomy known as Home Rule. He gained the support of the revolutionary leaders and of the Catholic hierarchy, especially of Archbishop Walsh of Dublin and Archbishop Croke of Cashel. Gladstone, returned to office in 1880, was sympathetic, but the English conservatives, including some prominent

---

[9] The failure of the university has often erroneously been ascribed to this last factor alone. Cullen and Newman had managed to cooperate, even if only with difficulty. "We were different," Newman wrote to C. W. Russell, the president of Maynooth, on 17 November 1878 after Cullen's death, "but I was always attached to him with love and gratitude, and because of his work regarded him very highly." Cullen also esteemed Newman and defended his orthodoxy when Newman was suspected by Rome (see F. McGrath, *Newman's University: Idea and Reality* [Dublin 1951], 503–4).

Catholics, depicted the Irish movement in Rome as revolutionary. Papal intervention and condemnation made life more difficult, but the movement held together until 1889, when Parnell was named a corespondent in a divorce suit. The bishops declared that he could no longer act as spokesman, and the consequent split led to a further period of political instability. When it was overcome, it was recognized that the involvement of the clergy in politics, peculiar to the 19th century, had also passed.

The United States

During the second third of the nineteenth century, the Catholic Church in the United States was able to record some significant progress. After 1870 it was not only numerically the largest English-speaking Catholic group in the world, but it was also during this time that American Catholicism acquired its peculiar characteristics.

Originally consisting of former English and French settlers, and former Spanish ones in the southern states, the Catholic community of the United States gradually assumed different characteristics with the immigration of Irish Catholics. The great famine between 1845 and 1847 in Ireland speeded up this movement, and additional German immigrants journeyed to the United States in the wake of the 1848–49 revolutions. This dual movement, which coincided with the rapid economic development of the country, continued during the two subsequent decades. The majority of the Irish were Catholics, and so were many Germans.[10] Although many of them, and especially their children, isolated in a Protestant environment, left the church of their fathers,[11] the immigration, together with the natural increase, resulted in a growth of the Catholic population which exceeded all expectations. According to Shaughnessy's findings, resting on a critical examination of the available data, there were in the United States in 1840 approximately 663,000 Catholics, i.e., 4 percent of the total population. Ten years later, they had increased by one million people, of whom 700,000 were immigrants from fourteen different countries; in 1860, there were 3,103,000 and in 1870 there were 4,504,000 Catholics, corresponding respectively to 7 percent, 10 percent, and 11 percent of the total population.

But the distribution of the Catholics was quite different from region to region. While around 1870 one out of nine Americans was Catholic,

[10] The number of Catholic immigrants during the years from 1820 to 1870 has been estimated at 1,683,791 Irish and 606,791 Germans.
[11] The significance of these departures during the second half of the century used to be overestimated, as the precise calculations by G. Shaughnessy, op. cit. prove.

the ratio in the southern states, which the immigrants avoided because of their black population, was only one in twenty-five or less. The immigration of Catholics benefited chiefly the states of the North, such as Pennsylvania, Ohio, Kentucky, Illinois, Wisconsin, Iowa, and Minnesota. The Germans, settling chiefly in the triangle between Cincinnati, Milwaukee, and Saint Louis, generally settled in rural areas, while the Irish, too poor for agrarian colonization,[12] and dependent on immediate employment as workers or domestics, congregated mostly in the port and industrial cities of the North. Inasmuch as the Irish were by far the largest group, American Catholicism for a long time had an urban, even proletarian, character.

The steady stream of immigrants from Ireland led to a rekindling of the nativist campaign which had been declining in the 1840s, and under the new name of Know-Nothingism anticlerical violence started again. It reached its apogee between 1854 and 1855 and only came to an end with the Civil War.[13]

The rapid increase of the Catholic population, together with the westward movement and the addition of Oregon, Idaho, Texas, New Mexico, and California, presented the ecclesiastical authorities with difficult problems of organization.

In the open areas of the Far West a new beginning had to be made, and in 1846 the Congregation for the Propagation of the Faith founded a new church province with Oregon City as its capital upon the instigation of the adventurous vicar apostolic Monsignor Blanchet.

Even in the former Mexican provinces a new beginning needed to be made, for the Church had had to suffer grievously in these seemingly Catholic areas as a consequence of Freemason-inspired government action against the regular clergy and from a corrupt clergy. Through the establishment of the dioceses of Galveston for Texas (1847), Santa Fe (1850) for New Mexico, Monterey-Los Angeles (1850) and San Francisco (1853) for California, the situation was mastered. This was facilitated by the freedom of religion which prevailed in the United States and which permitted the Franciscans to resume their missions to the Indians.

---

[12] There were some attempts to help them with settling, but the Irish did not like living in the countryside because of its isolation.

[13] One of the most spectacular episodes was the campaign of demonstrations directed at Monsignor Bedini, whom Pius IX had sent to the United States for the purpose of examining the possibility of establishing an apostolic delegation and who after a short stay was forced to flee. To xenophobia and antipapism was added in his case the rejection of the Italian immigrants because of the temporal power of the Pope (see J. F. Connelly, *The Visit of Archbishop G. Bedini to the United States* [Rome 1960] and R. Sylvain, *A. Gavazzi* II [Quebec 1962], 426–40.

In the largely rural areas of the Midwest and the South, in which the majority of the population lived dispersed in the country, the situation for a long time was similar to that of the missionary countries, as the few priests could travel through the vast areas only at long intervals. But with the active support of bishops like J. B. Purcell, from 1833 to 1883 archbishop of Cincinnati and, outside of the dioceses of the East Coast, the preeminent American prelate of his time, new dioceses were established with the growing cities as centers. In spite of the sparse financial means and the lack of priests (at the beginning hardly more than ten), gradually there were established Chicago, Milwaukee, and Little Rock in 1843; Cleveland in 1847; Saint Paul and Savannah in 1850; Springfield, Covington, and Alexandria in 1853; Marquette and Fort Wayne in 1857; and Green Bay, La Crosse, and Columbus in 1868.

In the states of the Northeast in which the majority of the immigrants was concentrated, the delicate question of trusteeism was only solved in the 1860s. His energy and his influence on the public enabled G. Hughes, from 1842 to 1866 bishop, then archbishop of New York, to obtain in 1860 a law for the state of New York which provided the Church with the desired degree of freedom and simultaneously maintained a sufficient degree of lay control over the property of the Church. Gradually the other states also adopted this law. But the main difficulty was posed for the Catholic authorities by the ever increasing stream of immigrants. The priests, although industrious and agile, could no longer do all of their work, and the great number of languages spoken by their flock confused matters totally. What is more, the poverty of the faithful, who earned their daily bread as workers or domestics, in spite of a high degree of altruism did not permit them to do more than supply a portion of the financial needs of the Church.

Fortunately, the American bishops, of whom two thirds came from Europe,[14] excelled with their sense of the practical and their enterprising spirit, and Europe responded generously to their appeals. Irish priests arrived in great numbers and placed themselves in the service of their emigrated brethren. In 1857, at the request of Monsignor Spalding, a college was established at Louvain for the purpose of training European seminarians who volunteered for the apostolate in the United

---

[14] Of the thirty-two bishops who attended the council of Baltimore in 1852, only nine were born in the United States; eight were of Irish, eight of French, two of Belgian, two of Canadian, one of Austrian, one of Spanish, and one of Savoyard extraction. Of the forty-five bishops attending the council of 1866, fourteen were born in the United States, eleven in Ireland, one in Belgium, one in Austria, one in Germany, and one in Savoy. Almost all metropolitan sees were in Irish hands, which in addition to other disadvantages to be mentioned later had the advantage of providing the American episcopate with a large degree of homogeneity in this difficult transition period.

States. By way of these additions and the slowly growing number of native priests,[15] the active number of clergy rose from about 700 at the time of the accession of Pius IX to 1320 in 1852, to 2,770 in 1866, and in 1875 reached 6,000. A good number of new parishes were founded, but the Irish character of the Church in the United States, and especially the tendency of the Irish priests to treat their flocks as minors and to leave only little initiative to laymen in religious matters, was strengthened by this development.

At the same time that the clergy was growing, the continuous arrival of regular clergy (both men and women) from France, Belgium, and Austria, and the financial assistance of French, German, and Austrian missionary societies made possible the building of Catholic schools, the creation of charitable institutions for the reception of the immigrants in the ports, and the organization of parish missions according to the method which had proved itself in Europe (the Austrian Jesuit Xavier Weninger after 1848 preached more than eight hundred sermons in such parish missions).

The Civil War, in which the southern states rose against the Union between 1861 and 1865, tested the mettle of the young American Church. The Church had never taken an unequivocal stand in the controversy over slavery. In the South, the ecclesiastical authorities were not completely opposed to slavery as long as it was humane, and even in the North, where the attitude of the Catholic clergy was virtually the same as that of the Protestant ministers, many Catholics were irritated by the alliance between the abolitionists and the nativists. The ideals as well as the practical consideration, touched by resignation, of America's most representative Catholic theologian of the time, P. Kenrick, which he presented in his *Theologia Moralis,*[16] are characteristic of the official attitude of the hierarchy. It left the faithful with the complete freedom of decision, and itself was completely engrossed in maintaining the political neutrality of the Church in temporal affairs, a tradition reaching back to Carroll.[17] The outbreak of the war, kindled less by slavery than by the concern to preserve national traditions, made the situation easier for the Catholics. Almost throughout, they followed the leaders of their

[15] In 1854 there were already thirty-four diocesan seminaries, but in 1860 only 15 percent of the active priests were born in the United States. In 1859, Pius IX opened the American College in Rome, so as to provide a number of young Americans with a higher theological education (see R. McNamara, *The American College in Rome* [Rochester 1956]).

[16] 1841. Last edition (Baltimore 1861), I, 166. See J. D. Brokhage, *Father P. Kenrick's Opinion on Slavery* (Washington 1955).

[17] As an example, see the pastoral letter of May 1840 following the Fourth Provincial Council of Baltimore (in P. Guilday, *The National Pastorals,* 142–43) and the observations by J. T. Ellis, op. cit., 68–75.

respective states, and Catholics fought in both armies. The absence of a clear position among the Catholics, in a question whose moral relevance was evident, engendered fresh attacks by the Yankees against the Roman Church. Yet its standing was enhanced by the charitable activity in which priests and cloistered women engaged in the Confederate states as well as in the Union states. It was furthermore aided by the fact that the Catholic Church was the only one among the various religious communities which managed to maintain its unity, even though its faithful and occasionally its pastors[18]—although on their own authority—declared themselves unequivocally for one camp or the other.

After the end of the war, the Catholics began immediately to heal the material and moral wounds. In this effort they were led by such bishops as Monsignor Verot, the vicar apostolic of Florida and one of the originators of the period of reconstruction in the South; not even his infantile behavior at the Vatican Council could overshadow the remarkable achievement of these chaotic times. There was also Monsignor Spalding, between 1864 and 1872 archbishop of Baltimore. He was a typical American, who combined the talents of the man of science, the ability to administer, advocacy of the Church, and concern for the nation.[19]

One of the first actions of the Church after the end of the war was the convocation of a plenary council.[20] It was held in October 1866 in Baltimore. Although it was able only partially to solve the difficulties confronting the Church in the United States during the last third of the nineteenth century, it at least strengthened the idea of a collegiate leadership of the Church. This was a concept rarely encountered in Europe at the time, but it became one of the characteristics of the American episcopate. In addition to many practical regulations, Spalding suggested the writing of a textbook-like explanation of the council, which amounted to a departure from earlier councils. The intention was to present the great topics raised in the encyclical *Quanta cura* and the *Syllabus* in a positive form and to adapt them to the American mentality,

[18] Thus, Bishop Hughes and Bishop Domenec in favor of President Lincoln and Bishop Lynch in favor of the Confederates.

[19] The biography by his nephew J. L. Spalding (1873) has not yet been replaced by a more recent one. See also A. A. Micek, *The Apologetics of M.J. Spalding* (Washington 1951).

[20] The first one took place in 1852 following the division of the Church province of Baltimore, which until then comprised the entire United States. It was replaced by five new provinces: in 1846 Oregon, in 1847 Saint Louis, in 1850 New York, Cincinnati, and New Orleans, and San Francisco in 1853.

especially with respect to the demands which the apostolate was making on the Church in a pluralistic society.[21]

Among the many council decrees, an entire chapter was devoted to the pastoral care of millions of blacks, whose sudden emancipation created great problems. The Protestant blacks suffered much less under the new situation, as their pastors belonged to their race. While in the South relations between black and white Catholics were cordial, the mutual embitterment carried separation of the races into the Church and resulted in a further decline of contacts. The blacks, constituting about 10 percent of the total population of the United States, were effectively lost to Catholicism in spite of the care which members of foreign orders lavished on them. Outstanding among them were the Fathers of Saint Joseph of Mill Hill, whom the future cardinal Vaughan had sent from England in 1871 at the behest of the Pope.[22]

Another difficult problem with which the council of 1866 had to grapple was the membership of Catholics in secret societies. In addition to the Irish societies connected with the Fenian movement, other groups with philanthropic aims grew considerably. Although these groups, unlike Freemasons in Europe, did not have any revolutionary or anti-Christian objectives, their indifferentism posed a real threat. The bishops could not agree on a united stand and the decree of the council of Baltimore which attempted to formulate binding regulations was not very suitable in practice. This was so in part because it occasioned constant inquiries in Rome, where no clear understanding of the American situation existed.

Most of the council's attention, however, was devoted to the problem of education. Since the constitution guaranteed religious freedom, the secretary of education, Horace Mann, at first attempted to include non-denominational religious instruction in the curriculum of the public schools. But in practice this plan encountered obstacles, and public instruction quickly developed in an almost exclusively laicistic direction. This convinced the Catholics that, following the Irish example, they had to organize their own schools, in spite of the heavy burden involved. The motto of Archbishop Hughes of "school before Church" was gradually accepted by most of the other bishops. The plenary council of 1866 referred to a decree of the provincial council of Cincinnati of 1858 and declared that the establishment of parish schools was a serious

---

[21] See the interesting article by J. Hennesey, "The Baltimore Council of 1866, an American Syllabus," *RACHS* 77 (1966), 1–18.

[22] It should be noted that almost all Indian missions were the work of foreigners, after 1830 especially of the Austrian priest A. F. Baraga and after 1838 of the Belgian Jesuit P. Desmet.

moral duty of parish pastors. Urgent appeals were directed to Catholic families to keep their children from attending public schools as much as possible. After 1870 some militant laymen, like the journalist J. McMaster—a second Louis Veuillot in the United States—and Miss Edes, who believed that some bishops were slack in implementing their demands, carried the matter to Rome. In November 1876 the American episcopate was informed by Rome that it must follow the same strict directives which then were valid in England and Ireland.

The emphasis with which the organization of Catholic schools was pursued was only one, albeit a fundamental, aspect of a more general policy, the objective of which was to keep the faithful in strictly closed communities, to avoid the use of Protestant institutions as much as possible, and to keep Catholics on the periphery of normal American society. Many priests and bishops, especially Monsignor Hughes, whose personal prestige among the Irish contributed to winning them to his side in opposition to the native American Catholics, thought that the faith of the immigrants, who in the majority were very simple people and in the past had been tied to the Church by environment and local traditions, was not capable of resisting the influence of a Protestant or indifferent environment. The inherited hostility of the Irish toward the Anglo-Saxons and the awareness of being a socially despised proletariat, an awareness that was constantly being nourished by the repeated attacks of the nativist movement, as well as the mistrust of the traditionalist German farmers of the materialistic character of the new American civilization, finally drove the Catholics into denominational ghettos. The enterprising spirit of the Irish coupled with the organizational talent of the Germans[23] resulted in the creation of a number of organizations, the listing of which in 1867 in the *National Catholic Almanac* covered nine pages of small print: charitable organizations, hospitals, newspapers and journals, and societies of all kinds. Their growth received a further boost by the arrival after 1870 of numerous nuns whom the *Kulturkampf* had driven out of Germany.

Their encapsulation compelled the Catholics to develop a degree of activity that had no equal in the European Churches; an activity which simultaneously strengthened the vitality of their faith. Beneficial for the moment, this separation in the long run produced serious problems. For one thing, it held the vast majority of the Catholics at a very low cultural level, as at this time their lack of money and people did not yet permit

---

[23] In 1855 they created a central organization, the German Roman Catholic Central Union, suggested by the Pius Association.

them to establish a system of higher education.[24] According to T. McAvoy it also delayed the upward mobility of the Irish immigrants by a whole generation. This low cultural and social level of the Catholic minority also explained its relatively weak ability to influence the society around it. As Comte de Meaux after a voyage to the United States noted, "the fear of sinking to a lower class kept many a prominent American from the Church of the Irish and domestics, in a country in which social and racial differences play a much greater role than is customarily believed in Europe."

As most of them came from countries in which for centuries they were looked upon as second-class citizens, the immigrants had a natural tendency not to proselytize. But the desire for a less passive attitude grew among the converts of American origin who also were influenced by the Oxford movement. One of the first to become engaged in this fashion was Orestes Brownson.[25] He was a genuine American, upset by the Irish predominance in the Church, often eccentric and obstinate, yet one of the guiding spirits of American Catholicism in the nineteenth century. He was the founder and from 1844 until 1875 the editor of Brownson's Quarterly, a nonconformist and lively journal. In 1859, another enterprising convert, Isaac Hecker,[26] together with some former Redemptorists who objected to the European mentality of their superiors, founded the congregation of the Paulists, whose chief objective was the proselytization of Protestants. But men like Brownson and Hecker were for a long time only exceptions.

It is part of the same development that the Catholics and above all the clergy in the United States did not participate in the solution of the great social problems. Reference to this fact was already made in connection with slavery. The same is true for the movements directed against alcoholism and the attempts to gain greater social justice for the workers. At first sight this particular failure appears most astonishing in view of the connection of American Catholicism with the lower social

[24] There were a number of attempts, especially by Jesuits, to establish Catholic colleges, but most of them survived only a few years. Also characteristic is the small interest shown by the bishops at the council of 1866 when Monsignor Spalding suggested the creation of a Catholic university.

[25] On Orestes Brownson (1803–76), see in addition to the biography by his son (3 vols. [Detroit 1898–1900]) the works by A. M. Schlesinger (Boston 1939) and T. Maynard (New York 1942), as well as T. McAvoy, RPol 24 (1962), 19–47. Edition: The Works of Orestes Brownson, 20 vols. (Detroit 1882–87).

[26] On Isaac Hecker (1819–88), see the biographies by W. Elliot (New York 1891) and J. McSorley, Father Hecker and his Friends (Saint Louis 1952). The book by V. F. Holden, The Yankee Paul, Isaac T. Hecker I (Milwaukee 1958) breaks off with the year 1853.

classes. But it must not be forgotten that the social programs were generally imported from Europe by anticlerical revolutionaries, whose radical proclivities seemed to threaten the Church.

The isolation of the Catholic minority in the United States on the periphery of American public life provided it with peculiar characteristics for a long time to come. Still, there was a gradual development after the Civil War; it began in the Midwest and spread to the East Coast. It was favored by the fact that in such places as New York and Baltimore the Irishmen Hughes and Kenrick were replaced in 1864 by the American-born McCloskey and Spalding. Simultaneously it became evident that the young American Church, which had so successfully applied the well-known formula of a free Church in a free state beyond all ideology, was beginning to assume a place of its own in the universal picture. The first time this happened was at the Vatican Council. When in 1875 McCloskey was elevated to cardinal, it was spectacular proof that the New World had at last outgrown the missionary phase.

Canada

The years after the Act of Union in 1840 were fruitful for Catholicism. The liberal inclinations of Governor Lord Elgin, embodied in the law of 1851, ended the official predominance of the Anglican Church, especially as the high birth rate of the French Canadians and the immigration of Irishmen into the Great Lakes area temporarily resulted in the numerical superiority of Catholics (650,000 vs. 550,000 in 1840). In the subsequent period, immigration favored the Catholics, but the absolute number of Catholics also continued to rise noticeably. The census of 1851 registered more than one million, and by 1881 there were 1,600,000, approximately 40 percent of the total population of 4,300,000. The numerical progression was reflected in the establishment of additional dioceses: four under Gregory XVI and five under Pius IX.[27] The Church province of Quebec, founded in 1844 after lengthy negotiations,[28] was gradually dismantled and three other dioceses took its place: in 1862 Halifax for the Maritime Provinces, in 1870 Toronto, and in 1871 Saint-Boniface in the West. Despite the

[27] At the same period in Newfoundland, which only joined the Canadian confederation a century later, the number of Catholics rose from fifteen thousand at the beginning of the century to sixty-four thousand in 1874; in 1847, 1856, and 1870, three new dioceses were established on the island (see M. F. Howley, *Ecclesiastical History of New Foundland* [Boston 1888]).

[28] The London government did not agree; additionally, the very ponderous bishop of Quebec, Monsignor Signay, who feared the responsibility of the metropolitans, sabotaged the plan as well as he could (see L. Lemieux, op. cit., 432–518).

premature attempt to establish a hierarchy on the Pacific Coast, which at the time of the death of Pius IX was inhabited by only a few thousand Catholics, and despite the missionary work of pioneers like Monsignor Provencher and Monsignor Taché, whom the Oblates of Immaculate Mary assisted in Manitoba, the essential strength of Canadian Catholicism remained concentrated in the area of the Saint Lawrence. But even there they were unevenly distributed. At the time of the formation of the Canadian confederation in 1867, which on the whole was well received by the Catholics,[29] they constituted 86 percent of the population in the province of Quebec, consisting of descendants of French settlers and fifty thousand Irish; they constituted 16 percent in Ontario, five-sixths of whom were English-speaking and economically weak; they were 24 percent of the population in Nova Scotia, chiefly of Scottish descent; and they constituted 33 percent of New Brunswick, largely as descendants of the French-speaking Acadians.

In the province of Quebec the development started at the end of the 1820s by Monsignor Lartigue,[30] the first bishop of Montreal (1821–40), continued. The young clerics, influenced by the theocratic direction of the French ultramontane school of the restoration period and its subliminal social thought, turned the nationalistic reaction, which lost its initial liberal ties, to their advantage. They became the propelling force of a clerically oriented society with focus on the rural population. In the decade from 1840 to 1850, the Church slowly and gradually grew to be the strongest institution in French Canada, largely as a result of the numerical and qualitative growth of the clergy. In contrast to the United States, the native recruitment of clergy in Canada was high even before the middle of the century, and between 1840 and 1880 the ratio of 1700 Catholics per priest decreased to 520. Coupled with rising standards of training in the seminaries, priestly exercises were reintroduced in 1840, and a short time afterwards periodical meetings for the purpose of studying theological questions were begun. The bishops did good work in establishing uniform regulations for the work of the priests, and the Canadian clergy, which at one time had been extremely independent, during the second half of the century became highly disciplined.

This change in the attitude of the clergy, and especially its "Romanization," were hastened by the arrival of many French members of reli-

---

[29] The support of the Catholics in favor of the confederation met a certain opposition by the French-Canadians and the Irish; but the majority of the bishops regarded the plan as a smaller evil, and those who were opposed, like Monsignor Bourget, were realistic enough not to oppose an unavoidable development (see W. Ullman, *Canadian Historical Review* 44 [1963], 213–34, and J. K. Farrell in *CHR* 55 [1969], 7–25.

[30] See F. Ouellet, *Histoire économique et sociale du Québec, 1760–1850* (Montreal 1966), 373, 476–77, 589–90.

gious orders, both male and female,[31] during the 1840s. They were invited by Monsignor Bourget, the enterprising, authoritarian bishop of Montreal (1840–76) and the outstanding ecclesiastical personality in Canada during the nineteenth century; for more than a generation he guided the religious fortunes of the province of Quebec in a strictly clerical sense. The enthusiastic ultramontanism and the reactionary political concepts of the regular clergy from France consolidated tendencies already present in Quebec. They fueled the embryonic religious-political struggles and led to difficulties with the native clergy. Their influence on the spiritual development was considerable; they were largely responsible for the acceptance of new forms of piety. They turned against the moralistic rigorism of the old priests; the establishment of new classical colleges contributed to the training of future clergy; and they promoted the founding and spreading of conventual orders like the Gray Sisters of Ottawa and the Daughters of Charity of Montreal,[32] who later spread to all of North America and attested to the vitality of the Canadian Church.

Within the entire Church, the province of Quebec constituted the unique case of a society which in the midst of the nineteenth century was formed by Catholic principles. In their desire to preserve their cultural heritage within an English-speaking and Protestant majority, the French-Canadians spontaneously accepted the influence of the Church in all areas of private, social, and political life. This became clear with the interference of the clergy in elections,[33] inspired by the fear of the radicalism of many liberals, and even Rome felt constrained to urge the bishops to exercise greater restraint. But this situation, in which the Church with a minimum of official privileges exercised an almost unlimited moral authority, also had its disadvantages. It very soon resulted in a clericalism which systematically prevented any efforts by laymen. Characteristic of this condition was the opposition of the hierarchy to the *Institut Canadien,* a series of public libraries organized by some young, liberal Catholics, and to the development of teacher associa-

---

[31] In 1841, the Oblates of Mary Immaculate (who became very active in the Saint Lawrence area as well as in northern Canada and western Canada), in 1843 the Jesuits (who in 1880 numbered 130 members, more than 100 of them natives); in 1847 the Clercs de Saint-Viateur and the Fathers of the Holy Cross, who grew better in Canada than in France. Among the conventuals were the nuns of the Sacred Heart of Jesus, the Sisters of the Good Shepherd, and many others.

[32] See M. A. Blanchard, *L'Institut de la Providence,* 6 vols. (Montreal 1925–40).

[33] A few examples are in C. Lindsey, *Rome in Canda. The Ultramontane Struggle for Supremacy over the Civil Authority* (Toronto 1877) and in J. Willison, *Sir Wilfrid Laurier and the Liberal Party* I (Toronto 1926).

tions.[34] This attitude encouraged the development of a strictly conformist Catholic civilization, in spite of the founding by the first provincial council (1851) of a Catholic university in Quebec which, in a province in which Louis Veuillot was regarded as an uncontested oracle, became one of the few centers of a moderate Catholic liberalism.

In the Maritime Provinces, P. C. Lefebvre was especially active; he placed himself in the service of the social improvement of the inhabitants of Nova Scotia. The brief struggle over education (1871–74) between the Catholics and the Protestant majority of New Brunswick is also noteworthy.

In the province of Ontario, where the Catholics constituted a minority, the bishops were confronted with two problems at the middle of the century. One of them was the necessity to integrate the stream of immigrants, especially in the countryside, and the difficulty of priests and nuns, imported from France and Quebec for that purpose, in adapting themselves to an environment so totally different from their native soil. The other great problem was the question of Catholic schools. The Catholic campaign for the improvement of the status of the schools was intensified after the passing of legislation in 1850 under the leadership of the Toronto Catholic Institute, but the bishops themselves disagreed on how much to demand.[35] The most active among them was the bishop of Toronto, Monsignor Charbonnel, who had recently arrived from France and whose sympathies in the discussions of the Falloux Law were more in keeping with the intransigence of Louis Veuillot than with the tempered realism of Dupanloup and Montalembert. Protracted negotiations with the government and Superintendent Ryerson[36] ultimately resulted in insufficient though noticeable improvements (in 1853 with the Taché Bill and in 1862 with the Scott Bill). In this instance as well as in the matter of Church property (clergy reserve) a solution was reached which combined the limited denominational protectionism desired by the Church with the American ideal of the complete neutrality of the state in religious affairs.

The appointment of an apostolic delegate in 1877 acknowledged the growing importance of Canadian Catholicism. Despite many problems which it had in common with the United States, such as immigration

---

[34] See A. Labarrère-Paulé, *Les instituteurs laïques au Canada français, 1836–1900* (Quebec 1963).

[35] See P. Hurtubize, "Monseigneur de Charbonnel et Monseigneur Guigues, La lutte en faveur des écoles séparées," *Revue de l'Université d'Ottawa* 33 (1963), 38–61.

[36] His enemies accused him of systematic hostility to the Catholics; but he pointed to the low standards of the rural Catholic schools.

and borders, the mixing of races and languages, and secularization, Canadian Catholicism came to have its own peculiar characteristics. The factor chiefly responsible for this separate development was the French element, which was determined to survive in an Anglo-Saxon world.

Australia

Although more modest than in America, the progress of Catholicism in Australia within a single generation resulted in the growth of a new Church with half a million faithful (25 percent of the total population).

Initially a penal colony, Australia gradually also attracted free immigrants; the Irish were especially strongly represented in both groups. After the turn of the century the government permitted the dispatch of clerics, who naturally also were Irishmen. But after the Emancipation Act of 1829, the government insisted that the chief representatives of the new Church be Englishmen. Benedictines, in the majority from Downside Priory, assumed this function. John Bede Polding, the first vicar apostolic, appointed in 1834 and archbishop of Sydney after 1842, was an energetic man and full of missionary zeal.[37] It was his intention to train the future clergy in a monastic environment in order to impress the Anglicans with its sense of liturgy and good education and the faithful with its detachment from the goods of the world. But the growth of the population made the realization of his dream impossible. At the time of his appointment in Sydney, 90 percent of the forty thousand Australian Catholics resided in New South Wales, but the increasing Irish immigration to other areas of Australia and the gold rush in 1851 in the area of Melbourne demanded an increase in the number of parishes and dioceses.[38] These were by necessity primarily staffed with Irish priests, and even the majority of the additional bishops were of Irish descent. These, however, followed pastoral principles which were quite different from those of the Benedictines, inasmuch as they emphasized education and an increase in the number of elementary schools. Frequent tensions among the bishops; conflicts between the bishops and their active and independent-minded priests; misunderstandings between the English Benedictines and the Irish clergy, which often placed its patriotic feelings above obedience to superiors; and the opposition of some liberal laymen desirous of a more democratic organization of the Church; all of these resulted in frequent disturbances of the Australian

[37] The establishment of the hierarchy in Australia, which was the first in the British Empire, caused a violent reaction on the part of the Anglicans of the colony; thanks to the tactful handling of the matter by Monsignor Polding, calm quickly returned.
[38] Six between 1842 and 1848 and five additional ones subsequently; a second Church province was finally established in Melbourne in 1874.

Church during the second third of the century.[39] But these troubles must not be permitted to overshadow the missionary efforts by all clergy, an effort which found a visible reward in the growth of religious activity. Nor should the devotion be forgotten of some lay people like Caroline Chisholm, whose charitable work for the immigrants (1838–57) was admirable.

As in many other countries, the problem of education assumed a central role in Australia after 1865. The increased withholding of state subsidies for parochial schools, which led to the closing of many Protestant schools, hardly affected the growth of the Catholic elementary schools, which bishops and priests regarded as one of the most important foundations of pastoral care.[40]

---

[39] And even later: Intrigues resulted in a petition to Rome to withdraw the nomination of the Benedictine R. W. Vaughan, who in 1873 was named Polding's coadjutor.

[40] In New Zealand, the organization of the Catholic Church was started much later. Although two dioceses were established in 1848 and entrusted to the Marists, there were only a few thousand Catholics of European descent; the uprising of the Maoris in 1859 put an end to all missionary activity for a decade. Only in 1887 was the Catholic hierarchy reorganized upon the suggestion of the plenary synod of Australia, which had met two years earlier (the archbishopric of Wellington with three suffragan dioceses). The number of white Catholics was hardly higher than one hundred thousand by the turn of the century (see A. Landes in *RHM* 6 [1929], 8–36, 220–59).

South Africa, as far as Catholics were concerned, remained a missionary area until the end of the century. When an apostolic vicariate was established there in 1837, there were only seven hundred Catholics who were organized in a system similar to that of trusteeism in the United States; it posed great difficulties for Monsignor Griffith (1837–62). There were about one thousand Catholics when the vicariate, in keeping with the political division, was divided into two vicariates (Englishmen in the West and Boers in the East; the Boers granted full religious freedom to the Catholics only after 1870) (see W. E. Brown, *The Catholic Church in South Africa* [New York 1960]).

CHAPTER 10

The Easing of Tensions in the Iberian World

Spain

Spain lost much of its significance for the Holy See when its former American colonies declared their independence. Even so, it remained one of the three great Catholic powers of Europe. In fact, until the accession of Pius IX Spain was of greater concern to Rome than the France of Louis-Philippe or the Josephinist Austria of Metternich.

The crisis began in 1833 upon the death of King Ferdinand VII. He had annulled the Salic law and assured the throne for his daughter

Isabella. But the "apostolic faction," afraid that the regency of María Cristina would return the liberals to power, supported the claims of Don Carlos, who was known for his reactionary political and religious views and also had the support of the regionalists of the northern provinces. The resulting dynastic war lasted until 1839, openly supported by most of the clergy of Navarre, León, and the Basque country. The war intensified the contrast between the liberals and the intransigent Catholics because Gregory refused to acknowledge Isabella. Partly out of a spontaneous sympathy for the traditionalist ideology represented by the Carlists, and partially under the pressure from Austria and Russia, Gregory openly took the side of Don Carlos.

Gregory was also motivated to do so by the anticlerical policy of the new government, even though during the first months of his regency the moderate Minister Martínez de la Rosa tried not to break with Rome and, without diverging from canonic forms, attempted to adjust the statute concerning the Spanish Church. This statute still conformed to the concordat of 1753 and corresponded neither to the ideas nor to the political realities of the present. But it was soon removed by the radicals. The change began with widespread outbreaks of violence, the burning of monasteries, the murder of regular clergy in Madrid, Saragossa, Murcia, and Barcelona, and violent acts aimed at the clergy in other cities. Beginning in 1835, the new minister, Mendizábal, proclaimed a number of anticlerical laws. The first, the confiscation of Church property, chiefly grew out of economic considerations and was an attempt to deal with the growing deficit in the state's budget. But all of the others had their origin in an ideology which combined the dreams of the Alumbrados of the eighteenth century and of the liberals of the nineteenth century. The laws effected the dissolution of all monasteries except those devoted to education and the care of the sick, the unconditional dissolution of the large orders,[1] the confiscation of the property of the parishes and chapters, and the abolition of the tithe, which constituted the chief source of income for the clergy (approximately 400 million reales). The state, now expected to assume the tasks hitherto performed by the Church, failed to live up to its public welfare obligations. The government passed punitive legislation against the "abuse" of pulpit and confessional, and expelled with military force the prelates accused of opposition to the government. In no time at all the most important episcopal sees such as Toledo, Valencia, Burgos, and Granada

---

[1] Between 1830 and 1835, the number of regular clergy declined from 61,723 to 52,627: 22,342 nuns and 30,285 monks (in 1898 convents and monasteries), among them 11,232 Franciscans, 3,202 Carmelites, 3,118 Dominicans, 2,829 Capuchins, but only 363 Jesuits. There were sixty Benedictine monasteries and fifty-three Cistercian monasteries.

were vacant. For the first time, the Protestants received permission to proselytize. Finally, a plan was conceived for a general reform of the Church according to the example of the French Civil Constitution of the Clergy of 1790.

The opposition of María Cristina resulted in three years of calm (1837–39) and an attempt to put the finances of the Church on a new footing. But eventually María Cristina was forced to flee the country, and under the regency of General Espartero (1840–43) anticlerical policy came to the fore again. Espartero not only refused to pay the clergy the salaries to which it had agreed in return for the confiscations, but also on his own authority established new parishes and without consulting the Holy See appointed administrators for forty-seven of the vacant sixty-two episcopal sees. His Catholic opponents, among them preeminently the Catalan canon Jaime Balmes,[2] based their opposition to his policies on Espartero's own principles of liberalism. There was no doubt that the radicalism of this religious policy began to worry a good number of moderates in a country in which the Catholic faith was still deeply rooted even among the bourgeoisie. The career of Donoso Cortés[3] was characteristic of this attitude.

After ten years of an uninterrupted degeneration of the old Spanish Church regimen, a relaxation of tensions set in with the return of the moderates. It lasted for a whole decade and began with the maturity of Queen Isabella, who had warm feelings for the Church. In 1844 the laws providing for the state's supervision of ecclesiastical activities were repealed. A short time later the expelled bishops returned and the court of the Rota was reinstated. The sale of Church property[4] continued for a while, but was fully stopped during 1845. While the government was revising its policies, some sensible bishops like P. P. Romo, the new archbishop of Seville, began to recognize that a regime willing to allow

[2] Jaime Balmes (1810–48), a powerful apologist, champion of Neo-Thomism, who nevertheless tried to maintain contact with modern philosophy, politically controversial and social activist, was the dominating intellectual figure of the Spanish clergy during the second third of the nineteenth century; nonetheless, his influence was limited during his lifetime (see I. Casanovas, *Balmes, su vida sus obras y su tiempo,* 2 vols. [Barcelona 1942] and *LThK* I, 1211–12).

[3] See E. Schramm, *Donoso Cortés. Leben und Werk eines spanischen Antiliberalen* (Hamburg 1935) and *DHGE* XIV, 668–71.

[4] While the sale of monastic property had begun in 1835, the land belonging to the secular clergy was not sold until 1842. All told, between 1835 and 1844, 76,734 pieces of property of the regular clergy were sold for 2,762,202,415 reales and 69,539 pieces of property of the secular clergy were sold for 774,983,086 reales. The tremendous transfer of property was very advantageous for the liberal aristocracy and the middle class, but, even more than during the French Revolution, it had grave social consequences, as on the whole it aggravated the situation of the peasants.

constitutional freedoms would permit the Church to have a degree of independence which would more than compensate for the loss of certain privileges. They began to draft a pastoral program which better corresponded to the new mentality and whose objective was freedom of education. This attempt was facilitated by the open atmosphere prevailing in Rome during the first months of the pontificate of Pius IX. After it failed, the Spanish Church limited itself to regain as fully as possible the restoration of the position earlier achieved in 1814 and 1825. But it was an erroneous expectation, as the change of thought among the middle class, especially among the university students, this time was much more profound.

In the meantime, negotiations with Rome had been started with a view toward restoring the relationship interrupted in 1835 and toward a new arrangement of ecclesiastical affairs. The most difficult point was the statute for the financing of the Spanish clergy, as it involved not only financial questions but fiscal ones as well. Additionally, the negotiations were handicapped by the mistrust of the Holy See toward a government which the papacy considered as too liberal and by some regalistic demands on the part of the Spanish government. A draft providing for some reforms was initialed in April 1845.[5] Among them were the reopening of a few monasteries and the return to the secular clergy of unsold Church property. But the Holy See did not want to acknowledge the sale of Church property officially until the question of paying salaries to the clergy had been answered satisfactorily by the parliament. But, faced with the demand of the liberals to have the sales officially accepted immediately, the Spanish government refused to ratify the treaty. The government was also disappointed in not seeing included in the treaty several clauses, included in the concordat of 1753, which granted the state a number of concessions, particularly in the matter of the *placet*.

Yet both sides were interested in finding a solution, and the negotiations were resumed. After being interrupted by the death of Gregory XVI, they were continued in 1847 on a new basis and with a willingness on both sides to compromise. After extremely frank exchanges of views, the delicate question of salaries for the clergy was settled by the law of April 1849.[6] Eventually the negotiations produced the concordat of 16 March 1851.[7] It was a partial success for the Holy See, because the events of 1848 produced a shift of the moderates to the right.[8]

[5] Text in Mercati I, 796–99.
[6] Text in J. Pérez Alhama, *La Iglesia y el Estado español,* 269–70.
[7] Text in Mercati I, 770–96.
[8] The intervention of Spanish, Austrian, French, and Neapolitan troops in 1849 for the purpose of restoring the temporal power of the Pope was significant.

The agreement, in spite of some concessions to the spirit of the times, indeed confirmed Spain's Catholic nature. It also differed from the concordat of 1753 in removing the interference by the state in purely ecclesiastical matters and in granting the Church a large degree of autonomy. It thus was the "most liberal" of all Spanish concordats. It should also be noted that the loss of the majority of Church lands was a liberating experience for the Church and that after fifteen years of troubles the clergy felt closer to the Holy See than before. At the same time, the excesses of the liberals convinced the clergy that a guarantee of religion and social order could only be expected from the conservatives. This conviction moved the Church closer to the parties of the right, on whom the fate of the concordat seemed to depend. This was demonstrated clearly in 1854 when Espartero returned to power and immediately repealed the concordat with accompanying transgressions against Church property and religious orders. The debates of the new parliamentary assembly were the opportunity "for the first real discussion of the relationship of Church and state in the history of Spain" (Kiernan). But in the fall of 1856 the government returned to the hands of the moderates under the leadership of Narváez. Until the revolution of 1868, the Church was permitted to live in relative peace, sanctioned by an agreement with the Holy See.[9]

The concordat granted the Church a decisive position in the state. It made possible a limited restoration of the Church, facilitated by the protection of Queen Isabella II. She was a narrow-minded bigot, who was advised by Antonio-Maria Claret,[10] her overly zealous father confessor. External reconstruction expressed itself in a high number of applicants for the seminaries, on whose reorganization the episcopate spent a large degree of effort. It was also shown by the founding of new active convents, especially in Catalonia, devoted to education and charity. But the underpinnings were provided by the genuine Christian sentiment among the masses. Unfortunately, the blossoming of the Church was only external. The clergy was still very numerous proportionally; despite a reduction of 20 percent since the time of Ferdinand VII, there was still one priest for every 380 people. Moreover, the clergy all too often was satisfied with a mere religion of rite and routine and frequently confused its apostolate with inflexibility. It maintained

[9] On 25 August 1859; Text in Mercati I, 920–29. Supplementary agreement concerning religious foundations, ibid., 18–24.

[10] On A. M. Claret (1807–70), founder of two missionary congregations, extremely active archbishop of Santiago de Cuba from 1850 to 1857, father confessor of the Queen from 1857 to 1868, see C. Fernández, *Antonio-Maria Claret,* 2 vols. (Madrid 1942) and J. M. Viñas, ed., *Escritos autobiográficos y espirituales* (Madrid 1959). Also, C. Fernández, *El confesor de Isabel II y sus actividades en Madrid* (Madrid 1964).

its claim to the moral leadership of the nation without justifying it with an adequate education, and by relying on an outdated Scholasticism which lacked any originality. The attempts by Balmes and Donoso Cortés to revive traditional apologetics were ignored.

While during the preceding generation many anticlericals had remained believing Christians, after 1860 the number of intellectuals whose faith was shaken increased. Romanticism was introduced in Spain only belatedly after 1833 by the exiles who returned from France, at a time when its chief proponents were already alienated from the Church. It opened the way to free thought and under the influence of post-Hegelian philosophies found its Spanish expression in "Krausism." Many of the intellectuals were discouraged by a Catholicism which, under the leadership of the Neo-Catholics of Nocedal, the spiritual heirs of the Carlists, and their paper *Pensiamento español,* was fanatically antimodern. Their noisy conduct, joyfully greeted by Pius IX, produced nothing but a stronger anti-clericalism among the educated middle class.

Portugal

The religious situation in Portugal during the pontificate of Gregory XVI developed parallel to that of Spain, just as had been the case during the restoration period. Portugal also had two pretenders: Don Miguel on one hand, and Don Pedro and his daughter Maria da Gloria on the other. The dynastic conflict was made graver by the ideological struggle between the absolutists, supported by clergy and Pope, and the constitutionalists, supported by the Freemasons. After the victory of Don Pedro in 1832, a number of anticlerical steps were taken: expulsion of the nuncio; establishment of a commission for the reform of the clergy, which in addition to sensible suggestions like a reduction of the overly large number of dioceses came up with projects of Gallican and Jansenist origin which were at direct variance with Roman ideas; suppression of the Jesuits, who had only just returned in 1829; and the closing of all monasteries, including those in the overseas possessions (in Spain, the liberals at least allowed the missions to continue). Even graver was the fact that Don Pedro refused to acknowledge bishops who between 1826 and 1832 had been appointed by his rival Don Miguel, while on their part the majority of the bishops refused to cooperate with the liberal government. Many episcopal sees were soon declared vacant, and the government proceeded to noncanonical elections of chapter vicars. These came in conflict with the legitimate Church authorities, and priests and faithful who refused to recognize them were subject to persecution. A virtually schismatic condition existed for several years.

But, as in Spain, the political developments produced a relaxation of tension, starting in 1835. Even so, the negotiations with Rome, skillfully conducted by Monsignor Capaccini since 1842, made only slow progress. An agreement was reached only in October 1848 after the death of Gregory XVI; it dealt primarily with the question of the seminaries and the ecclesiastical jurisdiction in law.[11] In 1857, the agreement was supplemented with a convention on the right of patronage by the Portuguese King with respect to the missions in India and China.[12] Seminaries were reformed, a matter of dire necessity in light of the low standards of training of the clergy, whose conduct and pastoral negligence the nuncios had frequently criticized in their reports. In spite of the obstacles put up by the Freemasons, the orders, including the Jesuits, gradually regained a foothold in the country after 1858. Even more than in Spain, the common people remained faithful to the traditions of Catholicism. But the rationalistic orientation of the educated middle class became more prominent, and the indifference of the Portuguese Catholics to the attacks by the antireligious press stood in uncomfortable contrast to the Spanish endeavors to create a Catholic press during the second third of the nineteenth century.

The Spanish American Republics

The dozen republics of former Spanish America were far from bringing much joy to the Holy See during the middle of the nineteenth century. While most of their constitutions continued to acknowledge Catholicism as the official state religion, the governments were unwilling to give up the tradition of a strict supervision of the Church and insisted that the Holy See recognize their right of patronage over the Church. At the same time they tried in the name of the new liberal ideology to reduce the influence of the clergy on the population, to do away with the clergy's legal privileges, and to incorporate the Church's considerable land holdings in the public economy. This attempt led to repeated conflicts and occasionally, as in Colombia and Mexico, to a rupture.

In some cases the conflicts were caused by the insistence of the Church on rejecting the state tutelage, which was incompatible with the new ultramontane ideas. But in most cases they resulted from a reactionary attitude of the clergy, which obstinately fought rearguard actions in defense of increasingly outmoded positions. Simultaneously, with the exception of Chile, the clergy, whose condition had changed radically, was no longer up to its tasks. There was a great lack of priests, especially

[11] Text in J. Ferreira Borges de Castro, *Coleição dos tratados* . . . VII (Lisbon 1856seqq.), 221f.
[12] Text in Mercati I, 844–52. It dealt with the termination of the so-called Goan schism.

in the rural areas.[13] It grew worse with the break with Spain, especially as the immigrants, in contrast to the United States, were almost never accompanied by priests from their native homelands. In addition, there was a lowering of morality, a lack of discipline, and the total loss of a pastoral dynamic, leading to the total abandonment of the Indian missions within fifty years. The religious orders, which had remained after the secularization at the beginning of the century, were in full decline. Thus, even with the assistance of foreign confreres, they were able to compensate the losses in the parish clergy only with limited success, the more so as they were constantly harassed and even expelled by the governments.

But after the deep crisis which had shaken these Christian communities during the wars of independence, a new beginning dawned by the middle of the century. It started with the pontificate of Gregory XVI. At first, the long-vacant episcopal sees were filled gradually. This was the prerequisite for establishing better ecclesiastical discipline. In South America, the dioceses of the colonial period were augmented by six additional ones, their number having become inadequate as a consequence of immigration from Europe and the steady increase in the population.[14] Apostolic visitors with extensive authorization were sent to restore discipline in the orders. The Jesuits settled again in some of the republics (in 1836 in Argentina, in 1842 in New Granada, and in 1843 in Chile).

Restoration proceeded slowly but steadily. Pius IX, who had a vivid interest in these countries ever since his trip to Latin America, supported the initiatives. Additional dioceses made possible closer contact between priests and their flocks; Church provinces were reorganized in order to adjust them to the new political borders; attempts were made to regain control over the local clergy through the appointment of delegates who tried to ameliorate the crassest abuses, although only with limited success; regular clergy from Europe were encouraged to open schools, and in spite of obstacles put up by the governments their number increased gradually, even though their influence was limited to the propertied people. In Rome, the *Collegio Pio latino-americano* was established in 1858, with the aim of training an elite clergy obedient to the Holy See.

[13] One example: In Mexico, the total number of priests in 1810 was 7,341 (4,229 secular and 3,112 regular clergy), but in 1850 it was only 3,275 (2,084 secular and 1,191 regular priests), while the population grew from 6 to 7.5 million.

[14] Twenty-four (without Brazil) in the south of the Gulf of Mexico in 1815, at a time when of the 15 million Spanish-Americans only a third lived south of Panama. While the population of Mexico and Central America until 1850 only increased by 30 percent (13 million), the population of South America grew by 250 percent, to 12.5 million, who resided in an area encompassing 5.8 million square miles.

To be sure, almost the entire pontificate of Pius IX passed before official diplomatic relations between Rome and the most important South American republics could be established; prior to 1877, there were only a few delegates apostolic. But between 1852 and 1862 the Holy See succeeded in negotiating seven concordats or conventions.[15] Some of them remained in effect only temporarily, but at least they brought about an improvement in the relations between the Church and the governments. This was usually the case both after the conservatives returned to power in the course of the second third of the century and after the subsequent triumph of the liberals during the final decades of the century.

This was especially true for Central America, where the dictator of Guatemala, General R. Carrera (1839–65), repealed the anticlerical laws introduced after 1829 by the liberal President Marazán. He restored the ecclesiastical privileges and the control of the clergy over the schools and the press, returned the land of the orders, and forced the smaller neighboring states to conclude concordats with the Holy See which were advantageous for the Church. This was also true, even though to a lesser degree, for Chile. There, Archbishop R. V. Valdivieso (1847–78), a diligent pastor, inflexible defender of the rights of the Church, and bitter antiliberal, complained unceasingly about the regalism of the government and the relief granted to the Protestants. But the Church received considerable compensation payments for the abolition of the tithe (1853), and during the twenty-five years that D. Portales was minister of education the influence of the Catholic Church in the schools was fostered, because Portales saw in it the best guarantee for public order. He also promoted the immigration of active orders from Europe, such as the Jesuits and the Ladies of the Sacred Heart.

In Venezuela the Church had to accept the loss of its own legal jurisdiction and of the tithe and the decision of the government to establish two new dioceses without consultation with Rome. But the conservative oligarchy which governed almost without interruption from 1830 to 1864 favored the clergy, culminating in the concordat of 1862. Bolivia almost concluded a concordat in 1851.[16] In view of the

---

[15] With Guatemala and Costa Rica in 1852 (Text in Mercati I, 800–821); with Honduras and Nicaragua in 1861 (Mercati I, 936–59); with San Salvador, Venezuela, and Ecuador in 1862 (Mercati I, 960–99). Negotiations for a concordat were also started with Bolivia (1851), Peru (1853), and Argentina (1855 and 1857), but were not concluded chiefly due to the demand concerning patronage. After half a century of tension and difficulties, a concordat was negotiated with the black republic of Haiti in 1860 (Mercati I, 929–36); Haiti's Church was reorganized by French missionaries (see A. Caron, *Notes sur l'histoire religieuse d'Haiti de la Révolution au concordat, 1789–1860* (Port-au-Prince 1933).

[16] Text in Mercati I, 3–14.

small influence of the Church in public life, the government was friendlier than in many other countries, but refused to ratify the treaty when Rome insisted on "granting" the government the right of patronage over the Church, while the government demanded this recognition as a matter of right. Relations nevertheless remained cordial, because Rome tolerated the exercise of the national patronage de facto, without recognizing it officially.

In Peru the moderate liberal President R. Castilla was able to effect a compromise solution with the assistance of the conciliatory Archbishops F. X. de Luna Pizarro (1845–55) and J. S. Goyeneche (1859–72), in spite of the protests of a group of priests connected with the conservative party who tried to impose their reactionary views on the government. It was not possible to save the legal jurisdiction of the Church, the tithe, and the control of the Church over education, but the Church retained the majority of its property. Chiefly, however, the Church enjoyed an independence from the state which went far beyond that in any other South American state. Even in Argentina the end of the "golden age of the clergy" came with the departure of dictator Rosas in 1852. There, the clerics had adjusted to a pronounced regalism, but it was favorable to them.[17] Still, the Church enjoyed another ten years of peace, because the constitution of 1853 contained several articles favoring the Church.

The Church registered a spectacular success in the years after 1860 in Ecuador. President García Moreno, a fiery but authoritarian Catholic,[18] admired by the ultramontanes of the world, between 1861 and 1875 attempted to mold his country into a model Christian state. Legislation was fashioned along the lines of the encyclicals of Pius IX and especially of the *Syllabus.* For the implementation of his ideal the president to a large degree relied on European orders, in which he saw the guarante for regeneration.

This policy clearly illuminates one of the principal weaknesses of Catholicism in Latin America throughout the nineteenth century. Social life, at least in those areas in which the Church had firm roots under the Old Regime,[19] was inherently Christian. But these Christian traditions were not capable of making necessary internal changes. Local Catholi-

[17] Many details concerning the relations between Rosas and the Church are found in the book of the anticlerical J. Ingenieros, *Evolución de las ideas argentinas: Obras completas* XVI, (Buenos Aires 1947), 99–142.
[18] Concerning the very controversial person of Gabriel Garcia Moreno (1821–75), see, in addition to R. Pattee, op. cit., P. H. Smith in *HAHR* 45 (1965), 1–24.
[19] Especially Mexico, Guatemala, Colombia, Peru, and Ecuador. But in the interior of Venezuela and Bolivia the institutional presence of the Church was almost completely absent, and it was very modest on the Rio de la Plata and in Chile.

cism, with few exceptions, like those of Bartolomé Herrera in Peru[20] for the clergy and of José Manuel Estrada, "the Argentinian Louis Veuillot," for the laity, was passive and without vitality or originality culturally, socially, and apostolically. The reason was the absence of a middle class in these countries, the social structure of which was hardly changed by the political revolutions. It is chiefly to be found in the fact that the Church until the end of the Old Regime had retained a colonial structure too dependent on Spain and had become sterile and incapable of thought or action. Additionally, there was a very individualistic mentality, which under the influence of Freemasonry neglected organized ecclesiastical life in order to find salvation in a pietistic attitude toward faith.

Brazil

The Empire of Brazil was the largest and most populated state in South America, with a size of 3.3 million square miles and 5.5 million inhabitants in 1830, who grew to more than ten million by the end of Pius IX's pontificate. Under the regency and long reign of Pedro II (1831–88), the Church lived in relative peace, even though the government, which, following the example of Pombal, desired to govern the Church by protecting it, periodically created tensions. For example, in 1834 it supported the attempts of the political priest D. A. Feijo, who strove for a legalization of priest marriages with the argument that celibacy of the clergy de facto did not exist in Brazil and that this fact favored public immorality to a high degree. In 1844 the government appointed the archbishop of the capital contrary to canon usage. The measures against the old orders, "victims of internal abuses which without radical reforms inevitably would lead to their dissolution" (Y. de la Brière), were intensified in 1855. On the other hand, however, new active congregations were founded,[21] and the European congregations which devoted themselves to education and charity were freely accepted. From the 1860s on, these congregations were able to conduct parish missions of several weeks duration, an undertaking very much needed, considering the profound religious ignorance of the people.

[20] See O. Barrenechea, *Bartolomé Herrera, 1808–64* (Buenos Aires 1947). The collection *Escritos y discursos*, 2 vols. (Lima 1929–30) gives insight into the thinking of this most highly qualified representative of the conservative clergy in Peru during the nineteenth century.

[21] See, for example, the biography of the founder of the congregation of N. -D. d'Amparo, devoted to the care of orphans (1871), *O Padre Siqueira, sua vida e sua obra* (Petropolis 1957).

The regalistic mentality of the government was approved by the clergy until about 1860, proof of which was the distribution of the handbooks by Monsignor M. de Araujo. But not everything was perfect. Freemasonry gained a considerable influence, even touching the religious confraternities. Another inheritance of the eighteenth century was the growth of rationalism and positivism among the educated and the deplorable situation of the clergy. The clergy was not only weak numerically; in 1872, there were fewer than one thousand priests. They were chiefly concentrated in the coastal cities, while in the interior of the country perhaps twenty parishes, covering thousands of square miles, were administered by a single priest and many faithful did not see a priest for ten years or longer. In addition, the morality of the clergy often left much to be desired, and their attitude also gave cause for alarm. Until 1850, many priests were influenced by the ideas of Rousseau and the encyclopedists, and even if a portion of them turned away from Freemasonry on account of its hostility to the Holy See, by 1870 approximately more than half of the clergy still belonged to its adherents. Some of the bishops, of whom there were only eleven, tried to strengthen the seminaries, and gradually the Catholic lay leaders became better educated also. But on the whole the period of the Empire was a time of stagnation behind a facade of peace and quiet. In fact, more to the truth, it was a period of decay for Catholicism.

CHAPTER 11

The Catholic Church in the Orthodox World

Unionist Prospects in the East

In the middle of the nineteenth century, two phenomena drew attention to the Eastern Churches. One was the development of the Eastern Question; the expected disintegration of the Ottoman Empire presaged profound political and religious changes. The other one was the clear recognition of the role which Russia's Pan-Slavic policy would play in connection with the budding nationalism of eastern Europe. Toward the end of the pontificate of Gregory XVI, a group led by Princess Volkonskaya, a wealthy convert residing in Rome since 1825, took up the question of the return of the separated Eastern Churches to Rome.[1] Among the members of the group were Monsignor Corboli-Bussi, Au-

[1] See C. Korolevsky in *Unitas* 2 (1949–50), 189–90.

gustin Theiner, Monsignor Luquet, a former French missionary,[2] several consultants of the Congregation for the Propagation of the Faith, a number of Uniates, and the founders of the Polish Resurrectionists. Under the presidency of the prefect of the Propaganda, the group in 1847 suggested to Pius IX that he address a solemn appeal to the separated brethren in the East. The Pope combined this plan with his own intention to send an apostolic visitor who was to inform himself of the prevailing conditions in the East. In January 1848 he directed the encyclical *In suprema Petri sede*[3] to the Eastern Christians. He informed the Uniates of the impending arrival of the apostolic visitor, who was well-known among the Catholic Armenians. He praised the customary advantages of the Catholic faith and invited the separated Uniates to join the Roman Church "as no conceivable reason could prevent their return to the true Church." The Uniates saw this document as a provocation. In May 1848 four partriarchs and twenty-nine archbishops wrote a negative reply in which they condemned Latin innovations, the pretensions of the Pope, and the proselytism of the Latin missionaries.[4]

This failure did not discourage those, however, who regarded the upper clergy of the Orthodox Churches as no longer representing the true feelings of the people, who were in turmoil as a result of changes. At first they looked toward Russia, where they believed they saw a tentative opening for a rapprochement in the reforms of Alexander II and in the growing interest in Roman Catholicism among some noblemen who were searching for an effective antirevolutionary ideology. With the covert and overt assistance of this nobility, the writings of Joseph de Maistre enjoyed renewed popularity in Russia for a number of years and occasioned a series of foundations after the Crimean War (1854–56). Under the patronage of the bishops of Münster and Paderborn, Baron von Haxthausen in 1857 founded the Saint Peter's Association in Germany, prayer groups for the conversion of Russia, and entered into correspondence with Metropolitan Philaret of Moscow. In Italy, the convert P. Schuvarov inspired Father Tondini to action on behalf of the cause of Christian unity, and Tondini founded a similar prayer organization.

---

[2] On his ideas, which were in advance of the time, see R. Roussel, *Un précurseur: Monseigneur Luquet* (Langres 1960), 83–89.

[3] *Acta Pii IX* I, 78–91. See A. Tamborra, "Pio IX, la lettera agli orientali del 1848 e il mondo ortodosso," *RStRis* 56 (1959), 347–67.

[4] Mansi XL, 377–418. See T. Popescu, *Enciclica Patriarhilor ortodosci dela 1848* (Bucharest 1935) and A. Tamborra, op. cit., 357–66. The Russian Church did not join in this protest, but A. Stourdza published another vehement book against Rome: *Le double parallèle ou l'Église en présence de la papauté* (Athens 1849).

But it was especially in the Austrian Empire and France that a vivid interest was awakened in the return of the Eastern Christians to Rome (the problem of union was always approached in this way, going counter to any ideas of ecumenism). In Austria an attempt was made to draw the Orthodox believers in the border areas away from Russian influence and to orient them toward Rome; Franz Joseph and his advisers in this instance were motivated by both genuine religious concerns and reasons of state. Such attempts were also aided by some Slavic clerics in the Empire. Monsignor A. M. Slomšek, the bishop of Lavant, in 1851 in Slovenia founded the Brotherhood of Saints Cyril and Methodius, which quickly grew in Moravia under the leadership of Father Sušil and also among the Ukrainians of Hungary and Galicia.

In France, the death of Madame Swetchine in 1857 led to the dissolution of her circle, but her work was continued even more systematically with the aid of the general of the Jesuits, Father J. Pierling, and her relative, Father I. Gagarin.[5] In his book *La Russie, sera-t-elle catholique?* (1856), which was translated into several other languages, Gagarin recommended a reconciliation which was not to end in the absorption of the Russian Church by the Roman Church; he thought that diplomatic negotiations between the Tsar and the Pope could bring about such a union. He was more realistic when, in 1856, being aware of the need for a fundamentally academic approach, he founded *Études de théologie, de philosophie et d'histoire* with the aid of his fellow countrymen Father J. Martinov and P. Balabin. The journal was designed to make the Orthodox understand Catholicism and Catholics to understand the Orthodox religion better. In the same climate of unionist ideas, but from a strongly apologetic point of view, Hergenröther wrote his books on Photius during the same period.[6]

After 1860, the expectations with respect to Russia gradually disappeared. They were replaced by a new interest in the potential return to the Roman Church of the Christian communities of the Ottoman Empire. Such expectations were raised as a result of French intervention in Syria, and the model thought of were the Uniate communities. Public

---

[5] Shortly after his conversion he wrote a memorandum in 1845 on "Das Wirken der Gesellschaft Jesu im Blick auf die Bekehrung des Orients und vor allem Rußlands" (printed in *SPM* 2 [1955], 205–28). In it he suggested the establishment of a school for Jesuits of the Eastern Rite for the apostolate in Russia; however, the general at the time, Philipp Roothaan, had little interest in this project.

[6] The three volumes of his *Photius,* published between 1867 and 1869, were begun in 1855 and indicated by his *Mystagogia* of 1857. See the praising review by Döllinger in J. Friedrich, *Ignaz von Döllinger* III, 444.

opinion was especially enthused by this question in France,[7] where interest in the Christian East had grown for the past two decades. The issue had been kept alive by the speeches of men like Monsignor Dupanloup, by publications like the bimonthly journal *La Terre Sainte et les Églises orientales,* founded in 1864 by C. R. Girard, and by the *Oeuvres des Écoles d'Orient,* founded in 1855 and given strong leadership by Lavigerie.[8] Finally, in 1862, Father d'Alzon, at the request of the vicar apostolic at Constantinople, Paolo Brunoni, and of Pius IX, engaged his Assumptionists under the leadership of Father Galabert in the unionist apostolate in the East. After a difficult beginning they played an important role for the next seventy-five years.

Rome could not remain indifferent to this interest in the East which agitated the Catholic world of the West, especially as the efforts of the Russians and chiefly the Protestant missions aided by the British were cause for concern. For several years, the rather simplistic efforts of J. G. Pitzipios, a Greek who thrived on intrigue,[9] were aided by Rome. His voluminous *L'Église orientale* was published by the Congregation for the Propagation of the Faith in 1855. Much more serious were the efforts of Cardinal Reisach, who became interested in the Slavic problem by way of his contacts with Austria. He acquainted the Pope with the necessity of having available in Rome a number of specialists for the East. Following his suggestion, the Benedictine Pitra was ordered to undertake a study trip to Russia (1859–60), during which he was also to gather material for a broad documentation of the sources of Orthodox canon law.[10] In 1862 Pius IX decided to divide the Congregation for the Propagation of the Faith into two sections, one of which was to concern itself with the affairs of the Churches of the Eastern Rite. Each cardinal belonging to the new section was assigned to a certain rite and asked to acquire competency in his area, and some of the best experts on the East were employed as consultants. There was no doubt that Pius IX and the leaders of the Propaganda genuinely desired to respect the different liturgical usages of the Eastern Churches, in contrast to many Western missionaries who were bent on forcing the Eastern Catholics into loyalty to Rome by making them replace their traditions with Latin customs, or

[7] Especially in France, but not exclusively: in Austria, the Association of the Immaculate Conception of Mary for the Support of the Catholics in the Turkish Empire, founded in 1857 for the mission in the Sudan, turned increasingly to the support of the Catholic Churches of the Eastern Rite.

[8] H. de Lacombe, *Note sur l'œuvre d'Orient* (Paris 1906) and de Montclos, 143–55.

[9] See A. Tamborra in *Balkan Studies* 10 (1969), 51–68.

[10] See A. Battandier, *Le cardinal Pitra* (Paris 1893), 351–440; F. Cabrol, *Histoire du cardinal Pitra* (Paris 1893), 220–40.

in contrast to men like Father d'Alzon, who were convinced that the advance of European ideas necessarily would be followed by the disappearances of the Eastern rites.

Rome also tried to reestablish the influence of the Curia over the life of these Churches and gradually to gain entry for the principles of post-Tridentine Catholicism into the canon law of the Eastern Churches. But the optimistic expectations of a mass return of the separated Eastern Churches to the Church of Rome were not realized. In fact, the extreme centralization policy of Cardinal Barnabo by 1870 resulted in serious crises in the Uniate communities, crises which were intensified by the Vatican Council. Only in southeastern Europe and the Near East was Catholicism able to register some rather superficial progress, while its position in Russia once again deteriorated.

The Russian Empire

Contrary to the expectations which Gregory XVI at the beginning of his pontificate attached to the condemnation of the Polish rebellion, Tsar Nicholas I did not change his policy toward the Catholic Church; in fact, its condition behind "a curtain of silence" (de Bertier) grew worse. The Section for Religion at Saint Petersburg openly promoted the conversion of three Uniate dioceses of the Empire (1839) to the Russian Orthodox Church. Measures limiting the freedom of action of the Latin Church and its contacts with Rome in Poland and in the Russian Empire intensified from year to year. It is not to say too much that the Catholic Church legally was so integrated in the Russian state that it did not differ at all from any other state religion. While papal diplomacy in 1840 took up contacts with Polish conservatives in exile, through whom pressure was to be exerted on Russia, Gregory XVI's violent dislike of any revolutionary enterprise[11] quickly regained the upper hand, and Rome returned to the usual method of secret negotiations through diplomatic channels.

In return for new concessions by Rome in 1841, Russia's envoy made some vague promises. In fact, however, nothing changed. The ukase of 25 December 1841, which secularized all property of the Churches in the western provinces and reduced still further the authorized number of regular clergy, only confirmed the failure of this method. Catholics in Russia, Austria, and western Europe could not understand the long silence of the Holy See. Incited by B. Kopitar, the leader of Austro-Slavism, Augustin Theiner and the Jesuit Secchi emphatically implored

---

[11] "The Pope had to condemn your revolution," Gregory XVI told the envoy of Prince Czartoryski on 7 May 1841, "and if necessary he will, with regret, condemn it again" (quoted in *RStRis* 51, [1964], 474).

the Pope. All questioned cardinals regarded a public protest as unavoidable. At this point, Gregory XVI again asked the Austrian Emperor and Metternich to mediate, only to learn that they were interested in a prolongation of the ecclesiastical abuses in the western provinces of neighboring and hostile Russia. This attempt having failed, the Pope in July 1842 published an address[12] in which he complained to the world about the repressive measures applied to Polish and Russian Catholics and about the disloyal conduct of the Tsar. The appeal, accompanied by a formal exposé of the Secretariat of State, received great attention, as everyone knew that the Pope would have preferred to protect the Tsar for political reasons.

Angry over the unexpected outburst, the Tsar, as many people had feared, began to intensify the measures against seminaries and orders. But upon the advice of Chancellor and Secretary of State Nesselrode, he started a policy of détente after a few months. He had two reasons. One was that at the very moment when Russia, in the eyes of a "revolutionary" Europe, tried to appear as a country in which, under the paternal authority of the Tsar, religion and order prevailed without compulsion, such an appeal to the world did not fit the Tsar's policy. He also feared that Austria would exploit the situation and would present itself to Rome as the only Christian great power. The recall of the Russian envoy from Rome (1843), his replacement by the moderate Butenev, and contacts made in 1844 through the mediation of the nuncios at Vienna and Munich paved the way for a personal encounter between Nicholas I and Gregory XVI. They met in December 1845, and Gregory XVI submitted to the Tsar an agenda which he had personally prepared.

Negotiations were started in November 1846 in Rome, after Nesselrode had made the necessary preparations first in Rome in talks with Monsignor Corboli-Bussi and Cardinal Lambruschini and then in Saint Petersburg with a special ministerial committee for Catholic affairs. Gregory XVI had died in the meantime, but Pius IX insisted that former Secretary of State Lambruschini, who was well versed in the problems, should continue to represent the Holy See. On the Russian side, negotiations were conducted by Bludov, former minister of the interior and justice, who was assisted by Butenev. The plenipotentiaries faced a difficult task; after all, they had to find solutions for the reconciliation of two powers with incompatible principles. Rome desired a total revision of Russian legislation, designed to return freedom to the Catholic Church. Saint Petersburg desired an improvement of its rela-

---

[12] *Acta Gregorii XVI* III, 224; see also *Allocuzione . . . ,* 3–4; the exposé of the secretariat of state, ibid., 5–19.

tions with Rome for the purpose of pacifying Polish agitation and winning the opinion of Europe for Russia. Russia was prepared to make some concessions, but was unyielding in the question of strict control over the Churches by the state. After twenty conferences (19 November 1846 to 1 March 1847), agreement was reached on some points, including the question of appointment of bishops. But the representatives of the Tsar again refused to discuss the suppression of the Uniate Church in the Ukraine. They insisted on demands unacceptable to Rome, among them those concerning mixed marriages and contacts of the bishops with Rome.

An impasse was reached, and both the Tsar and Lambruschini were willing to break off the negotiations. But the more conciliatory Nesselrode implored the delegates to resume their talks after a certain interval. At the same time the same opinion was voiced in Rome by a commission of cardinals headed by Pius IX. Considering that the Catholic Church in Russia was facing an extreme emergency situation, the opportunity for an ever so limited improvement should not be allowed to pass. Consequently, negotiations were resumed on 15 June and by 3 August 1847 led to a settlement. It listed all points on which the two parties had agreed, as well as those on which agreement had not been reached and which were reserved for future discussions.[13] A completely satisfying concordat was still a long way off, but at least a clear break was made with the policy of unilateral decisions, followed by the Tsars since the beginning of the eighteenth century. The agreement, which Nicholas I in the absence of a better one ultimately signed, could be viewed as a success by the Holy See.

Yet the particular conditions made normalization difficult, the more so as after initial proofs of good will the administrative chicaneries increased as soon as the fears raised by the revolutions of 1848–49 dissipated. Even graver was the government's tactic of appointing to higher offices prelates who for reasons of cowardice or ambition were willing to do the government's bidding. Finally, in the 1860s, after the Crimean War, slavophile influences replaced the party friendly toward Rome, and a campaign for the conversion of Latin Catholics to the

---

[13] Text in S. Olszamowska, op. cit., 790–802; attached documents, ibid., 779–807. The bull set the new diocesan areas in the Russian Empire by applying the Convention according to which the diocesan borders coincided with those of the provinces and a new diocese of Cherson for the south of Russia was created, where many Catholics of German extraction lived; it was published on 3 July 1848 (*Acta Pii IX*. I, 134–49). The agreement also regulated the condition of the Uniate Armenians, especially those living in the Caucasus (see Ammann, 517–18 and M. Tamarti, *L'Église géorgienne* [Rome 1910]).

Orthodox Church was begun.[14] There was no doubt that in the eyes of many Russians the western provinces of the Empire were seen as foreign bodies as long as Catholicism, which was called the "Polish faith," continued to exist. Even the insufficient attempts to adhere to the concordat were justification for the convinced Orthodox Russians to emphasize all those points which gave them reason for their opposition to "Romanism." This attitude produced a number of controversies among the intellectuals[15] until the end of the century. They are reflected in Dostoevski's *Idiot* (1868), where Prince Myshkin evaluates Catholicism as worse than atheism.

As for Poland, the tsarist government understood that it could not eliminate Latin Catholicism, but was nevertheless determined to control all ecclesiastical life as much as possible. It kept episcopal sees vacant and tried to limit the contacts between bishops and Rome to a minimum. It forbade the bishops to convoke their priests in synods and to make public appeals in pastoral letters to the faithful. It intervened in the running of seminaries, which were badly off in any case owing to insufficient funds, and limited the number of postulants admitted to orders. At the beginning of 1862 the government created a committee for religion which strictly separated Catholics, Orthodox, Protestants, and Jews and, ignoring canon law and the Convention of 1847, deprived ordinaries of a majority of their jurisdiction.

It was not so much a matter of persecution of a denomination as one of regalistic practices. These had been a matter of course during the Old Regime in all of Europe, but in view of the developments in the Catholic world, for which the Austrian concordat of 1855 was a benchmark, appeared anachronistic and offensive. Thus, it was not surprising that priests and regular clergy, who had expected a democratic government to free the Church from its fetters, increasingly made common cause with the leftist opposition, which in addition to propagating social reforms knew how to exploit the Polish nationalism of the lower clergy. In spite of the reserved attitude of the Holy See and the episcopate, these patriotic priests with their revolutionary agitation discredited the Catholic Church and strengthened the distrust of the Russian officials and encouraged them to take stronger action against the Church. Yet, in spite of the growing discontent, the resistance of the Catholic people was not strong enough. The mass of the rural population did not comprehend the extent of the violations of canon law brought about by governmental decrees. Most important, however, was

---

[14] Boudou II, 347–98.
[15] Some details in Winter, *Rußland* II, 274–78.

the absence of any foundation on which a movement analogous to the Irish struggle for the emancipation of Catholics or to the resistance of the German Catholics to the *Kulturkampf* after 1870 could have developed. In this police state there were no political platforms, no newspapers, nor any other means by which information could have been disseminated. Additionally, many episcopal sees were either vacant or occupied by incompetent men who were willing to accept a mutilated canon law to the extent that their ecclesiastical training was determined by Josephinism and Febronianism. Finally, a number of the upper clergy, often of aristocratic origin, partially for reason of social conservatism, partially for reason of hostility to the Germans, regarded collaboration with Russia as the lesser evil.

The Holy See, very well informed of the difficulties of the Church in Poland by emigrants[16] and its numerous contacts in the Hapsburg Empire, repeatedly protested to the Russian embassy at Rome against the violations of the 1847 agreement. At the same time, the Holy See tried to establish a nunciature at Saint Petersburg, in the expectation that it would facilitate the solution of many local problems and the supervision of the efforts of the Polish clergy, which the Holy See frequently regarded as unfortunate. The more liberal attitude of the new Tsar, Alexander II, seemed to justify such hopes during the initial period of his rule, and, in fact, negotiations had reached a promising state by 1862. But the Polish rebellion of 1863–64 once again put everything in question and thereafter relations between Rome and Saint Petersburg grew chillier.

The reaction by the Russian government to the assistance provided the rebels by the clergy was very strong[17] More than four hundred clerics, including several bishops, were deported to Siberia. Of 197

---

[16] In addition to the very active political role of the Polish emigrants during the second third of the nineteenth century, some efforts of a religious nature are notable, for example the founding of the Congregation of the Resurrectionists in 1836 in Paris, which set as its task the Christianization of socialist radicalism. Pius IX entrusted the Bulgarian mission to the Resurrectionists, who also became active among the Polish immigrants of the United States and Canada. They also originated the founding of the Polish College at Rome (1866) (see L. Long, *The Resurrectionists* [Chicago 1947] and W. Kwiatkowski, *O. Piotr Semenenco, C.R.* [Vienna 1952]).

[17] See, for example, K. Gadacz, "Capucins déportés pour leur participation à l'insurrection en 1863," *Miscellanea Melchor de Pobladura* II (Rome 1964), 455–82. On the national and religious agreement, see R. Bender in *Roczniki Humanistyczne* 7 (Lublin 1960), 257–88. Outside of the Church, Polish nationalism was born in Freemasonry, but it developed chiefly among the upper classes, from which, until the end of the nineteenth century, the majority of the clergy emerged. The clergy in turn increasingly influenced the rural population, which until then had shown little interest in national affairs.

monasteries, 114 were closed; because the regular clergy was strongly allied with the rebels, bans of processions and pilgrimages multiplied, as did police surveillance of sermons and the confessional. Between 1866 and 1869, three dioceses were dissolved without the consent of Rome and were attached to neighboring dioceses.

Pius IX harbored as little sympathy for revolutionaries as Gregory XVI; but the brutality of the Russian reprisals against the Church angered him. On 24 April 1864 he lodged a strong protest. A complete rupture of diplomatic relations was delayed by Austrian mediation, but when the situation continued to deteriorate, the Pope again complained in a speech on 29 October 1866. It had been drafted by a commission of cardinals and was accompanied by rich documentation for the press.[18] On 4 December the Russian government replied by revoking the concordat. In May 1867 it decreed that in the future all contacts of the bishops, including the Polish ones, with Rome were to be subject to official control by the Roman Catholic College at Saint Petersburg. The majority of the bishops was willing to comply with the new regulation, but the Pope described it as incompatible with the divine constitution of the Church.[19] In 1869 the administrator of Mogilev, Monsignor Staniewski, was excommunicated because he failed to take account of this condemnation. The Russian government in turn forbade the bishops of Russia and Poland to attend the Vatican Council. After the council, attempts were made by several factions to start a movement in favor of establishing a separate Slavic Catholic Church with a Latin rite, modeled after the Old Catholics. The project was utopian and the Russian government paid hardly any heed to it. On the other hand, it effectively assisted the campaign of some Ukrainian priests led by Michael Popiel. Blinded by the prestige of the Orthodox Church and their own anti-Polish sentiments, they tried to attach to the Russian Orthodox Church the only Uniate Church, that of Chelm, still existing in Poland.[20]

The matter was started in 1865 by a legitimate effort, but which, given the circumstances, was nothing more than a threadbare ruse. Initially, the Ruthenian rite was cleansed of all the Latinisms which had crept in since the Council of Zamosc. It was hoped that the removal of anything which provided the Uniates with a structure of their own would facilitate their conversion to Orthodoxy. The reforms were carried out without consideration of Roman objections. When the soil had been prepared, Popiel, whom the government had entrusted with the administration of the diocese, did not hesitate to call on the police in

[18] Text: *L'Esposizione documentata*, 303–6.
[19] Encyclical *Levate* of October 17, 1867: *Acta Pii IX* IV, 371–78.
[20] Details in Boudou II, 105–14, 263–74, 399–447.

order to break the resistance of some Catholics loyal to Rome. After a petition campaign which was supported by two-thirds of the clergy, he announced at the beginning of 1875 the "reunion of the Uniate Greeks with the Holy Orthodox Eastern Church, the Church of our forefathers."

The Russian government, which since 1870 seemed to be interested in improving relations with Rome, from which it expected a pacifying influence on Poland, made a gesture of good will. It announced its willingness to reform the Roman Catholic College at Saint Petersburg in a way acceptable to the Holy See. But renewed attempts in 1877 to introduce the Russian language into the religion, as well as the discovery by the British during the Russo-Turkish war of police measures against the Uniates who refused to bend to the dictates of the "robber synod of Chelm," occasioned another Roman protest.[21] It led to the final break between the two parties.

On balance, however, the situation was not as negative for Poland as it might seem. While the rationalistic influence of the Enlightenment was long in evidence among the educated people, the upper levels of society, who recognized the pacifying influence of the Church in relation to revolutionary social demands, experienced a development very similar to that which France had undergone a few decades earlier. This change of atmosphere, even though it was tied to certain interests, promoted a profound religious awakening. It was strengthened by the new wave of spirituality then coursing through all of Europe.

A more significant indication of the rejuvenation of the vitality of Catholicism was the development of the religious orders. Many among them bore unmistakable signs of decadence, which fully justified the measures taken by the Russian government. There were too many monasteries with too few people, and there was a lack of novice-masters. Violations of seclusion regulations and the vow of poverty and the admittance of candidates who had no real vocation and merely wished to escape military service were very frequent. On the other hand, the Capuchins, especially in Warsaw, performed extremely valuable work in the areas of piety—particularly as it concerned the Virgin Mary—charity, and social work. After the middle of the century, there were also numerous new foundings of women's congregations, as for example those of the Felicians[22] in 1856. The movement continued even after the setbacks of 1864. The Capuchin Honorat Kominski (1829–1916), for example, founded about twenty secret Tertian con-

---

[21] Memorandum by Cardinal Simeoni of 26 July 1877 on "the greatest injustices under which the Catholic Church suffers in Russia and Poland," and encyclical to the nuncios of 20 October 1877 (Text in *L'Univers,* 20 January 1878).
[22] *DHGE* XVI, 855–59; *CollFr* 37 (1967), 343–65.

gregations which, in order to avoid a ban by the government, wore civilian clothes while teaching and devoting themselves to the social apostolate among the workers.[23]

The Slavs in Austria-Hungary

As a country of nationalities on the borders of the Slavic world, the Hapsburg Empire was a place of encounter and also conflict between Eastern and Western Christendom. In 1870, the Empire comprised 24 million Latin Catholics, 3.5 million Protestants, 4 million Catholics of the Eastern rite, and 3 million Orthodox. The last two enjoyed freedom of religion and of organization, but both the government and the Catholic hierarchy hoped that they would return to Rome.

In Croatia, where the Orthodox comprised 30 percent of the population and were in close contact with their brethren still under Turkish domination, unionist efforts were embodied by Monsignor J. G. Stroßmayer, Bishop of Diakovar from 1849 to 1905. A conscientious prelate and ardent patriot, he had gradually become the moral leader of the Croatian opposition to the Magyar oligarchy. Instead of becoming involved in fruitless political battles, he preferred to advance the Slavic cause on the cultural level. He employed a majority of his high income to subsidize journals and publications on Slavic literature, history, and folklore and to give his country two important institutions, an academy (1867) and a university (1874). His contributions earned him an incomparable popularity among all Slavs of the south, Orthodox and Catholic alike. He intended to use his popularity to gain his second objective, the unification of the Churches. As far as he was concerned, this union was the prerequisite for the adoption of Western culture by the Slavs without risk. In order to facilitate an approach, he favored the Roman liturgy in Old Slavic and at the Vatican Council suggested a policy of decentralization of the Church. But his irenic way of approaching the problem of unifying the divided Christians met a favorable echo in Rome only during the pontificate of Leo XIII.

At the other end of the Empire, the growth of Pan-Slavism and the resultant tension between Austria and Russia had repercussions on the Ruthenian Church of Galicia. Its leader, Monsignor Lewicki, after 1813 archbishop of Lvov, was created cardinal in 1856; this dignity had not been awarded to a prelate of the Eastern rite since the sixteenth century. The clergy, cognizant since 1848 of the humiliating condition which Poland had imposed on the Ruthenian people, increasingly devoted itself to the political struggle in the name of Ukrainian nation-

[23] K. Gorski in *Roczniki teologiczno-kanoniczne* 11 (1964), 5–50.

alism. Some saw in it a means to regroup all Uniates on both sides of the border for a more effective resistance to the attractions of Russian Orthodoxy, but others, especially among the young, began to view Orthodox Russia as the protector of the Slavs. With the secret support of tsarist agents they viewed with sympathy the efforts of Michael Popiel in the diocese of Chelm, because after the concordat of 1855, which was binding for all Catholics of the Empire, the tendency to adjust Eastern ecclesiastical regulations to Latin canon law was intensified under pressure from the Vienna government.

In this atmosphere, the century-old controversies between the clerics of both rites could not but become aggravated,[24] but the resistance of the Ruthenian clergy to the Latin pressures of Poland served to tighten the connection between Church and people. With the consent of the nuncio, the Galician bishops worked out a sensible plan for an agreement, which was presented to the Holy See in 1853. Regrettably, Rome did not make an immediate decision, and soon the situation worsened again when both sides accused one another of proselytism, especially in connection with mixed marriages. Only in 1863, under the impact of the Polish revolution, was an agreement finally reached.[25]

The Ruthenian dioceses of Podcarpathia, living in complete peace until the middle of the century, now also began to feel the effects of nationalistic agitation. For it was at this time that an effort was started in liturgy to substitute Hungarian for those Magyars who no longer understood Old Slavic.[26] The government in Budapest, interested in weakening the influence of Slavism in its territory, supported these efforts, while the Russophile propaganda was encouraging the awakening of Slavic consciousness and obtained a number of conversions to the Orthodox religion.

The Uniate Rumanians of Transylvania had to thank the hostility to the Orthodox Serbs for many conversions. Upon the suggestion of the bishop of Grosswardein, Monsignor Erdeli (1843–62), two new dioceses were established together with an autonomous province with its capital at Fogaras.[27] The reorganization of this Church was undertaken in close cooperation between Rome and the Rumanian Uniate hierarchy. In 1858, the Congregation for the Propagation of the Faith directed three instructions concerning marriage law to the hierarchy, asking for urgent reforms.[28] A Roman delegation headed by the Vienna nuncio

---

[24] Some examples in Winter, *Byzanz,* 162–64.
[25] *ColLac* II, 561–66.
[26] C. Korolevský, *Liturgie en langue vivante* (Paris 1955), 44–46.
[27] Bull of 26 November 1853 (Mansi XLII, 619–26; see also 638–40).
[28] Mansi XLII, 645–708.

went to Transylvania in order to examine the situation which had become doubtful in light of the right of the Emperor, acknowledged in the concordat of 1855, to intervene in various matters, including the election of bishops. After conferences between Monsignor De Luca and the Rumanian bishops it was decided to hold a provincial council. After some delay, but well prepared by the new Metropolitan Ioan Vancea (1868–92), an extremely active prelate with Roman training, and Monsignor J. Papp-Szilaggi, the author of one of the few handbooks on Eastern canon law of the sixteenth century,[29] the council met in Blaj in May of 1872. Its decrees[30] were well considered and complete. In addition to this juridical rejuvenation, the clergy continued its efforts in the pastoral and cultural areas by becoming the ardent defender of the Rumanian language and national idea in the face of Magyar domination.

Progress of Catholicism in Southeastern Europe and the Levant

In 1860 it looked for a moment as though a new Uniate Church were to be established in Bulgaria. Faced with the consistent refusal of the Phanariot to allow the Bulgarians to have their own bishops as a first step to their cultural and political emancipation, the Polish Committee in Paris began to suggest that the Bulgarians could expect their religious emancipation only from the Pope; they propagated the union with Rome under the condition that Old Slavic be retained as the liturgical language. Pius IX was well disposed toward the suggestion; after he had personally consecrated the aged Hegumenos, J. Sokolski, as archbishop of the Uniate Bulgarians in April 1861, a conversion movement was started in which politics played as much of a role as did religion. But the intervention of Russia, which desired the emancipation of Bulgaria for Russia's benefit, and the tactlessness of the apostolic delegate, Monsignor Brunoni,[31] soon nipped the movement in the bud. After the mysterious disappearance of Sokolski only a small flock was left, entrusted by Pius IX to the Assumptionists of Father d'Alzon and to the Polish

---

[29] Published in Latin: *Enchiridion juris Ecclesiae orientalis catholicae* (Grosswardein 1862).
[30] Mansi XLII, 463–710. The Congregation for the Propagation of the Faith, which forbade any mention of the Councils of Photius, of the Nomokanones, and of the Byzantine canonists, finally gave its approval in 1881. The Roman authorities had already been dissatisfied with the positions of the diocesan synod of Blaj in 1868, a synod which pointed to the collegial structure of the Church and which assigned a significant role in the Church to the laity (see de Clercq II, 632–34).
[31] This story, writes C. Dumont, "makes clear the degree to which some persons in the Latin Church at that time failed to understand anything which legitimized the loyalty of our Eastern brethren to their own traditions" (I. Sofranov, op. cit., X).

Resurrectionists. When a new Bulgarian bishop was finally appointed four years later, the opportunity had passed.

During the events in Bulgaria, the conversion in 1861 of Archbishop Meletios in Greece raised hopes which were just as false, as the Greeks remained unshakeably true to their national religion. When as a consequence of the growing number of Catholics in Athens and Piraeus Pius IX in 1875 established an archbishopric in Athens, it was as a diocese with Latin rite, whose followers, overwhelmingly of Western descent, were viewed as an alien element by the Greeks.

In all areas which for centuries had been under Ottoman domination, Catholicism of the Latin rite made progress during the second third of the nineteenth century; today, this progress seems very questionable to us, but in its own time it was very significant.

In Rumania, autonomy grew until the establishment of an independent monarchy in 1866. In the same way the activity of the regular clergy in Moldavia increased in spite of the occasionally justified criticism leveled against it, and within a period of fifty years increased the number of faithful from forty-eight thousand to seventy-five thousand. In the liberal atmosphere prevailing in 1859 during the reorganization of the Polish status of the principalities, the Catholics were granted civil and political equality. In 1864 the government, which wished to end the Austrian protectorate over the Catholics, even planned a concordat with the Holy See. But sensitiviiy on the part of the Orthodox did not permit the replacement of the apostolic visitor by the establishment of a diocese at Jassy before 1884. In the preceding year an archbishopric had been established in Bucharest,[32] after the number of Catholics in Wallachia, insignificant until the middle of the century, had grown tenfold within a few decades. The reorganization of the Catholic Church in the new kingdom was facilitated by the benevolence of King Carol.

But this progress on the level of institutions should not lead to false conclusions. The spiritual tension between the national Orthodox Church and the Catholic minority continued. The majority of the Latin clergy were foreigners and the mission of the Conventuals in Moldavia was accused of being a tool of Magyarization. In fact, there were people who, with reference to the Hungarian descent of a part of the Catholic population, for a long time tried to entrust the mission to Hungarian members of the order and to withdraw it from the authority of the Congregation for the Propagation of the Faith in order to place it directly under the ecclesiastical administration of Hungary. The government of the new kingdom in its striving for national independence

[32] See *DHGE* X, 1011–12.

insisted on the training of a native clergy, a demand which as early as 1842 had been acknowledged as justified by the Congregation for the Propagation of the Faith. The Conventuals, however, jealous of their privileges, thwarted the opening of a seminary until 1866 by claiming to have financial difficulties. For some time in this area, in which the priests because of their low numbers were not able to minister regularly to the faithful, who lived dispersed in many villages, a native organization had grown, the lay didascales. These were not only catechists and sacristans, but they also conducted Sunday prayer services, conducted funerals, and took the place of missionaries in civil matters. But as most of them were former seminarians from Transylvania and partisans of the Hungarian cause, the efforts to train the Rumanian didascales was persistently thwarted by the Hungarian Conventuals. It was accomplished only in the final years of the century.

In Bosnia, which until 1878 belonged to the Ottoman Empire, the long conflict between Vicar Apostolic Barišić and the Croatian Franciscans, who defended the South Slavic idea against Austria's influence, was solved in 1847 by dividing the country into the two vicariates of Bosnia (one hundred twenty-five thousand faithful) and Herzegovina (thirty-five thousand faithful.)[33] In the expectation of the establishment of a regular hierarchy, which was erected between 1878 and 1881, an increase in the number of monasteries was allowed; in 1878 there were ten, instead of the four of thirty years earlier. However, the Catholics in these areas remained isolated and had only a small share in the improvement of the legal position of the Christians in the Ottoman Empire as a result of the decrees of 1839 and 1856.

At Constantinople and the ports of the Levant, the Catholic presence as well as the activity of Protestant missions was no longer concealed. In 1839, the new sultan, Abdul Mejid, following the advice of his liberal grand vizier, published the Hatti Sherif of Gulhané, which promised to all, regardless of religion or sect, complete safety of their lives, their honor, and their property. He wanted the Western powers to feel obligated and to assure himself of the loyalty of the Christians. The application of this regulation often was only theoretical, especially in the Balkan countries. But a first step toward emancipation had been taken, of particular benefit to the Uniate communities.

The Crimean War and the resultant Hatti-Humayun of 1856 produced another noticeable improvement in the legal position of the Christians, which improved even further after the Syria expedition of 1860. The holding of the regional Council of Smyrna in 1869, which

[33] See I. Kecmanovic, *Barisiceva afera* (Sarajevo 1957).

brought together the Latin episcopate of Greece and the Greek islands, the vicar apostolic of Constantinople, and the archbishop, would have been unthinkable twenty years earlier.[34] Nevertheless, the steady growth of the missions founded by religious congregations, most of which were of French origin, was surprising.[35] In close contact with the French consuls, who under the Third Republic were even more concerned with limiting Italian influence in the Near East than under the Second Empire, the activity of the Lazarists, of the Christian Brothers, of the Sisters of Charity, and of the Sisters of Saint Joseph increased; they were joined by the Assumptionists, the Ladies of the Sacred Heart, the Sisters of Notre Dame of Zion, and many other congregations. The Jesuits of Beirut were especially active. In an attempt to protect the educated classes from the Protestant influence, they founded a modern publishing company which published Arab translations of Western religious tracts; they also established a large Catholic newspaper, the *Al-Bashir* (1871), and finally a modern college which in 1881 became the University of Saint Joseph.

Incidentally, no matter how great the zeal of its members may have been, these missions contributed much more to the spread of French culture than of Christianity. And if their spiritual and intellectual abilities, coupled with the prestige of the West, enabled these institutions to take hold in the Eastern communities, it must still be admitted that the Latin Catholics of the Near East, whose numbers increased very satisfactorily, were for the most part foreigners. They came primarily from Malta and Italy, and as they grew in numbers they were increasingly regarded as alien intruders. But at the time their progress was greeted in Rome with joy, and the Holy See tended to see in their growth the future of Catholicism in the East. In order to coordinate the multifaceted missionary work and to assure Rome of control over the organization of the various Catholic communities in the Ottoman Empire, the Congregation for the Propagation of the Faith put its hope in the work of the apostolic delegates. It also continued to send out visitors who supervised the implementation of reforms and reported back to Rome. The most active representative of the Roman and Latin presence in the East was Monsignor Giuseppe Valerga,[36] after 1847 Latin patriarch of Jerusalem and after 1858 apostolic delegate to Syria; he bent

---

[34] *ColLac* VI, 565–91.

[35] See a concrete example of this growth by leaps and bounds of missionary congregations between 1840 and 1890 in the article "Alexandrie" in *DHGE* II, 364–65.

[36] On Giuseppe Valerga (1813–72), see the unedited dissertation of S. Manna (Pont. Istituto Orientale in Rome, 1969). Also, de Montclos, 533–34; Hajjar, 279–81.

all of his efforts toward a policy of centralization which the Holy See practiced with respect to the Uniate patriarchates.[37]

The Eastern Patriarchates

In the course of the third quarter of the nineteenth century two developments characterized the Uniate Churches. There was a quantitative growth and with it a continuation of institutional consolidation, but there was also the threat of new schisms as a result of Rome's intensified policy of centralization. This policy of the pontificate of Pius IX expressed itself in the interference of the Congregation for the Propagation of the Faith in the elections of patriarchs and bishops, in the alteration of decisions of the local synods, and in the introduction of reforms in traditional institutions. It also showed itself in the activity of the apostolic delegates in favor of an accommodation of Eastern ecclesiastical regulations to those of the Latin West.

This could be noted particularly in the Armenian Church. Numerous conversions, especially in Constantinople, raised the total number of the faithful in Turkey to about one hundred twenty thousand by 1870. Allowing for this progress, Pius IX in 1850 had created six new dioceses in northern Asia Minor and subordinated them to the primate archbishop of Constantinople. This archbishop, Monsignor Hassun, with enterprising energy and with the assistance of the Jesuits and other Western missionaries as well as the Armenian Congregation of Antonites, who were experiencing an incomparable growth, increased the number of churches and schools several times over. In order to crown this progress with a uniform canon discipline[38] and a further improvement in the relations between Turkey and Rome, the Holy See after the death of the patriarch of Cilicia decided in 1866 to fuse the two supraepiscopal jurisdictions by the election of Monsignor Hassun as patriarch. But this very step, which seen from the Roman point of view would promote the cohesion of the Armenian Church, in fact caused a

---

[37] He was also concerned with the return of a number of consecrated places in Palestine, which the Turks assigned to the Orthodox in the course of the eighteenth century. As is well known, the harsh discussions concerning the holy places were one of the reasons for the Crimean War, but de facto the status quo was maintained until the end of the nineteenth century (see B. Collin, *Les lieux saints* (Paris 1948); A. Popov, *La question des lieux saints de Jérusalem dans la correspondance diplomatique russe,* 2 vols. [St. Petersburg 1910–11]).

[38] A first step in this sense was attempted in 1851 by the patriarch of Cilicia, but the council convened by him for this purpose unified only the churches under his jurisdiction. The council's decrees (Mansi XL, 783–890), which strongly resembled those of the Maronite Council of 1736, were clumsily worded and thus not recognized by Rome.

great crisis. The reason was that the document which reorganized the Armenian patriarchate, the famous bull *Reversurus,* also and fundamentally altered the Eastern laws with respect to the privileges of the patriarch and the method of election of the bishops. The upper crust of the laity after 1850 repeatedly had complained about the virtual abolition of its right of participation; now it protested again, supported by clergy and bishops who also accused the patriarch of despotism in the leading of his Church and too much subservience to the Congregation for the Propagation of the Faith. The opposition became stronger at the council which the patriarch convoked at Constantinople from July to November 1869. While Hassun was attending the Vatican Council, a dissident movement was formed under the leadership of the superior of the Antonites, Monsignor Kasandschan. After the opposition declared Hassun deposed, it obtained recognition by the Turkish government as the true Armenian Church, and took over a number of churches and schools. The schism lasted for ten years, until Leo XIII in 1880 replaced Hassun, who had been created a Curia cardinal, with the more flexible Monsignor Azarian.

The Chaldean Church was fortunate in being led between 1847 and 1878 by Joseph Audo, an energetic and dynamic person, even though he was an only moderately educated patriarch. After 1856 it also had the assistance of the French Dominicans of Mossul. At the Council of Rabban Hurmuz[39] in 1853 the Church for the first time codified its canon discipline in a Latin form under the influence of the apostolic delegate, the Jesuit Planchet. Within a period of twenty-five years it grew from forty thousand members to sixty thousand, but was shaken after 1860 by the increasingly fierce conflict between Audo and the Congregation for the Propagation of the Faith. Rome objected to the patriarch extending his jurisdiction to the Chaldeans of Malabar, who since the seventeenth century had been under Latin sovereignty.[40] After a preliminary settlement of the question in 1863 and the recall of the apostolic delegate, who had exceeded his instructions, the struggle was renewed when the applicability of the bull *Reversurus* was extended to the Chaldeans by the constitution *Cum ecclesiastica disciplina*[41] of 31 August 1869. Furthermore, the resentment caused by the Vatican Council was still smoldering. The Chaldean episcopate split into two groups, and in 1876 the aged and ill-advised Audo was about to break with Rome. But the loyalty of the old patriarch to Catholicism and a gesture of peace by Pius IX were able to prevent this catastrophe at the last moment.

[39] J. Vosté, op. cit., 35–76.
[40] For details, see C. Korolevsky in *DHGE* V, 326–35, 343–49.
[41] De Martinis, *Ius pont.* VI/2, 32–35.

The Syrian Church did not have to go through such a crisis, even though a tense atmosphere lasted throughout the pontificate of Pius IX. The founding of the patriarchate by Antonius Samhiri (1854–66), which was occasioned by the Council of Sarfeh in 1853,[42] was accompanied by some disagreements and some new efforts. It laid the basis for the future of the Syrian Church, whose center was transferred from Aleppo to Mardin upon the request of Rome. But the succeeding patriarch, Philipp Arqus (1866–74), was hesitant and assumed a very vague and waiting stance in view of the uncertainties caused by the bull *Reversurus* and the Vatican Council.

The patriarch of the Melchites, Mazlum, heatedly opposed Roman interference with the rights of the patriarch. After the deaths of Gregory XVI and Cardinal Litta, who had personally known and trusted the patriarch, violent clashes took place, especially as the authoritarian and power-hungry Mazlum caused some of his opponents within his own Church to ally themselves with the Western partisans of a systematic Latinization. The Congregation for the Propagation of the Faith succeeded in having Clement Bahut (1856–64) chosen as Mazlum's successor. Bahut was very loyal to Rome, where he had studied, but he was more of an ascetic than a man of action. His ineptitude created a schism in his Church, but fortunately it was of short duration. It was caused by a question of seemingly secondary importance, but it once again illuminated the policy of adaptation to the Latin discipline which was pursued by the Congregation for the Propagation of the Faith. In 1836 and 1837, the Syrian and the Chaldean Church had adopted the Gregorian calendar in order to disavow the schismatics. Upon the request of the Propaganda, Bahut decreed the same step in 1857, but met strong opposition. The metropolitan of Beirut, Riachi, angry at Rome because he had not been chosen as patriarch, exploited the unrest and with the assistance of the Russian Orthodox mission formed his own community.

Fortunately, the massacres of 1860, in which the Druses were responsible for almost as many cruelties among the Melchites as among the Maronites, put an end to the squabbles. Everything was put right again by Bahut's conciliatory successor, the eminent Gregory Yussef (1864–97). One of his greatest concerns was the improvement in the education of the local clergy, which was still inadequate in spite of Mazlum's efforts. Through the establishment of native schools, designed as a counterweight to the education provided by the Protestants, he tried to counter the annoyance caused by the schools maintained by certain Latin missionaries for the Churches of the Eastern rite. But he did not

---

[42] Which, complemented by the Council of Aleppo (1866), attempted to achieve a certain uniformity in canonical and liturgical discipline, which until then was rather vague; but it did not produce final results (Texts in de Clercq II, 1037–72, 1072–93).

convene a council, in spite of the advantages which would have accrued to his reorganization, because he would have required the help of Rome and did not wish to ask for it. There was no doubt that Yussef, although he was a former student of the college of the Congregation for the Propagation of the Faith at Rome, was convinced by the bull *Reversurus* and the undifferentiated program of the neo-ultramontanes at the Vatican Council that Rome desired the destruction of the traditional privileges of the patriarchs. The reorganization of the Melchite Church had been started by the Council of Jerusalem, but its decrees had not been ratified by the Holy See during the time of the sharp conflict with Mazlum.

The Maronite Church suffered heavily from the revolt of the Lebanese peasants against the feudal domination of the sheiks and the Druse massacres in 1845 and 1860.[43] But the decline of the civilian leadership ultimately turned the patriarchate into the most important political power of the country. For half a century it was guided by Paul Masad (1854–1890), who combined great leadership qualities with considerable erudition. He opened his pontificate in 1856 with a national council[44] at Bkerke under the chairmanship of the apostolic delegate; the council was attended by the superiors of the three Maronite orders, which at this time comprised about eighteen hundred members and eight hundred priests. The long-standing and close connection with France, the strong protector of Lebanon, prepared the ground for a good understanding with the Latin missionaries. The disagreements caused by the bull *Reversurus* and by the definitions of the Vatican Council only slightly disrupted the Maronite Church, whose connection with the Holy See went much further back in history than that of the other Uniates.[45] Regrettably, little is known to this day about the inner life, the pastoral work of the clergy, the religious life of the faithful, and the development of the monastic customs of this vital Church, as well as of the other Uniate Churches. It is hoped that research in the archives of the Church by native historians will soon throw more light on these topics.

[43] Concerning their actual nature, see de Montclos, 144–54.

[44] Text in de Clercq II, 1093–1135. Its files, like those of most other Eastern councils of the time, were not acknowledged by the Congregation for the Propagation of the Faith; it was increasingly obsessed with the idea of a fundamental reordering of Eastern discipline and its accommodation to Latin canon law.

[45] The patriarch did not hesitate to point out to Pius IX in polite but unmistakable form that these steps contradicted the solemn promises of Benedict XIV.

The Missions between 1840 and 1870

CHAPTER 12

The Strengthening of the Gregorian Restoration

The long pontificate of Pius IX, seen from the missionary point of view, was essentially a continuation of the reforms of Gregory XVI, but also an amplification. The actual work was done by Alessandro Barnabo (1801–74). Serving the Congregation for the Propagation of the Faith since 1831, Pius IX in 1847 made him its secretary and chose him as its cardinal prefect in 1856. He had a strong sense of duty and was a conscientious administrator, but not even his contemporaries, let alone posterity, knew much about his many accomplishments.[1] Schmidlin mentions that Pius IX was responsible for the creation of thirty-three vicariates, fifteen prefectures, and three delegates for missions to the pagans, numbers which indicate the degree of Barnabo's intensive missionary activity.[2] Barnabo not only prepared all new foundings to the point of papal briefs and appointments, but also took care that missionary personnel were increased accordingly. Even the separation of the Eastern missions from the missions to the pagans, an act of importance for the future within the jurisdiction of the Congregation for the Propagation of the Faith, can be traced back to Barnabo's preparations and suggestions.[3]

While during the first half of the nineteenth century new missionary institutes were established chiefly in France, it was Italy which became very much engaged in this area of activity during the second half of the

---

[1] It is characteristic that there is no biography of this man who headed the Congregation for the Propagation of the Faith for so many years. His selfless nature and his devotion to the dissemination of the faith can be seen in the modest obituary of 2 March 1874 in the archives of the Congregation (*S. Cong. Cardinali, Segretarii* . . ., vol. 3, 1850–92, 253–55; see *DHGE* VI, 858).

[2] Schmidlin, *PG* II, 226.

[3] In 1862, the *Congregatio de Propaganda Fide pro negotiis ritus Orientalis* was established with its own administration and its own secretary. At first still a part of the Congregation for the Propagation of the Faith, it eventually became an independent body (*JP* VI/1, 381–86). Barnabo's obituary assigned responsibility for this change to him.

nineteenth century. Until the twentieth century, all of the Italian foundations were rooted in the renewal and intensification of the religious life of the closing eighteenth and beginning nineteenth centuries, carefully nurtured through generations of outstanding priests and bishops.[4] This explains the fact that all new religious foundations, created and carried by the secular clergy, had an apostolic-missionary character. Some of the institutions, owing to the Italian revolutions, could become active only after a long period of preparation. So, for example, the Milan mission seminary was founded in 1850 by Monsignor Ramazotti, named bishop of Pavia in 1849. This seminary in organization and spirit was a duplicate of the Paris mission seminary and retained its exclusively missionary nature.[5]

The foundations by Giovanni Don Bosco (1815–88) of the Oratory and in 1859 of the Society of Saint Francis de Sales (Salesians) were primarily directed to local religious and social needs, but the apostolic spirit soon carried members beyond the borders of Italy to all continents, where they took over individual missions and also worked successfully as educators and journalists.[6] Another institute, created solely for Africa, was that which Daniel Comboni founded in 1866 in northern Italy. It was the Mission Institute for Africa (Nigricia, as he called it), which later was transferred to Verona and in 1885 renamed the Society of the Sons of the Sacred Heart. The impetus for it came from the Sudan mission established in 1846 in central Africa and maintained largely by Austrian secular priests. Monsignor Comboni's interest was to provide it with a stable foundation.[7] In Rome in 1867, the papal seminary of Saints Peter and Paul was established; its members, active in China, were later combined with the Milan mission seminary.[8]

---

[4] A typical example are the *Amicizie,* religious secret societies which were modeled on the secret political and antireligious associations in Italy (C. Bona, I.M.C., *Le Amicizie. Società segreta e rinascita religiosa (1770 a 1830),* [Turin 1962]). The soul of these societies and this rejuvenation was the Swiss convert and ex-Jesuit N. J. A. von Dießbach (1732–98) (ibid., 1–230 [documents, 471–528]). The members of these secret religious societies of the eighteenth century became the initial promoters of the Italian missionary movement in the 19th century (C. Bona I.M.C., *La Rinascita missionaria in Italia dalle "Amicizie" all'opera per la Propagazione della Fede* [Turin 1964]).

[5] G. B. Tragella, *Le Missioni Estere di Milano* I (Milan 1950), 1–89.

[6] Heimbucher II, 392–99; E. Cervia, *Annali della Società Salesiana 1841–1888* (Turin 1941); Pietro Stella, *Don Bosco nella storia della religiosità cattolica,* 2 vols. (Zurich 1968–69); see F. Desramaut, *RHE* 65 (1970), 926–33.

[7] H. Wohnhaas, *Bischof Daniel Comboni, Apostolischer Vikar von Zentralafrika* (Ellwangen 1937); Streit XVI, 714–18; *Comboniani. Numero speciale di Nigrizia. Dic. 1962* (Verona).

[8] Other institutions of similar structure were created at Parma in 1895 (*Xaveriani*) and at Turin in 1901 (*Missionari della Consolata*) (G. B. Tragella, *Italia Missionaria* [Rome 1939]).

In France also new mission institutions came into being. Father Jules Chevalier in Issoudun established the Association of the Sacred Heart of Jesus, which devoted itself chiefly to the mission in the South Seas.[9] In 1856 some clerics at Lyon joined the former Paris missionary and bishop in India, Melchior de Marion Brésillac (1813–59), to form the Society for the African Mission for the conversion of the blacks. In 1858, the vicariate of Sierra Leone was entrusted to them, but within a year the bishop and his associates died of fever. Leadership at Lyon was assumed by the youthful Augustin Planque (1826–1907), who led the society through obstacles and sacrifices to a stable existence.[10] The Holy Ghost Fathers and the Lyon missionaries were able to send missionaries only to the coastal areas of East and West Africa, as they lacked the personnel for missions in the interior. The farseeing and energetic Cardinal Lavigerie (1825–92) became their apostle. In 1868 he established the Society of the White Fathers, organized their first caravans to the interior of the continent, and fostered the work of the missionaries with his practical and prudent directives.[11] In 1860 Pius IX confirmed the Society of Saint Francis de Sales (Salesians of Annecy), founded in 1833 at Annecy, which in 1845 had begun to send missions to Central Africa.[12]

The founding of two other important missionary societies took place at about the same time: the Belgian missionaries of Scheut and the English missionaries of Mill Hill. In 1862, a number of Belgian secular priests offered themselves to the Congregation for the Propagation of the Faith for work in the missions. With them Theophile Verbist founded the Congregation of the Immaculate Heart of Mary (at Scheut/Brussels) and selected Mongolia for its work; he died there in 1868.[13] The English Society of Saint Joseph (Missionaries of Mill Hill/ London), founded in 1866 by the future Cardinal Herbert Vaughan, concentrated on the mission to the blacks in the United States. In 1892 it became an autonomous organization in America, but also extended its work to British colonies.[14]

---

[9] G. Goyau, La France missionaire II, 393–458.

[10] Ibid. II, 255–302; F. F. Guilcher, Un apôtre d'Afrique au XIXᵉ siècle, Augustin Planque 1826–1907. Premier Supérieur Général de la Société des Missions de Lyon (Lyon 1928).

[11] G. Goyau, op. cit. II, 303–63; J. Perraudin, Lavigerie, ses principes missionaires (Fribourg 1941); X. de Montclos, Lavigerie, le Saint Siège et l'Église de l'avènement de Pie IX à l'avènement de Léon XIII (Paris 1965).

[12] G. Goyau, op. cit. II, 390–91.

[13] V. Rondelez, C.I.C.M. Scheut, Congrégation missionnaire. Ses origines—ses débuts (Brussels 1960); J. Fleckner, S.V.D., "Hundert Jahre Missionare von Scheut," NZM 18 (1962), 220–22.

[14] Heimbucher II, 621–23; H. Brugger, Der erste Josefs-Missionar und sein Werk (Brixen 1941; concerning Cardinal Vaughan and the development of the society).

Beginning in the middle of the nineteenth century, after freedom of religion and proselytization were guaranteed in a large number of Asian states, the emphasis of the missions was placed on education and charity. For this reason it was natural to involve the Christian Brothers, especially the followers of Saint Jean-Baptiste de la Salle, in the Asian missions. In 1859 they began to work in India and gradually extended their activity to other countries as well.[15]

The imposing number of new missionary institutions in this period could create the impression that the missions had enough personnel; comparisons with earlier periods show clearly, though, that these efforts were far from those of the Spanish and Portuguese during the sixteenth and seventeenth centuries.[16] Other mission areas were worked only feebly or not at all. For this reason it was significant that earlier orders, whose apostolic impulses had grown feeble, renewed their missionary spirit.[17] The activity of the Holy Ghost Fathers is a case in point. By opening apostolic schools, establishing a Portuguese province, and resuming missionary work in Angola, the Portuguese missions developed a fresh impetus.[18]

The Weakening of the Portuguese Patronage and the Reorganization of the Asian Missions

IN THE BRITISH SPHERE OF INFLUENCE

After the long period of struggle over the reorganization of ecclesiastical matters, especially in India, it could have been assumed that all seeds of discontent had been removed. Exactly the opposite occurred. The contrast between the patronage missionaries and the missionaries of the Congregation for the Propagation of the Faith grew increasingly intense. Even if the Goan unrest did not cause a schism in terms of canon law—obedience to the Pope was never in question—legal uncertainties

---

[15] G. Rigault, *Histoire générale de l'Institut des Frères des Écoles Chrétiennes VIII: L'Institut en Europe et dans les pays de Missions* (Paris 1951).

[16] For Spain, see L. de Aspurz, O.F.M.Cap., "Magnitud del esfuerzo misionero de España," *MH* III (1946), 99–173; for Portugal, J. Wicki, S.J., *Liste der Jesuiten-Indienfahrer 1541–1758. Aufsätze zur portugiesischen Kulturgeschichte* VII (Münster 1967), 252–450.

[17] The first reorganization of the Capuchin mission was conducted by Bishop A. Hartmann (W. Bühlmann, O.F.M.Cap. *Pionier der Einheit. Bischof Anastasius Hartmann* [Paderborn 1966], 200–210).

[18] A. Brasio, C.S.Sp., *Spiritana Monumenta Historica I. Angola* 2 (Pittsburgh-Louvain 1968). The Holy Ghost Fathers have been active in Portugal since 1869.

constituted a heavy burden, especially in those areas where the interests of the two authorities clashed. A conciliatory step was taken by Portugal in 1849 when it recalled da Silva Torres, the archbishop of Goa. After arrival at Lisbon, he directed a letter of apology to Pius IX, who read it in open consistory and sent a friendly reply.[19] During the vacancy of the see, the bishop of Macao, Jeronimo da Matta, exercised episcopal functions in the areas assigned to the vicars apostolic of Ceylon and Bombay, triggering a protest from them. The struggle between adherents of the patronage and adherents of the Congregation for the Propagation of the Faith reached its climax with the siege of the church of Upper Mahim, in which the vicar apostolic of Bombay, Anastasius Hartmann, remained confined for weeks. In a letter of 12 April 1853 he informed the vicars apostolic of India of the events, and after receipt of their replies he sent a letter of protest in all of their names to the Holy See.[20]

During the conflict the British authorities observed strict neutrality in keeping with their principle of not becoming involved in religious matters in India. Finally, though, they gave in to the pressures of the Goanese and denied Bishop Hartmann the church of Upper Mahim.[21] From Rome, the bishop had received only a temporizing reply which left him no option but to draw the consequences. "Inasmuch as they found support not even in Rome, the vicars apostolic could do nothing but resign."[22] In 1856 Bishop Hartmann returned to Europe. His willingness to turn over the vicariate of Bombay to the Jesuits and to devote himself to the organization of the Capuchin mission in the newly created position of a mission procurator allows the conclusion that this journey was the logical end result of the principles which he himself had enunciated in 1853. Was Bishop Hartmann the sacrificial victim for the complete reconciliation with Portugal? Based on the documents, the question can be answered neither in the negative nor in the affirmative. But certain indicators point in the direction of the affirmative, among them the quoted sentence from the letter of the bishop to Pius IX. He

[19] The various documents are in Streit VIII, 168ff. Archbishop da Silva Torres became suffragan of Braga. Anastasius Hartmann issued the papal address and his letters in Latin with English translation and explanations (*Monumenta Anastasiana* I [Lucerne 1939], 678–700).

[20] The most comprehensive collection of sources for this and the subsequent years is the *Monumenta Anastasiana* II (Lucerne 1940), 3–1054. It also contains the text of the encyclical, 149–51.

[21] Ibid., 197–205.

[22] "Sed vicarii apostolici jure canonico sese defendere nequeunt, quum proinde neque in Roma assistentiam inveniant, aliud haut remanet, quam ut resignent" (Letter of 11 February 1853 to Pius IX), ibid., 32.

spoke from his heart, as in the hour of his greatest need he had not even received an answer to his many letters and cries for help.[23]

The concordat of 21 February 1857 with Portugal settled the confusion in India, albeit in favor of Portugal's patronage. The efforts of Gregory XVI, the regulation by *Multa praeclare* (1838), and Bishop Hartmann's warnings were to no avail.[24] The Portuguese bishoprics of Cochin, Mylapur, and Malacca (in addition to the archbishopric of Goa) were restored, and the jurisdiction of the Congregation for the Propagation of the Faith was recognized only for China and individual parts of Malacca. In fact, Portugal obtained the concession of establishing additional patronage bishoprics in India.[25]

In spite of the one-sided emphasis of the rights of patronage, the concordat of 1857 did not have any deleterious results for the Indian mission, in part because of the discretion exercised by the vicars apostolic, who tolerated the Goan communities in their dioceses and treated them generously according to their needs, in part because of the lack of Portuguese priests who might have ministered to the already established Christian communities and might also have won additional believers. Furthermore, with the experience of a century behind them, the British would not have liked to see an increased activity of the Portuguese; they placed no obstacles in the way of native Goan priests.

In close connection with the work of Bishop Hartmann and his secretary, future Bishop and Cardinal Ignatius Persico (1823–95), occurred an event which guided the Indian Church for many decades: a papal visitation. On 1 June 1858 the two Capuchin bishops directed a memorandum to the Congregation for the Propagation of the Faith concerning the deficiencies of the Indian mission and the means of removing them.[26] In order to counter the lack of unity among the vicars apostolic and the missionaries of the Propaganda, they suggested a papal visitation. In August of the same year Pius IX appointed the vicar apostolic of Pondicherry from the Paris mission seminary, Clement

---

[23] This situation was not changed by the brief of 9 May 1853 and Hartmann's appointment as vicar apostolic of Bombay or by his appointment in 1856 as assistant to the papal throne. The most recent biographer of Bishop Hartmann, W. Bühlmann, O.F.M.Cap. (*Pionier der Einheit* [Paderborn 1966], 121f.), believes that Hartmann became a victim of the struggle and differences between the Congregation for the Propagation of the Faith and the Secretariat of State (Antonelli).

[24] The memorandum of 10 October 1856 concerning this question is in *Monumenta Anastasiana* III (Lucerne 1952), 668–87.

[25] T. Gentrup, S.V.D., *Jus Missionarium* I (Steyl 1925), 211f. The brief judgment of the legal historian is: "Tota res in favorem Portugalliae fuit ad statum pristinum reducta" (ibid., 212). Concerning the various text editions of the concordat, see Streit VIII, 226–28.

[26] *Monumenta Anastasiana* IV (Lucerne 1946), 151–55.

Bonnand (1796–1861), as his visitor.[27] He was charged with examining the deficiencies as well as determining the means of removing them in the areas subject to the Propaganda, all to be included in a detailed report of his own writing. He started upon his task with courage and optimism, but was not able to finish it because he died of cholera at Benares in March 1861.[28] The vicar apostolic of Mysore, Monsignor Étienne Charbonneaux, carried the visit to its conclusion.

This visit of inspection was necessary not only in order to bring about greater harmony and cooperation among the visitors apostolic of various nationalities and orders, but also to instill renewed courage to persevere in the representatives of the Congregation for the Propagation of the Faith, who after the victory of the Portuguese in the concordat of 1857 felt deserted and betrayed.[29] Within the Portuguese bishoprics there were at the time of the visitation the following dioceses under the direction of the Propaganda: in the west, Bombay and Poona under German Jesuits, whom Bishop Hartmann had invited in 1853, in the north the vast areas of the vicariates of Agra and Patna under Italian Capuchins, in the center Hyderabad and Visakhapatnam, the former under the new Milan mission seminary, the latter under the direction of the Oblates of Saint Francis de Sales of Annecy. In the south, the old Jesuit mission of Madura was revived; the Italian Jesuits worked in Mangalore. The Carmelites continued to minister to the two vicariates of Verapoly and Quilon, the Paris missionaries to Pondicherry, Mysore, and Coimbatore; there were also the earlier established vicariates of Madras, which later was taken over by Don Bosco's Salesians, and Calcutta under the Jesuits, who in 1856 were joined by the Holy Cross Fathers and in 1866 by the Milan missionaries in eastern Bengal. The suggestions of the visitors (establishment of a hierarchy and apostolic delegation) were implemented only after the pontificate of Pius IX.

Another point to which the visitors drew emphatic attention was the absence of a native clergy in the areas under the ministration of the

---

[27] JP VI/1, 292–93. Concerning the visitation, see J. Waigand, *Missiones Indiarum Orientalium S.C.P.F. concreditae, juxta visitationem apostolicam 1859–62* (Budapest 1940); A. Launay, *Histoire des Missions de l'Inde* II (Paris 1898), 356–427 (*Visite Apostolique par Monseigneur Bonnand, Fin de son Épiscopat 1858–61*).

[28] He was journeying to Patna, where A. Hartmann was working as vicar apostolic for the second time since 1860 (*Monumenta Anastasiana* IV [Lucerne 1946], 615).

[29] The assertion that Pius IX did not ratify the concordat of 1857 (Delacroix III, 212) out of consideration for the vicars apostolic does not agree with the bull of appointment of the new archbishop of Goa, J. C. d'Amorim Pessoa, and the accompanying letter of 22 March 1861, in which the concordat is not only cited as a fundamental agreement, but which gave the archbishop jurisdiction for six years over all areas which after the conclusion of the concordat were subject to the vicars apostolic (JP VI/1, 326–29).

Congregation for the Propagation of the Faith.[30] Aside from Pondicherry, where since the synod of 1844 the training of a native clergy was being undertaken with vigor and which at the time of the visitation numbered fifty Indian priests, seven vicariates had no native clergy, and the others only a few, most of them in the ranks of their own orders. Monsignor Bonnand in his visitation report deplored this fact with the words: *Monachi monachos gignunt.*[31] While this or that area doubtlessly still had to battle initial obstacles and for this reason could not yet engage in the training of a native clergy, the Propaganda acknowledged the justification of the reproof. On 8 September 1869,[32] in extensive instructions to the mission bishops, it reminded them not only of its own directives of 1845, but also demanded the formation of a capable native diocesan clergy.[33]

The lack of an Indian clergy had to be the more detrimental as the numerically strong Goan clergy theologically and ascetically held views which closely corresponded to those of the European missionaries. This was due chiefly to the excellent theological seminary at Rachol on the Salsette peninsula.[34] Its origins were the local Jesuit College of earlier times. After the expulsion of the Jesuits from India in 1759 by Pombal, Rachol became the central education institution for the clergy of Portuguese India. In spite of many a change in directors and occasional closings—depending on the political situation in Portugal—the seminary turned out a numerous and well-educated clergy. It was particularly the Archbishops da Silva Torres and d'Amorim Pessoa who introduced a better education. D'Amorim Pessoa reorganized the courses into a systematic three-year curriculum, wrote theological syllabi, and gave the seminary a library with seventy-three hundred volumes.[35]

The external difficulties of the Indian mission included the relationship to the colonial power. The English East India Company had absolutely no interest whatever in missionary activity. It required a direct order from London before the work of Anglican missionaries in 1833 and of non-British Protestant mission societies in 1834 was permitted. The Catholic Church, which had been active in the country for cen-

---

[30] C. Merces de Melo, S.J. *The Recruitment and Formation of the Native Clergy in India* (Lisbon 1955), 255–305; F. Coutinho, *Le régime paroissial des diocèses du rite latin de l'Inde* (Louvain 1958), 217–20; J. Humbert, S.J., *Catholic Bombay, her Priests and their Training,* 2 vols. (Bombay 1964; the 2nd volume deals with the priests between 1800 and 1928); E. Zeitler, S.V.D., "Die Genesis der heutigen Priesterbildung in Indien," *In Verbo Tuo (Festschrift),* (St. Augustin 1963), 321–53.

[31] F. Coutinho, op. cit., 219.

[32] *CPF* II, 21–28.

[33] Ibid., 21f.

[34] Merces de Melo, op. cit., 181–205.

[35] Ibid., 190.

turies, did not seem to exist at all. The unceasing efforts of the Capuchin Bishop Hartmann showed how difficult it was to obtain limited just treatment of the Catholics in India—there never was any talk of equality. In addition to personal representations in India, especially in Bombay, Hartmann in 1853 sent the English Jesuit G. Strickland and his secretary Ignatius Persico to Rome and London for the settlement of mission problems. Through oral and written efforts they obtained an official statement from the government in 1856 in the form of "Notes on the position of Roman Catholics in India."[36] In 1857 Hartmann journeyed to London and with his brochure *Remarks on the Resolution of the Government of India upon the Catholic Affairs in India* commented on the government's declarations.[37] Clearly and objectively he dealt with the question of the position of the Catholic bishops, the military chaplains and garrison priests, churches, schools, hospitals, and the unjust treatment of Catholic orphans. His efforts and those of other bishops were crowned with a minimum of success for the rest of the century.[38]

When in the course of reorganization in 1834 the vicariate apostolic of Ceylon was set up, there were only sixteen priests, Goan Oratorians, for two hundred fifty thousand Catholics. The first bishops came from their ranks, but the initial fervor of the Goan priests declined. As a result of English pressure—Ceylon was English after 1796—augmented by pressure from the Catholics of Colombo, Rome was compelled to appoint a European as suffragan bishop. Considerately, an Oratorian, Orazio Bettachini (1810–56), was selected. Soon the Pope gave him jurisdiction over the northern part of Ceylon, the vicariate of Jaffna, established in 1847. In that same year he succeeded in gaining the cooperation of the Oblates of Mary Immaculate.[39]

After Bettachini had finally been named vicar apostolic of Jaffna (1849), Rome appointed the Italian Silvestrin Giuseppe Bravi (1813–62) as suffragan bishop of Colombo. The Oblates worked principally in Jaffna, the remaining Oratorians of Goa principally in Colombo.[40] In spite of all machinations, the native vicars apostolic remained loyal to

---

[36] The text can be found in *Monumenta Anastasiana* II (Lucerne 1940), 238–53.

[37] Op. cit. III, (1942), 724–58.

[38] Thanks to his efforts, the monthly salary of the military chaplains was raised from 100 to 150 rupees, and a few decades later to 200–250, while in Hartmann's time the salary of a Protestant military chaplain or pastor was already 500–800 rupees (F. Coutinho, *Le régime paroissial*, 271–73).

[39] J. Rommerskirchen, O.M.I., *Die Oblatenmission auf der Insel Ceylon im 19. Jahrhundert, 1847 bis 1893* (Hünfeld 1931).

[40] S. Semeria (1811–68), the first superior of the Oblates, in 1856 became suffragan bishop and in 1857 vicar apostolic of Jaffna. He was particularly interested in training a native clergy (N. Kowalsky, O.M.I., "Monsignor Semeria [Apostolischer Vikar von Jaffna 1857–68] zur Pflege des einheimischen Klerus," *NZM* VII (1951), 273–81).

the Congregation for the Propagation of the Faith; but intrigues and messengers from Goa so poisoned the atmosphere that ultimately there was only one solution: the replacement of the decreasing number of Goan priests with European missionaries.[41] In 1857 Bravi was named vicar apostolic, and in 1863 his fellow-Silvestrin Hilarion Sillani succeeded him.

One reason for the decline of the once flourishing mission of the native priests was the inability of the Goans to adapt to new conditions. While the Catholics with increasing urgency asked for English schools and English education, their priests obstinately clung to the Portuguese language and culture. At the same time the Catholics faced the task of becoming better acquainted with the Sinhalese and Tamil cultures of the country. Credit is due principally to the Oblates, especially E. C. Bonjean (1823–93), who at first was vicar apostolic of Jaffna (1868–83) and then archbishop of Colombo, that this education was provided and fostered.[42]

In the Kingdom of Burma, which gradually fell to England in the course of the nineteenth century, Italian Barnabites were active from 1722 to 1832. Because of lack of personnel and means, they transferred the mission to the Oblates of Mary of Turin, who, for the same reasons, were forced to abandon the mission in 1856.[43] The Congregation for the Propagation of the Faith immediately assigned the vast territory to the Paris mission seminary and appointed A. T. Bigandet (1813–94) as vicar apostolic.[44] He excelled not only as organizer of the Burmese Church, but as a scholar highly esteemed by King and people he also wrote a number of important books on linguistics and religion.[45] The division of the area into three dioceses,[46] earlier decided upon by the Propaganda

---

[41] B. Barcatta Silv, O.S.B., "Lo Scisma del Padroado nel Ceylon fino al 1853," NZM V (1949), 241–57, VI (1950), 15–34. Additionally, in the course of the dissolution of orders by Portugal in 1834, the Oratory at Goa was also closed.

[42] J. Rommerskirchen, O.M.I., Die Oblatenmission auf der Insel Ceylon (Hünfeld 1931), 96–228. The papal visitation of Bishop Bonnand in 1860 was decisive for the progress of the northern area of Ceylon (N. Kowalsky, O.M.I., "Die Oblatenmission von Jaffna (Ceylon) zur Zeit der Apostolischen Visitation im Jahre 1860," ZMR 40 [1956], 209–13).

[43] This period is described by L. Gallo, La Storia del Cristianesimo nell'Impero Birmano (Milan 1862).

[44] A Launay, Mémorial II, 50–54.

[45] The good relations between court and people were mirrored by the briefs of Pius IX to the King in 1857 (JP VI/1, 273) and 1858 (JP VI/1, 287). P. Anatriello, P.I.M.E., calls the bishop the "principe dei classici cattolici sul Buddismo Birmano" ("I Cattolici ed il Buddismo Birmano," NZM, XXII [1066], 265).

[46] G. B. Tragella, P.I.M.E., Le Missioni Estere di Milano II (Milan 1959), 11–13.

in 1863, was implemented by him.[47] The Paris missionaries in northern and southern Burma were joined by the Milan missionaries in eastern Burma, where they were active among the Karens.[48]

After 1828, the Malay peninsula constituted a part of the British Empire. The bishopric of Malacca, established in 1558, did not have a bishop throughout the entire century. The activity of the patronage priests was limited to the Portuguese parishes in Malacca and Singapore.[49] The missionaries of the Paris mission seminary devoted themselves chiefly to the Chinese and Indian immigrants. The focus of their work in the vicariate, which was established in 1841, was the expansion of the seminary at Pulo-Penang. The vicar apostolic generally resided in a neighboring parish. The unique arrangement of the parallelity of a patronage bishopric and a vicar apostolic in Malacca continued in existence.

The Kingdom of Siam (Thailand) owed its independence during the nineteenth century to the fact that the two colonial neighbors England and France were unwilling to either share domination over the Thais or to leave it to only one of them. Catholic missionaries had been active in the area since the sixteenth century. Although they were not able to register noticeable successes, the tolerance of ruler and people allowed them to develop the country into an important missionary base. This was true especially for Vicar Apostolic Jean Baptiste Pallegoix (1802–62), an expert on Siamese language and culture, who established close ties to the Siamese court.[50] For fifteen years, Pallegoix maintained friendly relations with the abbot of a Buddhist monastery, who later ruled in Bangkok as King Mongkut (1851–68). His toleration and benevolence continued, with the result that the Catholic mission, almost at the point of extinction because of wars and lack of missionaries, revived again. Mongkut himself directed a friendly letter to Pius IX in March 1861; in October, Pius IX replied in the same vein, praising the tolerant

---

[47] *JP* VI/1, 442–43 (first establishment of the vicariates in 1866, which was not implemented), also VI/2, 93–94 (division of the country in 1870 into two vicariates and one prefecture).

[48] G. B. Tragella, op. cit., 371–400 ("La Missione della Birmania Orientale sotto il prefetto Biffi, 1868–81").

[49] M. Teixeira, *Macau e a sua Diocese* V: *Efemérides religiosas de Malaca*, VI: "A Missão portuguesa de Malaca" (Lisbon 1963). Until 1868, Portugal appointed regents for bishoprics. M. Teixeira, *The Portuguese Missions in Malacca and Singapore (1511–1959)* III: "Singapore" (Lisbon 1963). Jurisdictionally, Singapore at first was part of Goa, was placed under the Congregation for the Propagation of the Faith in 1884, and in 1886–87 became part of the diocese of Macao.

[50] A. Launay, *Mémorial* II, 482–85.

attitude of the monarch toward Christianity.[51] Yet with all of his gestures of goodwill to Christianity, Catholic and Protestant alike, the King remained a convinced Buddhist and used his newly won knowledge of Christianity for a thorough reform of Siamese and Hinayana Buddhism.[52]

The strengthening of the Catholic Church in Siam, begun by Bishop Pallegoix, has lasted to the present. Even if conversions among the Buddhist inhabitants of the country remained rare, an increasing number of Catholic communities were established among Chinese and Vietnamese immigrants, from whom a native clergy was recruited.

IN THE FRENCH SPHERE OF INFLUENCE

After the death of Emperor Minh Mang in 1841, the Tonkin Church enjoyed peace under his successor Thieu-Tri (1841–47). The indefatigable vicar apostolic of West Tonkin, Monsignor Pierre Retord (1803–58), used this period to reassemble the dispersed and frightened Christians.[53] But a new, even bloodier persecution afflicted the Church under Tu Duc (1847–82). Thousands of Christians had to pay for their faith with their lives, among them about fifty priests and five bishops. The first decree of persecution (1848) was directed against the European priests, the second decree (1851) against the Vietnamese priests, and the third one (1855) against all Christians. In order not to endanger their flocks directly, the missionaries had to live in the mountains and forests, where Bishop Retord, exhausted by flight and deprivation, died in 1858.

French intervention took place during this difficult period. After an initial failure, the French consul de Montigny asked Monsignor Pellerin, the vicar apostolic of North Cochin China (1813–62), who had fled to Hong Kong, to seek an audience with Napoleon III in order to obtain help for missionaries and Christians.[54] Because in 1857 a Spanish Dominican bishop, Monsignor Diaz, was executed, the two powers intervened together. In 1858, the port of Da Nang in Tonkin was taken, and in 1859 Saigon was occupied by French troops. This action was the first step in the gradual occupation of all of Indochina by the French, culminating with the seizure of Hanoi in 1873. Although religious free-

---

[51] *JP* VI/1, 349–50. The brief was accompanied by gifts and a portrait of the Pope. An earlier brief of thanks by the Pope is dated 20 December 1852 (*JP* VI/1, 153–54).

[52] G. Lanczkowski, "Das sogenannte Religionsgespräch des Königs Mongkut," *Saeculum* 17 (1966), 119–30; see G. Höltker in *NZM* XXII (1966), 300.

[53] A. Launay, *Mémorial* II, 550–53; A. Launay, *Monsignor Retord et le Tonkin catholique* (Lyon 1919).

[54] A. Launay , *Mémorial* II, 497–99.

dom was embodied in all treaties following each individual phase of the wars of conquest, the Church had to suffer its greatest loss of blood after the "pacification," especially in what is today Vietnam. It is not to be denied that missionaries caused the French intervention and that the suppressed and threatened Christians desired and expected it.[55] But it is also clear that most of the missionaries and Christians did not die because of these political events and wars, but because of their faith.[56] How little involved the missionaries in the interior of the country were with the political conflict was impressively demonstrated with the trial and subsequent beheading of Théophane Vénard (1829–61) in February 1861. It was confirmed by the letters which he wrote while kept in the bamboo cage in which he was confined until his execution.[57]

In spite of the almost incessant persecution, Christianity made progress. The number of missionary dioceses was doubled during this period and so was the number of native clergymen. The clergy had been taught at Pulo-Penang, which was known by the name of *Seminarium martyrium.* As soon as the south of Indochina was calm, the Christian Brothers began their work in Saigon; in 1861, the first Carmelite house was established there. Other houses at Hanoi, Hué, Phat Diem, and Thanh Hoa followed. The seventeenth century form of the lay apostolate, the *Domus Dei* existing in some areas, proved their worth during the persecutions.[58]

The development of the Church in China took place on two levels: on the political/ecclesiastical, and the missionary/religious one. The concordat of 1857 with Portugal dissolved the hitherto Portuguese dioceses of Peking and Nanking, with only Macao remaining under Portuguese patronage. The replacement of the patronage missionaries by representatives of the Congregation for the Propagation of the Faith occurred without stir and without injury to the areas concerned.[59] Nanking was

---

[55] E. Do Duc Hanh, *La place du catholicisme dans les relations entre la France et le Viet-Nam de 1851 à 1870,* 2 vols. (Leiden 1969).

[56] This fact was emphasized in the historical expert opinions in the course of the last beatifications (1951). B. Biermann, O.P., *De Martyribus tempore Tu-Duc Regis in Missionibus Ordinis Praedicatorum tunkinensibus profide occisis* (Rome 1937); O. Maas, O.F.M., "Die Christenverfolgung in Tongking unter König Tu Duc in den Jahren 1856–1862," *ZMR* 29 (1939), 142–53.

[57] Streit XI, 177–81, and T. Vénard, *Käfigbriefe. Bekenntnisse vor seiner Hinrichtung in Hanoi in Tonking 2.2.1861.* (translated into German by W. Stadler [Freiburg 1953]); on the martyrs beatified in 1951, especially the Dominicans, see B. Biermann, O.P., *Im Feuerofen. Glaubenszeugen unserer Zeit. Die Martyrer von Tongking* (Cologne 1951).

[58] Delacroix III, 239–44.

[59] J. Beckmann, *Die katholische Missionsmethode in China in neuester Zeit, 1842–1912* (Immensee 1931), 26f.

replaced by the vicariate apostolic of Kiangnan and transferred to French Jesuits, Peking was given to French Lazarists.[60] The Chinese provinces of Kwangtung and Kwangsi belonged to Macao; missionaries of the Paris seminary had been at work in them since the eighteenth century. Only in 1858 was this area also split from the mother diocese.[61] From then on, the entire China mission was directed by the Congregation for the Propagation of the Faith.

This development resulted in the virtual end of the Portuguese right of patronage in China. But the Treaty of Whampoa (1844) started a new political association, which, especially during the second half of the century, was to be unhappy: French patronage.[62] The contractually agreed freedom of religion was at first valid only for the five so-called treaty ports. Other military action (especially in response to the rebellion of Taiping)[63] led to the treaty of Tientsin (1858) and the peace treaty of Peking (1860). They extended religious freedom to the entire country and to all missionaries who carried a French document of protection. The Chinese were granted the freedom to accept and exercise the Christian faith. The weakness of these treaties and other agreements was, of course, that they were not concluded on the basis of equality but were imposed on the Chinese.[64] All disagreements and persecutions in the course of the century were, in the final analysis, only expressions of hate directed at foreigners and not at Christianity, which was hardly known.

This fact becomes evident from a study of Chinese sources.[65] The increasing number of "missionary incidents" after 1860 may occasionally have been caused by tactlessness, lack of comprehension, and pushy missionaries, but the real cause was the class of Confucian-trained gentry, mandarins, and large landowners. Ever since the seventeenth century they made common front against foreigners and Christianity and

[60] J. de Moidrey, *La Hiérarchie catholique en Chine, en Corée et au Japon* (Shanghai 1914), 97, 140.

[61] Ibid., 107.

[62] L. Wei Tsing-sing, *La politique missionnaire de la France en Chine, 1842–1856* (Paris 1960); J. Beckmann, op. cit., 14–23.

[63] *LTHK* IX, 1277, with literature. The Catholic missions had to suffer doubly from the social-religious movement of the fanatics, first from the killings and arson by the revolutionaries from Canton to Shanghai, then also, outside of the areas concerned, by the newly created mistrust, because the Christians were placed on the same level as the revolutionaries.

[64] T. Grentrup, S.V.D., *Die Missionsfreiheit nach den Bestimmungen des geltenden Völkerrechts* (Berlin 1928), 64.

[65] P. A. Cohen, *China and Christianity. The Missionary Movement and the Growth of Chinese Antiforeignism, 1860–1870* (Cambridge, Mass. 1963).

intensified their hostility during the nineteenth century.[66] By means of falsehoods and lies they tried to incite the ignorant masses against the strangers and the followers of foreign religions.[67] Violent incidents led to negotiations with the foreign powers which lasted for years. The hate of foreigners and Christians reached its first high point with the blood-bath of Tientsin on 21 June 1870, in which the French consul, other Europeans, a European and a Chinese Lazarist, and ten Sisters of Mercy were killed.[68]

Such setbacks did not prevent the missions from expanding far into the interior of the country. Externally this was evident in the increase of the vicariates apostolic: in 1846, North Kiangsi, Kweichow, and Tibet; in 1856 North Tscheli, West Tscheli, Southeast Tscheli (these three areas were formed from the former diocese of Peking), Kiangnan (for Nanking), East Szechwan, South Hunan, and the apostolic prefecture of Kwangtung; in 1860, South Szechwan. In 1870, the vicariate of Hupei was divided into three vicariates. From Fukien, the Spanish Dominicans in 1859 resumed the mission on the island of Formosa, interrupted since the seventeenth century. Those orders already present in China strengthened their ranks, among them the Franciscans, Dominicans, Paris missionaries, Lazarists, and Jesuits, In 1858, the missionaries of the Milan mission seminary began their work in Hong Kong and in 1869 in the province of Honan; the Belgian missionaries of Scheut after 1865 laid the foundation for new Christian communities in the vast provinces of Kansu and Mongolia.[69]

In its instructions of 1845 concerning the education and training of native clergy, the Congregation for the Propagation of the Faith had emphasized the importance of regular meetings of the superiors of orders at local synods for the preservation of ecclesiastical unity and discipline.[70] This general admonition was followed in June 1848 by an encyclical to the bishops of China and neighboring countries to gather for a synod at Hong Kong.[71] In spite of additional reminders such a

[66] For the year 1860 alone, the archives of the Foreign Office (Tshungli Yamen) contain 8000 pages on "missionary incidents," for the years 1860–1909 there are 910 volumes (it is the largest section of the archives of the Foreign Office) (P. A. Cohen, op. cit., 346).
[67] P. A. Cohen, op. cit., 77–99 (Gentry Opposition to Christianity).
[68] Ibid., 229–61. He concluded: "Each side operated on premises that it believed to be universally valid, and both were caught up in a clash of cultures over which neither had much control" (261). On missionary concerns, see J. Beckmann, *Missionsmethode*, XIVf.
[69] The decrees for the establishment of new vicariates are in *JP* VI/1 and VI/2.
[70] *CPF* I, 545.
[71] G. B. Tragella, P.I.M.E., "Il mancato Concilio di Hongkong 1950," *Missionswissenschaftliche Studien (Festschrift J. Dindinger)* (Aachen 1951), 347–60. The meetings of six bishops in Shanghai and of the superiors of the Lazarist mission in Ningpo were a substitute (J. Beckmann, *Missionsmethode* 10).

synod did not take place, primarily because to most of the bishops the conditions in the country for such a gathering were not favorable and the journeys too dangerous, but also because most of them did not see the need for such a meeting. Behind the scenes, the old protectionist power (Portugal) and the new one (France), insisted on their right to participate.

In the meantime, Rome tried to prepare for an eventual synod. Pius IX appointed Monsignor L. C. Spelta, O.F.M., the vicar apostolic of Hupei, as apostolic visitor.[72] Unfortunately, he was forced to terminate his inspection and died in 1862 at Wuchang. A stronger impression than this visit was made in Europe by the journey of two Lazarists, E. Huc and Joseph Gabet, through Mongolia to Tibet (1844–46).[73] After his return to Europe in 1848, Gabet directed a voluminous memorandum to Pius IX in which in plain language he told him the truth about China and the means whereby its conversion could be hastened. In essence, these consisted of drawing concrete consequences from the instructions of 1845 by the Congregation for the Propagation of the Faith.[74] When Father Gabet submitted his report, he could look back upon ten years of missionary experience; as the founder of the Catholic mission to Mongolia he had worked in Mongolia since 1837.[75]

In 1848 the first European sisters arrived in China. Their work in schools, hospitals, and orphan homes was the reflection of a profound change in missionary methods. Ever since persecutions had begun, es-

---

[72] *JP* VI/1, 308f. Pius IX also sent a letter to the Emperor of China in which he commended Monsignor Spelta and the Catholics of the Empire to the benevolence of the Emperor and referred to the beneficial doctrines of Catholicism for his Empire. It is not likely that the letter ever reached the addressee.

[73] E. Huc, *Souvenirs d'un voyage dans la Tartarie, le Thibet et la Chine pendant les années 1844, 1845, 1846* (Paris 1950). See Streit XII, 230–38 listing individual editions and translations. The French sinologist Paul Pelliot writes about the occasional doubts concerning the genuineness of the report in "Le voyage de MM. Gabet et Huc à Lhasa," *T'oung Pao* 24 (Leiden 1926), 133–78. According to him, the report is genuine in its essentials. But it was also edited by E. Huc for a broad public, and as a consequence the actual leader of the exploration, J. Gabet, was pushed to the background.

[74] *Coup d'oeil sur l'état des Missions de Chine présenté au Saint Père le Pape Pie IX* (Poissy 1848); Streit XII, 204–8. Monsignor Verrolles, vicar apostolic of Manchuria, protested the brochure, which in 1850 was condemned by the Congregation for the Propagation of the Faith. Gabet had the gift of seeing the situation in a way which was only acknowledged a hundred years later (see G. B. Tragella, "Le vicende di un opusculo sul clero indigeno e dul suo autore," in J. Beckmann, *Der einheimische Klerus in Geschichte und Gegenwart* [*Festschrift L. Kilger*] [Beckenried 1950], 189–202; N. Kowalsky, "Das 'verlorene' Manuskript zu Gabets Denkschrift über den einheimischen Klerus," *NZM* XIV (1958), 96–103.

[75] H. Verhaeren, C.M., "Un catéchisme mongol du lazariste Joseph Gabet?," *NZM* XXIII (1967), 150–51.

pecially during the past 150 years, the European missionaries had confined themselves to spreading the faith unobtrusively among moderate numbers of people. The pastoral care of families and women was left to Chinese girls. Beginning with the second half of the nineteenth century, the educational, social, and charitable institutions recruited members for the Christian faith indirectly. But it was precisely the (actually very beneficial) activity of European women which the Chinese regarded as alien and which they rejected. It is understandable, therefore, that the Chinese memorandum of 13 February 1871, which the government addressed to the foreign powers after the events of Tientsin, demanded more respect for Chinese sensibilities from the Europeans in general and the removal of the sisters in particular.[76] The demand was decisively rejected by foreign powers and missionaries alike.[77] The expansion of the missionary work was continued as before and characterized the Chinese mission until recently. In retrospect, the rejection of Father Gabet's recommendations by the mission superiors and the Congregation for the Propagation of the Faith was fatal.

Korea was established as a vicariate apostolic separate from Peking in 1831. The remoteness of the country and the long access journey meant that it was not until 1836 that the first European missionary, Pierre Philibert Maubant (1803–39), arrived. The vicar apostolic of Korea, Bishop Barth. Bruguière, had died in Mongolia in 1835 on the way to Korea. In 1837, Father Jaques Honoré Chastan (1803–39) reached Korea, soon followed by the second vicar apostolic, Laurent Joseph Marius Imbert (1796–1839). All three died a martyr's death after the bishop had been arrested and the two missionaries voluntarily had turned themselves in to the authorities in order to protect their communities from harassment.[78] During the next bloody persecution in 1846 the first Korean priest, Andreas Kim, became a victim. After finishing his theological studies at Macao, he had gone to Korea in 1845, accompanied by his bishop, J. Ferréol (1808–53), and a missionary. When new persecutions broke out in 1866, during which two bishops, seven missionaries, and about eight thousand Christians were slain, the young Korean Church numbered about twenty-five thousand members. It was to be ten years before the country would receive other missionaries and pastors.[79]

---

[76] Streit XII, 455, listing the various editions of this memorandum.
[77] Streit XII, 455f.: Reply by the Western powers. From the side of the missionaries, there was Le Memorandum Chinois ou violation du Traité de Peking. Par un missionnaire (F. Genevois, Rome 1872); Ibid., 476f.
[78] A. Choi, L'Érection du premier vicariat apostolique et les origines du Catholicisme en Corée (Beckenried 1961), 76–87.
[79] Delacroix III, 281.

Attempts to reestablish missions in Japan failed until the American admiral Matthew Perry opened the country in 1854.[80] In 1858 France obtained the concession from Japan to allow freedom of religion for foreigners in port cities and in Tokyo. Father Girard (1821–1867) became the first priest and interpreter of the French Society of Paris Missionaries to settle in the capital. For foreign Catholics, small churches were established at other places as well, but attendance was forbidden to the Japanese.[81]

Nagasaki allowed the presence of foreigners again in 1862, and the Paris missionaries built a small church. It was here that Father T. Petitjean in 1865 discovered surviving Christians, of whom about twenty-five thousand acknowledged themselves to the missionaries.[82] Such an event could not be concealed from the Japanese authorities in spite of all precautions on the part of the missionaries. Anti-Christian legislation was still in force and was strengthened in 1869 by an imperial edict. Another wave of persecutions swept over the newly organized Christian communities, culminating in mass deportations and exile to distant parts of the country. Only pressure by the European powers effected a gradual diminution of the persecutions.[83]

The discovery of the Old Christians produced internal difficulties, especially with respect to language. The faithful of Nagasaki still used prayers, hymns, catechisms, and religious literature in Spanish and Portuguese terminology. The muddled situation did not improve when Monsignor Petitjean, vicar apostolic of Japan after 1866, reissued old books from the Jesuit printing press. By about this time, Chinese terminology had become accepted in central and northern Japan, while the traditional Spanish-Portuguese terminology survived in southern Japan until the death of Bishop Petitjean.[84] The problem was attenuated in

---

[80] J. Jennes, C.I.C.M., *A History of the Catholic Church in Japan, 1549–1873* (Tokyo 1959); J. Van Hecken, C.I.C.M., *Un siècle de Vie Catholique au Japon 1859–1959* (Tokyo 1960); J. Beckmann, *Die katholischen Missionen in Japan und ihre Auseinandersetzung mit den japanischen Religionen. Priester und Mission* (Aachen 1960), 337–74.

[81] Van Hecken, op. cit., 11–13.

[82] Ibid., 14–16. A large number of the Old Christians did not trust the new times. As late as 1954 there were about thirty thousand secret Christians in the west of the island of Kyushu. In its essential parts they had adhered to the Catholic faith, but exercised their religious life only clandestinely (J. Van Hecken, C.I.C.M., "Les Crypto-chrétiens au Japon au XXe siècle," *NZM* XI, [1955], 69–70).

[83] If Japan was slow and hesitant in dismantling anti-Christian legislation, the reason was that the new state had to have time to organize the national religion of Shintoism, to consolidate it among the people, and thereby to erect a strong dam against the rise of Christianity (K. M. Panikkar, *Asien und die Herrschaft des Westens* [Zurich 1955], 392f.).

[84] J. Laures, S.J., "Das kirchliche Sprachproblem in der neuerstandenen Japanmission," *Monumenta Nipponica* III (Tokyo 1940), 630–36.

1876 by the division of Japan into two vicariates, North Japan and South Japan.

Philippines, Indonesia, Oceania, Africa

Although relatively autonomous and possessing their own religious administration, the Philippines until the nineteenth century were nothing more than an extension of Spanish-America to the Far East. Given this close association, the ideas of the French Revolution and of the American Independence movement could not but affect the islands. The first stirrings of political independence failed, in part because the dominant Spanish upper class was too weak to assume a leading role, in part because the Friars, especially the Augustinian Eremites, who since the end of the sixteenth century had carried the chief missionary and pastoral burden on the islands, maintained their strong position. Together with Franciscans and Dominicans they formed the most reliable pillar of Spanish rule. It was a paradox of history that Spain itself, expecially after the revolution and the dissolution of all orders in 1835, began to weaken its own position in the country through the positive support of Freemasonry. The association of Philippinos with lodge brothers of the United States in the neighboring Asiatic countries, who were to serve only as allies in the struggle against the Church, produced in the islands new sources of unrest, fostered the movement for independence, and ultimately, much to the surprise and disappointment of all parties concerned, brought about the American occupation of the country.[85]

Until the middle of the nineteenth century, the ranks of the Spanish missionaries could be filled with Spaniards, but after 1855 there were difficulties with recruitment. Queen Isabella II granted the reopening of the mission seminaries for the Philippines and the readmission of the Jesuits, whose first members arrived at Manila in 1859.[86] They performed their work primarily on the islands of Yolo and Mindanao, where the majority of the population was Muslim. In addition to the already mentioned political paradox, there was also an ecclesiastical-religious paradox with ominous consequences. The orders had done good work in training a native clergy, whose numbers had grown to impressive proportions by the nineteenth century. Unfortunately, they left this native clergy in subordinate positions, without raising its social

---

[85] A critical comprehensive treatment of recent Philippine Church history is unfortunately lacking, but a wealth of source material has been sorted and is cited by Streit IX (1937) in a volume of almost one thousand pages.
[86] J. A. Otto, S.J., *Philipp Roothaan*, 493.

or economic standing. Thus they forced this educated class into the ranks of the malcontents and rebels.[87]

A mission to Indonesia became possible only after 1807 when Louis Napoleon granted freedom of religion to Holland.[88] But even after the establishment of the vicariate apostolic of Batavia in 1842, missionary work remained limited to the pastoral care of white Catholics. The colonial legislation of 1854 made any expansion of such work dependent on specific permission by the government. Only gradually, step by step, did Catholics achieve their missionary right to exist. This was generally in response to particular events, such as in Borneo, where an apostolic prefecture was created in the northern part in 1857, and after 1860 in Flores.[89] In 1859 Portugal, in a peace treaty with Holland, ceded this island and others, but managed to insert a clause guaranteeing the care over native Christians. One of the outstanding missionaries of the early period was the Jesuit Le Cocq d'Armandville; the first Jesuits arrived in Batavia in 1859.[90] Further progress was made only during the subsequent mission period. The part of Timor remaining with Portugal and a few other small islands, raised to the bishopric of Dili in 1940, were administered by the diocese of Macao until recently.

The missions of Oceania continued to attract hosts of missionaries after the middle of the nineteenth century in spite of tremendous difficulties, such as immense distances, tropical diseases, and political and denominational contrasts.[91] With most of them, genuine religious motives determined their preference for the Pacific islands, but some of them were no doubt also influenced by romantic adventurism and the image of paradisiac conditions.[92] Missionary romanticism imbued the

[87] C. A. Majul, "Anticlericalism during the Reform Movement and the Philippine Revolution," in G. H. Anderson, *Studies in Philippine Church History* (Ithaca 1969), 152–71.

[88] A. Mulders, *De Missie in tropisch Nederland* ('s-Hertogenbosch 1940); A. Mulders in Delacroix III, 378–80. This suppression of the Catholic missions was tied to the Dutch colonial method of the time, about which the Indian historian K. M. Panikkar judges harshly: "The Dutch were the only one among the European nations in the East who lowered a whole population to the level of plantation coolies and who acknowledged for it neither a legal nor a moral obligation" (*Asien und die Herrschaft des Westens* [Zurich 1955], 103).

[89] Concerning the attempts of the Milan missionaries to gain a foothold in Borneo, see G. B. Tragella *Le Missioni Estere* I, 189–91.

[90] J. A. Otto, S.J., *Philip Roothaan*, 34.

[91] Streit XXI, C. R. H. Taylor, *A Pacific Bibliography*, 2nd ed. (Oxford 1965); see also the regular "Bibliographie de l'Océanie," *Journal de la Société des Océanistes* I (Paris 1945seqq.). On the whole matter, see also *Journal de la Société des Océanistes. Numéro spécial sur les missions du Pacifique* XXV (1969).

[92] J. Meier, M.S.C., "Primitive Völker und 'Paradies'-Zustand mit besonderer Berücksichtigung der früheren Verhältnisse beim Oststamm der Gazelle-Halbinsel im Bismarck-Archipel (Neu-Pommern)," *Anthropos* 2 (Vienna 1907), 374–86. The missionary utopias of the South Seas mission still need to be examined.

Society of Oceania; it existed from 1844 to 1854 for the support of the missions in Polynesia and trade with it. Even Pius IX and a number of other bishops joined it. But neither missions nor trade benefited from it, and the society was dissolved.[93] Polynesia remained the missionary field for the Picpus missionaries. Spreading out from Hawaii, they gained footholds on the Marquesas, Tahiti, and the Cook Islands, where independent vicariates were gradually erected. Subsequently, the missions gained world-wide attention through the heroic work of Father Damian de Veuster (1840–89), who, active in Hawaii since 1863, after 1873 worked among the lepers on Molokai.[94] Easter Island, where B. Eyraud began missionary work in 1864,[95] was also part of Polynesia.

When in 1836 the vicariate of Central Oceania, comprising all of Melanesia and Micronesia, was established and handed to the care of the Marist Fathers, ignorance of geographical realities allowed people to believe that enough had been done. But missionaries on the spot quickly realized that by themselves they would never be able to take care of such an immense area. Operating from the Solomon Islands, the Marist Fathers tried to deny Protestant missionaries access to New Guinea; but the deadly climate put an end to their efforts. Therefore their superior, Father J. U. Colin, welcomed the offer of the Milan missionaries to continue this work. The first group left Milan in 1852. But the young Italian missionaries also had to pay tribute to the tropical climate, and when in 1855 Father G. Mazzuconi was murdered by the natives, they left the unhealthy mission and retreated to Sydney to recover. The mission was not resumed,[96] and twenty-five years passed before fresh help arrived.

From their center in New Zealand, where they were trying to convert the Maoris, the Marist Fathers expanded their efforts to other, northern island complexes, especially to the Solomons,[97] to Tonga, Samoa, Fiji, New Caledonia, and the New Hebrides. Gradually, independent dioceses were established in this area. The vast distances and new languages promoted local printeries, especially by the Marist Fathers.[98]

[93] P. O. Reilly, S.M., "La Société des Océanie," *RHM* VII (Paris 1930), 227–62. Additional literature in Streit XXI, 130–32.

[94] Streit XXI, 225–42.

[95] S. Engler, O.F.M.Cap., *Primer siglo cristiano de la Isla de Pascua 1864–1964* (Villarrica 1964).

[96] G. B. Tragella, *Le Missioni Estere* I, 125–71.

[97] Hugh M. Laracy, *Catholic Missions in the Solomon Islands, 1845–1966* (Auckland 1969), diss., Canberra.

[98] P. O. Reilly, S.M. *Imprints of the Fiji Catholic Mission, 1864–1959* (London-Suva 1958); P. O. Reilly, S.M., "Premiers traveaux des presses de la mission catholique à Wallis, 1845–1849," *Journal de la Société des Océanistes* XIX (Paris 1963), 119–28. Earlier works by the same author in Streit XXI, XIII/XIV, 653–55.

The Marist Fathers never reached Micronesia, which had been assigned to them as missionary area as part of the vicariate of Central Oceania. These islands, especially the Mariana Islands, where Christianity survived even after the expulsion of the Jesuits, ecclesiastically belonged to the diocese of Cebu in the Philippines (1814–98). Their Christian communities were tended by the Augustinian Recollects.[99]

At this time, the Benedictines began their missionary work among the Australian aborigines. In 1859 the area became an apostolic prefecture, and later became an *Abbatia nullius.* The method employed by the Benedictines was the same as the one used by them in missionizing Germanic tribes during the Middle Ages.[100]

Although Africa was geographically closer to the European mission centers and thus could be reached much more easily than the Pacific islands, missionary settlements in the dark continent were established only slowly, under great sacrifices, and with only moderate success. The vicariate of Central Africa, established in 1846, had a stirring and sorrowful history.[101] Its establishment was suggested by A. Casolani, canon in Malta, who became its first vicar apostolic. He accepted the appointment on the condition that Jesuits accompany him as missionaries.[102] But to General Roothaan the enterprise appeared as rather romantic and vague, and he detached only two Jesuits for an initial exploration. When Bishop Casolani resigned from his post, the Congregation for the Propagation of the Faith appointed Father Ryllo as provicar, whom the bishop together with two other secular priests accompanied as a simple missionary.[103] By 1861, the new mission had cost the lives of forty missionaries. Only Daniel Comboni (1830–81), vicar apostolic of Central Africa after 1877, was able to create better conditions for his missionaries by moving his headquarters from Khartoum to Cairo. But the rising of the Mahdi in 1882 destroyed the entire mission.[104]

---

[99] C. Lopinot, O.F.M.Cap., "Zur Missionsgeschichte der Marianen und Karolinen," *NZM* XV (1959), 305–8.

[100] R. Salvado, O.S.B., *Memorias históricas sobre la Australia y la Misión de Nueva Nursia* (Madrid 1946). This Spanish edition of the original (Naples 1852) contains a good historical introduction to the Benedictine missionary work in New Nursia.

[101] E. Schmid, M.F.S.C., "L'erezione del Vicariato Apostolico dell'Africa Centrale," *ED* XXII (1969), 99–127, XXIII (1970), 87–110; M. B. Storme, C.I.C.M., "Origine du Vicariat Apostolique de l'Afrique Centrale," *NZM* VIII (1952), 105–18.

[102] M. B. Storme, C.I.C.M., "La renonciation de Monseigneur Casolani, Vicaire Apostolique de l'Afrique Centrale," *NZM* IX (1953), 290–305.

[103] J. A. Otto, S.J., *Philipp Roothaan,* 237–48. Father Ryllo, S.J., died in 1848 and his successor, the secular priest J. Knoblecher, in 1858.

[104] S. Santandrea, F.S.C.J., *Bibliografia di Studi Africani della Missione dell'Africa Centrale* (Verona 1948).

Thanks to the loyalty of the missionaries of Verona, the flourishing Sudan mission emerged from the vicariate apostolic of Central Africa. In 1868 the new apostolic prefecture of Sahara and Sudan was created and subordinated to the archbishop of Algiers, Charles Lavigerie, as apostolic delegate. It can hardly be assumed that Rome, when making out the decree, which is not contained in any official collection of documents of the Congregation for the Propagation of the Faith, seriously thought of converting the Sudan. But the man to whom the seemingly impossible task was entrusted conceived of a daring plan to achieve this objective with the aid of the White Fathers, whom he had founded. First attempts to penetrate to Central Africa from the Kabylia mission in Algeria failed. Only after much more careful preparations did the White Fathers make their way from the East African coast to the area of the great lakes.[105]

The areas which they had to cross in the east in order to reach their central African mission areas were under the jurisdiction of the Holy Ghost Fathers, who in 1863 worked in Zanzibar and after 1868 at Bagamoyo on the mainland. After the death of their founder, Franz Maria Libermann, Father Ignaz Schwendimann filled the office of superior general from 1852 until 1881. Under his leadership the young society was strengthened and took a firm foothold on the African mainland. In addition to their initial areas in western Africa (Senegal, Senegambia, Gabon), they were given the vicariate apostolic of Sierra Leone in 1864.[106] In 1849 the plan emerged to minister to the vacated Portuguese mission areas,[107] but it was not until 1866 that the first Spiritans arrived in the Portuguese Congo and in Angola. In the Congo, they found traces of the Italian Capuchins who had worked there earlier.[108] To the normal difficulties in tropical Africa was added the severe opposition of Portugal; only the tireless activity of Father Charles Duparquet (1830–88), residing after 1866 in Angola, effected the settlement of the Spiritans in Portugal and the establishment of a Portuguese province, thereby removing any obstacles.[109]

With the arrival of the Oblates of Mary Immaculate in Natal in 1852, the areas of South Africa saw their first missionaries; until this time the area's secular priests had been able to minister to the white settlers only.

[105] Streit XVII, 757–71.
[106] A. Engel, C.S.Sp., *Die Missionsmethode der Missionare vom Heiligen Geist auf dem afrikanischen Festland* (Knechtsteden 1932).
[107] *Spiritana Monumenta Historica. I. Angola 1.* Par António Brásio, C.S.Sp. (Pittsburgh and Louvain 1961), 30ff.
[108] Op. cit., 514–25.
[109] Volumes 2 and 3 of the *Spiritana Monumenta Historica* contain information on the work of C. Duparquet and the establishment of a Portuguese settlement and province.

In 1862 the Oblates made their way to Basutoland, which hitherto had been closed to Catholic missionaries, and eventually built up a flourishing mission. During subsequent decades they also became active in other areas of Africa.[110]

With the Jesuits active on the island of Réunion and the islands around Madagascar, they sought ways and means to penetrate the interior of the large island itself. But the political and denominational contrast (England/France) as well as the difficulties posed by France and the long-established colonial seminary in Paris were so strong that initial attempts failed. Only in 1861 did the Jesuits settle firmly at Tananarive and begin the establishment of the Church in Madagascar.[111]

It is perhaps astonishing that in a survey of missionary activity during the middle of the nineteenth century Africa occupies such a modest place. Of course, the difficulties to be overcome were great, but certainly not greater than in the Far East, the South Pacific islands, or in China and India. If the missions of the East were treated better, the reasons for this lie deeper. The optimistic missionary reports of the seventeenth and eighteenth centuries had surrounded the missions of the Far East with an attractive halo. The advanced cultures of these peoples, known particularly through the researches and reports of the missionaries, were valued as much as the tolerant character of the inhabitants. Unimaginable utopias exercised a great allure for the islands of the Pacific. Africa lacked such attractions. The great explorations of European investigators started only in the middle of the past century and were only cautiously exploited by Protestant and Catholic missionary circles.[112] The languages and cultures of Africa, aside from the west coast and Portuguese colonies, were largely unknown. Finally, the burden of earlier times still rested on the shoulders of the black race. The African was largely regarded as a slave in Europe and the New World, and this was also the view of the Church. The descriptions of slave hunters and traders remained alive, at least subconsciously.[113] To be sure, slavery was condemned and an attempt was made to lighten the lot of the blacks; but the continent exerted only minimal political and missionary appeal, a circumstance which explains the slow penetration of Africa.

---

[110] T. Ortolan, O.M.I., *Cent ans d'Apostolat dans les deux Hémisphères. II: En dehors de l'Europe, 1841–1861* (Paris 1914).

[111] J. A. Otto, S.J., *Philipp Roothaan*, 211–37; A. Boudou, S.J., *Les Jésuites à Madagascar au XIXe siècle*, 2 vols. (Paris 1952).

[112] T. Ohm, O.S.B., *Wichtige Daten der Missionsgeschichte* (Münster 1961), 193–95, listing dates of discoveries and missionization.

[113] Urs Bitterli, *Die Entdeckung des schwarzen Afrikaners. Versuch einer Geistesgeschichte der europäisch-afrikanischen Beziehungen an der Guinea-Küste im 17. und 18. Jahrhundert* (Zurich 1970).

CHAPTER 13

The First Vatican Council and the Missions

The first Vatican Council from 1869 to 1870 was a mirrored reflection of the laborious missionary effort during the nineteenth century. In contrast to the Council of Trent, missionary countries were represented, even though the presence of missionary bishops was controversial. As it was, their principal concerns were not dealt with at all, in part because of the early termination of the council and in part because of the lacking preparation and knowledge of the council participants.

Pius IX solemnly announced the impending council on 26 June 1867 in a public consistory, and a year later, on 29 June 1868, the bull *Aeterni Patris* invited the participants from throughout the world. Between these two events the decision was made to include the vicars apostolic, i.e., the missionary bishops. In its session of 17 May 1868 the preparatory central commission agreed that it would be proper to invite titular bishops to the council in keeping with the words "patriarchs, archbishops, and bishops" in the draft of the bull.[1] But the commission did not address the legality of participation.[2] This fact proved to be a hindrance for the position of the vicars apostolic at the council. Their position was inhibited by the polemics preceding and accompanying the council, denying the vicars apostolic the right to participate and mentioning their lack of education and manners.[3] From the words of some missionary bishops we know that they became aware of their second-class standing only at the council itself. Monsignor E. J. Verrolles (1805–78), the senior missionary bishop in China, who had administered the Christian communities in Manchuria since 1833 and had to undergo one of the most fatiguing journeys in order to reach the council, was furious when he learned upon arrival in Rome that French newspapers in particular disputed the right of vicars apostolic to partici-

[1] T. Granderath, *Geschichte* I, 93. Consequently, the text of the bull of appointment was printed in *JP* VI/2, 16–19.
[2] Granderath, op. cit., 93–97; Grentrup in *ZMR* 6 (1916), 30–32. Neither author dares to deal with the legal aspects. Granderath merely emphasizes that it would be unfair "to exclude from the Council the titular bishops of the mission countries which do not yet have an ordered hierarchy, who administer their dioceses like regular diocesan bishops, and on whose shoulders rest the largest of burdens."
[3] An examination of the importance of the actual pagan missions in the ultramontane-liberal polemics still needs to be written. A short synopsis is in Delacroix III, 81f. (L. Wei Tsing-sing, "Le Ier concile du Vatican et les problèmes missionnaires en Chine," *RHE* 57 [1962], 500–525).

pate in the council.[4] His fellow-brother from the Paris seminary, Monsignor Louis Faurie (1824–71), vicar apostolic in Kweichow since 1860, remarked sarcastically that some liberal papers seemed to think that "as barefoot ignoramuses and papal valets" they had been included among the worthy council fathers.[5] But the bad "missionary climate" at Rome was even more painful for the mission representatives than the journalistic sniping. The idea of forming preparatory commissions had first been raised in 1865. Cardinal Bizzarri, the chairman of the central commission, primarily moved to engage members of the Roman Curia, as they were most conversant with the problems to be treated and with the traditions of the Apostolic See. Additional theologians and canonists could then be made members as necessary. As a result of the chaotic conditions in Italy, it was not until 1867 that five preparatory commissions were formed and approved by Pius IX.[6]

In this context, the Commission for the Eastern Church and Missions is of primary interest.[7] The chairman of the commission was the prefect of the Congregation for the Propagation of the Faith, Cardinal Barnabo (1801–74). It consisted of seventeen members: eleven Italians, three Germans, and one Englishman, Russian, and Oriental each. Upon the urging of the cardinal, the commission, which initially comprised only members of the Curia, specifically of the Propaganda, was expanded with three men who had practical experience. These were Monsignor Giuseppe Valerga (1813–72), since 1847 the first Latin patriarch of Jerusalem; his brother, the Carmelite Leonardo di S. Giuseppe Valerga (1821–1903), at that time apostolic prefect of the Carmelite mission in Syria; and the Franciscan Paolo Brunoni (1807–75), after 1853 vicar apostolic of Aleppo and since 1858 vicar apostolic of Constantinople. Both the men of the Curia and those with practical experience counted among them outstanding Eastern experts such as the German Benedictine abbot D. B. Haneberg (1816–76) and the Russian Jesuit J. Martinov (1821–94).

For the mission bishops arriving at Rome it was disappointing and paralyzing to learn that there was not a single expert or representative of the actual pagan missions on the commission. Moreover, in the very first session Cardinal Barnabo announced that the primary task of the commission was the application of the disciplinary rules of the Council of Trent to the conditions of the Eastern Churches. Aside from a few

[4] A. Launay, *Monseigneur Verrolles et la Mission de Mandchourie* (Paris 1895), 397.
[5] A. Launay, *Histoire des Missions de Chine. Mission de Kouy-tcheou* II (Paris 1908), 596.
[6] R. Aubert, "La composition des commissions préparatoires du premier concile du Vatican," *Reformata reformanda (Festschrift Jedin)*, (Münster 1965), 447–82; Granderath, op. cit. I, 62–82.
[7] The following observations rest primarily on R. Aubert, op. cit., 473–77.

laudable exceptions, what was meant by this was a far-reaching Latinization of the Eastern Churches.[8] "Mission" meant for most of the members of the commission, aside from a few laudable exceptions, nothing more than the Near Eastern mission. This narrow interpretation resulted from the fact that the older missionary nations like Spain and Portugal were not at all represented on the preparatory commission, while the bishops of the Portuguese and Spanish patronage, respectively their American successor states, regarded themselves as belonging to the European residential bishops, i.e., to the bishops first class, and not to the barely tolerated vicars apostolic.[9] Only in January 1870 were two missionary bishops of the Paris mission seminary, Monsignor E. L. Charbonneaux, vicar apostolic of Mysore, and Father J. M. Laouënan, vicar apostolic of Pondicherry, appointed to membership on the commission. Both of them were renowned linguists and historians and had made names for themselves as associates of Visitor Monsignor Bonnand and continued his work.[10]

The principal task of the commission was the drafting of a schema to be presented to the council fathers. Cardinal Barnabo had written to Near Eastern and Austrian bishops as early as February and March 1868 and asked them for ideas and suggestions.[11] Of the replies, that of the Hungarian Bishop Roscovany demanded a thorough and effective promotion of the propagation of faith and a higher level of piety in the Christian countries.[12] Other demands or suggestions reached the commission during the council. Among the home Churches, only France submitted a valuable postulate pointing to the future (signed by thirteen participants). On 23 January 1870, 110 members asked for a solemn recommendation by the council of the Association for the Propagation of the Faith. Thirty-five vicars apostolic voiced a similar concern for the Childhood of Jesus Association, and two postulates, one signed by thirteen, the other signed by sixty-one participants, were in favor of

[8] J. Hajjar, "L'Épiscopat catholique oriental et le Ier Concile du Vatican (d'après la correspondance diplomatique française)," *RHE* 65 (1970), 423–55, 737–88; J. Hajjar, *Les chrétiens uniates du Proche-Orient* (Paris 1962); L. Lopetegui, *El Concilio Vaticano Primero y la Unión de los Orientales* (Berritz 1961).

[9] C. J. Beirne, "Latin American Bishops of the First Vatican Council," *The Americas* 25 (Washington 1968–69), 265–88. The conversion and pastoral care of the Indians, interrupted since the expulsion of the Jesuits and other orders from almost all Latin American countries, was no problem for the Latin American bishops, as little as the Indian and Negro missions were for the bishops of North America.

[10] A. Launay, *Mémorial de la Société des Missions Étrangères* II (Paris 1916), 119–21 (on Charbonneaux), 363–66 (on Laouënan), with bibliographies of their works.

[11] Ting Pong Lee, op. cit., 106. Similar letters to actual mission bishops are not known to me.

[12] Grentrup, op. cit., 32. Suggestions by Bishop Dupanloup and Cardinal Pecci (Leo XIII) point in the same direction.

supporting the Association for the Support of Schools in the Near East.[13]

By November 1869 a first draft of a mission schema was ready; it contained only one lengthy chapter on missionaries, their qualities, their education, and individual facets of their activity.[14] It was judged inadequate by the commission and in December 1869 replaced by a second draft with four chapters.[15] This schema also was rejected. Only the third draft of 26 June 1870 was accepted for distribution to those council fathers still at Rome.[16] Following an introductory letter from Pius IX, there were three chapters: 1. On Bishops and Vicars Apostolic, 2. On Missionaries, 3. On the Means of Spreading the Faith. Appended to the text were the *Adnotationes ad Schema Decreti de Apostolicis Missionibus*.[17]

The contents of the schema were probably the brainchild of the Latin patriarch of Jerusalem, Giuseppe Valerga. It ran to forty-four folio pages on the Uniate Churches of the Eastern rite and to thirty-five pages on the missionaries of the Roman-Latin rite in the countries of the Near East.[18] The reliance on one of the outstanding representatives of the Latin mission in the Near East and the objective of the commission as earlier defined by Cardinal Barnabo make clear why the schema was concerned principally with the mission to the Near East. Still, the intervention of the representatives of missions to the pagans succeeded in changing many passages in such a way that they applied to all messengers of the faith. Yet other long passages, concerning only the Church and pastoral and missionary care among the peoples of the Near East, remained intact.[19] That the second chapter "On the Apostolic Missionaries" conformed precisely to the initial intention, i.e., the implementation of Tridentine rules, was clearly shown by the *Adnotationes*,

---

[13] Grentrup, op. cit., 35–37; Ting Pong Lee, op. cit., 105–9. The number of signatures was not significant. According to the listing in Granderath (op. cit. I, 463–509), the number of cardinals, patriarchs, bishops, vicars apostolic, etc. who were obliged to participate in the council was 990.

[14] On the history of the schemata, cf. Ting Pong Lee, op. cit., 111–15. The author found two manuscript volumes with twenty opinions by the consultants of the mission commission *(Conc. Vat. Acta. Commissio pro Orientalibus)* and one volume of the *Conc. Vat. Comm. Orient. Studia praevia*, op. cit., 111–21, in the library of the Lateran University, Rome.

[15] List of contents of the two schemata in Ting Pong Lee, op. cit., 112–13.

[16] The text of the third schema was printed by Mansi, 53, and *ColLac* VII. I am quoting from the original imprint as distributed to the council fathers in 1870 (photocopy).

[17] Schema, Text 1–20, *Adnotationes* 21–32.

[18] Ting Pong Lee, 114. According to him, not only essential portions of the schema, but actual phrasings were taken from these expert opinions.

[19] Note the careful delineation of the jurisdictions of bishops (of the Eastern rite) and vicars apostolic (of the Latin rite) which, aside from the Near East, had no significance (Schema 9–10, *Adnotationes* 30–31).

which contain no fewer than nine concrete references to the Tridentine Council.[20]

This one-sided orientation toward the Near Eastern missions was further indicated by the writers listed in the *Adnotationes*. Writings concerning pagan missions were conspicuous by their absence. To be sure, the Carmelite Thomas a Jesu, whose mission theories drew upon the provincial of the Jesuits in Peru, José de Acosta, S.J.,[21] was mentioned twice for the purpose of cementing claims of papal and episcopal jurisdiction.[22] However, no instruction from the Congregation for the Propagation of the Faith was adduced, neither the fundamental one of 1659 nor the equally recognized handbook on missionary method, *Monita ad Missionarios* (1669). Two specifically cited chief witnesses of the schema were the canonists and experts on the canon law of the Eastern rite Churches: Angelo Maria Verricelli and his *Tractatus de Apostolicis Missionibus*[23] and the Franciscan Carolus Franciscus a Breno and his *Manuale Missionarium Orientalium*.[24]

Aside from the deficient treatment of the pagan missions and their problems, the centralistic orientation of the schema encountered opposition. It was less a question of papal infallibility, to which all representatives of the missions agreed, than of the concentration of jurisdiction and administration of the missions in the hands of the bishops and vicars apostolic, which implied the virtual exclusion of the orders. After the mission schema had been distributed toward the end of June 1870, twenty-seven council fathers submitted extensive observations. Almost all of them opposed the intended exclusion of the superiors of orders; this view was not only held by the generals such as the general of the Society of Jesus, Petrus Beckx, but also by representatives of the home episcopate of the secular clergy.[25] Behind the tendency toward centralization, no matter how carefully and cautiously it was formulated,

---

[20] While the text in the schema (10–17) is general, the *Adnotationes* 26–30 clearly refer to the clergy of the Near East, for in the real mission countries, including the patronage countries, the regulation of the Council of Trent had been in effect for centuries. They were also being followed for the education and training, and the conduct and work of the clergy.

[21] P. Charles, "Les sources de *De Procuranda salute omnium Gentium*," *Scientia Missionum Ancilla (Festschrift Mulders)*, (Nijmegen 1953), 31–63.

[22] Schema 24, 28.

[23] Venice, 1656.—That this book, according to the title of missionary character, was designed primarily to serve the Near Eastern missions, becomes clear from the appendix which examines the validity of the ordinations of bishops and priests in the Near Eastern Churches. (Streit I, 233).

[24] Venice, 1726. Streit I, 379–80.

[25] A. M. Hoffman, "Die Vollmachten der Missionsbischöfe über Ordensmissionare auf dem Vatikanischen Konzil," *NZM* 12 (1956), 267–75. Hoffman used the expert opinions which were published by Mansi in volume 53.

was concealed a noticeable rejection of the missionizing orders, especially of the Jesuits. After all, most of the members of the commission belonged to the Congregation for the Propagation of the Faith, and Monsignor Giuseppe Valerga, the Latin patriarch of Jerusalem, the most influential representative of the orders (O.F.M.), virtually spoke for the prefect of the Propaganda, Cardinal Barnabo.[26] For a specialist of missionary history, their aversion was clearly indicated by the positive evaluation of the disastrous actions of Bishop Juan de Palafox y Mendoza of Puebla in Mexico against the missionary orders.[27] Additionally, a mission directory was to promote uniformity of missions in all mission areas; its precise constitution was left to the Congregation for the Propagation of the Faith.[28] This suggestion also was made by Monsignor Valerga, who in his verdict acknowledged that while the *Monita ad Missionarios* contained valuable admonitions, it was incomplete and lacked the necessary authority.[29]

Faced with this atmosphere, which was not exactly favorable to the pagan missions, the missionary bishops resorted to a kind of self-help in regional bishops' conferences.[30] The Indian and Chinese bishops met separately. The eighteen vicars apostolic of India directed a petition to the Pope requesting him to do away with the Portuguese right of patronage, in which they saw the greatest obstacle to the conversion of India. But Pius IX did not think that he could accede to their request.[31] The gathering of the Chinese bishops developed into a kind of synod. The soul of these meetings, which from 22 December 1869 onward took place once a week and then twice a week, was the vicar apostolic of Kweichow, Monsignor Louis Faurie, who also acted as the secretary of the gatherings.[32] The basis of their discussions were seventy-two ques-

---

[26] R. Aubert, "La composition des commissions préparatoires du premier concile du Vatican," *Reformata reformanda* (Münster 1965), 473–77.

[27] Schema 25, where only the steps taken against the Jesuits are emphasized. The arguments by the canonist A. M. Verricelli, employed by him in his book of 1656 for the defense of the bishop of Mexico, were refuted by his very contemporaries, especially by the learned Jesuit Diego de Avendaño.

[28] Schema 20; P. Wanko, op. cit., 35–37.

[29] Ting Pong Lee, op. cit., 134–36.

[30] Pius IX specifically authorized such group meetings of the bishops (R. Aubert, *Le Pontificat,* 323).

[31] Delacroix III, 84. Even though he traces the instruction of the Congregation for the Propagation of the Faith of 8 September 1869 to the activity of the council participants from India, the indication can not be correct chronologically, as the Indian bishops had not yet arrived in Rome at that time. The document is a consequence of the papal visitation by Bishop E. Bonnand.

[32] A. Launay, *Histoire des Missions de Chine. Kouy-Tcheou* II (Paris 1908), 598–612 (Launay published the draft of the protocol from the archives of the Paris Mission Seminary); I. Ting Pong Lee, *De congressu praesulum Missionum sinensium Concilio Vat-*

tions submitted to the bishops by the Congregation for the Propagation of the Faith. In addition, the participants were chiefly concerned with the relationship of the Chinese missions to the French government, respectively to the French protectorate. Some of the non-French bishops absented themselves from the sessions dealing with a letter of gratitude to Napoleon III.[33] There was no doubt that all of the French missionaries recognized the protection by their government, whose effective strengthening was repeatedly mentioned in the sessions on the letter to Napoleon. The letter was sent on 10 March 1870.[34]

The questions of the Congregation for the Propagation of the Faith dealt with by the bishops of China concerned the establishment of an apostolic delegation or nunciature, to which the bishops reacted skeptically and negatively, as they were jealous of their independence; the division of the Chinese mission into five regions, specifically with respect to the holding of regional synods; the appointment of a council for the vicars apostolic and of another council for mission estates and the regular clergy in missions; the Chinese clergy, its education and training, which should be of a kind allowing them to administer a mission or become bishops;[35] liturgical questions; feast and fast days;[36] the significance and spread of Christian literature and schools; and the administration of the sacraments.[37]

icano durante. Commentarium pro Religiosis et Missionariis 29 (Rome 1948), 104–11 (according to the protocol in the archives of the Congregation for the Propagation of the Faith, vol. 242, 1874); L. Wei Tsing-sing, "Le Ier concile du Vatican et les problèmes missionnaires en Chine," *RHE* 57 (1962), 500–523, based on Launay, supplemented with documents of the Foreign Office in Paris.

[33] Wei Tsing-sing, op. cit., 513. Wei deals almost exclusively with the political side of the meetings, while Ting Pong Lee emphasizes the missionary and pastoral aspects.

[34] Unfortunately, Launay, op. cit., 607, published only a fragment of this letter. We do not know who signed this petition of thanks. The author was Monsignor A. Languillat, S.J., the vicar apostolic of Kiangnan.

[35] On the whole, the bishops reacted positively to this question, but were also in favor of proceeding slowly and cautiously. (A. Launay, op. cit., 602–3).

[36] The bishops preferred Chinese as the liturgical language, but were willing to leave the decision to the Congregation for the Propagation of the Faith. (Ting Pong Lee, op. cit., 108).

[37] With respect to the administration of baptism, the discontinuation of the baptismal ceremony according to the Roman rite and its distribution over the entire period of the catechumenate was rejected, but it was required that all questions should be put in the Chinese language (Ting Pong Lee, op. cit., 109). —This decision was a compromise, for the missionaries of the Paris Mission Seminary, most recently Monsignor Faurie, in the eighteenth century had introduced the division of the baptismal ceremony in their dioceses. But in 1866 this practice was expressly forbidden by the Congregation for the Propagation of the Faith (J. Beckmann, "Taufvorbereitung und Taufliturgie in den Missionen vom 16. Jahrhundert bis zur Gegenwart," *NZM* 15 [1959], 20–21).

On 14 July 1870 a final session of all Chinese bishops was called, the only one which was chaired by the cardinal prefect of the Congregation for the Propagation of the Faith. Thirteen problems were discussed; some of them had been discussed earlier, others were new, like the problem of opium and the use of Chinese hymns in liturgical and paraliturgical celebrations.[38] All decisions of the Chinese bishops were to be submitted to the council fathers for final disposition. Considering the second-class standing of the missionary bishops, it is not astonishing that not one of them played an eminent role at the Vatican Council.[39]

The weakness of the missionary climate of the council as a whole was shown by the single postulate on the African missions.[40] It was short and impressive, carried a brief rationale, and demanded effective steps on the part of the council for the conversion of the blacks, especially in central Africa. The author was Daniel Comboni, the founder of the Missionaries of Verona, missionary, and future vicar apostolic of central Africa. It is dated 24 June 1870 and was signed by seventy council fathers. These signatures, especially in the context of what was said above, present a clear picture of the lack of interest in missions. Although Comboni rushed from man to man like a beggar, appealing for the conversion of Africa, he only met large-scale incomprehension. He was best received by the representatives of the Near Eastern Churches; together with the missionary bishops of the Near East, they provided thirty-one signatures.[41] Of the residing bishops, twenty-five signed.[42] Even of the actual mission bishops only fifteen signed their names: six from India and nine from Far Eastern countries.

Given the lack of interest in missions among the council fathers and the almost systematic displacement of the pagan missions to the margin of the council, no profound reflections on the missions were produced. Nevertheless, the Vatican Council acted as a stimulant and guide for

[38] Ting Pong Lee, op. cit., 109–11.

[39] L. Wei Tsing-sing, op. cit., 508.

[40] P. Chiocchetta, "Il *Postulatum pro Nigris Africae Centralis* al Concilio Vaticano I e i suoi precedenti storici e ideologici," *ED* 13 (1960), 408–47 (text of the *Postulatum*, 409–11, signatures, 412–14).

[41] The absence of the signature of Monsignor Lavigerie, the bishop of Algiers, was particularly noticeable.

[42] Of these, six were North Americans, two were Brazilians, one was German, and the others were Italian. P. Chiocchetta (op. cit., 415ff.) somewhat artificially attempts to raise the significance of the individual signatures by drawing attention to their signers. But neither this positive evaluation nor the reference to the fact that the Sudan mission and Comboni's efforts were later promoted by Rome are a sufficient reason for his optimistic presentation. Comboni, who participated in the council as theologian for the bishop of Verona, was a "voice in the wilderness."

mission theory during the subsequent period.[43] Among the votes and postulates, especially of the French and Chinese bishops, there were programmatic suggestions, some of which were put into action under the more relaxed pontificate of Leo XIII, while others had to wait for the twentieth century and the Second Vatican Council. In their submission to the council, the French bishops considered deliberations on the dissemination of the faith as one of the primary, most significant and important matters with which the council ought to deal. At the same time, they anticipated their great responsibility for the missions. So that they could perform their tasks better, they asked for regular reports from the Congregation for the Propagation of the Faith concerning the status and problems of the pagan missions.[44]

[43] P. Wanko, op. cit., 16–23.
[44] J. Moreau, *L'Épiscopat français et les missions à l'heure du Ier Concile du Vatican: Missions de l'Église* (Paris 1962), 8–13; see also R. Aubert, *Vaticanum I* (Mainz 1965), 295.

Light and Shadows of Catholic Vitality

CHAPTER 14

Regular and Secular Clergy

Orders and Congregations

The pontificate of Pius IX saw a new and decisive phase in the internal reorganization of the old orders and an expansion of the new congregations. To be sure, the orders were hard hit by secularization measures in southeastern Europe, Poland, and Latin America, but in western Europe and in North America there was a continuing quantitative and qualitative growth. The orders constituted an essential factor in the flourishing of religious organizations and the intensification of spiritual life.

Pius IX himself was not a member of an order, but like his predecessors Pius VII and Gregory XVI concerned with the restoration of discipline. The consolidation during the first half of the century enabled him, with the assistance of Monsignor Bizzarri, the energetic and competent secretary of the *Congregatio Episcoporum et Regularium,* to raise his aspirations. Immediately after his election he established a commission of cardinals in September 1846 and charged it with restoring the life of the orders in those countries in which they had suffered as a consequence of disorder. In the next year he created the *Congregatio super statu regularium,* with the specific function of supervising the reforms.[1] Two decrees of 25 January 1848 strengthened the precautionary measures taken to prevent the admission of unworthy candidates to the novitiate.[2] An encyclical of 1851 tightened the requirements of communal life and of poverty (although prudently retaining the toleration of the *peculium*). The enclyclical *Neminem latet*[3] of 19 March 1857 extended a requirement to all monastic orders which heretofore was only applied to the

---

[1] *Collectanea in usum Secretariae S. Congr. Episcoporum et Regularium* (Rome 1863), 867–68, and *Acta Pii IX* I, 46–54.

[2] *Collectanea . . . ,* 882–902.

[3] *Collectanea . . . ,* 904–6. Twenty-four explanations by the congregation *Super statu regularium* from 1857 to 1882 supplemented the new rules (see also *Acta Pii IX* III, 417–20).

Jesuits: the obligation to precede the solemn profession of vows with temporary vows. In order better to counter the loosening of morals and customs which had crept in during the preceding centuries, Pius IX did not limit himself to encouraging centralization within the orders and to emphasizing more strongly their dependence on the Roman congregations; in several cases he did not hesitate to appoint their superiors himself. In 1850, for example, he designated the reformer Don Casaretto as abbot of Subiaco and assisted him during the following year in Casaretto's efforts to reorganize in a new province those monasteries which were desirous of returning to a stricter observance of the Benedictine rules.[4] In 1852 it was the Pope's admonition which induced the monastery of Monte Cassino, where discipline had become very lax, to reintroduce seclusion and communal life and to regroup the novitiates.

During his refuge at Gaeta Pius IX had noted the deplorable conditions prevailing among the Redemptorists in the Kingdom of Naples, where their generalate was located, in contrast to the progress of the congregation north of the Alps.[5] For this reason he decided in 1853 to move their headquarters to Rome and to appoint their general, a function which normally would have been exercised by the chapter general of the order.

In order to remove the decadent features which had begun to characterize the Dominicans, he decided in 1850 to abolish the election of the master general. Much to the dismay of the Italian members, he named Father Jandel, one of Lacordaire's early associates, as head of the order. Jandel remained master general until 1872 and finished the movement of restoration. Characteristically, his efforts were guided by the initial concepts of the order, which the historical research of the eighteenth century had brought to light again. Thus, the closings to which the order had been subjected since the French Revolution and which in some countries continued beyond 1870[6] at least had the advantage of completely clearing the slate of the most recent past. The fact that the provinces of the order had to be restored from new houses facilitated

[4] A few years later, in 1867, this province was raised to an independent congregation, the *Congregatio cassiniana primitivae observantiae,* which, like the modern orders, was divided into four provinces: Italy, Anglo-Belgium, France, and Spain (see I. Di Brizio, *L'Italia benedettina* [Rome 1929], 103–44).

[5] Despite some vicissitudes in Austria in 1850 (see E. Zettl in *Spicilegium historicum Congr. SS. Redemptoris* 6 [1958], 353–404; E. Hosp in ibid. 7 [1959], 260–354).

[6] Between 1844 and 1876, the number of Dominicans in Italy decreased from 1602 to 830, in Russia and Poland from 709 to 65, and in Latin America from 626 to 315. In spite of a regular increase in western Europe, especially France, the total number in 1876 was only 3,341 compared to 4,562 in 1844.

the return to the original guidelines. This was not as simple as it sounds, as Jandel, who tended to cling to traditional forms, came in opposition to Lacordaire, who had a better feeling for the necessity of accommodation to the requirements of modern times.

Pius IX also repeatedly (1856, 1862, 1869) intervened in the designation of the general of the Franciscan order; in 1856 it resumed the long interrupted practice of chapters general and revised its statutes. Gradually the order reestablished itself in the various countries of western and central Europe. But the order also suffered new and serious losses in consequence of the secularization in the Latin countries. At the chapter of 1856, ninety provinces were represented, but in 1882 only thirty were still in existence, and the number of members during this quarter of a century decreased from twenty-five thousand to fifteen thousand.

Even though the reform attempts instigated or encouraged by Pius IX produced good results fairly rapidly in the centralized orders, the same efforts met resistance from the abbeys, especially in central Europe, which had remained largely independent. The great canonical visitation conducted by Cardinals Schwarzenberg and Scitowsky in the Habsburg Empire between 1852 and 1859 had no noticeable results.[7] Yet the Premonstratensians gradually revived and in 1869 held their first chapter general since the French Revolution. Former Cistercian abbeys were reopened and regrouped in new congregations. The Belgian congregation was established in 1846, the Austro-Hungarian congregation in 1859,[8] and that of Sénanque in southern France in 1867. The young branch of the Benedictines, planted by Dom Guéranger at Solesmes, also began to bear fruit. While progress in France was slow and difficult and really came into its own only during the following pontificate, the brothers Wolter, who in 1863 founded the German abbey at Beuron,[9] completed their training at Solesmes. As early as 1872, Beuron founded a branch monastery at Maredsous in Belgium, and additional foundings were made in Austria-Hungary during the *Kulturkampf*.

The example of Beuron demonstrates that it did not always require the initiative of the Holy See to revive old orders and congregations. Some of them, in fact, made remarkable progress on their own. This was the case, for example, with the Christian Brothers, who under the prudent leadership of their general superior Philippe (1838–74) in-

---

[7] C. Wolfsgruber in *SM* 32 (1911), 304–29, 477–502, 665–92, 33 (1912), 109–30.

[8] N. Konrad, *Die Entstehung der österreichisch-ungarischen Zisterzienserkongregation, 1849–69* (Rome 1967).

[9] See *Beuron 1863–1963* (Beuron 1963), to be corrected in several points according to P. Wenzel, *Der Freundeskreis um Anton Günther und die Gründung Beurons* (Essen 1965).

creased their membership from twenty three hundred to more than ten thousand. While most of their members were recruited in France, they succeeded in establishing themselves all over the world. The same was true of the Passionists, who under the generalate of Antonio di San Giacomo (1839–62), known as the "Second Founder," tripled the number of their members and provinces and concentrated on missionary work (Rumania, Brazil, and Australia).

In particular, the Society of Jesus demonstrated its vitality. The first years of the pontificate of Pius IX were rather difficult for the order. On one hand the Jesuits had to meet general attacks on them in most of the European countries, and on the other they received only lukewarm support from the Pope. He was irritated by the covert resistance of many Jesuits to his concessions to the liberal cause. But the aftereffects of 1848 brought the Pope closer to the Jesuits again, especially after Father Roothaan, with whom the Pope did not get along too well, was replaced in 1853 by Father Beckx.[10] For more than thirty years he led the society with prudence and intuition and saw to it that the Jesuits refrained from any polemics and avoided involvement in politics. The frequency with which his intervention was required indicated, however, that not all Jesuits agreed with him on this issue. Although the Jesuits suffered from fourteen cases of expulsions and confiscations during a thirty-year period in all Catholic countries of Europe, with the single exception of Belgium, and especially in Latin America,[11] the society increased its membership from 4,540 in 1848 to 10,030 in 1878. The influence of the Jesuits steadily increased. On the level of the regional Churches they were effective in missions to the parishes and through other organizations; their colleges and sermons and their contacts with the upper classes were invaluable. On the level of the universal Church, the Gregorian University and the journal *La Civiltà cattolica* gave them an important voice. They also were involved in the Roman congregations, in which neither the secular nor the regular clergy had men as competent as the Jesuits. And finally there was the growing confidence of Pius IX, who after his earlier bias against them recognized the value of the discipline of their training and their devotion to the Holy See.

---

[10] On Petrus Beckx (1795–1887), Belgian, see K. Schoeters, op. cit., who confirms that in contrast to the frequent assertions during his lifetime, Beckx was basically a moderate.

[11] The systematic mistrust by the liberal bourgeoisie of the Jesuits is not sufficient to explain everything. Much is due to the ineptitude of the Jesuits themselves, who had difficulty, especially in the Latin countries, in adapting themselves to modern thinking (see, for example, J. Kennedy, *Catholicism, Nationalism, and Democracy in Argentina* [Notre Dame 1958], 61).

In comparison to the Jesuits, the new congregations and institutes attracted much less attention. Between 1862 and 1865, seventy-four new congregations and institutes received papal approbation, compared to forty-two such approvals between 1850 and 1860. Aside from the fact that many of them were destined to have a glorious future—the Salesians founded in Turin in 1857 by Don Bosco come to mind—the global significance of their capillary effectiveness in all areas of the apostolate must not be underrated. They were active in education, especially that of girls; the care of the sick; social work, which became increasingly specialized for orphans, old people, domestics, young working girls, prisoners, the blind, the deaf; catechetical instruction; publishing; and missions. The development, going hand in hand with the growth of the congregations founded during the first half of the century, was universal. There were the congregations of priests who followed the versatile guidelines of the sixteenth and seventeenth centuries in pursuing their many activities; the confraternity institutes, which were well attended at a time when admission to the high schools, which alone paved the way toward the priesthood, was still a privilege; and countless women's organizations, many of which placed themselves under the protection of the Virgin Mary (Daughters of the Heart of Mary, Daughters of the Immaculate Heart of Mary, Daughters of Mary Immaculate, Little Sisters of the Assumption, Oblate Sisters of the Assumption, and Praying Sisters of the Assumption).

Rome did its best to channel these forces and to limit the increase of tiny congregations, which occasionally created the impression of ecclesiastical anarchy. On the other hand, of course, they served the interests of many priests and of many women willing to place their energy in the service of charity, especially as they could do justice to the various needs on the local level. The *Congregatio Episcoporum et Regularium* continued to encourage especially those congregations which under a superior general could group together a number of communities whose activities were not confined to one diocese or even one country. But it also had to take account of the differences in languages and customs or of the objection that this necessitated excessively long journeys for the members of these congregations. Additionally, there was the fact that many countries objected to seeing their religious institutions under the control of foreigners. Monsignor Bizzarri knew how extraordinarily varied intentions and local customs were and was smart enough to avoid prescribing a uniform constitution. At least until 1860 he left it up to each congregation to draft its own statutes and limited himself to examining them and making occasional suggestions for change. In 1862 he then published a *Methodus quae a S. Congregatione Episcoporum et Regularium servatur in approbandis novis institutis votorum simplicium.*[12] It did not yet have the force of law, but was an attempt to lay down some common norms. Gradually and under the pressure of events a new rule for members of institutes emerged. It was codified only much later, as the Vatican Council, which was supposed to pass on it, did not have enough time to deal with the eighteen decrees prepared for the purpose.

While Rome proved itself flexible, many congregations considered it their obligation to come up with the regulation of minutiae. They were generally religiously inspired, but it was easy to place rules ahead of the gospel; it was a consequence of the general tendency of the spirituality of the time, which, devoid of solid doctrinal foundations, resorted to mere recipes. The education of women, as it was understood at that time, intensified such tendencies. Nevertheless, many people who were inspired by the Christian faith willingly accepted such completely superfluous restrictions in order to be able to devote themselves to the many needs of the daily life of the church. They constituted an impressive testament to the high-minded convictions of an age which in so many other respects was bourgeois and materialistic.

The Diocesan Clergy and Pastoral Work

Even though we have a number of biographies of priests, sociological studies of the middle level of clergy in the countries of the nineteenth century are still rare. Yet it is possible to arrive at some common denominators. Without a doubt there were substantial differences between a French village priest, the vicar in an industrial area of the Rhineland or Belgium, the owner of a benefice in Austria-Hungary, a Spanish dean, a Sicilian priest, and an immigrant pastor in the United States. Somehow, from the various national traditions and the different life styles, there emerged over the years the classical type of Catholic pastor. The worldly priest playing the role of an intellectual in the salons of Paris, the scholar whose benefice afforded him enough leisure to pursue his studies, the rural parish priest with loose morals only distinguishable by his habit from the mass of his flock, all of them became, especially in western Europe, exceptional cases after 1850. The distinct rise in the spiritual standards of the clergy was one of the most characteristic aspects of Church history in the course of the pontificate of Pius IX. This development was dear to the heart of the Pontiff and he constantly returned to it in his encyclicals, speeches, and especially in his private correspondence.

[12] *Collectanea in usum Secretariae S. Congr. Episcoporum et Regularium,* 828–66; see F. Callahan, *The Centralization of Government in Pontifical Institutes of Women* (Rome 1948), 43–68.

This development of the clergy was the result of education received in the seminaries. Most candidates for the priesthood now had to undergo such an education and training, often starting in childhood. This was, of course, a hothouse atmosphere, rather deficient in intellectual content (only a part of the German and Austrian clergy still attended the regular universities), even though the clergy was imbued with high spiritual and pastoral ideals. The ideal had been formulated by Saint Sulpice, which directly or indirectly served as model for all of Europe and America. The clergy's development was also the product of the systematic efforts of many bishops with high standards of office. While there was only one Manning to write a book like *The Eternal Priesthood,* many others in their revised diocesan statutes or at the provincial synods prescribed a variety of pious exercises, recommended weekly confession, the holding of periodical retreats and possibly monthly recollections.[13] These episcopal objectives corresponded to the spontaneous efforts of a growing number of priests who gathered in associations, better to promote their aims. Some of them soon acquired international renown, such as the Apostolic Union of Secular Priests, founded in 1862 by V. Lebeurier, a member of the Orléans cathedral chapter, and the *Associatio perseverantiae sacerdotalis,* founded in 1868 at Vienna by R. Koller.[14] At the same time, the influence of the regular clergy over the secular priests grew. The two branches of the clergy cooperated better and the secular priests relied on the publications of the orders for their spiritual guidance. Thus the regular clergy tended to intensify the tendency among the diocesan priests to an other-worldliness inculcated in them by the seminaries, even at the risk of losing touch with the people among whom they exercised their apostolate.

This was the obverse of the medal. It was less pronounced in the German-speaking countries than in the Latin countries in which the wearing of the soutane became a habit.[15] Thus, the question is legitimate whether ecclesiastical policy, followed by a large part of the Church with the more or less express encouragement of Pius IX, was not in fact ambivalent. Undeniably positive results, especially the raising of the spiritual quality of the clergy and a better understanding of the eminent dignity of the priestly function, were balanced by negative consequences. Father Martina was justified in asking whether the emphasis on clericalism resulting from this policy was not one of the causes of anti-

---

[13] *DSAM* IV, 1937–40. The thirty-six bishops consulted in 1865 with respect to the program of the Vatican Council were unanimously in favor of requiring the clergy to conduct retreats every two or at the most every three years.

[14] F. Beringer, *Die Ablässe* II (Paderborn 1921), 367–69.

[15] R. Rouquette, "Une centenaire, la soutane," *Études* 314 (1962), 32–48.

clericalism and the secularization of everyday life.[16] Daniel-Rops, a historian without any revolutionary proclivities, asked the pointed question: "Did the reaction to the excessive freedom of the period of crisis and the concern with discipline encourage the priests to live in a compartmentalized world, a world without windows on the real life of the people?" During the long years of training, except for Germany and Austria frequently starting at the age of thirteen, the teachers inculcated in the future priest the conviction that he had to become a man of prayer and live a withdrawn life of sacrifice. They taught him to celebrate the Mass correctly and to salve the pangs of conscience of his flock. It was therefore not surprising that priests frequently confined their activities to sacramental gestures and excluded themselves from everything that was not directly subject to their authority and might lead to abuses. When the priest kept away from popular festivals, he was not sufficiently aware that his distinction between what he considered to be good or bad was possibly nothing more than the difference between differing levels of culture, between the "bourgeois" and urban culture of the pastor and the culture of the broad masses of the people.[17]

But these aspects should not be generalized too much. Without a doubt, many priests in the villages and small towns everywhere confirmed the famous definition of Taine: "Loyal sentry duty in a guardhouse, obeying the watchword, and standing a lonely and monotonous guard." Their activity essentially consisted of celebrating the Mass—during the week only for a few women—of preaching the Sunday sermon, explaining the catechism to children, listening to confessions, and administering the last rites to the dying. But these conditions varied from country to country. A village priest in central or southern Italy was much more closely involved, occasionally much too much, in the daily lives of his flock than a French priest. In England and Ireland, the priests in the workers' quarters were not merely the spiritual fathers of their communities, but also acted as worldly advisers and occasionally were the leaders for their demands from the authorities. Even in those countries in which the restriction of the clergy to its purely ecclesiastical functions was most pronounced, there increasingly emerged, especially in the large city, an asceticism of action. It moved the clergy to engage in forms of the apostolate designed for conquest. Founders of religious congregations such as Father d'Alzon and Don Bosco clearly pushed their associates in this direction; but such thinking was not limited to the

---

[16] *RRosm* 62 (1968), 409.

[17] D. Julia and W. Frijhoff in *Concilium* 5 (1969), 560. In contrast to widely accepted opinion, the clergy was recruited primarily from the small towns. During the further course of the century, the share of the rural areas increased, but the young clerics were thoroughly influenced with respect to culture by their long stays at seminaries.

regular clergy. Dupanloup in his rural diocese encouraged his priests not to be content with waiting for the faithful in their churches, but to make home visits in order to arouse the indifferent; he tried to stimulate them to greater efforts through the introduction of social inquiries, of which he was a pioneer,[18] even though not the only one. Although the focus of priestly work continued to be the parish, a new type of priest in addition to pastors and vicars came into being: the leader of socio-religious organizations. This was by no means the beginning of the specialized apostolate of the twentieth century, but many priests began to suit the method of the apostolate to the various groups to which they ministered, such as craftsmen, the sick, women, and children. The phenomenon became so much common property that experiences were written up in such books as *Méthode de direction des œuvres de jeunesse* (1858) by Abbé Timon-David. The development was particularly strong in Germany, where after 1848 many different associations began to expand. While the proportion of laymen in them was rather high, many priests were very interested in them because they recognized them as a suitable means of the apostolate, in keeping with the requirements of modern times.

These efforts to reach the faithful more effectively unfortunately all too often suffered from a great deficiency. They were more oriented toward defense than to proselytization and urged the "good people" to withdraw unto themselves and to do nothing to shorten the gap between them and the bad Christians and the faithless. The latter were regarded as people without loyalty and faith, with whom any attempt at conversion would be fruitless.[19] The same threat of confining Catholicism in a kind of intellectual ghetto, with its consequences for the apostolate, was also evident in the considerable efforts to develop a Catholic school system. The problem of education had already been raised during the pontificate of Gregory XVI, but the more education became common property, the more the clergy viewed education in a positively Catholic spirit as a necessity justifying any sacrifice. While in the German-speaking countries a solution acceptable to the Catholics was reached, the disappearance of Christian content in the public schools in many Latin countries, or their Protestant character in the Anglo-Saxon countries, caused the ecclesiastical authorites (at different rates in different countries) to establish a network of free Catholic schools. This was done parallel to the public school system and often in competition with it. In Great Britain, the system of parochial schools

---

[18] Details in C. Marcilhacy, *Le diocèse d'Orléans sous l'épiscopat de Monseigneur Dupanloup* (Paris 1962).

[19] Note the fitting observations in W. Ward, *W.G. Ward and the Catholic Revival* (London 1912), 121–23.

was generally confined to the elementary level of the parishes, but also comprised high schools, as in France, and even a Catholic university, as in Belgium. These efforts, repeatedly encouraged by the Holy See, had undeniably positive results, in spite of the dangers already mentioned. C. Marcilhacy has pointed to the concordance between the establishment of parochial instruction and the growth of religious practice and noted that cause and effect became intertwined. "The Christian areas most readily accepted the religious teachers and they in turn strengthened the influence of religion on the population."[20]

The conscientious zeal with which many priests devoted themselves to the three-fold tasks of parish, organization, and education was unfortunately devoid of the pastoral imagination necessary to rethink classical methods, allowing for the changes which civilization was undergoing. The lack of initiative was particularly worrisome in light of the problems posed by the growth of the large cities. While at the beginning of the nineteenth century there were only 20 cities with more than one hundred thousand inhabitants, they numbered 149 at the end of the century, among them 19 cities with more than half a million inhabitants each. Together they housed 47 million people in contrast to only 5 million in 1801. Although ever larger numbers of people moved from rural to urban areas and were cooped up in them, new parishes were established only slowly and belatedly.

Of course, the situation was not the same everywhere. In Great Britain and the United States, where Catholicism as a consequence of Irish immigration had an essentially urban character, serious work was accomplished. But in France, Italy, Belgium, and Catalonia the considerable increase in the number of only nominal Catholics was not seen as a sufficient reason for the division of a parish. During the final years of the century evidently only distances and transportation difficulties were considered, and rural areas were assigned a clear preference in pastoral organization. Inasmuch as the ecclesiastical authorites were chiefly concerned with what were regarded as the irreducible needs of the rural population, from which the seminaries obtained a large number of their students, they raised the number of pastors in the growing urban parishes only meagerly. Needless to say, this neglect made personal contact between the priest and his flock increasingly difficult. Finally, looking at the continuing urban de-Christianization, which eventually could no longer be ignored, only very few leaders of the Church recognized that an increase in the number of churches or in the personnel of the parishes was much less important than the discovery and application of new methods of the apostolate, which alone would make it possible

[20] C. Marcilhacy, op. cit., 312.

to reestablish effective contact between the rootless masses of the proletariat and the Church.

Even though the clergy was very derelict in this respect, it at least quickly placed the periodical press in the service of the apostolate. During the second quarter of the century the clergy had encouraged the publication of periodicals for the educated class and had actively participated in such enterprises. Now a new, more popular type of publication was developed, the church newspaper, which indicated the hours of services in the various parishes of a district and listed the Catholic associations. This kind of publication had been in existence in Germany since the 1840s, including Catholic weeklies of general interest.[21] They appeared in France after 1850 and especially after 1862 (fifty-seven *Semaines religieuses* in twenty years).[22] In Belgium, the first religious weekly appeared in 1866 at Tournai and six others were added during the subsequent fifteen years. During the same time period there also appeared the first journals designed specifically for the clergy, such as the *Theologisch-praktische Quartalschrift* in 1848 in Austria, the *Mélanges théologiques* (concerned chiefly with practical questions of canon law) in 1847 in Belgium,[23] and the *Irish Ecclesiastical Record* in 1865. All of these initiatives bore witness to a rather active clergy increasingly cognizant of its responsibility.

[21] R. Pesch, *Die kirchlich-politische Presse der Katholiken in der Rheinprovinz vor 1848* (Mainz 1966); R. Pesch, "Das *Süddeutsche Katholische Kirchenblatt* 1841/45, ein 'klassisches' Beispiel für die Übergangssituation der katholischen Kirchenblattpresse vor 1848 in Deutschland," *FreibDiözArch* 86 (1966), 466–89.

[22] E. Poulat, *Les "Semaines religieuses". Approche historique et bibliographique* (Paris 1958); A. Boyer-Mas, *Centenaire de la "Semaine religieuse de Carcassone". Un siècle de vie diocésaine de l'Église 1868/1968* (Carcassone 1968).

[23] The *Mélanges théologiques* in 1869 became the *Nouvelle revue théologique* (see *NRTh* 56 [1929], 785–99).

CHAPTER 15

The Growth of Piety

The second third of the nineteenth century was accompanied by a profound and lasting change in piety, especially north of the Alps. Turning away from the strict and rather cold piety preached in Germany by Sailer and his people, in England by the former students of the seminary of Ushaw, in France by the products of Saint Sulpice, and in Italy by the spiritual heirs of the Jansenists of the Synod of Pistoia, within a decade or two there emerged a religiosity which was more sentimental and less rigoristic. It emphasized a more frequent reception of the sacraments and a greater exercise of external forms of piety. From now on piety was increasingly directed to the compassionate Christ pointing to his heart "which loves man," to Jesus, "the prisoner of love in the tabernacle," to Mary, among the more intuitive aspects of Notre-Dame de Lourdes, and to a number of popular saints like Saint Anthony and Saint Joseph, whom Pius IX in 1870 proclaimed as the patron of the Church. Pilgrimages, which had lost much of their importance in the eighteenth century, gained appeal again. In Germany, pilgrimages were made to Mariazell and Altötting; in Switzerland, to Einsiedeln; in France, to Chartres, Vézelay, La Sainte Baume, Rocamadour, La Salette, Lourdes, and Ars; in Spain, to Compostela, Montserrat, and Our Lady of Pilar; in Italy, to Assisi, Loreto, and Monte Gargano.

Several factors contributed to the change, beginning with the romantic enthusiasm for everything that was reminiscent of the Middle Ages: veneration of Mary, adoration of saints, veneration of reliquaries, processions, pilgrimages, and other public displays of faith. But a large role was also played by considered actions, such as the influence of Pius IX, who strongly promoted the new love of indulgences and who multiplied the opportunities for jubilee indulgences;[1] the influence of Roman-educated priests like the English Oratorian Frederick William Faber (1814–63) and the French prelate Gaston de Ségur (1820–81), who in many popular publications told the world why they were so delighted with expressions of popular piety in Italy; the influence of those who disseminated the works of Saint Alphonsus Maria de Liguori, which were suffused with confidence in divine providence, love for the Virgin Mary and the Eucharist; but chiefly the influence of the Jesuits with their optimistic and anti-Jansenist theology, whose impact was multiplied by the fact that they had become the chief preachers at retreats for secular and regular clergy.[2] It was partially owing to the Jesuits that piety became increasingly individualistic during the nineteenth century. But they also contributed much to the spread of the Sacred Heart of

---

[1] Jubilee indulgences were announced not only on the occasion of the Holy Years of 1850 and 1875, but also at the time of the elevation of Pius IX to the chair of Saint Peter (1846), at the time of the pronouncement of the Immaculate Conception (1854), after the journey of the Pope through the Papal State (1857), on the tenth anniversary of the definition of Immaculate Conception (1864), on the fiftieth anniversary of his ordination as a priest (1869), and on the twenty-fifth anniversary of his pontificate (1871).

[2] One example: In France, Pierre Chaignon (1791–1883) conducted more than three hundred retreats for priests. Chaignon also wrote a *Nouveau cours de méditations sacerdotales* (1857) in five volumes (see *DSAM* II, 438–39).

Jesus veneration, to the introduction of closed retreats, and to silent prayer according to the Ignatian method as interpreted by Father Roothaan.[3]

The new orientation of piety, branded by the adherents of the old customs as one of the main sins of ultramontanism,[4] naturally also had its drawbacks: it was frequently insipid and infantile, as many simplistic church hymns[5] and a whole range of devotional literature demonstrate; good intentions did not exclude mediocrity and bad taste. It allowed too much room for miracles, prophecies, reports of stigmatizations, and the so-called revelations of Anna Katharina Emmerick.[6] At the very time when German historians, with the tools of modern methodology, were in the process of rewriting Church history on the strict basis of authentic documents, devotional literature was written by authors who virtually had no such standards. According to the principle that any type of tradition must be accepted as long as it promotes piety, they became fervent defenders of the most improbable tales of saints, which the Bollandists and the Maurists had swept away a century earlier. The zeal with which piety was promoted narrowed even further the horizon of believers who had lost contact with Bible and liturgy. On the other hand it must be acknowledged that this development, no matter how inept, was the healthy reaction of Christian sentiment to an attenuated Christianity bordering on deism, which in the preceding century had gained many converts. Confessions on a regular basis and admonition to take Communion more frequently once again drew attention to the essentially sacramental character of Catholic life. The orientation of the new piety to the Christmas crib,[7] to the cross, to the heart of Jesus, and to the Eucharist once again placed into the limelight the central reality of Christianity: Christ as the true God and true human being, the incarnation of divine love, who is asking each person to love him.

---

[3] J. de Guibert, op. cit., 464–67.
[4] An especially aggressive example: E. Michaud, *L'esprit et la lettre de la piété* (Paris 1869). "This is the blemish of contemporary Phariseeism in the area of piety," he wrote to Döllinger (*ZSKG* 58 [1964], 313).
[5] C. Rozier, *Histoire de 10 cnatiques* (Paris 1966).
[6] They were first published by the poet Clemens Brentano, then by the Redemptorist K. E. Schmöger (3 vols. [Regensburg 1858–60]); immediately translated into several foreign languages, they were a great success. Concerning the question of to what extent Brentano interpolated the notes which he took at the bedside of the stigmatist with older writings (by Martin von Cochem, for example) and with his own imagination, historians are of divided mind. More recent historians are less strict than W. Hümpfner (See *DHGE* XV, 432–33).
[7] Concerning the veneration of the Childhood of Jesus in the 19th century, see *DSAM* IV 679–80.

Eucharistic piety as yet had no feeling for liturgical life as a community-embracing aspect; instead, Communion was seen as the wellspring of special grace and the real presence as the object of veneration. The reaction to the Jansenist strictures on Communion became increasingly pronounced after the middle of the century. In France, Monsignor de Ségur became the fervent and tireless herald of frequent Communion. His book *La très sainte communion* (1860), in which he advised the faithful to take Communion at least once a week and, if possible, every day or every second day, created a storm of indignation among the old clergy. But the book saw a printing of 180,000 copies in France, was translated into German, English, Spanish, Portuguese, and Flemish, and hailed in a papal brief (29 September 1860). The encouragement for such dissemination came chiefly from Italy. In his *Il convito del divino amore* (1868), Frassinetti defended frequent Communion in the name of Christian antiquity, and Don Bosco declared himself in favor of early Communion, which had been fashionable in southern Italy for a long time. In 1851 the Council Congregation corrected a chapter of the provincial synod of Rouen, which had forbidden children under thirteen to be admitted to Communion. In 1866 Cardinal Antonelli, in a letter to the French bishops, sharply condemned the custom of delaying First Communion until a later, precisely prescribed age.

Also from Italy came the various forms of venerating the sacrament of the altar. They became very popular during the second half of the nineteenth century and were adopted as their very own concern by a number of congregations founded during this period. The "Perpetual Adoration" officially recommended by Pius IX in 1851 was propagated in England by the two converts Faber and Dalgairns, was introduced in Canada by Monsignor Bourget, and was accepted in the United States in the decade between 1850 and 1860. In France, where it was already being employed in two dioceses at the time that Pius IX ascended the throne of Saint Peter, it was adopted by twenty dioceses between 1849 and 1860 and by another thirty-seven dioceses during the subsequent fifteen years. The Roman custom of nocturnal veneration was introduced in Germany by the Carmelite Hermann Cohen, a Jewish convert, famous preacher, and talented composer of several stirring hymns in honor of the Eucharist. In 1848 he introduced this custom in France with the assistance of Abbé de La Bouillerie; thirty years later the custom had been adopted by twenty dioceses and flourished particularly in northern France, thanks to the efforts of Philibert Vrau.

In the case of the veneration of the Sacrament of the Altar, emphasis for a long time had been placed on the atonement for the humiliation inflicted on Jesus Christ. In France, this concept received a new interpretation: Atonement should be made no longer merely for the lapses of individual sinners, but for the attitude of the authorities, who were surrendering society to laicism. Engendered by this view, there emerged, also in France, toward the end of the pontificate of Pius IX, the idea of holding international Eucharistic Congresses. The reason behind the idea was two-fold. The apathetic masses were to be brought closer to the Eucharistic Presence by the drama of grandiose rallies, and make Catholics, intimidated by anticlerical policies, aware of their numbers and their strength. The idea was inspired by the pious lay Christian E. Tamisier, who was encouraged by Monsignor de Ségur and two bishops from neighboring countries, Monsignor Mermillod (Fribourg, Switzerland) and Monsignor Doutrelouz (Liège, Belgium). The original thought was to exploit the new interest in pilgrimages for the staging of special pilgrimages of atonement to the major sites which had been honored by a Eucharistic miracle. Various experiments were conducted on the local level between 1874 and 1877 and, publicized by sermons and pamphlets, gradually acquainted Catholics with this new type of mass demonstration. E. Tamisier then conceived the idea of combining the rallies with scholarly conferences in order to fashion them into genuine congresses with an international reputation. This idea was first put into practice at Avignon in 1876 and at Lille in 1881.

The devotion to the Sacrament of the Altar emphasized an especially important aspect of nineteenth century piety: It was more attracted to a union with the suffering Christ than to the glorious mysteries of the Easter message. In the spreading devotion to the Sacred Heart of Jesus several facets of this form of piety were addressed: deep sympathy with the pain of the pitiable victim of Golgotha, as the Middle Ages had felt it; compensation for the betrayal and the grave insults of sinners in the spirit of love and atonement, in keeping with the message of Marguerite Marie Alacoque; and, finally, the apostolic desire to complete what was missing in the suffering of Christ by assuming, as Christ's successors, the sins of humanity and their consequences. All in all a rather paradoxical aspect of this bourgeois, individualistic, and positivist century. This atoning and apostolic longing unfortunately had a weak theological foundation, which took too little account of the Corpus Christi mysticism and was too sentimental; in France, furthermore, it also had political implications.[8] The parish missions of the restoration period had spread the devotion to the Sacred Heart of Jesus, until then limited to a

---

[8] The legitimists, whose influence in Catholic life was very great, did not forget that during his imprisonment Louis XIV had promised to dedicate France to the Sacred Heart and that the people from the Vendée went into battle with this divine emblem sewn to their chests. The papal Zouaves put it on their flag. But on the whole, the purely Christian zeal in connection with this veneration, which was growing more popular, won out over the monarchistic tendencies.

few elitist circles, to the parishes. The founding of Sacred Heart of Jesus associations, frequently encouraged by the bishops, often constituted the regular end or continuation of a parish mission. Many of the religious congregations founded during this period also emphasized the devotion to the Sacred Heart of Jesus.[9] But it was the pontificate of Pius IX which earned the nineteenth century the name of the "Century of the Sacred Heart," suggested by Monsignor d'Hulst. Actively promoted by the Jesuits, the Sacred Heart of Jesus devotion was eagerly taken up by the faithful. To them, the realistic mysticism of this veneration appeared as the best means to protest against the rationalistic and pleasure-seeking trends of their time. After 1870, a new element was added in France: the tendency to combine the atoning veneration of the Heart of Jesus with thinking of the "Prisoner in the Vatican" and with the recollection of national defeat. This dual aspect provided the grandiose demonstrations of Paray-le-Monial and, after 1876, of Montmartre, where the church of Sacré-Cœur in the first year of its existence witnessed the presence of three cardinals, twenty-six bishops, and 140,760 pilgrims, with a peculiar and frequently unpleasant coloration.[10]

Even if the impulse driving the masses to a veneration of the Sacred Heart of Jesus was emotional, a few theologians, following the example of Perrone, began to find a place for the idea of the Sacred Heart of Jesus piety in the doctrine of the "Word which had become man" and tried rather ineptly to define the theological basis for the devotion to the Sacred Heart of Jesus. Pius IX encouraged the movement. In 1856 he agreed to the wish of many French bishops and expanded the Sacred Heart of Jesus feast to the entire Church; in 1864 he beatified Marguerite Marie Alacoque.

The message of this mystic also contained a social element. Having long remained in the background, it was emphasized by ultramontane circles after the middle of the century. They tried to convince the entire world to acknowledge the absolute sovereignty of the Sacred Heart of

[9] See E. Bergh, "La vie religieuse au service du Sacré-Cœur," *Cor Jesu* II, 457–498. Two congregations specifically dedicated to the Sacred Heart were founded in 1800; they were the *Congregatio Sacrorum Cordium Jesu et Mariae* (Picpus Association) and Madeleine Barat's Society of Sisters of the Sacred Heart of Jesus. Between 1815 and 1846 there were: one congregation of priests, one congregation of brothers and fifteen congregations of sisters in France; two congregations of sisters and one of priests in Italy; and two congregations of sisters in Belgium. Under Pius IX, however, there were three congregations of priests and nine of sisters in France; one congregation of priests and ten of sisters in Italy; three congregations of sisters each in Belgium, Spain, and the United States; and one congregation of sisters each in Germany, Lebanon, and Australia. The first foundings in Austria and Latin America date from the pontificate of Leo XIII.

[10] See Lecanuet I, 208–11, 378–80.

Jesus and the obligation to strive for its social domination. In this context the musician Verboitte composed the famous motet: "Christus vincit, Christus regnat, Christus imperat." Two French Jesuits, F. -X. Gautrelets and H. Ramière, started the apostolate of prayer. They started an association whose members once a month prayed for a special and joint concern. The particular project was announced each month with the approval of the Pope and explained in the *Sacred Heart Messenger* (since 1861), a publication which twenty-five years later was issued in sixteen national editions and was duplicated in many other countries. The movement of the Consecration of the Sacred Heart was guided by the same considerations, although theocratic sympathies also played a role. After the consecration of individuals, families, and orders, states were also solemnly consecrated (Belgium in 1869, Ecuador and France in 1873), and the consecration of the entire world to the Sacred Heart of Jesus was also demanded. In 1875, Father Ramière accordingly handed the Pope a petition signed by 525 bishops. But Pius IX decided not to act hastily and merely asked the Congregation of Rites to send Father Ramière a dedication formula, approved by the Pope, and to encourage him to have it read publicly on 16 June 1875, the bicentennial of the appearance of Christ to the blessed Marguerite Marie Alocoque. The response which the proclamation received throughout the world was one of the most solemn events ever experienced by the Catholic world.

The rise in the devotion to Mary happened somewhat later than the Sacred Heart devotion. In Spain, the very strong current, sustained for two centuries, had grown feeble toward the end of the eighteenth century and was only revived in the twentieth century. In Italy, the few publications dealing with the matter were very weak from the theological point of view. In France, the Marian revival during the restoration period had remained superficial and without theological force, in spite of some pious initiatives like that of Pauline Jaricot's "Living Rosary." Then, within a quarter of a century, a complete turnabout occurred. It started with a number of appearances by the Virgin Mary.[11] In 1830 she appeared to Catherine Labouré,[12] signaling the beginning of the *Épopée de la medaille miraculeuse;* in 1836, also in Paris, she appeared to the pastor of Notre-Dame des Victoires, an appearance which resulted in

[11] It is remarkable that the nineteenth century saw the appearance of the Virgin Mary alone, without Christ.

[12] L. Misermont, *La blessée Catherine Labouré et la Médaille miraculeuse* (Paris 1933); W. Durrer, *Siegeszug der Wunderbaren Medaille* (Freiburg i. Br. 1947); M. Pélissier, *Le secret de la Reine* (Paris 1957).

the establishment of an archconfraternity which grew rapidly and within forty years numbered eight hundred thousand members;[13] in 1846 she appeared to two children at La Salette in Savoy;[14] and Bernadette Soubirous saw her at Lourdes in 1858.[15] Marian congregations sprang up in all countries and May prayers became very popular after the 1830s.[16] The discovery of Grignion de Montfort's manuscript on the *Traité de la vraie dévotion à la Sainte Vièrge,* the first publication of which took place in 1843, provided the cult of Mary with another impulse. The final impetus was the solemn definition of the Immaculate Conception in 1854, the product of a number of petitions.[17]

The intensity of the piety connected with Mary in the nineteenth century was also demonstrated by the names which religious congregations adopted when they were founded in this period. Between 1802 and 1898, not a single year passed that did not witness the founding of one or more congregations devoted to the Virgin Mary, with especially

---

[13] L. Blond, "L'abbé du Friche des Genettes" (unpubl. diss. [Paris 1960]); C. Savart, "Pour une sociologie de la ferveur religieuse, l'archiconfrérie de Notre-Dame des Victoires," *RHE* 59 (1964), 824–44.

[14] See E. W. Roetheli, *La Salette* (Olten 1945); La Bassette, *Le fait de La Salette* (Paris 1955); *Pour servir à l'histoire réelle de La Salette. Documents* I (Paris 1963); R. Laurentin in *RSPhTh* 48 (1964), 120–21.

[15] All earlier publications concerning Lourdes must be revised in light of the comprehensive documentation gathered by R. Laurentin in *Lourdes. Documents authentiques,* 7 vols. (Paris 1957–66); see also R. Laurentin, *Lourdes. Histoire authentique des apparitions,* 6 vols. (Paris 1961–64).

[16] In 1837, J. Beck published the first edition of *Der Monat Mariae;* by 1853 it had gone into its 5th edition.

[17] The petitions for the new dogma began in 1840 (fifty-one French prelates). The appeals resumed with the elevation of Pius IX in the face of resistance by Jansenist circles and German departments of theology. In response to an important memorandum by Perrone, Pius IX in June 1848 established a commission. In 1849, all bishops were consulted, and 90 percent of them were in favor of the petitions. The preparation of the bull of definition was rather difficult, and the bishops present in Rome participated in the final formulation. The definition was proclaimed on 8 December 1854 and occasioned rallies in the entire Catholic world (concerning some obstacles, see Aubert, *Pie IX,* 279, n. 3). Sources and literature: *Pareri dell'Episcopato cattolico, di capituli, di congregazioni, di università . . . etc., sulla definizione dogmatica dell'immacolato concepimento della B.V. Maria,* 10 vols. (Rome 1851–54); V. Sardi, *La solenne definizione del dogma dell'immacolato concepimento di Maria santissima, Atti e documenti* (Rome 1905); *DThC* VII, 1189–1218; Giulio da Nembro, *La definibilità dell'Immacolata Concezione negli scritti e nell'attività di Giovanni Perrone* (Milan 1961); W. Kasper, *Die Lehre von der Tradition in der Römischen Schule* (Freiburg i. Br. 1962), 231–66; G. Frenaud: *Virgo Immaculata. Acta Congressus 1954* II (Rome 1956), 337–86; J. Alfaro in *Virgo Immaculata. Acta Congressus 1954* II (Rome 1956), 201–75; R. Aubert in *EThL* 31 (1955), 63–99; G. Russo in *Asprenas* 10 (1963), 59–93.

numerous foundings in the decades 1830–40 and 1850–60.[18] But there were dark sides to the cult of Mary as well. The forms assumed by the Marian rejuvenation were extremely uneven, sometimes infantile, and sometimes of such a nature that the Holy Office was compelled to take action. Mariological writings were of sad mediocrity.[19] Only a few theologians came up with valuable contributions, among them Passaglia and Malou on the occasion of the definition of Immaculate Conception, and Newman and Scheeben somewhat later. But theirs were isolated accomplishments and received little attention at the time.

However, not only Mariological literature was generally mediocre. This was true as well for all of the spiritual literature of that time, especially in the Latin countries, where the tastelessness of the "art of Saint Sulpice" had its counterpart in the "ghastly pamphlets of piety," so aptly castigated by Ernest Hello. The best pieces that showed up in France prior to 1860 were the many reprints of works of the French school of the seventeenth century, moderately well adapted to the prevailing taste of the common people. The works of the Jesuit Jean Nicolas Grou, a disciple of Jean Joseph Surin, fell into the same category. After 1860, the situation gradually improved thanks to the efforts of Lacordaire, Gratry, Perreyve, and Monsignor de Ségur. De Ségur was inspired by Saint Francis de Sales, whom A. J. M. Hamon had brought back into favor. Of great significance was Monsignor Charles Gay,[20] whose great book *De la vie et des vertus chrétiennes* (1874), imbued with the spirituality of Saint Paul and Saint John, experienced an unexpected and encouraging success.

The situation was somewhat better in England and Germany. England produced some original works, generally written by converts whose Anglican background had given them a much more pronounced knowledge of the Bible and patristics than was the case with most Catholics on the continent. Newman, Manning,[21] Dalgairns, and Faber deserve mention. Faber's book especially, translated into various languages, spread

---

[18] See E. Bergh in *Maria* III, 465–88. France is in the lead, followed by Belgium, Italy, and Spain. Record years were 1850 and 1854; the former saw sixteen new congregations devoted to the Virgin Mary, the latter, fourteen.

[19] This remark was made by R. Laurentin (*Maria* III, 19). It had earlier been made by an unquestionable witness: Louis Veuillot (*Mélanges:* 2nd ser., V [Paris 1860], 605–6); confirmation in J. Pintard, *Bulletin de la Société française d'études mariales* 17 (1960), 119–50.

[20] On Charles Gay (1815–92), see B. du Boisrouvray, *Monseigneur Gay,* 2 vols. (Tours 1922).

[21] He emphasized the working of the Holy Ghost in the leadership of the Church and in the sanctification of souls; *The Temporal Mission of the Holy Ghost* (1865); *The Internal Mission of the Holy Ghost* (1875).

in all of Europe and the Anglo-Saxon countries a spirituality which was inspired by the Italian school of Saint Liguori and the great Oratorians of the seventeenth century. In Germany, Görres's important book *Die Christliche Mystik* inspired a series of scholarly works on speculative mysticism. Scheeben's first books, *Natur und Gnade* (1861) and *Die Herrlichkeiten der göttlichen Gnade* (1863), were actuated by the Greek Fathers, with whom his teacher Johannes Franzelin had acquainted him. But these were publications which were hardly accessible to the broad public. Yet, Germany could take the credit for introducing liturgical piety to the large mass of the faithful.

The liturgical renewal took its rise from the French Benedictine Dom Guéranger. The treasures which he collected in the volumes of his *Année liturgique*[22] unfortunately remained restricted to a small elite in his country, probably because his perspective, as well as that of his contemporary in the field of architecture, Viollet-le-Duc, too strongly reflected the interests of an archeologist who was interested in the most complete restitution of the Middle Ages possible.[23] In the German-speaking countries, the liturgical question had been raised in the 1830s and 1840s from the pastoral point of view by men like A. A. Hnogek, whose Josephinist *Christkatholische Liturgik* (5 vols. [Prague 1835–42]) is still of interest even today, and Anton Graf and Johann Baptist Hirscher, whose attempts to have laymen admitted to the chalice and to use vernacular languages in the Mass met strong opposition. The return to liturgical piety occurred in Germany during the following generation in a form which closely corresponded to medieval tradition. In 1864, Maurus Wolter, one of the founders of Beuron Abbey, translated into German the famous *Exercitia spiritualia* by Saint Gertrude von Helfta, which were oriented toward annual and daily spiritual observations. In a long enthusiastic introduction, Wolter acquainted the German public with the movement started by Dom Guéranger in France and explained its principles. In the following year he published the small book *Choral und Liturgie,* quoting whole pages from the introduction to *L'année liturgique,* and devoting a large amount of space to a summary of Guéranger's principal thought concerning the incomparable wealth of the spiritual food involved in liturgy. His booklet had a great response among large segments of the population. Parallel to it, Wolter wrote a patristic commentary on the Psalms, *Psallite sapienter* (5 vols. [1871–

---

[22] The reprints indicate a stronger interest only after 1875. See C. Savart, "Vie spirituelle et liturgie au XIXe siècle," *MD* 69 (1962), 67–77.

[23] The positive aspects of the liturgical impact of Dom Guéranger are treated in O. Rousseau, op. cit., 1–24, 45–65, and F. Cabrol in *Liturgia* (Paris 1930), 864–72; the negative aspects are dealt with by H. Leclercq, *DACL* IX, 1636, and L. Bouyer, *La vie de la liturgie* (Paris 1960), 23–29.

90]), for monks in order to induce them to bring their spiritual life in step with liturgical life. What appears to us as a matter of course was very necessary at that time, for the influence of Ignatian methods had so profoundly affected the spiritual atmosphere of most of the Benedictine monasteries that worship often completely lacked the liturgical spirit. Following the example of his teacher Maurus Wolter, Dom Gérard van Caloen, a monk at Maredsous, in 1871 published the first *Missel des fidèles* in Belgium.[24]

[24] O. Rousseau, "L'œuvre liturgique de Monseigneur Van Caloen," *QLP* 17 (Louvain 1932), 79–91; A. Haquin, *Dom Lambert Beauduin et le renouveau liturgique* (Gembloux 1970), 8–13.

CHAPTER 16

The Backwardness of Religious Studies and the Controversy about the "German Theologians"

In his famous lectures to a gathering of Catholic scholars at Munich in 1863, Döllinger stated that only Germany was "tending the two eyes of theology, history and philosophy, with conscientiousness and thoroughness." Comparing the two competing schools of thought, the "German" one and the "Roman" one, he asserted that the former was defending Catholicism with rifles, while the latter was still using bows and arrows. His allegation created consternation in many circles. Today, with the benefit of a century of perspective, it must be admitted that Döllinger was right. Even if the erudite historian exaggerated the theological decadence of the Latin countries slightly, it can not be denied that it was in a wretched condition. Although the efforts of the German scholars in teaching and research were not totally perfect, there is no doubt that the departments of religious studies in German universities were able to maintain and to enlarge the lead which they had gained during the first half of the century. Outside of Germany there were hardly any centers of Catholic scholarship which could measure up to the achievements of Protestants and rationalists.

Religious Studies Outside of Germany

All observers, including those most devoted to the Holy See, were unanimous in deploring the extraordinary nadir of scholarship in Rome under Pius IX, the absence of organized libraries, and the lack of interest on the part of the papal leadership in teaching and research.[1] Yet, as paradoxical as it may sound, it was in Rome that the most serious work outside of Germany was conducted. This was in part due to foreigners working in Rome. One of them was the French Benedictine Pitra, who published patristic editions (philologically not entirely free of errors), and numerous important works on Eastern canon law and Byzantine hymnology. Another was the German Oratorian Augustin Theiner,[2] prefect of the Vatican Archives, a somewhat sloppy and restless spirit, who published several editions of sources which have been useful to this day. But there were not only foreigners. An associate of Cardinal Mai, the Barnabite Vercellone (1814–69), published some valuable Biblical textual criticisms. Christian archeology was Rome's very own science. It had awakened to new life under the pontificate of Gregory XVI, encouraged by this far-seeing Pope, Canon Settele, and the Jesuit Giuseppe Marchi. After the reorganization of the Museum Kircherianum, Marchi somewhat clumsily had begun the scientific exploration of the catacombs, which had been totally neglected since the seventeenth century. Pius IX sanctioned the new beginning with the creation of the *Commissione di archeologia sacra* in 1852. Marchi's work was continued by Father F. Tongiorgi, until 1886 professor at the Roman College, but Marchi's preferred student was Giovanni Battista De Rossi.[3] Even though after Fausti's evaluation he can no longer be regarded as the originator of Christian archeology, De Rossi was responsible for its strict scientific methodology, and he defined the rules of Christian epigraphy to such an extent that he became its virtual originator. After he had published the *Inscriptiones christianae Urbis Romae* (1857) and founded the *Bollettino di archeologia cristiana* in 1863, De Rossi wrote the comprehensive *Roma Sotteranea cristiana*. It revived the whole history of the Roman Church from its beginnings, dealing with its doctrine, its hierarchy, its liturgy, and its art. According to Cardinal Pie it was a new *locus theologicus*, but with exemplary scholarly scrupulousness De Rossi refused to exaggerate the meaning of facts for apostolic purposes. His treatment was the best possible one at that time, and H. I. Marrou said: "The great Mommsen acknowledged his work by refusing

---

[1] Some quotes are listed in Aubert, *Pie IX,* 184–85. In a letter of 25 February 1861 Ventura stated: "Everything of a scholarly nature emanating from Rome is wretched and proves that Rome has not the slightest understanding of the great questions of our time."

[2] On Augustin Theiner (1804–74), see H. Jedin in *ArSKG* 11 (1953), 247–50; see also the biography of his brother Anton by H. Hoffmann in *ArSKG* 9 (1951), 74–143, 10 (1952), 226–78, 11 (1953), 169–209, 12 (1954), 199–232, 13 (1955), 228–67.

[3] On Giovanni Battista De Rossi (1822–94), see *LThK* IX, 58–59 and H. Leclercq in *DACL* XV, 18–100.

to include the Christian inscriptions of Rome in the program of the *Corpus inscriptionum latinarum.* It was the greatest honor that an Italian, Roman, and Catholic scholar could be accorded."[4]

There was also the Roman College. If its teaching was more akin to that of high schools than that of German universities,[5] and if the majority of the faculty was not known for its excellence, dogmatic theology at least was brilliantly represented. Passaglia,[6] Perrone's best-known student and, according to W. Kasper, one of the most brilliant theologians of the nineteenth century, taught at the college from 1844 to 1858. His theology rested on an infinite knowledge of the Greek Fathers, and was also influenced by Petau, Thomassin, and J. A. Möhler. He made up for his unfamiliarity with German by having his young colleague Clemens Schrader keep him informed of the important studies appearing in German.[7] Subsequently, Schrader largely followed the doctrines and methods of his older confraternity brother, albeit more scholastically and rigorously. When Schrader was appointed professor at Vienna (1857) and Passaglia was forced to leave Rome because of his involvement in the Italian cause, their work at the Collegium Romanum was carried on by the Austrian Johannes Baptist Franzelin.[8] He worked out a theology less striking than Passaglia's, but one that was more elegant and exact. It was based on criticism of the texts, monuments, and facts, utilizing the latest archeological discoveries, and employing his thorough knowledge of Eastern languages and the products of the German historical school. The solid and original works of these three teachers gave large room to positive theology and to speculation; their speculative theology was more concerned with an organic synthesis of the facts of faith based on the Bible than with a philosophical exploration of the truths of revelation.

Compared to their work, the *Instructions synodales sur les erreurs du temps présent* by Monsignor Pie,[9] long regarded as one of the masterworks of French theology in the nineteenth century, made a pitiful impression. Fighting against the naturalism of the time by presenting

[4] *Aspetti della cultura cattolica nell'età di Leone XIII* (Rome 1961), 81.

[5] Interesting details in the memoirs of Franz Hettinger, who studied there from 1841 to 1845: *Aus Welt und Kirche* I (Freiburg i. Br. 1911), chap. 1.

[6] On Carlo Passaglia (1812–87), see *LThK* VIII, 133. C. G. Arévalo drew attention to the significance of his book *De Ecclesia Christi,* in which he emerges as a precursor of the doctrine of the Mystical Body.

[7] Concerning Clemens Schrader (1820–75), see *LThK* IX, 482; *DThC* XIV, 1576–79; F. van der Horst, *Das Schema über die Kirche auf dem I. Vatikanischen Konzil* (Paderborn 1963), 52–56, 153–60.

[8] On Johannes Baptist Franzelin (1816–86), see *LThK* IV, 272–73, and G. Bonavenia, *Raccolta di memorie intorno alla vita dell'Em. card. Franzelin* (Rome 1877).

[9] Concerning his theological work, see Hocedez II, 265–67 and passim.

the supernatural aspects of Christ's passion and salvation, Pie's instructions were long on beautiful rhetoric and short on scholarly spirit. They were written in order to oppose writers like Cousin, who as yet had little influence on the younger generation. Although imbued with great powers of persuasion, they are a testament to the tremendous weakness of Catholic thought in France under the Second Empire. The theologians were still using the oratorical methods of romanticism, while the thinkers of this period were increasingly influenced by the results of the positive sciences and the detailed analyses of historical criticism. Characteristic in this context is the weakness of the refutation of Ernest Renan's basically rather superficial *Vie de Jésus* (1863).

In the field of Church history, the inferiority of Catholics during the pontificate of Pius IX, with the exception of Germany, was most clearly visible. In Spain, the tradition of Flórez and Villanueva was interrupted for almost a hundred years. Italy also, aside from Christian archeology, lagged behind the eighteenth century. Even respectable scholars like C. Cantù and L. Tosti did not progress beyond the old concepts of *historia magistra vitae* with its emphasis on presentation at the price of critical content. True, there were in France two or three good books on positive theology. This does not include Freppel's studies of the Church Fathers, which were nothing more than eloquent popularizations, but refers to the *Histoire du dogme catholique pendant les trois premiers siècles* (1852) by Ginoulhiac and the two volumes of Monsignor Maret's *Du concile général* (1869), which displayed a good knowledge of Christian antiquity and some critical faculties. But Maret, like Bossuet, whom he followed without being too dependent on him, did not have sufficient talent for a genuine scholar and tended more toward synthesis than toward analysis.[10]

A good number of clerics used their free time for scholarly activity; most of them confined themselves to local researches and historiography, and as a consequence of their faculty training they rarely produced anything that exceeded the mediocre. More serious was the fact that the idea of apostolicity of the French Church, which had been discredited by the scholars of the seventeenth and eighteenth centuries, was taken up again in 1835 by the Sulpician Faillon, was again taught in the seminaries, found entrance in the history books, was supported by many bishops, and seemed to triumph with the appearance in 1877 of *Les Églises du monde romaine* by the Benedictine Chamard.[11] At the same time, the lack of associates forced the monks of Solesmes to discontinue

[10] R. Thysman in *RHE* 52 (1957), 401–65.
[11] A. Houtin, *La controverse de l'apostolicité des Églises de France au XIXe siècle* (Laval 1900).

the publication of *Gallia christiana*. This backwardness in the scholarly field was not even balanced by acceptable works of synthesis. The *Histoire générale de l'Église depuis la création jusqu'à nous jours* by Abbé Darras (1825–78) in forty-four volumes, enjoying great popularity in seminaries and parish houses with the blessing of *L'Univers,* revealed a total ignorance of the most elementary principles of the historical method.[12]

The situation was somewhat better in Belgium. The university of Louvain continued to produce respectable studies in the areas of Eastern studies, patrology,[13] and historical evaluations of canon law. The Bollandists, after having been restored in 1837, published six volumes of the *Acta sanctorum* between 1845 and 1867 and included Slavic sources and Celtic hagiography in their fields of endeavor. Their inspiration, however, the tireless V. de Buck, remained a gifted improvisor; only after his death in 1876 was the work of the group placed on a firm foundation by his successor, Charles de Smedt.[14]

In philosophy, the "other eye" of theology, the situation was more complex. The systems which in their struggle against rationalism denigrated the powers of reasoning to an excessive degree lost a part of their prestige after the condemnation of Lamennais and the difficulties experienced by Bautin. But many Catholics saw the interventions of the Holy See merely as warnings against excesses, and traditionalism continued to exist in attenuated form until the Vatican Council. This was the case especially in Italy and France, where traditionalism was represented by A. Bonnetty and the brilliant Italian polemicist Ventura,[15] whom the events of 1848 had forced to take refuge in France. In his *Annales de philosophie chrétienne,* Bonnetty continued to pursue his intention of proving the continued existence of original revelation. He sharply criticized the fateful influence of Aristotelian rationalism on the "hardly Christian" language of scholastic theology. Ventura conceded that the existence of God, the immortality of the soul, and the foundations of morality, once they are established, can also be proved by reason, but in contrast to the "Semi-Pelagians of Philosophy" argued the necessity of revelation for their primary knowledge and the importance of God-given language for the thorough study of these concepts. Traditionalism continued to be successful in spite of the criticism ad-

[12] *DHGE* XIV, 89–91.
[13] See *EThL* 9 (1932), 663–70, 678–80, 689–92. Concerning Henri Feye (1820–94), professor of canon law from 1850 until 1885, who supervised several doctoral theses which attracted the attention of the academic world, see *DHGE* XVI, 1359–60, and Schulte III, 295.
[14] P. Peeters, *Figures bollandiennes contemporaines* (Brussels 1948), 11–26.
[15] L. Foucher, op. cit., 238–49.

vanced by the defenders of the rights of reason from among the Jesuits[16] and the Sulpicians and in spite of a very hesitant renewed intervention of Rome.[17] Its success stemmed not only from the continuing fascination exercised by Lamennais upon his followers, but also from the agreement of the traditionalist system with an ultramontane attitude and the authoritarian inclinations of many Catholics after 1848. It was from this perspective that the attempts of the French ontologists derived their meaning, even though in contrast to Rosmini's system theirs found only limited acceptance. It started with a group of intelligent priests,[18] who recognized the danger posed by the growth of an authoritarian principle in philosophy for the future of Catholicism in a society determined to have intellectual autonomy. Dissatisfied with both the idealistic German systems and a positivism which closed its eyes to metaphysical problems, they attempted to restore intellectualism in a Platonic and Augustinian tradition. But the general of the Jesuits in 1850 put a quick end to the success of the ontological doctrines at the training center at Vals.[19] While the attacks against Rosmini twice, in 1854 and 1876, ended with a preliminary acquittal,[20] the Neo-Scholastic opposition in 1861 succeeded in obtaining from the Holy Office the condemnation of seven characteristic theses of French ontologism[21] and, somewhat later, of the writings of professor Ubaghs.[22] Ubaghs was the chief representative of ontologism coupled with traditionalism, which had become the dominating doctrine in the departments of theology and philosophy at the University of Louvain.

[16] P. M. A. Chastel, S.J. (1804–61), was particularly fierce and received the approval of Liberatore and Passaglia and of the *Magister Sacri Palatii* for his book *De la valeur de la raison humaine* (1854) (see L. Foucher, op. cit., 250–52, and Sommervogel II, 1089–91).

[17] Bonnetty was asked in 1855 to agree to four theses (see *ASS* III, 224), the first three of which were determined by those which Bautain had signed twenty years earlier. The fourth thesis acknowledged the value of Scholastic philosophy.

[18] The most important among them were Baudry and Branchereau at Saint Sulpice and Maret and Hugonin at the Sorbonne; the system was accorded great sympathy by the Jesuits of Vals, several Sulpician seminaries, and, thanks to *Ami de la religion* and *Correspondant,* by the educated public (see L. Foucher, op. cit., 176–95).

[19] Burnichon III, 140–61.

[20] H. Reusch, *Der Index* II (Bonn 1885), 1142–44; also Aubert-Martina, 812–19.

[21] See *ASS* III, 204–6. On the discussions following these interventions, see *DThC* XII, 1047–55, and J. Kleutgen, *L'ontologismo e le sette tesi censurate dalla S. Inquisizione* (Rome 1867).

[22] See *ASS* III, 206–24. On the beginnings of Ubaghs' case, see above, chap. 3, n. 34. The question was raised again in 1858 by the bishops of Liège and Bruges, former students at the Gregoriana; they wished to counteract Cardinal Sterckx, whom they accused of not taking account of the views of the other bishops in the matter of supervising the orthodox direction of the Catholic university. They assured themselves of the

The reaction to traditionalism and ontologism was a result of the renascence of Scholasticism. It was promoted by the conservative wing of romanticism, which was captured by the ideas and institutions of the Middle Ages. Prior to 1870, many adherents of a return to Scholasticism were not yet genuine Neo-Thomists. Rather they were eclectics, desirous of a return to the philosophy of the Middle Ages, who wanted to rethink this philosophy, in the light of Suarez in Spain, and in the light of Cartesianism in France and Italy. Gradually the number of people desiring a return to a genuine Thomism increased. In Germany, this was the case from the 1850s onward; in Spain, there was the circle led by the Dominican Gonzalez, who founded the journal *La ciencia cristiana* in 1873; in France, there was Abbé Hulst's circle; in Belgium, there was the group led by the Dominican Lepidi, professor and regent of the research department at the training center at Louvain. The main impact occurred in Italy. While the Roman College remained a citadel of Suarezianism until the election of Leo XIII, the Jesuits of the *Civiltà cattolica* became fervent propagandists of Thomism, especially Father Liberatore. The two chief centers of Thomism were the Collegio Alberoni at Piacenza and the Jesuit Collegio Massimo and the Liceo arcivescovile at Naples. In 1846, G. Sanseverino[23] established the Accademia tomista there and published the journal *Scienza e fede;* after his death in 1865, S. Talamo filled his place. There were also other centers, at Bologna for example, where the Jesuit Cornoldi published the journal *La Scienza italiana.* He was particularly interested in the harmony of science and faith. In Perugia, Cardinal Pecci, assisted by his brother, a Jesuit, and some Dominicans, founded the Accademia San Tommaso, where he pursued his program of reforming ecclesiastical studies.

From the quantitative point of view, it must be noted that the Catholic authors of the third quarter of the nineteenth century devoted their best efforts to apologetics. For after the revival of religiosity and of sympathy for the medieval Church, characteristics of the generation of romantics, the intellectual world, beginning with the middle of the

---

support of P. Perrone and the *Civiltà cattolica.* The Pope was persuaded to transfer the examination of the case from the Congregation of the Index to the Holy Office because Cardinal D'Andrea, the prefect of the Index, was an opponent of the Jesuits and too favorably disposed toward the people at Louvain. Interventions by Cardinal Sterckx, who wanted to save the reputation of the university, delayed a decision by several years. But in 1864 the Holy Office declared the corrections made by Ubaghs as insufficient and in 1886 condemned his books for good, referring to the condemnation of the seven ontological theses in 1861.

[23] His *Philosophia christiana cum antiqua et nova comparata* (7 vols. [Naples 1862–72]), finished by his student N. Signoriello, is a remarkable work of clarity, depth, and historical information.

century, experienced a quick and different type of development. The historical claims of Christianity and the traditional authority of the Bible were questioned in the name of historical criticism and as a result of the discoveries of paleontology and Near Eastern archeology. The problem of the transcendence of Christianity was immediately raised by the comparative history of religions, and soon the foundations of theism and the idea of religion were attacked by Feuerbach and the liberal Hegelians. Materialistic explanations of the universe were widely disseminated in Germany by men like Ludwig Büchner, Karl Vogt, and Ernst Haeckel. Spencer continued the traditions of English empiricism and propagated the Darwinian evolutionary interpretation of the world, which theologians rejected categorically.[24] In the France of the Second Empire, Auguste Comte's thoughts combined with English agnosticism and German materialism and were exported under the name of "positivism."

Under these circumstances it was not surprising that apologetics increased in significance in the course of the nineteenth century. The study of dogma, hitherto regarded as the essential task of theologians, began to appear to most Catholic thinkers as less urgent than the defense of religion and the foundations of Christianity. Even when they studied theology, they did so from an apologetic perspective. The speculations of Hermes and Günther, formally belonging to the field of dogmatics, were in reality guided by the aim of making dogma acceptable for people who had been won by modern philosophy. The scholarly studies at Tübingen and Munich as well were more directed toward a defense of the great Christian and Catholic theses against rationalistic and Protestant criticism than they were concerned with the origins of the Bible of the Fathers.

To be sure, apologetic works continued to be written and testified to the apostolic zeal of their authors; but most of them suffered from a total lack of adaptation. Elegantly in Germany, more superficially elsewhere, they incessantly repeated the same classical arguments. In view of the intellectual atmosphere of the time, they no longer had any impact; people were no longer receptive to them. It is sad to note the paucity of Catholic studies prior to the final twenty years of the century which competently treated the principal problem of adapting the Christian faith to the new science-based thinking. A first step was taken in 1875 by the Jesuit Carbonelle with the founding of the Scientific Soci-

---

[24] The first intervention by the ecclesiastical magisterial office concerning the theory of evolution was the declaration of the Cologne provincial synod of 1860. It stated that the view that the human body had emerged from an earlier natural state was clearly at variance with Holy Scripture and the faith.

ety of Brussels, which drew together Catholic scientists from various countries. Two years later, the *Revue des questions scientifiques* was established as the organ of the society.

Among the apologists who endeavored to understand the views of those whom they wished to convince was G. Bonomelli, whose *Il giovane studente* (3 vols. [1871–74]) was one of the best books of this type at the time.[25] In Belgium, the Redemptorist Victor Dechamps[26] developed the so-called *Méthode de la providence,* which between 1857 and 1874 he presented in a number of books and vigorously defended against sharp criticism. In France, there were Father Félix and Alphonse Gratry. Between 1853 and 1869, the Jesuit Félix preached the conference sermons at Notre-Dame in Paris[27] and in them developed an apologetics which took account of contemporary realities. He analyzed the trends of the time with astuteness, especially the enthusiasm with which progress was regarded. He tried to show that Christianity, far from hindering any legitimate striving of humankind, was actually the only way for it to achieve what it was blindly seeking. Gratry[28] tried in vain to realize an idea by Lamennais to gather a number of priests in a kind of *atelier apologétique* by reestablishing the *Oratoire de France*[29] in 1852. In many of his publications he anticipated the path taken during the next generation by Ollé-Laprune and Blondel. According to L. Foucher, Gratry's was the best and most comprehensive attempt at a Catholic philosophy in France during the 19th century, but Antonin Gilbert Sertillanges judged that he formulated too much like a writer and thought too much like a poet to be numbered among the great philosophers.

One man surpassed all others by the power and force of his genius and his ability to look into the future: John Henry Newman.[30] Even

---

[25] C. Bello, *G. Bonomelli* (Brescia 1961), 52–55.

[26] On Victor Dechamps (1810–83), one of the most famous Belgian preachers, who in 1867 became archbishop of Mechelen, see M. Becqué, *Le cardinal Dechamps* (2 vols. [Louvain 1956]) and *L'apologétique du cardinal Dechamps* (Paris and Louvain 1949). The core of his thought was presented in the *Entretiens sur la démonstration catholique de la révélation chrétienne* (1857).

[27] P. Fernessolle, *Les conférenciers de Notre-Dame* II (Paris 1936), 59–136.

[28] On Alphonse Gratry (1805–72), see A. Chauvin, *Vie du Père Gratry* (Paris 1911) and L. Fouché, op. cit., 197–236.

[29] See in addition to the biography of Gratry (136–90: "L'idéal," "La réalité"), A. Perraud, *L'oratoire de France au XVIIᵉ et au XIXᵉ siècle* (Paris 1866) and G. de Valroger, *Le Père de Valroger* (Paris 1911). He managed to gather a few young people around him, but Abbé Pététot, in charge of the organization, in spite of Gratry's protests preferred to emphasize high school instruction.

[30] On John Henry Newman (1801–90), who in 1845 converted to Catholicism, see volume VII in this series, p. 406. On his theological concepts: R. A. Dibble, *John Henry Newman. The Concept of Infallible Doctrinal Authority* (Washington 1955); J. Stern, *Bible*

more than Möhler he paved the way for the acceptance of new demands and fresh values of human reason in the service of faith. In his *Essay on the Development of Christian Doctrine* (1845) he emphasized the value and the need for historical thought; in his *Grammar of Assent* (1870) he wrote of the value of the spontaneous power of reason, based on a convergence of judgments and practical life experience; he demanded a "Dialectic of Conscience" and the psychological preparation of people for the acceptance of faith justified by reason. In his essay *On Consulting the Faithful in Matters of Doctrine* (1859), the *Letter to the Duke of Norfolk* (1875), and two volumes of the *Via Media* (1877) he brought out the importance of the meaning of Holy Scripture and the Christian Fathers for the Christian mystery as the basis of all religious knowledge. Unfortunately, there was no one at the time to follow him on the paths whose importance for the future Newman anticipated. Moreover, his employment of the essay made his studies less accessible to professional theologians. Lastly, there were the suspicions which were cast on his orthodoxy. They were one of the most unpleasant aspects of the intellectual policy of the Roman Curia under Pius IX and persisted until the elevation of Leo XIII.

Scholastics and Germanics vs. the "German Theologians"

One of the major achievements of the Tübingen School was that Catholic dogma was rethought with pronounced attention given to the historical dimension, the discovery of which was a main characteristic of the intellectual life of the nineteenth century. What counted from now on was not merely critical scholarship or chronology, but a sense of becoming and the awareness that events, institutions, and doctrines are what they really are only when they are placed in the context of time and when their historical development is taken into consideration. Following the example of Drey and Möhler, theologians increasingly discussed the consequences of seeing Christian events and Christian revelation in the context of history. This did not mean that speculative considerations disappeared, not even among those who remained tied to Scholastic tradition. This was shown by the enthusiasm displayed for Günther's ideas as well as by the teachings of Kuhn at Tübingen. Still, as the century advanced, theological sciences became more concerned with historical theology and became more interested in the vitality of dogma than its metaphysics. The redirection to a less speculative theol-

---

et tradition chez Newman. Aux origines de la théorie du développement (Paris 1967); B. D. Dupuy, *Textes newmaniens. VII. Lettre au Duc de Norfolk* (Bruges and Paris 1970); L. Bouyer, *L'Église de Dieu* (Paris 1970), 135–52.

ogy than had been pursued during the first half of the nineteenth century was hastened by apologetic interests. While Protestant historians developed a critical method which enabled them to question many traditional attitudes toward the origins of Christianity and the Middle Ages, some university departments, especially at Tübingen, developed a radical exegesis and a Hegelian interpretation of the history of dogma, originated by Ferdinand Christian Baur. In close contact with their opponents at the universities, Catholic theologians grasped quickly that it was essential to enter the arena on which the battle was fought, to fight them with the same weapons employed by them, i.e., with facts, texts, and documents, and to revise positions incompatible with the facts.

In the field of exegesis, the following people were active: August Bisping,[31] whose *Exegetisches Handbuch zum Neuen Testament* (9 vols. [1854–76]) remained for long the only complete commentary from the Catholic point of view, even if it lacked originality; the Munich professors for Old and New Testament studies, Daniel-Bonifaz Haneberg[32] and Franz Xaver Reithmayr;[33] and Peter Johann Schegg,[34] who wrote a *Leben Jesu* (2 vols. [1874–75]). There were also two rather lackluster treatments of biblical theology, P. Scholz's *Handbuch der Theologie des Alten Bundes* (2 vols. [1861–62]), and J. Lutterbeck's *Die neutestamentlichen Lehrbegriffe* (2 vols. [1852]). These publications were rounded out by some essays written with the intention of reconciling the reports of Genesis with modern scientific discoveries.[35] Among them were *Bibel und Natur* (1860, 1870) by Franz Heinrich Reusch, and *Die biblische Schöpfungsgeschichte* (1867, 1872) by Johann Baptist Baltzer. However, seen as a whole, the achievements of Catholics, even though not insignificant, remained far behind those of the Protestants.

In the area of the history of dogma and Church history, on the other hand, good work was done. This was the case at Tübingen, where Karl Joseph Hefele[36] worked on studies ranging from the apostolic Fathers to Cardinal Ximenes and wrote his monumental *Conciliengeschichte* (7 vols. [1855–74]). Also at Tübingen there was a group of young scholars who wrote for the *Theologisches Quartalschrift* and

---

[31] On August Bisping (1811–84), professor at Münster, see *DHGE* IX, 10–11.

[32] Concerning Daniel Bonifaz Haneberg (1816–76), see *100 Jahre St. Bonifaz in München* (Munich 1960), 29–36, 61f.

[33] On Franz Xaver Reithmayr (1809–72), see *LThK* VIII, 1155.

[34] On Peter Johann Schegg (1815–85), see *LThK* IX, 379f.

[35] *DThC* VI, 2340–46.

[36] On Karl Joseph Hefele (1809–93), professor of Church history and patrology from 1840 until 1869, when he was appointed bishop of Rottenburg, see A. Hagen, *Gestalten aus dem schwäbischen Katholizismus* II (Stuttgart 1950), 7–58.

employed the new critical methods in order to delineate the stages of progress in Christian thought. Another center of activity was Munich, thanks to the great influence of Ignaz Döllinger, the uncontested leader of the German Catholic historical school.

In the course of the events of 1848, Döllinger emerged as one of the most important Catholic leaders both with respect to politics and religion. But he was disappointed by the trends of the Catholic movement under the leadership of the men from Mainz and the growing influence of the Jesuits in the Church. He withdrew from public life and devoted himself to scholarly work, always from an apologetic point of view. *Hippolytus und Callistus* (1853), a masterful example of historical criticism receiving the acclaim of all German scholars, was designed to shore up the Catholic conscience in the face of objections to the papacy which Protestants like Christian Karl von Bunsen believed to have found in the recently discovered *Philosophoumena*. Similarly, *Heidentum und Judentum. Vorhalle zur Geschichte des Christentums* (1857), the first scholarly Catholic attempt to present the origins of Christianity within their historical context. He wanted to demonstrate that, historically speaking, no development of Greek or Jewish origin could explain the rise of Christianity. His *Christentum und Kirche in der Zeit der Grundlegung* (1860), a book with a genuine religious flair, contained a number of passages concerning the papacy which were clearly directed against Protestants.[37] Even more than through his publications, Döllinger's influence, whose tremendous extent it is difficult to understand today, was spread by his lectures and was carried by his students to many professorships at universities in Germany, Austria, and Switzerland. In his personal contacts, the richness of his thought, the clarity of his views, and the simple demeanor of the man captured his discussion partners, and his correspondence touched upon the scholarly works written in German, English, and French.

Döllinger, Hefele, Kuhn, Günther, and most of their colleagues and students who were in close contact with the academic world were primarily animated by the desire to liberate Catholic intellectuals from the inferiority complex which the flowering of Protestant and rationalistic scholarship had given them. They expected to accomplish their aim by suggesting to them to compete with the same weapons and to give them the feeling of complete intellectual freedom, aside from the relatively few questions of dogma. They hoped to win a degree of influence for the Church in the world of the mind which corresponded to the influence which the Church was in the process of gaining through public political action.

---

[37] The 2nd edition (1868) was revised in a direction less favorable to the papacy.

But a part of the German clergy, among them Bishop Ketteler of Mainz and his advisers Lenning, Heinrich, and Moufang, saw matters differently. They had in mind the mass of the Catholics, the peasants, the craftsmen, and tradesmen, whose Christian beliefs, consolidated by a pious and active clergy, was to find expression in a mighty movement of well-disciplined associations. These were to subordinate themselves to the Holy See, able to carry out the decisions of the hierarchy down to the lowest levels of society. The supporters of this movement were more interested in having good priests than educated ones, and there-fore were very much opposed to the German system, which forced young clerics to study in the departments of theology attached to public universities. They wanted to replace this system with the system of diocesan seminaries used in France and Italy, the same system which Ketteler had reintroduced in his diocese. Beyond this, many of them wished to withdraw young laymen from the atmosphere of public uni-versities, where the vast majority of the faculty were Protestant.[38] They called for the creation of a Catholic university[39] which for the German Catholics was to play the same role as the University of Louvain in Belgium.[40] These plans were supported by all people and publications associated with Bishop Ketteler. Headed by Döllinger, Ketteler and his supporters were opposed by all other German Catholics who realized that the faith needed clergy completely conversant with the latest knowledge. They also recognized the danger of educating young Catholics in complete isolation, as it would deny them access to all of the scholarly tools which only the universities could provide. They feared the cutoff of Catholics from the intellectual life of their time, if the point of view of Ketteler should prevail. Döllinger's fear was the

[38] Prussia in 1864, with a population of 7 million Catholics and 10 million Protestants, had only 55 Catholic professors among its 556 university professors.

[39] The idea of a Catholic university was raised in 1848 and assumed tangible form by 1861. But several obstacles and, after 1870, the *Kulturkampf* led to an abandonment of the plan (see G. Richter, *Der Plan zur Errichtung einer katholischen Universität in Fulda* [Fulda 1922]).

[40] A similar aim was pursued at this time in other countries as well. In Great Britain, the Irish bishops with the support of Wiseman founded a Catholic university at Dublin in 1851, but the enterprise failed after a few years in spite of Newman's efforts (see F. McGrath, *Newman's University, Idea and Reality* [London 1951] and A. Gwynn in *Newman-Studien* III [Nuremberg 1957], 99–110); Manning attempted to found a Catholic college at Kensington, but it also existed only for a few years (see E. Purcell, *Life of Cardinal Manning*, I, 495–505). In France the Catholics succeeded, especially due to the efforts of Monsignor Dupanloup, in obtaining permission through the law of 12 July 1875 for the establishment of free universities. They immediately founded five universities at Paris, Lille, Angers, Lyon, and Toulouse (see Lecanuet I, 251–68, 501–10, and A. Baudrillart, *Vie de Monseigneur d'Hulst* I [Paris 1912], 277–382).

greater as his opponents openly demanded a return to Scholasticism, failed to comprehend the urgency of the problems raised by historical criticism, and believed that speculative thought in Germany had reached a dead-end street with Kant's philosophy.

A return to Scholasticism was the major concern of the Mainz journal *Der Katholik,* which was edited by professors appointed by Ketteler in 1849 when he reopened the Mainz seminary. The pioneers of German Neo-Scholasticism were the dogmatist Johann Baptist Heinrich[41] and the philosopher Paul Leopold Haffner.[42] At Bonn, the movement was supported by the young belligerent layman Franz Jakob Clemens.[43] At Munich, the *Historisch-politische Blätter,* Archbishop Reisach, a former student at the German College in Rome, and Vicar General Windischmann were behind the movement. Windischmann had long pointed to the dangers of Güntherianism. In Austria Neo-Scholasticism was encouraged by Cardinal Rauscher, who in 1857 appointed the Jesuit Schrader and the Dominican Guidi to positions at the University of Vienna. After 1857 Neo-Scholasticism had an active center in the department of theology at the University of Innsbruck, which was directed by the Jesuits. It was in fact the Jesuits who everywhere became the most ardent supporters of the Neo-Scholastic restoration, assisted by the success of Kleutgen's books *Die Theologie der Vorzeit vertheidigt* (5 vols. [1853–70]) and *Die Philosophie der Vorzeit vertheidigt* (2 vols. [1860–63]).[44] In an original and thorough fashion, Kleutgen rethought the doctrines of Saint Thomas, but he also tackled problems which Thomas had not foreseen, and occasionally was guided by Suarez as well. He demonstrated that Thomas's traditional doctrines could be applied to new problems and how they fit into other great philosophical systems. It was his great achievement that he cleared away antiquated methods which made them unacceptable to modern minds.

The fact that many people favored this Scholastic orientation is in part explained by the real weaknesses of theological instruction at the universities, as for example in the rationalistic and historicistic approach of some professors, but especially in the neglect of the leadership role,

[41] Johann Baptist Heinrich (1816–91). His *Dogmatische Theologie* (6 vols. [Mainz 1873seqq.] indicates the dual purpose of making theology kerygmatic and of supplementing scholastic presentations with a serious study of Holy Scripture and the Fathers.
[42] On Paul Leopold Haffner (1829–99), see L. Lenhart in *Jahrbuch für das Bistum Mainz* 8 (1958–60), 11–117.
[43] On Franz Jakob Clemens (1815–62), active member of the Catholic Association, see *Der Katholik* 42 (1862), I, 257–80 and *LThK* II, 1230.
[44] On Joseph Kleutgen (1811–83), a German Jesuit residing in Rome, see F. Lakner in *ZKTh* 57 (1933), 161–214 and *LThK* VI, 340. Even if his books were largely ignored by the academic world, they nonetheless found a great echo among Catholics. His impact was strengthened by the translation of *Philosophie der Vorzeit* into Italian and French.

which in theology must be assigned to the magisterial office of the Church guided by the Holy Spirit. In the subsequent generation, Matthias Joseph Scheeben showed that Neo-Scholasticism was not only of defensive utility in the fight against the excesses of the "German theologians", but also produced works of real spiritual and religious value. Karl Werner's books proved that adherence to Scholasticism did not have to exclude solid historical scholarship.[45] Yet it must be conceded that most of the products of Neo-Scholasticism remained on a rather low level. Even when they attempted to integrate historical knowledge—which almost always was only secondhand—with the speculative treatises of classical authors, they failed to integrate them truly and to evaluate them historically and theologically. The retreat to the bastion of a timeless valid system cost theology its actuality and representation in the modern world. L. Scheffczyk was totally correct when he wrote: "There is no possible doubt that in comparison with the youthful freshness, the variety, and the enthusiasm of theological thought in the time of Johann Sebastian Drey and Anton Günther, the products of Neo-Scholasticism are cautious, uniform, and sober; a coldly didactic method of interpreting eternal truths replaced original and subjective thought; speculation designed to create unity and an organic overview was replaced with objective detail studies, and a universal openness to all currents of the spirit gave way to defense and polemicism."

This last aspect was particularly regrettable, as the opposition to university theology came in part from men who were not merely worried by the occasional excesses of "German scholarship," but were indifferent or hostile to scholarship in general. This was, of course, not true of all of them. Some harbored genuine admiration for scholarship, as long as it was orthodox; but many former students of the Collegium Romanum, called "Germanics" because they had resided in the Collegium Germanicum when they were in Rome, failed to make use of the perspectives which the teaching of Passaglia and Franzelin had made available to them. They refused to acknowledge that the advances of historical methods required new attitudes in many different areas. Even less did the survivors of the fideistic and traditionalist currents, influential in Archbishop Geissel's circle, favor the aim of the "German theologians" of confronting Christian thought with the great Neo-Kantian philosophical systems. They refused to undertake a serious review of the texts which modern historical criticism required. These texts were

---

[45] On Karl Werner (1821–88), see *LThK* X, 1056, He was professor of moral theology and exegesis at Sankt Pölten and Vienna and was known chiefly as a historian of medieval thought.

usually adduced by the Catholics for the defense of their traditionalist positions, but were too often confused by them with ecclesiastical tradition itself.

More serious was the fact that many defenders of Neo-Scholasticism, irritated by the contempt in which the academic world held them, tried to strengthen their arguments and objections by an appeal to the supreme foreign ecclesiastical authority. The notes which they increasingly sent to Rome were not always generated by the desire for truth but stemmed from personal intrigues and rivalries. In 1854, unjustified accusations on the part of the Mainz circle forced one of the best Church historians, Schwartz, to resign from his chair at Würzburg. The first great success of the scholastic reactionaries was the condemnation of Güntherianism in 1857. The Neo-Scholastics were supported by the nuncio at Munich in their increasingly bitter attacks, and in the Roman Curia they found allies in Cardinal Reisach and Kleutgen. As consultant to the Congregation of the Index, Kleutgen was particularly influential.

Günther's condemnation encouraged the ultramontanes to attack those theologians and philosophers who insisted on continuing their studies without taking account of ecclesiastical directives. F. J. Clemens's *De sententia scholasticorum philosophiam esse theologiae ancillam* (1856) became the manifesto of this faction. When Kuhn asserted the right of philosophy to be independent, Clemens was assisted by *Der Katholik,* which kept a close eye on doctrinaire currents.[46] The front of the universities was breached in 1854 with the appointment of Heinrich Denzinger, a former student at the Gregoriana, to the chair of dogmatics at Würzburg.[47] He was soon joined by two other "Romans": by the Church historian Joseph Hergenröther[48] and the apologist Franz Hettinger.[49] All three of them worked in the spirit of total subjection to ecclesiastical authority. Denzinger's collection of ecclesiastical decisions, *Enchiridion Symbolorum et Definitionum* (1854), reminded the

[46] G. B. Guzzetti, op. cit., 79–86.

[47] On Heinrich Denzinger (1819–83), see the memoirs of his brother in *Der Katholik* 63 (1883), I, 428–44, 523–38, 638–49, and *NDB* III, 604.

[48] On Joseph Hergenröther (1824–90), see S. Merkle, *Aus der Vergangenheit der Universität Würzburg* (Berlin 1932), 186–214, and *LThK* V, 245–46. He was not very good in the classroom but a worthy scholar who complemented his Roman studies with doctoral work at Munich under Döllinger. His 3 volumes on Photius established him as a scholar. His *Handbuch der Kirchengeschichte* (3 vols. [1876–80]) was "generally admired because of his sovereign mastery of the material, even if the apologetic direction and the dependence on other treatments of Church history were criticized" (Bigelmair).

[49] On Franz Hettinger (1819–90), a well-balanced personality of universal erudition, acuity of mind, and great writing ability, see A. Chroust, ed., *Lebensläufe aus Franken* II (Munich 1921), 202–15. His *Apologie des Christentums* (2 vols. [1863–67]) deservedly remained a classic for more than sixty years.

German theologians of the importance of the decisions of the magisterial office, including those which were not infallible.

Numerous German professors in the name of academic freedom refused to bow to the authority of the Church, unless it was a question of defined dogma. Their attitude created consternation in Rome, where academic concerns were of little interest and the struggle against liberalism was in full swing. In this connection, many works were placed on the Index after 1857.[50] In 1862, Pius IX directed a letter to the archbishop of Munich in which he discussed the errors of the Munich professor Jakob Frohschammer[51] and lamented that Frohschammer was not the only one who demanded "a freedom to write and to teach with which the Church hitherto had been unacquainted."[52] Separated by the geographical distance, Rome's distrust of German academics increased and eventually encompassed even Germany's leading professors, including Döllinger.

For several years, the eminent historian had been the subject of accusations.[53] He, in turn, was offended by Rome's centralizing tendencies, which coincided with the aggressive behavior of the Neo-Scholastics. The most zealous among the ultramontanes suspiciously watched this theologian, who used such un-Roman methods, tended to think that serious ecclesiastical studies were only conducted at the German universities, and considered the growing influence of the former students of the Collegium Romanum in Germany's ecclesiastical life as a victory of obscurantism. For the time being, however, at least until his two lectures which he gave in 1861 at Munich, the ecclesiastical authorities respected his stance. The two lectures had essentially a pastoral goal. Convinced of the impending decline of the Papal State, he wanted to calm the Catholics with the assertion that by no means would such a decline constitute a decline of the papacy as such, no matter what the Protestants were saying. But he did not confine himself to the presentation of positive views concerning the importance of papal primacy and the recognition of the attempts by Pius IX to bring about

---

[50] F. H. Reusch, *Der Index* (Bonn 1885), 1125–32. Compared to the indictments, the number of condemnations was relatively small and the caution of the Congregation of the Index was acknowledged by scholars who held little sympathy for the Scholastics, such as Flir (*Briefe aus Rom* 47) and Kuhn (*ThQ* 108 [1927], 215).

[51] On Jakob Frohschammer (1821–93), professor of philosophy, who after his indictment in 1857 defended positions held by liberal Protestants and subsequently became an Old Catholic, see *LThK* IV, 397; Hocedez II, 60–68; and J. Stracke, "Ecclesiae judicium de Jakob Frohschammer doctrina circa mysteria" (unpubl. diss., Rome 1934). His real attitude toward the freedom of Christian philosophers probably should be reexamined.

[52] Brief *Gravissimas inter* (11 December 1862) in *Acta Pii IX,* 548–56.

[53] Aubert, *Pie IX,* 203–4.

improvements in the Papal State. He explained the hostility toward the secular power of the papacy with the obvious deficiencies of the archaic and clerical papal government. Many observers interpreted Döllinger's remarks as open support for Cavour and some seized this opportunity to take action against him. They organized a protest campaign and tried to discredit the scholar in the eyes of the Catholic people, who were still devoted to the Pope in spite of his shortcomings. Dismayed, Döllinger tried to correct the situation, but was not successful in eradicating the initial negative impression. Subsequently, criticism of his theological positions became more overt, the critics being secure in the knowledge of having the ear of all those who placed the defense of the privileges of the papacy at the top of their objectives.

It annoyed Döllinger that his prestige among Catholics had been hurt and it displeased him that his academic work was questioned by absolutely incompetent people. Yet in spite of his growing hostility to the policies of the Curia, he remained a devoted son of the Church. But it bothered him that the German Catholic intellectuals were fighting one another instead of making common front against the increasingly radical attacks by secular academics. Thus, a reconciliation of the two Catholic groups was urgently necessary. For years the idea of a congress of German Catholic scholars had been in the air. Therefore Döllinger, Alzog, and Haneberg, ignoring the skepticism of the Tübingen group, the reserve of the Mainz circle, and the open hostility of the Jesuits, invited the Catholic scholars of Germany, Austria, and Switzerland to gather in Munich in September 1863.[54] In the meantime, unfortunately, the distrust of Döllinger had grown, primarily because of his book *Die Papstfabeln des Mittelalters* (1863). In it he revealed the legendary character of some of the traditions of the medieval papacy and used the weaknesses of Pope Liberius and Pope Honorius as arguments against the thesis of papal infallibility.

In his remarkable opening address on "The Past and Present of Theology,"[55] justifiably described by Goyau as a "Declaration of Rights" of theology, Döllinger described various methods of theology and demanded complete freedom of movement whenever faith was not directly affected. "For scholarship, such freedom is as essential as air is for the body," he said, and called for purely scholarly weapons in the struggle against theological error, instead of ecclesiastical censures. Just as among the Hebrews prophets and priestly hierarchy had existed side

---

[54] On this congress, see *Die Verhandlungen der Versammlung katholischer Gelehrter in München* (Regensburg 1863). Also: J. Friedrich, *Ignaz von Döllinger* III, 270–354; K. Müller, *Leben und Briefe von J. T. Laurent* III (Trier 1889), XIII–XXVIII; H. Lang in *HJ* 71 (1952), 246–58; G. Martina in *AHPont* 6 (1968), 350–51, n. 39.

[55] Slightly weakened text in *Verhandlungen . . . ,* 25–29.

by side, there should be in the Catholic Church as well an extraordinary power in addition to regular authority. This, he asserted, is public opinion, the molding of which was a matter for theologians. Inasmuch as at the same time he spoke of the complete decline of theology in the Latin countries, he created the impression that he was demanding the actual intellectual leadership of the Church by the German theologians. The theologians from Mainz and Würzburg did not allow such assertions to pass without protest, but finally a vague compromise concerning the rights of authority and of liberty was formulated.

Many participants returned home convinced that the chief objective of the congress of scholars, namely an understanding with the "Romans," had been effected. The first reaction of Pius IX, who had feared that the congress might degenerate into a declaration of war against the Roman congregations, also was rather favorable. But the reports of the nuncio and other opponents of Döllinger about the atmosphere at the congress, at which the students of Döllinger constituted a majority, and the text of Döllinger's addresses produced an immediate change in the attitude of the Pope. For a time, placing the proceedings of the congress on the Index was even considered. Ultimately, however, Pius IX only sent a brief[56] to the archbishop of Munich in which he denounced the attacks on Scholasticism and deplored that a gathering of theologians had taken place without explicit request from the hierarchy, "whose task it is to guide and supervise theology." He stated further that Catholic scholars were not only bound by solemn definitions, but actually were obligated to take into consideration the magisterial office, the decisions of the Roman congregations, and the common doctrines of theologians. His disapproval was supplemented a few months later by a regulation which made future gatherings of this kind virtually impossible.

Döllinger's attempt at conciliation had failed, and the tone of the polemics of the two camps immediately doubled in stridency. On one side were the men who were convinced that the chief task was to regain the respect of the educated Catholics for the Church by painstaking applications of the historical method and by a presentation of Catholic dogma convincing for modern philosophical attitudes. The Tübingen group also shared this dual ideal, but disapproved of the radicalism of the Munich group and assumed a more passive stance. The aggressive vanguard of the Munich group consisted of Döllinger's friends. Soon they had their own journal, the *Theologisches Literaturblatt,* founded in 1865 by the Bonn professor Franz Heinrich Reusch. On the other side was the "Roman" party, which thought that the chief task was to pro-

[56] Brief *Tuas libenter* (21 December 1863) in *Acta Pii IX* III, 636–45.

vide Catholics with a complete doctrinary system of unquestionable orthodoxy. Their main centers were the seminary at Mainz, the seminary at Cologne, where Scheeben taught dogmatics, the seminary at Eichstätt, where Albert Stöckl inaugurated philosophical instruction of not only a Scholastic but of a Thomist character, and the training center of the Jesuits, where Joseph Florian Riess in 1864 founded the *Stimmen aus Maria Laach* for the purpose of commenting on the *Syllabus.*

Only a few people succeeded in maintaining good relations with both sides. Even rarer were the men like Karl Werner, A. Schmidt, and Franz Xaver Dieringer, who attempted to mediate between the two parties. Tension increased from year to year and the smallest incident gave rise to sharp polemics which held no trace of disinterested scholarship or of the milk of human kindness.

Döllinger, constantly worried about the serious threat to the freedom of Catholic scholars, grew bitter when he noticed that his popularity was disappearing. It looked as though he himself were trying to justify the attacks of his opponents by announcing loudly his compromises with Protestant scholars and anticlerical administrators and by his malicious comments on everything that emanated from Rome. Some of his disciples, like Johann Nepomuk Huber, Johannes Friedrich, and Alois Pichler, the "young Munich School," as it was called, created consternation through their arrogance and their lack of Catholic sympathies.

The responsibility for these conditions was to be found on both sides. The intransigence and narrow-mindedness of many defenders of the Roman position contributed a great deal to worsening an already delicate situation. There were indeed moderate men among them, people like Joseph Hergenröther, Franz Hettinger, and Matthias Joseph Scheeben. But there were also men whose fanaticism had deplorable consequences. They included Kuhn in their attacks and thus carried suspicion to the Tübingen school. They prevented the Tübingen group from exercising the moderating influence of which it would have been capable. It did not suffer from the historicism and the rationalism of the Munich school and could have supplied what the Neo-Scholastics lacked in the way of Biblical and historical thought and a sense of mystery.

The Altercation between Catholicism and Liberalism

The confrontation of liberal ideas with the traditional positions of the Church, which had started in the 18th century and continued to grow with the Declaration of the Rights of Man and the Citizen in 1789, reached its peak under the pontificate of Pius IX. Shortly after the end of the idyll of 1848, the antagonism on both sides increased on the ideological and practical levels. The revival of the Roman Question could not but inflame the hostility further. Even though its true roots were found in the national enthusiasm of the Italians and partially also in the political ambitions of Piedmont, the sovereignty of the Pope was officially questioned in the name of the new freedoms—the right of peoples to self-determination and the liberal concept of the state. The two problems could very well have been kept separate, as proved by the attitude of the people led by Montalembert and Dupanloup; but in fact they were looked upon as intertwined.

CHAPTER 17

The Roman Question

From the Papal Restoration to the Italian War

The restoration of the authority of the Pope in the Papal State after the brief interlude of the Roman Republic had taken place in a clearly reactionary atmosphere. The new form of government, worked out by Cardinal Antonelli in a number of laws passed between 10 September and 24 November 1850 followed the principles of Cardinal Bernetti. The secretary of state subsequently regarded him as his mentor in political matters. He envisioned a number of reforms, but they consisted exclusively of improvements of existing institutions and produced no genuine changes in structure. In the failure of 1848 Antonelli saw final proof of the incompatibility of the maintenance of the temporal power of the Pope with even only a partial liberalization of the governmental system. For this reason he rejected all entreaties by the Paris and the Vienna governments at least to take the path of a moderate constitutional reform. Yet it must be acknowledged that Antonelli's government had its merits on the level of administrative accomplishments. De

Rayneval,[1] French ambassador to Rome, mentioned that Antonelli started or inspired a number of steps which demonstrated great vitality and good will. This view was confirmed by the investigation of Dalla Torre,[2] even if he is too apologetic. Other foreign observers also noted with satisfaction that some of Antonelli's measures were far-sighted. But many of these endeavors were only partially realized and remained on the level of the enlightened despotism of the eighteenth century and were not able to prevent people's minds from being dominated by the two thoughts of a liberal growth of political institutions and the realization of Italian unity.

The first years were relatively calm. But after the Congress of Paris (1856) the problem of necessary reforms in the Papal State was pushed into the foreground of the concerns of the Italian public by the skillful propaganda organized by Cavour and supported by England. In spite of the misbehavior of the Austrian troops charged with maintaining order in the northern provinces, the common people, who could note a slight increase in their standard of living and appreciated the popular modesty of the Pope, actually were not terribly dissatisfied. The middle class, on the other hand, found it increasingly more difficult to endure a government which not only denied it any political responsibility but also filled all important positions with clerics, and whose legislation was still oriented to medieval canon law. This was clearly demonstrated to the West in 1858 with the unfortunate Mortara case.[3]

That was the situation in the summer of 1859 when the Italian war broke out. Several provinces revolted, encouraged by the Austrian defeat, and demanded to be annexed to the Kingdom of Piedmont, in which throughout the entire country all those people had placed their hopes who wished to see a unified Italy governed according to modern constitutional requirements. Assured of the support of Napoleon III, who for several reasons wanted to see the temporal power of the Pope maintained, albeit in a smaller, essentially only symbolic state,[4] the

---

[1] His report of 1856 was printed in *Recueil des traités . . . concernant l-Autriche et l'Italie* (Paris 1859); see A. M. Ghisalberti in *ADRomana* 75 (1952), 73–101.

[2] *L'opera riformatrice e amministrativa di Pio IX fra il 1850 e il 1870* (Rome 1945); see also M. Roncetti, *Bolletino della Deputazione di storia patria per l'Umbria* 43 (1966), 139–74. An example on the local level: M. Pellegrini, *Le condizioni economiche, sociali, culturali e politiche di Jesi dal 1849 al 1859* (Jesi 1957).

[3] On the case itself, see R. De Cesare, *Roma e lo Stato del Papa* I (Rome 1907), 278–94 and G. Masetti Zannini, *RSTI* 13 (1959), 239–79. On the reaction: G. Volli in *Bolletino del Museo del Risorgimento* 5 (Bologna 1960), 1085–1152; J. Altholz in *Jewish Social Studies* 23 (1961), 111–18 (for England); G. Braive in *Ris* 8 (1965), 49–82 (for Belgium); B. Korn, *The American Reaction to the Mortara Case* (Cincinnati 1957).

[4] As it was expressed in the pamphlet *Le Pape et le Congrès*, which Viscount de la Guéronnière wrote in December 1859 according to his instructions: "The city of Rome has this connotation . . . that the smaller the territory, the greater the ruler."

Piedmontese government tried to exploit the situation to the utmost. Victor Emmanuel demanded from Pius IX not only that he accept the situation in the Romagna, which spontaneously had placed itself under Piedmontese sovereignty, but he also asked him to turn over effective governmental powers in Umbria and the Marches, which were to remain under the nominal sovereignty of the Pope. But the Vatican refused any accommodation. On 19 January 1860[5] Pius IX in his encyclical *Nullis certi verbis* exposed to the eyes of the Catholic world "the sacrilegious attack on the sovereignty of the Roman Church" and demanded the "unlimited restitution" of the Romagna. After the Pope had been assured once more by Cardinal Antonelli that there was only one solution, i.e., "to restore what had been taken," he on 26 March placed under the ban the usurpers who had violated the laws of the Holy See.[6]

The Roman Question had now become acute. Even though it was more a problem for diplomacy than for the Church, it was nevertheless a heavy psychological burden for the remaining eighteen years of the pontificate of Pius IX. The opposition of the Vatican, which was more one by Antonelli than by Pius IX, to any compromise could do nothing but confirm the attitude of those who suspected the Church of being fundamentally opposed to the ideas of the modern world. It contributed its considerable share to the further reduction of papal prestige in non-Catholic and indifferent circles. Additionally, the Roman Question preoccupied the energies of the most dynamic Catholics in France and Italy with a political problem and for a whole generation distracted them from religious concerns. To be sure, the Roman Question contributed to tying all engaged Catholics even more closely to the Pope, and in this way it played an important role in the ultimate defeat of Gallican and Josephinist tendencies; but it did so in an atmosphere of passionate involvement, which on its part contributed to giving the ultramontanism of the time an emotional coloration which was rather objectionable from the doctrinal point of view.

From the Establishment of the Kingdom of Italy to the Occupation of Rome

While Antonelli, in the hope of saving what could be saved, cautiously engaged in diplomatic negotiations with the French government, his attempts were compromised by the Pope himself. The plan was hatched by Monsignor de Merode, a decided opponent of Napoleon who was destined to raise the ante in the ambiguous game which Napoleon III

[5] *Acta Pii IX* III, 129–36.
[6] *Ibid.* III, 137–47.

during the past months had played with the Holy See. For several months de Merode had tried to convince the Pope to give up the protection of the French troops and to raise his own army by recruiting volunteers from the entire Catholic world. Antonelli was too much the realist to approve of this plan. But Pius IX, deeply disappointed by Napoleon's unreliable policy, was not prepared in this time of crisis to heed the cautious secretary of state. He did not remove him, as was expected by many, from the general direction of affairs, but ordered his opponent Merode, together with the legitimist French general Lamoricière, to organize the new army.[7] But within a few months the campaign of Garibaldi and the fall of the Kingdom of Naples hastened events. Italian troops quickly occupied Umbria and the Marches after they had defeated the small army of Lamoricière at Castelfidardo. A short time later a national parliament proclaimed Victor Emmanuel King of Italy.

The Papal State was now reduced to Rome and its environs (about seven hundred thousand inhabitants contrasted to the earlier 3 million), and there was little hope of ever regaining the lost provinces. The moment seemed to have come to bow before the inevitable and to seek a reasonable compromise. This was the opinion of the French government, but also of many Italian Catholics and even clerics. Cavour, who could count on active sympathy in the Curia, was eager to complete his work by offering Rome an agreement on the following basis: the Pope was to renounce voluntarily any temporal power, which in any case would soon be a matter of the past; Italy in turn would renounce the last remaining traces of regalistic influence on ecclesiastical life and replace earlier legislation by the concept of a free Church in a free state. But from the beginning the negotiations suffered from a lack of willingness on the part of Antonelli and in March 1861 ended in total failure.

The position of the Holy See was now determined for a long time to come: it consisted of total rejection. Antonelli, failing to recognize the degree to which political conditions and ideas had changed during the preceding ten years, was still hopeful of saving the Pope's temporal power. He expected to be able to do so through a repetition of the policy which had been successful at Gaeta, namely an appeal to the Catholic powers on the basis of legitimacy and the immutable right of the Pope to his state. But for this policy to be effective it was necessary to remain on the foundations of international law without causing the impression that the possibility of a compromise would be considered.

---

[7] See G. Carletti, *L'esercito pontificio dal 1860 al 1870* (Viterbo 1904). On the regiment of papal Zouaves, see E. de Barral, *Les zouaves pontificaux* (Paris 1932) and Cerbeland-Salagnac, *Les zouaves pontificaux* (Paris 1963).

By assuming this strictly legalistic position one could gain time by placing the European governments in a difficult position. The secretary of state, secretly encouraging Neapolitan resistance, probably hoped, as did so many others at the time, that the young Italian state would quickly break apart again and present new possibilities.

For Pius IX the problem was of a totally different nature. In contrast to his secretary of state, he had preserved deep sympathies for the national aspirations of Italy. But for him the question was not one of the independence of Italy from Austria, but the enforced centralistic unification under the leadership of anticlerical Piedmont which led to the dissolution of the Papal State. Pius IX was not so much concerned with temporal power for its own sake as that he saw in it the indispensable guarantee of his spiritual independence, and the outraged reaction of Europe's ultramontane press confirmed him in the belief that this power was something for which he had to answer to the Catholics of the whole world and of which he could not dispose according to his private wishes. He confronted the realists, who tried to convince him that it would not be possible to avoid the necessity of negotiations for long, with a mystical confidence in providence. It was fed by the conviction that the political upheavals, which included him, were merely another episode in the great struggle between God and Satan, which, of course, could only end with the victory of the former.

The conflict between a liberal Italy and the Pope's temporal power was transformed in his eyes into a religious war in which resistance to what increasingly he liked to call "the revolution" was no longer a question of the balance of diplomatic, military, and political forces, but a question of prayer and trust in God. The almost mystical fervor with which some of the leaders of the *Risorgimento* conducted the struggle against the demands of the Church confirmed him in the conviction that all of this was preeminently a religious problem. In order to emphasize in solemn fashion the religious character of the Roman Question, he in May 1862 convoked a gathering of more than three hundred bishops.[8] In response to a papal allocution, in which Pius IX attacked the rationalism and materialism of the period and sharply criticized the Italian government, they agreed to an address which, while it did not condemn liberalism as unequivocally as the Pope had desired, described papal temporal power as an indispensable institution of providence for the well-being of the Church. It refrained, however, from raising temporal power to a dogma of faith.

---

[8] Concerning this assembly, see in addition to N. Wiseman, *Rome and the Catholic Episcopate* (London 1862) and *CC* 5. R. II (1862), 705–46; Aubert, *Pie IX*, 96–97, 248–49; J. Maurain, *La politique ecclésiastique du Second Empire*, 612–15; de Montclos, 184–87.

But neither the protests of the bishops nor the on the whole rather sparse recruitments of papal mercenaries could stop the unavoidable course of events. Nor could this be done by the protestations of the Catholic press, which only with difficulty could conceal[9] the indifference of the Catholic masses or the more or less open sympathies of a number of Italian faithful or even priests who were forced into a painful conflict of conscience between their patriotic strivings and the directives of the Church. The unexpected death of Cavour on 6 June 1861 and the fact that his successors lacked diplomatic skill, together with the hesitant policy of France, effected a brief delay of the decision. Napoleon III, forced to take account of Catholic agitation and hoping for the election of a Pope more willing to make concessions than the ailing Pius IX, did not wish to offend anyone. But finally, on 15 September 1864, he signed a convention with the government at Turin[10] in which it obligated itself to respect the remnants of the Papal State; the agreement included the possibility of the recall of the French garrison from Rome.

[9] With respect to the "conciliatory" movement, varying in temperament and orthodoxy, which with the support of Minister Ricasoli spread among a part of the Italian clergy after 1860, see the balanced and well-documented article by M. -L. Trebiliani in *RStRis* 43 (1956), 560–75 and the treatment by M. Themelly, "La riforma cattolica dell'Italia moderna prima del Sillabo," *XIIe congrès international des Sciences historiques* (Vienna 1965), I, 161–75.

The movement of patriotic priests, which was successful especially among those who had been involved in the events of 1848 as well as among the lower clergy in the south, centered on the ex-Jesuit Passaglia and his newspaper *Il Mediatore* (1862–66) in the north, and on L. Zaccaro in the south. A petition to the Pope in 1862 contained 8,943 signatures, including 767 of regular clergy; but in the following year, disavowed by the bishops, it experienced a noticeable decline. Concerning the attitude of the clergy to Italian unification and to the question of temporal power, which differed according to region, see M. Bertazzoli, "I conciliatoristi milanesi," *SC* 110 (1962), 307–30; C. Castiglioni in *Memorie stor. della dioc. di Milano* 9 (1962), 9–39; E. Passerin d'Entrèves, "Il clero lombardo dal 1848 al 1870," *Il movimento unitario nelle regioni d'Italia* (Bari 1962), 44–49; A. Pesenti in *Bergomum* 33 (1959), 45–67; A. Gambasin, *Il clero padovano e la dominazione austriaca 1859–1866* (Rome 1967), 255–300; L. Briguglio, "Questione romana e clero veneto," *Ateneo veneto* 151 (1960), 49–61; C. Cannarozzi, "I frati minori di Toscana el il Risorgimento italiano," *StudFr* 52 (1955), 394–425, 54 (1957), 199–249; A. Berselli, "Aspetti e figure del movimento conciliatorista nelle ex-legazioni," *AstIt* 112 (1954), 84–108; F. Manzotti in *RStRis* 48 (1961), 271–93; M. Fanti, *Strenna storica bolognese* 10 (1960), 3–26; A. Cestaro, *Rassegna di politica e di storia* 9 (1963), 6–23; P. Sposato in *Atti del 2° congresso stor. calabrese* (Naples 1961), 368–405; F. Brancato, "Riflessi delle vicende del '59 sul clero siciliano," *Bolletino del Museo del Risorgimento* 5 (Bologna 1960), 365–85; F. Brancato, "La participazione del clero alla rivoluzione siciliana del 1860," *La Sicilia verso l'unita d'Italia* (Palermo 1960), 6–33; F. Brancato, *La dittatura garibaldina nel Mezzogiorno* (Trapani 1964), 41–45, 216–20.

[10] Text in Bastgen III, 350–51. See P. Pirri, op. cit. III/1, 1–56; R. Mori, *La questione romana,* 162–269.

The agreement, concluded without knowledge of the Pope, appeared as a hardly concealed disavowal, and the defeat of Austria at Königgrätz in 1866, which destroyed any remaining expectations from this side, caused ultimate despair for the defenders of temporal power. The French intervention at Mentana, 3–4 November 1867, which blocked an attempt by Garibaldi to seize Rome,[11] and the categorical declaration of Minister Romher[12] were a pleasant surprise, but the extremely reserved attitude of most of the European powers, including Austria, confirmed that the days of temporal power were numbered. Less than three years later the collapse of the French Empire at Sedan opened the way for the Italians to Rome; on 20 September 1870 they entered the city,[13] and a few days later they annexed it.

In spite of the advice of some hotheads, Pius IX obediently followed Antonelli's advice not to leave Rome. But his reactions to the new accomplished fact produced, as could have been predicted, fresh excommunications, diplomatic protests, an appeal to the Catholic and conservative powers,[14] and a repeated invocation of the immutable rights of the Holy See. Similarly, he refused to accept in the following year the law of 13 May 1871 "for the guarantee of the independence of the Pope and the free exercise of the spiritual authority of the Holy See," because the guarantee appeared to him as absolutely inadequate. In fact it must be noted that to contemporary liberals, even the moderate ones, the necessity of an unconditional renunciation of temporal power, no matter in what form, appeared as an absolutely untouchable "dogma," and a solution of the type of the Lateran treaties of 1929 would not have been acceptable to them. In order to do justice to the intransigence with which Pius IX repeatedly presented demands to the world which today seem immoderate to us, one must be aware of this lack of understanding on the part of official Italy for the concerns of the Holy See for independence in the exercise of its spiritual mission. But the senescent Pope was again and again buoyed in his hopes for a "miracle" by the illusionary thoughts of his entourage and the enthusiastic demonstrations of the

[11] See Della Torre, *L'anno di Mentana* (Turin 1938); R. Di Nolli, *Mentana* (Rome 1966); R. Mori, *Il tramonto,* 207–307.

[12] "In the name of the French government we declare: Italy will not seize Rome. France will never tolerate such an affront against its honor and its Catholicity." Until then, the French government had consistently refused publicly to take on such a commitment; it was forced into it by the development of domestic policy which required the support of Catholicism on the parliamentary level.

[13] Literature in Mollat, 357–58. Concerning the hesitation of Pius IX with respect to resistance, see P. Pirri, op. cit III/1, 310–16.

[14] Among others Prussia, where it was hoped to exploit legitimist arguments. See P. Pirri, op. cit. III/1, 294–302, 317–24; A. Constable, *Die Vorgeschichte des Kulturkampfes* (Berlin 1956), 29–37.

growing numbers of pilgrims who cheered "the Prisoner of the Vatican." He was equally angered by the narrow-minded fanaticism of Italian religious policy. Increasingly he connected his demands for the spiritual freedom of the Holy See with growing radical criticism of liberal assumptions, which he untiringly castigated as the source of the misfortunes of the Church. Such an attitude could not but strengthen the belief of those who held that in its innermost core the Church was in solidarity with the governments which had been swept away by the progress of the centuries and that it was still striving for the general restoration of a theocratic regime. But it must be conceded that, although the undifferentiated declarations of Pius IX against governments which were based on modern freedoms contributed to alienating many minds from the Church during the third quarter of the nineteenth century, the practical attitude of most of the governments, which appealed to liberal principles, frequently justified the irritation of the Pope. They make more easily understandable the growing intransigence of his views.

CHAPTER 18

The Offensive of the Liberal Governments in the Non-German-Speaking Countries

The Secularization Policy in Italy

Until 1860 Italy was nothing more than a geographical expression; its religious-political condition as well as the religious life and the mentality of the clergy varied greatly among the different states.

In the Kingdom of the Two Sicilies the Church maintained its privileged position, and the reaction after 1848 only served to strengthen the tutelage of education by the Church. Yet, in spite of the cordial relations between the court at Naples and the Holy See, the regalistic attitude of the civil servants diminished only very gradually, especially as the local episcopate, in contrast to the bishops of the north, was quite content with this situation. Moreover, the anti-Roman traditions of the eighteenth century were still quite alive in many seminaries, and the very specific conditions under which priests were recruited in the south exemplified the lack of discipline and the lax morals of a still numerically strong clergy. Side by side with wealthy, almost empty monasteries there existed a clerical proletariat, consisting of parsons in small villages, priests without a clearly defined function, Capuchins and others. Many of these deserted their spiritual calling after the arrival of Garibaldi.

In Tuscany, on the other hand, the standards of the also numerically very strong clergy were clearly above the average; but its frequent attempts at reform often disregarded the boundaries of orthodoxy. Under pressure from the Grand Duke, who had shared exile with Pius IX in Naples and revered him, the government in 1851 reluctantly signed a concordat;[1] it put an end to the regalistic legislation which had come down from Pietro Leopoldo. But Rome's success was more theoretical than practical, for while the Tuscan bureaucracy had made concessions in principle, it regained a great portion of its earlier control over religious matters. For eight years both sides conducted an unreal and fruitless dialogue: Florence continued to deliberate from the perspective of the eighteenth century and Rome did so from the standpoint of the medieval Church. Characteristic in this connection were the attempts by the Vatican to prevent the emancipation plans of the Jews.[2] Symptomatic of the progress of ultramontanism was the fact that a few bishops, especially Cardinal Corsi, gradually began to resist the government.

In 1857 an agreement was reached with the Duke of Modena[3] which effected a limitation of the right of asylum by the Church and in return made concessions on mortmain, a problem which had become acute on account of the many monasteries on the peninsula.

In the Lombard-Venetian kingdom the dislike by many clerics of the Austrian government sprang from Italian national feelings and the hostility toward the Josephinist system. Subsequent to the concordat of 1855, the Church regained some of its freedom of movement. This development was noticeable especially in Venetia, where the clergy had little contact with the lay world, even though the examination by A. Gambasin of the diocese of Padua shows that the neoguelf movement had many adherents until 1862. In Lombardy, where the priests were better educated and less open to authoritarian arguments, many of them continued to sympathize even after 1848 with the national and liberal aspirations of the middle class, and after annexation to Italy they constituted a strong bloc of resistance to Roman directives.

In Piedmont—according to Doubet "the people which in Italy took

---

[1] Text in Mercati I, 767–69. Cf. A. Bettanini, *Il concordato di Toscana* (Milan 1933); R. Mori in *AstIt* 98 (1940), 41–82, 99 (1941), 131–46, to be complemented by G. Martina, *Pio IX e Leopoldo II,* 142–94.

[2] On the problem of the emancipation of the Jews in Italy during the middle of the nineteenth century, see G. Martina, *Pio IX e Leopoldo II,* 195–227 (the bibliography is very extensive, pp. 195–97).

[3] Text in Mercati I, 876–80. Cf. P. Forni in *RSTI* 8 (1954), 356–82.

Catholicism most seriously"—apostles like Don Bosco, Cafasso, and Murialdo[4] were only the most outstanding examples of a great number of pious and diligent priests who, thanks to their education in the Ecclesiastical Convent of Turin,[5] clearly surpassed all of the Italian clergy, including the Papal State. Charitable and apostolic works continued to flourish and often imitated French examples; the brilliant figure of Rosmini was surrounded by a veritable elite of intellectuals drawn from the laity and the clergy. But under pressure from a middle class increasingly hostile to ecclesiastical privileges, even though it was a more devout middle class than in France, the state was subjected to a policy of secularization against which the clergy, especially in Savoy, fought in vain. The initial steps taken by the moderate government of Massimo d'Azeglio, especially Siccardi's legislation (9 April 1850) which repealed the jurisdiction of the Church and noticeably restricted mortmain, were in no way extreme. Despite Rome's opposition in principle, which was based on the clauses of the concordat, a majority of the Catholic public approved of the legislation. The people were irritated by the clumsy obstinacy of the archbishop of Turin, Fransoni, and in any case were used to accepting papal directives with simultaneous emphasis of their own independence. But the atmosphere was poisoned by the inept conduct of the Turin government, the inflexibility of the Roman canonists, who had no feeling for the spiritual situation, and the Machiavellianism of Cardinal Antonelli, who thought it fitting to exploit the case of Fransoni (at first imprisoned and then expelled) for the benefit of his political design, but in the process neglected to take account of long-range religious concerns. The situation worsened when Cavour allied himself with the anticlerical left. The latter demanded civil marriage, began the secularization of education, and forced, over the hesitation of the King, the passage of the law of 22 May 1855, which dissolved a number of monasteries. While the Vatican broke off diplomatic relations and excommunicated the authors of the law, there also grew a Catholic opposition. Following the example of Montalembert in France, it attempted in part to gain strength on the parliamentary level, but principally was concerned with stirring up public opinion with the

[4] On Saint Giovanni Don Bosco (1815–88), see P. Stella, *Don Bosco nella storia della religiosità cattolica,* 2 vols. (Zurich 1968–69). On Saint Giuseppe Cafasso (1811–60), see J. Cottino, *San Giuseppe Cafasso, il piccolo prete torinese* (Turin 1947). On Saint Leonardo Murialdo (1828–1900), see A. Castellani, *Il beato Leonardo Murialdo,* 2 vols. (Rome 1966–68).
[5] Concerning this institution, founded in 1817 by Bruno Lanteri, see G. Usseglio in *Salesianum* 10 (1948), 453–502.

aid of newspapers organized along the lines of Louis Veuillot's *L'Univers.*[6]

Cavour was reluctant to enlarge the struggle. He had supported the more regalistically than liberally inspired policies of the anticlerical left only in order to gain its parliamentary support for his Italian policy. He had no intention of limiting the activity of the clergy, provided that they confined themselves to purely religious work. His goal was a mutually agreed-upon separation of Church and state, with the Church having the freedom to regulate itself autonomously.[7] In Rome, where Pius IX had resumed the concordat policy of Pius VII and Consalvi, minds were not yet open to a solution of this nature. Without a doubt, however, a modus vivendi would eventually have emerged if the development of the Roman Question after 1859 had not irrevocably disposed the government of Turin against the Holy See.

In fact, from now on Piedmontese religious legislation was applied in all of Italy, and its quick application in the former papal provinces was the more painful to Rome as the reformist tendencies of Cavour's successor, Ricasoli, who belonged to the Tuscan group of Raffaele Lambruschini, produced the unfounded suspicion that he intended to Protestantize the country.[8] But there still existed possibilities for a rapprochement. On the Italian side many moderates, although forced to make concessions to the radicals, in all seriousness wished to find a basis for agreement with Rome. They desired it in part because of their religious convictions and emotional traditions, in part because they regarded the activity of the Church as a guarantee of social stability. On his part, Pius IX was of the opinion that a satisfactory regulation of Italy's ecclesiastical affairs was more important for the Church than the restitution of the provinces annexed in 1860. He was sensitive to the dangers which would accompany a permanent break: denial of approval of new bishops by the government and thus an annual increase in the number of vacant episcopal sees (in 1864 this was true for 108 out of

[6] Especially *L'Armonia della Religione colla Civiltà* of Turin which was under the editorship of the priest G. Margotti (1823–87); in the field of dailies, it fought the same battle which *Civiltà cattolica* conducted in Rome (see B. Montale in *RStRis* 43 [1956], 474–84). One of the most important initiators of the Catholic press, especially of brochures, was Monsignor M. Moreno, from 1848 until 1878 bishop of Ivrea.

[7] The origins of Cavour's famous formula "A free Church in a free state" have been much debated. See F. Ruffini, *Ultimi studi sul conte di Cavour* (Bari 1936), 19–124 (the phrase was coined by Vinet); E. Passerin d'Entrèves in *RStRis* 41 (1954), 494–506 (it stems from Montalembert); U. Marcelli in *RStRis* 43 (1956), 449–55 (Jansenist influences).

[8] See S. Marchese, *La riforma mancata, le idee religiose di B. Ricasoli* (Milan 1961). Also: *Bolletino storico pisano*, 3rd ser. 30 (1961), 418–25; P. Gismondi, *RStRis* 24 (1937), 1071–1113, 1256–1301; F. Fonzi in *Humanitas* 6 (Brescia 1951), 65–83.

225); disturbance of seminaries and diocesan life in consequence of arrests of refractory priests; flooding of secondary and high schools with infidels and apostate priests;[9] and other actions. The mutual hostility of the anticlerical left in Florence, which had become the capital of the Kingdom, and of the bitter opponents of the new Italy in Rome, in the spring of 1865 brought about the failure of Vegezzi's mission. But the protracted hesitation of the government to apply the law of 7 July 1866, which dissolved religious corporations and confiscated ecclesiastical property,[10] demonstrated clearly that the bridges had not yet been burned. After Tonello's mission at the beginning of 1867[11] Rome harbored the justified expectation of a mutually acceptable agreement, especially as there grew in some Roman circles the willingness to reconcile. But the opposition of the radicals, who desired no separation on a friendly basis, but rather a throttling of the Church, which in their eyes constituted an obstacle on the way to progress, made a failure also of this renewed attempt. The second Ratazzi cabinet initiated a new period of a bitter anticlericalism. It produced the law of 15 August 1867, which was clearly Jacobin-oriented and whose consequences were to be a heavy burden on religious policy for years. This was especially the case after 1870 when sectarian elements forced the King and the government, in spite of their desire for a pacific development, to enforce this law with increased harshness, and thereby hurled fresh insults at Pope and clergy.[12]

It was in this tense atmosphere, in which liberalism appeared as the oppressor of Church and even of Christian values, that the Catholic press developed and the Italian Catholic Action had its beginning. Ever since the restoration there had existed a number of Catholic periodicals, but daily newspapers were published hardly at all. In 1860 there were

[9] See G. Talamo, *La Scuola dalla legge Casati alla inchiesta del 1864* (Milan 1964). According to the Casati Law of 13 November 1859, teachers were to be laicized, but it could hardly be implemented because of the low salaries for elementary teachers (by 1864 two-thirds of the teachers were still clerics); in the secondary school system, however, two thirds of the instructors were laymen within five years, and together with the personnel the spirit was also quickly laicized.

[10] See G. Jacquemyns in *Revue belge de philologie et d'histoire* 42 (1964), 442–94, 1257–91. The real property of the Church was estimated at 2 billion lire (more than 15 percent of all real property). It becomes increasingly clearer that the motives for the dissolution of religious corporations were more often financial requirements than ideological principles, and in many instances the religious were permitted covertly to buy back their monasteries. Still, the dissolutions led to the secularization of numerous regular clergy, whose numbers were reduced from 30,632 in 1861 to 9,163 in 1871 (despite the annexation of Rome).

[11] E. Del Vecchio in *Studi Romani* 16 (1968), 315–43.

[12] See P. Gismondi, *Il nuovo giurisdizionalismo italiano* VI/1 (Milan 1946).

only seven on the entire peninsula. Now, within five years, their number doubled, and by 1874 there were eighteen of them.[13] But while in other countries Catholic newspapers were generally under the guidance of laymen, in Italy the founders were almost invariably priests. In fact, frequently they were directly dependent on a bishopric, a characteristic which tended to strengthen their clerical orientation. This remained a peculiarity of the Italian press far into the twentieth century. The vast majority of those who shared the opinion of the Holy See about the new government withdrew resentfully and passively awaited the impending collapse of the Kingdom, which daily was prophesied by an increasingly aggressive press. A few irreconcilable laymen from Bologna, led by the lawyer Casoni, wanted to take action. Dusting off the slogan "neither cast a ballot nor allow yourself to be elected," which a few years earlier had been used in Piedmont to keep people from voting, they wanted to organize in all of Italy an extraconstitutional movement with the aim of first re-Catholicizing society and then of seizing political power. The idea gained ground only slowly. It was supported by the founders of the Society of Italian Catholic Youth, Count G. Acquaderni from Bologna and the young Roman M. Fani. Led by the Venetian G. B. Pagganuzzi, it was to lead in 1874 to the convening of the first Italian Catholic Congress, modeled after the German Catholic Conferences and the congresses of Mechelen. Confronted with a middle class which increasingly turned away from a Church which seemed to disapprove of modern trends, the militant wing of Italian Catholicism decided against compromises along the line of Catholic liberalism and in favor of a militant movement on the basis of the principles of the *Syllabus,* whose anathema against liberal society had reawakened the energies of the intransigents. They could count on the strong support of a new generation of clerics, faithful to Rome, which had taken the place of the numerous conciliatory priests who were the heirs of the neoguelf illusions of 1848.

This change of mind in the clergy in the 1860s was the result of systematic action on the part of the episcopate. With the support of the Holy See it throttled in sometimes despotic fashion the liberal tendencies and the strivings for a democratic reform of the Church which could frequently be observed among the priests of the 1848 generation.[14] Much absorbed by these attempts and numerous administrative

[13] On the Catholic press, see Aubert-Martina, 15–16, 832–38 biblio.
[14] See M. Bertazzoli, "I riformisti milanesi del 'Carrocio' 1863–64," *SC* 92 (1964), 123–53; A. Gambasin, *Il clero padovano 1859–66* (Rome 1967), especially 25–36, 117–69; N. Cavaletti, *L'abate G. a Prato* (Trentino 1967); M. Themelly, "La riforma cattolica nell'Italia moderna prima del Sillabo," *XIIe Congrès international des sciences historiques. Rapports* I (Vienna 1965), 161–75.

difficulties which governmental policy imposed upon them and even though there often were agreements on the local level, the bishops—among whom were such able and open-minded men as Charvaz in Genoa, Arrigoni in Lucca, Pecci in Perugia, and Riario Sforza in Naples—were unable to deal with other tasks which by themselves would have been enough to absorb their energies. To be sure, the question of de-Christianization was not yet as acute as in France, but there were other problems: the disappointing condition of the old religious orders, which at least in the north was partially compensated for by the founding of some very dynamic new congregations such as the Salesians of Don Bosco and the African missionaries of Comboni; the backwardness of Italy in the number of female religious;[15] the unpleasant behavior of many priests, particularly noticed by foreigners, and the high number of apostates; the extremely inadequate education of the clergy (worse in the south), which to a large degree had not attended any seminaries at all; and the low standards of these seminaries. This was in part caused by the small size of some dioceses (the concept of interdiocesan seminaries, voiced since 1849, was only realized by Pius X); the frequently still very archaic forms of pastoral methods, which rested on an external control of religious practices and which left the Christian masses to their own devices when they were confronted with the secularization of public life and especially of schools, although there were a number of significant private initiatives, such as Ramazotti's in Milan, Fra di Bruno's in Turin, Frassinetti's and Alimonda's in Genoa, and Mazza's in Verona; and finally, with the exception of a few centers[16] which actually had been more active in the 1850s than they were in 1870, the recognizable lack of a Catholic culture of a genuine Italian and simultaneously truly Christian character. In this connection, the reaction of the Jesuits to the adherents of Rosmini, who were suspected of liberal sympathies, passed up an opportunity which would not soon

---

[15] In contrast to all neighboring countries, they were far less numerous than male religious and in spite of a gradual increase they surpassed the males only at the beginning of the twentieth century. The increase resulted primarily from the founding of teaching orders in some of the dioceses of the north. In 1871 there were in the province of Genoa 1,324 sisters compared to 3,301 clerics; in the diocese of Turin there were 577 nuns compared to 827 priests.

[16] Naples, for example, where two very active reviews, *La scienza e la fede* (after 1841) and *La Carità* by P. Ludovico de Casoria (1865–73), appeared. On the Catholic circles of Naples during the nineteenth century, which retained the traditions of Vico and Gioberti, see P. López, *E. Cenni e i cattolici napoletani dopo l'unità* (Rome 1962) and F. Tessitore, *Aspetti del pensiero neoguelfo napoletano dopo il Sessanta* (Naples 1962).

261

present itself again.[17] The delay of the solution of these urgent problems in part doubtlessly resulted from the inadequate structure of the Italian Church, which, like many European countries at this time, had too few centers of pastoral reflection and remained split in too many small dioceses. But to a substantial degree it was also the indirect consequence of the long political-religious conflict which agitated Italy during the entire pontificate of Pius IX, a consequence which was much graver than the loss of obsolete privileges, on whose defense the ecclesiastical authorities vainly concentrated their best energies.

Anticlericalism in Belgium and in the Netherlands

The Church of Belgium in the middle of the nineteenth century "through its strength and independence had become a model, a kind of ideal for the other European Churches" (Pouthas). The continuing growth of the secular and regular clergy[18] throughout the pontificate of Pius IX made possible the encouragement and development of all kinds of activities in addition to the ordinary and regular growth in the number of parishes and in Catholic education. Despite some differences between several bishops and the Jesuits, who in the view of some people had gained much too much influence, their cooperation was generally excellent. Charitable efforts, in continuation of the Vincent conferences, were made to ameliorate the suffering of the industrial workers and to influence the youth of the lower classes in the cities. Four hundred twenty-two such works were undertaken in 1863, more than half of them in Flemish and Walloon Flanders. Publishing companies and newspapers tried to make up for bad literature.[19] After 1850 there were

[17] See, for example, the clear-sighted observations by P. Scoppola, *Crisi modernista e rinnovamento cattolico in Italia* (Bologna 1961), 20–42. Concerning the mistrust of the clerics vis-à-vis Manzoni's work, which was regarded as insufficiently conformistic, see, for example, R. Comandini, "Della varia fortuna dell'opera manzoniana in Romagna," *Collana di Monografie* (del Istituto tecnico di Rimini), ed. by R. Pian, 5 (1962), 5–60.
[18] The increase in the numbers of the diocesan clergy was slower than the increase of the population, but the annual number of deaths remained below that of ordinations. There were fewer than one thousand souls per parish priest. If one adds the priests engaged in teaching school, auxiliary pastors, and regular clergy, the ratio becomes a very good one. For example, in the diocese of Mechelen in 1862, to which the two cities of Brussels and Antwerp belonged, there were 2,200 priests for 1,100,000 inhabitants. The number of regular clergy had doubled in fifteen years from 4,791 in 1829; in 1866 it reached the figure of 18,196 and in 1880 25,326. More than one hundred sixty new houses were opened in the diocese of Mechelen between 1832 and 1867.
[19] After they had been devoted during the first half of the century to the Indian mission in America, attention was now turned to the East: Belgian Jesuits in 1855 settled in Bengal, and in 1862 a priest from Brussels, Théophil Verbist, founded the missionary congregation of Scheut, to which Mongolia was entrusted (see E. de Moreau-J. Masson, *Les missions belges de 1804 jusqu'à nos jours* (Brussels 1944).

also an increasing number of works of an edifying nature, thanks to the initiative of young ultramontane laymen who through the deepening of their own religious life and through publicly witnessing their faith intended to re-Christianize all social and cultural life.

But while the Catholics thought it the most natural thing in the world that under the protection of freedom the Church de facto, if not de jure, was able to exercise a growing influence in the country, the liberals soon became convinced that matters could not be allowed to proceed in this fashion. In order to return to what they justifiably considered the letter of the constitution, they held a congress in June 1846 at which they unequivocally presented their program: "actual independence" of the civil power from the Church and especially "the establishment of a comprehensive system of public education under the exclusive authority of the civil power . . . and rejection of the interference of priests on the basis of their jurisdiction in a school system organized by the civil power."[20]

The first indication of this new secularization policy was the law of 1 June 1850 dealing with secondary schools.[21] It was far less favorable for the Church than the law of 1842 dealing with elementary education. Without intending to exclude religion from education, the new law provided for public education totally independent from any ecclesiastical control. Many liberals, who in the future wanted to pay their respects to religion, had hoped to effect their policy of secularizing institutions through a friendly agreement with the Church. But the implacable attitude of most of the bishops, in spite of the willingness to compromise on the part of Cardinal Sterckx, to the new education legislation destroyed such illusions, and the attitude of Rome deepened the disappointment. Inasmuch as the liberals had lost the hope for a reasonable agreement with the Church and as before were determined to carry out their intention to secularize without the hierarchy or, if necessary, in opposition to it, they now increasingly chose the way of radicalization. In 1857 they succeeded in voting down the "Monastery Law" and with it the last attempt by the Catholics to amend the constitution in a direction favorable to them. Then, egged on by the Freemasons and supported by an electorate whose suspicions of the wealth of the orders and the "excesses of the clergy" they knew how to exploit, the liberals proceeded to restore the "independence of lay authority" in order "to protect society against a repetition of the abuses of an earlier age." The government of Rogier-Frère Orban, in office from 1857 to 1870, passed

---

[20] Le congrès libéral de Belgique (Brussels 1846), especially ARTICLES 2 and 3.
[21] See W. Theuns, De organieke wet op het middelbaar onderwijs (Louvain 1959) and especially Simon, Sterckx I, 469–501; Simon, Réunions des évêques I, 102–13; Becqué I, 97–106; H. Fassbender in BIHBR 40 (1969), 469–520.

a number of laws which, supplemented by administrative decisions, dealt in secular fashion with the problems of charitable foundations, cemeteries, and church boards. In the eyes of the bishops these were nothing but falsifications of constitutional freedoms. Simultaneously the liberals, encouraged by such radical groups as the Education League, which was founded in 1864 in advance of a similar organization in France, intensified their efforts in the communities with a liberal majority for a "correction" of the law of 1842 through administrative decisions. Their purpose was to limit the rights which had been conceded to the clergy in the area of elementary education.

While liberalism thus was increasingly more determined and militant, the Catholics defended every foot of the religious bastions which they had succeeded in restoring or maintaining within the civil institutions. Their resistance was weakened, however, by lack of unity in their ranks and the diffusion of their efforts. Disregarding the exhortations of his colleagues, at first by Van Bommel and then also by the young militant bishops who had been appointed after 1850 and received their directives from Rome, Cardinal Sterckx refused to unify Catholics in a denominational political party, for fear of strengthening liberal suspicions even further. He preferred the individual activity of laymen on the parliamentary level and within the framework of ecclesiastical works. On the other hand, the sympathies of a part of the Catholic population for the intransigent attitude of Louis Veuillot, which admittedly was largely identical with that of the Pope, after twenty years of quiet had once again fanned the discussions between ultramontanes and Catholics loyal to the constitution. The debates grew more bitter by the year, because the ultramontanes went so far as to declare that Catholics loyal to the constitution were more dangerous and damaging to the Church than admitted anticlericals.

In the expectation of being able to unify all Catholic forces in practical matters, some laymen, led by E. Ducpétiaux,[22] in the years 1863, 1864, and 1867 organized large Catholic congresses, designed to coordinate the activity of ecclesiastical works which had grown without guidance, and to inspire a powerful movement of public opinion for the support of Catholic resistance on the parliamentary level. Encouraged by the aged cardinal and, in spite of the caution of the ultramontanes, effected through the spectacular intervention in 1863 of Montalembert, these congresses undeniably contributed to awakening Catholic energies. An attempt was made to make up for omissions in the area of the

---

[22] On Édouard Ducpétiaux (1804–64), whose influence on the reorganization of the Catholic forces was decisive, see E. Rubbens, *Édouard Ducpétiaux,* 2 vols. (Louvain 1922–34) and *BnatBelg* XXXII, 154–76.

press[23] and to establish immediately—at least in the dioceses of Bruges, Ghent, and Tournai—a network of free schools directly under the authority of the clergy. They were intended to counter public instruction, whose ideological tendencies were, with a good deal of exaggeration, regarded as fundamentally incompatible with the Catholic faith. They also changed the status of the "Catholic Circles," chartered by the state, into political organizations and united them in a national federation. It produced the electoral victory of the Catholics in 1870 which kept them in power until 1878.

This amounted only to a delay on the parliamentary and legislative levels, however, for the situation in the country had become increasingly worse since the beginning of the 1860s. As in all of western Europe, the gap between the masses of the workers and the Church had widened, indifferentism made progress in the rural settlements, which were strongly affected by Freemasonry, and religious practice was retrogressive in the large population centers. Much graver, however, was the fact that while a portion of the Catholic middle class was much more willing to testify to its faith, the new liberal generation after 1860 increasingly tended toward a militant anticlericalism. The reason for this was the conviction that there was an incompatibility not only between the Church and modern freedoms (this was underscored in 1864 by the *Syllabus*), but also between science and faith.[24] The young generation instead turned in part to a demythologized Protestantism, but more frequently to a scientific and a religious humanism—the first society of this kind, Free Thought, was founded in 1863—and also to a socialistic atheism. For these young liberal intellectuals it was no longer simply a matter of liberating the civil power from the grasp of the Church, but of "rescuing intelligence from the darkness of obscurantism." In order to achieve this goal, they called for public control of all Catholic activities.

In view of the development of liberalism in the direction of intolerance, the Catholics once more were split in two camps. While one group, as before, saw the only effective protection against the aims of the radicals in the constitutional freedoms, the others responded that this was nothing more than a fool's paradise in that the state was actually under the control of the enemies of the Church. This second group, led by Professor Périn (Louvain), who was being encouraged by Pius IX, started a campaign against the constitution and its "freedom to be de-

---

[23] Reorganization of the *Journal de Bruxelles* (cf. M. Blampain, *Le Journal de Bruxelles, histoire interne de 1863 à 1871* [Louvain 1965]) and the founding in 1865 of the *Revue générale* (cf. N. Piepers, op. cit., General Bibliography).

[24] The condemnation of the rationalistic instruction by two professors at the University of Ghent (1856) by the bishops contributed to deepening the gap.

stroyed."[25] It was only a minority, but a very vocal minority, which around 1875 made many people believe that at the moment that liberalism under the influence of the radicals would turn away from the compromise solution which was hailed in 1830, the Church also would turn away from it, but in the opposite direction, in order to regain at least partially the standing which it had enjoyed under the Old Regime. This, in turn, enraged the liberals and the moderates as well. Thus, the situation was extremely tense and the entire relationship between Church and state once again seemed to be in question.

In the Netherlands, the situation developed quite similarly, even though somewhat more slowly and although the position of the Catholics in the state was rather different. The parliamentary alliance between Catholics and liberals lasted until 1866; but more so than in Belgium the rapprochement was determined by tactical considerations rather than by a change of conscience. Soon wide differences of opinion surfaced, additionally strengthened by the general development of ideas during the third quarter of the century. On one side stood the intolerant behavior which a liberal anticlericalism adopted in all European countries and which in the Netherlands was enhanced by the continuation of an abiding hostility to the Pope. On the other side stood the increasingly reactionary orientation of the pontificate of Pius IX and the influence of the antiliberal polemics of Veuillot, which Cramer echoed in the *Tijd* by making it virtually obligatory for Catholics to divorce themselves from modern civilization. While a generation earlier Broere and Van Bommel had been responsible for some efforts at rethinking Catholicism with a view toward new ideas, the condemnation of Lamennais had interrupted this first attempt at intellectual modernity, and the excesses of the anticlerical polemics on the occasion of the publication of the *Syllabus* confirmed those in their views who insisted on the incompatibility of Catholic philosophy and the principles of 1789. The example of liberal Protestantism, which in the Netherlands assumed a peculiarly radical position, also confirmed many Dutch Catholics in their conviction that it was dangerous for the faith to have too much of an open mind for modern ideas. Together with such doctrinal factors the Dutch Catholics, who were strongly tied to the papacy, were offended by the sympathies of the liberal press for the machinations of Piedmont against the Holy See. It was the problem of education over which the final break occurred.

The Catholics did not have enough money to establish their own school system and therefore had to choose between those who wanted to preserve the Calvinist character of the public schools and the liberals

[25] Concerning Charles Périn (1815–1905), see *BnatBelg* XXX, 665–71.

who demanded the neutrality of public instruction. Preferring the latter to a Protestant parochial school and hoping that in the end it would be characterized by the Christian spirit, many Catholics, not without criticism by other members of their faith, supported the liberals. Together they passed the law of 13 August 1857, which in addition to some noticeable pedagogical innovations for the first time in Europe introduced absolute neutrality in education. But after a few years hard facts could not be denied: neutral education in reality had turned largely into a completely secular, even a religious type of instruction. Now the bishops, encouraged by the encyclical *Quanta cura,* at first at the Provincial Council in 1865 and then in a joint pastoral letter in July 1868, proclaimed the right of a Catholic child to be raised in a Catholic school. The right of the child had its complement in a corresponding obligation of the parents, and the bishops legally began to increase the number of free schools. In order to meet the tremendous expenditures which this policy necessitated, the parishes organized active school boards; the joint demand for public money for the free denominational schools brought Catholics and Protestants closer to one another. Such cooperation would have been unthinkable twenty years earlier, and even now it was undertaken by many Catholics only with the greatest reluctance. Now that the liberals had replaced the religious outlook of 1850 with a rationalistic and positivist attitude, the "common foundation" (A. Kuyper) of Calvinists and Roman Catholics was suddenly discovered; while it was not yet strong enough to form the basis of an ecumenical dialogue, it was sufficient for a "Christian coalition" to gain religious objectives. However, the goals were not achieved immediately. To the contrary: inasmuch as the elections of 1877 gave the liberals a strong majority, the radicals became eager to translate their ideas into reality and managed to pass a law which tightened the clauses of the law of 1857 and jeopardized free education.

It was a severe defeat for the defenders of Christian schools and impressed upon the Catholics the necessity of having an organization of their own and of closing ranks in a political party. The idea was broached as early as 1877 by the *Tijd,* citing the German Center Party as an example; following the law of 1878, it was masterfully realized by the young priest Abbé Schaepman.

The Confused Situation in the Iberian Peninsula

In Spain as well as in Portugal the situation of the Church had improved since the unrest which it had experienced under the pontificate of Gregory XVI, but peace was only temporary and was constantly endangered. In Portugal there were repeated scandalous interferences by the government in ecclesiastical affairs. In 1864 the government forced a reduction in the number of parishes; in 1862, 1866, and 1869 there were new secularizations of ecclesiastical estates and the expulsion of foreign nuns (the case of the Daughters of Charity in 1861 created quite a disturbance); and after 1865 the Freemasons under the leadership of Count Paraty started a campaign in favor of civil marriage.

In Spain serious disturbances took place. The liberals refused to accept the predominance of the Church, which it had regained with the concordat, and their hostility was heightened when the clergy attempted to arrange itself with the increasingly reactionary Narvaez government. Between 1854 and 1856, when Espartero was in power, this hostility had known no bounds; but it was even worse after the revolution of 1868, when the Provisional Government quickly fell under the influence of the radicals; it meant the end of intellectual and political moderation. There was not only the immediate repeal of the concordat; much more serious was that as a result of acts of violence by the people against priests and regular clergy the growing gap between the proletariat of the large cities and the Church became visible. The evolution of a part of the liberal middle class from a simple political and economic anticlericalism to an antichristian rationalism clearly came to the fore in the debates on the new constitution of 1869. It subjected the Church to a number of legal restrictions, introduced civil marriage and a relative freedom of religion,[26] and contained measures directed against the orders, especially the Jesuits, and the Vincentian Conferences. Much more significant than these obstacles, however, was the spirit in which they were rooted. The highly solemn civil funeral in 1869 of Sanz del Río, who had introduced positivism to Spain, and that in 1874 of his friend F. de Castro, a priest in open rebellion against the Church and president of the central university, underscored the power which the new antireligious current had gained. It was actually strengthened by the obstinate reaction of the hierarchy to the anticlerical steps which followed one another after October 1868, as well as by the declaration of the infallibility of the Pope in 1870.

After the fall of the republic in 1874 Canovas del Castillo was interested in reinstituting the concordat, but considering the confusion it seemed impossible to him to return without adjustments to the conditions which had existed before 1868. Consequently, the constitution of 1876 included the principle of freedom of religion, despite the vehement protests of the clergy and of Pius IX. If one takes into consideration that the constitution, among other things, left the Church in control

---

[26] It was granted only to foreigners. The Protestant English missionaries derived the greatest benefit from it, but their successes remained limited. By 1874 there were about two thousand five hundred adherents.

of education, even at the universities, religious freedom was only a minor concession to the liberals. Still, it was one more defeat for those who saw in the *Syllabus* the ideal of a Christian society, a defeat for which to a large degree the antiliberal Catholics were responsible. By insisting on placing their hopes in a chimeric Carlist restoration and by virtually isolating themselves from public life by their antidynastic opposition, which grew even more pronounced after 1870, the "traditionalist" Catholics had robbed the moderate conservatives of the support of a strong Catholic government party. Their cooperation would have enabled them better to resist the parties of the left and even to achieve objectives of their own. This was the solution suggested in 1848 by Balmes. Instead, they forced the Catholics who were actively engaged in the government to collaborate with the liberals, and unavoidably this led to agreements and concessions which were despised by these irreconcilables.

Regalistic Liberals and Freemasons in Latin America

The relative easing of tension, noticeable in many Latin American states by the middle of the nineteenth century, was not universal. Especially in two countries, Mexico and Colombia, in which the Church ever since colonial times held a particularly strong position, the liberals incessantly and successfully tried to break its power, a power which benefited the large landowners, who in turn relied on the army.

In Mexico, the most densely settled republic in Spanish America, where the conflict was aggravated by the racial hatred harbored by the Indians against the Spanish, V. Gómez Farias as early as the 1830s had attacked the orders and the privileges of the clergy and had secularized a part of its great wealth. The principal consequence was that the flourishing missions of the Franciscans in California were almost totally destroyed, but the economic and political power of the Church was hardly affected. After a conservative interlude, the success of the reform movement, which had grown since 1845 under the leadership of the Indian Benito Juárez, a convinced Freemason and anticlericalist, led to the resumption of an earlier policy. Its aim was to replace the corporate society, in which denominational groups and especially the orders occupied a privileged position, with a regime of individual rights. Its ultimate aim was to laicize the state, which in spite of earlier disputes was still subject to the Church.[27] The recalcitrance of the clergy, which

[27] Concerning the spirit which inspired the reforms introduced by the laws of 1857, 1859, and 1860, in which the old regalistic traditions, the natural mistrust of Rome, and liberal individualism joined, while intending to respect the principles of Christianity, see the work by one of the most important ministers of Juárez, M. Ocampo, *La religión, la Iglesia y el clero* (new ed., Mexico 1965).

on its own had been incapable of introducing unavoidable reforms and correcting the most flagrant abuses, could not have been more pronounced. Utilizing the tenuous pretext of the utopian character of the democratic program and its evident social failure in a preindustrial society, the clergy continued to place all of its hopes in the vain attempts by the conservative reaction. In its intransigence, encouraged by Nuncio Meglia and the new archbishop, P. A. Labastida (1863–91), it refused to support Emperor Maximilian (1864–67) when he wanted to maintain freedom of religion and the press and to ratify the nationalization of Church estates in the hope of winning the moderate liberals to his side. After his return to power, Juárez, aware of the slumbering strength of Catholic traditions in the common people, was sensible enough to enforce anticlerical legislation with moderation. But after his death in 1872, his successor, S. Lerdo de Tejada, wanted to strengthen them through incorporation in the constitution. Subsequently, civil marriage, laicized education on all levels, separation of Church and state, and the nationalization of Church lands, having been embodied in articles of the Mexican constitution, became sacrosanct. But considering the close ties which a majority of the population still had with Catholicism—provided that its demands were not excessive—and considering the generosity of the faithful, the reality was much less tragic than it appeared according to the law; but there was no question that the secular power of the Church finally had been broken.

In Colombia also the situation, which, with the exception of the presidency of General Alcántara Herrán (1842–45), who invited the Jesuits to return, had not been good under Gregory XVI, became increasingly worse during the pontificate of Pius IX. After 1845 anticlerical steps followed in quick succession: abolition of the tithe and of canonical jurisdiction; expulsion of priests and bishops, especially Monsignor M. J. Mosquera (1834–53), the remarkable archbishop of Bogotá, if they attempted to resist this legislation;[28] separation of Church and state in 1843, the first decision of this kind in Latin America; nationalization of Church property; and the dissolution of all monasteries in 1861. These measures were accompanied by extensive restrictions on the activity of the clergy, in spite of the contradiction that was involved with respect to the official separation of Church and state. This genuine *Kulturkampf* lasted until 1880.

The other South American republics, with the exception of Bolivia and Peru, after 1870 also experienced a revival of militant anticlericalism and secularization policies. It was now no longer merely a

---

[28] Personally moderate, but compromised by a largely reactionary clergy. With respect to him, cf. *Antología del Il. Señor M.J. Mosquera y escritos sobre el* (Bogotá 1954).

matter of the nationalization of Church property, the abolition of canonical jurisdiction, or the control over the appointment of bishops and parish priests, but of the introduction of civil marriage, freedom of religion for the Protestants (whose numbers in some countries increased because of immigration), reduction of the influence of the Church on education, and total separation of Church and state. Just as in the preceding generation, the rationale of these policies was the attempt of the liberals, who almost everywhere had regained power, to reduce the political and social influence of the clergy. This was the result, in part, of the clergy's support of the conservative parties in the interest of defending the "established order" and its hierarchical and paternalistic concept of society. It was in part also caused by the introduction of two new elements which created hostility to the Church: the influence of the members of orders who had come from Europe and who advocated ultramontane ideas which conflicted with an increasingly sensitive nationalism, and the unmitigated claim by the Church to regulate the life of civil society as recently laid down by the *Syllabus;* also there was the progress of Comte's positivism, which in some instances changed the church-political conflict into a regular battle against the Christian faith, which a part of the educated middle class was beginning to reject. In Venezuela President Guzmán Blanco, a fanatic sectarian, in 1870 began the fight for laicized schools and attempted to create a national Church totally dependent on the state, in which the archbishop would be elected by the parliament and the parish priests by their parishes. In Guatemala the sentiment was not quite so radical, but here also there began after the fall of President Cerna (1871), the great protector of the Jesuits, a policy of laicization which reached its apogee in the constitution of 1879 and soon was imitated by the other republics of Central America (except for Costa Rica). Chile followed the same path under the presidency of Errazuriz (1871–76), as did Argentina after the success of the National Autonomist Party in 1874. It was centered on the landed gentry, which makes evident that the roots of South American anticlericalism were not only of a social nature; Ecuador after the assassination of García Moreno in 1875 also took this direction.

In Brazil, where the legal status of the Church hardly changed during the period of imperial government, i.e., until 1888, the hardening of the fronts between Freemasonic liberals and ultramontane Catholics was shown in an incident which, although limited in time and space, found an echo even in Europe. Influenced by the increasingly unequivocal positions taken by Pius IX, several bishops were worried about the toleration by the Emperor of Protestant missions, the acceptance of rationalistic doctrines from Germany by educated people, and the growing anti-Christian attitude of the Freemasons. In 1872 the Capuchin bishop of Olinda, Monsignor V. de Oliveira, who had been trained in France, and one of his brethren, Monsignor A. de Macedo Costa, bishop of Para, ordered their priests and the members of the parishes with threat of punishment to leave Freemasonic lodges. The government, however, arguing that the papal bulls against the Freemasons had never received the approval of the state, annulled the episcopal decisions. When the prelates denied the right of the civil authority to interfere in religious questions, they were imprisoned. The horrified Catholic world press celebrated the bishops as martyrs in the cause of ecclesiastical independence. The other bishops actually supported their colleagues only moderately, but this case was the starting point for a mobilization of public opinion which caused the most energetic Brazilian Catholics to call for the spiritual freedom of the Church in the face of abusive interference by the civil authority.

C H A P T E R 19

Preliminary Phases of the Kulturkampf *in Austria, Bavaria, Baden, and Switzerland*

During the 1860s the conflict between liberalism and the Catholic Church in several German-speaking countries reached that ideological confrontation which Rudolf Virchow characterized as *"Kulturkampf."*[1] Consequently, liberalism, which had grown to be the predominant political power, began to implement one of its central concerns: the liberation of state and society from ecclesiastical tutelage. The chief opponent seemed to be Catholicism with its ultramontane coloration, highlighted by the dogma of Immaculate Conception and the *Syllabus,* which had been augmented by the dogma of papal infallibility. The contrast emerged particularly sharply in countries with mixed denominations. German and Swiss liberalism, having grown out of Protestantism and being especially doctrinal, considered a frontal attack necessary. In the process, the power of the state was often ruthlessly applied, in violation of liberal principles. To the ideological contrast there was frequently added an economical-social one: the liberal urban middle class con-

---

[1] In the programmatic speech in which Virchow, the famous pathologist and left-liberal politician, on 17 January 1873 in the Prussian House of Representatives expressed himself in favor of the bill concerning the education and employment of clerics. The speech is excerpted in Franz-Willing, *Kulturkampf gestern und heute,* 9f.—Concerning occasional earlier uses of the word *"Kulturkampf,"* see ibid., 11f.

fronted the lower middle class and rural populations, who had close ties to the Church and felt disadvantaged by the beginning industrialization.[2]

Both sides were responsible for aggravating the situation. Neither was prepared to recognize the autonomy of the other in its own area; liberal politicians and Church leaders attempted to define "the borderline between state and Church"[3] in such a way as to be most beneficial to each group.

Catholic states on the whole were content to acquire sovereignty over the borderline areas claimed by the Church, such as education and civil registries, and to retain the surviving parts of the system of state Churches. Non-Catholic politicians went much further; they wanted to replace the cooperation for which the Church had fought with a complete return to the earlier state Church, a move which they justified with the claim to the absolute legal authority of the modern state. Frequently these liberals, imbued by national ideologies, tried to substitute such national Church organizations for the supranational principle of Catholicism.

In Austria, the denominational laws of the year 1868 continued to undermine the concordat but did not affect the inner sphere of the Church. Emperor Franz Joseph endeavored to avoid a break with Rome,[4] yet could not prevent the extremely sharp condemnation of the laws by the Pope.[5] In Austria itself voices were raised in objection and not only by conservatives. The belligerent Bishop Franz Joseph Rudigier of Linz (1811–84)[6] became the focal point of a popular opposition movement. Such a development was new for Austria, but it found imitation in other states where the struggle against the liberals was being waged; the Catholic faction in the parliament at Vienna also grew stronger. Because he exhorted people to disregard the law, Rudigier was found guilty by a court in 1869, but was immediately pardoned by the Emperor; nevertheless, the brief imprisonment of the bishop had a jolting effect on the Catholic masses. Rudigier was supported by Bishop

[2] This aspect of the *Kulturkampf,* generally neglected in treatments of the period, is brought to light in the essay by L. Gall, even though he overemphasized it.
[3] This was the programmatic title of a *Kulturkampf*-promoting work by the liberal canon lawyer Emil Friedberg (Tübingen 1872).
[4] The Emperor tried in vain to convince the Pope of the necessity of a modification of the concordat. Franz Joseph to Pius IX on 16 February 1868; handwritten remarks by Pius IX, no date. Texts: Engel-Janosi, *Politische Korrespondenz* nos. 130, 130a; see also nos. 133, 134.
[5] Allocution of 22 June 1868. Text: *Acta Pii IX* IV, 407ff.
[6] Biography by K. Meindl (2 vols. [Linz 1891–92]); J. Lenzenweger in *LThK* IX, 85.

Johann Baptist Zwerger[7] (1824–93) of Seckau and Bishop Josef Fessler[8] (1813–72) of Sankt Pölten.

The Emperor continued to effect a moderate application of the laws, and his constant communication with Cardinal Rauscher also had a calming effect. Although polemics from both sides continued with unabated stridency and the liberals in 1869 succeeded in passing a national elementary school act which reduced the number of denominational schools, Emperor and cardinal working together prevented the outbreak of a real *Kulturkampf*. Rauscher's suffragan Johann Rudolf Kutschker[9] contributed greatly to his cardinal's policy of understanding. He was also in charge of Catholic ecclesiastical matters in the Ministry of Education, a dual position which can only be comprehended by looking at Josephinist traditions. In the question of appointment of bishops, agreement was generally also reached on candidates willing to compromise.

The constant objective of Chancellor Friedrich Ferdinand von Beust was revenge for Prussia's victory in 1866. For this purpose he needed both the support of the liberals and an alliance with antipapal Italy. Among other matters, the concordat was an obstacle to such goals, but all attempts to move the Curia to a voluntary renunciation of the treaty were in vain. In the summer of 1870 Beust finally used the dogma of papal infallibility as a pretext for disavowing the concordat and was supported in this move by the liberal minister of religion, Stremayr. After some hesitation, Emperor Franz Joseph on 30 July 1870 declared the concordat as no longer valid. He argued that as a consequence of the dogma the Roman partner had changed his character, that a contractual relationship was impossible with a partner who claimed to be infallible, and that it was the state's responsibility to counteract the dangerous consequences of the new dogma. This legally untenable step rested on a much too broad interpretation of the dogma, although it was plausible as a result of ultramontane declarations. It can be assumed that the Emperor resorted to it only because he was deeply disappointed by the results of the Vatican Council and the Curia's hardening attitude, both of which harmed ecclesiastical peace. His disappointment was

---

[7] Biography by F. von Oer (Graz 1897); J. Köck in *LThK* X, 1430.

[8] Biographies by A. Erdinger (Brixen 1874); M. Ramsauer (Würzburg 1875); F. Grass in *LThK* IV, 95; *ÖBL* I, 305.

[9] Johann Rudolf Kutschker (1810–81), 1857–76 ministerial councilor in the Ministry of Education, after 1862 simultaneously suffragan bishop and vicar general in Vienna, 1876 as successor of Rauscher archbishop of Vienna, 1877 cardinal (biography by A. Eitler [diss., Vienna 1956]); H. Erharter in *LThK* VI, 699.

deepened by the resigned attitude of the Austrian bishops when they returned from Rome.[10]

The attempts of the liberals to intensify the struggle after Beust's resignation were only partially successful. They reached their legislative peak with the religious laws which were introduced in 1874 by the liberal ministry of Auersperg and accepted by the Emperor.[11] The passage of the laws was preceded by intense arguments in which the Pope intervened in the form of an encyclical to the Austrian bishops and a letter to the Emperor.[12] While Cardinal Schwarzenberg favored vocal protests, Rauscher and Kutschker negotiated quietly and succeeded in the striking of several unpalatable clauses.

The laws strengthened the state's supervision of the Churches and effected the equality of denominations, without, however, crossing the line established by the legislation of 1868. They left to the Catholic Church the position of a privileged public corporation and assured it of freedom of education and worship, the free exercise of its jurisdiction in the ecclesiastical sphere, and the free development of the orders and parochial school systems. The ecclesiastical part of the public schools was merely placed under state supervision. Thus, the Austrian laws were considerably milder than the *Kulturkampf* legislation in Baden and Prussia. Additionally, transgressions required neither prosecution by the state nor a "dismissal" of the offending cleric; at most, the offices of such clerics had to cease public activity.

Emperor Franz Joseph was convinced that these laws adequately protected the rights of the state and resisted all additional anticlerical legislation. A law in the spring of 1874 which established the state's right to dissolve monasteries was not sanctioned by him. The Curia also was willing to be flexible, not least thanks to the judicious reports of Nuncio Jacobini, who had been sent to Vienna in 1874. It was recognized that

[10] In a letter of 25 August 1870 to his mother, Archduchess Sophie, Franz Joseph wrote (among other matters); "It is also my most fervent desire again to come to an agreement with the Church, but that is impossible with the current Pope. When one sees the embitterment and hopelessness with which our bishops returned from Rome . . . one can almost despair of the future of the Church if one is not firm in the faith and in the confidence that God will preserve the Church from further disaster" (Weinzierl-Fischer, op. cit., 117).

[11] Three laws were passed: one regulated the external legal relationships of the Catholic Church; the second dealt with the amount of contribution of the benefice property to the religious fund; and the third treated the recognition of religious corporations.

[12] Pius IX to Franz Joseph on 7 March 1874. Only in this letter did the Pope protest the termination of the concordat. Text: Engel-Janosi, *Politische Korrespondenz* no. 139.—In his reply (n.d. ibid., no. 140), the Emperor refuted the papal accusations and assured the Church of his continuing protection.

the Austrian laws struck a balance between state and Church and that despite a premature papal complaint conditions in Austria were not the same as in Germany. This did not mean that the ideological struggle between liberals and Catholics ceased; it continued and damaged not only the Church. The Catholic ability to resist, exemplified especially in the Christian-Socialist Party, founded in 1880, proved to be far stronger than opponents had assumed.

Prince Chlodwig of Hohenlohe-Schillingsfürst (1819–1901),[13] after 1866 Bavarian minister president, was a Catholic, but just as antiultramontane as his brother, who resided in Rome as a Curia cardinal.[14] He clung tenaciously to the remainders of a state Church. It was his intention to transform Bavaria with the aid of an emphatic liberal domestic policy and to strengthen South German autonomy. Only when this proved to be unattainable was he willing to enter into a closer relationship with the North German Confederation. In 1868 the right of the Church to supervise schools, which had been conceded in 1852, was repealed and the entire elementary school system was taken over by the state; Jesuit missions were banned. 1869 also saw theological and political resistance to the dogma of infallibility emanating from Munich. Hohenlohe, extensively but one-sidedly informed of the Roman happenings by his brother and Döllinger, tried to persuade the other powers to take a collective stand against the planned definition. As was the case with other liberals, Hohenlohe feared that the dogma would not be confined to the theological sphere but would claim papal jurisdiction over princes and states in nonreligious questions as well. But because of the disinterest of most of the governments, Hohenlohe's initiative failed; Beust as well as Bismarck, who at that time still pursued a dilatory policy toward the Catholic Church, replied evasively.

---

[13] After 1870 Hohenlohe occupied high offices in the service of the German Empire, from 1894–1900 he was reich chancellor and Prussian minister president. (Clodwig zu Hohenlohe-Schillingsfürst, *Denkwürdigkeiten* I–II, ed. by F. Curtius [Stuttgart and Leipzig 1907], III, ed. by K. A. von Müller [Berlin 1931]; O. Pfülf in *StZ* 72 [1907]; Kißling, *Kulturkampf* I, 423f., 427ff., II, 1f., 16–19, 22, 122, III, 162, 249; K. A. von Müller, *Der dritte deutsche Reichskanzler* . . . [Munich 1931]).

[14] Gustav Adolf Fürst zu Hohenlohe-Schillingsfürst (1823–1896), after studies in Munich in communication with Döllinger, after 1846 in the Roman Academia dei Nobili. Initially favorite of Pius IX, 1857 titular archbishop, 1866 cardinal. The good relationship with the Pope was not lasting when Hohenlohe proved to be a violent opponent of the Jesuits and became a member of the opposition at the Vatican Council; after 1870 he was isolated in the Curia (F. X. Kraus, "Cardinal Hohenlohe," in F. X. Kraus, *Essays* 2 [Berlin 1901]; R. Lill, *Vatikanische Akten zur Geschichte des deutschen Kulturkampfes. Leo XIII.* I [1878–80] [Tübingen 1970], 7f.; G. Böing in *LThK* V, 431; H. Jedin, "Gustav Hohenlohe und Augustin Theiner," *RQ* 66 [1971]).

Opposition to Hohenlohe's Little German and anticlerical policy in 1869 led to the founding of the Patriotic People's Party under the leadership of Joseph Edmund Jörg. Its membership was almost exclusively Catholic, and on the first try it won the majority of the seats in Bavaria's parliament. Its rapid successes rested on the support given to it by the Catholic associations, a lesson which was applied shortly afterwards in the foundings of Catholic parties in Baden and Prussia. The Patriots, whose agitation very much contributed to making the liberal press equate Catholic with particularistic, in January 1870 achieved the fall of Hohenlohe. The government's course did not change, however, as the new administration, backed by King Ludwig II, was under the influence of the National Liberal minister of religion Baron Johann von Lutz (1826–90).[15] He resolutely continued Hohenlohe's religious policy and even intensified it after the publication of the dogma of papal infallibility. He protected the incipient movement of the Old Catholics, and on 9 August 1870 he decreed that the new dogma could not be announced from the pulpits; owing to the objections of the bishops, the decree could not be implemented. However, in 1871 Lutz introduced a bill in the Federal Council of the new German Empire which outlawed the misuse of the pulpit for political purposes; it became law on 10 December 1871. The Bavarian government also played a leading role in the passing of the second imperial law of the *Kulturkampf,* which allowed the dissolution of the Jesuit organization and the expulsion of Jesuits from Germany. Yet Lutz did not openly endorse the conflict in Prussia; he was satisfied with conducting a kind of creeping *Kulturkampf.* Its apogee was a royal edict of 20 November 1873 which annulled the edict of 6 April 1852 and restored the previous supervision of the state over the Churches. Considerable tension, especially in connection with the appointment of bishops, continued for a long period of time. But an open break was avoided, as both King and government honored the concordat. The government tolerated that Bavaria's bishops temporarily gave refuge to Prussian priests and students of theology to whom the May Laws had denied the exercise of office and the opportunity to study.

The majority of the bishops appointed by the King, under the leadership of Archbishop Gregor von Scherr of Munich-Freising, assumed a conciliatory stance. Only Archbishop Michael Deinlein of Bamberg (1800–1875) agreed to the veto right of the government. Bishop Ignatius von Senestréy of Regensburg (1818–1906), whose strictly ul-

---

[15] F. von Rummel, *Das Ministerium Lutz und seine Gegner* (Munich 1935); W. Grasser, *Johann Freiherr von Lutz. Eine politische Biographie (Misc. Bavarica Monacensia* no. 1 [Munich 1967]).

tramontane attitude was shared by Bishop Baron Franz von Leonrod of Eichstätt (1827–1905), remained an intransigent fighter against liberalism and the state Church.[16]

Earlier and more completely than in any other German state, middle-class and Little German liberalism had assumed a dominant role in Baden. After 1860, the administrations of Lamey and Jolly, in cooperation with the liberal parliamentary majority, determined domestic policy and fashioned the relationship to the Churches. The law of 9 October 1860, which took the place of the concordat rejected by the Chamber, formed the foundation; still, the majority of the liberals was not satisfied with it and neither were many Catholics. In 1864 a struggle over education erupted. Especially among the active liberals in Baden there were eminent proponents of the principle of the absolute legal authority of the state, such as the jurists Bluntschli,[17] Friedberg,[18] and Jolly;[19] inasmuch as Jolly headed the government after 1866, they were able to implement their program. The religious legislation of Baden in the years 1868–76 transferred to the state many duties hitherto exercised by the Churches and subjected the Churches to a far-reaching system of state supervision. The laws of Baden influenced the *Kulturkampf* legislation of Prussia and other German states; conversely, the laws passed in Baden after 1871 followed the example of the legislation of Prussia and the German Empire.

From beginning to end, religious legislation in Baden[20] was characterized by the claim of the liberals to jurisdiction over education. The elementary school law of 8 March 1868 changed parochial schools into nondenominational schools and made the establishment of parochial schools dependent on a special law; eight years later, the education law

---

[16] Staber, *Kirchengeschichte des Bistums Regensburg,* 190–97; *Festschrift zur 150. Wiederkehr des Geburtstages Senestréys,* ed. by P. Mai (Regensburg 1968); P. Mai in *Annuarium Historiae Conciliorum* I (1969), 399–411.

[17] Johann Caspar Bluntschli (1808–81), 1833 professor of law in Zurich, 1848 in Munich, 1861 in Heidelberg, in 1864 cofounder of the Protestant Association (H. Fritzsche, *Schweizer Juristen der letzten 100 Jahre* [Zurich 1945]; H. Mitteis in *HDB* 2, 337f).

[18] Emil Friedberg (1837–1910), 1868 professor of law in Freiburg, 1869 in Leipzig (cf. n. 3 above, A. Erler in *NDB* 5, 443f.).

[19] Julius Jolly (1823–91), assistant professor of law in 1847 at Heidelberg, 1861 government councilor, 1862 ministerial councilor in the Baden Ministry of the Interior, 1866 its president, 1868–76 leading minister of state (biography by H. Baumgarten, *L. Jolly* [Tübingen 1897]; J. Heyderhoff, *ZGObrh* 86–87 [1934–35]).

[20] The texts of the laws are largely reproduced in Friedberg, *Staat und katholische Kirche in Baden,* supplements no. XXff., as well as in Stadelhofer, *Abbau der Kulturkampfgesetzgebung in Baden,* 394–403.

of 16 September 1876 made nondenominational schools mandatory. On 21 December 1869 a civil marriage law was passed which, like the first of the two education laws, was more a legal consequence of the secularization of society than a belligerent measure. The same could not be said of the foundation law of 5 May 1870. It arbitrarily differentiated between secular Catholic foundation property (school and charitable foundations), which was transferred to the administration of the municipalities, and actual church property, the administration of which was merely placed under supervision by the state.

The most trenchant incursions in ecclesiastical life took place in 1872 and 1874. Regulations concerning the religious orders of 2 April 1872 forbade members of orders to teach school, and forbade any pastoral activity to members of orders which were not legally registered in Baden. The law of 15 June 1874 concerning Old Catholics was based on the fact that the anti-Roman traditions of a minority of Baden Catholics had led a number of clerics and laymen to join the protest movement. The members of the new community were assured of all rights which they had held as Catholics. Clerics turned Old Catholic were allowed to retain their benefices and income; Old Catholic communities were permitted to use Catholic churches and were granted a share of the community property, the extent of which was determined rather arbitrarily by the state authorities. The high point of *Kulturkampf* legislation occurred with the law of 19 February 1874 on the legal position of the Churches in the state. After an academic examination according to the law of 1860 had been ordered in 1867, admission to a clerical office was now made dependent on graduation from a secondary school and a three-year course of study at a German university, as well as on a discriminating public examination in the fields of philosophy, history, and German and classical literature (ARTICLE 1).[21] The Churches were permitted to retain only institutions for the theological-practical preparation of prospective clerics; hostels for theology and secondary school students, which the liberals accused of isolating the students from the national education of the German youth, were closed (ART. 2). For transgressions, ART. 3 decreed fines and imprisonment, in severe cases also withholding of salaries and removal from office; in addition, the attempt to influence elections by clerics was also made subject to fines.

Ecclesiastical opposition to this law was led by the aged Archbishop von Vicari, whose last years were also filled with a battle over the appointment of his cathedral dean, whom he also wanted to act as his

---

[21] ARTICLE I of the law closely followed the Prussian law concerning education and employment of clerics (11 May 1873).

suffragan bishop. In 1867 Lothar von Kübel (1823–81)[22] was named director of the hostel, and after Vicari's death in 1868 headed the archdiocese as chapter vicar for thirteen years. The election of the archbishop foundered on the rejection by the government of all but one of eight candidates nominated by the cathedral chapter. Kübel filed legal objections to all of the laws.[23] Together with a large majority of the clergy he also passively resisted them, a resistance which was not even broken by the law of 25 August 1876 which suspended all financial subventions by the state. Chapter vicar and clergy refused any cooperation in implementing the religious law of 1874; jailing of clerics, numerous vacancies, and growing pastoral emergency conditions were the result.

Liberal anticlericalism in Baden also affected the political activation of Catholics. The Catholic People's Party, founded in 1869 by Jakob Lindau, sent five delegates to the Chamber and two years later raised this number to nine; its chief publication was the *Badischer Beobachter,* founded in 1863. In opposition to the oligarchical structure of the liberal system and in accordance with the democratic traditions of Baden, the party demanded not only religious freedom but also liberal and democratic basic rights which the liberal government had delayed, such as the universal, equal, and secret right to vote.

The irreconcilability of the opposing positions, the failure of many state regulations, and the renewed hardening of the fronts caused by the introduction of the obligatory nondenominational school, actually not desired by Jolly but forced upon him by the liberal majority in the Chamber, moved Grand Duke Friedrich I to be more reasonable. The administration of Turban-Stösser, installed in 1876, was charged with continuing established policies in most areas, but was also instructed to search for a modus vivendi in religious policy without surrendering the rights of the state.

Jolly's first religious law found a positive echo among the liberals outside of Baden. There was no change in the official religious policy of Prussia before 1871–72, but to the degree that Bismarck's alliance of 1866 with the liberals became firmer their anticlericalism also spread. When in the spring of 1869 Rome's intention to seek definition of papal infallibility at the impending council was made public, liberal declarations became angry and Protestant-conservative warnings added to the furor. As for the German Catholics themselves, the passionately discussed issue of infallibility divided them into two camps.

[22] Biographies by J. Schober (Freiburg 1911) and A. Schill in *Badische Biographien* IV, 230–41; W. Müller in *LThK* VI, 655.
[23] In this he was assisted by his office manager, the jurist Heinrich Maas (1826–95), who similarly had assisted Vicari.

It was in this tense atmosphere that the German bishops gathered at Fulda in September 1869.[24] Other urgent items on the agenda, such as Ketteler's social solutions, receded into the background behind the question of infallibility; the latter forced the episcopate into a one-sided and unnecessary fighting posture. But the conference at least discussed the events in Baden and declared its solidarity with Kübel.

As for the definition urged by Rome, the majority were disinclined to agree with it; of twenty bishops present or represented at Fulda, fourteen presented their views to Pius IX in vain. Their joint letter to the Pope was drafted by the recently appointed bishop of Rottenburg, Hefele, who together with Ketteler lectured on the issue of infallibility. Ketteler actually anticipated some postulates of the minority at the Vatican Council by demanding that the evidence of tradition in the definition meet scientific criteria and that the infallibility of the Pope be proved in connection with that of the Church. Hefele used historical arguments, denying a positive cause for the definition as well as its timeliness. If the dogma of infallibility were accepted, he said, it would make a reunification of the divided denominations much more difficult, would weaken the unity of German Catholicism, and would intensify the religious struggle in the political arena.[25] The waves of controversy which after the summer of 1870 broke over German Catholicism justified his views.

In Switzerland, the battle between liberalism and strict Church adherents and between the liberal minority and the ultramontane majority of the Catholics ever since the 1840s was marked by a *Kulturkampf* intensity which grew even more bitter in the decade before the Vatican Council.[26] The basic disagreement there also was the council itself and the issue of papal infallibility. The official announcement of the dogma was made more difficult in some cantons, in others it was forbidden altogether. On the other hand, the agitation against the council, which prepared the ground for the Old Catholics, was allowed to unfold un-

---

[24] Lill, *Bischofskonferenzen,* 80–95. Concerning Ketteler's Fulda paper on the question of infallibility, see also Freudenberger, *Universität Würzburg und erstes vatikanisches Konzil,* 166ff.

[25] The Catholic representatives of the Customs Parliament (between 1866 and 1870 the only all-German parliamentary body), among them Peter Reichensperger and Ludwig Windthorst, in a confidential advisory for the episcopate viewed the definition of papal infallibility as unnecessary and inopportune. Text: *ColLac* VII, 1185f.; cf. Granderath-Kirch I, 223–27.

[26] This had not only theological but also political reasons. For example, the Confederation did not stop the external jurisdiction of the bishops of Milan and Como over Ticino until 1859, when Lombardy, which until then had been Austrian, fell to Italy and there was reason to fear irredentist agitation.

hindered, initially in the "Freethinking Catholic Associations" in which political motives often outweighed religious ones. The reason for this was that many Catholics, whom the *Syllabus* offended in the core of their thought and action and whom it completely alienated from an authoritarian Church, saw in the opposition to the dogma a welcome opportunity to move the Church in the direction of a democratic and national Church. Only in 1873 was a theologian, the former Lucerne professor of theology Edward Herzog (1841–1924, after 1875 bishop of the Christian Catholic Church of Switzerland),[27] enabled to assume the leadership of the protest movement. It was largely due to him that the movement excluded the radical elements and as the Christian Catholic Church followed the tradition of Wessenberg's reform program.

Bishop Eugène Lachat of Basel (1819–86),[28] whose seminary was closed in the spring of 1870, in 1873 was "dismissed" and expelled from five of the seven cantons which comprised his bishopric because of his advocacy of the new dogma and the excommunication of Christ Catholic opponents; he withdrew to Lucerne. In the overwhelmingly Catholic Jura the Berne government expelled all pastors when they sided with Lachat. They were replaced with clerics loyal to the state, among them several foreigners, but were rejected by the parishes so that a schism was avoided. Pius IX acted very unwisely in 1873 when he appointed the suffragan Gaspard Mermillod as vicar apostolic of Geneva. He liked Mermillod because of his unquestioned ultramontanism, but his appointment partially anticipated the establishment of a bishopric, an action illegal under the constitution. Mermillod was immediately expelled by the Federal Council. To the papal condemnation of the injustices inflicted on the Church in the encyclical *Etsi multa luctuosa* (21 November 1873),[29] the Federal Council replied by completely severing diplomatic relations with the Vatican.[30]

The *Kulturkampf* was carried over into the new federal constitution[31] of 29 May 1874. The establishment of new dioceses was made dependent on permission by the Confederation. Confederation and cantons received summary authorization to preserve peace among the denominations and to take the requisite steps to prevent violations of the rights of citizens and state by ecclesiastical authorities (ART. 50). The events

---

[27] Biography by W. Herzog (1935). See also F. Heiler, *Evangelische Katholizität* (1926), 9ff.; W. Küppers in *RGB* III, 287f.

[28] Biographies by E. Hornstein (Lucerne 1873), T. Scherer-Boccard (Würzburg 1873), and E. Folletête (Paris 1925); A. Chèvre in *ZSKG* 58 (1964); J. B. Villiger in *LThK* VI, 723.

[29] *Acta Pii IX* VI, 253–73.

[30] The nunciature in Switzerland was not reopened until 1920.

[31] Text: G. Franz, *Staatsverfassungen* (Munich 1964), 584–627.

of 1870 had shown that even the publication of principles of faith and the excommunication of opponents were viewed as such violations. The Society of Jesus and all organizations "affiliated" with it were excluded from the entire territory of Switzerland and its members were forbidden to be active in church and school (ART. 51). The establishment of new monasteries and the restoration of closed ones was also declared impermissible (ART. 52). The maintenance of civil registries was turned over to the exclusive care of the government (ART. 53), canonical jurisdiction was declared abolished (ART. 58), and elementary education was placed exclusively in the hands of the state (ART. 27).

Although the *Kulturkampf* politicians quickly had to acknowledge that the National Church-Old Catholic movement constituted no more than a minority, anti-Catholic legislation was dismantled only slowly; fundamental moves for a relaxation of tension in Switzerland were made only under the pontificate of Leo XIII.

CHAPTER 20

Internal Catholic Controversies in Connection with Liberalism

Catholicism and Liberalism after 1848

The crisis of 1848, which pointed out the degree to which the traditional order of society had been shaken, and the subsequent wave of reaction only intensified the great problem which had confronted Catholic thought for half a century. What was to be the attitude to the world which had emerged from the revolution and its advertised governmental form of freedom? Could one reconcile with it or did its nature require that it be rejected? Many Catholics were fascinated by the memory of the Christian Middle Ages, which a Catholic Romanticism had impressively displayed before their eyes in idealized fashion, were haunted by the thought of a recurrence of the unrest which once again had troubled Europe, and were profoundly disappointed by the failure of the attempts by Pius IX to guide liberal demands into acceptable channels through concessions. They were also troubled by the almost universal decline of religious practice, in which—as moralists and not as sociologists—they saw a consequence of the errors spread by an "evil press." Thus, they gradually became more and more convinced that the restoration started at the beginning of the century could only be successful if one resolutely forgot about the social philosophy of the eighteenth century and returned to those concepts on which the strength and greatness of the "century of faith" rested. Justification and confirmation for this mistrust of liberal principles existed in the continuance of the political philosophy which the Scholastics of the Spanish Counter-Reformation had developed. It was also found in the still strong influence of Maistre and Bonald, which was used to counter the seditious character of the rationalistic Cartesian-inspired systems, and in the aversion of many clerics to the new bourgeois society, which was identified with excessive stock market speculations and the search for material pleasures. In short, political and social notions, pastoral prejudices and traditional thought combined in varying proportions to lead a considerable number of the clergy and a few militant laymen to an authoritarian Catholicism. Its aim was to preserve and to regain privileges and external prestige for the Church within Catholic states freed from the pressure of anti-Christian currents, such as in the Spain of Isabella II, in the Empire of the Habsburgs, and until 1859 in several Italian states. The official publication of this intransigent Catholicism was the *Civiltà cattolica,* published by the Roman Jesuits. Its guiding principles were those outlined in the essay "Ensayo sobre el catolicismo, el liberalismo y el socialismo" (1851) by the Spaniard Donoso Cortés,[1] which also became available soon thereafter in French and German. *Civiltà cattolica,* founded in 1849, had as its principal goal the complete restoration of Christian principles in the life of the individual, of the family, and of society. In some countries the Society of Jesus was responsible for the view held by many people that these principles were the only ones which were acceptable to Catholic orthodoxy.

In contrast to 1815, the monarchical and reactionary governments which were totally devoted to the Church by the middle of the century had lost the support of the young. Thus, there were many Catholics who, deeply sympathetic with the currents of their century, attacked the intransigent group by arguing that the attempt to return to the concepts of the restoration period was not only dangerous but also futile. Not all of them agreed with Montalembert's *Intérêts catholiques au XIXe siècle* (1852), in which he took the position that the religious renascence of the first half of the century was the exclusive result of the liberties which the Church enjoyed under a parliamentary regime. But most of them pointed out that a significant number of the leaders in the state no longer practiced their religion and that for this reason it was utopian to expect disinterested aid and protection from the state; at best the Church could hope for a benevolent neutrality. Some of them went further. In light of the genuine values and of the real humanitarian progress which liberalism in spite of some excesses had produced, they were prepared to accept the modern concept of greater rights for the

---

[1] Concerning Juan Donoso Cortés (1809–53), see J. Schramm, *Donoso Cortés* (Madrid 1936) and J. Chaix-Ruy, *Donoso Cortés, théologien de l'histoire et prophète* (Paris 1956).

individual. It hardly needs mentioning that they were not always aware of the danger that the excessive autonomy of the individual could result in the claim of man's total independence from God.

Gradually there arose two opposing Catholic groups which, while both were intent on serving the Church, completely differed in how best this could be accomplished. One group saw the modern world of its century as an historical epoch with its own peculiar organizational form and thought it necessary to be its advance guard. Tactfully the members of this group threw a veil over the condemnations in the encyclical *Mirari vos,* the memory of which was beginning to pale, and demanded that the Church embrace liberalism just as in earlier times it had done with Greco-Roman civilization, the reaction of the parishes to the feudalism of the Middle Ages, and the humanistic endeavors of the Renaissance. The others, regarding the modern world as the anti-Christian legacy of the revolution, preferred to avoid error by breaking off all contacts and desired a tightening of prohibitions in order to avoid infection. They insisted on the solemn repetition of the earlier condemnation of liberalism and other modern errors by the magisterial office. They were oblivious of the dangers of such a course of action, which could only intensify the ambiguities as a result of which many liberals had come to the firm conviction that a society in keeping with the demands of the time could only be built if the Catholic Church was deprived of all influence.

Conflicts between the two groups were unavoidable. They were aggravated at the same time by the intrusion of additional debates which split the Catholic elite in many countries. In France, where political problems easily assumed an ideological and religious character, it was the question of reconciliation with the Empire after the coup d'état; in Italy it was the Roman Question; in Germany it was the growing contrast between university theologians and defenders of Scholasticism, in which could be seen the same spiritual opposition which separated the believers in progress with their sense of history from those who preferred to trust the methods which previously had been approved by a hierarchical authority.

The Division of the Catholics in France

Internal Catholic controversies over modern liberties reached their high point in France. Elsewhere the problem was dealt with as a practical one. Rome conceded under Pius IX as well as under Gregory XVI that on this level attitudes could be different, depending on each case. While liberal legislation in Piedmont was formally condemned, it was tolerated in Belgium and even appreciated in countries with a Catholic minority, such as the United States, England, and the Netherlands. But such practices confused the French, who with their logical bent desired coherent theories which could be raised to the level of universal validity. Revived by the differences of opinion swirling around the Falloux Law, whose proponents and opponents indulged themselves in treating the matter on the level of fundamentals, the old debates over the ideal Christian society, which ever since the condemnation of Lamennais had receded into the background, once again began to agitate some people. Numerically weak, their influence nevertheless stretched far beyond the borders of France.[2]

The Catholics who believed in freedom in turn were divided over several important issues. There was the group which in 1855 had reorganized the newspaper *Le Correspondant*. It was headed by a few anti-Bonaparte laymen who were closely allied with Orléanist circles: Falloux, Albert de Broglie, Cochin, and primarily Montalembert, who thanks to their personal qualities, their social position, their influence in political life, and their great services in the cause of Catholicism also influenced people who did not sympathize with all of their ideas. This group, "academic and in vogue" (Planque), which in some respects approached the ideal of "devout humanism," was also represented in the provinces[3] and in the great orders. Among the Dominicans its views were championed by Lacordaire, among the Oratorians by Gratry, and even among the Jesuits by P. de Ravignan and the first editors of *Études*. But above all it profited from the support and the growing prestige of Monsignor Dupanloup, the eloquent and active bishop of Orléans, whom his defense of the temporal position of the Pope after the Italian War placed in the forefront of Europe's religious politics. In contrast to Montalembert, who just as during the time of *L'Avenir* unreservedly continued to rely on freedom in Church as well as in state, Dupanloup's liberalism was highly relative. Basically his aim, as that of the Belgian bishops and of Ketteler, was to employ new methods and institutions which corresponded to liberal aspirations and under the circumstances were the only possible ones, in order to create a modernized Christian

---

[2] P. Sylvain wrote about Veuillot, the chief enemy of Catholic liberalism: "No other French writer contributed as much to the forming of the French-Canadian mentality" ("Quelques aspects de l'antagonisme libéral—ultramontain au Canada français," *RSoc* 8 [1967], 275–97). The few Spanish liberal Catholics like Mañé y Flaqeur, the manager of the *Diario* of Barcelona, the founders of the *Revista mensual* (1868), and the chief representative of the liberal current in Hungary, Baron J. Eötvös, looked to Montalembert for inspiration.

[3] Among others in Nancy, with focus on Guerrier de Dumast (cf. de Montclos, 241–42).

society in which liberty "was regarded as the guarantee for the activity of the Church" (Gadille). Yet he was viewed by the ultramontane press as the religious leader of the "liberal Catholic faction," while conversely many moderate Catholics, convinced that they were in agreement with the spirit of the century, accused him of a lack of logic precisely because he refused to apply liberal principles to the solution of the Roman Question.

A much more consistent liberalism was represented by the clerics led by Monsignor Maret, the dean of the theological faculty at the Sorbonne.[4] On the one hand, they did not hesitate to proclaim a "Catholic and liberal reform" within the Church, which was to rejuvenate the old institutions like synods and councils which limited authority and to free Catholic research from the stranglehold of the Index. They made no secret of their sympathies for the constitutional efforts of the Romans or of their conviction that the temporal power of the Pope was more damaging than useful for the exercise of his spiritual mission. On the other hand, in the question of the relation between the two powers, they openly adhered to the concept of the modern state, which was allied with the principles of 1789, which, "correctly understood, were rooted in Christianity just as much as in philosophical reason" (Maret). These neo-Gallicans saw in the concordat an instrument of cooperation in freedom between the Church and a secularized society. But such also were the ideas of a majority of the Catholic middle class which was frequently willing either to exclude or to ignore of the official doctrines of the Church whatever happened to be too much of a burden for its intellectual and political concepts. "The very small number of consciously liberal Catholics and the high number of moderate, i.e., unwittingly liberal, Catholics, were indeed two significant characteristics of French Catholicism" (Maurain).

These groups were opposed by those who in contrast to the liberal Catholics proudly designated themselves as "nothing but Catholics" and thereby emphasized their loyalty to the Roman standpoint, whose hard line they wanted to strengthen. They remained faithful to the counter-revolutionary traditionalism of the first third of the century and lacked the power of discrimination to detect the kernel of truth inherent in liberalism. They tended to judge political decisions according to absolute principles, from which they deduced their logical consequences, instead of searching for compromises adapted to concrete situations varying according to time and place. The leader of this group was Mon-

---

[4] On this group, which received less attention than the more brilliant, as well as more superficial, one of *Le Corespondant,* see de Montclos, 130–32, 225–27, 287–323; J. Gadille, op. cit., 89–108, 134–39.

signor Pie,[5] who in his *Instructions synodales sur les erreurs du temps présent* (1855–71) ceaselessly pilloried naturalism, which wanted to alienate God and the Church from the concerns of the world. Inspired especially by Dom Guéranger, he developed a political supernaturalism which was based on the Kingdom of Jesus Christ in this world and the glorification of the Pope-King. He did not advocate theocracy as such, i.e., the exercise of direct political power by the Church, but while admitting that the complete attainment of a Christian society would not come before the end of time, he nevertheless demanded the renewal of faith in the individual and the family as well as the Christianization of the state and the state's agencies. Overly zealous admirers became even more reactionary, however, and ignoring the eschatological perspectives and the reservations of the bishop of Poitiers with respect to too much of a direct political engagement, exaggerated the secularization of the supernatural. They did not hesitate to proclaim the direct sovereignty of Church and Pope over all of civil society. They expected that with the aid of Bourbon President Chambord a Christian state, as the Middle Ages had seen it, would soon be established.

These extreme ideas were spread with an absolute lack of differentiation and were often accompanied by unjust condemnations of Catholics who thought differently. The leading journalist who acted in this fashion and intensified the polarization was Louis Veuillot. Veuillot's achievements are undeniable: his devotion to the Pope, his personal altruism, and the great accomplishment when through his sarcastic contempt of anticlericals he helped to free the average Catholic from the inferiority complex which had burdened him for so long. But he also did more than anyone else to poison the atmosphere. The intransigence of his Catholicism—that of a convert—all too often made him forget the requirements of Christian charity and led him to a wholesale condemnation of modern civilization, for which he held the foolishness of the freethinkers of his time responsible. While the bishops were reluctant to admonish this journalist who often criticized them for what he regarded as their lack of orthodoxy, he quickly became an oracle for the provincial clergy, which valued his popular language and his massive criticisms. With this clergy acting as an intermediary, Veuillot's influence was effective with a limited, but not to be underestimated, number of the faithful. For a long time they maintained a stance of clerical intolerance and systematic defamation of civil authority.

[5] On Louis Pie (1815–80), after 1849 bishop of Poitiers, see L. Baunard, *Histoire du cardinal Pie,* 2 vols. (Paris 1893); E. Catta, *La doctrine politique et sociale du cardinal Pie* (Paris 1959), which needs to be read in conjunction with J. Gadille, op. cit., 48–59.

Catholic Liberalism outside France around 1860

The debates in Belgium proved most similar to those in France. There also around 1860, under the influence of the bitter press polemics which agitated French Catholicism and of the domestic political situation, the question about the bearable extent of Catholic accommodation to the system of modern freedoms was translated from the level of tactics to the level of ideas. While those with personal contacts to Montalembert and his friends continued to praise the extremely liberal constitution as the ideal, others began to worry over the change of Belgian liberalism to an anticlerical radicalism which no longer had anything in common with the unionism of 1830. They raised the point that the traditional privileges of the Church had been surrendered and that the opponents had gained freedom for the unlimited propagation of their ideas, but that they, after having achieved the legal majority, now systematically prevented the Church from taking advantage of the concessions which it had been promised in return. Even if the Catholics should regain the majority in the parliament, they argued, it would be impossible for them to conduct an unequivocally Catholic policy as long as they were obligated to respect the freedom of evil. Without agreeing in all points with the extreme positions of Veuillot—a comparison between the newspapers *L'Univers* and *Le Bien Public,* the chief paper of the Belgian ultramontanes founded in 1853, is very revealing—and clearly distancing themselves from the antiparliamentarism of the French polemicist, they began to talk of the necessity of amending the constitution as soon as circumstances permitted it. Between these two extremes stood Cardinal Sterckx and the canonists of Louvain, who drew attention to the practical advantages of the constitution, which guaranteed the Church a unique independence from the civil authority. They had to overcome the growing resistance of many younger bishops, trained in Rome, who regarded the Catholicization of some aspects of liberalism as impossible.

In Italy the problem was quite different. After the collapse of the neoguelf movement, which by many had been seen as the meeting point of the Catholic sentiment and the liberal sentiment, the development of the Roman Question made a reconciliation between liberal endeavors and Catholic loyalty to the faith much more difficult. The idea, propagated by Montalembert and the Belgian Catholics, of a Christian reconquest of society with the help of political freedoms found only few adherents in Italy. On the one hand, many patriotic and constitutional Catholics, disappointed by the "betrayal" of Pius IX, without reservation joined the liberal camp, i.e., the moderates, and for the achievement of their political ideals allied themselves with the anticlerical left "by leaving everything religious behind them and being concerned with it only in the last hour when the priest is called" (Curci). On the other hand, the indignation of many over the more statist than truly liberal policy of the Turin government, which de facto constituted a serious infringement of the rights of the Church and a limitation of its freedom even in the spiritual sphere, led to a reaction of embitterment and an indiscriminate condemnation of liberalism, no matter how moderate it might be. This intransigent direction enjoyed the complete approval of Rome and was spread throughout the country by such belligerent newspapers as Don Margotti's *Unità cattolica* and Don Albertario's *Osservatore cattolica*. Under the pontificate of Pius IX, after the passing enthusiasm of the "mediating" priests immediately after 1860,[6] it won most of Italy's clerics and militant Catholics.[7]

But even if the circumstances in Italy prevented the formation of a liberal Catholic party which, like those in France and Belgium, could have been politically influential, a Catholic liberal spirit, which believed in the possibility of a reconciliation of the Catholic faith with constitutional institutions and modern civilization, had not quite disappeared. This was especially so as the memory of the first two years of the pontificate fostered the conviction that such a reconciliation was not a doctrinal matter but merely a matter of timing with respect to the Roman Question. This liberal Catholic spirit, strongly determined by the differences of cultural traditions in the various parts of Italy and the preferences of individuals, could be found in many groups: among moderate constitutionalists like C. Balbo; among the genuinely faithful like A. Manzoni who were of the opinion that it was permissible to disagree with Rome politically; among Catholics like Minguetti who were disconcerted by the inflexibility of the Papal State; among utopians like the Tuscans Ricasoli and Capponi who stood on the outer fringes of orthodoxy; among reformers of a certain unconditional faith like Rosmini, whose influence lasted far beyond his death (1855); among histo-

---

[6] Concerning the liberal tendencies among the clergy, see G. Martina, op. cit., 765–68, and for an individual, but very significant case, A. Gambasin, *Il clero padovano* (Rome 1967), 117–69, 279–300; also A. Fappani, *Il clero liberale bresciano negli anni dell'unità d'Italia* (Brescia 1968); R. Fantini, "Sacerdoti liberali bolognesi dal 1848 all'unità nazionale," *Bolletino del Museo del Risorgimento* 5 (1960), 453–84.

[7] It must be noted, however, as Spadolini has shown, that the intransigents of the period after 1860, in contrast to those of the first half of the century, were not necessarily political reactionaries and that as justification for their refusal to cooperate with the liberals they no longer cited the principle of legitimacy and of divine right of sovereigns, but placed the rights of God and the Church above society and subjected politics to morality. The political philosophy developed by P. Taparelli d'Azeglio in the *Civiltà cattolica* is symptomatic of the new attitude.

rians of the tradition of Catholic Romanticism like the Lombard Cantù[8] and Tosti, the monk of Monte Cassino;[9] among admirers of Montalembert, like the future cardinal Capecelatro of Naples; and among the small Genoese group of the *Annali cattolici* which, encouraged by Archbishop Charvaz, in 1866 renamed its newspaper *Revista Universale* in order to attract more readers through this less denominational title, and wanted to bring into existence a Catholic party which, following the example of the Belgians and the Germans, alike was to be loyal to Pope, King, Catholic orthodoxy, and constitutional institutions.[10] Behind these leading figures was ranged the great number of those who continued to receive the sacraments, but who on the religious level combined the principle of authority with freedom of conscience and wanted to assure the independence of civil society within its own sphere. They were also the ones who, openly acknowledging the historical benefits which the Church had bestowed on Italy, were yet of the opinion that the status under which the Church had existed since the Middle Ages was not sacrosanct and that it was perfectly legitimate to adjust it to the requirements of the nineteenth century. This adjustment meant for some a clearer demarcation between the realms of religion and politics and, despite the protests of the Holy See, the cancellation of archaic ecclesiastical privileges, and for others the introduction of separation of Church and state and the renunciation of the exercise of the temporal power of the Pope.

In Germany the reconciliation between Church and state within a liberal framework occasioned fewer dramas of conscience than in the Latin countries. The reason for this was in part the fact that the German Catholics as a minority demanding religious freedom, unlike France or Belgium, did not seem to favor error but to the contrary seemed to support Catholicism. Furthermore, the German Catholics, influenced by Catholic Romanticism, in their praise of freedom harked back less to the principles of 1789 than to corporative freedom as it had existed prior to the absolute monarchy. Finally, unlike the Latin countries, religious freedom for them did not include the freedom of unbelief, but simply implied a nondenominational state with a Christian way of life. Despite

[8] Concerning Cesare Cantù (1804–95), see F. Bertolini, *Cantù e le sue opere* (Florence 1895); P. M. Manfredi, *Cesare Cantù* (Turin 1905); ECatt III, 646–49; also *Carteggio Montalembert Cantù*, ed. by F. Kancisvili (Milan 1969).

[9] On Luigi Tosti (1811–97), see A. Capecelatro, *Commemorazione di Luigi Tosti* (Monte Cassino 1868) and A. Quacquarelli, *Il Pater Tosti nella politica del Risorgimento* (Genoa 1945).

[10] Concerning these two journals, see O. Confessore: *Annali dell'Univ. di Lecce, Fac. di Lettere* 2 (1964–65), 158–210; O. Confessore in *SpAzLCIt* I, 141–76.

a certain worry in conservative circles and some reservations in Austria[11] and Bavaria, the disagreeableness of the petty bureaucratic interferences in the life of the Church was considered fairly balanced by the official recognition which the support of the state lent to the Church. Thus, the militant Catholics and the defenders of the principles, strengthened by the experience of Prussia after 1848, agreed to acknowledge the religious advantages of constitutional freedom, which they were careful not to label "freedom to lose," even though this did not keep them from directing fierce attacks on the anti-Christian character of ideological liberalism. This moderate position, represented by Ketteler in his work *Freiheit, Autorität und Kirche* (1862), for a long time was accepted by the large majority of German Catholics[12] and even at the time of the *Syllabus,* when only a few extreme voices on the right (Austrian Jesuits, among others) and on the left (Döllinger's group) muddied the waters of unity.

But violent controversies took place in the German-speaking countries over the question of academic freedom and ecclesiastical authority. Some representatives of the Catholic renascence, led by Döllinger, wanted to free Catholic intellectuals from the inferiority complex which a flourishing Protestant and rationalistic scholarship had given them. They thought it absolutely necessary to provide them with complete freedom of research, aside from the few questions which touched upon defined dogma and which they tried to avoid as much as possible.

Their intentions were genuine and their attempt to withdraw scholarly work from the control of the Inquisition was justified. But they insisted on seeing only one aspect of a complex situation. A reaction was therefore unavoidable; unfortunately it originated with men who often were ignorant of the new methods of scholarship and in some instances were actually hostile to them. Friction resulted inevitably when the narrowmindedness of one side provoked the free attitude of the other. Some people now opposed any intervention by the ecclesiastical magisterial office on principle and wanted to escape from all control by the ecclesiastical authorities. In this way there developed on the soil of

---

[11] After 1855 there is hardly any mention of the small group of Güntherians, so active in 1848; for this time they were very representative of the Viennese middle class with respect to politics and culture; at the same time they were hostile to democracy and autocracy, and were believers in a free Church in a free state and in intellectual freedom (see T. Simons in *CHR* 55 [1969], 173–94, 377–93, 610–26).

[12] This was also the position of the Catholics in Alemannic Switzerland (see W. Ganz, "Philipp Anton von Segesser als Politiker," *Schweizerische Zeitschrift für Geschichte* 1 [1951], 245–74). Monsignor Mermillod defended a similar position in Romansch Switzerland.

classical liberal Protestantism a tendency among Catholic intellectuals which had its equal only in the small English group of *The Rambler.*

The journal *The Rambler* was founded in England in 1848 by the convert Richard Simpson[13] with the objective of countering the intellectual inferiority of English Catholicism. Repeatedly the journal was the outspoken advocate for a limited autonomy of laymen in the Church. Its iconoclastic tendencies were reinforced in 1859 when the young John Acton assumed the directorship.[14] He was a student of Döllinger's and for a period of fifteen years embodied English Catholic liberalism. He characterized himself as "a man who has renounced everything that is incompatible with freedom in Catholicism and with the Catholic faith in politics." The independent position of the journal (and also that of *Home and Foreign Review,* which followed it in 1862) with respect to academic freedom, the Roman Question, and numerous other burning religious issues provoked the reaction of Wiseman and Manning, both of whom were avidly supported by W. G. Ward, the English emulator of Veuillot, and his *Dublin Review.* One of the saddest consequences of this controversy was the fact that it compromised Newman, who could not be further away from religious and political liberalism and who had attempted the role of mediator in vain.[15]

The *Syllabus* and Its Consequences

The different manifestations of liberalism in Catholic life, often incautiously expressed and occasionally accompanied by openly equivocal conduct, were an irritant for the men of faith. Confronted with this "religion of freedom" and a "religion of learning," they endeavored once again to confirm the "rights of God over minds and society." They were deeply worried because, as conservatives almost instinctively tied to the past, they had great difficulty distinguishing between eternal

---

[13] On Richard Simpson (1820–76), see D. McElrath, *Richard Simpson. Study in English Liberal Catholicism* (Louvain 1972); D. McElrath is preparing an edition of his correspondence.

[14] There is not yet a good document-based biography of John Acton (1834–1902). But consult: H. Butterfield, *Lord Acton* (London 1948); D. Matthew, *Lord Acton and his Times* (London 1968); G. Himmelfarb, *Lord Acton. A Study in Conscience and Politics* (London 1954); also E. Watts in *RPol* 28 (1966), 493–507; U, Noack, *Katholizität und Geistesfreiheit. Nach den Schriften von John Dalberg-Acton* (Frankfurt 1947); D. McElrath, *Lord Acton. The Decisive Decade 1864–1874* (Louvain 1970). With respect to his correspondence, see O. Chadwick in *JEH* 16 (1965), 114f.; D. McElrath in *RHE* 65 (1970), 87–89.

[15] In addition to H. McDougall, op. cit., see the excellent introduction by J. Coulson to the new edition of Newman's, at the time very controversial, article "On consulting the Faithful in Matters of Doctrine," (New York 1961).

verities which must be preserved at all cost and contingent structures of the ecclesiastical and civil order. Many others were additionally shaken by the fact, no longer to be glossed over by 1860, that whenever liberals came to power, anticlerical legislation soon followed. This aspect worried the Romans especially, whom the events after 1848 in Italy confirmed in the belief of a close connection between the principles of 1789 and the destruction of traditional values in the social, moral, and religious order. Pius IX came to believe that he had to take action so that his silence would not discourage the few Catholic nations which to some degree had remained faithful to the—in his eyes best—system of a privileged Church protected by the state. Inasmuch as circumstances had forced him to make practical concessions in several countries, he now considered it so much more urgent unmistakably to draw attention to principles. To the extent that concepts condemned by his predecessors Pius VI, Pius VII, Leo XII, and Gregory XVI took root in officially Catholic countries like Spain, the Latin American republics and Italy, he seized every opportunity to emphasize the corresponding classical doctrine of the Church.[16] Additionally, however, the idea of a comprehensive condemnation of all ideas of modern society regarded as erroneous gained ground gradually. It was started in 1849 by Cardinal Pecci and later taken up by the *Civiltà cattolica.* After the revival of the Roman Question in 1859 it was promoted again, and in the fall of that year the Vatican asked some trusted churchmen like Monsignor Pie, Dom Guéranger, and the president of the University of Louvain, Xavier de Ram, for suggestions as to which errors ought to be condemned and which points of doctrine ought to be emphasized.

On the basis of the replies, a first draft of the *Syllabus errorum in Europa vigentium* with seventy-nine propositions was prepared by the spring of 1860. But in the fall Rome received a long pastoral letter from Bishop Gerbet of Perpignan. Gerbet was a former collaborator of Lamennais, but he now fulminated against what he once had revered. The document under the title of "Instruction sur les erreurs du temps présent," contained a list of eighty-five erroneous statements and appeared to the Pope as an even better basis for his own solemn project. According to P. Martina, he did so wrongly, as the first draft dealt more with principles and had a more comprehensive character. Several successive commissions of theologians and cardinals, whose work was closely observed by the Pope, for more than a year worked on the theological justification of Gerbet's propositions. Disregarding the pronounced reserve of many Curia cardinals, who would have preferred a

---

[16] Encyclicals, but also briefs to authors who defended the "right principles," and especially many addresses. Their listing in *Acta SS. D. N. Pii IX ex quibus excerptus est Syllabus* (Rome 1865).

return to the first draft, Pius IX decided to present the new list of sixty-one propositions to the bishops who visited Rome in the summer for the purpose of lending support for the Pope's temporal power. The list was based on Gerbet's pastoral letter and summarized the most important modern efforts to liberate philosophy, morals, and politics from the control of religion. Although the information was provided on a confidential basis, some of it was leaked. The premature disclosure of the document occasioned a storm of indignation in the anticlerical press against Rome's obscurantism. Episcopal reactions, few in number, were rather reserved. Nonetheless, the Pope insisted on his original idea and the commission continued work on Monsignor Gerbet's propositions. Still, it proceeded so slowly that it seemed that the great condemnation of modern errors was being postponed to a later day; some hoped it was sine die.

But in the summer of 1863 two unfortunate speeches once more brought the problem to the fore. One was the apology which Montalembert, impatient with the "timidity" of his friends, made at the international congress of Belgian Catholics in Mechelen in defense of a "free Church in a free state."[17] The other one was Döllinger's bold demand for the independence of Catholic scholars from the ecclesiastical magisterial office, which he presented in Munich. The first speech received a strong echo and was a challenge to all those who saw the chief danger of their time in liberal Catholicism. They now insisted that Rome react clearly and unequivocally. Several interventions spared Montalembert a public censure, but Pius IX more and more became convinced that he needed to take a solemn step in order to calm the excited spirits. Several factors then delayed his pronouncement by a full year. The French intervened diplomatically, fearing that public opinion would be offended; the Belgians were worried that it might look as though Rome condemned the constitution, and just before elections this would only play into the hands of the liberals; and finally there were the apprehensions of Cardinal Antonelli that some non-Catholic defenders of the temporal power of the Pope, like Adolphe Thiers, might become discouraged. Pius IX was not deaf to these considerations, but this so very impressionable man was also subject to other influences. There was the increasing tendency of many Italian Catholics to take a neutral position; there was the success of Renan's book *Vie de Jésus*, which graphically made evident the dangers of freedom of the press; there were the recent violations of the rights of the Church in Poland and Mexico; there were Ketteler's warnings of the spiritual indepen-

---

[17] R. Aubert in *Collectanea Mechliniensia* 20 (1950), 525 51. On the occasion of this speech, *Civiltà cattolica* for the first time suggested a distinction between "thesis" and "hypothesis," which was to become classic (cf. J. Leclerc in *RSR* 41 [1953], 530–34).

dence of the German theologians; and, more generally, there was the threat of promoting radicalism through passivity on the part of the Catholics. The convention of September 1864 was then the final straw which decided Pius IX to hesitate no longer.[18]

Consulted again in August 1864, the cardinals of the Inquisition had renewed their objections to the list of Gerbet's propositions and had suggested a different approach. They thought the Pope should repeat his earlier condemnations in summary form. The Pope decided to follow the new suggestion and within a few weeks there was drafted, with the special assistance of the young Barnabite L. Bilio, an encyclical and a list of excerpts from addresses and writings of the Pope which he had made since the beginning of his pontificate and in which he had already condemned the various "modern errors." At the end of December the encyclical *Quanta cura* was published; appended to it was a catalog of eighty unacceptable propositions under the title of *Syllabus errorum*.[19] In it the Pope condemned pantheism and rationalism; indifferentism, which regards all religions as equal in value; socialism, which denies the right to private property and subordinates the family to the state; the erroneous concept regarding Christian marriage; Freemasonry; the rejection of the temporal power of the Pope; Gallicanism, which wanted to make the exercise of ecclesiastical authority dependent on the authorization by the civil power; statism, which insists on the monopoly of education and dissolves religious orders; and naturalism, which regards the fact that human societies no longer have respect for religion as progress and which demands laicization of institutions, separation of Church and state, and absolute freedom of religion and the press. The last aspect in particular impressed the public, as the propositions of the *Syllabus,* taken out of context, often were bewildering and justified the evaluation of Dom Butler that "it was a most inopportune" document.

The majority of non-Catholics at first were confirmed in their belief in the incompatibility of an ultramontane Church with the ways of life and habits of thought of the nineteenth century. The ultramontane press, jubilant over the *Syllabus,* heightened the impression to the point that many Catholics began to ask themselves whether conditions were really as they were depicted.

Actually, though, excitement was not very strong everywhere. In Italy, the press engaged in verbal skirmishes but the public remained calm, some because long ago they had stopped paying attention to the strictures of the Vatican in political questions, and others because they

[18] See R. Mori, *La Questione Romana 1861–65* (Florence 1963), 331, 338.
[19] Text in *Acta Pii IX* III, 687–700 *(Quanta cura),* 701–11 *(Syllabus).* Commentary in L. Choupin, *Valeur des décisions . . . du Saint-Siège* (Paris 1928), 187–415.

realized that an exact interpretation of the Roman document required careful exegesis. Generally the document was debated in connection with the Roman Question, and was seen less as a stand against modern society than against the convention of September. In Great Britain the non-Catholic public was virtually unanimous in finding the Pope's campaign against modern society totally ridiculous, primarily because he had condemned virtually everything. English Catholics, on the other hand, attempted, not very successfully, to argue that Pius IX had condemned the doctrinal errors and excesses of liberalism, and not the liberal institutions as England knew them. A similar situation prevailed in the Netherlands. Although there the Catholic newspapers also adopted this interpretation, the papal document contributed to increasing Protestant hostility to the papacy and to the hastening of the break between Catholics and liberals in parliament.

The situation was different in the German-speaking countries. The Austrian government initially feared that, emboldened by the encyclical, the clergy would demand an even more favorable application of the concordat. Döllinger and friends deplored the *Syllabus;* but the Mainz faction, whose influence reached the broad mass of the Catholics beyond the range of the intellectuals, noted the condemnation of atheistic philosophers and of bold theologians with satisfaction. With few exceptions, however, they took the justified position that the rejection of anti-Christian liberalism was no obstacle to continued exploitation of constitutional liberties. This interpretation also quickly gained ground in Belgium, even among the ultramontanes, but in the initial period the despondency of the constitutionally inclined Catholics was very great. In France agitation lasted for several weeks. Many moderate liberal Catholics were severely shaken in their convictions. Others were aware that the reminder of the principles on the whole did not really change the situation, but they also were despondent as the exaggerated comments of Veuillot's press forced them to observe the widening gap which separated the skeptics from the Church. Many bishops immediately wrote to Rome, pointing to the dangers of ambiguity, and demanded a clarification. Some of the others, among them Darboy and Maret, in the interest of preventing extreme interpretations on the part of their colleagues, persuaded the government to forbid the official publication of the encyclical under the pretext that its condemnations were directed against the constitution of the Empire. With the genius of the born polemicist, Dupanloup, assisted by Cochin, used this antiliberal measure to write a mitigating commentary on encyclical and *Syllabus* in the form of a defense of the Pope, who was being unjustly attacked by a hostile press and equally hostile cabinet ministers. Beyond this he was sufficiently skillful to woo the Romans by adding to his commentary an eloquent indictment of the recent convention in which the French imperial government had promised the Italian government to evacuate Rome.[20] This "translation of the encyclical into contemporary language" (A. Dechamps), in which the severity of the original was attenuated somewhat, was highly successful in Europe and even in America and within a few days persuaded public opinion to reject anticlerical criticisms. Pius IX, grateful to Dupanloup for his sharp attack on the imperial government, sent him a brief of commendation. The brief was very carefully formulated, but in conjunction with the praises of numerous bishops it gave Dupanloup's pamphlet the veneer of a more or less official interpretation of the *Syllabus,* even though many who disagreed with it attempted to belittle its significance.[21] This fact has a certain importance for the later history of Catholic liberalism, and for this reason Dupanloup's brochure deserves more than a merely anecdotal interest.

For the moment the storm subsided and theoretically both factions were back where they had started, inasmuch as Dupanloup's action had saved the liberal Catholics from seemingly inevitable retreat. For this reason they were able to maintain their position until the accession of Leo XIII, even if in the meantime they were forced to strike their sails. Many also acknowledged, in consequence of the papal condemnation, that in their utterances they occasionally had been too radical or imprecise. Above all they recognized the necessity of discretion[22] in order not to anger the aging Pope, who was increasingly irritated by the growing sectarianism of those who called themselves liberals. Toward the end, Pius IX, who almost daily condemned liberalism as the "error of the century," was no longer able to see the radical difference between Catholic liberalism and liberalism as such.[23] While regular liberalism, even if its adherents practiced their religion, was naturalistic and wanted to separate man as much as possible from his religious ties, liberal Catholics both intellectually and practically were guided by the demands of their faith and accepted, sometimes somewhat unwillingly, their subjection to the decisions of the Church. Pius IX admitted the

---

[20] *La Convention du 15 Septembre et l'Encyclique du 8 Decembre.* Concerning the preliminary work on this brochure, published on 24 January 1865, see R. Aubert, *RHE* 51 (1956), 83–142.

[21] Emphasizing the fact that Pius IX congratulated Veuillot and Schrader, who had interpreted the *Syllabus* much more strictly, in even warmer terms.

[22] At least the majority. Montalembert, embittered by disappointment and illness, charged his former supporters with avoiding hot issues (See A. Latreille in *RHEF* 54 [1968], 281–314).

[23] See the inspired "Considérations sur le libéralisme" by A. Simon in *Ris* 4 (1961), 3–25.

difference, but only unwillingly. "Catholic liberalism," he declared in 1874, "has one foot in the truth and one foot in error, one foot in the Church and one foot in the spirit of the century, one foot on my side and one foot on the side of my enemies." He was willing in many cases to tolerate the "hypothesis," but could not refrain from showing his dislike of those who in his eyes too easily decided for this option and now could proceed from practically admissible concessions to a surrender of principles. The full favor of the Pope was reserved for the "Knights of the Absolute," who, without consideration of intellectual developments or of local requirements, maintained what was supposed to be the "right of a Christian society." The frequent encouragements which Rome sent to their leaders finally convinced them that the Pope had entrusted them with a genuine mission.[24] Liberal Catholics had escaped condemnation, but they were clearly aware that they were in disfavor. For the next fifteen years the scene was dominated by extremists—liberal radicals and intransigent ultramontanes—who were equally intolerant and wanted to force their thinking upon everyone else.

Antiliberalism and Social Catholicism

Recent investigations have revealed that the Catholic opposition to liberalism was not always only confined to negative criticism. To be sure, there were among the opponents of the liberal Catholics many closed minds without any understanding of the times; but the more flexible among them, who succeeded in gaining the attention of a considerable segment of the Catholic public, were imbued with a two-fold positive ideal. For one, they wanted to react to the timidity of many of their brethren who seemed to be reconciled with the liberal view that religion was a private matter without any impact on social life. For another, they demanded the right to the "actual state," compared to the "legal state," which was dominated by a numerically small oligarchy. This makes understandable why from the second third of the nineteenth century onward these "reactionaries" in particular undertook more social initiatives than the liberal Catholics, of whom it might have been thought that they had more in common with democratic ideals. It also explains why these efforts were primarily directed toward the immediate amelioration of the poverty of the working class rather than to a solution of its real problems through structural reforms. The intention was to obtain the sympathy of the workers and their support in the battle against the

---

[24] Very characteristic in this respect is the document published by A. Louant, "Charles Périn et Pie IX," *Bulletin de l'Institut historique belge de Rome* 27 (1952), 181–220.

anticlerical bourgeois state. It finally also makes clear why these efforts were more often inspired by the nostalgic ideal of a return to an idealized, patriarchal, and corporative past than by a realistic accommodation to the new situations created by the Industrial Revolution.

The connection between antiliberalism and social efforts was shown early in the *Civiltà cattolica*,[25] in which, for example, Father Taparelli in 1852 held the view that the corporations dissolved by the French Revolution were rooted in natural law. Pius IX devoted one paragraph of the encyclical *Quanta cura* to the unmasking not only of the illusions of socialism, which wants to put the state in the place of providence, but also of the pagan character of economic liberalism, which in the relationship between capital and labor eliminates the moral factor.

Such ideas inspired several of the first initiators of the Catholic movement in Italy, who in this as yet hardly industrialized state were concerned chiefly with the pitiful situation of the rural masses, and whose initiatives actually reached their full effectiveness only under the subsequent pontificate.

In France during the July Monarchy there had existed an early form of Christian socialism in addition to the *Société d'économie charitable,* in which Viscount Armand de Melun had gathered legitimate representatives of social work who, while genuinely touched by the misery of the proletariat, were also rather reticent to call for an intervention by the state in economic life. Christian socialism could be traced to converted followers of Saint-Simon and Fourier, to former readers of *L'Avenir* who remembered the bold and social views of Lamennais, and to some members of the Society of Saint Vincent de Paul who had realized that alms were not the only solution. But the movement received a mortal blow by the general reaction to everything which resembled the kind of socialism which developed after the crisis of 1848. Thus, for a period of twenty years social Catholicism was represented almost exclusively by conservatives who were decided followers of the paternalistic approach. They tried less to change the condition of the workers for reasons of justice than to lead the workers back to the Church and to maintain the established order at the price of a few improvements in their material situation. The majority of the engaged men of the Second Empire, who were often met with the indifference and even the mistrust of the broad masses of the faithful and of the clergy, were inspired by the theories of

---

[25] P. Droulers, "Question sociale, État, Église dans la *Civiltà cattolica* à ses débuts," *ChStato* I, 123–47. Concerning the reinstallation of the corporations by Pius IX in 1852, see E. Lodolini in *RstRis* 39 (1952), 664–82; L. Dal Pane in *Giornale degli economisti, n.s.* 8 (1949), 603–8.

Le Play,[26] whose scholarship left much to be desired and which, in conjunction with a narrow interpretation of the *Syllabus,* served to lead these social Catholics to a "counterrevolution" opposed to the doctrine of human rights and democratic egalitarianism. In this fashion much personal generosity was wasted without actually reaching the working class. On the contrary, the working class now strove to take its fate and the battle for its liberation into its own hands.

In Belgium the situation was hardly any different. The few progressive Catholics who, together with E. Ducpétiaux, suggested a few hesitant legal measures in favor of the workers met general rejection at the congress of Mechelen. The man who set the tone in this question was Charles Périn, from 1845 until 1881 professor of economics at the University of Louvain, whose work *De la richesse dans les sociétés chrétiennes* (1861) was translated into most of the European languages. But while this champion in the ideological and political struggle against liberalism energetically drew attention to the exploitation of the workers by the new middle class and, based on the doctrine that moral laws should also be valid in the economic world, demanded a more humane division of labor, he also denied the state the right to intervene and expected the solution of the social problem only and exclusively from private initiative and growth of the Christian spirit among the employers.

It is paradoxical that the origin of a more realistic Catholic social movement lay in Germany, although its industrial development started only later. The German social movement had an open mind toward labor unions and approved of a restriction of economic liberalism through social legislation, the first steps toward which were outlined in the encyclical *Rerum novarum* of Leo XIII. There was no denying that the German Catholics, like the others, were at first primarily interested in maintaining order, but what they desired—in contrast to France, where all too many Catholics only wanted to preserve external order and to subjugate the workers to the current situation—was a traditional order, the organized society of the "good old days," which no doubt was not at all democratic but which at least had the advantage that it protected the little people against an unlimited exploitation by the rich. At first, until about 1870, most German Catholics in their attempt to bring the Church to the people and the people to the Church were mostly concerned with the defense of the independent artisans and the organi-

[26] On the sociologist and founder of the *Société internationale des hautes études d'economie sociale,* Frédéric Le Play (1806–82), see Duroselle, 672–84 and D. Herbertson, *Frédéric Le Play* (Ledbury 1952).

zation of the farmers. But gradually attention was paid to the problem of the workers. In 1837, the militant Catholic Franz Josef von Buß of Baden pointed to the dangers of uncontrolled industrialization and demanded action by the state in order to improve the situation of the workers. In his opinion it was up to the Church to assume the defense of the workers, who had no official representation.[27]

In 1846 Adolf Kolping,[28] a former shoemaker's apprentice turned priest, founded the first journeymen's association. Thanks to outstanding collaborators and the active participation of the journeymen themselves, whom Kolping allowed broad participation, the organization grew rapidly with the support of Cardinal Geissel of Cologne. From the Rhineland it spread throughout Germany and to Austria and Switzerland. Gradually other social institutions were founded in the industrial areas of the Rhineland, culminating in the founding of the People's Association of Mönchen-Gladbach. To the care and saving of souls and amelioration of need there was now slowly added the effort to establish a professional organization and a solid action foundation for the activity of the workers. These, it was hoped, would lead to a change of working conditions.

In this development, which presented the problem of the workers to the German Catholics more as a question of institutional reform and less as a matter of mere charitable help, the dynamic Bishop Ketteler of Mainz played a significant role.[29] He was frequently misunderstood and the prelate was often depicted as a pioneer of Christian democracy and as initiator of the booming social works in Germany during his life. Actually, many of these activities, started in the Cologne area, were begun without him. Even if Ketteler in his practical work was occasionally inspired by socialist doctrines, especially by the form which Lassalle had given them, and even if he adopted some of Lassalle's arguments and indictments of capitalism, he harbored no sympathies for modern democracy. Speaking out against the oppression of the economically weak, which society permitted, this Westphalian aristocrat had in mind a return to the corporative society as it had existed in the Holy Roman Empire of the Middle Ages. Yet Ketteler's influence on the social Catholicism of his time was tremendous. In his book *Die Arbeiterfrage*

[27] Cf. Schnabel, *G* IV, 202–7.
[28] On Adolf Kolping (1813–65), see F. G. Schaffer, *Adolf Kolping,* 8th ed., revised by J. Dahl and B. Ridder (Cologne 1961), as well as D. Weber, ed., *100 Jahre Kolpingfamilie 1849–1949* (Cologne 1949). Additional literature in *LThK* VI, 401.
[29] On Ketteler's social activity, see, in addition to the biography by Vigener (which, however, downplays his role), M. Spahn, *Hochland* 22 (1925), 144–46; T. Brauer, *Ketteler. Der deutsche Bischof und soziale Reformer* (Hamburg 1927) and especially L. Lenhart, *Bischof Ketteler* I–II (Mainz 1966–67).

und das Christentum (1864), the fruit of fifteen years of reflection, he did not limit himself to proposing a few concrete reforms, but attempted to demonstrate that the solution of the workers' problems was only possible by a cooperation of state and society, acting in direct opposition to liberal individualism and to the totalitarianism of the modern centralized state. Energetically he attacked the solutions suggested by middle-class capitalism and statist socialism. Instead, under the influence of Catholic Romanticism, which had marked him deeply in his youth, he glorified society as a living hierarchical organism, strongly molded by the unity of faith, in which the artisans were organized with a view toward the general welfare and economic life was freed from the iron law of greed and profits. Thus Ketteler was the first theoretician of a social order based on corporatism, which for more than half a century formed the basis of Catholic social doctrine. Its opposition to the individualistic ideal of economic liberalism after 1870 in more than one case—especially in the social wing of the Center Party, in the Austrian School, and with La Tour du Pin—was more unequivocal than the practical mistrust of and the theoretical objections to socialism.

The Victory of Ultramontanism

CHAPTER 21

Ultramontane Progress and Final Gallican Resistance

The Ultramontane Movement around 1850

As has been shown, the fifteen years of Gregory XVI's pontificate were a decisive phase in the progress of ultramontanism. Yet not all resistance had been removed. The great mass of the clergy and of the faithful were convinced of the advantages which accrued to the Church as a result of its liberation from the tutelage of the governments and of closing Catholic ranks around the Pope. Still, the question was occasionally asked whether it was at all advisable to have such a concentration of power in consequence of this rather extreme centralization. Such a centralization inevitably had to result in a reduction of the authority of the bishops, in uniformity of Church discipline and liturgy, even piety, all of which would mean the complete renunciation of revered local customs and the adoption of a "religious way of life" for the entire Church, analogous to Italy's.

It is of great importance not to lose sight of the complex character of the ultramontane movement and its concrete reality. Its adherents propounded theological and canonical doctrines concerning the special privileges of the Pope and the prerogatives of the Church over the civil power, developed a program for turning the ecclesiastical organization into a more authoritarian and centralistic one, favored restriction of the freedom of scholarship in philosophy and theology, and demanded a new outlook on piety which consisted less in an inner attitude than in frequent receipt of the sacraments and an increase in external devotions. While the ultramontane movement and its opposition to the heritage of the regalism of the Old Regime met with general acclaim, it encountered various forms of resistance because of the ecclesiastical problems posed by it. The resistance originated with the theologians whose minds were closed to dogmatic progress and who refused to see why the Pope now should occupy a more important place in the Church than during the first centuries. But there was also resistance by people who, tied to old religious customs, preferred the particularism of the past to a future with a predominantly supranational character. And finally there was also the opposition of upper clergymen who feared the loss of their historical rights and occasionally wondered whether the traditional character of an episcopate based on divine right was still safe.

Such pockets of resistance could be seen almost everywhere. They could be found in England, where among some Old Catholics the insular thinking of the eighteenth century lived on, and in Lombardy and in Poland, where Josephinist thought continued to be propounded in the seminaries and universities. They held on especially strongly in France and the German-speaking countries, where latent opposition was incited by the very excesses of the ultramontane faction. In essence, though, these were no more than rearguard skirmishes, incapable of stopping the victory of the ultramontane movement.

In France during the Second Republic, the ultramontanes became stronger, ably assisted by Nuncio Fornari. The bishops appointed by Falloux largely thought "Roman" thoughts and helped them to victory at the various provincial councils. At these councils the Holy See succeeded in having some decrees changed and thereby implicitly achieved recognition of its claim to such control. The newspaper *L'Univers,* edited by Parisis and Gousset, eagerly supported every move made by the Holy See in this connection, and thereby strengthened the impulse with which Catholics had looked toward Rome for years.

The defenders of ultramontanism found considerable support among the lower clergy, which was dissatisfied with the arbitrariness of many bishops. In order to protect themselves, the priests were demanding the restoration of church tribunals, which had been abolished after the French Revolution; the provincial councils of the middle of the century met some of their demands through the reinstitution of officialates. Often this was only illusory, however, and many tribunals existed only on paper. Dissatisfied with the way and methods of episcopal jurisdiction, the parish priests began to turn to the Roman tribunals even in the smallest of episcopal decisions whenever they did not meet the approval of the pastors. The tribunals in turn were only too happy to oblige and to interfere in the internal affairs of French dioceses, going over the heads of the bishops.[1] The tendency to resort to Rome was promoted by some canonists like Abbé André[2] and publications like *Le Rappel* and *La Correspondance de Rome,* which in France publicized the decisions favorable to the lower clergy which the Roman congregations had made in the name of universally valid canon law.

[1] Cf. J. Vernay, "Un aspect du mouvement ultramontain dans l'Église de France au XIXe siècle," *Bulletin des Facultés catholiques de Lyon,* n.s. 34 (1963), 5–18.
[2] On him, see *DDC* I, 516–19.

Returned to Rome at the beginning of 1851, Cardinal Fornari emphatically continued to support the attempts of the ultramontanes by defending the papers *L'Univers* and *La Correspondance de Rome* against the attacks of some bishops, and by promoting the inclusion of Gallican-oriented works in the Index. Between 1850 and 1852 several textbooks employed by the seminaries were condemned. Included were Bailly's *Théologie,* even though it had been revised as late as 1842, and Lequeux's *Traité de droite canonique,* which strongly favored episcopal autonomy and common law.

The vociferous enthusiam with which the ultramontane press greeted these steps, and the application of often rather insensitive methods led to a counterreaction. In 1852, a Paris theologian wrote *Mémoire sur la situation présente de l'Église gallicaine relativement au droit coutumier,* which concerned itself with the most important questions discussed at the time, such as the problem of particular rights as against the universal right of the Church, the reform of liturgy, and the interference by Roman congregations. At the same time, steps were taken to silence those journalists who expressed themselves too loudly in favor of the ultramontane cause. The time was well chosen, inasmuch as many, even non-Gallican, bishops were becoming concerned about priestly agitation; they detected in it the spirit of rebellion which, by appealing to Roman authority, was trying to escape from the supervision of the bishops at home. Additionally, they were shocked by the action of Catholic laymen who presumed to substitute a learning Church for the teaching Church, and became angry over the arrogance with which some journalists assumed they could dictate how the bishops should carry out their duties. Pius IX himself was required to counsel Veuillot to moderation. Errors in leadership by Dupanloup and Sibour, the archbishop of Paris, necessitated the Pope's intervention. In April 1853 he published the encyclical *Inter multiples,*[3] concerning the problems raised in France. It was a clear disapproval of Gallicanism, even in its moderate form, and of all those who, for whatever reasons, were resisting the ultramontane current.

Rome's Systematic Activity

The publication of the encyclical *Inter multiples* signified a change in the attitude of Rome. Like most of the great movements in Church history, the ultramontane movement had started from below. Initially the Holy See had confined itself to noting its progress without active interference on its part. But during the final years of Gregory XVI a development

---

[3] Text in *Acta Pii IX* I, 439–48.

was initiated which became notably intensified under the pontificate of Pius IX.

The personality of the Pope alone contributed to it. His charm and open nature, so different from the reserved behavior of his predecessor, together with the aura of a "martyr," which the problems arising from the Roman Question lent him, gradually gave him among the Catholic peoples of the world a popularity such as no Pope had known before him. This, in Church history, singular phenomenon explains in part the enthusiasm with which all of the clergy and of the faithful accepted the doctrine of papal infallibility after it had been unclear for centuries. It also explains the favorable reception of ecclesiastical centralization, which, as everyone knew, also was desired by the Pope.

But Rome was not satisfied with allowing favorable circumstances alone to do the work. The course of the 1848 revolution inevitably meant that at the close of the crisis a systematic plan would be developed to prevent future revolutionary attempts. In its implementation the Jesuits, who had become very influential in the Curia, played a great role. In 1847, Ballerini's *Vindiciae,* one of the works which was directed against Febronianism and on which ultramontane propaganda was very strongly based, was published again. A short time later Gallican and Febronian textbooks were suppressed, an action which made a deep impression on contemporaries. Parallel with it, the professors at the Gregoriana in their works emphasized the classical theses of the primacy and infallibility of the Pope. Like Passaglia in his *Commentarius de prerogative B. Petri* (1856), which served as the model for analogous publications, they strove for a more scholarly foundation by returning to the Scripture and the Fathers. Or, like Schrader, they developed the ultramontane positions to an extreme, giving them a clearly theocratic perspective. The number of their students continually grew, thanks to the increase in the national seminaries at Rome,[4] and they in turn spread these ideas throughout the world. *Civiltà cattolica* effectively popularized them. The proclamation of the Immaculate Conception (1854) can also be seen from the perspective of the increasingly emphasized infallibility of the Pope. This event, which strongly influenced the Catholic world, in singular fashion affirmed the prerogatives of the Pope and his growing importance in the life of the Church.[5]

---

[4] To the old colleges (German-Hungarian, English, Scottish, Irish, Greek, and that of the Congregation for the Propagation of the Faith), the following seminaries were gradually added: the Belgian seminary in 1844, the Beda Seminary for English-speaking converts in 1852, the French seminary in 1853, the Latin American Pius seminary in 1858, the North American seminary in 1859, the Illyrian seminary in 1863, and the Polish seminary in 1866.

[5] See *EThL* 31 (1955), 83–86.

Even more than on the doctrinal level, Roman activity proceeded systematically in the practical area of discipline. Rome seized every opportunity to support and strengthen the efforts that were being made by ultramontanes in the various countries to effect closer ties to the center of Christianity and a strengthening of papal power. While nuncios in earlier times had acted as diplomatic liaisons to governments, they now also took a hand in the internal affairs of the Churches in the countries to which they had been assigned. Pro-Roman priests were supported and, if necessary, protected against the accusations of their bishops; frequently they were appointed as prelates in order to raise their standing. The obligation for periodic visits, which had fallen into disuse, was revived, and the increasing contacts with the bishops were augmented by the large assemblies of 1854, 1862, and 1867.[6] Hundreds of bishops gathered in Rome and each time the assemblies appeared as the apotheosis of papal power and Catholic unity. Everything possible was done to stifle regional differences in ecclesiastical life by discouraging all calls for the convocation of national councils, by favoring a return to the integral observation of universal canon law, and by recommending appeals to the Curia, even in unimportant matters. The Pope increasingly appointed bishops without considering the opinions of the local higher clergy, and more than once gave preference to mediocre men of whom he could be sure, rather than appoint able men with an independent view; what made the difference was the Roman education and pliability of the candidates. It was a grave matter that the one-sided reports by ultramontanes about clergymen suspected of lukewarmness toward Rome were uncritically accepted. Such a policy of denunciation developed particularly in France. Until 1860 Pius IX and Antonelli, desirous not to increase internal tensions, assumed a reserved attitude and pointed out to the governments that "it was paradoxical to expect the Holy See to keep within limits a movement from which it could only gain." But the extremely half-hearted attitude of the Gallicans in the Roman Question and their liberal sympathies caused high indignation in Rome and the Pope began to favor their opponents.

It was even attempted to increase Roman influence in the election of Eastern bishops. The opportunity for this move was provided by the Ottoman government when it withdrew Catholics of the Eastern Rite from the civil jurisdiction of schismatic patriarchs and thus made sure that the election of bishops and patriarchs had secular significance. It was necessary to take steps to prevent the elections from taking place

---

[6] Concerning the assembly of 1867, at which according to Manning "the martyrdom of Peter and his primacy over the world" was celebrated (Saint Paul was neglected, see *Irenikon* 40 [1967], 43), see P. Karlbrandes, *Der heilige Petrus in Rom oder Rom ohne Petrus* (Einsiedeln 1867) and Aubert, *Pie IX* 309f.

under the pressure of influential laymen who conceivably had their material interests more in mind than the spiritual welfare of the Church. The Armenian patriarch Hassun suggested to Rome a transitional solution which would simultaneously enhance the role of the apostolic delegate and preserve the essentials of the traditional system. The majority of the consulted cardinals in Rome agreed with this approach, but Cardinal Barnabo, the prefect of the Congregation for the Propagation of the Faith, and some of his supporters tended to see a schismatic factor in the slightest autonomy in ecclesiastical discipline and were unwilling to grant the Uniates more than their liturgical peculiarities.[7] Pius IX, personally agreeing with Barnabo, consulted Valerga, the Latin patriarch of Jerusalem, on the matter; Valerga came out in favor of a radical reform of the Eastern patriarch statute in order to give it a centralistic tone. The Pope used the presence of all patriarchs during the festivities of 1867 in Rome to inform them of his intentions. From now on, the lower clergy and laymen would no longer participate in elections, the patriarch elected by the bishops alone would assume his position only after being confirmed by the Pope, and the appointment of bishops would be in the hands of the Holy See. It would select one candidate from a list of three names submitted by the patriarch, the bishops, and the Congregation for the Propagation of the Faith. The immediately following protest by the Maronite and Melchite patriarchs resulted in a postponement of the application of the measure in the jurisdictional area of the two patriarchates; but for the Armenian Church it went into effect immediately with the papal bull *Reversurus* of 12 July 1867.[8] The announcement that these steps, amounting to a reversal of the status expressly granted by Benedict XIV, would soon also be extended to other patriarchates created profound consternation in all Uniate Churches. This worry was added to the displeasure with the pressure which increasingly was applied in favor of an adaptation of Eastern Church discipline to the canon law of the Latin Church. It became evident in the commission which was charged with preparing the decrees of the Vatican Council for the Uniate Churches.[9] The attempts violated the venerable traditions of the East too much not to cause considerable resistance, but in Europe they could easily be enforced through the joint actions of the nuncios, bishops, Catholic movements, and ecclesiastical press.

[7] With respect to this point, the Roman officials were in fact less radical than Dom Guéranger, in whose view liturgical uniformity had to be a normal consequence of the unity of the Church. In his encyclical of 8 April 1862 (*Acta Pii IX* III, 424–36), Pius IX unequivocally affirmed his intention to respect the Eastern liturgies.

[8] See *JP* VI/1, 453–65. The discussions occasioned by the bull are treated in Mansi XL, 745–1132; *DThC* I, 1914–15; *DHGE* IV, 338–42, 679–80, V, 337–38, 345.

[9] See Hajjar, 292–300.

In Austria, the concordat of 1855 had liquidated Josephinist laws and had made possible the reorganization of the educational system in keeping with the wishes of the Holy See. Consequently, Cardinal Rauscher, the archbishop of Vienna, together with the support of his colleagues Rudigier, Gasser, and Fessler, was able to influence the numerous Catholic associations in an ultramontane direction and to promote the activity of the Jesuits and Redemptorists. In Innsbruck, whose department of theology was entrusted to the Jesuits in 1857, Moy and Vering established the Archives for Catholic Canon Law as a strong outpost of Roman ideas, in Budapest F. Hovanyi made the theology department into a center for the reaction to the Josephinist tentacles in Hungary, and in Vienna the most radical ultramontane theses were defended at the University of Vienna by the Jesuit theologian Clemens Schrader[10] and the canonist George Phillips.[11] In his *Kirchenrecht* (7 vols. [1845–72]), Phillips, like Schrader, betrayed an unabashed romantic enthusiasm for medieval theocracy, identified the Pope with the Church, and expressed a rather legalistic and superficial view of the Church and its unity. The work was only second-rate from an academic point of view, but is proof of an educated mind; it was largely responsible in the German-speaking countries for widely popularizing the doctrine of the infallibility of the Pope and of his universal episcopal office and the doctrine of the indirect sovereignty of the Church over the state.

In Germany, Ketteler assumed the leading position, which Geissel held until his death in 1864. Mainz was still the vanguard of the movement, but Moufang and Heinrich, assisted by the nuncio in Munich and Reisach, who in 1854 had become a Curia cardinal, elsewhere also had supporters who worked toward the same goal: the Jesuits with their increasing numbers and influence, the Germanists, and the priests trained in Innsbruck under the guidance of the Jesuits. All of them, who liked to think of themselves as the sole possessors of the Catholic spirit, gradually impressed their views on the Catholic masses. They imparted to them their ideas about the prerogatives of the Pope and the authority of the Roman congregations in the life of the national Churches, as well as about the ideal image of a good Catholic. Within the span of a few decades they produced a profound change in German Catholicism. The place of the old view of piety, centered around inner spirituality and the

---

[10] Clemens Schrader (1820–75), professor of dogmatics at the Roman College from 1852 to 1857 and at the Department of Theology of the University of Vienna from 1857 to 1870.
[11] On George Phillips (1804–72), from 1834 to 1847 professor at the University of Munich and from 1851 until his death professor at the University of Vienna, see J. von Schulte, *Die Geschichte der Quellen und Literatur des canonischen Rechts* III/1 (Stuttgart 1880), 375–87, and *LThK* VIII, 468.

exercise of virtue, was taken by a new way of religious life which emphasized superficial exercises, membership in confraternities, and the strict observation of church regulations. Sailer's irenics yielded to an attitude which emphasized the gap between Catholics and non-Catholics by once again applying the old maxim of "Extra Ecclesiam nulla salus." Instead of working for a strengthening of religious convictions by appealing to church history and philosphy, all too often there was nothing more than the demand blindly to bow to the authority of the Church, mention of whose preeminence over the state was never omitted in the process.

In England, the persistent Manning, assisted by the *Dublin Review,* succeeded within a few years in winning the majority of the Catholic faithful to a very unpretentious and radical ultramontanism, in spite of the opposition of the liberals at the *Rambler* and the hesitant stance of Newman and other traditionalist bishops. In Ireland, Cardinal Cullen, who was a total adherent of the centralistic plans of the Holy See, carried the day for the Roman concepts.

In France the encyclical *Inter multiples* played a decisive part in the victory of ultramontanism. It became possible because of the benevolent neutrality of the government at the beginning of the Second Empire, the extension of Dom Gúeranger's campaign in favor of the Roman liturgy, the Rome-oriented development of Saint Sulpice, which trained a majority of the young clergy, and the establishment of the French Seminary at Rome. The last was accomplished in 1853 with the support of Monsignor de Ségur,[12] whose writings greatly helped in spreading the "Roman spirit" in France. Louis Veuillot's newspaper *L'Univers,* like *L'Avenir* twenty years earlier, grew into a battle instrument of the movement. It started a campaign to win the lower clergy for a theocratic concept of society in which politics would be in the service of religion, and for a Church in closer contact with the papacy; in this way it would be better prepared to withstand the dangers of "revolution." Ultimately Veuillot succeeded in creating among French Catholics a "cult of the papacy" as could be found in no other country. At the same time the works of Bossuet, of the Maurists and their students, and of the Jansenists,[13] which in earlier generations had formed the foundation for the training of the clergy, were replaced by an ecclesiastical literature whose academic content was virtually nonexistent, but whose orientation was clearly ultramontane.

[12] Cf. M. de Hédouville, op. cit., 208–27.
[13] This reaction is explained by the connection which in the course of time sprang up between Gallicanism and Jansenism. It was reflected in part in the attacks against the Jansenists by Sainte-Beuve (1840–59) and the publication of the hitherto unpublished memoirs of the Jesuit Rapin (Paris 1861–65).

The Excesses of Neo-Ultramontanism and the Reaction in Germany and France

As all other movements, ultramontanism also was not able to avoid excesses. Thoughtful ultramontanes clearly recognized the weaknesses of Gallicanism. More clearly than their opponents they realized that the development of ecclesiastical institutions had not come to an end with the conclusion of the patristic period. They were of the opinion that Rome's intervention in the affairs of the national Churches, which would be able to resist the encroachments of the governments only with difficulty, was justified. They desired a clear centralization, convinced that it was indispensable for the solution of religious problems on the only level where this was possible, namely on the supranational one. But they also often lacked moderation and occasionally a sense of the fitting in their methods and ideas. (Reference was already made above to the abusive practice of secret denunciations made with irresponsible frivolousness). After 1860 certain tendencies became clear which Wilfrid Ward and Dom Butler suggested be termed "neo-ultramontanism." Some people wanted to see the role of the bishops reduced to an intolerable point; some portrayed the most extreme theses of medieval theocracy as divine law; others wished to extend the infallibility of the Pope to all of his pronouncements, even those which concerned religious policy, or they developed forms of papal veneration which amounted to "idolatry of the papacy." The Pope was referred to as the "Vice-God of Mankind" and as the "Permanent Word Incarnate." Monsignor Mermillod preached on the "three incarnations of the Son of God" in the womb of the Virgin Mary, in the Eucharist, and in "the old man in the Vatican." The *Civiltà cattolica* went so far as to write that "when the Pope meditates, it is God who is thinking through him." All of these exaggerations and flatteries, to which Pius IX did not object, were splashed throughout the Catholic press, to the great disgust of those who were incapable of realizing that these unfortunate formulations were not merely thoughtless expressions emerging from the simple soul of the masses. They certainly did their part in fortifying the last remaining centers of resistance.

The stupidities of neo-ultramontanism angered the German professors the more as they already had great difficulty in swallowing the more moderate views of Bellarmine's followers. As they tended to see ecclesiastical reality only in historical terms, their view in general was too retrospective. They ignored that, considering its involvement with history, the Church perforce had to adapt its institutions to contemporary times. As experts on Christian antiquity, they refused to recognize as legitimate the development of papal prerogatives in the course of the centuries. Their view was supported by the questionable nature of many of the arguments advanced by the representatives of ultramontanism, whose scholarly pronouncements often were not able to keep pace with Catholic thought. They were accused of being a group of fanatics who, while they had a certain power as a result of the support of a considerable number of pious laymen, nevertheless were discrediting the standing of the Church in the eyes of society's leaders. Additionally, there was the hostility between the "German theologians" and the representatives of Scholasticism, which had assumed the form of conflict between Rome and Germany. It was incited by the condemnations and occasionally broad-based criticisms which Rome hurled against these German theologians; it involved accusations which not only offended the German scholars' sense of academic superiority, but also their national pride.

The opposition of the Catholic scholars to the growth of ultramontanism could have confined itself to the type of passive resistance which the professors at Tübingen exercised. But under the influence of Döllinger, the intellectual leader of the movement of reaction to the incursion of the "Romans" into Catholic scholarship and the administration of the Church in Germany, it assumed the character of an open battle. The last word on Döllinger's development during these years, which step by step led him from a theological to a dogmatic opposition, has not yet been spoken; there can be no doubt, however, that on the Catholic side there was too much of a tendency to simplify matters. Once Döllinger had become suspicious of the centralizing tendencies of the Romans, which were in line with the aggressive orientation of the Neo-Scholastics, his apprehension of papal absolutism made him increasingly fearful. The *Syllabus* confirmed his fears of the dangers to academic freedom and of the introduction of a medieval theocratic system as an article of faith. He was convinced that the future of Catholicism itself was in danger if there was no change in the behavior of the Church. At the convention of Catholic scholars in 1863 in Munich he collided with the Neo-Scholastics. His indignation reached its peak in 1867 when Inquisitor Arbues was canonized. Now there arose the question of whether the ultramontane faction, disregarding ecclesiastical institutions, was not in fact falsifying the religious ideal of Christianity. But the very virulence of his polemics against the "papal system," which he portrayed as a creation of the Middle Ages, incited the bishops against him, including those who, like Rauscher and Ketteler, also regarded certain forms of Roman centralization as excessive. Thus, open resistance to ultramontanism in Germany remained essentially restricted to the universities.

In France, on the other hand, a group of decided opponents of ultramontanism within the episcopate once again came to the fore during
the final years of the Second Empire. It had two different roots. The
dean of the theological faculty at the Sorbonne, Monsignor Maret,[14]
who identified with the ecclesiological views of Bossuet, was deeply
concerned about the absolutist and theocratic manipulations of the
neo-ultramontanes. He surrounded himself with a small group of intelligent priests with liberal and moderately Gallican views,[15] and through
his close relationship with Napoleon III succeeded in having several of
them appointed as bishops. Although the effectiveness of these bishops
was limited by the Roman enthusiasm of their clergy and a majority of
their flocks, they nonetheless constituted a very intimate association of
opponents of Roman policies. They were led by Monsignor Darboy,[16]
archbishop of Paris after 1863. Indignant about the behavior "of these
strange Catholics whose piety consisted mainly of greeting the Pope
from afar in order to insult the bishops near by," Darboy several times,
and with a frankness to which Rome was no longer accustomed, informed the Pope of his profound consternation with regard to the interference of the Roman congregations in episcopal administrations. He
condemned this as an attempt to introduce in France "the regimen of
mission countries."

Raised in a totally different theological climate and having long been
cool toward the Bonapartist bishops, the liberal Catholics of the *Correspondant,* who once had seen in ultramontanism the guarantee for the
freedom of the Church, now began to move closer to the group around
Maret and Darboy. They saw ultramontanism represented and per-
sonified in *L'Univers* and the *Civiltà cattolica,* in men, that is, who had
not the slightest inkling of the true requirements of modern society and
who favored absolutism in Church and society. Even men as devoted to
the Holy See as Dupanloup, who more than once had stated his belief in
the infallibility of the Pope, now began to fear its final formulation.
They feared that it would lead to a consolidation of the positions of the

---

[14] With respect to his theological position, see, in addition to the biography by G. Bazin
(3 vols. [Paris 1891]), R. Thysman in *RHE* 52 (1957), 401–65 and *DThC* IX, 2033–37.
[15] The future Cardinal Lavigerie belonged to them until 1866. He tried to keep the
excesses of Roman centralization within limits and to preserve the originality of national
modes of thought; in 1862 he submitted a plan to the French government in which he
suggested the inclusion of men from the large Catholic countries in the Roman congregations and in the college of cardinals of the Curia (see de Montclos, 200–223).
[16] On Georges Darboy (1813–71), one of the smartest French bishops, a good biography is still lacking. For the time being, consult those by J. Foulon (Paris 1889), *DHGE*
XIV, 84–86, and J. -R. Palanque, op. cit., 21–25.

Syllabus and other documents which assumed religious-political views incompatible with the modern mind. Thus, the extent of the ultramontane victory in France led to the formation of a new Gallican front, whose most active members were precisely those men who twenty years earlier had been the champions of this victory.

CHAPTER 22

The Vatican Council

Preparation

The decision of Pius IX to convoke a council must be seen from the pastoral perspective of the reaction to naturalism and rationalism which he had pursued since the beginning of his pontificate. As painful and retrogressive the modalities occasionally might be, essentially it was his intention once again to provide Catholic life with a focus on the fundamental events of revelation. Additionally, he intended to undertake the highly necessary adaptation of canon law to the profound changes which had taken place during the past three centuries since the last ecumenical council.

The idea of a council as a cure for the crisis from which the Church was suffering had been suggested to Pius IX as early as 1849, and slowly matured. At the end of 1864 he consulted a number of cardinals, who happened to be in Rome, about the advisability of the matter. In spite of some qualifications, their opinion on the whole was rather positive, and the Pope decided to pursue the issue carefully. He asked about forty bishops, selected from the most important Catholic countries, and a few bishops who held offices in Churches of the Eastern Rite to submit suggestions for an agenda. Gradually he then formed four commissions, which he charged with working out the details of the program. A majority of the Curia, however, was not very enthusiastic about the papal plan, and their reticence caused the Pope to hesitate for more than two years. He was also moved by the not totally unjustified fear that the contrasting tendencies evident in the Church in many areas, such as the question of modern freedoms and the growing Roman centralization, might come to a head at the council. But finally, encouraged by a number of respected bishops, the Pope on 26 June 1867 publicly made known his intention, and one year later he invited to Rome for 8 December 1869[1] all Catholic bishops and those people who had the right to participate in a council.[2]

During the consultative deliberations, more than one bishop suggested that the council be used to attempt contacts with the separated Christians. This was in part based on the hopes of a return of the Orthodox, which grew out of the changes in the Slavic world and the Near East. Similarly, with respect to the Reformed Churches, the continuation of the Oxford Movement in the Anglo-Saxon countries and the crisis which the progress of liberal Protestants had caused in the German Lutheran Church had occasioned unionist thoughts on all sides.[3] It is true that the Holy See reacted rather reservedly and during the 1860s, especially under the influence of Manning, several times stiffened its attitude.[4] Nevertheless, Pius IX and several of his advisers continued to hope for a return of the separated Christians and they believed that at least in the Near East there were some opportunities which should not be allowed to pass. With this possibility in mind, a letter was directed to all Orthodox bishops in September 1868, in which they were asked to return to Catholic unity in order to be able to participate in the council; a few days later a global letter was sent to Protestants and Anglicans.[5] But this clumsy and double procedure was generally badly received and to us, today, from an ecumenical point of view appears as one of the saddest cases of missed opportunities.[6]

In the Catholic world the announcement of the council quickly intensified the opposition between the currents which for a number of years had been facing one another: Gallicans and liberal Catholics on one side, ultramontanes and opponents of the modern freedoms on the other.[7] The selection of the consultants who were supposed to prepare the conciliar decrees—sixty Romans and thirty-six foreigners, almost all of them known for their unequivocally ultramontane and antiliberal

[1] Bull *Aeterni Patris* of 29 June 1868 (Mansi L, 193–200).
[2] In this group were ultimately also included the bishops *in partibus,* notwithstanding the reluctance of the Pope, who would have preferred to exclude Monsignor Maret (see J. Hamer in *RSPhTh* 44 [1960], 40–50). It is to be noted that, contrary to repeated assertions at the time of the council, the number of vicars apostolic did not exceed 10 percent of the total number of fathers.
[3] See the information in Aubert, *Pie IX,* 478f., 484–86, 564.
[4] Ibid., 479–85. Concerning the decrees of 1864 and 1865, which forbade English Catholics to participate together with the Anglicans in the Association for the Promotion of the Union of Christendom (A.P.U.C.), see E. Purcell, *Life and Letters of A. Phillips de Lisle* I (London 1900), 346–422 and C. Butler, *Life and Times of Bishop Ullathorne* I (London 1926), 334–68.
[5] Text of the letters of 8 and 13 September 1868 in Mansi L, 199–205.
[6] See F. de Wyels in *Irenikon* 6 (1929), 488–516, 655–86.
[7] See Aubert, *Vat.,* 84–101. Also R. Lill, "Die deutschen Theologieprofessoren im Urteil des Münchener Nuntius," *Reformata reformanda* II (Münster 1965), 483–507.

views[8]—worried those who had hoped that the council would give the bishops who stood on the periphery the long-awaited opportunity to achieve a limited opening of the Church to modern ideas. Instead they believed that they saw a certain tactic at work: a secret preparation of the council beyond all conflicting debates and only with exclusive consideration of the point of view of the Curia, and then discussionless acceptance by the council fathers of all proposals, worked out beforehand down to the smallest detail. A misunderstood piece of news, the "Correspondance de France," which on 6 February 1869 was published in the newspaper of the Jesuits, the *Civiltà cattolica,* seemed to confirm this prognosis by announcing the definition of papal infallibility by acclamation and therefore without any possibility of clarifying the matter through discussion. Reactions were violent, especially in the German-speaking countries and even in the circles which normally could not be accused of harboring any systematic hostility toward Rome.[9] Döllinger, whose hostility to the Curia had grown noticeably during the last several years, under the pseudonym of Janus published a critical and partisan book attacking the primacy of the Pope and the Roman centralization.[10] In France also press polemics appeared, somewhat milder in tone, because the liberal Catholics considered a definition of papal infallibility as inopportune and the ultramontanes viewed it as desirable. In this fashion the problem, initially virtually not intended to be on the program, during the months preceding the council moved into the foreground of activity. Several respected bishops like Monsignor Dechamps, archbishop of Mechelen, and Monsignor Manning, archbishop of Westminster, demanded immediately that the council be utilized solemnly to define the truth of this publicly contested point. Monsignor Dupanloup, on the other hand, after a long silence came out against the definition because he deemed it inopportune. The majority of the German bishops at their annual conference at Fulda in September 1869 also expressed reservations about the future definition of the personal infallibility of the Pope.[11]

Several governments on their part feared decisions of the council concerning civil marriage, secular education, and constitutional freedoms, and were apprehensive over a possible reconfirmation of certain medieval prerogatives of the Church over the civil authority. The request by some bishops, which was received positively by Rome, to make the *Syllabus* of 1864 the basis for council deliberations, could not

---

[8] See R. Aubert, "La composition des commissions préparatoire du Ier Concile du Vatican," *Reformata reformanda* II (Münster 1965), 447–82.

[9] Cf. J. Granderath, op. cit. I, 187–246.

[10] *Der Papst und das Conzil* (Leipzig 1869).

[11] R. Lill, *Die ersten deutschen Bischofskonferenzen* (Freiburg i. Br. 1964), 80–91.

but intensify such fears. All those in the Church who were afraid of the triumph of the ultramontanes at the council tried to reinforce the suspicions of the governments, hoping thereby to cause diplomatic admonitions and warnings. For a while France considered appointing an ambassador extraordinary for the council as it had done for the Council of Trent,[12] and in April the minister president of Bavaria, Prince Chlodwig zu Hohenlohe-Schillingsfürst, tried to bring about a joint intervention of the European governments;[13] they, however, preferred to barricade themselves behind an attitude of watchful waiting.

Infallibilists and Anti-Infallibilists

The council opened on 8 December 1869 in the presence of about seven hundred bishops, i.e., of more than two-thirds of those entitled to participate. Among them were 60 prelates of Eastern Rites, for the most part from the Near East, and almost 200 fathers from outside of Europe: 121 from America, 49 of these from the United States, 41 from India and the Far East, 18 from Oceania, and 9 from the missions in Africa. It should be noted, however, that while the prelates from the other parts of the world amounted to about one-third of the council, many of them, especially the missionaries, in reality were European, and that with the exception of the bishops of the Eastern Rites there were no native bishops from Asia and Africa. Within this European predominance there was a Latin predominance. There were some significant English-speaking groups (among them the Irish element predominated) and about seventy-five Germans and Austrians, but disregarding the Spaniards and Latin Americans, who comprised about one hundred members, the French constituted about 17 percent of the assembly (for many missionaries hailed from France) and the Italians constituted a whopping 35 percent, so that the French and Italians together amounted to more than half of the council fathers. The overwhelming Italian predominance, which was strongly criticized, interestingly enough had no tactical rationale; it was merely the result of historical circumstances. In antiquity the number of dioceses established in southern and central Italy was high, in more recent times a large part of the Catholic apostolate in the Greek and Turkish islands was entrusted to Italian missionaries, and Italians occupied a large number of the positions in the Curia. The Italian prelates by themselves constituted not only one-third of the assembly, they also provided two-thirds of the consultants and experts, all of the secretaries, and all five presidents;

[12] The detailed treatment by E. Ollivier, op. cit. I, 403–536 has been revised in this instance by de Montclos, 391–405.
[13] See J. Grisar, *Bayern, Staat und Kirche* (Munich 1961), 216–40.

318

only one important position, that of secretary general, was entrusted to a foreigner, to the Austrian Fessler.

The controversies which in the course of 1869 swirled around papal infallibility and especially the clumsy interference of Monsignor Dupanloup in the middle of November soon after the opening of the council resulted in the replacement of national groupings, which had begun in the first few days, with an ideological grouping.[14] On one side stood the fathers who did not doubt, who in fact expected, that the council would again emphasize those principles which in their view in an ideal Christian society had to form the foundation for the relationship between Church and state and who desired a solemn definition of the infallibility of the Pope. Even if they were not in agreement with all of the centralizing steps of the Roman Curia and thought of some manifestations of papal veneration as ludicrous, many fathers were convinced that the Gallican and Febronian theses which called for a limitation of the papal primacy in favor of the episcopate would be a regression. It would go counter to the old traditions favored by a number of unequivocal statements in Scripture (for example: "Tu es Petrus"), by some formulations stemming from the time of the church Fathers (for example: "Roma locuta est, causa finita est"), and by all of the great Scholastic teachers, from Thomas Aquinas to Bellarmine and Alphonsus Liguori. Confronting some of the difficulties of a historical nature with the living faith of the Church, they were especially impressed by the almost universal agreement of the Church of their time with the thesis of the personal infallibility of the Pope, a concept which in the preceding twenty years had been affirmed by provincial councils several times. Under such circumstances it appeared quite normal to them that controversies which they considered fruitless should be nipped in the bud. Extratheological reasons lent additional weight to the conviction of many prelates. In addition to their veneration of Pius IX, they were convinced that emphasis on the monolithic character of the Roman unity would send non-Catholics to the Church, because they were confused by the hesitation of the Churches separated from Rome or by the contradictions in modern philosophical systems (this aspect was emphasized particularly by the convert Manning). Noticeable also was their endeavor to emphasize the principle of authority as strongly as possible in a world undermined by democratic efforts, which in their eyes were nothing more than a milder form of anarchy, inspired in the main by Protestantism. Finally, given the developing crisis before their eyes, they desired

[14] See R. Aubert, "Motivations théologiques et extrathéologiques des partisans et des adversaires de la définition dogmatique de l'infaillibilité du pape à Vatican I," *L'infaillibilité*, ed. by E. Castelli (Paris 1970), 91–103.

to see an increasingly centralized organization for the offensive and defensive strategy of the Church.

Precisely the same mixture of considerations of a theoretical-doctrinal kind and extratheological factors brought other bishops to the conviction that such plans would be a shock for the traditional constitution of the Church and threaten civil society in its most legitimate aspects. The number of these bishops was relatively small and for this reason they were known as the "minority," but they enjoyed a high prestige because of the sees[15] which they occupied and because of their theological scholarship. Some—they were actually more numerous than an apologetically oriented historiography later wanted to admit—continued to adhere to the semi-Gallican concept of the ecclesiastical magisterial office, the starting point of which was that the Pope could never treat a question of doctrine independently from ratification by the episcopate. The influence of the tradition of Bossuet, the episcopal mentality passed down from the Febronian theologians and the canonists of the preceding century, historical difficulties such as the condemnation of Pope Honorius, an archaic theological attitude which clung too much to the sources and had little understanding for dogmatic developments, led them to the conclusion that either the Pope did not possess the privilege of personal infallibility or that the problem at best was still obscure and its treatment therefore premature.

More widespread seemed to be the legitimate, albeit occasionally exaggerated worry about the second element in the divine structure of the ecclesiastical hierarchy. The proposed definition of the infallibility of the Pope appeared to many fathers as the separation of a partial aspect from an indivisible whole, the effect of which would result in the virtual abolition of the episcopate.[16] The way in which the council had been prepared seemed to justify their apprehensions. Did the agenda,[17] determined by the Pope and, in contrast to the Council of Trent, not by

---

[15] Almost the entire Austro-Hungarian episcopate under the leadership of Cardinal Rauscher, a renowned patrologist and fervent defender of the rights of the Holy See against Josephinist and liberal demands; all of Germany's sees; a considerable number of French prelates, among them the archbishops of Paris and Lyon; several North American archbishops; the archbishop of Milan, the most populous Italian diocese; and three Eastern patriarchs.

[16] This appears to have been Ketteler's view. Concerning his attitude (very characteristic of those bishops who were devoted to Rome and open toward the idea of the infallibility of the Pope, but who rejected the definition in the context in which it was offered to them), see the balanced treatment by V. Conzemius, "Acton, Döllinger und Ketteler," *AMrhKG* 14 (1962), 194–238, which corrects the exaggerated thesis put forth by F. Vigener in his biography of the prelate.

[17] Text in Mansi L, 215–22. See Aubert, *Vat.*, 78–83 on the development of the regulation. It was modified by the Pope on 20 February 1870 in a way which displeased the

the fathers, sufficiently respect their freedom of action? And could the bishops expect to play more than the role of extras in a scene staged in advance by the Curia? The bad acoustics of the council auditorium, which did not satisfy minimum requirements for holding genuine debates, was a further case in point.

There was additional concern about the fact that several of the best-known supporters of the definition wanted to include in the subject area of the infallibility of the Church, i.e., of the Pope, a number of "Catholic truths" which did not belong to the *depositum fidei* and had only indirect connection with it. This was particularly the case in the religious-political area. Many people indeed noted that the definition of papal infallibility in the extensive form suggested by its proponents would strengthen the authority of such documents as the bull *Unam sanctam,* the declaration of Sixtus V concerning the right to depose sovereigns, and especially the *Syllabus,* whose judgments were a special burden for the council. Both European and American newspapers were extensive witnesses to this concern. Besides, the way in which the question of infallibility was being dealt with by the ultramontane papers was enough to justify the belief of those who were convinced "that it was the intention to declare the Pope infallible in matters of faith in order to give him the appearance of infallibility in other matters as well" (Leroy-Beaulieu). It was expected that the governments would not tolerate such a course of events without voicing their opposition, but of course this would be to the disadvantage of the local Churches. Beyond the question of immediate tactics there was also a question of principle. It was raised by those who believed that the political future belonged to the liberal institutions, and that the Church, as long as it showed itself as a defender of an autocratic authoritarianism, stood to lose everything. Finally, there were the ecumenical aspects: the proposed definition would add to the difficulties of establishing closer relations with the separated brethren, especially of the Christians in the East; it would promote the aggressiveness of certain Protestants; and could even provide a new schism in the intellectual circles of Germany which were strongly impressed by Döllinger's arguments.

If the feeling of discontent which showed itself at the beginning of the council rapidly resulted in an organized opposition, this was in part the result of some misunderstandings, but to an overwhelming degree it was the result of a regrettable maneuver of the infallibilists. For the purpose of preparing the election of the dogmatic commission, the so-

---

minority even more (see Mansi L, 854–55 and C. Butler, op. cit., 243–53). Cf. H. Jedin, "Die Geschäftsordnungen der beiden letzten ökumenischen Konzilien in ekklesiologischer Sicht," *Cath* 14 (1960), 105–18.

called *deputatio de fide,* which was to deal with the question of papal infallibility, two different election committees had been formed: one by Dupanloup, the other one by Manning. The latter insisted on the exclusion from the deputation of all fathers who were suspected of opposing the definition. A list compiled under his supervision and approved by one of the council presidents was distributed to the fathers. For the most part they had no personal knowledge of the other members of the council and on 14 December elected the proposed members in good faith. This procedure, which excluded from the deputation such competent men as Cardinal Rauscher and Monsignor Hefele, the learned author of the *Conciliengeschichte,* was a gross mistake. It put an end to the possibility of a dialogue between the two opposing positions and by its partisanship angered the members of the minority who, erroneously, believed that this maneuver by Manning's group had been engineered by the Curia. Even more, it created the impression outside of the assembly that the elections had only been a guise. From this moment on there were many who began to doubt the freedom of the council.

First Council Debates

After three weeks of exhausting formalities, the discussion concerning the first constitutional draft "against the many errors stemming from modern rationalism" was begun on 28 December.[18] It immediately became the object of strong criticism. To many fathers it was obscure, insufficiently pastoral and too aggressive, and went far beyond the points that had been discussed freely by the theologians. Criticism originated both from the infallibilists and the minority, an advantageous fact in that it gave hope that the council would proceed less inhibitedly than had been feared. After six sessions of debate, the presidents announced on 10 January that the schema was being returned to the deputies for revision. Some men were astonished that the decision was made without prior advice from the assembly, which in its majority probably would have adopted the draft with only minor changes. That this was not done shows clearly that the Roman leaders—contrary to the intention of which they were accused even before the opening of the council—were far from exploiting the obedient majority and that they tried to achieve the best possible result even at the cost of some humiliations.

[18] Mansi L, 58–119, 122–276. The protracted drafting of this schema can be followed in the minutes of the preparatory commission for doctrinal questions (ibid. XLIX, 617–736). See also L. Orban, *Theologia Güntheriana et Concilium Vaticanum,* 2 vols. (Rome 1942–49) and, with respect to the atmosphere of this commission, the letters of the American consultant Corcoran, edited by J. Hennesey in *CHR* 48 (1962), 157–81.

In order to occupy the fathers during the time which the revision of the first doctrinal schema required, discussions were begun on the schemata concerning church discipline and the adaptation of canon law. Many of the fathers believed that this adaptation to the new circumstances of the nineteenth century was the principal task of the council. For this purpose, twenty-eight schemata or draft proposals had come from the disciplinary commission, even though most of them were of a picayune nature and failed to display any openness to the future or any pastoral imagination in the search for truly new formulations;[19] eighteen additional ones had been worked out by the commission dealing with the religious orders,[20] which thanks to the leadership of its authoritarian and effective president, Cardinal Bizzarri, had done fruitful work. Furthermore, the preparatory commission for the missions and the Churches of the Eastern Rite had prepared three schemata[21] and the commission for political-ecclesiastical problems had worked out eighteen schemata[22] which concerned topics of genuine interest and often were more timely than the ones which had been prepared by the commission for church discipline.[23] Only a few of the eighty-seven schemata were distributed to the fathers during the council and ultimately there was not enough time to pass even one of them.

For an entire month, beginning on 14 January, the first four schemata were debated.[24] Because no time limit existed, many fathers were tempted to lose themselves in details and to discuss purely local problems. Many also—misunderstanding the topic—confined themselves to tiresome homilies concerning the sanctity of priests and the ecclesiastical spirit, which of course did not help progress at all. A number of interjections were of interest, however. Some of the Eastern bishops, for example, raised the question, one which did not seem to have occurred to anyone, as to what extent the disciplinary schemata were relevant to the Eastern Churches. Once again it was realized that seemingly quite neutral questions could involve ecclesiology. This became even more

---

[19] Text in Mansi LIII, 721–81; minutes of the discussions in the preparatory commission, ibid. XLIX, 748–932.

[20] Mansi LIII, 783–854; minutes, ibid. XLIX, 940–79.

[21] Mansi LIII, 45–61, 893–914; minutes, ibid. XLIX, 985–1162.

[22] Mansi LIII, 854–94. The pertinent minutes are no longer extant; some documents, ibid XLIX, 1171–1211 and in addition some indications in the diary and the correspondence of the consultant Moufang, edited by L. Lenhart in *AMrhKG* 3 (1951), 323–54, 9 (1957), 227–58.

[23] Especially those "de pauperum operariorumque miseria sublevanda" (Mansi LIII, 867–72).

[24] "De episcopis, de synodis et de vicariis generalibus" and "De sede episcopali vacante" (Mansi L, 339–52; 359–518); "De vita et honestate clericorum" (ibid., 517–22, 522–700); "De parvo catechismo" (ibid., 699–702, 703–853).

evident in the course of the discussions of the fourth project, dealing with the expediency of the drawing up of a universal catechism which was to take the place of the numerous diocesan catechisms: the proposal, which had not originated with the Roman Curia, was viewed as a sign of mistrust of the bishops.[25]

The dissatisfaction of many fathers with this proposal was aggravated by the distribution on 21 January of the constitutional draft *"De Ecclesia Christi."*[26] The draft had its good qualities—the patristic sources of its chief author, Clemens Schrader, were clearly discernible—but it also had regrettable weaknesses, especially in the disproportional number of passages devoted to the episcopate and to the papacy, a deficiency which was noted with regret even by some members of the majority. The final chapters as well, concerning the relationship between Church and state, were rejected by many because of strongly theocratic views offensive to the modern mind.[27]

Work on the schema on rationalism, which had been revised by Kleutgen, was resumed on March 18, after the sessions had been interrupted for three weeks to make needed improvements in the acoustics. The new version[28] was favorably received by the fathers, and only small details needed to be ironed out. Aside from a violent incident, caused by the passionate remarks of Monsignor Stroßmayer, and some complaints about the unseemly hurry with which ballots were taken on requests for amendments, the discussions took place in an atmosphere of equanimity. On 24 April the council, despite the last-minute hesitation of the most mistrustful of the minority, solemnly and unanimously approved the first dogmatic document, the constitution *Dei Filius.*[29] It opposed pantheism, materialism, and modern rationalism with a com-

---

[25] The revised text of this schema was again discussed by the fathers from 29 April until 13 May (Mansi LI, 454–85) and accepted with 491 *placet* votes against 56 *non placet* and 44 *placet juxta modum* votes, but was never officially promulgated. The majority of the fathers were particularly receptive to the reference to the disadvantages of the multiplicity of the catechisms in a world which evinced strong population movements from rural areas to industrial cities and from Europe to other parts of the world. But some opponents of the draft, such as Dupanloup for France and Rauscher for the German-speaking countries, pointed out that, aside from the respect for the episcopal magisterial office, circumstances needed to be considered which demanded the adaptation of catechisms to the prevailing situations in the various areas.

[26] Text in Mansi LI, 539–636. Observations by the fathers, ibid., 731–930. See F. Van der Horst, *Das Schema über die Kirche auf dem 1. Vatikanischen Konzil* (Paderborn 1963).

[27] See C. Colombo, "La Chiesa e la società civile nel Concilio Vaticano I," *SC* 89 (1961), 323–43.

[28] Text in Mansi LI, 31–38; minutes of the discussions of the commission, ibid. LIII, 177–94; speeches at the sessions, ibid. LI, 42–426.

[29] Text in Mansi LI, 429–36. Among the historio-theological commentaries see especially A. Vacant, *Études théologiques sur les constitutions du concile du Vatican*, 2 vols. (Paris

pact and enlightened presentation of the Catholic doctrine concerning God, revelation, and the faith. For almost a century it was to be the basis of standard theological textbooks.

Agitation concerning Papal Infallibility

While inside the council auditorium texts were prudently debated which caused little excitement, outside of it the discussions concerning infallibility, which soon became the center of attention, were in full sway. During the last days of December, Manning, Dechamps, and some German-speaking bishops began to circulate a petition which asked the Pope to put the item on the council agenda. The preparatory commission, however, was not disposed to placing the issue on the agenda itself. During January the petition was signed by more than four hundred fifty people.[30]

This maneuver, organized by a group acting independently from the Curia, was the occasion for the opponents of the definition to organize resistance from among splinter groups which had not yet clearly articulated their views. Monsignor Dupanloup labored under the illusion that his appearance alone would suffice to make him the center of the various discontented groups, but even the feverish activity in which he plunged himself after his arrival in Rome had only very limited success.[31] The actual leader of the minority was a layman, John Acton. As a historian he shared with his teacher Döllinger the objections to the new proposed dogma, but even more than Döllinger he feared the potential indirect consequences on the future development of Catholicism in a society whose preoccupation with the idea of freedom was growing. The recent publication of Acton's correspondence with Döllinger has confirmed the assertions of the English diplomat Odo Russell concerning the preeminent role played by the young English lord in the organizatin of the council minority. Thanks to his numerous international connections and his linguistic abilities he was largely responsible for the fact that at the very beginning of the council the most important leaders of the opposition, many of whom hardly knew one another, were brought together. His acquaintance with parliamentary procedure allowed him to point out to them the possibility of joint action, suggest several operations to them, draw their attention to several intrigues which were being hatched in the opposing camp, supply them with historical documents

---

1895), to be supplemented and corected by *De doctrina Concilii Vaticani Primi* (Vatican City 1969), 3–281 and H. Pottmeyer, *Der Glaube vor dem Anspruch der Wissenschaft* (Freiburg i. Br. 1968).

[30] List in Mansi LI, 650–63.

[31] R. Aubert in *Miscellanea historiae ecclesiasticae* (Louvain 1961), 96–116.

for the buttressing of their position, and play the role of mediator between the leaders of the minority and several foreign governments. It was due to his initiative that together with Archbishop Haynald—a member of the Hungarian House of Lords and therefore also familiar with parliamentary practices—an international committee was formed which was to guarantee the collaboration of the various opposition groups. Several times a week it served as a meeting place for about ten Austrian, German, French, British, Italian, and American bishops. The committee circulated a counterpetition which demanded from the Pope that he forego the definition of his infallibility. The counterproposal garnered 136 signatures, i.e., one-fifth of the assembled fathers.[32] It did not, however, prevent Pius IX from deciding on 1 March to include a formal definition of the infallibility of the Pope in the draft of the "Dogmatic Constitution of the Church."

The leaders of the minority did not confine themselves to increased personal contacts with those fathers whom they hoped to win for their cause. Convinced of the disastrous consequences for the Church of the proposed definition, and believing that they were justified in using all possible means of preventing it, some of them thought it advisable to mobilize public opinion in the hope that it would exert the necessary pressure on the council leaders from the outside. Several Roman salons turned into veritable snake pits of intrigue in the service of this or that view, for the proponents of the definition quickly, with the agreement of the Vatican, imitated the tactics of their opponents. But if in this still very aristocratic society the salons occupied a very important place, the newspapers constituted an even more potent instrument. Both camps tried to enlist the press, especially as the interest of the public in the affairs of the council had become evident.

Among the journalist polemics, particularly those of Louis Veuillot in favor of the definition and those of Monsignor Dupanloup in opposition to it, the "Roman Letters" assumed a special place. Döllinger published them in the *Allgemeine Zeitung* of Augsburg under the pseudonym of Quirinus. As a kind of council chronicle they were designed, by way of a tendentious depiction of participants and events, to discredit from the beginning all the decisions at which the assembly might arrive. Acton supplied Döllinger with the necessary information,[33] which he received

---

[32] List in Mansi LI, 677–86.

[33] The considerable contributions of Acton's to the "Römische Briefe," which had been suspected, was made clear by V. Conzemius (*JEH* 20 [1969], 267–94; *ThQ* 140 [1960], 428–32; *RQ* 59 [1964], 186–229, 60 [1965], 78–119), who also succeeded in differentiating the concepts of the two men, who, both searching for the best method to serve the cause of the minority, grew more and more apart. See also D. McElrath, op. cit.

from some bishops who did not consider the obligation of secrecy, which the Pope had unilaterally decreed, as binding.

The feuds of the press were augmented on both sides by continuing publications of brochures which, like those of Dechamps or Gratry, were identified by name, but which more often remained anonymous. There were also attempts by some members of the minority to enlist the support of the governments in Vienna, Munich, London, and especially Paris. Everyone was aware of the tremendous weight of Napoleon III, whose military and diplomatic support was absolutely essential for the survival of the remnants of the Pope's temporal power.[34] The various attempts by some bishops to cause their governments to intervene were a failure with respect to placing the item of papal infallibility on the agenda, but it can justifiably be assumed that they were not quite without influence. Cardinal Antonelli was in any case concerned with the matter, but now the attention of several members of the Curia and a number of the majority moderates was drawn to the influence which the agitation occasioned by the proposed definition had in the secular world on the discussions concerning the legitimacy of modern freedoms and the right of the Church to intervene in civil affairs. An effort was made to restrict the question of infallibility to the strictly doctrinal area in order to dispel the worries of any who were afraid that, once the Pope was acknowledged as infallible, he would be in the position, as one of them said, "in the future to decree [as infallible] any syllabus, even the most controvertible one."

With public and governmental concern growing on the fringe of the council, the assembly continued its work; but it soon became clear that, considering the speed with which progress was made, the chapter dealing with the primacy and the infallibility of the Pope would reach the discussion stage in the following spring at the earliest. Therefore, new petitions in March demanded that this chapter, which greatly disturbed the council, be dealt with immediately after the conclusion of the discussion on the constitution concerning rationalism. Although three out of the five council presidents were reluctant to do so because they did not wish to anger the minority,[35] Pius IX, whose irritation with the opposition was growing, decided in favor of the petition.

---

[34] On the political aspects of the council see: for France, E. Ollivier, op. cit., to be supplemented by J. Gadille, A. du Boÿs. L'intervention du gouvernement impérial à Vatican I (Louvain 1968) and de Montclos, 446–70; for Austria, Engel-Janosi I, 156–70; for Germany, E. Weinzierl-Fischer in MÖSTA 10 (1957), 302–21; for England, A. Randall in Dublin Review 479 (1959), 37–56 and especially D. McElrath, op. cit., 141–83; for Switzerland, V. Conzemius in Schweizerische Zeitschrift für Geschichte 15 (1965), 204–27.
[35] Their moderation, especially that of Cardinal Bilio, was clearly demonstrated by M. Maccarrone, op. cit. The intransigence of Cardinal Capalti, on the other hand, becomes clear from his Diario, recently published by L. Pásztor.

The Constitution *Pastor Aeternus*

In order to gloss over the extraordinary procedure involved in giving chapter 11 priority, it was decided to reformulate it in such a way that it became a small constitution, especially devoted to the Pope.[36] The discussion was opened on 13 May by the moderate expert opinion of Monsignor Pie. The general discussion, even at this early stage, essentially reduced itself to a debate of the expediency of the definition and in places was conducted with great passion. After about fifteen sessions, in which the presentations of Manning and Dechamps and the criticisms of Hefele, Stroßmayer, Maret, and Darboy stood out, the assembly proceeded to a discussion of the details of the text. It was especially concerned with the fourth chapter, which contained a definition of papal infallibility which the commission had already improved, but which failed to take sufficient account of the legitimate role of the episcopate, in addition to the Pope and in conjunction with him, as part of the supreme magisterial office of the Church. Fifty-seven members addressed the measure, presenting theological arguments and historical difficulties, and pointing up the practical advantages and disadvantages of a definition under the prevailing conditions. These often tiring debates, which took place in increasingly unbearably hot weather, at least permitted more precise formulations and removed some obstacles. A few suggestions stood out from the monotony of the debates, such as the formula which Rauscher had proposed on the very first day as a basis for compromise between majority and minority; it was taken from the formula suggested by S. Antonin of Florence in the fifteenth century.[37] There was also the proposal by Ketteler, who, in keeping with his views of the corporative constitution of the Church, insisted on the necessary cooperation between the Pope and his natural advisers, the bishops; and there was especially the proposal by the Dominican Cardinal Guidi, whom Pius IX rewarded with severe reproaches for his pains.[38]

In the meantime the negotiations in the hallways outside of the auditorium had grown in intensity and it was hoped that a compromise formula could be found which would prevent the divisions within the assembly from becoming known to the public. Indeed, many defenders of infallibility in the meantime had acquired a better grasp of the complexity of the problem and the necessity of greater differentiation, while the opponents learned that the faith of the Church in this matter was

---

[36] The various developmental phases of the text and the discussion in the public session as well as in the commission in Mansi LII, 4–1253, LIII, 240–83.

[37] Concerning this formula, often mentioned in these debates, see U. Betti in *Memorie domenicane* 76 (1959), 173–92.

[38] On the speech and the reactions to it, see M. Maccarrone, op. cit. I, 424–232.

broader and firmer than many of them had thought at the beginning. But primarily the greatest part of the fathers—standing between the two extremes of the enthusiasts of the majority and the diehards— basically consisted of moderates for whom all of the agitation was painful and deeply worrisome. Far from being intent on the destruction of the opponents, they desired only to find a middle ground on which a compromise was possible. This was especially true for the majority of the Italians, who constituted one-third of the council participants and who had not taken a definite position in the initial maneuvering to include the infallibility issue on the agenda. By dint of their numbers they lent decisive support to the informal compromise faction. This group, conciliatory from the outset, finally succeeded in having a more flexible formula accepted, which occupied a middle ground between the neo-ultramontane and the anti-Curial extremists, and which allowed for adjustments in the future. It is quite likely that an even greater portion of the minority would have voted for the ultimately adopted solution if Pius IX, who in the course of the last months had intervened increasingly openly in favor of the definition,[39] had not been so intransigent.

Whatever the extent of his personal responsibility, it is a fact that the attempts at achieving a reconciliation with the opponents failed, in spite of the good impression made by the summary which Monsignor Gasser had prepared in the name of the theological commission. It was an authorized commentary which even today is of essential importance in grasping the nuances of the council text.[40] In the preliminary balloting, 451 *placet* votes were cast, together with 88 *non placet* and 62 *placet juxta modum* votes. Hoping that the size of the opposition would provide a reconsideration, the minority made a final appeal to Pius IX in order to obtain the elimination of a controverted expression in the canon concerning papal primacy and the addition of a few words in the definition of the infallibility of the Pope which would imply the close cooperation of the Pope with the Church as a whole. But Pius IX, who was pressured in the opposite direction by the extremists of the majority, proved unyielding and inflexible. For this reason about sixty bishops decided to leave Rome before the final vote in order to avoid having to cast their *non placet* in front of a Pope who was personally affected by the issue. The other members of the minority believed that, despite the inclusion of an unfortunate phrase which designated the Pope infallible

[39] C. Butler already demonstrated several instances of exertion of pressure by Pius IX. M. Maccarrone (op. cit., especially 350–52, 395, 409–13, 464–77), by using hitherto ignored documents, has shown more precisely how Pius IX repeatedly during the final negotiations intervened personally on behalf of the ultras among the majority.
[40] Mansi LII, 1204–30.

"ex sese, non autem ex consensu Ecclesiae"[41]—designed to dispel the slightest suspicion of Gallicanism—the most serious objections had been removed as a result of the various textual improvements and Monsignor Gasser's commentary. They decided to approve the final version, which on 18 July was solemnly and almost unanimously passed by the members present.[42]

During the subsequent weeks the council continued its work at a slower pace; because of the heat and of the Franco-Prussian War, most of the fathers left Rome during the summer. The occupation of Rome by Italian troops on 20 September terminated the council, and on 20 October the Pope announced its adjournment sine die.

The end of the debates, however, did not produce an immediate acquiescence. Agitation continued for some time[43] and there occurred some regrettable apostasies, especially in the German-speaking countries. Led by university professors who took their cue from Döllinger, the so-called Old Catholic schism came into existence. Among the bishops of the minority some, like Hefele and Stroßmayer, hesitated for a while, but ultimately none of them denied his approval of the new dogma.

[41] On the precise meaning of this phrase, see G. Dejaifve in *Salesianum* 24 (1962), 283–95 and H. Fries in *Volk Gottes. Festgabe J. Höfer* (Freiburg i. Br. 1967), 480–500.
[42] Text in Mansi LII, 1330–34. Among the historio-theological commentaries see especially U. Betti, *La costituzione dommatica "Pastor aeternus"* (Rome 1961); G. Thils, *Primauté pontificale et prerogatives épiscopales. "Potestas ordinaria" au concile du Vatican* (Louvain 1961); U. Betti, *L'infaillibilité pontificale* (Gembloux 1969); U. Betti, *De doctrina Concilii Vaticani I* (Vatican City 1969), 285–575.
[43] Aubert, *Pie IX*, 359–67, 546f.

CHAPTER 23

The Rise of the Old Catholic Community

The internal Catholic protest movement against the dogma of the universal episcopate and the infallibility of the Pope spread after the summer of 1870, especially in Germany and Switzerland. It experienced several stages, and contrary to the initial intentions of its leaders culminated in the establishment of its own Church. The nucleus was formed by the university theology professors Döllinger, Johannes Friedrich, and J. A. Messmer of Munich, G. J. Hilgers, F. P. Knoodt, J. Langen, and Franz Heinrich Reusch of Bonn, Johann Baptist Baltzer, Joseph Hubert Reinkens, and T. Weber of Breslau, A. Menzel and Friedrich

Michelis of Braunsberg, Eduard Herzog of Lucerne, and a layman, the Prague canonist and legal historian J. F. von Schulte. Sectarian radicalism, which had characterized German Catholicism, was at first alien to the professors. They regarded themselves as conservatives adhering to the old Catholic faith in the face of erroneous innovations;[1] some of them had been close to Günter's theology.

At the council, primarily historical objections had been raised against the doctrine of infallibility and the way it was dealt with. The protesting theologians were now joined by some noted historians who as Catholics in a liberal age had earned their right to academic equality. Among them were F. W. Kampschulte and C. A. von Cornelius with his students A. von Druffel, M. Ritter, and F. Stieve.

The professors were joined virtually only by academicians and middle-class citizens. Some of them were guided by the same religious and scholarly impulses, others more by a religious liberalism which had begun to split away from the Church even before 1870. This burdened the movement as much as the nationalism of many of its members which reflected the climate of the founding of the German Empire. Old Catholicism was and remained an elitist movement; in the 1870s it reached its peak in Germany with about sixty thousand members. After all, the Catholic masses and their organizations had contributed to the development which culminated in the Vatican Council; after the annexation of the Papal State they felt even more impelled to stand by the imperiled Pope. The political leaders, who prior to 1869 had warned against the dogma, also made their peace with the decrees of the council.

In August 1870 more than one thousand three hundred Rhenish Catholics protested against the council; in Nuremberg thirty-two professors appealed to an "ecumenical council, true and free, and therefore to be held not in Italy but on this side of the Alps."[2] Expectations of support by the episcopate diminished when at the end of August the majority in Fulda agreed on a pastoral letter, temperately defending council and dogma;[3] they disappeared totally only in April 1871, when Hefele as the last German bishop published the council decrees.[4]

---

[1] Cf. the statement by the Bonn professor Reusch: "Our Catholic conscience forbids us the acceptance of the two doctrines because in word and tradition they contradict the old Church to which we are connected as Catholic priests." Conzemius, *Katholizismus ohne Rom,* 63.

[2] The texts of the protest declarations: *ColLac* VII, 1731f.

[3] Text: *ColLac* VII, 1733ff.; Butler-Lang, 455–58; Lill, *Bischofskonferenzen,* 95–112.

[4] Some of the opponents of the dogma who were willing to act only in conjunction with the bishops thereupon withdrew from the movement, such as the dogmatist Kuhn (Tübingen) and Dieringer (Bonn), who resigned from his teaching position.

The agitation over council and dogma, in which the entire liberal press took the side of the opponents, experienced a renewed intensification after the temporary diversion of the Franco-German War. The reason was that several bishops after the fall of 1870 proceeded against the opponents of the council by withholding the *missio canonica,* suspension, excommunication, and denial of the sacraments. The victims appealed to the state for assistance. The governments granted them protection and guaranteed them the continuation of temporal and ecclesiastical offices; the ensuing feud with the bishops led to the *Kulturkampf.*

In September 1870 the first congress of Old Catholics was held in Munich with three hundred delegates from Germany, Switzerland, and Austria. The participation of guests from the Orthodox and Anglican Churches and the small Utrecht Church signified not only the joint opposition to Rome which the Vatican Council had intensified, but also a novel ecumenical content which Döllinger and his friends consciously promoted by appealing to the common Christian tradition of old. Döllinger's program underscored the conservative nature of the protest movement and claimed for it the right to continued equal membership in the Catholic Church. Döllinger passionately advised against division, and he himself never formally joined the Old Catholic Church. Schulte, Friedrich, Michelis, and Reinkens, on the other hand, called for the establishment of an emergency community, and the majority of the congress participants agreed with them.

In Rome, the momentous decision, which, like the whole movement, confirmed old prejudices against the German professors, determined future development. At first local Catholic Associations were formed. The Second Congress in 1872 in Cologne, which officially adopted the name "Old Catholic," decided to establish regular pastoral care and appointed a commission for the preparation of the election of a bishop. On 14 June 1871 the Breslau professor Joseph Hubert Reinkens was chosen. He was consecrated by a bishop of the Utrecht Church[5] and thus entered into the apostolic succession.[6]

Reinkens, placed under interdict by Pius IX, established an episcopal administration in Bonn, assisted by Reusch as vicar general. He was acknowledged as a Catholic bishop by Prussia, Baden, and Hessen-Darmstadt; legislation passed in these states during the *Kulturkampf* assured the Old Catholics of their share of Catholic Church property

---

[5] The consecration followed the rite prescribed in the *Pontificale Romanum.*
[6] Reinkens perpetuated the succession. In 1876 he consecrated E. Herzog as bishop and in 1895 his vicar general T. Weber, who one year later became his successor.

and use of Catholic churches.[7] Only to the extent that the *Kulturkampf* was acknowledged as a mistake and was dismantled after 1878 did the support of the states flag; earlier than other proponents of the *Kulturkampf*, Bismarck recognized that as an ally against Rome Old Catholicism was too weak.

The constitution drafted by Schulte according to old Christian models granted legislative powers and the right to elect bishops to the synods, formed of representatives of the clergy and laymen. After approval by the Third Congress in 1873 in Constance, it was ratified by the first synod in 1874 in Bonn. The synods of the subsequent years with respect to doctrine remained based on the undivided Church of the first millenium; tempered and timely reforms were introduced into worship and after 1880 German was employed in the liturgy of the Mass. Against the will of Reinkens, Reusch and other fellow champions, liberal forces in 1879 succeeded in abolishing celibacy.

In Switzerland, where the conditions were particularly favorable, Reinkens and Michelis actively participated in the establishment of a Church. In 1875 the first synod gathered in Olten and established the "Christ Catholic Church of Switzerland." In doctrine it followed the German model, in its constitution it was more democratic. In 1876 Eduard Herzog was elected bishop and during almost fifty years of work established a Church oriented to Bible and Eucharist. The theological university established in 1874 in Berne by the government as an instrument in the *Kulturkampf*, with Herzog's authoritative assistance grew into a considerable theological center which after the turn of the century was influential far beyond the borders of Switzerland.[8] The reason for this was that the German leadership came to an end with the expiration of the outstanding scholarship of that generation. All attempts to maintain the theological faculty at Bonn, which, except for one member, was totally Old Catholic, failed; after the death of Reusch (1900) and Langen (1901) the remaining chairs were filled again with Catholics.[9]

In Austria, where the government remained passive and where the bishops, especially Rauscher, avoided a confrontation by extremely lenient treatment, the protest movement developed very slowly. After 1872 there existed four Old Catholic communities, to be officially rec-

[7] The Catholic bishops refused this arrangement and under protest stopped services in the churches allotted to the Old Catholics.

[8] Since 1893 the department has issued the scholarly quarterly *Internationale kirchliche Zeitschrift* (until 1910 *Revue Internationale de Théologie*).

[9] In 1902 a chair for Old Catholic theology was created at the University of Bonn, directly responsible to the university president.

ognized by the state in 1877. An increase occurred during the 1890s in consequence of the more nationally than religiously inspired Away-from-Rome Movement. In 1879 its first synod took place and it adopted the German patterns. After 1881 the small Church, whose constitution was also drafted by Schulte, was guided by an episcopal administrator.

The Old Catholic bishoprics and the Utrecht Church, which prior to 1870 had been totally isolated, in 1889 formed the Union of Utrecht. It is an autonomous union of national Churches free from Rome, whose honorary primate is the archbishop of Utrecht. A joint declaration again accepted the faith of the first millenium and the kind of Roman primacy which then prevailed. It repeated the protest against the dogmas of 1854 and 1870, as well as its readiness for the "removal of the differences existing since the schism."[10] Döllinger's internationally recognized scholarship and his ecumenical efforts[11] in 1874–75 resulted in the Bonn conferences of union consisting of Old Catholic, Russian Orthodox, and Anglican theologians. In the nineteenth century they were a bold attempt at interdenominational theological discussions and thus a precursor to ecumenism, in the service of which the future international congresses of Old Catholics placed themselves. But the practical result of the conferences was small; they suffered from their small basis and from the resentful and antiecumenical polemics against Rome, which for a long time characterized Old Catholicism.

[10] On the future development of Old Catholicism, which in the countries of its roots has declined but which as a consequence of the adherence of new national Churches (Poland, U.S.A.) has grown in absolute terms, see Algermissen, op. cit; Conzemius, *Katholizismus ohne Rom,* 55, 68ff., 79ff., 81–102; K. Algermissen in *LThK* I, 398–402; W. Küppers in *RGG* I, 295–99.

[11] After Döllinger grew out of the combative attitude of his earlier years, theological scholarship and ecumenical interest were essentially one to him. At the Munich assembly of scholars he characterized the impartial examination of denominational doctrinal differences as an urgent task of theology.

BIBLIOGRAPHY

GENERAL BIBLIOGRAPHY

I. GENERAL HISTORY

WORLD HISTORY: O. Westphal, *Weltgeschichte der Neuzeit. 1750–1950* (Stuttgart 1953); F. Valjavec, ed., *Historia Mundi* IX and X (Berne 1961); G. Mann, ed., *Propyläen-Weltgeschichte* VII and VII (Berlin 1960); D. K. Fieldhouse, *Die Kolonialreiche seit dem 18. Jahrhundert (Fischer-Weltgeschichte 29)*, (Frankfurt am Main 1965); G. N. Clark, ed., *The New Cambridge Modern European History* VII, IX, and X (Cambridge 1960, 1960, 1965).

EUROPE: B. Croce, *History of Europe in the 19th Century* (New York 1963); W. Mommsen, *Geschichte des Abendlandes von der Französischen Revolution bis zur Gegenwart, 1789–1945* (Munich 1951); H. Herzfeld, *Die moderne Welt. 1789–1945*, 2 vols. (Braunschweig 1966); L. Salvatorelli, *Storia del novecento* (Florence 1957); C. Zaghi, *Napoleone e Europa* (Naples 1969); R. R. Palmer, *The Age of Democratic Revolution*, 2 vols. (Princeton 1959–64); M. Beloff, ed., *L'Europe du XIXᵉ et du XXᵉ siècle* I (Paris 1959); J. B. Duroselle, *L'Europe de 1815 à nos jours. Vie politique et relations internationales (Nouvelle Clio 38)*, (Paris 1964); G. A. Craig, *Europe since 1815* (Englewood 1966); G. Lefebvre, *La Révolution Française (Peuples et Civilisations 13)*, (Paris 1968); G. Lefebvre, *Napoléon (Peuples et Civilisations 14)*, (Paris 1953); F. Ponteil, *L'Éveil des Nationalités et le Mouvement Libéral, 1815–1848 (Peuples et Civilisations 15)*, (Paris 1968); C. H. Pouthas, *Démocraties et Capitalisme, 1848–1860 (Peuples et Civilisations 16)*, (Paris 1948); H. Hauser et al., *Du Libéralisme à L'Impérialisme (Peuples et Civilisations 17)*, (Paris 1952); E. Weis, *Der Durchbruch des Bürgertums, 1776–1847 (Propyläengeschichte Europas 4)*, (Frankfurt am Main 1978). T. Schieder, *Staatensystem als Vormacht der Welt, 1848–1918 (Propyläengeschichte Europas 5)*, (Frankfurt am Main 1977); A. Sorel, *L'Europe et la Révolution française*, 8 vols. (Paris 1885–1911); J. L. Godechot, *La grande nation. L'expansion révolutionnaire de la France dans le monde de 1789 à 1799*, 2 vols. (Paris 1956); E. Naujoks, *Die Französische Revolution und Europa* (Stuttgart 1969); L. Bergeron, F. Furet, and R. Koselleck, *Das Zeitalter der europäischen Revolution 1780–1848 (Fischer-Weltgeschichte 26)*, (Frankfurt am Main 1969); L. Salvatorelli, *La rivoluzione europea. 1848–1849* (Milan 1949); P. Robertson, *Revolutions of 1848* (New York 1960); A. J. P. Taylor, *The Struggle for Mastery in Europe, 1848–1918* (Oxford 1954); C. Brinton, *A Decade of Revolution, 1789–1799* (New York 1934); G. Bruun, *Europe and the French Imperium, 1799–1814* (New York 1938); F. B. Artz, *Reaction and Revolution, 1814–1832* (New York 1934); W. F. Langer, *Political and Social Upheaval, 1832–1852* (New York 1969); R. C. Binkley, *Realism and Nationalism, 1852–1871* (New York 1935).

FRANCE: *Nouvelle histoire de la France*, vols 1–10. Editions du Seuil (Paris 1972); P. Gaxotte, *La Révolution française.* Nouvelle edition avec Jean Tulard (Paris 1977); M. Vovelle, *Religion et Révolution: La dechristianisation de l'An II* (Paris 1976); P. H. Beik, *The French Revolution Seen from the Right* (New York 1970); J. N. Moody, *French Education since Napoleon* (Syracuse 1978); F. Furet and D. Richet, *The French Revolution* (London 1970); J. Godechot, *The Counter-Revolution* (New York 1971); G. de Bertier de Sauvigny, *The Restoration* (New York 1967); R. Rémond, *La vie politique en France depuis 1789*, 2 vols. (Paris 1965–69); R. Rémond, *La Droite en France de 1815 à nos jours*

(Paris 1963); J. L. Godechot, *Les révolutions, 1770–1799* (Paris 1965); J. L. Godechot, *L'Europe et l'Amérique à l'époque napoléonienne, 1800–1815* (Paris 1967); B. Groethuysen, *Philosophie de la Révolution française* (Paris 1956); I. Kaplow, ed., *New Perspectives on the French Revolution* (New York 1965); A. Gérard, *La Révolution française, mythes et interprétations, 1799–1970* (Paris 1970); J. Chastenet, *Histoire de la Troisième République*, 7 vols. (Paris 1952–63); G. Dupeux, *La Société française, 1789–1960* (Paris 1964); J. L. Godechot, *Les institutions de la France sous la Révolution et l'Empire* (Paris 1968); F. Ponteil, *Les institutions de la France de 1814 à 1870* (Paris 1966); A. Prost, *L'enseignement en France 1800–1967* (Paris 1968); L. Duguit, H. Monnier, R. Bonnard, *Les constitutions et les principales lois politiques de la France depuis 1789* (Paris 1952); *Le Moniteur Universel* (1799–1868) and *Journal officiel* (Paris 1869seqq.) for legislation and parliamentary debates.

BELGIUM, NETHERLANDS, LUXEMBURG: S. Schama, *Patriots and Liberators: Revolution in the Netherlands, 1780–1813* (New York 1977); C. H. E. De Wit, *De Strijd tussen Aristocratie en Democratie in Nederland, 1780–1848* (Heerlen 1965); P. Gerin, S. Vervaeck, J. De Belder, J. Hannes, *Bibliographie de l'histoire de Belgique, 1789–1914*, 3 vols. (Louvain 1960–66); H. Pirenne, *Histoire de Belgique* VI/VII (Brussels 1926–32); J. Van Houtte, ed., *Algemene Geschiedenis der Nederlanden* VIII/XII (Antwerp and Zeist 1955–58); J. Deharveng, ed., *Histoire de la Belgique contemporaine, 1830–1914*, 3 vols. (Brussels 1928–30); T. Luykx, *Politieke geschiedenis van Belgie van 1789 tot heden* (Brussels 1969); A. Simon, *Le parti catholique belge* (Brussels 1958).

SPAIN AND PORTUGAL: M. Artola, *Los origines de la España contemporanea*, 2 vols. (Barcelona 1958); F. G. Bruguera, *Histoire contemporaine d'Espagne. 1789–1950* (Paris 1953); R. Carr, *Spain, 1808–1939* (Oxford 1966); M. Fernández Almagro, *Historia política de la España contemporánea*, 2 vols. (Madrid 1956–59); H. V. Livermore, *A New History of Portugal* (Cambridge 1966);

ITALY: C. Spellanzon, *Storia del Risorgimento e dell'unità de'Italia*, 5 vols. (Milan 1932–40); W. Maturi, *Interpretazioni del Risorgimento* (Turin 1962); L. Salvatorelli, *Spiriti e figure del Risorgimento* (Florence 1962); D. Mack Smith, *Italy. A Modern History* (Ann Arbor 1959).

GERMAN STATES AND SWITZERLAND: B. Gebhardt, H. Grundmann, *Handbuch der deutschen Geschichte* I and II (Stuttgart 1960); L. Just, ed., *Handbuch der deutschen Geschichte* III (Constance 1956); H. Holborn, *A History of Modern Germany* II and III (New York 1959); E. Marcks, *Der Aufstieg des Reiches, 1807–78*, 2 vols. (Stuttgart 1936); A. H. Springer, *Geschichte Österreichs seit dem Wiener Frieden 1809*, 2 vols. (Leipzig 1863–65); G. Mann, *Deutsche Geschichte im 19. und 20. Jahrhundert* (Frankfurt am Main 1966); A. Ramm, *Germany, 1789–1919* (London 1967); T. S. Hamerow, *Restoration, Revolution, Reaction. Economics and Politics in Germany, 1815–71* (Princeton 1958); H. Hantsch, *Die Geschichte Österreichs* II (Graz 1962); G. A. Craig, *Germany, 1866–1945* (New York 1978); F. Schnabel, *Deutsche Geschichte im 19. Jahrhundert*, 4 vols. (Freiburg 1929–37); V. Valentin, *Geschichte der deutschen Revolution von 1848–49*, 2 vols. (Berlin 1930–31); R. Charmatz, *Österreichs innere Geschichte von 1848 bis 1895*, 2 vols. (Leipzig 1918); V. Bibl, *Der Zerfall Österreichs*, 2 vols. (Vienna 1922–24); H. v. Srbik, *Deutsche Einheit*, 4 vols. (Munich 1935–42); E. Fueter, *Die Schweiz seit 1848* (Zurich 1928).

GREAT BRITAIN: G. M. Trevelyan, *British History in the Nineteenth Century and after* (London 1937); E. Halévy, *History of the English People in the Nineteenth Century*, 6 vols. (London 1949–52); L. Woodward, *The Age of Reform, 1815–70* (Oxford History of England), (Oxford 1962).

UNITED STATES OF AMERICA: H. G. Dahms, *Geschichte der Vereinigten Staaten von Amerika* (Munich 1953); E. Samhaber, *Geschichte der Vereinigten Staaten von Nordamerika* (Munich 1954); E. Angermann, "Die Vereinigten Staaten von Amerika," *Historia Mundi* X (1961), 253–331; R. Hofstadter, W. Miller, D. Aaron, W. Jordan, and L. Litwack, *The United States* (Englewood Cliffs 1976); J. A. Garraty, *The American Nation* (New York 1979); J. M. Blum, E. S. Morgan, W. L. Rose, A. M. Schlesinger, Jr., K. M. Stampp, C. Vann Woodward, *The National Experience: A History of the United States* (New York 1973); R. N. Current, T. H. Williams, F. Freidel, *American History: A Survey* (New York 1979); B. Bailyn, D. B. Davis, D. H. Donald, J. L. Thomas, R. H. Wiebe, G. S. Wood, *The Great Republic: A History of the American People* (Lexington, Mass. 1977).

LATIN AMERICA: S. de Madariaga, *The Fall of the Spanish American Empire* (London 1947); H. V. Livermore, ed., *Portugal and Brazil* (Oxford 1953); A. P. Whitaker, "Die iberoamerikanische Welt von 1825–1920," *Historia Mundi* X (1961), 332–57.

II. CHURCH HISTORY

1. GENERAL CHURCH HISTORY

L. A. Veit, *Die Kirche im Zeitalter des Individualismus* II: *1800 bis zur Gegenwart* (Freiburg im Breisgau 1933); L. Rogier, R. Aubert, D. Knowles, *Geschichte der Kirche* IV (Einsiedeln 1966); E. E. Y. Hales, *The Catholic Church in the Modern World. A Survey from the French Revolution to the present* (London 1958); K. S. Latourette, *Christianity in a Revolutionary Age. A History of Christianity in the 19th and 20th Centuries,* 5 vols. (New York 1958–62); J. Lortz, *Geschichte der Kirche in ideengeschichtlicher Betrachtung* II (Münster 1964); L. Girard, *Le catholicisme en Europe de 1814 à 1878* (Les Cours de Sorbonne), (Paris 1962); Daniel-Rops, *L'Église des Révolutions,* 2 vols. (Paris 1960–63); H. Hermelink, *Das Christentum in der Menschheitsgeschichte von der Französischen Revolution bis zur Gegenwart,* 3 vols. (Stuttgart 1951–55); K. D. Schmitt, *Grundriß der Kirchengeschichte* IV: *Geschichte der Kirche im Zeitalter des Individualismus und des Säkularismus* (Göttingen 1960); K. D. Schmitt, E. Wolf, *Die Kirche in ihrer Geschichte. Ein Handbuch* IV, Part 1; F. Heyer, *Die katholische Kirche vom Westfälischen Frieden bis zum ersten Vatikanischen Konzil* (Göttingen 1963); A. Fliche and V. Martin, *Histoire de l'Église,* vols. 20 and 21, (Paris 1949, 1964); K. Bihlmeyer and H. Tüchle, *Church History,* 3 vols. (New York 1979).

2. PAPACY

J. Schmidlin, *Papstgeschichte der neuesten Zeit,* 4 vols. (Munich 1933–39); F. X. Seppelt, G. Schwaiger, *Geschichte der Päpste* (Munich 1964); P. Paschini, P. Brezzi, *I papi nella storia* II (Rome 1961); C. Ledré, *Un siècle sous la tiare. De Pie IX à Pie XII* (Paris 1955); G. Mollat, *La Question romaine de Pie VI à Pie XI* (Paris 1932); V. Del Giudice, *La Questione romana* (Rome 1948); C. Berthelet, *Conclavi pontifici e cardinali nel secolo XIX* (Rome 1903); E. De Marchi, *Le Nunziature apostoliche dal 1800 al 1956* (Rome 1957); *Notizie dell'anno* (until 1860); *Annuario pontificio* (1861–70, 1912seqq.); *La Gerarchia cattolica* (1872–1911).

3. THE HISTORY OF THE CATHOLIC CHURCH IN INDIVIDUAL COUNTRIES

GERMANY: H. Brück, *Geschichte der katholischen Kirche in Deutschland im 19. Jahrhundert* (Mainz 1902–3); G. Goyau, *L'Allemagne religieuse. Le Catholicisme*, 4 vols. (Paris 1905–9); F. Schnabel, *Deutsche Geschichte im 19. Jahrhundert IV: Die religiösen Kräfte* (Freiburg i. Br. 1937); P. Funk, *Von der Aufklärung zur Romantik* (Munich 1925); F. Heyer, *Die katholische Kirche von 1648 bis 1870* (Göttingen 1963); H. Schrörs, *Die Kölner Wirren. Studien zu ihrer Geschichte* (Berlin and Bonn 1927); H. Bastgen, *Die Verhandlungen zwischen dem Berliner Hof und dem Heiligen Stuhl über die konfessionell gemischten Ehen* (Paderborn 1936); H. Bastgen, *Die Besetzung der Bischofssitze in Preußen in der ersten Hälfte des 19. Jahrhunderts*, 2 parts (Paderborn 1941); R. Lill, *Die Beilegung der Kölner Wirren* (Düsseldorf 1962); J. -B. Kißling, *Geschichte der deutschen Katholikentage*, 3 vols. (Münster 1920–21); R. Lill, *Die ersten deutschen Bischofskonferenzen* (Freiburg i. Br. 1964); A. K. Huber, *Kirche und deutsche Einheit im 19. Jahrhundert* (Königstein 1966); K. Buchheim, *Ultramontanismus und Demokratie. Der Weg der deutschen Katholiken im 19. Jahrhundert* (Munich 1963); K. Bachem, *Vorgeschichte, Geschichte und Politik der deutschen Zentrumspartei* I (Cologne 1927, reprint Aalen 1967); F. Hanus, *Die preußische Vatikangesandtschaft, 1747–1920* (Munich 1954); G. Franz-Willing, *Die bayerische Vatikangesandtschaft, 1803–1934* (Munich 1965); F. Engel-Janosi, *Österreich und der Vatikan 1846–1918* I (Graz, Vienna and Cologne 1958); R. Hacker, *Die Beziehungen zwischen Bayern und dem Heiligen Stuhl in der Regierungszeit Ludwigs I.* (Tübingen 1967); H. Schiel, *Johann Michael Sailer*, 2 vols. (Regensburg 1948–52); W. Schellberg, *Johann Görres* (Cologne 1926); J. Janssen, *Friedrich Leopold Graf zu Stolberg* (Freiburg i. Br. 1877); E. Hosp, *Hofbauer* (Vienna 1951); R. Till, *Hofbauer und sein Kreis* (Vienna 1951); O. Pfülf, *Kardinal Johannes von Geissel*, 2 vols. (Freiburg i. Br. 1895–96); L. Lenhart, *Bischof Ketteler*, 3 vols. (Mainz 1966–68); L. v. Pastor, *August Reichensperger*, 2 vols. (Freiburg i. Br. 1899); F. Schmidt, *Peter Reichensperger* (Mönchen-Gladbach 1913); S. J. Schäffer, J. Dahl, *Adolf Kolping* (Cologne 1961); J. Friedrich, *Ignaz von Döllinger*, 3 vols. (Munich 1899–1901).

AUSTRIA: F. Engel-Janosi, *Österreich und der Vatikan*, 2 vols. (Graz 1958–60); F. Engel-Janosi, *Die politische Korrespondenz der Päpste mit den österreichischen Kaisern 1804–1918* (Vienna 1964); J. Grisar, *De historia Ecclesiae catholicae austriacae saeculi XIX* (Rome 1936); A. Hudal, *Die österreichische Vatikanbotschaft 1806–1918* (Munich 1952); C. Wolfsgruber, *Joseph Otmar von Rauscher* (Vienna 1888); C. Wolfsgruber, *Kardinal Schwarzenberg*, 3 vols. (Vienna 1905–17).

FRANCE: A. Latreille, *L'Église catholique et la révolution française*, 2 vols. (Paris 1950); G. Bourgin, "Les sources manuscrites de l'histoire religieuse de la France moderne," *RHEF* 10 (1924), 27–66, 172–206, 333–58, 466–92; J. Gadille, "Les sources privées de l'histoire contemporaine du catholicisme en France," *RH* 238 (1967), 333–46; G. Weill, "Le catholicisme français au XIXe siècle," *Revue de synthèse historique* 15 (1907), 319–56; A. Latreille, J. -R. Palanque, É. Delaruelle, R. Rémond, *Histoire du catholicisme en France* III (Paris 1962); W. Gurian, *Die politischen und sozialen Ideen des französischen Katholizismus, 1789–1914* (Freiburg i. Br. 1929); A. Dansette, *Histoire religieuse de la France contemporaine*, 2 vols. (Paris 1948/51); A. Debidour, *Histoire des rapports de l'Église et de l'État en France de 1789 à 1870*, 2 vols. (Paris 1891); A. Debidour, *L'Église catholique et l'État sous la IIIe Republique, 1870–1906*, 2 vols. (Paris 1906); A. Rivet, *Traité du culte catholique et des lois civiles d'ordre religieux* (Paris 1947); J. Brugerette, *Le prêtre français et la société contemporaine*, 3 vols. (Paris 1933–38); F. Boulard, *Essor ou déclin du clergé français* (Paris 1950); L. Baunard, *L'Épiscopat français depuis le Concordat jusqu'à la*

Séparation (Paris 1907); L. Baunard, *Un siècle de l'Église de France, 1800–1900* (Paris 1901); L. Grimaud, *Histoire de la liberté d'enseignement en France*, 6 vols. (Grenoble and Paris 1944–54); P. Nourisson, *Histoire légale des congrégations religieuses en France depuis 1789*, 2 vols. (Paris 1928); G. Le Bras, *Études de sociologie religieuse*, 2 vols. (Paris 1955–56); G. Weill, *Histoire de l'idée laïque en France au XIXe siècle* (Paris 1929); A. Mellor, *Histoire de l'anticléricalisme français* (Paris 1966); P. Droulers, *Action pastorale et problèmes sociaux sous la Monarchie de Juillet chez Monseigneur d'Astros* (Paris 1954); E. Sevrin, *Un évêque militant et gallican au XIXe siècle, Monseigneur Clausel de Montals*, 2 vols. (Paris 1955); F. Lagrange, *Vie de Monseigneur Dupanloup*, 3 vols. (Paris 1883–84); *DHGE* XIV, 1070–1122); A. de Falloux, *Mémoires d'un royaliste*, 2 vols. (Paris 1888); E. Veuillot, *Le comte de Falloux et ses Mémoires* (Paris 1888); C. de Ladoue, *Monseigneur Gerbet, sa vie, ses œuvres*, 3 vols. (Paris 1870); F. Gousset, *Le cardinal Gousset* (Besançon 1903); P. Delatte, *Dom Guéranger, abbé de Solesmes*, 2 vols. (Paris 1909–10); J. Paguelle de Follenay, *Vie du cardinal Guibert*, 2 vols. (Paris 1896); T. Foisset, *Vie du R. P. Lacordaire*, 2 vols. (Paris 1870); L. Baunard, *Le cardinal Lavigerie*, 2 vols. (Paris 1896); X. de Montclos, *Lavigerie, le Saint-Siège et l'Église, 1846–78* (Paris 1965); G. Bazin, *Vie de Monseigneur Maret*, 3 vols. (Paris 1891–92); F. Besson, *Vie de S. É. le cardinal Mathieu*, 2 vols. (Paris 1882); J. Leflon, *Eugène de Mazenod*, 3 vols. (Paris 1896–1902); A. d'Andigné, *Un apôtre de la charité, Armand de Melun* (Paris 1962); E. Lecanuet, *Montalembert*, 3 vols. (Paris 1896–1902); C. Guillemant, *P. -L. Parisis*, 3 vols. (Paris 1916–25); L. Baunard, *Histoire du cardinal Pie*, 2 vols. (Paris 1893); C. -J. Destombes, *Vie de S. É. le cardinal Régnier*, 2 vols. (Paris 1885); M. de Hédouville, *Monseigneur de Ségur, sa vie, son action* (Paris 1957); F. Poujoulat, *Vie de Monseigneur Sibour* (Paris 1857); M. J. Rouet de Journel, *Une russe catholique. La vie de Madame Swetchine* (Paris 1953); E. and F. Veuillot, *Louis Veuillot*, 4 vols. (Paris 1902–13).

ITALY: *Archiva Ecclesiae* 3/4 (1960–61), 87–179, 223–87; Silvino da Nadro, O.F.M.Cap., *Sinodi diocesani italiani. Catalogo bibliografico degli atti a stampa, 1574–1878* (Vatican City 1960); A. -C. Jemolo, *Chiesa e Stato in Italia negli ultimi cento anni* (Turin 1963); P. Scoppola, *Chiesa e Stato nella storia d'Italia. Storia documentaria dall'Unità alla Repubblica* (Bari 1967); P. Scoppola *Dal Neoguelfismo alla Democrazia cristiana* (Rome 1957); A. Della Torre, *Il cristianesimo in Italia dai filosofisti ai modernisti* (Milan 1912); G. De Rosa, *Storia del movimento cattolico in Italia*, 2 vols. (Bari 1966); *I cattolici italiani dall'800 ad oggi* (Brescia 1964); T. Chiuso, *La Chiesa in Piemonte dal 1797 ai giorni nostri*, 4 vols. (Turin 1888); T. Salvemini, *La statistica ecclesiastica con speciale riguardo al clero in Italia* (Ferrara 1941); G. Spini, *Risorgimento e protestanti* (Naples 1956); C. Castiglioni, *Gaysruck e Romilli, arcivescovi di Milano* (Milan 1938); C. Castiglioni, *Monsignor Nazari di Calabiana* (Milan 1952); E. Federici, *Sisto Riario Sforza* (Rome 1945); G. Russo, *Il cardinale Sisto Riario Sforza e l'unità d'Italia* (Naples 1962); J. E. Borrel, *Vie de Monseigneur Charvaz* (Chambéry 1909); P. Stella, *Don Bosco nella storia della religiosità cattolica*, 2 vols. (Zurich 1968–69); A. Castellani, *Il b. Leonardo Murialdo*, 2 vols. (Rome 1966–68).

SPAIN: J. del Burgo, *Fuentes de la Historia de España. Bibliografía de las guerras carlistas y de las luchas políticas del siglo XIX*, 4 vols. (Pamplona 1954–60); V. de la Fuente, *Historia eclesiástica de España* VI (Barcelona 1875); P. Gams, *Die Kirchengeschichte von Spanien* III/2 (Regensburg 1872, reprint Graz 1956); E. A. Peers, *The Church in Spain, 1737–1937* (London 1938); E. A. Peers, *Spain, the Church, and the Orders* (London 1939); J. M. Cuenca, *La Iglesia española ante la Revolución liberal* (Madrid 1971); J. Becker, *Relaciones diplomáticas entre España y la Santa Sede durante el siglo XIX* (Madrid 1909); M. Menéndez y Pelayo, *Historia de los heterodojos españoles* VII (Madrid .1932).

BELGIUM: *Sources de l'histoire religieuse de la Belgique. Époque contemporaine. Colloque de Bruxelles 1967* (Louvain 1968); A. Simon, *Réunions des évêques de Belgique. Procès-verbaux, 1830–83,* 2 vols. (Louvain 1960–61); A. Simon, *Instructions aux nonces de Bruxelles, 1835–89* (Brussels 1961); R. Aubert, "Kirche und Staat in Belgien im 19. Jahrhundert," W. Conze, ed., *Beiträge zur deutschen und belgischen Verfassungsgeschichte im 19. Jahrhundert* (Stuttgart 1967); V. Mallinson, *Power and Politics in Belgian Education, 1815–1961* (London 1963); A. Tihon, *Le clergé et l'enseignement moyen pour garçons dans le diocèse de Malines, 1802–1914* (diss., Louvain 1970); "Prêtres de Belgique, 1838–1930," *NRTh* 57 (1930), 617–744; S. Scholl, ed., *150 jaar katholieke arbeidersbeweging in Belgie, 1789–1939,* 3 vols. (Brussels 1963–66); N. Piepers, *La "Revue générale" de 1865 à 1940* (Louvain 1968).

PORTUGAL: F. de Almeida, *Historia da Igreja em Portugal* IV, 1/4 (Coimbra 1917–23); M. de Oliveira, *Historia eclesiástica de Portugal* (Lisbon 1940).

GREAT BRITAIN AND IRELAND: J. H. Whyte, "Historians of XIXth-century English Catholicism," *Clergy Review* 52 (1967), 791–801; G. A. Beck, ed., *The English Catholics, 1850–1950* (London 1950); D. Mathew, *Catholicism in England* (London 1936); P. J. Corish, ed., *A History of Irish Catholicism* IV/V (Dublin 1968seqq.); A. Bellesheim, *Geschichte der katholischen Kirche in Schottland* (Mainz 1883); P. Thureau-Dangin, *La renaissance catholique en Angleterre au XIXe siècle,* 3 vols. (Paris 1899–1906); O. Chadwick, *The Victorian Church,* 2 vols. (London 1966–70); C. Butler, *The Life and Times of Bishop Ullathorne,* 2 vols. (London 1926); W. Ward, *The Life and Times of Cardinal Wiseman,* 2 vols. (London 1897); W. Ward, *The Life of John Henry Cardinal Newman,* 2 vols. (London 1912); E. Purcell, *Life of Cardinal Manning,* 2 vols. (London 1895).

THE NETHERLANDS: L. J. Rogier, N. De Rooy, *In vrijheid herboren. Katholiek Nederland, 1853–1953* (The Hague 1957); P. Albers, *Geschiedenes van het herstel der hiërarchie in de Nederlanden,* 2 vols. (Nijmegen and The Hague 1903–04); A. Commissaris, *Van toen wij vrij werden, 1795–1903,* 2 vols. (Groningen 1929); J. Witlox, *De Katholieke Staatspartij,* 2 vols. ('s-Hertogenbosch 1919–27); J. A. De Kok, *Nederland op de breuklijn Rome-Reformatie. Numerieke aspecten van protestantisering en katholieke herleving in de Noordelijke Nederlanden, 1580–1880* (Assen 1964).

SWITZERLAND: A. Büchi, *Die katholische Kirche in der Schweiz* (Munich 1902); T. Schwegler, *Geschichte der katholischen Kirche in der Schweiz* (Stans 1945); K. Müller, *Die katholische Kirche in der Schweiz seit dem Ausgang des 18. Jahrhunderts* (Einsiedeln 1928); F. Strobel, *Die Jesuiten und die Schweiz im 19. Jahrhundert* (Olten 1954).

SCANDINAVIA: A. Palmqvist, *Die römisch-katholische Kirche in Schweden nach 1781,* 2 vols. (Upsala 1954–58); K. Kjelstrup, *Norvegia catholica, 1843–1943* (Rome 1947); J. Metzler, *Die apostolischen Vikariate des Nordens* (Paderborn 1919).

RUSSIA AND POLAND: A. M. Ammann, *Abriß der Ostslawischen Kirchengeschichte* (Vienna 1950); A. Boudou, *Le Saint-Siège et la Russie,* 2 vols. (Paris 1922–25); E. Winter, *Rußland und das Papsttum* II (Berlin 1961); W. Urban, *Ostatni etap dziejów Kościola w Polsce przed nowym tysiacleciem, 1815–1965* (Rome 1966); O. Beiersdorf, *Papietswo wobec sprawy polskiej w latach 1772–1864 wybor źródel* (Wroclaw 1960); J. Wasilewski, *Arcybiskupi i administratorowie archidiecezji Mohylowskiej* (Pinsk 1930); J. A. Malinowski, *Die deutschen katholischen Kolonien am Schwarzen Meere* (Stuttgart 1927); S. Zaleski, *Jezuici w Polsce* V (Cracow 1907); J. Bjelogolovov, *Akten und Dokumente in Bezug auf die Organisation und Verwaltung der römisch-katholischen Kirche in Rußland* (St. Petersburg

1905); A. Welykyj, *Documenta Pontificum Romanorum historiam Ukrainiae illustrantia* II (Rome 1954); S. Olszamowska-Skowronska, *La correspondance des papes et des empereurs de Russie (1814–78) selon les documents authentiques* (Rome 1970).

SOUTHEASTERN EUROPE AND THE NEAR EAST: G. G. Golubovich, *Biblioteca biobibliografica della Terra Santa e dell'Oriente cristiano,* 8 vols. (Karachi 1906–30); E. von Mülinen, *Die lateinische Kirche im Türkischen Reiche* (Berlin 1903); F. W. Hasluck, *Christianity and Islam under the Sultans,* 2 vols. (Oxford 1929); A. Schopoff, *Les Réformes et la protection des chrétiens en Turquie, 1673–1904* (Paris 1904); G. Goyau, *Le protectorat de la France sur les chrétiens de l'Empire ottoman* (Paris 1895); J. Friedrich, *Die christlichen Balkanstaaten in Vergangenheit und Gegenwart* (Munich 1916); B. Rupčič, *Entstehung der Franziskanerpfarreien in Bosnien und Herzegowina und ihre Entwicklung bis zum Jahre 1878* (Wroclaw 1937); I. Simrak, *Graeco-catholica Ecclesia in Jugoslavia* (Zagreb 1931); P. Tocanel, *Storia della Chiesa cattolica in Romania* III: *Il Vicariato apostolico e le missioni dei Frati Minori Conventuali in Moldavia,* 2 vols. (Padua 1960–65); K. Lübeck, *Die katholische Orientmission in ihrer Entwicklung dargestellt* (Cologne 1917); Hilaire de Barenton, O.F.M.Cap., *La France catholique en Orient durant les trois derniers siècles* (Paris 1912); *Les jésuites en Syrie, 1831–1931* (Paris 1931); A. Posseto, *Il patriarcato latino di Gerusalemme* (Milan 1938); F. de Portu, *Notice sur le diocèse de Smyrne et le vicariat apostolique de l'Asie Mineure* (Smyrna 1908).

UNITED STATES: J. T. Ellis, *A Guide to American Catholic History* (Milwaukee 1959); C. R. Fish, *Guide to the Materials for American History in Roman and other Italian Archives* (Washington 1911); T. McAvoy, "Catholic Archives and Manuscript Collections," *The American Archivist* 24 (1961), 409–14; P. Cadden, *The Historiography of the American Catholic Church, 1785–1943* (Washington 1944); H. J. Browne, "American Catholic History, A Progress Report, Research and Study," *CH* 26 (1957), 372–80; J. G. Shea, *History of the Catholic Church in the United States,* 4 vols. (New York 1886–92); T. McAvoy, *A History of the Catholic Church in the United States* (Notre Dame 1969); J. T. Ellis, *American Catholicism* (Chicago 1956); L. Hertling, *Geschichte der katholischen Kirche in den Vereinigten Staaten* (Berlin 1954); R. F. McNamara, "Etats-Unis," *DHGE* XV, 1109–47; A. Greeley, *The Catholic Experience. An Interpretation of the History of American Catholicism* (Garden City 1968); F. Kenneally, *United States Documents in the Propaganda Fide Archives,* 2 vols. (Washington 1966–68); J. T. Ellis, *Documents of American Catholic History* (Milwaukee 1956); D. Shearer, *Pontificia Americana. A Documentary History of the Catholic Church in the United States, 1784–1884* (Washington 1933); P. Guilday, *The National Pastorals of the American Hierarchy, 1792–1910* (Washington 1923); P. Guilday, *A History of the Councils of Baltimore* (New York 1932); E. Shaughnessy, *Has the Immigrant kept the Faith? A Study of Immigration and Catholic Growth in the United States* (New York 1925); J. A. Burns, *The Growth and Development of the Catholic School System in the United States* (New York 1912); J. A. Burns, J. Kohlbrenner, *A History of Catholic Education in the United States* (New York 1937); D. T. McColgan, *A Century of Charity: the first one hundred Years of the Society of St. Vincent de Paul in the United States,* 2 vols. (Milwaukee 1951); P. J. Dignan, *A History of the Legal Incorporation of Catholic Property in the United States, 1784–1932* (Washington 1933); F. McDonald, *The Catholic Church and the Secret Societies in the United States* (New York 1946); R. Corrigan, *Die Propaganda-Kongregation und ihre Tätigkeit in Nord-Amerika* (Munich 1928); T. Roemer, *The Ludwig-Missionsverein and the Catholic Church in the United States, 1838–1918* (Washington 1933); R. Clarke, *Lives of Deceased Bishops of the Catholic Church in the United States,* 3 vols. (New York 1888); J. B. Code, *Dictionary of the American Hierarchy* (New York 1940); R. Baudier, *The Catholic Church in Louisiana*

(New Orleans 1939); W. Casper, *History of the Catholic Church in Nebraska,* 3 vols. (Milwaukee 1960–66); R. Trisco, *The Holy See and the Nascent Church in the Middle Western United States* (Rome 1962); W. Schoenberg, *A Chronicle of the Catholic Historiography of the Pacific Northwest, 1743–1960* (Spokane 1962); E. V. O'Hara, *Pioneer Catholic History of Oregon* (Portland 1907); C. Blanchard, *History of the Catholic Church in Indiana,* 2 vols. (Logansport 1898); H. H. Heming, *The Catholic Church in Wisconsin* (Milwaukee 1895–98); J. F. Kempker, *History of the Catholic Church in Iowa* (Iowa City 1887); J. H. Lamott, *History of the Archdiocese of Cincinnati* (New York 1921); M. J. Hynes, *History of the Diocese of Cleveland* (Cleveland 1953); G. Garraghan, *The Catholic Church in Chicago* (Chicago 1921); G. Paré, *The Catholic Church in Detroit* (Detroit 1951); J. Smith, *The Catholic Church in New York,* 2 vols. (New York 1905); L. J. Kirlin, *Catholicity in Philadelphia* (Philadelphia 1909); F. J. Magri, *The Catholic Church in the City and Diocese of Richmond* (Richmond 1906); J. H. Bailey, *A History of the Diocese of Richmond, the Formative Years* (Richmond 1956); J. E. Rothensteiner, *History of the Archdiocese of St. Louis,* 2 vols. (St. Louis 1928); J. M. Reardon, *The Catholic Church in the Diocese of St. Paul* (St. Paul 1952); F. Parkman, *The Jesuits in North America* (Boston 1963); V. O'Daniel, *The Dominican Province of St. Joseph* (New York 1942); G. Herbermann, *The Sulpicians in the United States* (New York 1916); A. Gabriel, *The Christian Brothers in the United States* (New York 1948); M. de L. Walsh, *The Sisters of Charity of New York, 1809–1959,* 3 vols. (New York 1960); T. P. McCarty, *Guide to the Catholic Sisterhoods in the United States* (Washington 1964); W. Sweet, *The Story of Religion in America* (New York 1950); C. Olmstead, *History of Religion in the United States* (New Jersey 1960); S. Ahlstrom, *A Religious History of the American People* (New Haven 1972); S. Ahlstrom, *Theology in America: The Major Protestant Voices from Puritanism to Neo-Orthodoxy* (Indianapolis 1976); N. Burr, *A Critical Bibliography of Religion in America* (New Jersey 1961); N. Burr, *Religion in American Life* (New York 1971); L. Loetscher, *American Christianity: An Historical Interpretation with Representative Documents,* 2 vols. (New York 1960–63); J. Brauer, *Reinterpretation in American Church History* (Chicago 1968); E. Gaustad, *Historical Atlas of Religion in America* (New York 1962); R. Handy, *A History of the Churches in the United States and Canada* (Oxford 1976); M. Marty, *Righteous Empire: The Protestant Experience in America* (New York 1970); A. Stokes, *Church and State in the United States,* 3 vols. (New York 1950); S. Mead, *The Lively Experiment: The Shaping of Christianity in America* (New York 1963); E. Humphrey, *Nationalism and Religion in America* (New York 1965); W. McLoughlin, *Modern Revivalism: Charles Grandison Finney to Billy Graham* (New York 1959); W. Kennedy, *The Shaping of Protestant Education: An Interpretation of the Sunday School and the Development of Protestant Educational Strategy in the United States, 1789–1860* (New York 1966); R. Billington, *The Protestant Crusade, 1800–1860: A Study of the Origins of American Nativism* (New York 1938); C. Griffin, *Their Brother's Keepers: Moral Stewardship in the United States, 1800–1865* (New Brunswick 1960); D. Riemers, *White Protestantism and the Negro* (New York 1975); R. Michaelson, *Piety in the Public Schools: Trends and Issues in the Relationship Between Religion and the Public School in the United States* (New York 1970); R. Handy, *A Christian America: Protestant Hopes and Historical Realities* (New York 1971); K. Bailey, *Southern White Protestantism in the Twentieth Century* (New York 1964); P. Gaston, *The New South Creed, A Study in Southern Mythology* (New York 1970); G. Lenski, *The Religious Factor: A Sociological Study of Religion's Impact on Politics, Economics, and Family Life* (New York 1961); M. Ewens, *The Role of the Nun in Nineteenth-Century America* (University of Minnesota 1971); B. J. Meiring, *Educational Aspects of the Legislation of the Councils of Baltimore, 1829–1884* (diss., University of California 1963); P. Gleason, ed., *Documentary Reports on Early American Catholicism*

(New York 1978); A. H. Dorsey, *The Flemmings* (New York 1869); J. England, *The Works of the Right Rev. John England, First Bishop of Charleston,* 5 vols. (New York 1849); A. M. Greeley, "Catholicism in America: 200 Years and Counting," *The Critic* XXXIV (1976), 14–47, 54–170; H. J. Nolan, ed., *Pastoral Letters of the American Hierarchy, 1792–1970* (Huntington 1971); R. F. Hueston, *The Catholic Press and Nativism, 1840–1860* (New York 1976); W. B. Faherty, *Dream by the River. Two Centuries of Saint Louis Catholicism, 1766–1967* (St. Louis 1973); J. P. Gallagher, *A Century of History: the Diocese of Scranton, 1869–1968* (Scranton 1968); R. H. Lord, J. E. Sexton, E. T. Harrington, *History of the Archdiocese of Boston in the various Stages of its Development 1604 to 1943,* 3 vols. (New York 1944); G. J. Garraghan, *The Jesuits of the Middle United States,* 3 vols. (New York 1938); J. Rippinger, "Some Historical Determinants of American Benedictine Monasticism, 1846–1900," *American Benedictine Review* XXVII (1976), 63–84; T. Radzialowski, "Reflections on the History of the Felicians in America," *Polish-American Studies* XXXII (1975), 19–28; J. M. Daley, *Georgetown University: Origin and Early Years* (Washington 1957); J. T. Ellis, *The Formative Years of the Catholic University of America* (Washington 1946); M. H. Sanfilippo, "Personal Religious Expressions of Roman Catholicism: A Transcendental Critique," *Catholic Historical Review* LXII (1976), 366–87; J. Dolan, *Catholic Revivalism in the United States, 1830–1900* (Notre Dame 1977); J. P. Gaffey, "Patterns of Ecclesiastical Authority: The Problem of the Chicago Succession," *Church History* XLII (1973), 257–70; D. Spalding, "Martin John Spalding's 'Dissertation on the American Civil War,'" *Catholic Historical Review* LII (1966), 66–85; J. R. G. Hassard, *Life of the Most Reverend John Hughes, D. D., First Archbishop of New York* (New York 1969); T. W. Spalding, *Martin John Spalding: American Churchman* (Washington 1973); T. R. Ryan, *Orestes A. Brownson* (Huntington 1976); R. M. Leliaert, "The Religious Significance of Democracy in the Thought of Orestes A. Brownson," *Review of Politics* XXXVIII (1976), 3–26; P. H. Lemcke, *Life and Work of Prince Demetrius Augustine Gallitzin* (London and New York 1940); J. Oetgen, *An American Abbott: Boniface Wimmer, O.S.B., 1809–1887* (Latrobe, Pa. 1976); P. L. Johnson, *Crosier on the Frontier: A Life of John Martin Henni, Archbishop of Milwaukee* (Madison 1959); P. L. Johnson, *Stuffed Saddlebags: The Life of Martin Kundig, Priest, 1805–1879* (Milwaukee 1942); P. Horgan, *Lamy of Santa Fe; His Life and Times* (New York 1975); V. R. Greene, *For God and Country: The Rise of Polish and Lithuanian Ethnic Consciousness in America, 1860–1910* (Madison 1975); W. Galush, "The Polish National Catholic Church: A Survey of its Origins, Development and Missions," *Records of the American Catholic Historical Society of Philadelphia* LXXXIII (1972), 131–49; A. Kuzniewski, "The Polish National Catholic Church—The View From People's Poland," *Polish-American Studies* XXXI (1974), 30–34; H. B. Leonard, "Ethnic Conflict and Episcopal Power: The Diocese of Cleveland, 1847–1870," *Catholic Historical Review* LXII (1976), 388–407; D. P. Killen, "Americanism Revisited: John Spalding and Testem Benevolentiae," *Harvard Theological Review* LXVI (1973), 413–54; A. I. Abell, *American Catholicism and Social Action; A Search for Social Justice* (Garden City 1960); T. O. Hanley, ed., *The John Carroll Papers,* 3 vols. (Notre Dame 1976); P. Gleason, "The Main Sheet Anchor: John Carroll and Catholic Higher Education," *Review of Politics* XXXVIII (1976), 576–613; J. W. Sanders, *The Education of an Urban Minority: Catholicism in Chicago, 1833–1965* (New York 1977); V. P. Lannie, "The Emergence of Catholic Education in America," *Notre Dame Journal of Education* III (1973), 297–309.

CANADA: M. Sheehan, *A Current Bibliography of Canadian Church History: Canadian Historical Association Report;* D. de St-Denis, O.F.M.Cap., *L'Église catholique au Canada. Précis historique et statistique* (Montreal 1956); H. H. Walsh, *The Christian Church in*

Canada (Toronto 1956); J. S. Moir, *Church and State in Canada, 1627–1867. Basic documents* (Toronto 1967); L. Pouliot, "Canada," *DHGE* XI, 675–98; A. de Barbézieux, O.F.M.Cap., *Histoire de la province ecclésiastique d'Ottawa,* 2 vols. (Paris 1925); W. P. Bull, *From MacDonnell to McGuignan. The History of the Growth of the Roman Catholic Church in Upper Canada* (Toronto 1939); A. Morice, *Histoire de l'Église catholique dans l'Ouest canadien* III/IV (Winnipeg 1928); A. A. Johnston, *A History of the Catholic Church in Eastern Nova Scotia* (Antigonish 1963); H. Têtu, *Les évêques de Québec. Notices biographiques* (Québec 1889); Mgr. Tangay, *Répertoire général du clergé canadien* (Montréal 1893); L. E. Hamelin, "Évolution numérique du clergé catholique dans le Québec," *Recherches sociographiques* 2 (1961), 189–243; *Mandements, lettres pastorales et circulaires des évêques de Québec,* 9 volumes (Québec 1887–98). *Mandements, lettres pastorales et circulaires des évêques publiés dans le diocèse de Montréal,* 13 vols. (Montréal 1887–1926); J. Grant, *A History of the Christian Church in Canada,* 3 vols. (Toronto 1966–72); J. Moir, *Church and State in Canada, 1627–1867: Basic Documents* (Toronto 1967); P. Carrington, *The Anglican Church in Canada: A History* (Toronto 1963); W. Reid, *The Church of Scotland in Lower Canada: Its Struggle for Establishment* (Toronto 1936); M. Armstrong, *The Great Awakening in Nova Scotia, 1776–1809* (Hartford 1948); E. Norman, *The Conscience of the State in North America* (Cambridge 1968); S. Crysdale, *The Industrial Struggle and Protestant Ethic in Canada* (Toronto 1961); J. Grant, *The Canadian Experience of Church Union* (London 1967); C. Silcox, *Church Union in Canada: Its Causes and Consequences* (New York 1933); C. Sissons, *Church and State in Canadian Education* (Toronto 1959).

AUSTRALIA: P. F. Moran, *History of the Catholic Church in Australasia,* 2 vols. (Sydney 1896); P. O'Farrell, *The Catholic Church in Australia, 1788–1967* (London 1968); P. O'Farrell, ed., *Documents in Australian Catholic History,* 2 vols. (London 1969).

LATIN AMERICA: R. Streit, J. Dindinger, *Bibliotheca Missionum* III (Freiburg i. Br. 1927); J. L. Mecham, *Church and State in Latin America* (Chapel Hill 1966); E. Ryan, *The Church in the South American Republics* (New York 1932); F. B. Pike, ed., *The Conflict between Church and State in Latin America* (New York 1964); J. J. Kennedy, *Catholicism, Nationalism and Democracy in Argentina* (Notre Dame 1958); J. S. Campobassi, *Laicismo y catolicismo en la educación pública argentina* (Buenos Aires 1961); F. López Menéndez, *Compendio de la historia eclesiástica de Bolivia* (La Paz 1965); P. F. da Silveria Camargo, *Historia eclesiástica do Brasil* (Petropolis 1955); J. Dornas Filho, *O padroado e la Igreja brasileira* (São Paulo 1939); Julio Maria, *A Religiâo: Livro do Centenario* I (Rio de Janeiro 1900); C. Silva Cotapos, *Historia eclesiástica de Chile* (Santiago de Chile 1925); M. Cruchaga Montt, *De las relaciones entre la Iglesia y el Estado en Chile* (Madrid 1929); J. M. Groot, *Historia eclesiástica y civil de Nueva Granada,* 4 vols. (Bogotá 1889–93); J. P. Restrepo, *Le Iglesia y el Estado en Colombia* (London 1885); B. E. Haddox, *Sociedad y religión en Colombia* (Bogotá 1965); J. Maramillo, *El pensiamento colombiano en el siglo XIX* (Bogotá 1964); J. T. Donoso, *La Iglesia ecuatoriana en el siglo XIX,* 2 vols. (Quito 1934–36); M. Cuevas, *Historia de la Iglesia en México,* V (Mexico 1928); J. Bravo Ugarte, *Diocesis y obispos de la Iglesia mexicana, 1519–1939* (Mexico 1941); J. Ramírez Cabañas, *Las relaciones entre México y el Vaticano* (Mexico 1928); G. Decorme, *Historia de la Compañia de Jesús en la República Mexicana durante el siglo XIX,* 2 vols. (Guadalajara 1914–21); R. Vargas Ugarte, *Historia de la Iglesia en el Perú,* V (Burgos 1962); A. Watters, *A History of the Church in Venezuela, 1819–1930* (Chapell Hill 1933); F. B. Pike, "The Catholic Church in Central America," *RPol* 21 (1959), 83–113.

4. CATHOLIC CHURCHES WITH EASTERN RITE

J. Hajjar, *Les chrétiens uniates du Proche-Orient* (Paris 1962); J. Hajjar, *L'apostolat des missionnaires latins dans le Proche-Orient selon les directives romaines* (Jerusalem 1956); S. Sidarous, *Les patriarcats dans l'Empire ottoman et spécialement en Égypte* (Paris 1907); *Statistica con cenni storici della gerarchia e dei fedeli di rito orientale* (Vatican City 1932); C. de Clercq, *Conciles des Orientaux catholiques,* 2 vols. (Paris 1949–52); *S. Congregazione per la Chiesa Orientale. Codificazione canonica orientale. Fonti,* 3rd ser. (Rome 1931seqq.); C. Charon (= C. Korolewski), *Histoire des patriarcats melkites* II/III (Rome and Paris 1910–11); A. D'Avril in *ROC* 3 (1898), 1–30, 265–81; T. Anaissi, *Bullarium Maronitarum* (Rome 1911); G. Beltrami, *La Chiesa caldea nel secolo dell'unione* (Rome 1933); M. Cramer, *Das christlich-koptische Ägypten einst und heute. Eine Orientierung* (Wiesbaden 1959); V. Inglisian, *Hunderfünfzig Jahre Mechitaristen in Wien, 1811–1961* (Vienna 1961); The articles "Maronites," "Nestorienne (Église)," "Roumanie," "Syrienne (Église)," *DThC;* The articles "Alep," "Antioche," "Antonins," "Arménie," "Audo," "Beyrouth," "Constantinople," "Égypte," *DHGE*. E. Likowski, *Dzieje Kosciola unickiego na Litwie i Rusi w XVIII i XIX wieku,* 2 vols. (Warsaw 1906); A. Korczok, *Die griechisch-katholische Kirche in Galizien* (Leipzig 1921); N. Nilles, *Symbolae ad illustrandam historiam Ecclesiae in terris Coronae S. Stephani,* 2 vols. (Innsbruck 1885); I. Radu, *Istoria diocezei romane-unite a Orazü-Mari* (Oradea Mare 1930).

5. MISSION HISTORY

Bibliotheca Missionum, R. Streit, J. Dindinger, eds. (Freiburg im Breisgau 1916seqq.), VIII, XII–XIV, XVII–XXI, XXVII; *Collectanea S. Congregationis de Propaganda Fide* I (1622–1866), II (1867–1906), (Rome 1907); S. Delacroix, *Histoire Universelle des Missions Catholiques* III: *Les Missions Contemporaines* (1800–1957), (Paris 1958); K. S. Latourette, *A History of the Expansion of Christianity* IV/VI: *The Great Century* (New York 1941); A. Launay, *Histoire Générale de la Société des Missions Étrangères,* 3 vols. (Paris 1894); F. Schwager, *Die katholische Heidenmission der Gegenwart* I–IV (Steyl 1907).

6. ORDERS AND CONGREGATIONS

M. Heimbucher, *Die Orden und Kongregationen der katholischen Kirche,* 2 vols. (Paderborn 1932–34); M. Escobar, ed., *Ordini e Congregazioni religiose,* 2 vols. (Turin 1951–53); C. Tyck, *Notices historiques sur les congrégations et communautés religieuses et les instituts missionnaires du XIXe siècle* (Louvain 1892); H. C. Wendlandt, *Die weiblichen Orden und Kongregationen der katholischen Kirche und ihre Wirksamkeit in Preußen von 1818 bis 1918* (Paderborn 1924); S. Hilpisch, *Geschichte des benediktinischen Mönchtums* (Freiburg i. Br. 1929); P. Schmitz, *Histoire de l'Ordre de S. Benoît* VI/VII (Maredsous 1948–56); P. Weissenberger, *Das benediktinische Mönchtum im 19./20. Jahrhundert* (Beuron 1958); L. F. Lekai, *Geschichte und Wirken der Weißen Mönche. Der Order der Cisterzienser* (Cologne 1958); N. Backmund, *Monasticon Praemonstratense,* 3 vols. (Straubing 1949–56); A. Walz, *Compendium historiae Ordinis Praedicatorum* (Rome 1948); A. Mortier, *Histoire des Maîtres généraux de l'ordre des Frères Prêcheurs* VII (Paris 1915); H. Holzapfel, *Manuale historiae Ordinis FF. Minorum* (Freiburg i. Br. 1909); M. de Pobladura, *Historia generalis Ordinis Fratrum Minorum capucinorum* III (Rome 1951); R. Villoslada, *Manual de historia de la Compañia de Jesús* (Madrid 1954); P. Albers, *Liber saecularis historiae Societatis Iesu ab anno 1814 ad annum 1914* (Rome 1914); H. Azzolini in *AHSI* 2 (1933), 88–92; J. Burnichon, *La Compagnie de Jésus en France. Histoire d'un siècle.*

1814–1914, 4 vols. (Paris 1914–22); L. Frias, *Historia de la Compañia de Jesús en su Asistencia moderna de España,* 2 vols. (Madrid 1923–44); B. Basset, *The English Jesuits* (New York 1968); P. Galletti, *Memorie storiche intorno alla Provincia Romana della Compagnia di Gesù, 1814–1914* (Prato 1914); A. Monti, *La Compagnia di Gesù nel territorio della Provincia torinese* V (Chieri 1920); A. Aldegheri, *Breve storia della Provincia veneta della Compagnia di Gesù, 1814–1914* (Venice 1914); Volpe, *I Gesuiti nel Napoletano, 1804–1914,* 3 vols. (Naples 1914–15); F. Strobel, *Die Jesuiten und die Schweiz* (Olten 1955); G. Decorme, *Historia de la Compañia de Jesús en la República mejicana durante el siglo XIX* (Guadalajara 1914); T. Hugues, *History of the Society of Jesus in North America* II/IV (New York 1908–14); A. Brou, *Cent ans de missions, 1815–1934. Les jésuites missionnaires au XIX*e *et XX*e *siècle* (Paris 1935); E. Hosp, *Die Kongregation des Allerheiligsten Erlösers* (Graz 1924). M. de Meulemeester, *Histoire sommaire de la Congrégation du T. S. Rédempteur* (Louvain 1958); G. Rigault, *Histoire générale de l'Institut des Frères des Écoles chrétiennes,* 9 vols. (Paris 1936–53); K. Zähringer, *Die Schulbrüder* (Freiburg i. Br. 1962); H. Neufeld, *Die Gesellschaft Mariens* (Munich 1962); P. Coste, G. Goyau, *Les Filles de la Charité* (Paris 1933). J. F. Devaux, *Les Filles de la Sagesse* II (Cholet 1955); L. Ziegler, *Die Armen Schulschwestern von Unserer Lieben Frau* (Munich 1935); A. Hillengass, *Die Gesellschaft vom heiligen Herz Jesu* (Stuttgart 1917).

7. HISTORY OF THEOLOGY

E. Hocedez, *Histoire de la théologie au XIX*e *siècle* 3 volumes (Brussels 1947–52); M. Grabmann, *Die Geschichte der katholischen Theologie seit dem Ausgang der Väterzeit* (Freiburg i. Br. 1933); L. Scheffczyk, *Theologie in Aufbruch und Widerstreit. Die deutsche katholische Theologie im 19. Jahrhundert* (Bremen 1965).

BIBLIOGRAPHY TO INDIVIDUAL CHAPTERS

Part One
Between the Revolutions of 1830 and 1848

SECTION ONE

The Continuation of Catholic Renewal in Europe

1. *The Progress of Ultramontanism and the Growth of the International Orders*

LITERATURE

On the further development of ultramontanism there are several references in the tendentious work by J. Friedrich, *Geschichte des Vaticanischen Conzils I: Vorgeschichte* (Bonn 1877), 96–142, 200–226. Comprehensive descriptions by R. Aubert and Y. Congar in *L'Ecclésiologie au XIXe siècle* (Paris 1960), 11–35, 97–104.

ON FRANCE: see vol. VII in this series, pp. 400–1, for the works by J. Martin and P. Poupard on the activity of the nuncios, as well as biographies of Guéranger, Montalembert, Gousset, and Parisis.

ON GERMANY: H. Becher, *Der deutsche Primas* (Colmar 1943), 175–223; F. Vigener in *HZ* 111 (1913), 565–81; the biographies (listed in the General Bibliography) of Geissel and Döllinger.

ON AUSTRIA: E. Winter, *Der Josephinismus* (Vienna 1962), 222–98 and F. Maaß, *Lokkerung und Aufhebung des Josephinismus 1820–50* (Vienna 1961).

ON THE GROWTH OF THE SOCIETY OF JESUS UNDER THE GENERALSHIP OF P. ROOTHAAN: his biography by P. Albers (2 vols. [Nijmegen 1912]) to be supplemented by those by P. Pirri (Isola del Liri 1930) and R. G. North (Milwaukee 1944), and by *Io. Ph. Roothaan. Testimonia aequalium* (Rome 1935), the edition of his correspondence (5 vols. [Rome 1935–40]) and his *Opera spiritualia* (2 vols. [Rome 1936]). Also J. A. Otto, *Gründung der neuen Jesuitenmission durch General P. J. P. Roothaan* (Freiburg i. Br. 1939) and J. de Guibert, *La spiritualité de la Compagnie de Jésus* (Rome 1953), 461–68. With respect to national developments, see the works (General Bibliography) by J. Burnichon for France, L. Frias for Spain, P. Galetti and Volpe for Italy, and F. Strobel for Switzerland.

On the Restoration of the Dominicans in France: in addition to the biographies of Lacordaire (see above, chap. 1, n. 16), those of P. Jandel (by H. Cormier [Paris 1890]) and P. Besson (by E. Cartier [Paris 1865]), a collection of documents by R. Devas, *Ex umbris. Letters and Papers hitherto unpublished of the Fathers Lacordaire, Jandel, Danzas* (Hawkesyard 1920); also *Année dominicaine* 1921, 118–20 and A. Duval in *AFP* 36 (1966), 493–542.

On the Restoration of the Benedictines in France: the works on Guéranger (chap. 1 above, n. 17) as well as the biographies of Dom Pitra (by F. Cabrol [Paris 1891] and by A. Battandier [Paris 1896]), of Dom Couturier (by A. Houtin [Angers 1899]) and of Dom Gauthey (by R. B. Laure [Grenoble 1944]).

2. Old and New in Pastoral Care and Moral Theology

LITERATURE

F. X. Arnold, *Grundsätzliches und Geschichtliches zur Theologie der Seelsorge* (Freiburg i. Br. 1949); F. X. Arnold, *Seelsorge aus der Mitte der Heilsgeschichte* (Freiburg i. Br. 1956), 152–95; H. Schuster, *Handbuch der Pastoraltheologie,* ed. by F. X. Arnold et al., I (Freiburg im Breisgau 1964), 47–76; H. J. Müller, *Die ganze Bekehrung. Das zentrale Anliegen des Theologen und Seelsorgers J. M. Sailer* (Regensburg 1949); A. Schrott, *Seelsorge im Wandel der Zeiten* (Graz 1949), 153–266; Schnabel, *G* IV, especially 50–56, 270–76; M. H. Vicaire in *Histoire illustrée de l'Église* II (Geneva 1948), 261–326; P. Broutin, "L. Querbes. Recherches sur l'évolution de la pastorale au XIXe siècle," *NRTh* 81 (1959), 696–720; E. Vercesi-E. Santini, *La sacra eloquenza dal sec. XVII ai nostri giorni* (Milan 1930).

On Catechetics: *DThC* II, 1951–67; F. H. Thalhofer, *Entwicklung des katholischen Katechismus in Deutschland von Canisius bis Deharbe* (Freiburg i. Br. 1899); F. X. Arnold, *Dienst am Glauben* (Freiburg i. Br. 1948), 31–92; B. Dreher, *Die biblische Unterweisung im evangelischen und katholischen Religionsunterricht* (Freiburg i. Br. 1963), 9–55; H. Kreutzwald, *Zur Geschichte des biblischen Unterrichts* (Freiburg i. Br. 1957), 107–79; J. Hofinger, *Geschichte des Katechismus in Österreich* (Innsbruck 1937), 238–77; P. Broutin, "Le mouvement catéchistique en France au XIXe siècle," *NRTh* 82 (1960), 494–512, 607–32, 699–715.

On Moral Theology during the First Half of the Nineteenth Century: B. Häring, *Das Gesetz Christi* I (Freiburg i. Br. 1961), 62–64; J. Diebolt, *La théologie morale catholique en Allemagne 1750–1850* (Strasbourg 1926), 166–354; P. Hadrossek, *Die Bedeutung des Systemgedankens für die Moraltheologie in Deutschland seit der Thomas-Renaissance* (Munich 1950); 76–214; F. Steinbüchel, *Der Zerfall des christlichen Ethos im 19. Jahrhundert* (Frankfurt 1951).

On the Progress of the Liguoric Moral: I. von Döllinger and F. H. Reusch, *Geschichte der Moralstreitigkeiten in der römisch-katholischen Kirche* I (Nördlingen 1889); 462–76; G. Cacciatore, *S. Alfonso de'Liguori e il Giansenismo* (Florence 1944), 440–59; J. Guerber, "Le rôle de P. B. Lanteri dans l'introduction de la morale ligorienne en France," *Spicilegium Historiae Congreg. SS. Redemptoris* 4 (1956), 343–76; M. de Meulemeester, "Introduction de la morale de S. Alphonse de Liguori en Belgique," *EThL* 16 (1939), 468–84.

3. *Catholic Thought Searching for New Ways*

LITERATURE

Hocedez II; J. Bellamy, *La théologie catholique au XIXe siècle* (Paris 1904); L. Scheffczyk, *Theologie im Aufbruch und Widerstreit. Die deutsche katholische Theologie im 19. Jahrhundert* (Bremen 1925); C. Werner, *Geschichte der katholischen Theologie. Seit dem Trienter Concil bis zur Gegenwart* (Munich 1867).

HERMESIANISM: H. Schrörs, *Ein vergessener Führer der Rheinischen Geistesgeschichte des 19. Jahrhunderts* (Bonn 1925); H. Schrörs, *Die Kölner Wirren 1837* (Cologne 1927); H. Schrörs, "Hermesianische Pfarrer," *Annalen des Historischen Vereins für den Niederrhein* 103 (1919), 76–183; H. Bastgen, *Forschungen und Quellen zur Kirchenpolitik Gregors XVI.* (Paderborn 1929), 18–74, 245–77, 437–548; S. Merkle in *HJ* 60 (1940); 179–220; J. Pritz, *Franz Werner* (Freiburg i. Br. 1957); G. Schönig, *A.J. Binterim* (Düsseldorf 1933); Hocedez I, 195–203, II, 37–39; B. Guzzetti, *La perdita della fede nei cattolici* (Venegono 1940), 41–73; D. Gla, *Repertorium der katholisch-theologischen Literatur* I/2 (Paderborn 1904), 355–70.

GÜNTHERIANISM: F. P. Knoodt, *A. Günther,* 2 vols. (Vienna 1881; tendentious, but well-informed); E. Winter, *Die geistige Entwicklung Anton Günthers und seiner Schule* (Paderborn 1931); P. Wenzel, *Das wissenschaftliche Anliegen des Güntherianismus* (Essen 1961); P. Wenzel, *Der Freundeskreis um Anton Günther* (Essen 1965; consult also U. Engelmann in *Erbe und Auftrag* 42 [1966], 240–45); J. Pritz, *Glauben und Wissen bei Anton Günther. Eine Einführung in sein Leben und Werk* (Vienna 1963); A. Dempf, *Weltordnung und Heilsgeschichte* (Eichstätt 1958); K. Beck, *Offenbarung und Glaube bei Anton Günther* (Vienna 1967); Hocedez II, 39–59.

TÜBINGEN AND MUNICH: in addition to the general works listed above: J. R. Geiselmann, *Die katholische Tübinger Schule* (Freiburg im Breisgau 1964); M. Miller, "Die Tübinger katholisch-theologische Fakultät und die württembergische Regierung 1835–46," *ThQ* 132 (1952), 22–45, 213–34; S. Lösch, "Die katholisch-theologische Fakultät zu Tübingen und Gießen 1830–50," *ThQ* 108 (1927), 159–208 (about Gießen); A. Schuchert, "Die katholisch-theologische Fakultät an der Universität Gießen", *Jahrbuch für das Bistum Mainz* 1 (1946), 64–75; H. Witetschek, "Die Bedeutung der theologischen Fakultät der Universität München für die kirchliche Erneuerung in der letzten Hälfte des 19. Jahrhunderts," *HJ* 86 (1966), 107–37; A. Lauscher, *Die katholisch-theologische Fakultät der Universität zu Bonn* (Düsseldorf 1920); S. Lösch, *Professor A. Gengler. Die Beziehungen der Bamberger Theologen zu Döllinger und Möhler* (Würzberg 1963; letters from the years 1827–43); J. Friedrich, *Ignaz von Döllinger* I/II (Munich 1899; numerous documents); J. Zinkl, *Magnus Jocham. Ein Beitrag zur Geschichte der katholischen Theologie und Frömmigkeit im 19. Jahrhundert* (Freiburg i. Br. 1950).

THE CATHOLIC UNIVERSITY OF LOUVAIN: Simon, *Sterckx* I, 260–93; L. van der Essen, *L'Université de Louvain* (Brussels 1945), 279–81; *EThL* 9 (1932), 608–704; A. Franco, "Geschiedenis van het traditionalisme aan de Universiteit te Leuven 1835–67" (typed diss., Louvain 1956); J. Henry, "Le traditionalisme et l'ontologisme à l'Université de Louvain," *Annales de l'Institut supérieur de philosophie* 5 (Louvain 1922), 42–149; A. Simon, "Le cardinal Sterckx et al condamnation de Ubaghs en 1843," *Collectanea Mechliniensia* 16 (Mechelen 1946), 639–44.

TENTATIVE INITIATIVES OF CATHOLIC INTELLECTUALS IN FRANCE: J. R. Derré, *Lamennais, ses amis et le mouvement des idées à l'époque romantique* (Paris 1962), 461–728; L. Foucher, *La philosophie catholique en France au XIXe siècle avant la renaissance thomiste* (Paris 1955), 51–195; N. Hötzel, *Die Uroffenbarung im französischen Traditionalismus* (Munich 1962), 115–384; Brugerette I, 84–97; H. Bremond, *La littérature religieuse d'avant-hier et d'aujourd'hui* (Paris 1906), 3–21; P. Moreau, *Le Romantisme* (Paris 1932), 296–317; P. Fernessole, *Les conférenciers de Notre-Dame I: Genèse et fondation* (Paris 1935); *Lettres de Frédéric Ozanam II: Premières années à la Sorbonne,* ed. by J. Caron (Paris 1971).

The Ascension of Pius IX and the Crisis of 1848

4. *The First Years of the Pontificate of Pius IX: From the Neoguelf Mythos to the Roman Revolution*

LITERATURE

ON THE REVOLUTION OF 1848: an excellent comprehensive treatment is that by L. Salvatorelli, *La rivoluzione europea 1848–49* (Milan 1949). Also Hermelink II, 40–95. On the shifting fortunes of the Church during this period, there are Aubert, 11–71, 505–10; Schmidlin, *PG* II, 6–45; Hales, 17–133.

ON GIOVANNI MASTAI BEFORE HIS ELECTION: in addition to the biographies mentioned below on p. 357, A. Serafini, *Pio nono* I (Rome 1958; numerous letters and other documents); G. Pontrandolfi, *Pio IX e Volterra* (Volterra 1928); G. L. Masetti-Zannini in *Bolletino del Mueso del Risorgimento di Bologna* 2 (1957), 91–148; G. L. Masetti-Zannini in *RSTI* 14 (1960), 283–98; L. Valentini in *SC* 87 (1959), 321–43; P. Leturia, "El viaje a América del futuro Pio IX," *Xenia Piana* (Rome 1943), 367–444; G. Margotti, *Pio IX ed il suo episcopato nelle diocesi di Spoleto e Imola* (Turin 1877); L. Rivera in *RStRis* 19 (1932), 205–20; F. Minoccheri, *Pio IX ad Imola e a Roma. Memorie,* ed. by A. M. Bonetti (Naples 1892); *Pio IX da vescovo a pontefice. Lettere al cardinale Amat 1832–48,* ed. by G. Maioli (Modena 1949); R. Fontini in *Archiginnasio* 57 (1962), 274–98.

ON THE CONCLAVE OF 1846: T. Buttini in *RStRis* 27 (1940), 41–68; Engel-Janosi I, 4–19.

ON THE FIRST TWO YEARS OF THE PONTIFICATE: A. -M. Ghisalberti, *Nuove ricerche sugli inizi del pontificato di Pio IX* (Rome 1940); P. Pirri, "L'amnistia di Pio IX," *RSTI* 8 (1954), 207–32; P. Pirri, "Massimo d'Azeglio e Pio IX al tempo del quaresimale della moderazione," *RSTI* 3 (1949), 191–234; R. Quazza, *Pio IX e Massimo d'Azeglio nelle vicende romane del 1847,* 2 vols. (Modena 1957); R. Lefèvre, "Le riforme di Pio IX e la liberta di stampa," *Studi romani* 3 (1955), 667–94; Jemolo, 13–48; A. Anzilotti, *La funzione storica del giobertismo* (Florence 1924); L. de Ruggiero, "Inghilterra e Stato pontificio nel primo triennio del pontificato di Pio IX," *ADRomana* 76 (1953), 51–172; L. P. Wallace, *Pius IX and Lord Palmerston 1846–1849: Power, Public Opinion and Diplomacy* (Durham 1959), 3–46; A. Filipuzzi, *Pio IX e la politica austriaca in Italia dal 1815 al 1848 nella relazione di R. Weiss* (Florence 1958); Engel-Janosi I, 20–37; M. Gualdi, *I primi anni del pontificato di Pio IX, la celebre benedizione e la questione romana* (Carpi 1952); G. Quazza, "Sull'origine della proposta di Pio IX per la Lega doganale," *RStRis* 40 (1953), 357–70; P. Pirri, "La politica unitaria di Pio IX dalla lega doganale alla lega italica," *RSTI* 2 (1948), as well as the other two articles by the same author in the same journal, 1 (1947), 38–84, and 4 (1950), 399–446; J. Anelli Stefanutti, *La lega italica promossa da Pio IX* (Tarcento 1951; on the role of Monsignor Corbolli-Bussi); R. Cessi, *Il mito di Pio IX* (Udine 1953); F. Carollo, *La missione de Antonio Rosmini a Roma nel 1848* (Palermo 1942); A. Baviera, "La corrispondenza diplomatica del P. Ventura incaricato del governo siciliano a Roma," *Miscellanea Di Carlo II* (Trapani 1960), 7–60; C. Riva, "La missione diplomatica di Rosmini a Roma nel 1848–49," *Studium* 63 (1967), 13–27.

THE ROMAN REVOLUTION AND ITS CONSEQUENCES: A. de Liedekerke, *Rapporti delle cose di Roma 1848–1849,* ed. by A. M. Ghisalberti (Rome 1949); *La diplomazia del Regno di Sardegna durante la prima guerra d'independenza II: Relazioni con lo Stato pontificio,* ed. by C. Baudi de Vesme (Turin 1951); E. Brazão, *Relações diplomáticas de Portugal com a Santa Sede. Um ano drámatico, 1848* (Lisbon 1969); A. Capograssi, *La conferenza di Gaeta del 1849* (Rome 1941; to be complemented by A. Ghisalberti in *RStRis* 40 [1953], 235–37); P. Pirri, *Pio IX e Vittorio Emanuele II dal loro carteggio privato I* (Rome 1944), 1–49, 1–83; E. di Carlo, "Lettere inedite del P. Ventura a Rosmini, nov. 1848–gen. 1849," *Regnum Dei* 20 (1964), 5–43; M. Degros, *Rome et les États pontificaux sous l'occupation étrangère* (Paris 1950).

In addition to general works, especially C. Spellanzon, *Storia del Risorgimento* IV, V, VII (Milan 1938–61) and G. J. Berkely, *Italy in the Making 1846–48* (Cambridge 1936–40), see especially G. Quazza, *La questione romana nel 1848–49* (Modena 1947); D. Massé, *Pio IX e il gran tradimento del '48* (Alba 1948); D. Demarco, *Pio IX e la rivoluzione romana del 1848* (Modena 1947; on economic and social causes); C. Minnocci, *P. Sterbini e la rivoluzione romana* (Maricianise 1967); J. Leflon in *AHPont* 1 (1963), 385–402; Engel-Janosi, 38–60; L. Rodelli, *La Repubblica romana del 1849* (Pisa 1955); M. Cessi Drudi, "Contributi alla storia della Conferenza di Gaeta," *RStRis* 46 (1959), 219–72; A. M. Ghisalberti, *Roma da Mazzini a Pio IX* (Rome 1958; the best treatment of the restoration of papal power); L. Pásztor, "La Segreteria di Stato di Pio IX durante il triennio 1848–50," *Annali della Fondazione italiana per la storia amministrativa* 3 (1966), 308–65.

5. *The Consequences of the Events of 1848 in France*

SOURCES

In addition to the *Moniteur universel* (for parliamentary debates), *Univers, Ami de la Religion,* and *Ère nouvelle,* see especially the memoirs of A. de Falloux (Paris 1888) and of A. de Melun II (Paris 1891) as well as the notes and letters of Montalembert, ed. by A. Trannoy in *RH* 192 (1941), 253–89.

LITERATURE

In addition to the biographies of Montalembert, Veuillot, Dupanloup, Lacordaire, Maret, Melun, Sibour, Parisis, and Clausel (General Bibliography), see J. Leflon, *L'Église de France et la révolution de 1848* (Paris 1948); Aubert, *Pie IX,* 40–57, 508–9; Gurian, 185–210; Duroselle, 291–490; H. Cabane, *Histoire du clergé de France pendant la Révolution de 1848* (Paris 1908); R. Limouzin-Lamothe and J. Leflon, *Monsigneur Denis Auguste Affre* (Paris 1971), 301–61; F. Isambert in *ArchSR* 6 (1958), 7–35; M. Vincienne, *Notes sur la situation religieuse de la France en 1848;* R. Rancoeur, *Bibliographie des traveaux publiés sur le centenaire de 1848* (Paris 1949).

ON THE PROVINCIAL COUNCILS: their decrees are published in *ColLac* IV. See G. Darboy in *Le Correspondant* 27 (1851), 193–218; E. Sevrin, *Monsigneur Clausel* II, 539–56.

ON THE FALLOUX LAW: H. Michel, *La Loi Falloux* (Paris 1906); F. Ponteil, *Histoire de l'enseignement* (Paris 1966), 227–45; A. Prost, op. cit. (General Bibliography), 173–77. On the preparation: *La commission extra-parlementaire de 1849. Texte intégral inédit des procès-verbaux,* ed. by G. Chenesseau (Paris 1937).

6. The Consequences of the 1848 Revolution in the States of the German Confederation and the Netherlands

SOURCES

Verhandlungen der ersten Versammlung des katholischen Vereins Deutschlands . . . (Mainz 1848); *ColLac* V, 941–1126 (Würzburg Bishops' Conference); L. Bergsträsser, *Dokumente des politischen Katholizismus* I (Munich 1921); Huber, *Dokumente I* (see bibliography chapter 7). Selections: E. Heinen, *Staatliche Macht und Katholizismus in Deutschland* I (Paderborn 1969).

LITERATURE

GENERAL: Brück, *Geschichte der katholischen Kirche in Deutschland im 19. Jahrhundert* III (Mainz 1902), ed. by J. B. Kißling (Münster 1905); Schmidlin, *PG* II, 135f., 162ff.; Aubert, *Pie IX* (Fliche-Martin 21), 57–63; Huber, *Deutsche Verfassungsgeschichte seit 1789* II (Stuttgart 1960), 685ff., 703ff., 778ff., III (Stuttgart 1963), 105ff., 114–20, 155; Bihlmeyer-Tüchle III, 329, 333, 335f., 337; Buchheim, *Ultramontanismus und Demokratie. Der Weg der deutschen Katholiken im 19. Jahrhundert* (Munich 1963); 55–72; Hubert Jedin, "Freiheit und Aufstieg des deutschen Katholizismus 1848–70," *Ausgewählte Aufsätze und Vorträge* II (Freiburg 1966), 469–84. For Austria: Maaß, *Josephinismus* V; E. Tomek, *Kirchengeschichte Österreichs* III, 686–713; E. Weinzierl-Fischer, *Die österreichischen Konkordate von 1855 und 1933,* 26–59; F. Engel-Janosi, *Österreich und der Vatikan 1846–1918* I (Graz, Vienna, and Cologne 1958), chaps. 3, 4; M. Hussarek, "Die Verhandlung des Konkordates vom 18. August 1855," *AÖG* 109 (1921).

BIOGRAPHIES: Andlaw: by F. Dor (Fribourg 1910); Binterim: C. Schönig, *Anton Josef Binterim (1779–1855) als Kirchenpolitiker und Gelehrter* (Düsseldorf 1933); Buß: by F. Dor (Fribourg 1910); Diepenbrock: by H. Förster (Wroclaw ³1878), by J. H. Reinkens (Leipzig 1881); Döllinger: J. Friedrich, *I. v. Döllinger* I, II (Munich 1889), G. Schwaiger, *I. v. Döllinger* (Munich 1963), J. Finsterhölzl, *I. v. Döllinger* (Graz, Vienna and Cologne 1969); Geissel: by J. A. F. Baudrie (Cologne 1881), by O. Pfülf (2 vols. [Fribourg 1895–96]); Radowitz: E. Ritter, *Radowitz* (Cologne 1948); Rauscher: C. Wolfsgruber, *Joseph Othmar Cardinal Rauscher* (Fribourg 1888).—F. Vigener, Ketteler. *Ein deutsches Bischofsleben des 19. Jahrhunderts* (Munich 1924); L. Lenhart, *Bischof Ketteler,* 3 vols. (Mainz 1966–68); H. Brück, *Adam Franz Lenning* (Mainz 1870); L. von Pastor, *August Reichensperger,* 2 vols. (Fribourg 1899); F. Schmidt, *Peter Reichensperger* (Mönchen-Gladbach 1913); C. Wolfsgruber, *Friedrich Kardinal zu Schwarzenberg,* 3 vols. (Vienna and Leipzig 1906–17).

UNION MOVEMENT, CATHOLIC CONGRESSES: J. B. Kißling, *Geschichte der deutschen Katholikentage* I (Münster 1920); L. Lenhart, ed., *Idee, Gestalt und Gestalter des 1. deutschen Katholikentages in Mainz 1848* (Mainz 1948); K. Buchheim in *LThK* VI, 69–72.

POLITICAL CATHOLICISM: Bergsträsser, *Studien;* F. Schnabel, *Der Zusammenschluß des politischen Katholizismus in Deutschland im Jahre 1848* (Heidelberg 1910); Bachem, *Vorgeschichte, Geschichte und Politik der deutschen Zentrumspartei* II (Cologne 1927; Reprint Aalen 1967), 1–95; K. Repgen, *Märzbewegung und Maiwahlen des Revolutionsjahres 1848 im Rheinland* (Bonn 1955); K. Repgen, "Klerus und Politik 1848," *Festschrift für F. Steinbach* (Bonn 1960); K. Repgen in *LThK* IV, 259ff.

BISHOPS' CONFERENCES: F. H. Vering in *AkathKR* 21, 22 (1869); H. Storz, *Staat und katholische Kirche in Deutschland im Lichte der Würzburger Bischofsdenkschrift von 1848* (Bonn 1934); P. Leisching, *Die Bischofskonferenz. Studien zu ihrer Rechtsgeschichte mit besonderer Berücksichtigung ihrer Entwicklung in Österreich* (Vienna and Munich 1963), 76–149; R. Lill, *Die ersten deutschen Bischofskonferenzen* (Freiburg 1964), 14–56.

THE NETHERLANDS: Rogier, *KathHerleving* 50–275 (also *Schrikbeeld van een staatsgreep in 1853* [Amsterdam 1959]) and Albers, *Herstel* are the main sources, to be complemented by J. Witlox, *Studien over het herstel der hierarchie in 1853* (Tilburg 1928) and A. Bronkhorst, *Rondom 1853. De Aprilbeweging* (The Hague 1953); A. Commissaris, op. cit. (General Bibliography); J. M. Gijsen, *J.A. Paredis, bisschop van Roermond* (Assen 1968); G. Homan in *CHR* 52 (1966–67), 201–11; J. Schokking, *Historisch-juridische schets van de wet van 10.9 1853* (Amsterdam 1894); J. B. van Hugenpoth, *De kloosters in Nederland in 1861* (Utrecht 1861; polemical); D. van Wely in *Bijdragen voor de geschiedenis van de prov. der Minderbroeders in de Nederlands* 14 (1964), 101–259; L. Rogier, "A. Thijm en de katholieke herleving," *Annalen van het Thijmgenootschap* 37 (1949), 1–23.

Part Two
The Catholic Reaction to Liberalism

Introduction: *Pius IX after 1848*

SOURCES

Acta Pii IX, 7 vols. (Rome 1854–78); *Atti del S.P. Pio IX,* 2 vols. (Rome 1857); A. Marcone, *La parola di Pio IX ovvero discorsi e detti di S. Santità,* 2 vols. (Genoa 1864–71); *ASS,* Yearbooks beginning 1865; P. Pirri, *Pio IX e Vittorio Emanuele dal loro carteggio privato,* 3 vols. (Rome 1944–61; also extensive correspondence with persons other than Victor Emmanuel); S. Jacini, *Il tramonto del potere temporale nelle relazioni degli ambasciatori austriaci a Roma 1860/70* (Bari 1931); N. Blakiston, *The Roman Question. Extracts from the Despatches of O. Russell from Rome 1858/70* (London 1962); *Romana . . . Beatificationis et Canonizationis servi Dei Pii IX S.P. Tabella testium et Summarium. Positio super introductione causae,* 2 vols. (Rome 1954); *Elenchus scriptorum quae in Santa Sedis archivis adservantur* (Rome 1954), *Appendix ad Elenchum scriptorum* (Rome 1955), *Positio super virtutibus,* 3 vols. (Rome 1961–62).

LITERATURE

In addition to the general church histories (see General Bibliography), consult Schmidlin, *PG* II, 1–330; Aubert, *Pie IX;* C. Pouthas, *Le pontificat de Pie IX* (Cours de Sorbonne, 1945); E. Hales, *Pius IX. A Study in European Politics and Religion in the XIXth Century* (London 1954); *DThC* XII, 1686–1716; *ECatt* IX, 1510–23.

BIOGRAPHIES OF PIUS IX: There exists as yet no critical biography of Pius IX. Most of the descriptions of his life which appeared during the nineteenth century are nothing more than panegyrics; among those to be mentioned are L. Wappmannsperger, (Regensburg 1879), J. M. Stepischnegg (2 vols. [Vienna 1879]); C. Sylvain (3 vols. [Paris 1885]) and A. Pougeois (6 vols. [Paris 1877–86]). Among more recent works there are A. Monti, *Pio IX nel Risorgimento italiano* (Bari 1928); F. Hayward, *Pie IX et son temps* (Paris 1948); D. Massé, *Pio IX papa e principe italiano* (Modena 1957); P. Fernessole, *Pie IX, pape,* 2 vols. (Paris 1960–63, in need of criticism; also *CivCatt* [1961] II, 63–64 [1964], II, 59–60; *RHE* 59 [1964], 198–204); Aubert-Martina, 839–48.

THE ROMAN CURIA UNDER PIUS IX: In addition to Aubert, *Pie IX,* 280–86, S. Nigro, *Seconda Roma 1850/70* (Milan 1941) and F. Hayward, op cit., see the memoirs of contemporaries, especially A. Flir, *Briefe aus Rom* (Innsbruck 1864); H. d'Ideville, *Journal II Rome 1862/64* (Paris 1873); K. von Schlözer, *Römische Briefe 1864/69* (Stuttgart 1913); J. Acton in *Cambridge Historical Journal* 8 (1946), 186–204; *La Curia romana e i Gesuiti* (Florence 1861; polemical); *La Crise d'Église* (Paris 1878; polemical).

The Temporary Improvement in the Situation of the Church

7. *The Seeming Success of the Church in France during the Second Empire and the "Moral Order"*

SOURCES

Pastoral letters of bishops in J. -P. Migne, *Orateurs sacrés,* 2nd Ser. (Paris 1856–66); the correspondence of L. Veuillot (12 vols. [Paris 1931–32]), A. Cochin (2 vols. [Paris 1926]), Lacordaire (see *LThK* VI, 726), Montalembert (see *LThK* VII, 294); the memoirs of Monsignor Mabile (ed. by P. Mabile, 2 vols. [Paris 1926]), A. de Melun (2 vols. [Paris 1891]), M. du Camp (*La charité privée à Paris, 1885*), A. de Broglie (2 vols. [Paris 1938]), H. Loyson (A. Houtin, *Le Père Hyazinth dans l'Église romaine* [Paris 1920]), H. Taine (*Carnets de voyage, 1863–65* [Paris 1897]), Abbé Frémond (ed. by A. Siegfried, I [Paris 1933]); the Catholic press (especially *L'Univers, Le Monde, L'Ami de la religion, Le Français, Annales de la charité, Revue de l'enseignement chrétien, Correspondant, Études,* and *La France ecclésiastique*); the *Journal officiel* (for the discussion of those laws after 1870 concerning religious affairs).

LITERATURE

Basic are J. Maurain, *La politique ecclésiastique du Second Empire* (Paris 1930, complementing the anticlerical work by Debidour, *Histoire*); J. Gadille, *La pensée et l'action politique des évêques français au début de la IIIe République,* 2 vols. (Paris 1976); Lecanuet I (liberal-Catholic point of view); Debidour, *IIIe République* I (a layman's view); E. Barbier, *Histoire du catholicisme libéral et du catholicisme social en France 1870–1914* I (Paris 1924, antiliberal point of view); the Sorbonne lectures by C. Pouthas, *L'Église et les questions religieuses en France de 1848 à 1877* (Paris 1945). In addition to the two works by L. Baunard and the works by G. Rigault and J. Burnichon, see Aubert, *Pie IX,* 108–31, 373–84, 517–19, 549–50; Schmidlin, *PG* II, 120–29; *HistCathFr,* 297–415; Gurian, 210–49; Brugerette I, 165–294, II, 3–151; C. A. Gimpl, *The "Correspondant" and the Founding of the French Third Republic* (Washington 1959); the biographies listed in the General Bibliography of Dupanloup, Gerbet, Guéranger, Guibert, Lacordaire, Lavigerie, Maret, Montalembert, Parisis, Pie, Regnier, Ségur, and Veuillot; to be added are J. Foulon, *Histoire de Monseigneur Darboy* (Paris 1899) and *DHGE* XIV, 84–86; H. Boissonot, *Le cardinal Meignan* (Paris 1899); G. Gautherot, *E. Keller* (Paris 1922); M. de Marcey, *Ch. Chesnelong,* 3 vols. (Paris 1903); L. Baunard, *Kolb-Bernard* (Paris 1899).

ON WORKS AND MANIFESTATIONS OF CATHOLIC LIFE: Duroselle, 495–710; H. Rollet, *L'action sociale des catholiques en France* I (Paris 1947), 11–65; A. de Melun, *Manuel des œuvres* (Paris 1878); E. Keller, *Les congrégations religieuses en France* (Paris 1880; statistical indices); L. Baunard, *E. Lelièvre* (Paris 1907); J. Schall, *A. Baudon* (Paris 1897); A. d'Andigné, *A. de Melun* (Paris 1962); M. Lynch, *The Organised Social Apostolate of A. de Mun* (Washington 1952).

ON THE CLERGY: F. Garilhe, *Le clergé séculier français au XIXe siècle* (Paris 1898); L. Bougaud, *Le grand péril de l'Église de France au XIXe siècle* (Paris 1878) and the work by F. Boulard listed in the General Bibliography; J. -F. Six, *Un prêtre, A. Chevrier, fondateur du Prado* (Paris 1965).

ON DENOMINATIONAL INSTRUCTION: Maurain, op. cit.; A. Prost, op. cit., 177–90 and J. Rohr, *V. Duruy. Essai sur la politique de l'Instruction publique au temps de l'Empire libéral* (Paris 1967).

ON RELIGIOUS PRACTICE: In addition to the works by G. Le Bras (General Bibliography), see especially C. Marcilhacy, *Le diocèse d'Orléans au milieu du XIXe siècle* (Paris 1964) and *Le diocèse d'Orléans sous l'épiscopat de Monseigneur Dupanloup* (Paris 1962); G. Duveau, *La pensée ouvrière sur l'éducation pendant la IIe République et le Second Empire* (Paris 1948), especially 185–96; P. Pierrard, *La vie ouvrière à Lille sous le Second Empire* (Paris 1965), 362–427; F. A. Isambert, *Christianisme et classe ouvrière* (Paris and Tournai 1960); Y. -M. Hilaire in *L'information historique* 25 (1963), 57–69, 29 (1967), 31–35; by the same author, "Les missions intérieures durant la seconde moitié du XIXe siècle dans la région du Nord," *Revue du Nord* 46 *(1964), 51*–68 and "Remarques sur la pratique religieuse dans le bassin houiller du Pas-de-Calais dans la seconde moitié du XIXe siècle," *Charbon et sciences humaines* (Paris and The Hague 1966), 265–79.

ON THE PROGRESS OF ANTICLERICALISM: Mellor, 286–318; Weill, *Idée laïque,* 121–244; A. Dessoye, *Jean Macé et la fondation de la Ligue de l'enseignement* (Paris 1883); G. Duveau, *Les instituteurs* (Paris 1954); L. Capéran, *Histoire contemporaine de la laïcité française* I (Paris 1958), 1–94.

8. *The States of the German Confederation and Switzerland, 1848–70*

SOURCES

Amtliche Tagungsberichte der Generalversammlungen (Katholikentage) 1849seqq.; ColLac V (Provincial Councils and Bishops' Conferences); *Aktenstücke betreffend die Fuldaer Bischofskonferenzen 1867–88* (Cologne 1889); Bergsträsser, *Dokumente* I (see biblio. chapter 6); *I. v. Döllinger-Lord Acton, Briefwechsel,* ed. by V. Conzemius, I:1850–69, II: 1869–70 (Munich 1963, 1965); Heinen, *Staatliche Macht und Katholizismus in Deutschland* I (Paderborn 1969).

LITERATURE

GENERAL: Brück, *Geschichte der katholischen Kirche in Deutschland im 19. Jahrhundert* III, ed. by J. B. Kißling (Münster 1905); J. B. Kißling, *Geschichte des Kulturkampfes im Deutschen Reich I: Die Vorgeschichte* (Freiburg 1911); Bachem, *Zentrumspartei* II, 96–410; Schmidlin, *PG* II, 136–41, 162–79, 191ff.; Aubert, *Pie IX* (Fliche-Martin 21), 132–53, 176–79; Bihlmeyer-Tüchle III, 321, 337, 403–6, 413f.; Buchheim, *Ultramontanismus und Demokratie,* 72–219; Heyer, *Die katholische Kirche von 1648 bis 1870,* 94, 129ff., 140–44; Huber, *Verfassungsgeschichte* III (Stuttgart 1963), 158f., 174ff., 180, 190f., 194–98, 200–203, 665; Jedin, *Freiheit und Aufstieg des deutschen Katholizismus;* K. H. Grenner, *Wirtschaftsliberalismus und katholisches Denken. Ihre Begegnung und Auseinandersetzung im Deutschland des 19. Jahrhunderts* (Cologne 1967); R. Lill, *Die deutschen Katholiken und Bismarcks Reichsgründung: Reichsgründung 1870/71,* ed. by T. Schieder and E. Deuerlein (Stuttgart 1970), 345–65.

ON THE CHURCH POLICY OF THE INDIVIDUAL STATES: PRUSSIA: J. Bachem, *Preußen und die katholische Kirche* (Cologne 1887), 71–85; B. von Selchow, *Der Kampf um das Posener Erzbistum 1865* (Marburg 1923); H. Schrörs, "Die Kölner Erzbischofswahl nach Geissels Tode," *AHVNrh* 108 (1926), 103–40; Constabel, *Vorgeschichte des Kulturkampfes;* Conzemius, *Briefe Aulikes an Döllinger. Ein Beitrag zur Geschichte der "Katholischen Abteilung" im preußischen Kultusministerium* (Rome, Freiburg and Vienna 1968).

AUSTRIA: Hussarek, *Die Verhandlung des Konkordats;* Weinzierl-Fischer, *Konkordate,* 60–111; Engel-Janosi, *Österreich und der Vatikan* I, 61–148; Leisching, *Bischofskonferenz,* 150–250.

BAVARIA: Doeberl-Spindler, *Entwicklungsgeschichte Bayerns* III; the corresponding sections of the works by A. Wendehorst, *Das Bistum Würzburg 1803 bis 1957* (Würzburg 1965) and J. Staber, *Kirchengeschichte des Bistums Regensburg* (Regensburg 1966); for the sixties, see also Brandmüller, *Publikation des 1. vatikanischen Konzils in Bayern.*

STATES OF THE UPPER RHENISH CHURCH PROVINCE: I. v. Longner, *Beiträge zur Geschichte der oberrheinischen Kirchenprovinz* (Tübingen 1863); H. Brück, *Die oberrheinischen Kirchenprovinz* (Mainz 1868); H. Maas, *Geschichte der katholischen Kirche im Großherzogtum Baden* (Freiburg 1891); H. Lauer, *Geschichte der katholischen Kirche im Großherzogtum Baden* (Freiburg 1908); A. Hagen, *Geschichte der Diözese Rottenburg II (Stuttgart 1958); C. J. Reidel, Die katholische Kirche im Großherzogtum Hessen* (Paderborn 1904); M. Höhler, *Geschichte des Bistums Limburg* (Limburg 1908); L. Golther, *Der Staat und die katholische Kirche im Königreich Württemberg* (Stuttgart 1874); A. Hagen, *Staat und katholische Kirche in Württemberg 1848–62,* 2 vols. (Stuttgart 1928); H. Färber, *Der Liberalismus und die kulturpolitischen Fragen in Baden 1850–70* (diss., Freiburg 1959); E. Will, "Die Konvention zwischen dem Heiligen Stuhl und der Krone Baden vom 28. Juni 1859," *Baden im 19. und 20. Jahrhundert. Verfassungs- und Verwaltungsgeschichtliche Studien,* ed. by K. S. Bader, III (1953), 99–188. See also the literature on the Baden Kulturkampf listed in chapter 19.

BIOGRAPHIES: In addition to those listed in the bibliography for chapter 6, there are also L. von Pastor, *Johann Baptist Heinrich* (Fribourg 1925); F. X. Zacher, *Heinrich von Hofstätter, Bischof von Passau 1839–1875* (Passau 1940); J. Nattermann, *Adolf Kolping als Sozialpädagoge* (Cologne 1959); S. J. Schäffer and J. Dahl, *Adolf Kolping* (Cologne 1961); O. Pfülf, *Hermann von Mallinckrodt* (Fribourg 1901); J. Götten, *Christoph Moufang, Theologe und Politiker 1817–90* (Mainz 1969); O. Pfülf, *Joseph Graf von Stolberg* (Fribourg 1913).

FORMATION OF ASSOCIATIONS, POLITICAL CATHOLICISM, BISHOPS' CONFERENCES: Kißling, *Katholikentage* I; Bachem, *Zentrumspartei* II; Buchheim, *Ultramontanismus und Demokratie;* Buchheim, *Der deutsche Verbandskatholizismus;* Lill, *Bischofskonferenzen,* 56–95; M. Schmolke, *Adolf Kolping als Publizist. Ein Beitrag zur Publizistik und Verbandsgeschichte des deutschen Katholizismus im 19. Jahrhundert* (Münster 1966); Lucas, *Joseph Edmund Jörg. Konservative Publizistik zwischen Revolution und Reichsgründung 1852 bis 1871* (diss., Cologne 1969).

BATTLES OVER "ROMAN" AND "GERMAN" THEOLOGY: Literature in chapter 16; the biographies of Döllinger, Heinrich, Ketteler, Moufang, Rauscher, Schwarzenberg; A. Hagen, "Hefele und das Vatikanische Konzil," *ThQ* 123 (1942), 223–52; H. Lang, "Die Versammlung katholischer Gelehrter in München . . . 1863," *HJ* 71 (1952), 246–58; R. Lill, "Die deutschen Theologieprofessoren vor dem Vatikanum I im Urteil des Münchener Nuntius", *Reformata Reformanda, Festgabe für Hubert Jedin* II (Münster

1965), 483–508; B. Schneider, "Der Syllabus Pius' IX. und die deutschen Jesuiten," *AHPont* 6 (1968), 371–92; T. Freudenberger, *Die Universität Würzburg und das erste vatikanische Konzil* I (Neustadt/Aisch 1969).

SWITZERLAND: Literature in vol. VII, chapters 7 and 20, also C. H. Marmier, *La convention du 23 avril entre l'évêque de Lausanne et Genève at l'État de Fribourg* (Fribourg 1925); V. Conzemius, "Der geistesgeschichtliche Hintergrund des Christkatholizismus . . .," *ZSKG* 60 (1966), 112–59; V. Conzemius, *Katholizismus ohne Rom. Die altkatholische Kirchengemeinschaft* (Zürich, Einsiedeln and Cologne 1969), 70–81. See also chapter 8, ns. 52–57.

9. *The Rise of Catholicism in the Anglo-Saxon World*

GREAT BRITAIN AND IRELAND (AFTER 1848)

LITERATURE: P. F. Moran, ed., *The Pastoral Letters and other Writings of Cardinal Cullen,* 3 vols. (Dublin 1882); E. S. Purcell, *Life of Cardinal Manning,* 2 vols. (London 1896); S. Leslie, *Henry Edward Manning* (London 1921); C. Butler, *The Life and Times of Bishop Ullathorne,* 2 vols. (London 1926); P. J. Walsh, *William J. Walsh, Archbishop of Dublin* (Dublin 1928); D. Gwynn, *A Hundred Years of Catholic Emancipation* (London 1929); C. Butler, *The Vatican Council,* 2 vols. (London 1930); J. E. Handley, *The Irish in Modern Scotland* (Cork 1947); G. A. Beck, ed., *The English Catholics 1850–1950* (London 1950); P. MacSuibhne, *Paul Cullen and his Contemporaries,* 3 vols. (Naas 1961–65); V. A. McClelland, *Cardinal Manning* (London 1962); E. R. Norman, *The Catholic Church and Ireland in the Age of Rebellion 1859–73* (London 1965); J. H. Whyte and P. J. Corish, *Political Problems 1850/78* (Dublin 1967).

THE UNITED STATES

SOURCES: F. Kenneally, *United States Documents in the Propaganda Fides Archives* II (Washington 1968); Ellis, *Documents, 252–424;* D. Shearer (see General Bibliography), 173–375; P. Guilday, *The National Pastorals* (see General Bibliography), 120–225; *ColLac* III (Provincial and National Councils); *Relazione . . . da Monsignor Bedini* (Rome 1854; republished in J. F. Connelly, *The Visit of Archbishop G. Bedini to the United States* [Rome 1960], 190–287); H. Browne, "The Archdiocese of New York a Century ago, a Memoir of Archbishop Hughes," *Historical Records and Studies,* 39–40 (1952), 129–90. Also Catholic journals, especially *The Metropolitan,* 1852–58 and *Brownson's Quarterly Review,* 1844–64, and newspapers, especially *The Freeman's Journal, The Catholic Telegraph,* and *The Catholic Vindicator.*

LITERATURE: Schmidlin *PG* II, 207–11; Aubert, *Pie IX,* 427–36, 559–60; Latourette, *Christianity* III, 4–246; M. Hoffman, *The Church Founders of the Northwest* (Milwaukee 1937); R. Bayard, *Lone Star Vanguard. The Catholic Reoccupation of Texas 1838–48* (St. Louis 1945); L. Lyons, *Father N. Blanchet and the Founding of the Oregon Missions 1838–48* (Washington 1940); J. Pillar, *The Catholic Church in Mississippi 1837–65* (New Orleans 1964); M. Schroeder, *The Catholic Church in the Diocese of Vincennes 1847–77* (Washington 1946); J. McSorley, *Father Hecker and his Friends* (St. Louis 1952); J. B. Code, "Bishop Hughes and the Sisters of Charity," *Miscellanea hist. L. van der Essen* (Louvain 1947), 991–1038; C. Walworth, *The Oxford Movement in America* (New York 1893); F. MacDonald, *The Catholic Church and the Secret Societies in the United States* (New York 1946); W. D'Arcy, *The Fenian Movement in the United States 1858–86*

(Washington 1947); P. G. Rahill, *The Catholic Indian Missions and Grant's Peace Policy 1870–74* (Washington 1953).

ON IMMIGRATION: a field which requires much more examination, see in addition to the work by Shaughnessy (General Bibliography) T. McAvoy, "The Formation of the Catholic Minority in the United States, 1820–60," *RPol* 10 (1948), 13–34; E. Rothan, *The German Catholic Emigrant in the United States 1830–60* (Washington 1946); M. Kelly, *Catholic Immigrant Colonization Projects in the United States, 1815–60* (New York 1939); J. P. Shanon, *Catholic Colonization in the Western Frontier* (New Haven 1957).

ON THE SECOND PHASE OF NATIVISM: J. Higham, *Strangers in the Land. Pattern of American Nativism, 1860–1925* (New Brunswick 1955); R. Lord et al., *History of the Archdiocese of Boston* II, 648–703.

ON CATHOLIC EDUCATION AND THE TRAINING OF THE CLERGY: J. A. Burns, *The Growth and Development of the Catholic School System in the United States* (New York 1912); E. Connors, *Church-State Relationship in Education in the State of New York* (Washington 1951); J. M. Campbell, "The Catholic Contribution to the American College," *Vital Problems in Catholic Education in the United States,* ed. by R. Deferrari (Washington 1939), 84–107; J. McCadden in *CHR* 50 (1965), 188–207; T. McAvoy in *RPol* 28 (1966), 19–46; J. M. Daley, *Georgetown University. Origin and Early Years* (Washington 1957); J. T. Ellis, *The formative Years of the Catholic University of America* (Washington 1946), 15–86; W. Morris, *The Seminary Movement in the United States, 1833–66* (Washington 1932); J. Sauter, *The American College of Louvain, 1857–78* (Louvain 1959).

ON THE CIVIL WAR: M. Rice, *American Catholic Opinion in the Slavery Controversy* (New York 1944); B. Blied, *Catholics and the Civil War* (Milwaukee 1955); C. Dunham, *The Attitude of the Northern Clergy toward the South, 1860–65* (Toledo 1942); W. Wight in *CHR* 44 (1958), 290–306; L. Stock in *CHR* 16 (1930), 1–18.

BIOGRAPHIES: those of the bishops M. Spalding (by J. L. Spalding, Baltimore 1873), McQuaid (by F. Zwierlein, 3 vols. [Rochester 1925–27]), Father Kenrick (by H. Nolan [Washington 1948]), Hughes (by J. Hassard [New York 1865]), Verot (by M. Gannon [Milwaukee 1964]), Bailey (by M. H. Yeager [Washington 1947]), Neumann (by M. Curley [Washington 1952]), Miles (by V. O'Daniel [Washington 1926]), Baraga (by C. Verwyst [Milwaukee 1900]), Purcell (by M. McCann [Washington 1918]), McCloskey (by J. Farley [New York 1918]), Eccleston (by C. Halsey in *RACHS* 76 [1965], 69–128, 77 [1966], 131–56), and J. O'Shea, *The Two Kenricks* (Philadelphia 1904).

CANADA

Aubert, *Pie IX,* 436–41; Latourette, *Christianity* III, 247–76; L. Pouliot, *Monseigneur Bourget et son temps,* 2 vols. (Montreal 1955–56), and the biographies of the bishops de Charbonnel (by C. Causse [Gembloux 1931]), Lynch (by H. McKeown [Toronto 1886]), Laflèche (by R. Rumilly [Montreal 1938]), Provencher (by D. Frémont [Winnipeg 1935]), and P. Lefebvre (by P. Poirier [Montreal 1898]); F. H. Walker, *Catholic Education and Politics in Upper Canada* (Toronto 1955); J. Moir, *Church and State in Canada West* (Toronto 1959); P. Savard, "La vie du clergé québecois au XIXe siècle," *Recherches sociographiques* 8 (1967), 259–73; P. Sylvain, "Quelques aspects de l'antagonisme libéral-ultramontain au Canada français," *Recherches sociographiques* 8 (1967), 279–97; G. Carrière, *Histoire documentaire de la congrégation des missionnaires Oblats de Marie Immaculée dans l'Est du Canada,* 6 vols. (Ottawa 1957–67); G. Carrière, *La*

Compagnie de la Baie d'Hudson et les missions catholiques dans l'Est du Canada (Ottawa 1957); G. Carrière, "L'Honorable Compagnie de la Baie d'Hudson et les missions catholiques dans l'Ouest canadien," *Revue de l'Université d'Ottawa* 36 (1966), 15–39, 232–57; E. Lamirande, "L'implantation de l'Église catholique en Colombie britannique, 1838–1848," *Revue de l'Université d'Ottawa* 28 (1958), 213–25, 333–63, 453–89; C. Roy, *L'Université Laval* (Québec 1903); P. Savard in *Culture* (Québec), 26 (1965), 64–83; J. B. Meilleur, *Mémorial sur l'éducation au Bas-Canada* (Québec 1876).

AUSTRALIA

E. O'Brien, *The Dawn of Catholicism in Australia,* 2 vols. (London 1930); H. Birt, *Benedictine Pioneers in Australia,* 2 vols. (London 1911); T. L. Suttor, *Hierarchy and Democracy in Australia, 1788–1870* (Melbourne 1965).

10. *The Easing of Tensions in the Iberian World*

LITERATURE

SPAIN: Schmidlin, *PG* I, 614–23, II, 143–48; F. Izaguirre Irureta, "Las relaciones diplomaticás de la Santa Sede con el gobierno español durante la prima guerra carlista," *Universidad* 35 (Salamanca 1958), 564–93; P. Pérez Embid, "Los católicos y los partidos políticos españoles a mediados del siglo XIX," *Nuestro tiempo* 5 (Pamplona 1958), 387–409; V. G. Kiernan, *The Revolution of 1854 in Spanish History* (Oxford 1966); F. Costadellas, *El arzobispo Costa y Borrás, 1848–1864* (Barcelona 1947); J. Goñi Gaztámbide, "S. Adriani, obispo de Pamplona," *HS* 21 (1968), 179–312; C. Fernández, *El confesor de Isabel II y sus actividades en Madrid* (Madrid 1964); J. M. Cuenca Toribio, "La desarticulación de la Iglesia española del antiguo régimen, 1833–40," *HS* 20 (1967), 33–98; J. M. Cuenca Toribio, "La tercera restauración religiosa del siglo XIX," *Anales de la Universidad Hispalense* 26 (1966), 1–11; J. M. Cuenca Toribio, "La Jerarquía eclesiástica en el reinado de Isabel II," *Atlantida* 6 (1968), 600–621; J. M. Cuenca Toribio, *Apertura e integrismo en la Iglesia española decimo-nonica* (Seville 1970); J. M. Cuenca Toribio, "El pontificado pamplonés de D. P. C. Uriz y Labayru," *HS* 22 (1969), 129–285; E. Federici, *Santa Gioacchina De Vedruna, fondatrice delle Carmelitane della carità* (Rome 1958); L. Frías, *Historia de la Compañia de Jesús en su Asistencia moderna de España II, 1835–68* (Madrid 1944); P. Jobit, *Les éducateurs de l'Espagne contemporaine, les Krausistes* (Paris 1936); J. Gorricho, "Epistolario de Pío IX con Isabel II," *AHPont* 4 (1966), 281–348.

On the secularization of the property of the Church, see J. M. de Antequera, *La desamortización eclesiástica* (Madrid 1885); J. Vicens Vivés, *Historia económica de España* (Barcelona 1959), 560–71; J. Porres Martin, *La desamortización del siglo XIX en Toledo* (Madrid 1966).

On the concordat of 1851, see J. Pérez Alhama, *La Iglesia y el Estado español* (Madrid 1967); F. Suárez: *Ius canonicum* (Pamplona) 3 (1963), 65–249.

PORTUGAL: Schmidlin, *PG* I, 623–27, II, 148–50; L. Frías, op. cit. II, 574–644.

SPANISH AMERICAN REPUBLICS: F. B. Pyke, "Heresy, Real and Alleged, in Peru. An aspect of the conservative-liberal struggle, 1830–75," *HAHR* 47 (1967), 50–74; F. B. Pyke, "Church and State in Peru and Chile since 1840, a Study in Contrasts," *AHR* 73

(1967), 30–50; R. Sotomayor Valdés, *Historia de Chile, 1831–71,* 2 vols. (Santiago 1875–76; concerning the activities of Monsignor Valdivieso); C. Oviedo Cavada, *La misión Irarrazaval en Roma 1847–50. Estudios de los relaciones de Iglesia y Estado en Chile* (Santiago 1962); C. Oviedo Cavada, "El gobierno chileno y el concepto misionero del Estado, 1832–61," *Historia,* 5 (Santiago 1966), 197–214; R. Pattee, *García Moreno y el Ecuador de su tiempo* (Mexico City 1941); W. Promper, *Priesternot in Lateinamerika* (Louvain 1965); L. Zea, *Dos etapas del pensamiento en Hispano-américa. Del romanticismo al positivismo* (Mexico City 1949); R. Pérez, *La Compañia de Jesús en Colombia y Centro América después de su restauración* (Valladolid 1896); R. Pérez, *La Compañia de Jesús restaurada en la República Argentina y Chile, Uruguay y Brasil* (Barcelona 1931); W. Loor, *Los jesuítas en el Ecuador* (Quito 1959); C. A. González, *F. de P. González Vigil, el precursor* (Lima 1961).

BRAZIL: F. Guerra, *A questão religiosa do segundo imperio brasileiro* (Rio de Janeiro 1952); M. E. Scherer, *D. Machado* (Munich 1965), 7–162; M. C. Thornton, *The Church and Free Masonry in Brazil, 1872–75. A Study in Regalism* (Washington 1943); M. Melo, *A Maçonaria no Brazil* (Recife 1909); T. Assis Bastes, *O positivismo e a realidade brasileira* (Belo Horizonte 1965); A. Rubert, "O bispado do Rio Grande do Sul e a nomeaçao de seu primo bispo 1848–1853," *Revista eclesiastica brasileira,* 28 (1968), 88–99; J. C. Fernandes Pinheiro, "Dom Manuel do Monte Rodriguez de Araújo," *Revista do Instituto histórico e geográfico brasileira* 27 (1867), 194–217; O. T. de Sousa, *Diogo Antonio Feijó* (Rio de Janeiro 1942); S. Elsner, *Die deutschen Franziskaner in Brasilien* (Trier 1912).

11. *The Catholic Church in the Orthodox World*

LITERATURE

UNIONIST PROSPECTS: Aubert, *Pie IX,* 478–84, 564; C. Korolevsky in *Unitas* 2 (Paris 1949–50), 189–205; Winter, *Rußland* II, 287–308; J. G. Remmers, *De herenigingsgedachte van I. Gagarine* (Tilburg 1951); M. J. de Rouët de Journel in *Études* 291 (1956), 171–95; M. J. de Rouët de Journel, *Une Russe catholique. La vie de Madame Swetchine* (Paris 1953); M. J. de Rouët de Journel in *Revue des études slaves* 3 (1923), 90–104; V. Laurent in *Mélanges E. d'Alzon* (St. Gérard and Namur 1952), 281–302; A. Tamborra, "Crisi d'Oriente, guerra di Crimea e polemiche politico-religiose fra cattolici e ortodossi, 1853–1856," *Clio* (Rome 1969), 169–91.

RUSSIA: *Allocuzione della Sant. di N. S. Gregorio XVI seguita da una Esposizione corredata di documenti* (Rome 1942); S. Olszamowska-Skowrońska, "Le concordat de 1847 avec la Russie d'après les documents authentiques," *SPM* 8–9 (1962), 447–877; *Esposizione documentata sulle costanti cure del S. P. Pio IX a riparo dei mali che soffre la Chiesa cattolica nei dominii di Russia e Polonia* (Rome 1866) and the Russian reply: *Résumé historiques des Actes de la Cour de Rome* (St. Petersburg 1867); A. Welykyj, *Documenta* (General Bibliography), II, 381–450 and the collection by Bjelogolovov. The Vatican Archives contain numerous pertinent material in the Russian files of the Congregation for Extraordinary Religious Affairs and the correspondence of the nuncios at Vienna. Schmidlin, *PG* I, 632–39, II, 213–23; J. Helfert, *Rußland und die Katholische Kirche in Polen* (Vienna 1867); R. Lefèvre, "Santa Sede e Russia e i colloqui dello Czar 1843–46," *Gregorio XVI* (Rome 1948), II, 159–293; J. S. Pelczar, *Pius IX a Polska* (Cracow 1914); Dmitri A. Tolstoi, *Rimskij Katolitsizm v Rossii,* 2 vols. (St. Petersburg 1914); A. van de Waal in *Het christelijk Osten en hereeniging* 8 (1955–56), 152–62, 303–12; R. Lubienski, *Vie de Mon-*

seigneur C.I. Lubienski (Roulers 1898); *DHGE* XVI, 867–70, 1471–72; *Suppression des couvents dans le Royaume de Pologne* (Paris 1865); A. Petrani, *Kolegium duchowne w Petersburgu* (Lublin 1950); Z. Olszamowska, "La suppression des diocèses catholiques par le gouvernement russe, 1866–69," *Antemurale* 9 (1965), 41–130; Z. Olszamowska, "Tentatives d'introduire la langue russe dans l'Église latine de la Pologne orientale," *Antemurale* 11 (1967), 47–169; A. Petrani in *Nasza przeszlosc* 27 (1967), 215–33; M. E. Jablonska in *Roczniki humanistyczne* 12 (Lublin 1964), 142–94; M. E. Jablonska in *Wiez* 3 (Warsaw 1960), 53–70; M. E. Jablonska in *Sprawozdania . . . Towarzystwa Naukowego Kathol. Uniw. Lublin* 14 (1963–64), 183–88; M. E. Jablonska in *Znak* 17 (1965), 1653–88; E. M. de Beaulieu, *Le Père Honorat de Biala, capucin* (Toulouse 1932); A. Szelggiewicz, *E. Bojanowski* (Poznan 1966); K. Gadacz, *Les capucins de la province polonaise dans l'insurrection de 1863–64* (Rome 1963).

THE HABSBURG EMPIRE: On the activity of Monsignor Stroßmayer, see N. Lalic in *Le Monde slave*, n.s. 6 (1929), 442–50; C. Loiseau, *Le Monde slave*, n.s. 4 (1927), I, 379–405; C. Loiseau, *Le Correspondant* 219 (1905), 251–71; A. Fortescue in *Dublin Review* 163 (1918), 234–57; K. Krzanič in *Nova revija* 20 (Markarska 1941), 1–28; Winter, *Rußland* II, 364–65, 382–90, 500–503; *DThC* XIV, 2630–25; H. Wendel, *Der Kampf der Südslawen um Freiheit und Einheit* (Frankfurt 1925), II, 377–81; R. Rißling, *Die Kroaten* (Graz 1956).

ON THE RUTHENIANS IN GALICIA: M. Malinowski, *Die Kirchen-und Staatssatzungen bezüglich des griechisch-katholischen Ritus der Ruthenen* (Lemberg 1861); Ammann, 644–59; N. Miko in *ZKTh* 79 (1957), 467–83.

ON THE UNIATE RUMANIANS OF TRANSYLVANIA: I. Moldovanu, *Acte sinodali ale baserecei romane de Alba Julia*, 2 vols. (Blaj 1869–72); G. Filip, *Pio IX e i Romeni* (Rome 1956); G. Filip, *De concilio provinciali Alba-Juliensi et Fagariensi A.D. 1872* (Rome 1954); G. Filip in *Acta historica* 4 (Munich 1965), 107–41; I. Gorgescu, *Mitropolitul Ioan Vancea* (Nagyvárad 1952); de Clercq II, 628–55.

SOUTHERN EUROPE, EASTERN EUROPE, AND THE LEVANT: See General Bibliography; Schmidlin, *PG* II, 230–33; Aubert, *Pie IX,* 410–15; *Papers relating to the Condition of Christians in Turkey* (London 1861; consular reports).

ON THE BULGARIAN MOVEMENT OF 1860: I. Sofranov, *Histoire du mouvement bulgare vers l'Église catholique au XIXᵉ siècle* (Rome 1960); G. Eldarov in *MF* 60 (1960), 426–54; Patriarch Cyrill, *Die katholische Propaganda unter den Bulgaren während der 2. Hälfte des 19. Jahrhunderts* I (Sofia 1962; in Bulgarian with French synopsis). On Catholicism in Bulgaria, see also B. Ristewski in *Razgledi* 2 (1960), 908–36, 1005–29, 3 (1960), 72–90, 158–89.

ON CATHOLICISM IN RUMANIA: P. Tocanel (General Bibliography).

BOSNIA: I. Kecmanović, *I. F. Jukič* (Belgrade 1963).

THE LEVANT: S. Salaville, "Monseigneur Hillereau, vicaire apostolique de Constantinople," *Union des Églises* 5 (1926), 134–39; *DHGE* XIII, 748–49, VIII, 1326–35; M. Julien, *La nouvelle mission de la Compagnie de Jésus en Syrie, 1831–95* (Tours 1898); J. Tagher, "Les rapports entre l'Égypte et le Vatican," *Cahiers d'histoire égyptienne* 2 (1949), 259–71; A. Martini, "La Santa Sede e la questione d'Oriente nel 1854," *CivCatt* (1958) IV, 169–81; *Les PP. Ratisbonne et N.-D. de Sion* (Paris 1928); J. Hajjar, *L'apostolat des missionnaires latins dans le Proche-Orient selon les directives romaines* (Jerusalem 1956); P. Médebielle, *Le diocèse patriarchal latin de Jérusalem* (Jerusalem 1963).

BIBLIOGRAPHY

THE UNIATE PATRIARCHATES: Among the general works, see in addition to Aubert, *Pie IX*, 415–425, especially Hajjar, 263–309, and Hajjar in *RHE* 65 (1970), 423–55, 737–88.

ON THE ARMENIANS: de Clercq II, 503–42; *DHGE* III, 867–70, IV, 338–42; D. Urquart, *Le patriarche Hassoun* (Geneva 1872); T. Lamy in *Revue catholique* 38 (Louvain 1874), 153–75, 583–603, 39 (1875), 34–63; M. Ormanian, *Le Vatican et les Arméniens* (Rome 1873).

ON THE CHALDEANS: B. M. Goormachtigh, "Histoire de la mission dominicaine en Mésopotamie," *AOP* 3 (1897–98), 141–58, 197–214, 533–45; J. Vosté, Les actes du synode de Rabban Hormizd," *S. Congr. per la Chiesa orientale. Cod. Can. Orient. Fonti* II/17 (Vatican City 1942); de Clercq II, 543–61; *DDC* III, 375–85; *DHGE* V, 317–56; J. C. Panjikaran, *Christianity in Malabar* (Rome 1926).

ON THE SYRIANS: Mamarbashi, *Les Syriens catholiques et leur patriarche Samhiri* (Paris 1855); P. Bacel in *ÉO* 14 (1911), 293–98; de Clercq II, 570–98; *DHGE* IV, 676–81.

ON THE MELCHITES: J. Hajjar, *Le patriarche Maximos III Mazloum* (Harissa 1957); de Clercq I, 390–414, II, 562–66; *DHGE* III, 652–63; IV, 229–36.

ON THE MARONITES: *DThC* IX, 104–07; de Clercq II, 667–82; Churchill, *The Druses and Maronites under the Turquish Rule from 1840 to 1860* (London 1862).

The Missions between 1840 and 1870

12. *The Strengthening of the Gregorian Restoration*

SOURCES AND LITERATURE

A. Brou, S.J., *Les Jésuites missionnaires au XIXᵉ et XXᵉ siècles* (Paris 1935); *Collectanea S. Congregationis de Propaganda Fide.* II. (1867–1906) (=CPF); G. Goyau, *La France missionnaire dans les cinq parties du monde,* 2 vols. (Paris 1948); *Juris Pontificii de Propaganda Fide* VI/1, 2, VII (Rome 1884–87) (=JP); A. Launay, *Mémorial de la Société des Missions-Étrangères* II (Paris 1916); J. A. Otto, S.J., *Gründung der neuen Jesuitenmission durch General P. Johann Philip Roothaan* (Freiburg 1939) (=J. A. Otto, *Roothaan*); G. B. Tragella, *Le Missioni Estere di Milano nel quadro degli avvenimenti contemporanei,* 3 vols. (Milan 1950–63); G. B. Tragella, *Italia Missionaria* (Milan 1939).

13. *The First Vatican Council and the Missions*

SOURCES

Mansi, 49–53; *ColLac* VII (Freiburg 1892); *Juris Pontificii de Propaganda Fide* VI/2 (Rome 1895 = JP); *Schema constitutionis super missionibus apostolicis* (Rome 1870 = Schema).

LITERATURE

T. Grentrup, "Die Missionen auf dem Vatikanischen Konzil," *ZMR* 6 (1916); I. Ting Pong Lee, *De jure missionario in Concilio Vaticano. Commentarium pro Religiosis et Missionariis* 14 (Rome 1944–46), 107–37; P. de Mondreganes, "Las Misiones en las actas del Concilio Vaticano," *ED* 1 (1948), 231–43; A. Santos, S.J., *Aspecto misional del concilio I. Estudios Eclesiasticos* 45 (Madrid 1970), 491–532; P. Wanko, *Kirche, Mission, Missionen. Eine Untersuchung der ekklesiologischen und missiologischen Aussagen vom 1. Vatikanum bis "Maximum illud"* (theol. diss., Münster 1969); T. Granderath, *Geschichte des Vatikanischen Konzils,* 3 vols. (Freiburg 1903–06); Schmidlin, *PG* II, 255–92; R. Aubert, *Le Pontificat de Pie IX* (Paris 1952), 311–67; R. Aubert, *Vaticanum I* (Mainz 1965).

SECTION THREE

Light and Shadows of Catholic Vitality

14. *Regular and Secular Clergy*

ORDERS AND CONGREGATIONS

LITERATURE: Aubert, *Pie IX,* 456–61; Schmidlin, *PG* II, 309–13; C. Tyck, *Notices historiques sur les congrégations et communeautés religieuses* (Louvain 1892), 324–334.

ON THE SOCIETY OF JESUS: Burnichon III and VI (for France, 1845–80), Frías (for the Iberian Peninsula and Latin America), Galleti, Monti, Volpe, and Aldegheri (for Italy), Hughes (for the United States), all listed in the General Bibliography. Also K. Schoeters, *P.J. Beckx en de "Jesuiten-politiek" van zijn tijd* (Antwerp 1965); B. Duhr, *Aktenstücke zur Geschichte der Jesuiten-Missionen in Deutschland 1848–1872* (Freiburg i. Br. 1903); A. Pina, *Carlos Rademaker, Restaurador dos Jesuitas em Portugal* (Porto 1967).

ON THE BENEDICTINES: P. Schmitz, *Histoire de l'ordre de Saint Benoît* (Maredsous 1948), 175–212.

ON THE DOMINICANS: Walz, 517–657; H. Cormier, *Vie du R.P. Jandel* (Paris 1890).

ON THE FRANCISCANS: H. Holzapfel, 331–34, 360–71; Frédégand (Callaey) d'Anvers, *Le Tier Ordre de Saint François d'Assise* (Paris 1923); on their restoration in France in 1851, see P. Sagues, *El P.J. Areso* (Madrid 1960).

ON THE REDEMPTORISTS: M. De Meulemeester, *Histoire sommaire de la Congrégation du T.S. Rédempteur* (Louvain 1958), 139–73.

ON THE SALESIANS: *LThK* IX, 263–64.

ON THE SCHOOLBROTHERS: G. Rigault, *Histoire générale de l'Institu des Frères des Écoles chrétiennes* V and VI, *L'Ére du Frère Philippe* (Paris 1945/48).

THE DIOCESAN CLERGY AND PASTORAL WORK

LITERATURE: Aubert, *Pie IX,* 451–56; C. Marcilhacy, *Le diocése d'Orléans sous l'épiscopat de Monseigneur Dupanloup* (Paris 1962), 48–191; P. Broutin, "Pastorale épiscopale au XIX*e* siècle," *RAM* 35 (1959), 60–77; Daniel-Rops, *L'Église des révolutions* I (Paris 1960), 882–97; P. Pierrard, *Le prêtre français* (Paris 1969), 101–28; Baunard, 133–44; C. Kempf, *Die Heiligkeit der Kirche im 19. Jahrhundert* (Einsiedeln 1928), 77–122. Several biographies of bishops contain details about the development of diocesan organizations and pastoral practice.

15. *The Growth of Piety*

LITERATURE

K. Kempf, *Die Heiligkeit der Kirche im 19. Jahrhundert* (Einsiedeln 1928); M. Nédoncelle, *Les leçons spirituelles du XIXe siècle* (Paris 1936); J. Friedrich, *Geschichte des Vaticanischen Concils I* (Nördlingen 1877), chap. 15 (tendentious); Aubert, *Pie IX,* 461–76, 563; Baunard, 197–244, 486–508; Daniel-Rops I, 921–55; H. Pourrat, *Histoire de la spiritualité IV* (Paris 1930), 505–658; J. de Guibert, *La spiritualité de la Compagnie de Jésus* (Rome 1953), 459–522; R. Chapman, *Father Faber* (London 1961).

ON EUCHARISTIC PIETY: *DSAM* III, 1282–85, IV, 1614–53; M. de Hédouville, *Monseigneur de Ségur* (Paris 1957); J. Vaudon, *L'œuvre des congrès eucharistique, ses débuts* (Paris 1910); L. de Paladini, *Die eucharistischen Kongresse. Ursprung und Geschichte* (Paderborn 1912).

ON THE VENERATION OF THE SACRED HEART OF JESUS: A. Hamon, *Histoire de la dévotion au Sacre-Cœur IV* (Paris 1931); A. Hamon in *DSAM* II, 1037–42; *Cor Jesu II Pars historica et pastoralis,* ed. by A. Bea et al. (Rome 1959), especially H. Holstein (291–340), E. Bergh (457–98), and R. Tucci (538–71); F. Degli Esposti, *La teologia del S. Cuore di Gesù* (Rome 1967), 11–18.

ON DEVOTION TO MARY: *Maria. Études sur la Sainte Vierge,* ed. by H. du Manoir, 7 vols. (Paris 1949–64), especially III (1954); B. Saint-John, *The Blessed Virgin in the XIXth Century: apparitions, revelations, graces* (London 1903); B. Metzler, "Die Marien-Maiandacht in ihrer historischen Entwicklung und Ausbreitung," *Der Katholik* (1909) I, 100–125, 177–88, 262–82.

ON THE ORIGINS OF THE LITURGICAL MOVEMENT: P. W. Trapp, *Vorgeschichte und Ursprung der liturgischen Bewegung* (Regensburg 1940); O. Rousseau, *Histoire du Movement liturgique* (Paris 1945), 1–185; O. Rousseau, "L'œuvre liturgique de Monseigneur Van Caloen," *QLP* 17 (Louvain 1932), 79–91; *Maurus Wolter, dem Gründer Beurons* (Beuron 1945), 93–109.

16. *The Backwardness of Religious Studies and the Controversy about the "German Theologians"*

LITERATURE: Hocedez II; Aubert, *Pie IX,* 184–223, 526–31; J. Bellamy, *La théologie catholique au XIXe siècle* (Paris 1904); Grabmann, *G,* part 3; Schmidlin, *PG* II, 315–30; F. Russo, "Cent années d'un dialogue difficile entre la science et la foi," *Recherches et débats du C.C.I.F.* 4 (1953), 7–30. Useful references in Hurter and Sommervogel.

ON THE RATIONALISTIC MOVEMENT: A. D. White, *A History of the Warfare of Science and Theology,* 2 vols. (London 1896); J. Maurain, "Le conflit de la science et de la croyance," *Peuples et civilisations,* ed. by L. Halphen and P. Sagnac, XVII (Paris 1939), 303–18; J. M. Robertson, *A History of Free Thought in the XIXth Century,* 2 vols. (London 1929); Weill, *Idée laïque,* 147–78; A. Della Torre, *Il cristianesimo in Italia dai filosofisti ai modernisti* (Palermo 1912); A. Schweitzer, *Geschichte der Leben-Jesu-Forschung* (Tübingen 1913).

RELIGIOUS STUDIES OUTSIDE OF GERMANY

LITERATURE: L. Foucher, *La philosophie catholique en France au XIXe siècle* (Paris 1955); E. Vacherot, "La théologie catholique en France," *Revue des deux mondes* 70 (1868), 294–318; C. Pouthas, *L'Église et les questions religieuses en France de 1848 à 1877* (Cours de Sorbonne 1954), 223–60; A. Houtin, *La question biblique chez les catholiques de France au XIXe siècle* (Paris 1902); *DThC* VIII, 235–42, Tables générales 2356–58 (for Italy); P. Barbaini, "Cultura teologica e cultura generale nell'epoca del Risorgimento," *SC* 89 (1961), 411–43; K. Werner, *Die italienische Philosophie des 19. Jahrhunderts,* 5 vols. (Vienna 1884–86), especially vol. I, *Rosmini and His School;* C. D. Fonseca, *La formazione del clero a Napoli nel sec. XIX* (diss., Naples and Posilippo 1955); E. Van Roey, *Les sciences théologiques: Le mouvement scientifique en Belgique 1830/1905* II (Brussels 1908), 488–523.

ON CHRISTIAN ARCHEOLOGY: G. Ferretto, *Note storico-bibliografiche di archeologia cristiana* (Vatican City 1942); R. Fausti, *Il P.G. Marchi e il rinnovamento degli studi di archeologia cristiana: Xenia Piana Pio XII dicata* (Rome 1943), 445–514.

ON THE THEOLOGY AT THE ROMAN COLLEGE: *L'Università Gregoriana del Collegio Romano* (Rome 1925); H. Schauf, *Carlo Passaglia and Clemens Schrader* (Rome 1938); H. Kerkvoorde in *EThL* 22 (1946), 174–93; C. G. Arevalo, *Some Aspects of . . . the Ecclesiology of Perrone, Passaglia and Schrader* (Rome 1959); W. Kasper, *Die Lehre von der Tradition in der Römischen Schule* (Freiburg i. Br. 1962).

ON THE THOMIST RENASCENCE: A. Masnovo, *Il neotomismo in Italia. Origini e prime vicende* (Milan 1923); P. Dezza, *Alle origini del neotomismo* (Milan 1940); C. A. Walz, "Il tomismo dal 1800 al 1879", *Angelicum* 20 (1943), 300–326; Aubert-Martina, 808–11; *G. Sanseverino nel 1. centenario della morte* (Rome 1965); P. Orlando, *Il tomismo a Napoli nel sec. XIX. La scuola del Sanseverino* I (Rome 1968); F. Duranti, "La rinascita del tomismo a Perugia," *Aquinas* 2 (Rome 1962); 249–94; R. Pizzorni in *Aquinas* 8 (1965), 423–58.

SCHOLASTICS AND GERMANICS VS. THE "GERMAN THEOLOGIANS"

SOURCES: In addition to Döllinger's correspondence, among it *Briefwechsel mit Lord Acton,* ed. by V. Conzemius, I (Munich 1963), see A. Flir, *Briefe aus Rom* (Innsbruck 1864); *Janssens Briefe,* ed. by L. Pastor (Freiburg i. Br. 1920); *Briefe von und an Ketteler,* ed. by I. Raich (Mainz 1879); A. M. Weiß, *Lebensweg und Lebenswerk* (Freiburg i. Br. 1925), chaps. I. and II; G. von Hertling, *Erinnerungen* (Freiburg i. Br. 1919); J. F. von Schulte, *Lebenserinnerungen* I/II (Giessen 1908–09); F. X. Kraus, *Tagebücher,* ed. by H. Schiel (Cologne 1957), 1–276. Also the journals *Der Katholik, Stimmen aus Maria Laach, Theologisches Literaturblatt,* and *La Civiltà cattolica,* as well as the contemporary summaries by A. von Schmid, *Wissenschaftliche Richtungen auf dem Gebiet des Katholizismus in der neuesten und gegenwärtigen Zeit* (Munich 1862) and K. Werner, *Geschichte der katholischen Theologie* (Munich 1866), 342–642.

LITERATURE: Basic, even though partial, is the work of the Old Catholic J. Friedrich, *Ignaz von Döllinger* III (Munich 1901). Among the more recent works, there are Scheffczyk, XXXVI–IL, 261–522; F. von Bezold, *Geschichte der rheinischen Friedrich-Wilhelm-Universität zu Bonn 1818–1918* (Bonn 1920); S. Merkle, "Die Vertretung der Kirchengeschichte in Würzburg bis zum Jahre 1879," *Aus der Vergangenheit der Universität Würzburg* (Berlin 1932), 146–214; T. Funk in *ThQ* 108 (1927), 209–20 (for Tübingen); G. B. Guzzetti, *La perdita della fede nei cattolici* (Venegono 1940), 75–175;

R. Lill, "Die deutschen Theologieprofessoren im Urteil des Münchener Nuntius," *Reformata reformanda. Festgabe für Hubert Jedin* II (Münster 1965), 483–508.

ON NEO-SCHOLASTICISM: F. Buuck in *Scholastik* 18 (1943), 54–77; M. Schmaus, *Die Stellung Scheebens in der Theologie des XIX. Jahrhunderts: Matthias Joseph Scheeben. Der Erneuerer der katholischen Glaubenswissenschaft* (Mainz 1935), 31–54; A. Kerkvoorde, *Scheeben et son époque: Matthias Joseph Scheeben. Le Mystère de l'Église* (Paris 1946); 5–34; B. Welte, "Zum Strukturwandel der katholischen Theologie im 19. Jahrhundert," *Freiburger Dies Universitatis* 2 (1953–54), 25–55; T. Schäfer, *Die erkenntnis-theoretische Kontroverse Kleutgen-Günther. Ein Beitrag zur Entstehungsgeschichte der Neuscholastik* (Paderborn 1961); W. Bartz, *Das Problem des Glaubens in der Auseinandersetzung mit Joseph Kleutgen* (Trier 1950).

The Altercation between Catholicism and Liberalism

17. The Roman Question

SOURCES

DIPLOMACY: B. Bastgen, *Die Römische Frage,* 3 vols. (Freiburg i. Br. 1917–19); *I documenti diplomatici italiani,* 1st ser. I–III/XIII, 2nd ser. I–II (Rome 1952–66); *Carteggi di Cavour,* 16 vols. (Bologna 1926–62); *Les origines diplomatiques de la guerre de 1870–71,* 28 vols. (Paris 1910–31); L. Thouvenel, *Le secret de l'empereur, 1860–63,* 2 vols. (Paris 1889); S. Jacini, *Il tramonto del potere temporale nelle relazioni delgi ambasciatori austraci a Roma 1860–70* (Bari 1931); N. Blakiston, *The Roman Question. Extracts from the Despatches of Odo Russell 1858–70* (London 1962); M. Gabriele, *Il carteggio Antonelli-Sacconi 1858–60,* 2 vols. (Rome 1962); G. Bandini, "Roma nel 1860, dalla corrispondenza diplomatica spagnuola," *RStRis* 24 (1937), 3–50, 194–230, 369–404; E. Brazão, *A unificação de Italia vista pelos diplomatas portugueses 1848–70,* 2 vols. (Coimbra 1963–66); E. Brazão, *Relações diplomáticas de Portugal com a Santa Sé a queda de Roma 1870* (Lisbon 1970; August 1870 to July 1871); N. Miko, *Das Ende des Kirchenstaates,* 4 vols. (Vienna 1962–70; to September 1871).

CORRESPONDENCE: especially P. Pirri, *Pio IX e Vittorio Emanuele II dal loro carteggio privato,* 5 vols. (Rome 1944–60); *La Questione Romana negli anni 1860–61,* 2 vols. (Bologna 1930; to be complemented by *Carteggio inedito fra M. d'Azeglio e D. Pantaleoni,* ed. by G. Faldella [Rome 1888] and by A. Berselli in *AstIt* 113 [1955], 73–100); *Carteggi del P. L. Taparelli d'Azeglio,* ed. by P. Pirri (Turin 1933; valuable for the attitude of the *"intransigenti"* in the period 1850–1862); F. Quintavalle, *La conciliazione fra l'Italia e il Papato nelle lettere di P. Tosti al senatore Casati* (Milan 1907; valuable for the attitude of the *"conciliatoristi"*); *Lettere e documenti del Barone B. Ricasoli,* ed. by M. Tabarrini and A. Gotti, 11 vols. (Florence 1886–96), and *Carteggi di Ricasoli,* ed. by M. Nobili and S. Camerani, 23 vols. (Rome 1939–68; continuing); B. Ferrari, *E. Rendu e M. d'Azeglio. Il Risorgimento italiano visto da un cattolico liberale francese 1849–65* (Santena 1967); on the correspondence of M. d'Azeglio, see A. M. Ghisalberti in *RStRis* 30 (1943), 398–403.

SPEECHES: C. de Cavour, *Discorsi parlamentari,* 11 vols. (Turin 1863–72; new edition by A. Omodeo and L. Russo, Florence 1932seqq.); *Scritti e discorsi politici di M. d'Azeglio,* ed. by M. De Rubris, 3 vols. (Florence 1931–38); *Discorsi di U. Rattazzi,* 8 vols. (Rome 1876–80).

MEMOIRS: G. Pasolini, *Memorie* (Turin 1887); M. Minghetti, *I miei ricordi* (Turin 1889; new edition by A. M. Ghisalberti, Turin 1948; see A. M. Ghisalberti in *RStRis* 34 [1947], 159–96); N. Roncalli, *Diario dall'anno 1849 al 1870,* ed. by A. De Magistris (Turin 1887); G. Margotti, *Memorie per la storia dei nostri tempi 1856–63* (Turin 1863).

JOURNALS AND NEWSPAPERS: *La Civiltà cattolica* (1850seqq.) and *L'Osservatore Romano* (1861seqq.) from the Roman point of view; *L'Univers* and *Le Monde* from the French point of view; for Italy, *L'Armonia* (1846–66), *L'Unità cattolica* (1863seqq.), *L'Osserva-*

tore cattolico (1864seqq.), and *Il Veneto cattolico* from the papal point of view, *Gli annali cattolici* (1862–66) and *La Rivista Universale* (1866–79) from the liberal Catholic point of view, and *La Gazzetta del Popolo* (1848seqq.) and *La Nuova Antologia* (1860seqq.) from the liberal point of view.

LITERATURE

Many bibliographic references are in B. Bastgen, op. cit. III, 841–64, Mollat passim, and *Nuove questioni di storia del Risorgimento* (Milan 1961), 377–80. Mollat's work, the standard for a long time, must be supplemented with P. Pirri, op. cit. II–1, III–1; J. Maurain, *La politique ecclésiastique du Second Empire* (Paris 1930), L. Case, *Franco-Italian Relations 1860–65* (Philadelphia 1932), Engel-Janosi I, 61–197, R. Mori, *La Questione Romana 1861–65* (Florence 1963), and *Il tramonto del potere temporale 1866–70* (Rome 1967).

MONOGRAPHS: "Il problema religioso del Risorgimento," *RStRis* 43 (1956), 191–345, 411–589 (=Congress of Messina in 1954); "L'unità d'Italia e i cattolici italiani," *Vita e pensiero* 42 (1959), 858–1010; *I cattolici e il Risorgimento* (Rome 1963); L. Salvatorelli, "Roma e la Questione Romana nella politica europea del sec. XIX," *Il Risorgimento e l'Europa* (Rome 1964), 39–134; on Cavour and the Roman Question, literature in *Il Diritto ecclesiastico* 75 (1964), 415, n. 18; W. Hancock, *Ricasoli and the Risorgimento in Tuscany* (London 1926; also C. Pischeda in *RSIt* 68 [1956], 37–81); L. Lipparini, *Minghetti,* 2 vols. (Bologna 1942–47); R. Aubert, "Pio IX et le Risorgimento," *Ris* 4 (1961), 51–74; R. Aubert, "La chute de Monseigneur de Merode en 1865," *RSTI* 9 (1955), 331–92; R. Aubert, "La Chiesa cattolica in Italia e la questione dell'unità politica," *Humanitas* 16 (Brescia 1961), 682–709; G. De Rosa, "Il 'non expedit' e lo Stato unitario italiana," *Humanitas* 16 (Brescia 1961), 709–32; F. Fonzi, "Echi e reazioni del mondo cattolico all'unificazione italiana," *RStT* 6 (1960), 247–71; N. Miko, "Österreich-Ungarn und der Untergang des Kirchenstaates im Jahre 1870," *RömHM* 1 (1958), 130–76; J. M. Goñi Gastambide, "El reconocimiento de Italia y monseñor Claret, confesor de Isabel II," *Anthologica annua,* 17 (1970), 369–462; A. Graham, *The Rise of the Dual Diplomatic Corps in Rome 1870–75* (The Hague 1952); L. P. Wallace, *The Papacy and European Diplomacy 1869–78* (Chapel Hill 1948); A. Vigevano, *La fine dell'Esercito pontificio* (Rome 1920); D. McElrath in *RHE* 65 (1970), 86–113.

18. *The Offensive of the Liberal Governments in the Non-German-Speaking Countries*

THE SECULARIZATION POLICY IN ITALY

SOURCES: G. D'Amelio, *Stato e Chiesa. La legislazione ecclesiastica fino al 1867* (Milan 1961); *ColLac* VI (provincial councils); *Memorie biografiche di S. Giov. Bosco* I–IX, ed. by G. B. Lemoyne (Turin 1898–1917), X–XX, ed. by E. Ceria (Turin 1940–48); Silvino da Nadro, *Sinodi diocesani italiani* (Vatican City 1960); for pastoral letters, see Aubert-Martina, 14–15. A good anthology is P. Scoppola, ed., *Chiesa e Stato nella storia d'Italia. Storia documentaria* (Bari 1967), 3–138.

LITERATURE: There is an especially rich bibliography. A good start can be made with F. Fausti, *I cattolici e la società italiana dopo l'Unità* (Rome 1960), 111–18 and *Stato e Chiesa: Nuove questioni di storia del Risorgimento* (Milan 1961), II, 325–35.

GENERAL: Aubert-Martina, 119–33, 163–82, 563–73, 761–838; Jemolo, 13–264; Jemolo, *La questione della proprietà ecclesiasticha 1848–88* (Turin 1911); S. Jacini, *La politica ecclesiastica italiana da Villafranca a Porta Pia* (Bari 1938); the files of the congresses of Messina in 1954, *Il problema religioso nel Risorgimento* (Rome 1958) and of Castiglioncello in 1958, "Il problema politico del cattolicesimo nel Risorgimento (=*RStT* 4 [1958], 213–407); A Della Torre, *Il cristianesimo in Italia dai filosofisti ai modernisti* (Milan 1912); G. Spini, *Risorgimento e protestanti* (Naples 1958), 257–369; A. Luzio, *La massoneria e il Risorgimento italiano* (Bologna 1925).

THE CONFLICT BETWEEN THE HOLY SEE AND PIEDMONT: C. Magni, *I Subalpini e il concordato. Studio storico-giuridico sulla formazione delle leggi Siccardi* (Padua 1967; also, *Humanitas* 17 [1962], 686–89 and *RSIt* 82 [1970], 256–59); V. Gorresio, *La lotta per lo stato laico: Saggi storici sul liberalismo italiano* (Perugia 1953), 373–458; F. J. Coppa in *CHR* 54 (1969), 579–612; A. M. Ghisalberti, *M. d'Azeglio, un moderato realisatore* (Rome 1953), especially 187–92, 199–223; A. C. Jemolo, *Scritti vari* (Milan 1965), 277–395; B. Ferrari in *Aevum* 32 (1958), 262–70; M. F. Mellano, *Il caso Fransoni e la politica ecclesiastica piemontese 1848–50* (Rome 1964; also G. Griseri in *BStBiS* 64 [1966], 375–492); A. Bozzola and T. Buttini in *Il Risorgimento italiano* 13 (1920), 217ff., 14 (1921), 81ff.; G. Biagio Furiozzi, "P. di Santa Rosa e il cattolicesimo liberale in Piemonte, 1850," *RStRis* 58 (1971), 21–47; M. Hudry in *ChStato* I, 327–54; M. Hudry, "Charvaz e Cavour 1852–61," *Miscellanea Cavouriana* (Turin 1964), 117–208; V. Eligio, *Il tentativo di introdurre il matrimonio civile in Piemonte* (Rome 1951); G. Ferroglio, "Per la storia della legge del 29.5.1855," *Il Diritto ecclesiastico* 63 (1952), 3–42; E. Borghese, "La crisi calabiana [1855] sec. nuovi documenti," *BStBiS* 55 (1957), 425–81; C. Pischeda, "Documenti sulla questione ecclesiastica in Piemonte, 1857," *Critica storica* 3 (1964), 764–91.

ON THE OTHER ITALIAN STATES: I Arcuno, *Il Regno delle Due Sicilie nei rapporti con lo Stato pontificio 1846–50* (Naples 1933); G. Martina, *Pio IX e Leopoldo II* (Rome 1967; see also A. Salvestrini in *Studi storici* 6 [1965], 55–98); G. Ferroglio, "I provvedimenti in materia ecclesiastica dei governi provvisori parmensi 1859," *Raccolta di scritti in onore di C.A. Jemolo* I (Milan 1963), 489–519; L. Briguglio, "Patriarcato di Venezia e governo austriaco," *Nova historia* 13 (Verona 1961), 3–30; L. Briguglio, "Lo spirito religioso nel Veneto durante la terza dominazione austriaca," *RStRis* 42 (1955), 22–57; G. De Rosa, "La crisi della parrochia nel Veneto dopo il 1866," *Fonti e ricerche di storia ecclesiastica padovana* (Padua 1967), 205–21; A. Gambasin, "Orientamenti spirituali e stati d'animo di cattolici intransigenti veneti," *ChStato* I, 243–96; G. Mantese, "La cultura religiosa a Vicenza negli anni dell'unificazione italiana," *ChStato* II, 391–419; A. Agazzi, "E. Tazzoli e il clero del Lombardo-Veneto," *Bergomum* 28 (1954), 25–47.

ON THE CLERGY: Aubert-Martina, 761–807; S. Bruno, *Ordini religiosi e clero in Basilicata 1861–70* (Matera 1964); X. Toscani, "Indicazioni sul clero bergamasco," *RSTI* 21 (1967), 411–53; A. Gambasin, *Il clero padovano 1859–66* (Rome 1967); B. Bertoli, *Il clero veneziano dopo il 1848; Rassegna di politica e di storia* (1964), 7–25.

BIOGRAPHIES: (one of the most neglected areas of ecclesiastical historiography in Italy). G. Russo, *Il cardinale S. Riario Sforza e l'unità d'Italia* (Naples 1962; also, G. Russo in *Asprenas* 11 [Naples 1964], 225–319, 14 [1967], 66–162, 324–90); A. Fermi, *Monsignor A. Ranza, vescovo di Piacenza,* 2 vols. (Piacenza 1956–66); C. Castiglione, *Gaysruck e Romilli arcivescovi di Milano* (Milan 1938); C. Castiglione, *Vita di Monsignor Nazari di Calabiana* (Milan 1952); T. Lecisotti, *Il cardinale Dusmet* (Catania 1962); M. Maccarrone, *Il Concilio Vaticano I* (Padua 1966), 3–132 (on Archbishop Arrigoni). Other references in Aubert-Martina, 18–20.

ON THE ORIGINS OF THE CATHOLIC MOVEMENT: L. Bedeschi, *Le origini della gioventù cattolica* (Bologna 1959); G. De Rosa, *Storia del Movimento cattolico in Italia* I (Bari 1966), 39–120; G. De Rosa, *Le Associazioni cattoliche dal Neoguelfismo all' Unità: I cattolici italiani dall 800 ad oggi* I (Brescia 1964), 95–150; A. Berselli, *Alle origini del movimento cattolico intransigente* (Livorno 1954); B. Bertoli, *Le origini del movimento cattolico a Venezia* (Brescia 1965); G. Griseri in *BStBiS* 11 (1963), 257–97 (on Piedmont between 1849 and 1861); S. Sciortino: *La Sicilia e l'unità d'Italia* (Milan 1962), 562–92; C. Marsilli in *Aurea Parma* 47 (1963), 127–45; M. Stranghellini in *RStRis* 43 (1956), 547–56 (on Lucca); P. Borzomati, *Aspetti religiosi e storia del movimento cattolico in Calabria 1860–1919* (Rome 1967), 7–182. See also Aubert-Martina, 563–64.

ANTICLERICALISM IN BELGIUM AND IN THE NETHERLANDS

BELGIUM: In addition to pastoral letters of bishops and A. Simon, *Réunions des évêques de Belgique. Procès verbaux,* 2 vols. (Louvain 1960–61), see information in the files of the congresses of Mechelen (=*Assemblée générale des catholiques en Belgique,* 1864, 1865, and 1867), in the *Journal historique et littéraire* (to 1867), the *Revue catholique* (1843–84), the *Revue générale* (1865seqq.), and the two most important daily newspapers, *Le Journal de Bruxelles* (1840seqq.) and *Le Bien public* (1853seqq.). See also C. Woeste, *Mémoires* (from 1859) I (Brussels 1927), 53–144; M. Becqué and A. Louant, "Le dossier 'Rome et Louvain' de Charles Périn," *RHE* 50 (1955), 36–124; and the documents published by A. Simon in *Catholicisme et politique* (Wetteren 1955) and *L'hypothèse libérale en Belgique* (Wetteren 1956); D. De Haerne, *Tableau de la charité chrétienne en Belgique* (Brussels 1857); E. Banning, *L'épiscopat et l'instruction publique de 1830 à 1879* (Brussels 1879); E. Banning, *Exposé historique des rapports entre le gouvernement belge et le Saint-Siège de 1830 à 1880* (Brussels 1881); A. Simon, ed., *Instructions aux nonces de Bruxelles 1835–1889* (Brussels 1961); K. van Isacker, *Werkelijk en wettelijk land 1863–84* (Antwerp 1955; see *Revue nouvelle* 23 [1956], 250–57 and A. Simon in *RHE* 51 [1956], 231–34); A. Simon, *Le parti catholique belge* (Brussels 1958); S. Balau, *70 ans d'histoire contemporaine de Belgique* (Brussels 1889), 89–376; A. Erba, *L'esprit laïque en Belgique 1857–70* (Louvain 1967); M. Defourny, *Les congrès catholiques en Belgique* (Louvain 1908; to be complemented with A. Delmer in *Revue générale* 90 [1909], 317–52); A. Rubbens, "De bezorgdheid van de Belgische Katholieken voor het onderwijs vanaf het Mechels Congres van 1863 tot aan de schoolwet van 1879," *Collationes brugenses et gandavenses* 13 (1967), 518–33, 14 (1968), 103–29, 243–69; P. Gérin, *150 Jaar katholieke Arbeidersbeweging in Belgie,* ed. by S. Scholl, I (Brussels 1963), 245–319; A. Verhaegen, *J. Lammens et les œuvres catholiques* (Ghent 1909); J. Daris, *Le diocèse de Liège sous Monseigneur de Montpellier* (Liège 1892). In addition to the biographies of cardinals Sterckx and Dechamps (General Bibliography) and of bishops Van Bommel and Ad. Dechamps, see also H. de Trannoy, *Jean-Baptiste Malou* (Brussels 1905; to be complemented with the articles by the same author in *Revue générale* 115 [1926], 513–22, 141 [1939], 1–18); J. Garsou, *Frère-Orban de 1857 à 1878* (Brussels 1946); E. Rubbens, *E. Ducpétiaux,* 2 vols. (Louvain 1922–34); R. Warlomont, *F. Laurent* (Brussels 1948).

NETHERLANDS: D. Langedijk, *De schoolstrijd in de eerste jaren na de wet van 1857* (Kampen 1937); C. Brok, *Openbaar en bijzonder onderwijs in Breda* (Tilburg 1964); J. M. Gysen, *J.A. Paredis, bischop van Roermond* (Assen 1968); 399–431.

THE CONFUSED SITUATION IN THE IBERIAN PENINSULA

SPAIN: J. López Órtiz, *Los cien años de la vida del concordato de 1851: El concordato de 1953* (Madrid 1956), 41–64; J. M. Cuenca Toribio, *La Iglesia española ante la revolución liberal*

(Madrid 1970), 197–290; J. M. Cuenca Toribio in *HS* 22 (1969), 129–285; V. Cacho Vía, *La Institución Libre de Enseñanza I: Orígenes* (Madrid 1962; on Sanz del Río and the progress of positivism); C. J. Bartlett, "The Question of Religious Toleration in Spain in the XIXth Century," *JEH* 8 (1957), 205–16 (on the difficult entrance of Protestantism, supported by English diplomacy); G. Barberini, "El article ll de la Constitución de 1876. Controversia diplomática entre España y la Santa Sede," *Anthologica annua* 9 (1961), 279–409 (on freedom of religion); M. Menéndez y Pelayo, *Los heterodoxos españoles* (Edition BAC, Madrid 1956) II, 946–1119.

PORTUGAL: X. Coutinho, "A descritianização de Portugal no seculo XIX," *Miscellanea historiae ecclesiasticae III* (Louvain 1970), 359–79.

REGALISTIC LIBERALS AND FREEMASONS IN LATIN AMERICA

MEXICO: W. H. Callcott, *Church and State in Mexico 1822–57* (New York 1926); W. H. Callcott, *Liberalism in Mexico 1857–1929* (Stanford 1931); G. García Cantú, *El pensamiento de la revolución, historia documental, 1810–62* (Mexico City 1966); W. V. Scholes, *Mexican Politics during the Juarez Regime 1855–72* (Columbia 1957); cf. *CHR* 51 (1965), 509–28; M. A. Cleven, "The Ecclesiastical Policy of Maximilian," *HAHR* 9 (1929), 317–60; G. Martina, "La corrispondenza tra Pio IX e Massimiliano," *AHPont* 5 (1967), 373–91; De Cosío Villegas, ed., *La historia moderna de México*, I (Mexico City 1956; from 1867); L. Zea, *Apogeo y decadencia del positivismo en Méjico* (Mexico City 1944).

COLOMBIA: A. Pérez Aguirre, *25 años de historia colombiana 1853 a 1878* (Bogotá 1959); J. Jaramillo Uribe, "Romanticismo, utopismo y positivismo en el pensamiento social y político colombiano del seculo XIX," *Revista Bolivar* 13 (1960), 117–44.

VENEZUELA: J. Nava in *HAHR* 45 (1965), 527–43.

BRAZIL: M. C. Thornton, *The Church and Free Masonry in Brazil, 1872–75. A Study in Regalism* (Washington 1943); R. D. Oliveira, *O Conflicto maçonico-religioso de 1872* (Petropolis 1952).

19. *Preliminary Phases of the* Kulturkampf *in Austria, Bavaria, Baden, and Switzerland*

LITERATURE

G. Franz, *Kulturkampf, Staat und katholische Kirche in Mitteleuropa von der Säkularisation bis zum Abschluß des preußischen Kulturkampfes* (Munich 1954); G. Franz-Willing, *Kulturkampf gestern und heute. Eine Säkularbetrachtung* (Munich 1971).

AUSTRIA: M. Hussarek, "Die Krise und die Lösung des Konkordats vom 18. August 1855," *AÖG* 112 (1932); K. Eder, *Der Liberalismus in Alt-Österreich* (Vienna 1955); N. Miko, "Der Untergang des Kirchenstaates und Österreich-Ungarn im Jahre 1870," *Römische Historische Mitteilungen* 1 ((1956–57); Karl Eder, "Die katholische Kirche in Österreich-Ungarn um 1870," *Festschrift für Karl Eder* (Innsbruck 1959); Engel-Janosi, *Österreich und der Vatikan 1846–1918* I (Graz, Vienna and Cologne 1958), 143–97; F. Engel-Janosi, *Die politische Korrespondenz der Päpste mit den österreichischen Kaisern 1804–1918* (Vienna and Munich 1964), 35–46, nos. 124–42; Weinzierl-Fischer, *Die österreichischen Konkordate von 1855 und 1933* (Vienna and Munich 1960), 112–24; E. Sauer, *Die politischen Aspekte der österreichischen Bischofsernennungen 1867–1903* (Vienna and Munich 1968).

BAVARIA: J. Grisar, "Die Circulardepesche des Fürsten Hohenlohe vom 9. April 1869 über das bevorstehende Vatikanische Konzil," *Bayern. Staat und Kirche, Land und Reich, Gedenkschrift für Wilhelm Winkler* (Munich 1961); D. Albrecht, "Döllinger, die bayerische Regierung und das erste Vatikanische Konzil," *Spiegel der Geschichte. Festgabe für Max Braubach* (Münster 1964); Franz-Willing, *Die bayerische Vatikangesandschaft 1803–1934* (Munich 1965), 52–68; W. Brandmüller, "Die Publikation des 1. Vatikanischen Konzils in Bayern. Aus den Anfängen des bayerischen Kulturkampfes," *ZBLG* 31 (1968); M. Weber, *Das I. Vatikanische Konzil im Spiegel der bayerischen Politik (Miscellanea Bavarica Monacensia* no. 28 [Munich 1970]).

BADEN: E. Friedberg, *Der Staat und die katholische Kirche im Großherzogtum Baden seit dem Jahre 1860* (Leipzig 1874); J. Becker, "Staat und Kirche in Baden in der 2. Hälfte des 19. Jahrhunderts. Bericht über den Stand der Vorarbeiten an einer geplanten Quellenpublikation," *ZGObrh* 111 (1963); L. Gall, "Die partei- und sozialgeschichtliche Problematik des badischen Kulturkampfes," *ZGObrh* 113 (1965); L. Gall, *Der Liberalismus als regierende Partei. Das Großherzogtum Baden zwischen Restauration und Reichsgründung* (Wiesbaden 1968); M. Stadelhofer, *Der Abbau der Kulturkampfgesetzgebung im Großherzogtum Baden 1878–1918* (Mainz 1969).

SWITZERLAND: P. Gschwind, *Geschichte der Entstehung der christkatholischen Kirche der Schweiz,* 2 vols. (Solothurn 1904–10); V. Conzemius, "Eugène Michaud, ein katholischer Reformator des 19. Jahrhunderts?" *ZSKG* 58 (1964); V. Conzemius, "Der schweizerische Bundesrat und das erste Vatikanische Konzil," *SZG* 15 (1965).

20. *Internal Catholic Controversies in Connection with Liberalism*

LITERATURE

FRANCE: Aubert, *Pie IX,* 224–61, 531–37; C. de Montalembert, *Catholicisme et liberté. Correspondance inédite 1852–1870* (Paris 1970); Weill, *Cath. lib.,* 91–202; Gurian, 210–38; M. Prelot, *Le libéralisme catholique* (Paris 1969), 14–33, 190–237; J. Maurain, *La politique ecclésiastique du Second Empire* (Paris 1930); J. Gadille, *La pensée et l'action politique des évêques français au début de la troisième République* (Paris 1967) I, 46–142; J. Fèvre, *Histoire critique du catholicisme libéral en France jusqu'au pontificat de Léon XIII* (Paris 1897; a partisan, but well-informed indictment); and the biographies (see General Bibliography) of Montalembert, Veuillot, Dupanloup, Pie, Maret, Guéranger, and Lacordaire; *DHGE* XIV, 1117–19 (on Dupanloup); L. de Lanzac de Laborie, *Le comte de Falloux* (Paris 1912; see also *DHGE* XVI, 1499–1513); H. Boissard, *T. Foisset* (Paris 1891; see also *DHGE* XVII, 1392–96); J. de Pange in *Le Correspondant* 317 (1929), 113–37 (on the years 1855–64); J. Lecler: *Études* 291 (1956), 196–211 (concerning the Jesuits).

ITALY: *Carteggi di L. Taparelli d'Azeglio e di B. Ricasoli;* the files of the council of Castglioncello, "Il problema politico dei cattolici nel XIX secolo," *RStT* 4 (1949), 215–407; G. Martina, *Il liberalismo cattolico ed il Sillabo* (Rome 1959); Jemolo, 87–264; Jemolo, *Scritti vari* (Milan 1965), 397–454; E. Passerin in *RSTI* 20 (1966), 500–506; G. Spadolini, "L'intransigentismo cattolico dalla 'Civiltà cattolica' al 'Sillabo,'" *RStT* 4

(1956), 309–32; F. Fonzi in *Itinerari* 4 (Genoa 1956), 603–23; E. Passerin d'Entrèves, *Nuove Questioni di storia del Risorgimento* (Milan 1961), 565–606.

BELGIUM: A. Simon, *L'hypothèse libérale en Belgique* (Wetteren 1956); A. Simon, *Catholicisme et politique* (Wetteren 1955); A. Simon, *Le cardinal Sterckx* I (Wetteren 1950), 209–56; E. de Moreau, *A. Dechamps* (Brussels 1911), 423–78; K. van Isacker, *Werkelijk en wettelijk Land* (Antwerp 1955), 1–85.

GERMANY: In addition to the general works by Goyau, Schnabel, Brück, and Kißling, and the biographies of Döllinger and Ketteler (see General Bibliography), see J. Rovan, *Le catholicisme politique en Allemagne* (Paris 1956), 46–78.

ENGLAND: In addition to the general works by W. Ward, *W.G. Ward and the Catholic Revival* (London 1893), 130–210, and M. Ward, *The W. Wards and the Transition* (London 1934), 1–53, and the biographies of Manning, Newman, and Ullathorne (cited in the General Bibliography), see J. Altholz, *The Liberal Catholic Movement in England* (London 1962); H. MacDougall, *Acton-Newman Relations* (New York 1962); A. Gasquet, *Lord Acton and his Circle* (London 1906; see also *Cambridge Historical Journal* 10 [1950], 77–105, where attention is drawn to grave gaps in the edition of the letters).

ON THE SYLLABUS: C. G. Rinaldi, *Il valore del Sillabo* (Rome 1888); *DThC* XIV, 2877–2923; G. Martina, "Osservazioni sulle varie redazioni del "Sillabo," *ChStato* II, 419–523; G. Martina, "Nuovi documenti sulla genesi del Sillabo," *AHPont* 6 (1968), 319–69; R. Aubert in *Revue Nouvelle* 40 (Brussels 1964), 369–85, 481–99; R. Aubert, "Monseigneur Dupanloup et le Syllabus," *RHE* 51 (1956), 79–142, 471–512, 837–915; R. Aubert, *Scrinium Lovaniense* (Louvain 1961), 543–60 (on the reaction in Belgium); R. Aubert, *Gesammelte Aufsätze zur Kulturgeschichte Spaniens* 19 (Münster 1962), 291–304 (on the reaction in Spain); E. Papa, *Il Sillabo di Pio IX e la stampa francese, inglese e italiana* (Rome 1968); D. McElrath, *The Syllabus of Pius IX. Some reactions in England* (Louvain 1964); B. Schneider, "Der Syllabus und die deutschen Jesuiten," *AHPont* 6 (1968), 371–92.

ANTILIBERALISM AND SOCIAL CATHOLICISM: General description and bibliography in *Die Katholische Arbeiterbewegung in Westeuropa,* ed. by S. Scholl and G. Mees (Bonn 1966). Useful information in R. Kothen, *La pensée e l'action sociale des catholiques* (Louvain 1945).

BELGIUM: R. Rezsohazy, *Origines et formation du catholicisme social en Belgique* (Louvain 1958), 1–98; P. Gérin in *150 Jaar Katholieke Arbeidersbeweging in Belgie,* ed. by S. Scholl, I (Brussels 1963), 223–319.—Germany: M Moennig, *Die Stellung der deutschen katholischen Sozialpolitiker des 19. Jahrhunderts zur Staatsintervention in der sozialen Frage* (Münster 1927); E. Ritter, *Die katholische soziale Bewegung Deutschlands im 19. Jahrhundert und der Volksverein* (Cologne 1954).

The Victory of Ultramontanism

21. *Ultramontane Progress and Final Gallican Resistance*

LITERATURE

ON THE MOVEMENT IN GENERAL: Aubert, *Pie IX,* 262–310, 537–41; R. Aubert, *La géographie ecclésiastique au XIXe siècle: L'ecclésiologie au XIXe siècle,* 36–55; C. Butler, *The Vatican Council I* (London 1930), 23–78; J. Friedrich, *Geschichte des Vaticanischen Concils I: Vorgeschichte* (Nördlingen 1877); W. Ward, *W. G. Ward and the Catholic Revival* (London 1893), chap. V.

FRANCE: See in addition to the biographies of Maret, Guéranger, Veuillot, Clausel, Sibour, Gousset, Mathieu, and Darboy (General Bibliography), J. Maurain, *Le Saint-Siège et la France de décembre 1851 à avril 1853* (Paris 1930); J. Maurain, *La politique ecclésiastique du Second Empire* (Paris 1930), chaps. III, V, IX, XVI, XVIII, XXI, XXII, XXIV, XXVII; P. de Quirielle, "Pie IX et l'Église de France," *Annales de l'École des sciences politiques* 5 (1890), 490–514, 6 (1891), 111–48; A. Houtin, *Un dernier gallican, H. Bernier* (Paris 1904); A. Houtin, *Le P. Hyacinthe dans l'Église romaine* (Paris 1920); A. Ricard, *L'abbé Combalot* (Paris 1891); M. de Hédouville, *Monseigneur de Ségur* (Paris 1957), 174–227, 485–534; de Montclos, 107–33, 200–321, 405; J. Gadille, "Autour de Louis Veuillot et de l'*Univers*," *Cahiers d'histoire* 14 (1969), 275–88; "Monseigneur Darboy et le Saint-Siège," *RHLR* 12 (1907), 240–81 (also R. Durand in *Bulletin de la Société d'histoire moderne* 7 [1907–08], 6–10); P. Mabile, *Vie de Monseigneur Mabile* (Paris 1926); J.-R. Palanque, *Catholiques libéraux et gallicans en France face au concile du Vatican* (Aix 1962), 5–32.

GERMANY: In addition to the biographies of Geissel, Ketteler, and Döllinger (General Bibliography), see Goyau IV, 201–90; V. Conzemius, "Aspects ecclésiologiques de l'évolution de Döllinger et du vieux-catholicisme," *L'ecclésiologie au XIXe siècle,* 247–79; S. Loesch, *Döllinger und Frankreich* (Munich 1955).

ENGLAND: See the biographies of Wiseman and Ullathorne (General Bibliography), W. G. Ward (see above), Newman, and Manning.

22. *The Vatican Council*

SOURCES

The majority of the official files were published by L. Petit and J.-B. Martin in *Mansi* XLIX–LIII. Concerning the reliability of the stenographic records of the debates, see the diary by Dehon (below), 5–10, 60f., and C. Mirbt in *HZ* 101 (1908), 546–48. But in order to write a history of the council, the official files must be complemented by other categories of sources still partly unpublished. Nearly six hundred documents (newspaper articles, manifestoes, diplomatic telegrams, letters of bishops, etc.) were printed in the second part (*Documenta historica*) of Volume VII of the *Collectio Lacensis* (Freiburg i. Br. 1892). E. Cecconi, *Storia del Concilio Vaticano,* 4 vols. (Florence 1872– 79) contains 308 documents dealing with the preparation of the council. A number of polemical writings were reprinted in J. Friedrich, *Documenta ad illustrandum Concilium Vaticanum,* 2 vols. (Nördlingen 1872) and E. Friedberg, *Sammlung der Aktenstücke zum I. Vatikanischen Konzil,* 2 vols. (Tübingen 1872–76).

MEMOIRS AND COLLECTIONS OF CORRESPONDENCE: L. Pásztor, "Il Concilio Vaticano I nel diario del cardinale Capalti," *AHPont* 7 (1969), 401–90; J. Friedrich, *Tagebuch während des Vaticanischen Concils* (Nördlingen 1873); E. Donckel, ed., *Reise nach Rom zum I. Vatikanischen Konzil. Tagebuch von Monsignor Adames* (Luxemburg 1963); V. Carbone, *Diario del Concilio Vaticano di L. Dehon* (Rome 1962); L. Veuillot, *Rome pendant le concile,* 2 vols. (Paris 1872); V. Conzemius, ed., *Ignaz von Döllinger - Lord Acton, Briefwechsel* II (Munich 1965); H. J. Browne, "Letters of Bishop McQaid," *CHR* 41 (1956), 408–41; L. Lenhart in *AMrhKG* 4 (1952), 307–29, 6 (1954), 208–29 (letters of Ketteler and his secretary Raich); F. Guédon in *Les Lettres* (1928) II, 19–34, 190–206, 314–31 (letters of Monsignor Foulon); P. Batiffol in *RHEF* 13 (1927), 199–213 (letters of Monsignor Devoucoux); J. Nasrallah, "Monseigneur Grégoire 'Ata et le concile du Vatican," *PrOrChr* 11 (1961), 297–330, 12 (1962), 97–122; R. Aubert, "Documents concernant le Tiers Parti au concile du Vatican," *Abhandlungen über Theologie und Kirche* (Düsseldorf 1952), 241–59; S. Jacini, *Il tramonto del potere temporale nelle relazioni degli ambasciatori austriaci a Roma* (Bari 1931); N. Blakiston, *The Roman Question. Extracts from the Despatches of Odo Russell from Rome* (London 1962); V. Conzemius in *ThQ* 140 (1960), 427–62 (letters of the Bavarian diplomat Arco Valley); A. Tamborra, *Imbro I. Tkalac e l'Italia* (Rome 1966), 123–44, 225–338; R. Aubert and J. -R. Palanque, "Lettres de Lady Blennerhasset au lendemain du concile du Vatican," *RHE* 58 (1963), 82–135.

LITERATURE

The best treatment is that by C. Butler, *The Vatican Council. The Story told from inside in Bishop Ullathorne's Letters,* 2 vols. (London 1930, 1965); the most recent treatment is by R. Aubert, *Vatican I* (Paris 1964); the most comprehensive treatment from the Catholic point of view is that by T. Granderath, *Geschichte des Vatikanischen Konzils,* 3 vols. (Freiburg i. Br. 1903–06, too apologetic); the best treatment from the point of view of the Old Catholics is by J. Friedrich, *Geschichte des Vaticanischen Concils,* 3 vols. (Nördlingen 1877–87, partisan); E. Mourret, *Le concile du Vatican* (Paris 1919) is of lasting value because of its use of the diary of M. Icard; H. Rondet, *Vatican I* (Paris 1962) concerns itself chiefly with the neglected aspects (preparation of the schemata, working methods, unimplemented projects). For the diplomatic aspects and impressions, see É. Ollivier, *L'Église et l'État au concile du Vatican,* 2 vols. (Paris 1877). From the Protestant point of view, C. Mirbt in *HZ* 101 (1908), 529–600.

ON NATIONALITIES: J. J. Hennesey, *The First Council of the Vatican. The American Experience* (New York 1963); F. J. Cwiekowski, *The English Bishops and the First Vatican Council* (Louvain 1971); M. Maccarrone, *Il Concilio Vaticano e il "Giornale di Monsignor Arrigoni,"* 2 vols. (Padua 1966), on the Italian episcopate; J. -R. Palanque, *Catholiques libéraux et gallicans en France face au Concile du Vatican* (Aix-en-Provence 1962; see also *RHEF* 48 [1962], 54–79); M. Martin Tejedor, "España y el Concilio Vaticano," *HS* 20 (1967), 99–175; J. Hajjar, "L'épiscopat catholique oriental et le Ier Concile du Vatican," *RHE* 65 (1970), 423–55, 737–88; M. Mac Suibhne, "Ireland at the Vatican Council,"

Irish Ecclesiastical Records 93 (1960), 209–22, 295–307; U. Betti, "I Frati minori al Concilio Vaticano," *Antonianum* 32 (1957), 17–26.

ON THE DOGMATIC CONSTITUTIONS: J. P. Torrell, *La théologie de l'épiscopat au Ier concile du Vatican* (Paris 1961); G. Dejaifve, *Pape et évêques au Ier concile du Vatican* (Bruges and Paris 1961); G. Dejaifve in *NRTh* 82 (1960), 787–802; G. Dejaifve, *L'épiscopat et l'Église universelle* (Paris 1962), 639–736; R. Aubert, "L'ecclésiologie au concile du Vatican," *Le concile et les conciles* (Paris and Chevetogne 1960), 245–84; R. Aubert in *Lumière et Vie* (St. Alban) 14 (1954), 21–52; A. Alsteen in *EThL* 38 (1962), 461–503; W. Dewan in *EThL* 36 (1960), 23–56. A number of historio-systematic works were reprinted thanks to the efforts of the Vatican Library in *De doctrina Concilii Vaticani Primi* (Vatican City 1969).

SPECIAL ASPECTS: J. Gadille, *Albert Du Boÿs. Ses "Souvenirs du Concile du Vatican". L'intervention du gouvernement impérial à Vatican I* (Louvain 1968); F. Engel-Janosi in *MÖSTA* 8 (1955), 223–35; L. Pásztor in *RSTI* 23 (1969), 441–66; H. J. Pottmeyer in *Annuarium Historiae Conciliorum* 2 (1970), 87–111 (on the method in the constitution *Dei Filius*); A. Hagen in *ThQ* 123 (1942), 223–52, 124 (1943), 1–40, 148 (1968), 403–28 (on Hefele's attitude); T. Freudenberger, *Die Universität Würzburg und das erste Vatikanische Konzil I* (Neustadt 1969); R. Lill, "Zur Verkündigung des Unfehlbarkeitsdogmas in Deutschland," *GWU* (1963), 469–83.

23. *The Rise of the Old Catholic Community*

LITERATURE

J. F. von Schulte, *Der Altkatholizismus* (Gießen 1887, reprint Hildesheim 1965); J. F. von Schulte, *Lebenserinnerungen* I (Gießen 1908); J. Troxler, *Die neuere Entwicklung des Altkatholizismus* (Cologne 1908); P. Gschwind, *Geschichte der Entstehung der christkatholischen Kirche der Schweiz,* 2 vols. (Solothurn 1904–10); M. Kopp, *Der Altkatholizismus in Deutschland 1871–1912* (Berne and Kempten 1913); K. Algermissen, *Konfessionskunde* (Celle 1957), 745–63; C. B. Moss, *The Old Catholic movement, its origins and history* (London 1964); U. Küry, *Die altkatholische Kirche* (Die Kirchen der Welt 3 [Stuttgart 1966]); Conzemius, *Katholizismus ohne Rom. Die altkatholische Kirchengemeinschaft* (Zurich, Einsiedeln and Cologne 1969); A. Lauscher, *Die katholisch-theologische Fakultät der Universität zu Bonn* (Düsseldorf 1920); P. Wenzel, *Der Freundeskreis um Anton Günther* (Essen 1965); E. Kleineidam, *Die Katholisch-Theologische Fakultät der Universität Breslau* (Cologne 1961).

INDIVIDUALS: Baltzer: A. Franz (Breslau 1873); Döllinger: Friedrich, *Döllinger* III (Munich 1901); Friedrich: F. H. Hacker (Kempten 1918); Reinkens: F. Nippold (Leipzig 1896); J. M. Reinkens (Gotha 1906); B. Poll in *AHVNrh* 155/56 (1954), 392–410; V. Conzemius: *Rheinische Lebensbilder* 4 (Düsseldorf 1970), 209–33; Reusch: L. K. Goetz (Gotha 1901); Schulte: R. von Scherer (Vienna 1915); N. Hilling in *AkathKR* 95 (1915), 519—27.

INDEX

Abdul Mejid, sultan 169
Abel, Carl August von 110
Academic freedom 291f, 304
Achterfeld, J. A. 32, 35
Acquaderni, G. 260f
Acton, John Emmerick Edward 124, 293, 320, 325
Ad limina visits 308
Affre, Denis Auguste, archbishop of Paris 6, 15, 49, 66, 68, 103
Africa mission 196ff
Agnosticism, English 235
Alacoque, Marguerite Marie 222, 224
Al-Bashir 170
Alberdingk Thijm, Joseph 79
Albertario 290
Alcántara Herrán 270
Aleppo, national council of Melchites (1866) 173
Alexander II, tsar of Russia 155, 162
Alimonda, Cajetan, cardinal 261
Allemand, J. J. 25
Allgemeine Zeitung (Augsburg) 326
Allioli, Joseph Franz von 42
Altar sacrament, form of veneration 221f
Alzog, Johann Baptist 245
Alzon, Emmanuel d' 104, 157, 158, 167, 215
Amberger, J. 22
America, see Latin America, United States of America
American College in Rome 133
Amicizie 176
Amorim Pessoa, John Chrysostom d', archbishop of Goa 181, 182
Ancaroni, master general O.P. 11
Andlaw-Birseck, Heinrich Bernhard von 7, 71
André, abbé 305
Andrea, d', cardinal 234
Anglicans and First Vatican Council 315f
Annales de philosophie chrétienne 50, 55
Annali cattolici 291
Annam, see Indochina
Anticlericalism 214
—in Baden 278ff

—in Belgium 262ff, 265, 289
—in Colombia 270
—in France 68f, 93, 100f
—in Italy 289
—in Latin America 269ff
—in Mexico 269
—in Netherlands 265ff
—in Portugal 148, 267
—in Prussia 280
—in Spain 144f, 148
Antiliberalism and social Catholicism 299ff
Antonelli, Giacomo, cardinal 61, 63, 64, 87, 88, 127, 180, 221, 248, 250, 251, 252, 254, 257, 295, 308, 327
Antonin of Florence 328
Antonio di S. Giacomo, general superior of the Passionists 211
Antonites 171
Apologetics 234ff
Apostolate 215
—methods 217
Apostolic Union of Secular Priests 214
April Movement (Netherlands 1853) 78
Araujo, M. de 154
Arbues 313
Archeology, Christian 229
Arendt, W. 44
Argentina 150f, 152, 271
Armenian Uniate Church 160, 171, 309
Arqus, Philipp, Syrian patriarch 173
Asia, reorganization of missions 178ff
Association of Sons of Mary the Immaculate 24
Associatio perseverantiae sacerdotalis 214
Association for the Support of Schools in the Near East 202
Association of Ladies of the Children of Mary 25
Association of the Immaculate Conception of Mary for the Support of the Catholics in the Ottoman Empire 157
Association of the Sacred Heart of Jesus 177
Assumptionists 98, 157, 167
—in Turkey 170
Aeterni Patris, bull (1868) 199f, 316

Atonement, pilgrimages of 222
Audo, Joseph, Chaldean patriarch 172
Auersperg, Austrian minister 275
Augustinians (Hermits, Recollects) 11
—in Micronesia 196
—in the Philippines 193
Aulike, Matthias 107
Australia 89
—clergy 142
—education 143
—episcopate 142
—establishment of hierarchy 142
—immigration 142
—progress of Catholicism in 19th century 142f
Austria
—all-Austrian bishops' conference at Vienna
  (1849) 76f
—and Near Eastern Churches 157
—and orthodoxy 156
—antiliberalism 108
—catechesis 17
—Catholic association movement 76, 309
—Christian Socialist Party 276, 161, 166f,
  273f, 310
—concordat (1855) 17, 76, 91, 108f
—defeat at Königgrätz (1866) 254
—ecclesiastical development 1848–70 108ff
—ecclesiastical laws (1874) 274f
—education 109
—expulsion from the German Confederation
  (1866) 116
—National Elementary School Law (1869) 274
—people's missions 23
—State and Church 272ff
—ultramontanism 310f
Austria-Hungary
—Slavs in Austria-Hungary 165ff
Avendaño, Diego de, S. J. 204
Away-from-Rome Movement 334
Azarian, Stephen, Armenian patriarch 172
Azeglio, Cesare d' 26
Azeglio, Massimo d' 59, 257

Baader, Franz von 38
Baden, grand duchy 119
—Catholic People's Party 280
—Church regulation (1868—76) 278
—civil marriage law (1869) 279
—concordat (1859) 91, 112
—Kulturkampf 277ff
—law on foundations (1870) 279
—law on religious orders (1872) 279
—liberal anticlericalism 278ff
—Old Catholics Law (1874) 279
—religious development after 1848 112f
—school dispute 278
—school regulation (1876) 278
—nondenominational schools 278, 280
Badischer Beobachter 280
Bahut, Clement, Melchite patriarch 173
Bailly, E. 306

Balabin, P. 156
Balbo, Cesare 290
Balmes, Jaime 45, 145, 148, 269
Baltzer, Johann Baptist 37f, 238, 330
Baraga, A. F. 135
Barat, Madeleine Sophie 223
Barberi, Dominicus 24
Barnabites
—in Burma 184
Barnabo, Alessandro, cardinal 88, 158, 175f,
  200f, 202, 204, 309
Baudry, C. 49, 233
Bauerband 72
Baur, Ferdinand Christian 238
Bautain, Louis Eugène Marie 32, 33, 47ff 102,
  232
Bavaria 276ff
—concordat (1871) 277
—creeping Kulturkampf 277f
—first bishops' conference at Freising (1850)
  110
—movement of Catholic associations 277
—Patriotic People's Party 277
—religious policy after 1848 110
—secularization 276ff
Beckx, Petrus, general superior, S. J. 203, 211
Beelen, T. 44
Belgium 25, 91, 286
—and Syllabus 297
—anticlericalism 262ff, 265, 289
—Catholic congresses (1863, 1864, 1867), 264
—Catholic publications 55, 265
—Catholic social movement 301
—education policy 263f
—episcopate and liberalism 263
—moral theology 31
—ultramontanism and Catholics loyal to
  constitution 264
Bellarmine 312, 319
Benedict XIV, pope 174, 309
Benedictines 9, 12f, 209, 210
—in Australia 142f, 196
—in Spain 144
—liturgical renewal 227f
Bergier, Nicolas Sylvestre 51
Berlage, Anton 40
Bernetti, Tommaso, cardinal 57, 248
Bertier, Ferdinand de 26
Bertier, G. de 158
Bettachini, Orazio, vicar apostolic of Jaffna 183
Beuron, abbey 210
Beust, Friedrich Ferdinand von 109, 274f, 276
Bible 21
—in catechesis 17ff
Bigandet, A. T., vicar apostolic in Burma 184
Bigelmair, Andreas 243
Bilio, L., cardinal 88, 296, 327
Binterim, Anton Josef 7, 32, 75
Bishops' conferences at Rome (1854, 1862,
  1867) 308
Bismarck, Otto von 117, 276, 280, 333

Bisping, August 238
Biunde, F. X. 34
Bizzarri, cardinal 200, 208, 212, 323
Bkerke, national council of Maronites (1856) 174
Black and White Penitents 24
Blaj, synod (1868) 167
Blanchet, vicar apostolic in the United States 131
Blanco, Guzmán, president of Venezuela 271
Blondel, Maurice 236
Bludov, Russian minister 159
Blum, Peter Joseph, bishop of Limburg 112
Bluntschli, Johann Caspar 278
Bofondi, secretary of state 88
Bolivia 150, 151, 152, 270
—concordat (1851) 91
Bollandists 44, 51, 220
Bolletino di archeologia cristiana 229f
Bolzano, Bernhard 36
Bommel, C. van, bishop of Liège 77, 264, 266
Bonald, Louis Gabriel Ambroise de 284
Bonald, Louis Jacques Maurice de, cardinal 14, 94
Boniface Association 114
Bonjean, E. C., archbishop of Colombo 184
Bonnand, Clement, vicar apostolic of Pondicherry 181, 182, 184, 201
Bonnechose, Henri Marie Gaston de, cardinal 94
Bonn union conferences of Old Catholic, Russian Orthodox, and Anglican theologians (1874–75) 334
Bonnetty, Augustin 50, 232
Borret, Theodor 79
Borromeo 86
Bosnia 169
Bossuet, Jacques Bénigne 6, 231, 311, 314, 320
Bourbons 61
Bourget, bishop of Montreal 139, 221
Bouvier, J. B. 30
Brazil
—celibacy and marriages of priests 153
—church and state 271
—clergy 153f
—concordat (1862) 91
—ecclesiastical situation and stagnation under Pedro II 153f
—liberalism and ultramontanism 271
—people's missions 153
Braun, G. 27
Braun, Johann Wilhelm Joseph 34, 35, 54
Bravi, Giuseppe 183
Brentano, Clemens 220
Brière, Y. de la 153
Broglie, Jacques Victor Albert de, duke 103, 286
Broere, C. 266
Brother institutes 212
Brotherhood of Sts. Cyril and Methodius 156

Brotherhood of the Sacred Childhood of Jesus 24
Brothers of Christian Schools, see Christian Brothers
Brothers of Our Lady of Mercy (Belgium) 13
Brothers of Our Lady of Mercy (Netherlands) 13
Brothers of the Immaculate Conception 13
Brownson, Orestes 137
Brownson's Quarterly 137
Bruckner, Anton 105
Bruguière, Bartholomew, vicar apostolic in Korea 191
Brunner, Franz Sales 23
Brunner, Sebastian 76
Bruno, Fra di 261
Brunoni, Paolo, vicar apostolic 167, 200
Buchner, A. 41
Büchner, Ludwig 235
Buck, V. de 232
Buddhism in Siam 185
Bufalo, Gaspare del 23
Bühlmann, W., O.F.M.Cap. 180
Bulgaria 162
—mission to 162
—union attempts 167
Bunsen, Christian Karl von 35, 239
Buß, Franz Josef von 7, 26, 71, 72, 73, 302
Butler, C. 87, 296, 312, 329

Canada 89
—Catholicism (1840–70) 138ff
—clergy and training of priests 139f
—clericalism 140
—founding of dioceses 138f
—immigration 138
—school dispute (1871–74) 141
—Union Act (1840) 138
Caloen, Gérard van 228
Canovas del Castillo 268
Cantù, Cesare 231, 291
Capaccini, Francesco, cardinal 35, 149
Capecelatro, cardinal 291
Capes, John Moore, 124
Capitanio, B. 13
Capponi, Gino 290
Capuchins 178
—in Africa 197
—in India 181
—in Poland 164
—in Spain 144
Carbonelle 235
Cardinals, college of, under Pius IX 87f
Carol I, King of Rumania 168
Carmelites
—in India 181
—in Spain 144
Carmelites, female congregations
—in Cochinchina 187
Carolus Franciscus a Breno, O.F.M. 203
Carrera, Rafael 151

Carroll, John, S. J., bishop 133
Cartesianism 234
Casaretto, abbot of Subiaco 209
Casolani, A., vicar apostolic in Central Africa 196
Casoni, lawyer 260
Cassino Congregation, O.S.B. 209
Castelfidardo, defeat of papal army (1860) 251
Castiglioni, Francesco Saverio, see Pius VIII
Castilla, R. 152f
Casuistry 27f, 29
Catacombs 229
Catholic associations 332
Catholic Association of Germany 74
Catholic Club 72
Catholic faction (in Prussia) 107f
Catholic labor organizations 114
Catholic Organization (Ireland) 74
Catholicism
—and ecclesiastical (Roman) authority 310
—and liberalism after 1848 283ff
—internal Catholic controversies regarding liberalism 283–303
Cavaignac, Eugène Louis 67
Cavour, Camillo Benso 245, 249, 251, 253, 257
—Italian policy 257
—separation of church and state 258
Cerna, president of Venezuela 271
Ceylon 183
Chaignon, Pierre, S. J. 219
Chaldeans, Uniate 172
Chamard, O.S.B. 231
Chambord, Count 103, 288
Chaminade, Guilleaume Joseph 26
Charbonneaux, Étienne, vicar apostolic of Mysore 181, 201
Charbonnel, Armand François M. de, bishop of Toronto 141f
Charvaz 261, 291
Chastan, J. H. 191
Chateaubriand, François René de 41
Chevalier, J. 177
Chevrier, P. 20
Chiaramonti, Luigi Barnaba, see Pius VII
Childhood of Jesus Association 201
Chile 151, 152, 271
China 93
—bloodbath of Tientsin (1870) 188f
—establishment of vicariates apostolic 189
—missionary and ecclesiastical development 187ff
—persecution of foreigners and Christians 188f
—religious freedom 187f
China mission, at First Vatican Council 204ff
Christian Brothers 178, 210
—in Cochinchina 187
—in Ottoman Empire 169
Christian Catholic Church of Switzerland 282, 333
Church, established 273
Church history 220, 231f

—in France 231f
—in Germany 238
—in Italy 231
—in Spain 231
Cistercians 144, 210
Claret, Antonio-Maria 147
Clausel de Montals, bishop of Chartres 68
Clemens, Franz Jakob 38, 241, 243
Clercs de St. Viateur 140
Clericalism 214
Clergy 14f, 86
—diocesan clergy and its pastoral activity in 19th century 213ff
—regular and secular clergy 214
Cochin, A. 88, 286, 297, 301
Cochin China, mission and Church 186
Cohen, Hermann, S. J. 221
Colin, J. U., superior general of Marists 195
Collegiality 134
Collegio Pio latino-americano in Rome 150
Collegium Germanicum, Rome 242
Collegium Romanum 45f, 230, 242, 244
Cologne, provincial synod (1860) 235
Cologne dispute 33, 73
Colombia 152, 270
—clergy 270
—liberalism 269, 270
—secularization 270
—separation of church and state 270
Combalot, Théodore 4, 14
Comboni, Daniel, vicar apostolic in Central Africa 176f, 196, 206, 261
Commissione di archeologia sacra 229
Commissio pro Ecclesia Orientali et pro Missionibus at the First Vatican Council 200ff
Comte, Auguste 235
Congregatio cassiniana primitivae observantiae 209
Congregatio Sacrorum Cordium Jesu et Mariae, see Picpus Society
Congregation of St. Peter 11, 30
Congregation of the Immaculate Heart of Mary (Missionaries of Scheut/Brussels) 177
Congregatio super statu regularium 208
Concordat policy 91
Congregations, religious 212f
—dedicated to the Heart of Jesus 222
—dedicated to the Virgin Mary 225
—for education and care of the sick 13f
—in Italy 261
Consalvi, Ercole, cardinal, secretary of state 258
Constantinople, council (1869) 172
Coventuals, in Moldavia 168f
Conzemius, V. 320, 326
Corboli-Bussi, adviser to Pius IX 58, 60, 65, 154, 159
Cornelius, C. A. von 331
Cornoldi, Johann Maria, S. J. 234
"Correspondance de France" 317
Corsi, Cardinal 256
Cortés, Juan Donoso 26, 45, 145, 148, 284

Costa Rica 271
—concordat (1852) 91, 151
Counterrevolution 301
Cousin, Victor 47, 69, 231
Coux, Charles de 43
Cox, E. 3
Cramer, J. W. 266
Crimean War 169f
Croatia, unionist striving 165
Croke, archbishop of Cashel 129
Crolly, George 129
Cullen, Paul, cardinal 123, 125, 127ff
Cum ecclesiastica disciplina, constitution (1869) 172
Curci, Carlo Maria, S. J. 65, 290
Customs Parliament
—and infallibility 280f
Czartoryski, prince 158

Dalgairns, Bernard (John Dobree) 221, 226
Dalwigk 112
Daniel-Rops, Henri 215
Darboy, Georges, archbishop of Paris 297, 314, 328
Darras, Abbé 232
Darwin, Charles Robert 235
Daughters of Charity of Montreal 140
Daughters of Charity of St. Vincent de Paul 13, 24, 170, 268
Daughters of the Immaculate Heart of Mary 212
Dechamps, A. 298
Dechamps, Victor, cardinal 236, 317, 325, 327f
Dechristianization, urban 217
Deharbe, Joseph, S. J. 18
Dei Filius, constitution (1870) 324
Deinlein, Michael, archbishop of Bamberg 277
Deism 243
De Katholiek 55, 79
Democracy 67
Denzinger, Heinrich, S. J. 243f
Der Katholik (Mainz) 7, 32, 54, 71, 105, 241, 243
Derré, J. R. 52
Desmet, P., S.J. 135
De Tijd 55, 266, 267
Deutinger, Martin 29
Deutsches Volksblatt (Stuttgart) 71
Devie, bishop of Belley 20, 30
De Wachter 79
Diepenbrock, Melchior von, Prince-bishop of Breslau 37, 72, 76f, 106
Dieringer, Franz Xaver 38, 39, 54, 247
Dogma 235, 237, 239
—and morals 27f
Dogmatics 37, 235, 246
Dogmas, history of 237, 238
Döllinger, Ignaz von 42f, 50, 54, 72, 73f, 75, 110, 114, 115, 116, 118, 124, 228, 239ff, 243, 244ff, 292, 295, 297, 313, 317, 320f, 326, 330, 332, 334

Domenec, bishop 134
Dominicans 9, 11f, 144, 172, 209
—in China 189
—in Formosa 189
—in France 286
—in Philippines 193
Don Bosco, Giovanni 25, 176, 215, 221, 257
Don Carlos 144
Donnet, suffragan bishop of Nancy 48
Dostoevski, F. M. 161
Doutreloux, bishop of Liège 222
Drey, Johann Sebastian 29, 40, 242
Droste zu Vischering, Clemens August von, archbishop of Cologne 33f
Druffel, A. von 331
Dublin, Catholic university 128f
Dublin Review 56, 293, 311
Dubois, H. 22
Ducpétiaux, E. 264, 301
Dum acerbissimas, brief (1835) 33ff
Dumont, C. 167
Dupanloup, Félix 19, 68f, 69f, 94f, 102, 103, 141, 157, 216, 248, 286, 297f, 306, 314, 319, 322, 325f
Duparquet, C. 197
Dupin, André 5
Dupont des Loges, bishop of Metz 99
Duruy, Victor 96

Eastern missions at Vatican I 200ff
Eastern patriarchates 171ff
Eastern Question 154
Ecclesiastical Titles Bill (1851) 121
Ecclesiology 237, 323
Economic liberalism 300, 301f
Ecuador 152, 271
—concordat (1862) 91, 151
Edes, Miss 136
Education Bill (1870) 123
Education League (Belgium) 264
Education, religious 16ff
Einsiedeln, abbey 120
El Diario 286
Electoral Hesse 111
Elgin, Lord 138
El Pensamiento de la Nacion 56
Elvenich, P. J. 27, 33f, 35
Émery, Jacques-André 19
Emmerick, Anna Katharina 220
Empiricism, English 235
England, see Great Britain
English Historical Review 124
Eötvös, J. 286
Epigraphy, Christian 229
Episcopalism 320
Episcopate 14ff, 304, 324
—and clergy 14f
—and council preparation 315ff
—and infallibility 319f
—and training of priests 214
Erdeli, bishop of Grosswardein 166
Errazuriz, president of Chile 271

Errington, George 122
Espartero, Spanish general 145, 147, 268
Estrada, José Manuel 153
Etsi multa luctuosa, encyclical (1873) 282
Études de théologie, de philosophie et d'histoire 156, 286
Eucharistic congresses 222
Europe, continuation of Catholic renewal 3–56
Eternal veneration 221
Exauvillez, P. d' 55
Exegesis 238f, 243
Eximiam tuam, brief 39
"Extra Ecclesiam nulla salus" 311
Eyraud, B. 195

Faber, Frederick William 219, 221, 226
Faillon, Sulpician 19, 231
Faith and natural sciences 235
Falloux, Alfred de 67f, 286, 305
Falloux Law (1850) 69, 94, 95, 141, 286
Fani, M. 260
Fathers of the Holy Cross 140, 181
Faurie, Louis, vicar apostolic in Kweichow 200, 204f
Fausti, P. 229
Febronius, Justinus 307
Félix, P., S.J. 236
Felicians 164
Fenian Movement 127
Ferdinand VII, king of Spain 147
Ferréol, J., bishop of Macao 191
Ferretti, secretary of state 88
Fessler, Josef, bishop of St. Pölten 274, 310, 319
Feuerbach, Ludwig 36, 235
Feye, Henri 232
Fideism 32, 33
First communion 20, 24, 221
Fleury, Claude 4
Flir, A. 244
Florentini, Theodosius, O.F.M.Cap. 120
Flórez 231
Fornari, R., cardinal 5, 44, 305
Foucher, L. 236
Foulon, bishop of Nancy 94
Fourier, François Charles 300
France 4, 31, 285, 305
—academic freedom 5
—and Near Eastern Churches 156f
—and Roman Question 250ff
—and *Syllabus* 297
—apostolicity of Gallican Church 231
—Catholic Church during Second Republic 65ff, 69
— — apparent successes of the Church during Second Empire and "Moral Order" 92–104
— — ambivalence of actual religious situation 98ff
—Catholic press 55
—Catholic social movement 299f
—Catholic universities 97, 102
—Catholicism and anticlericalism 104
—care of the poor and hospitals 96
—charitable works 96
—Church and industrial workers 100f
—clergy 92ff
—clerical intolerance 288f
—concordat between Napoleon I and Pius VII (1801) 14f
—coup d'état (1851) 67
—debates over Christian society 286
—education 69, 95
—episcopate 305f
—industrialization and proletariat 100f
—intellectual defects of Catholicism 102
—internal contradictions of Catholicism 102ff
—mission institutes 175f
—mission works 97
—missions to the people 23f
—moral theology 29f
—neo-Gallicans 287
—neo-ultramontanism 102, 314f
—oratory 102
—pastoral theology and practice 22
—pastoral and catechesis 19
—piety 96ff
—priest training 49
—priests, supply of 94
—provincial councils 69, 305
—rationalism and positivism 101
—renewal of philosophical and theological thought during July monarchy 47
—results of 1848 revolution 66–70
—revolution (1848) 66ff
—romanticism 101f
—Second Republic 66ff
—social question 100
—splitting of Catholics 285ff
—ultramontanism 3ff, 94, 305, 311f, 313
Franchi, cardinal 88
Francis de Sales 226
Franciscans 11, 144, 210
—in China 189
—in California 269
—in Croatia 169
—in Philippines 193
—in USA 131
Frankfurt National Assembly (1848) 70ff
—ecclesiastical demands and satisfaction 72ff
Fransoni, archbishop of Turin 257f
Fransoni case 257
Franz II (I), emperor of Austria 76f
Franzelin, Johannes B., S.J. 47, 227, 230f, 242
Franz Joseph I, emperor of Austria 108, 156
—and Austrian Catholicism 273ff
—concordat policy 108
Frassinetti, Giuseppe 221, 261
Frayssinous, Denis 19
"Free church in a free state" 251, 258, 295
Free Press, Glasgow 125
Freemasonry 296
—in Belgium 263f
—in Brazil 154, 271
—in France 101

—in Italy 259
—in Latin America 153, 269ff
—in Portugal 148, 268
—in Spain 193
—in USA 131
Free Thought (Belgium) 265
French seminary in Rome 94, 311
Freiburg im Breisgau, department of theology 41
Freppel, Charles Émile 95, 231
Freidberg, Emil 273, 278
Friedrich I, grand duke of Baden 280
Friedrich, Johannes 118, 247, 330, 332
Frohschammer, Jakob 244
Fuchs, Bernhard 29

Gabet, Joseph 190f
Gadille, J. 287
Gaeta, conference (1849) 64
Gagarin, I. (J.X. S.J.) 156
Gagern, M. von 72
Gallicanism, Gallicans 4ff, 29, 94, 102, 296, 312
—and Roman Question 766
Galicia 165
Gallitzin, Amalie, princess 26, 33
Galura, Bernhard 17
Gambasin, A. 256
Gangauf, abbot, O.S.B. 455
García Moreno, Gabriel 152
Garibaldi, nuncio in France 5
Garibaldi, Giuseppe 251, 254, 255
Gasser, Vinzenz, bishop of Brixen 310, 329f
Gaude, cardinal 88
Gaultier, P. 4
Gaume, Abbé 70
Gautrelets, F.-X. 224
Gay, Charles 226
Geissel, Johannes von, archbishop of Cologne 8, 14, 15, 38f, 39, 71f, 74, 75f, 106, 107, 242, 302, 310
Genga, Annibale della, see Leo XII
Genoude, Antoine de 51
Gentili, L. 24
Gerbet, Philippe 50, 294f
—and the *Syllabus* 294
Geritz, bishop of Ermland 72
German bishops' conferences
—in Fulda (1867) 118
—in Fulda (1869; infallibility question) 281, 317
—in Würzburg (1848) 74f
German Catholic Conferences 113ff
—in Breslau (1849) 74
—in Cologne (1858) 115
—in Innsbruck (1867) 117
—in Mainz (1848) 73f
—in Regensburg (1849) 74
Germanics 242, 310
German National Association 115
German Roman Catholic Central Union 136
"German Theologians"

—Scholastics and Germanics vs. the "German Theologians" 237ff
Germany 3, 31, 89, 285
—academic freedom 292f
—associative Catholicism 115
—catechesis, catechetical instruction 16f, 18f
—Catholic activity after 1848 70ff
—Catholic association movement 71, 106, 114, 216
—Catholic movement 116
—Catholic press 54
—Catholic scholars and ultramontanism 313
—Catholic social movement 114, 300f
—Catholicism and liberalism 290ff
—Catholicism and ultramontanism 312f
—church and state 290ff
—civil marriage 73
—contrast between liberalism and Catholicism in middle of 19th century 105
—economic liberalism 105
—effects of 1848 revolution 70ff
—end of German Confederation 116f
—episcopate 106, 117f
— — and problem of laborers 114
—episcopalism 6
—integration of Catholicism in North German Confederation 117
—internal contrasts in Catholicism 115
—missions to the people 23
—moral theology 27ff
—national assembly at Frankfurt (1848) 70
—pastoral theology 20ff
—piety 106
—project of a Catholic university 115
—religious education 16, 73
—Romanization of German Catholicism 116
—striving toward a national church (1848) 75
—theologians and neo-scholasticism 313f
—theologians' congress at Munich (1863) 245ff, 295, 313
—ultramontanism 6f, 115, 311, 312f
Gertrud von Helfta 227
Ghisalberti, A. M. 64f
Gießen, department of theology 41
Ginoulhiac, Jacques Marie Achille 231
Gioberti, Vincenzo 10, 46, 61, 65
Girard, C. R. 157
Girard, P. 192
Gizzi, cardinal secretary of state 57ff, 88
Gladstone, William Ewart 128, 129f
Glaire, Abbé 55
Glorieux, Abbé 13
Gómez Farias, V. 269
Gonzalez, Z., O.P., cardinal 234
Gorham, J. C. 122
Gorham judgment (1851) 122
Görres, Johann Joseph von 26, 37, 41, 42, 227
Görres Society 115
Gousset, archbishop of Rheims 5f, 30, 305
Goyau, Georges 245
Goyeneche, J. S. 152
Graf, Anton 22, 40, 227f

Gratry, A. J. Alphonse 102, 226, 236, 286, 327
Gray Sisters of Ottawa 140
Gravissimas inter, brief (1862) 244
Gray, John 125
Great Britain 89, 91, 286, 293f, 305, 316
—and Pius IX 58
—and *Syllabus* 296
—Catholic press 56
—Catholicism after 1848 121ff
—education 123f
—Old Catholics group (Newman) and ultramontanism (Manning) 123
—Oratory in Birmingham 123
—provincial synods (1852, 1855, 1859) 122
—reestablishment of hierarchy (1850) 121f
—ultramontanism 3, 311
Greater German Party 115
Gregorian calender 173
Gregorian University in Rome 211
Gregory XVI (Bartolomeo Alberto Cappellari, Fra Mauro), Pope 3, 7f, 10f, 30, 31, 46, 51, 57, 59, 61, 64, 83, 87, 138, 144, 146, 148, 149f, 154, 158f, 163, 173, 180, 208, 216, 229, 267, 270, 285, 294, 304, 306
—and orders 9
—and Russian church policy 158ff
—and Tsar Nicholas I 159
Greith, K. J., bishop of St. Gallen 120
Griffith, Raymond, vicar apostolic 143
Grignion de Montfort, Louis Maria 225
Grou, Jean Nicolas, S.J. 226
Gruber, A., archbishop of Salzburg 17
Guatemala 151, 152
—concordat (1832) 91
—concordat (1852) 151
Guéranger, Prosper Louis Pascal 4, 6, 9, 12f, 51f, 210, 227f, 288, 294, 309, 311
Guerber, J. 29
Guerrier de Dumast 286
Guidi, O.P., cardinal 241, 328
Guizot, F. P. G. 45
Günther, Anton 31, 35, 36, 235, 237, 239, 243
Güntherianism 241, 243, 292
—rise and fall of Güntherianism 35ff
Gury, P., S.J. 30f

Haeckel, Ernst 235
Haffner, Paul Leopold 118, 241
Haiti, concordat (1860) 91
Hamon, A. J. M. 226
Haneberg, Daniel Bonifaz von, O.S.B., abbot 42, 118, 200, 238, 245
Häring, Bernhard 28
Hartmann, Anastasius, O.F.M.Cap., vicar apostolic of Bombay 178, 179ff, 181, 183
Hassun, Antonius, cardinal 171f, 309
Haxthausen, Werner von 155
Haynald, Ludwig, cardinal 326
Hecker, Isaac 84, 13f
Hefele, Karl Joseph von, bishop of Rottenburg 40, 113, 118, 238f, 322, 328, 330, 331
—and infallibility 281

Hegel, Georg Wilhelm Friedrich 36, 40, 235
Hegelianism 37
Heinrich, Johann Baptist 71, 105, 112, 118, 240, 241, 310
Hello, Ernest 226
Herbst, Johann Georg 40f
Hergenröther, Joseph, cardinal 118, 156, 243, 247
Hermes, Georg 7, 27, 31f, 35, 235
Hermesianism, Hermesians 48
Herrera, Bartolomé 153
Herzegovina 169
Herzog, Edward 282, 331, 332, 333
Heß, Johann Jakob 28
Hesse-Darmstadt 111
Hesse-Nassau 112
Hettinger, Franz 118, 243, 247
Hilgers, G. J. 330
Hirscher, Johann Baptist 18, 22, 28f, 40f, 75, 227f
Historical school of law 42
Historisch-politische Blätter für das katholische Deutschland 32, 38, 54, 105, 241
Hnogek, A. A. 227
Hofbauer, Clemens Maria 36
Hohenlohe-Schillingsfürst, Gustav Adolf, prince, cardinal 86, 276f
Hohenlohe-Schillingsfürst, Chlodwig, prince 276f, 318
Home and Foreign Review 293
Home Rule 129
Honduras, concordat (1861) 91, 151
Hovanyi, F. 310
Huber, Johann Nepomuk 247
Huc, E. 190
Hughes, G., archbishop of New York 132, 134, 135f, 138
Hugonin 233
Hulst, Maurice d' 223, 234
Hurter, Friedrich 22

Illuminism, illuminati 103
Il Mediatore 253
Imbert, L. J. M. vicar apostolic of Korea 191
Immaculate Conception of Mary, dogma (1854) 272, 307
Index of Forbidden Books, 287
Indian missions 131, 135
—dissolution 150
India
—lack of a native clergy 181
India mission 178ff
—and English colonial power 182
—papal visitation (1859–62) 181
Indifferentism 296
Indochina 93
—French-Spanish intervention (1858) 186
—mission and persecution of Christians 185ff
—occupation by France 186
Indonesia mission 194
Indulgences 219
Industrialization and problem of workers 299ff

Infallibility, papal 3, 6, 114, 125, 203, 245, 268, 274, 280f, 307, 312, 317ff, 319, 330
—at the First Vatican Council 325ff
—infallibilists and anti-infallibilists 318ff
—political resistance to dogma 276
Innsbruck, department of theology 118, 241
Institutes, religious 212f
In suprema Petri sede, encyclical (1848) 155
Inter multiples, encyclical (1853) 306, 311
Intermediate Education (Ireland) Act (1878) 128
Internationale kirchliche Zeitschrift 333
Intransigents (Italy) 57, 260, 290
Irish 136, 142
Irish Ecclesiastical Record 129, 218
Ireland 122
—Catholicism after 1848 126ff
—education and Catholic University at Dublin 128f
—Queen's Colleges 127f
Isabella II, Queen of Spain 144, 145, 147
Italy 31, 57, 274, 285, 289ff
—and Austria 57ff, 252
—and Papal States 117, 248
—and Pius IX 59
—and *Syllabus* 296
—anticlericalism 289
—Catholic movement 300
—Catholic press 56
—clergy 255, 263
— — and Roman Question 253
— — liberal tendencies 289
—ecclesiastical policy of the kingdom 258f
—first Catholic congress (1874) 260
—from establishment of kingdom to occupation of Rome 250ff
—mission institutes 175f
—missions to the people 23
—occupation of Rome (1870) 254
—secularization policy 255ff
—separation of church and state 291
Italian war (1859) 249

Jacobi, Friedrich Heinrich 27
Jacobini, Ludovico, nuncio in Vienna 275
Jandel, Alexander Vincent, master general O.P. 12, 209
Jansenism, Jansenists 311
Japan
—free exercise of religion for foreigners 192
—mission and persecution of Christians 192f
Jarcke, Carl Ernst 32, 38, 43, 54
Jaricot, Marie Pauline 26, 224
Jerusalem
—council of Malchites 174
Jesuits, see Society of Jesus
Jesuit law (1872) 277
Jews
—in Italy 256
—in Prussia 108
Jocham, Magnus 29
Jolly, Julius 113, 278, 280

Jörg, Joseph Edmund 105
Josephinism 108
Joseph, veneration of 219
Journal de Bruxelles 265
Journal des personnes pieuses 55
Journal historique et littéraire 55
Journeymen associations 25, 114, 302
Juárez, Benito 269
Jugan, Jeanne 13
Juilly, college 50

Kabylia mission 197
Kaiser, bishop of Mainz 73
Kampschulte, F. W. 331
Kasandschan, general superior of the Antonites 172
Katerkamp, Theodor 22
Katholische Zeitschrift für Wissenschaft und Kunst 39
Kenrick, P., archbishop of Baltimore 133, 138
Kersten, Pierre 55
Ketteler, Wilhelm Emmanuel von, bishop of Mainz 41, 72, 73, 106, 111f, 117, 240f, 286, 292, 295, 310, 313, 320
—and infallibility 281
—and social Catholicism 303
Kiernan 147
Kim, Andreas 191
Kingsley, Charles 124
Klee, Heinrich 6, 39
Kleutgen, Joseph, S.J. 118, 241, 243, 324
Knoodt, F. P. 37f, 330
Know-nothingism 131
Kohlmann, S.J. 32
Koller, R. 214
Kolping, Adolf 25, 114, 302
Kominski, Honorat 164
Kopitar, B. 158
Korea, mission and persecution of Christians 191
Kött, Christoph Florentius, bishop of Fulda 111
Kraus, Franz Xaver 75
Krausism 148
Kreuzlage, A. 33
Kübel, Lothar von, suffragan of Freiburg 280f
Kuhn, Johannes Evangelist 33, 40f, 118, 237, 239, 243, 244, 247
Kulturkampf 89, 332f
—preliminary stages 272–283
Kutschker, Johann Rudolf, cardinal 274f
Kuyper, A. 267

Labastida, P. A., archbishop of Mexico 270
Labor union movement 301
La Bouillerie, François A.R. de 221
Labouré, Catherine 24, 224
Lachat, Eugène, bishop of Basel 282
La ciencia cristiana 234
La Civilizacion 56
La Civiltà cattolica 65, 211, 234, 258, 284, 290, 294f, 300, 307, 312, 314, 317

Lacordaire, Henri Dominique 9, 11, 27, 48, 53, 66f, 70, 209, 226, 286
La Correspondance de Rome 305
Laity
—active in pastoral and charitable work 24ff
Lambruschini, Luigi, cardinal secretary of state 35, 57f, 159
Lambruschini, Raffaele 258
La Mennais (Lamennais), Hugo Félicité Robert 5, 7, 30, 32, 34, 43, 44, 49, 102, 232, 236, 266, 286, 294, 300
Lamennais, Jean Marie 30
Lamey, August 113, 278
L'ami de la religion et du roi 233
Lamorcière, general 251f
Langen, J. 330, 333
Languillat, A., S.J., vicar apostolic of Kiangnan 205
L'année liturgique 227f
Lanteri, Pio Brunoe 30
Laouënan, J. M., vicar apostolic of Pondicherry 201
L'Armonia della Religione colla Civiltà 258
Lartigue, bishop of Montreal 139
La Salette, pilgrimage 98, 225
Lasaulx, Peter Ernst von 72
La Scienza italiana 234
La Sociedad 56
Lassalle, Ferdinand 302
Latin America 89
—Catholicism in the 19th century 149ff, 152f
—clergy and lack of priests 149
—regalistic liberals and Freemasons 269ff
La Terre Sainte et les Églises orientales 157
La Tour du Pin 303
Latreille, A. 97, 104
L'Avenir 55, 286, 300, 311
Lavigerie, Charles, cardinal 94, 157, 177, 197, 314
Lay apostolate 26
Lazarists 170
—in China 188, 189
Lebanon 174
Lebeurier, V. 214
Le Bien Public 289
Le Bras, G. 98
Le Cocq d'Armandville, S.J. 194
Le Correspondant 55, 102, 233, 286f, 314
Ledóchoswki, Mieczyslaw Halka von, cardinal, 107
Lefebvre, P. C. 141
Lenhart, Ludwig 39
Lennig, Adam Franz 54, 71, 73, 112, 240
Leo XII (Annibale della Genga), pope 24, 30, 294
Leo XIII (Gioacchino Vincenzo Pecci), pope 83, 85, 89, 90, 125, 165, 172, 207, 223, 234, 237, 261, 283, 294, 298, 301
Leonrod, Franz von, bishop of Eichstätt 278
Le Pappe de Trévern, Jean François, bishop of Strasbourg 47f
Lepidi, Alban, O.P. 234

Le Play, Frédéric 301
Lequeux 306
Le Rappel 305
Lerdo de Tejada 270
L'Ère Nouvelle 66
Leroy-Beaulieu 321
Levant, Catholic missions 169ff
Levate, encyclical (1867) 163
Lewicki, M., cardinal 165
Liberalism 85, 89, 298, 331
—and infallibility dogma 276
—Catholic reaction to liberalism 83
—condemnation by the *Syllabus* 116
—in Baden 278
—in Germany 104f, 272
—in Italy 259
—in Netherlands 266ff
—in Portugal 267ff
—in Spain 144f, 267ff
—in Switzerland 119f, 272, 281
—in Venezuela 271
—increasing gravity of conflict of Catholic Church in German-speaking areas and *Kulturkampf* 272ff
—offensive by the liberal governments 255ff
—state church tendencies 273
—struggle between Catholicism and liberalism 248ff
Liberalism, Catholic 298f
—in Belgium 262ff, 289
—in Canada 140
—in England 293
—in France 69, 101ff, 286f
—in Germany 104, 291ff
—in Italy 289f
Liberatore, P. 234
Libermann, Franz Maria 197
Liebermann, Bruno Franz Leopold 6
Ligue française pour l'enseignement public 96
Liguori, Alphonsus Maria de 29ff, 219, 227, 319
Lincoln, Abraham 134
Linde, Justin T. B. 72
Lingard, J. 3
Lipp, Joseph, bishop of Rottenburg 112f
Litta, cardinal 173
Little Sisters of the Assumption 212
Little Sisters of the Poor 13
Liturgy 3, 4f, 21, 227, 311
Liturgical renewal 227
Liturgies, Eastern 309
Lombardy 61, 256, 281, 305
Louis Napoleon, see Napoleon III
Louis XIV, king of France 222
Louis-Philippe, king of France 60
Lourdes, pilgrimage 97, 98
Louvain, Catholic University 31, 43ff, 233
Löwe, professor 37
Luca, Antonio de, cardinal 167
Lucas, F. 56
Ludwig II, king of Bavaria 110, 277
Luna Pizzarro, F.X. de 152

L'Univers 5, 55, 70, 94, 232, 258, 289, 305, 311, 314
L'Université Catholique 50f, 55
Luquet, bishop 155
Lutterbeck, A. 41
Lutterbeck, J. 238
Lutz, Johann von, baron 277
Lydia, journal 38
Lynch, James, C.M. 126
Lynch, John Joseph, bishop of Toronto 134
Lyon, Association for the Propagation of the Faith 201
Lyon Missionaries 177

Maaß, F. 8
Maccarrone, M. 329
Macé, Jean 96
Macedo Costa, A. de, bishop of Para 272
MacHale, John, archbishop of Tuam 127
Madagascar mission 198
Mai, Angelo, cardinal 45, 229
Magisterial office of the Church 242, 292, 320
Maignen, Abbé 100
Mainzer Journal 71
Mainz Catechism 18
Mainz circle 7, 71, 118
—and *Syllabus* 297
Mainz seminary 41
Maistre, Joseph de 7, 155
Malabar 172
Malaya, mission and Church 185f
Mallinckrodt, Hermann von 108, 117
Malou, Jean Baptiste, bishop of Bruges 44, 226
Mañe y Flaqeur 286
Mann, Horace 135
Manning, Henry Edward, cardinal 87, 122ff, 124, 125, 214, 226, 293, 316, 317, 322, 325, 328
Manteuffel, Otto von 107
Manzoni, Alessandro 290
Maori 195
Marazán, president of Guatemala 151
Marc-Bonnet, H. 90
Marches 250, 251
Marchi, Giuseppe, S.J. 229
Marchilhacy 217
Maret, Henri Louis Charles 50, 231, 233, 287, 297, 314f, 328
Margotti 290
Maria II da Gloria, Queen of Portugal 148
María Cristina, regent of Spain 144f
Marian congregations 24, 224
Marilley, Étienne, bishop of Lausanne-Geneva 119f
Marion Brésillac, Melchior de 177
Marists, in Oceania 195
Maronites, Maronite Church 173f
Marrou, H. I. 229
Martin, K. 31
Martina, G. 61, 86, 214, 294
Martínez de la Rosa, Francisco 144
Martinov, J., S.J. 156, 200

Mary, appearances of 224
Mary, veneration of 24, 219, 224f
—in France 98
—in Poland 164
Masad, Paul, Maronite patriarch 174
Mastai-Ferretti, Giovanni Maria, see Pius IX
Mathieu, Adrien Jacques Marie, archbishop of Besançon 14
Matta, Jerome Joseph de, bishop of Macao 179
Maubant, Pierre Philibert 191
Maurain, J. 287
Maurists 52, 220, 311
Maximilian, emperor of Mexico 93, 270
Maximos III Mazlum, Melchite patriarch 173
Maynooth, seminary 129
May prayers 225
Mazzini, Giuseppe 64
Mazzuconi, G. 195
McCloskey, Cardinal 138
McMaster, J. 136
Meaux, count 571
Mechelen, congress of Belgian Catholics (1863) 295f, 301
Mechelen School 77
Meglia, nuncio in Mexico 270
Mélanges théologiques 218
Melchers, Paulus, cardinal 107
Melchites, Uniate 173
Melchite schism 173
Meletios, archbishop in Greece (1861) 168
Melun, Armand de 25f, 96, 300
Mendicant orders 9f, 10
—see also Dominicans, Franciscans
Mendizábal, Spanish minister 144
Menzel, A. 330
Mermillod, Gaspard 120, 222, 282, 312
Merode, Xavier de 86, 250
Mertel, cardinal 88
Messmer, J. A. 330
Metternich, Klemens, prince 8, 35, 59, 76
Mexico 93, 152, 269, 295
—Catholicism and liberalism 269f
—civil marriage 270
—clergy 269
—race problem 269
—secularization 269
Mey, Gustav 18
Michael Confraternity 116
Michelis, Friedrich 118, 331, 332f
Micronesia 196
Migne, Jacques-Paul 51f, 55
Miguel, Don M., king of Portugal 148f
Milan missionaries
—in Burma 185
—in China 189
—in India 181
—in Polynesia 195
Milan mission seminary 176
Milde, Vincenz, archbishop of Vienna 17, 76
Minh Mang, emperor of Tonkin 186
Minguetti 290
Mirari vos, encyclical (1832) 285

Missionaries of the Precious Blood 23
Missionaries of Mill Hill (London) 135, 177f
Missionaries of Scheut, in China 189
Missionari della Consolata 176
Mission(s) 91
—First Vatican Council and missions 199ff
—missions 1840–70 175–207
—under Pius IX 89f
Missions to the people, parish missions 211, 222
—in Austria 24
—in Brazil 153
—in England 122
—in France 23ff, 99
—in Germany 24, 106
—in Italy 23
—in USA 133
Mission directory 204
Mission Institute for Africa 176f
Mission works, in Belgium 262
Modena, duchy 256f
—concordat (1857) 91
Modernism 89
Möhler, Johann Adam 29, 40f, 41, 42, 48, 50, 230, 237
Moldavian monasteries 168f
Molé, Louis Mathieu 67
Moeller, J. 44
Mommsen, Theodor 229
Mönchen-Gladbach, movement 302
Mongkut, king of Siam 185
Mongolia mission 189
Montalembert, Charles René Forbes 5, 10, 26f, 52, 55, 67f, 69, 103, 141, 248, 264, 284, 286, 289, 295, 298
Montclos, X. de 49
Montigny, de, French consul 186
Moral theology, reaction to rationalism of the Enlightenment and rigorism 27ff
—and Holy Scripture 28f
Morel, Gall, O.S.B. 120
Moreno, García 271
Moreno, M., bishop of Ivrea 258
Mortara case 249
Mosquera, M. J., archbishop of Bogotá 270
Moufang, Franz Christoph 105, 112, 115, 118, 240, 310
Moy de Sons, Karl Ernst von 310
Müller, Johann Georg, bishop of Münster 72, 107
Multa praeclare, decree (1838) 180
Mun, Albert de 100
Munich, university 41ff
Munich circle, Görres circle 31, 41, 43
Munich School 50f, 235, 246f
—young Munich School 247
Murdoch, Dr. 125
Murialdo, Leonardo 257
Murray, Patrick 129

Naples, kingdom (of Two Sicilies) 61, 251, 255
Napoleon III (Louis Napoleon), emperor of

France 64, 67, 87, 92, 103, 186, 194, 205, 249, 251, 253, 314, 327
Narváez 147, 268
National Catholic Almanac 136
National seminaries at Rome 307
Neminem latet, encyclical (1857) 208
Neo-Gothic 79
Neo-Guelfism 256, 289
—from neoguelf myth to Roman revolution 57ff
Neo-Scholasticism 18, 118, 233, 241ff, 313f
Neo-Thomism 45, 234
Nesselrode, Karl Robert 159ff
Netherlands 89, 91, 286
—and Indonesia 194
—and *Syllabus* 296
—anticlericalism 265ff
—Catholic association movement 79
—Catholicism in isolation 79
—Catholic press 55
—clergy, monasteries, and orders 79
—effects of revolution (1848) 77ff
—first provincial council (1865) 78
—free Catholic schools 266f
—Jansenist Church 78
—liberal education policy 266ff
—liberalism and Catholicism 265ff, 297
—religious freedom and equality of religion after 1848 77ff
—reestablishment of an episcopal organization 77f
Nève, F. 44
Newfoundland 138
New Granada, see Colombia
Newman, John Henry, cardinal 49, 123ff, 128, 129, 226, 236f, 293f, 311
Nicaragua, concordat (1861) 91, 151
Nickes, H. 37
Nicolas, Auguste 50
Nicholas I, tsar of Russia 59, 158
—religious policy 158ff
Niederbronn Sisters 13
North German Confederation 117
Notre-Dame de Lourdes 219
Nullis certi verbis, encyclical (1860) 250
Nunciatures, nuncios, papal 88, 308
Nuns
—in China 190f
—in Italy 261

Oblates of Mary Immaculate
—in Africa 197
—in Ceylon 183
Oblates of Mary of Turin, in Burma 184
Oblates of St. Charles 122
Oceania, mission 194ff
O'Connell, Daniel 26, 56, 74, 125, 127
Oehler, vicar general of Rottenburg 112
Old Catholicism 39, 119, 277, 330ff
—Old Catholic congresses (1870, 1872, 1873) 332f
—episcopal election (1873) 333

—first synod (1874) 333
—in Baden 279
—in Germany 330ff
—in Switzerland 281f, 333
—international congresses 334
—origin of Old Catholic Church community 330–34
Olier, J.-J. 19
Oliveira, V. de, O.F.M.Cap., bishop of Olinda 272
Ollé-Laprune, Léon 236
Ontologism 232f
Oratoire de France 236
Oratorians 286
Oratorians of Goa 183
Orders 89, 92, 296
—growth of large international orders 9ff
—in Austria 275
—in Baden 279
—in Belgium 262ff
—in Brazil 153
—in Canada 139
—in China 189f
—in Cochin China 187
—in England 122
—in France 69, 93, 95, 97
—in Germany 106, 113
—in Italy 261
—in Mexico 269
—in Philippines 193
—in Poland 164f
—in Portugal 148f
—in Russia 158, 162
—in Spain 144, 268
—in Switzerland 283
—in Turkey 169
—in USA 133, 135
— — pastoral care of blacks 135
—orders and congregations 208ff
—significance for Roman unity, centralization, and ultramontanism 9ff
Orders, women in
—in China 190f
—in Italy 261
Order, Moral 97
Organic Articles 5, 14, 16, 68, 92
Orthodox Christians at First Vatican Council 315f
Osterrath 72
Ottoman Empire, see Turkey
Oudinot, general 64
Oeuvre des cercles 100
Oeuvres des Ècoles d'Orient 157
Overberg, Bernard 117
Oxford Movement 316
Ozanam, Frédéric 25, 52f, 59, 66f

Pabst, J. H. 36
Pagan Mission, at First Vatican Council 200ff
Pagganuzzi, G. B. 260
Palafox y Mendoza, Juan de, bishop of Puebla 204

Palestine 171
Pallegoix, J. B., vicar apostolic in Siam 185
Pallotti, Vincenzo 26
Panikkar, K. M. 194
Pan-Slavism 165f
Pantheism 296
Pappalettere, Simplicio 38
Papp-Szilaggi, J. 167
Papacy, pope
—and collegiality 3
—and election of Eastern Uniate bishops 308
—and episcopate 328
—and growth of ultramontanism 9
—and Papal State 90, 244
—and secular power (Papal States) 248ff, 296
—attempts at union with Eastern Churches 156ff
—Austrian policy 273
—centralization policy 171, 304ff
—French "cult of papacy" 311f
—growing importance after middle of century 307
—reduction of prestige 250
—universal episcopate 310, 330
Papal elections 57f
Papal Seminary of Sts. Peter and Paul 176
Papal States 57f, 60, 87, 90, 101, 116
—from papal restoration to Italian War 248ff
—missions to the people 23
—restoration under Pius IX 64
—under Pius IX 57ff, 248f
Paraty, count 268
Paray-le-Monial, pilgrimage 98, 223
Paris congregation 92
Paris Congress (1856) 249
Parisis, Pierre Louis, bishop of Arras 5f, 99, 305
Paris missionaries
—in Burma 185
—in China 188, 189
—in India 181
—in Japan 192
—in Malaya 185
Parnell, Charles Stewart 129f
Passaglia, Carlo 47, 226, 242, 253, 307
Passionists 211
Pastoral theology
—and professional ethics 21
—and pastoral practice in 19th century 20ff
Pastor aeternus, constitution (1870) 328ff
Patrizi, Costantino, cardinal 88f
Patrizi, F. X. 46
Patronage, right of
—French patronage in China 187f
—Portuguese 149
— — in China 187
— — in India 204
— — patronage priests in Malaya 185
— — reduction 178ff
—Spanish in Spanish America 149ff
Paulists 137
Pecci, Vincenzo Gioacchino, see Leo XIII
Pedro II, emperor of Brazil 153

Pedro IV, Don Pedro, king of Portugal 148
Peking, peace treaty (1860) 188
Pellerin, vicar apostolic of North Cochin China 186
Pelliot, Paul 190
Pensamiento español 148
People's Association, Catholic 302
Pérez Alhama 146
Périn, Charles 265, 301
Permaneder, Franz Michael 42
Perreyve, Henri 226
Perrone, Giovanni, S.J. 33, 46f, 223, 234
Perry, Matthew, admiral 192
Persico, Ignatius, cardinal 621
Persico, J., S.J. 180
Peru 151, 152f, 270
Petau, Dionysius, S.J. 230
Peter's Pence 116
Petitjean, T., vicar apostolic of Japan 192
Pfordten, Ludwig von der 110
Philaret, metropolitan of Moscow 155
Philippe, general superior of Christian Brothers 210
Philippines, missions and ecclesiastical development 193
Phillips, George 6, 42, 43, 54, 72, 310
Philosophy 232f
Pichler, Alois 247
Picpus Association 223
—in Polynesia 195
Pie, Louis, bishop of Poitiers 102, 230, 288, 294, 328
Piedmont 60f, 248, 249, 252, 256, 266, 285
—policy of secularization 256
—ultramontanism 3
Pierling, J. 156
Pietro Leopoldo, grand duke of Tuscany 256
Piety 304
—development of forms in 19th century 218–228
—Eucharistic 221
—in Belgium 262
—liturgical 227
Pitra, Jean-Baptiste, O.S.B., cardinal 51, 157, 229
Pitzipios, J. G. 157
Pius VI (Gianangelo Braschi), pope 294
Pius VII (Luigi Barnaba Chiaramonti), pope 3, 23, 30, 208, 258, 294
Pius VIII (Francesco Saverio Castiglioni), pope 30
Pius IX (Giovanni Maria Mastai-Ferretti), pope 9, 12, 24, 26, 35, 39, 47, 57ff, 60, 66, 75, 86, 103, 111, 117, 120, 121, 122, 133, 138, 146, 148, 150, 152, 155, 159, 163, 167, 172, 174, 179, 180, 195, 219, 221, 223, 229, 273, 244, 248, 262, 268, 270, 276, 281, 283, 285, 289, 297, 298, 300, 306f, 308, 309, 312, 326, 328f, 332
—and China mission 190f
—and Emperor Franz Joseph 274
—and German Congress of Theologians (1863) 245
—and Heart of Jesus piety 222f
—and Italian ecclesiastical policy 258ff
—and Josephinist religious policy in Austria 61
—and liberalism 255
—and missions at Vatican Council 200ff
—and papal sovereignty 252
—and Piedmontese religious policy 256f
—and *Risorgimento* 60
—and Russian ecclesiastical policy 162f
—and Siam mission 185
—and Switzerland 282
—and *Syllabus* 293ff
—and Uniate Churches in the East 155
—and union of Eastern Churches 156f
—and Vatican Council 315ff
—ascension and crisis of 1848 57–79
—activity after 1848 83–90
—bishops' meeting (1862) 252
—centralization policy 171
—characteristics of personality and activity 83ff
—concordat policy 258
—confirmation of Gregorian mission restoration 175–198
—first years of pontificate 57–65
—flight to Gaeta (1848) 62ff
—mission activity 175ff
—nadir of scholarly activity in Rome 228
—on tasks of theology 245f
—reorganization and centralization of the old orders and founding of new congregations 208ff
—Roman Question 250ff
—spiritual elevation of clergy 213f
Pius X, pope 261
Pius Associations 108, 115
Pius Association for Religious Freedom 71
Planchet, S.J. 172
Planque, Augustin 177
Placet, by the state 73, 76, 119, 146, 276f
Podcarpathia 166f
Poland 162, 295, 305
—Catholic Church under Russian domination 158ff
—rebellion (1863–64) 162
—religious awakening of Catholicism 164f
Polding, John Bede, O.S.B., archbishop of Sydney 142f
Polish College in Rome 162
Pombal, Marquis de 182
Popiel, Michael 163, 166
Portales, D., Chilean minister 151
Portugal
—and Africa mission 197f
—anticlericalism, dissolution of monasteries and suppression of Jesuits 148, 267ff
—concordat (1857) 91, 180f, 187
—development of religious situation during second third of the 19th century 148f
—missions 178ff

—secularizations 268
Positivism 235, 271
—in Spain 268
Pouthas, C. 94, 262
Pouthas, M. 97
Powondra, T. 21
Praying Sisters of the Assumption (Orantes) 212
Press, publications, Catholic 32
—and apostolate 217
—growth 53ff
—in Belgium 262, 264
—in England 56
—in France 55
—in Germany 54
—in Italy 55, 259
—in the Netherlands 55
Press, freedom of 295f
Priests, congregations of 212
Primacy, papal 244, 307, 327
Probabiliorism 30f
Probabilism 27, 46
Probst, Ferdinand 29
Processions 219
Propagation of the Faith, Congregation for the 170ff
—and missions in China 187
—and Portuguese patronage in China 187
—and question of missions at Vatican Council 200ff
—and union of Eastern Churches 157ff
—centralizing Latinization policy in Eastern patriarchates 170ff
—dispute with Portugal over patronage in India 178ff
Protestantism
—and Vatican Council 316f
—in Spain 144
Provencher, Monsignor, missionary 139
Prussia 71, 73, 91, 254, 280
—and Austria 117
—constitutional conflict (1862–67) 108f
—ecclesiastical development after 1848 105ff
—free exercise of religion 72
—freedom of belief and conscience 72
—Raumer's decrees (1852) 107
—religious paragraphs of the constitution (1848–50) 73
—religious policy 280
Purcell, J. B., archbishop of Cincinnati 132

Quanta cura, encyclical (1864) 134, 296, 300
Quebec, bishopric 138f
Quélen, de, archbishop of Paris 19
Quin, M. 56
Qui pluribus, encyclical (1846) 35, 58

Radowitz, Josef Maria von 72
Ram, Xavier De 43
Ramazotti, patriarch of Venice 176, 261
Ramière, H. 224

Ranke, Leopold von 43
Rapin, René, S.J. 311
Räß, Andreas, bishop of Strasbourg 18, 49
Rationalism 268, 296, 324
Ratio studiorum of the Jesuits 10
Raumer, Friedrich von 107
Rauscher, Josef Otmar von, cardinal 38, 76f, 108f, 117, 241, 274f, 310, 313, 320, 322, 328, 333
Ravignan, P. de 286
Rayneval, de 249
Redemptorists 31, 209f
—in Austria 310
Reichensperger, August 72, 108, 114, 117
Reichensperger, Peter 72, 107, 117, 281
Reinkens, Joseph Hubert 37f, 330, 332f
Reisach, Karl August von, cardinal 8, 32, 39, 75, 88, 110, 112, 157, 241, 243, 310
Reithmayr, Franz Xaver 42, 238
Religion, freedom of 91, 296
Religion, history of 234
Reliquaries, veneration of 219
Renan, Ernest 44, 101, 231, 295
Rerum novarum, encyclical (1891) 301
Resurrectionists 162, 168
Retord, Pierre, vicar apostolic of West Tonkin 186
Reusch, Franz Heinrich 238, 330, 332f
Revelation 232, 237, 315
Reversurus, bull (1867) 172ff, 174, 309
Revista mensual 286
Revolution of 1848: effects in Germany, Austria, and the Netherlands 70–79
Revue catholique 44
Revue des questions scientifiques 236
Revue européenne 55
Revue générale (Belgium) 265
Revue Internationale de Théologie 333
Rheinische Volkshalle, Cologne 71
Rheinisches Kirchenblatt 54
Rhineland 25
Riachi, metropolitan of Beirut 173
Riancé, Henri de 50
Riario Sforza 261
Ricasoli, Bettino 258, 290
Ricci, Scipione de, bishop 86
Riegler, G. 27
Riess, Joseph Florian, S.J. 247
Riffel, Kaspar 71
Rigorism 30
Rio, Alexis-François 52
Rio de la Plata 152
Risorgimento 252
Ritter, Joseph Ignaz 35
Ritter, M. 331
Rivista Universale 291
"Robber synod of Chelm" 164
Rock, D. 3
Rogier-Frère Orban 263
Rohrbacher, René François 4, 50
Romagna 250

Romanticism
—in Spain 148
Romher, minister 254
Roman Question 248–255, 285, 287, 289ff
Roman congregations under Pius IX 88
Roman republic (1848) 64
"Roman School" of German theology 242ff
Roman College, see Collegium Romanum
Romo, P. P., archbishop of Seville 145
Roothaan, Philipp, general S.J. 9f, 23, 34, 156, 196, 211, 220, 233
Rosary, living 224
Rosas, Juan Manuel 152
Roscovany, bishop 201
Rosmini-Serbati, Antonio 13, 15, 45f, 62, 65, 233, 257, 261, 290
Rossi, Giovanni Battista De 229f
Rossi, Pellegrino 62, 65
Rouland, French minister 93, 96
Rozaven, P., S.J. 47f
Rudigier, Franz Joseph, bishop of Linz 273, 310
Rumania
—mission of Moldavian monasteries 168f
—reorganization of the Catholic Church 167f
Russell, C. W. 129
Russell, Odo 127, 325
Russia 154, 155
—agreement (concordat) with Rome (1847) 160
—and Bulgaria 167
—Catholic Church under Tsar Nicholas I 158ff
—religious policy after 1847 160ff
—return of the Uniate Greeks to Orthodoxy 164
Ryerson, Canadian superintendent 141
Ryllo, P., S.J. provicar 196

Sacconi, Carlo, cardinal 75, 92
Sacred Heart associations 223
Sacred Heart Messenger 224
Sacred Heart veneration 98, 219, 222ff
Sailer, Johann Michael 17, 21, 28f, 41f, 89, 218, 311
Sainte-Beuve, Charles Augustin de 311
Saint-Simon, Claude Henri de, count 300
Saint Sulpice 311, 94, 214, 218, 233, 311f
Saints, cult of 219
—in France 98
—legends of 220
Saint Joseph of Mill Hill, Fathers of 135, 177f
St. Peter's Association 155
Salat, Jakob 27
Salesians
—in England 124
—in India 181
Salesians of Annecy 177
—in India 181
Salle, Jean Baptiste de la 178
Samhiri, Antonius, Syrian patriarch 173
San Salvador, bishopric

—concordat (1862) 91, 151
Sanseverino, G. 234
Sarfeh, Council of (1853–54) 173
Sausen, Franz J. 71
Schaepman, Abbé 267
Scheeben, Matthias Joseph 118, 226f, 242, 247
Scheffczyk, L. 40, 242
Schegg, Peter Johann 238
Schenkl, Maurus von, O.S.B. 28
Scheppers, bishop 13
Scherer-Boccard, Theodor von, count 120
Scherr, Gregor von, archbishop of Munich-Freising 111, 277
Schleiermacher, Friedrich 28
Schmid, Christoph von 18
Schmid, Heinrich, abbot, O.S.B. 120
Schmid, L. 459
Schmidlin, Joseph 175
Schmidt, A. 247
Schmöger, K. E. 220
Schnabel, Franz 7
Scholasticism 37, 40, 566, 241
Scholz, P. 238
School of La Chênaie and Malestroit 47
School of Molsheim 47f
Schrader, Clemens, S.J. 230, 241, 298, 307, 310, 324
Schreiber, H. 27
Schrörs, Heinrich 34
Schüch, I. 22
Schulte, J. F. von 331, 333
Schuster, Ignaz 18
Schwarzenberg, Felix zu 76
Schwarzenberg, Freidrich zu, cardinal 37, 74, 76, 210, 275
Schwendimann, Ignaz, general superior of Holy Ghost Fathers 197
Schwetz, Johannes Baptist 38
Scientific Society of Brussels 235
Scienza e fede 234
Scitowsky, cardinal, primate of Hungary 108, 210
Scotland
—reestablishment of hierarchy 126
—rise of Catholicism after 1848 125f
Secchi, Angelo, S.J. 158
Secularization 215
Sedlag, bishop of Kulm 72
Segesser, Anton Philipp von 119
Ségur, Louis Gaston Adrien de 96, 219, 221, 222, 226, 311
Semaine religieuse (France) 218
Semaine religieuse (Tournai) 218f
Semeria, St., vicar apostolic of Jaffna 183
Senestréy, Ignatius von, bishop of Regensburg 277
Serbs, Serbia 166
Sermon 21f, 53
Sertillanges, Antonin Gilbert 236
Settele 229
Shaughnessy 130

Siam, mission and Church 185
Sibour, archbishop of Paris 15, 68, 306
Siccardi 257
Signay, bishop of Quebec 138
Signoriello, N. 234
Silesia 37
Sillani, Hilarion 184
Silva Torres, José Maria da 179, 182
Simeoni, Cardinal 164
Simon, Jules 97, 101
Simpson, Richard 124, 293
Sisters of Charity 13
Sisters of Joseph of Cluny 170
Sisters of Notre Dame of Zion 170
Sisters of Providence 13f
Sisters of the Good Shepherd 140
Sixtus V, pope 321
Slavery 133f, 198
Slomšek, A. M. bishop of Lavant 156
Slovenia 156
Smedt, Charles de, S.J. 232
Smyrna, regional council (1869) 169
Social Catholicism 299ff
Socialism 296, 300
Social doctrine, Catholic 303
Société d'économie charitable 96, 300
Société hagiographique 51
Society for the African Mission 177
Society of Italian Catholic Youth 260
Society of Jesus 9ff, 23, 44f, 46f, 62, 65, 107,
   203, 211f, 233, 241, 284, 310
—and ultramontanism 307
—in Africa 196
—in Argentina 150
—in Austria 310
—in Belgium 262
—in Canada 139
—in Chile 150f
—in China 188, 189
—in Colombia 270
—in France 286
—in Germany 292
—in India 179, 181
—in Indonesia 194
—in Italy 261
—in Madagascar 198
—in New Granada 150
—in Philippines 193
—in Portugal 148
—in Spain 144, 268
—in Switzerland 283
—in Turkey 169, 171
—in USA 137
—instruction in piety 219f
—persecutions and expulsion from European
   countries (1830–48) 10f
—readmission under Pius VII and
   reestablishment of former provinces in
   Europe and overseas (1830–51) 9f
—sermons at retreats of priests 219
—Sacred Heart veneration 223

Society of Oceania 195
Society of St. Vincent de Paul 25, 96, 300
Society of White Fathers 177, 712
—in Africa 197
Society of Sisters of the Sacred Heart of Jesus
   223
Society of the Daughters of the Sacred Heart of
   Mary 212
Society of the Sons of the Sacred Heart 176f
Soglia, Giovanni, cardinal 88
Solesmes, abbey 112, 210, 231
Sophie, archduchess of Austria 275
Sorbonne 49f
Sorg, P., O.S.B. 38
Soubirous, Bernadette 225
South Africa 143
South America, establishment of new dioceses
   150
South American republics
—clergy 270
—civil marriage 271
—freedom of religion for Protestants 271
—liberalism 270f
—separation of Church and state 270
Spadolini, G. 290
Spalding, Martin John, archbishop of Baltimore
   132, 134, 137
Spain
—agreement with the Holy See (1859) 147
—anticlericalism 144f, 148, 268
—Carlist wars 144
—Catholic press 56
—Catholicism and liberalism 268f
—Church and state 143ff
—clergy 146
—clergy, training 147f
—concordat (1753) 144, 146f
—concordat (1851) 91, 146f
—dissolution of monasteries and orders 144
—ecclesiastical development after Ferdinand
   VII's death (1833) 143ff
—freedom of religion 268f
—hierarchy and liberalism 268
—liberals and intransigent Catholics 142
—nationalization of ecclesiastical estates 144
—revolution (1868) 268
—state and Church 268
—theological studies 45
Spelta, L. C., O.F.M., vicar apostolic of Hupei
   190f
Spencer, George 235
Spiegel, Ferdinand August, archbishop of
   Cologne 32
State church, established church 273
Staniewski, administrator of Mogilev 163
Stapf, J. A. 28
Staudenmaier, Franz Anton 41
Stella 86
Sterckx, E., cardinal archbishop of Mechelen
   14, 263f, 289
Stieve, F. 331

Stifter, Adalbert 105
Stimmen aus Maria Laach 247
Stöckl, Albert 247
Stolz, Alban 41, 114
Stösser, Franz Ludwig von 735
Strasbourg, School of 47
Strauß, David Friedrich 40
Stremayr, Austrian minister of religion 274
Strickland, G., S.J. 183
Stroßmayer, J. G., bishop of Diakovar 165, 324, 328, 330
Suarez, Francisco de, S.J. 234, 241
Sudan, missions 176, 197, 206
Sulpicians 47
Surin, Jean Joseph, S.J. 226
Sušil, F. 156
Swetchine, Madame 156
Switzerland 292
—antiultramontanes 119
—break in diplomatic relations with Rome 282
—Catholic association movement and charitable works 120
—federal constitution (1847) 282
—"Freethinking Catholic Associations" 282
—*Kulturkampf* 281f
—liberalism and Catholicism 281
—narrow ecclesiastical policy after 1848 119
—National Church-Old Catholic movement 283
—ultramontanism 281
—Wessenbergians 119f
Syllabus of Pius IX (1864) 65, 101, 104, 105, 118, 127, 134, 152, 266, 269, 271f, 272, 282, 292, 294f, 301, 313f, 317, 321
—and its consequences 293ff
Syria 93
Syrian Uniate Church 173f

Taché, Alexander Antonin, O.M.I. 139
Taiping rebellion 188
Talamo, S. 234
Talbot de Malahide, George 86f, 124
Tamisier, E. 222
Taparelli d'Azeglio, Luigi, S.J. 46, 300
Taparelli d'Azeglio, Massimo, see Azeglio
Tarnoczy, cardinal 37
Textual criticism 242
Teysseyrre 19
Thailand, see Siam
Theiner, Augustin 155, 158, 229
The Lamp 56
Theocracy 310, 312
Theology 36, 245
—Anton Günther's 36
—backwardness of ecclesiastical studies and the controversy over the "German theologians" 228–247
—Catholic thought and the search for new ways 31–56
—ecclesiastical studies outside of Germany 228ff

—freedom, academic 245
—G. Hermes 31ff
—in France during Second Empire 230
—scholarly work in Rome 228ff
—scholastics and Germanics vs. "German theologians" 237ff
Theologisches Literaturblatt 246
Theologisch-praktische Quartalschrift 218
The Rambler 293, 311
The Tablet 56
Thiers, Louis Adolphe 67, 295
Thieu-Tri, emperor of Tonkin 186
Thomas a Jesu, Carmelite 203f
Thomas Aquinas 241, 319
Thomassin, Louis de 230
Thomism 234f
Thorbecke, Jan Rudolf 77
Thun, count 109
Tientsin, treaty (1858) 188
Tierney, M. A. 3
Timon-David 20, 25, 216
Tits, Arnould 44
Tocqueville, A. C. de 91
Tondini, P. 155
Tonello 259
Tongiorgio, F. 229
Tonkin, mission and Church 186f
Toronto Catholic Institute 141
Torre, P. dalla 249
Tosti, Luigi 231, 291
Traditionalism 47, 231ff, 287
Transylvania 166
—provincial council at Blaj (1872) 167
Transcendence of Christianity 235
Trévern, see Le Pappe
Trusteeism, trustees 132
Tuas libenter, brief (1863) 246f
Tübingen, faculty 48
Tübingen School 222, 31, 39f, 235, 237, 246f
Tübinger Theologische Quartalschrift 238
Turban, Ludwig Karl F. 280
Turkey, Turks
—Catholic presence 169ff
—religious freedom 169
Tuscany, grand duchy 60, 256
—concordat (1851) 91, 256

Ubaghs, Gerhard Casimir 43, 44, 233
Ukraine, Uniate Church 160
Ullathorne, William, bishop of Birmingham 124f
Ultramontanism 29, 31, 89, 118, 256, 272
—excesses of neo-ultramontanism and reaction in Germany and France 312ff
—progress 3ff
— — and remaining Gallican resistance 304–315
—systematic activity by Rome 306ff
—ultramontane movement around 1850 304ff
—victory of ultramontanism 304ff

Umbria 250, 251
Unam sanctam, bull (1302) 321
Uniate Churches
—and papal jurisdiction 308
—Uniate Church of Chelm 163f
—Uniate Rumanians in Transylvania 166
Unita cattolica 290
United States of America 89, 91, 286
—Catholic isolation 135ff
—Catholicism and social questions 137
—Catholic parish schools 135
—Catholics and Civil War (1861–65) 133f
—clergy 132f
—education, question of 135ff
—episcopate 132
—founding of new dioceses 131f
—Irish and German immigration 130f
—plenary council of Baltimore (1852) 134f
—plenary council of Baltimore (1866) 132, 135
—priests, training of 133
—Provincial Council of Baltimore, Fourth (1841) 133
—race problem 135
—religious freedom 135
—rise of Catholicism during second third of 19th century 130ff
Upper Rhenish Bishops' Conference (1851) 111
Utrecht, Church 332, 334
Utrecht, union 334f

Valdivieso, R. V., archbishop of Chile 151
Valerga, Giuseppe, Latin patriarch of Jerusalem 170, 200, 202, 204, 309
Valerga, Leonardo di S. Giuseppe, O.Carm. 200
Vancea, Ioan 167
Vatican Council, First (1869–70) 315–330
—and the missions 199–207
—announcement by Pius IX (1868/69) and preparation 117f, 199, 315ff
—first council debates 322ff
— — catechism 324
— — church discipline and canon law 323
— — modern errors 322
—French episcopate and pagah missions 201, 206f
—lively actions concerning infallibility of the Pope 325ff
—opening and composition 318f
Vaughan, Herbert, cardinal 135, 177
Vaughan, Roger William, O.S.B., archbishop of Sydney 143
Vegezzi 259
Veith, Johann Emanuel 32, 36, 76
Vénard, Théophane 187f
Venetia 256
Venezuela 151, 152
—concordat (1862) 91, 151, 152
—constitution (1879) 271

—laicization policy 271
Venice, republic 257
—concordat (1855) 256
Ventura, Gioacchino 58, 59, 65, 229
Verbist, Theophil 177
Verboitte, musician 224
Vercellone, Barnabite 229
Vering, Friedrich 310
Verot, vicar apostolic of Florida 134
Verricelli, Angelo Maria 203f
Verrolles, E. J., mission bishop in China 190, 199
Veuillot, Louis 26f, 55, 67, 70, 94, 101f, 141, 226, 258, 264, 266, 286, 288f, 293, 297f, 306, 311, 326
Veuster, Damian de 195
Viale-Prela, Michele 8, 108
Vianney, Jean Marie (Curé d'Ars) 435
Vicari, Hermann von, archbishop of Freiburg 111, 279
Victor Emmanuel II, king of Italy 250, 251
Vietnam 186
Vigener, F. 320
Villanueva, Joaquin 231
Vincentian Brothers of Abbé Glorieux 13
Vincent associations, conferences 25f, 113f, 262
—in Belgium 262
Viollet-le-Duc 227
Virchow, Rudolf 272
Vogt, Karl 235
Volkonskaya, princess 154
Vows, simple 655
Vrau, Philibert 221

Wagner, bishop of St. Pölten 8
Waibel, A., O.F.M. 31
Walsh, William, archbishop of Dublin 129
Walter, Ferdinand 72
Ward, Wilfred P. 312
Ward, William George 124, 293
Warmond 77
Weber, Beda 72
Weber, T. 330, 332
Weis, Nikolaus, bishop of Speyer 8, 18, 111
Weninger, F. X., S.J. 24, 133
Wenzel, P. 36, 38
Werner, Franz 33f
Werner, Karl 29, 242, 247
Wessenberg, Ignaz Heinrich von 119, 736
William II, king of the Netherlands 502
Wilhelm I, king of Württemberg 113
Windischmann, Karl Joseph 32, 44, 110, 241
Windthorst, Ludwig 117, 281
Wiseman, Nicholas 3, 56, 121ff, 293
Witetschek, H. 36
Wolter, Maurus, O.S.B. 37, 210, 227
Wolter, Plazidus, O.S.B. 37, 210
Workers, problem of 299ff, 301
—pastoral care 114

Württemberg
—concordat (1857) 91, 112f
—ecclesiastical development after 1848 112f

Youth hostels 25
Yussef, Gregory, Melchite patriarch 173f

Zaccaro, L. 253
*Zeitschrift für Philosophie und katholische
Theologie* 32, 54
Zukrigl 37
Zwerger, Johann Baptist, bishop of Seckau 274
Zwijsen, Johannes, bishop of Utrecht 77